BEGINNER'S
LITHUANIAN

LEONARDAS DAMBRIŪNAS
ANTANAS KLIMAS
WILLIAM R. SCHMALSTIEG

HIPPOCRENE BOOKS
New York

Hippocrene paperback Edition, 1999.

Copyright © 1966 by Franciscan Fathers.

For information address:
HIPPOCRENE BOOKS, INC.
171 Madison Avenue
New York, NY 10016

ISBN 0-7818-0678-X

Printed in the United States of America

Foreword

Lithuanian is the language of the people of Lithuania and of about a million Americans of Lithuanian origin. Along with Latvian (Lettish) and the now extinct Old Prussian it belongs to the Baltic branch of the Indo-European family of languages. The Baltic languages are noted for their extremely conservative and philologically interesting linguistic forms. Thus a knowledge of Lithuanian is almost a "must" for any linguist who works in comparative Indo-European linguistics. The need for such a book is felt both among language scholars who wish to familiarize themselves with Lithuanian and among those Americans of Lithuanian descent who wish to know something of the language of their ancestors. Up to now, unfortunately, the number of grammars of Lithuanian available has been very small indeed. There are not more than two or three available in English, and these are obsolete.

This grammar is designed not for young children, but rather for those who have already reached a certain stage of maturity. The method is traditional, but there are some conversations and pattern drills in the text and it would be possible to use the book with an audio-lingual approach.

The book has 40 lessons in its main part. A typical lesson has a reading selection, vocabulary list, grammar, exercises and a topical, usually connected conversation of 10 utterances. No effort was made to make the lessons even in length and difficulty. By reason of the grammatical topic, some lessons are very long (e.g. Lesson 24, where *all* cardinal numerals are discussed with examples), while others are rather short. With this kind of arrangement, the instructor will have all kinds of teaching possibilities: he can stress either the aural-oral approach, or the reading-grammar-translation method.

Each fifth lesson (i.e. Lessons 5, 10, 15, 20, 25, 30, 35, 40) is a "Review Lesson". These lessons are "review" lessons only in the sense that they do not introduce any new grammatical material which the student should learn. But they vary very much in the supplementary reading items, lists, charts, graphs, etc. Almost every one of these review lessons has some drill patterns (either *combination drill* or *variation drill* types mostly) which partly review some main grammatical points covered in the previous four lessons. If there is a need to supplement these drills, any teacher can devise a great number of them, using the basic patterns and vocabulary given. The review lessons may be omitted, if the student wishes only to get acquainted with the grammatical structure of Lithuanian.

After the 40 main lessons, there is the grammatical appendix where the total grammar of Lithuanian is given. It is presented in the "classical" pattern: the nouns, adjectives, verbs, etc. At the end there is a chapter on verbal prefixes and a chapter on verbal aspects.

Then follows a very short chapter of extra reading selections: a folk tale, a few short selections on Lithuanian history, an editorial from a Lithuanian newspaper, a few folk songs and poems. All these selections are heavily annotated, and their vocabulary is included in the Lithuanian-English vocabulary.

The next part comprises the Lithuanian-English vocabulary which includes all the words used in the lessons and in the readings. We have provided a rather large vocabulary, since, for some time at least, this grammar will have to be a primer, a review grammar, a little reader and . . . a dictionary.

The English-Lithuanian vocabulary contains only those words which are needed for the translations from English into Lithuanian.

The best way to get a good pronunciation is to try to imitate the pronunciation of a native Lithuanian. The descriptions of the sounds given in the text are only an approximation and nothing can replace the careful guidance of a trained native Lithuanian. It is suggested that the student make every effort to find someone to help him. Eventually it is hoped that tapes to accompany this textbook will be available for sale or hire.

In learning to converse in Lithuanian the student should try to memorize the conversations rather than the grammatical rules. After memorizing the conversations he may then learn exactly why each word is put in the form in which he finds it. He may then substitute other words having similar meanings. In doing the exercises the student should follow as closely as possible the examples given in the reading and the grammatical explanations. Initiative and originality have no place for the beginner in a foreign language. Parrot-like imitation is preferable to incorrect original formulations.

In the future, we plan to prepare a key to all the exercises in this book, which will be available for teachers and bona-fide self-teachers of Lithuanian. As mentioned above, tapes will also be made for the entire book, i.e., for the pronunciation exercises of the introductory lesson, and for most of the basic reading selections, conversations, etc.

The authors wish to express their grateful thanks to Rt. Rev. Msgr. J. A. Karalius, for his great moral and financial help in making the publication of this book a reality. We are also indebted to Mr. William Babcock for making the map on the inside covers and also doing the drawings for the Introductory Lessons, to Mr. Paulius Jurkus for doing drawings for lessons 20, 25 and 35, and to Mr. V. Augustinas for the photographs. Finally, the authors express their thanks to the University of Rochester which allocated funds for helping with the typing of the original manuscript.

Leonardas Dambriūnas
Formerly Lecturer in Lithuanian
at the University of Kaunas

Antanas Klimas
Associate Professor of German
University of Rochester

William R. Schmalstieg
Associate Professor of
Slavic Languages
The Pennsylvania State University

CONTENTS

Introductory Lesson

I. THE ALPHABET

Lithuanian uses the Latin alphabet with some additions and modifications. There are 32 letters in the Lithuanian alphabet. This includes most of the letters of the Latin alphabet as used in English with the exception of *w*, *x* and *q*, which we do find, however, in foreign names such as *Quito*, *Wallace*, etc.

Lithuanian letters which differ from English are: ą, ę, ė, į, ų, ū, č, š, ž. The sounds which these letters represent are discussed in section III.

In the sequence of the Lithuanian letters there are some differences from the arrangement in English:

a) the *y* is considered as a type of *i* and it goes right after *į* so that the three *i*'s of Lithuanian occur in the following order: i, į, y.

b) the four vowel groups with diacritic signs are all treated as one letter, i.e. *a* and *ą* go together as do *e*, *ę* and *ė*; *i*, *į* and *y* go together as do *u*, *ų* and *ū*. Of course, we will do the same in this book.

c) if the *q* is ever used, it is placed (as, for example, in a dictionary of proper names) right after the *p*, the *w* right after the *v* and the *x* would be the last letter in the alphabet.

In print the Lithuanian alphabet appears almost the same as the English alphabet, except for the above-mentioned differences. In the written form there are other differences. (See Table 1)

1

Table 1: Standard Lithuanian Letters:

A a *Aa*	Ą ą *Ąą*	B b *Bb*
C c *Cc*	Č č *Čč*	D d *Dd*
E e *Ee*	Ę ę *Ęę*	Ė ė *Ėė*
F f *Ff*	G g *Gg*	H h *Hh*
I i *Ii*	Į į *Įį*	Y y *Yy*
J j *Jj*	K k *Kk*	L l *Ll*
M m *Mm*	N n *Nn*	O o *Oo*
P p *Pp*	R r *Rr*	S s *Ss*
Š š *Šš*	T t *Tt*	U u *Uu*
Ų ų *Ųų*	Ū ū *Ūū*	V v *Vv*
Z z *Zz*	Ž ž *Žž*	

Block (printed) letters are practically never used in regular Lithuanian writing, and all letters in individual words are usually connected.

EXERCISE:

A. Write out the Lithuanian alphabet. Practice especially the following letters: A a; Ą ą; Č č; Ę ę; Ū ū; Ž ž.

B. Write out the basic reading selection of Lesson 5.

II. STRESS AND INTONATION

The stressed syllable is that syllable of a word which receives special emphasis and the intonation is the manner of pronouncing that syllable. Since there are three types of pronunciation of a single syllable there are therefore three separate signs with which Lithuanians denote these intonations. (In the United States the term *pitch-stress* is sometimes used to denote what European scholars call intonation, but we will use the term *intonation*, since this is traditional in Baltic scholarship.) The stress can fall on almost any syllable of a word and sometimes one form of a word may carry the stress on a certain syllable whereas another form of the same word will carry the stress on another syllable. In this book almost all Lithuanian words are marked with the intonation, although in regular Lithuanian texts these are not used.

The intonation marks are as follows:

` — this is called the grave stress (*kairìnis kir̃tis*) or the short intonation (*trumpìnė priēgaidė*). A vowel marked with this stress is pronounced with more force or amplitude, but it is not lengthened. Even when stressed a Lithuanian short vowel remains short. Examples: *mamà*, *nè* 'no', *ìki* 'until', *tù* 'you (familiar form)', *pùpos* 'beans'.

´ — this is the acute or falling intonation (*tvirtaprādė priēgaidė*), known in German as the *Stosston*. This occurs with long vowels or diphthongs. A long vowel with this sign is always stressed more heavily on the first part than on the second part. In the case of a diphthong the first part of the diphthong receives a heavier stress and is held longer than the second part of the diphthong.
Examples with vowels: *ą́žuolas* 'oak', *sprę́sti* 'to decide', *dė́ti* 'to put', *į́rašas* 'inscription', *ýpač* 'especially', *óras* 'air', *bū́ti* 'to be'.
Examples with diphthongs: *káimas* 'village', *áuksas* 'gold', *méilė* 'love', *píenas* 'milk', *úostas* 'harbor'.

~ — this is the circumflex intonation (*tvirtagālė priēgaidė*), known in German as the *Schleifton*. A long vowel with this sign is always stressed more heavily on the second part than on the first part. In the case of a diphthong the second part of the diphthong receives a heavier stress and is held longer than the first part.
Examples with vowels: *tą̃* (acc. sing.) 'that', *ēglė* 'spruce', *manę̃s* (gen. sing.) 'of me', *katė̃* 'cat', *į̃prastas* 'usual, accustomed', *jõs* (nom. plur. fem.) 'they', *jų̃* (gen. plur.) 'of them'.

III. THE SOUNDS
and Their Representations by Letters

A. VOWELS

All vowels in Lithuanian are distinguished by length, i.e. there are short and long vowels. Contrary to the English situation where most vowels are diphthongized, or have some kind of off-glide, Lithuanian vowels are never diphthongized, and they are somewhat more tense than those of English.

Aa. Short Vowels

a — this letter may denote a short, more or less tense, un-rounded, open central vowel. It may be stressed or unstressed, but even when stressed it will be shorter than the normal stressed vowel of English. Under certain circumstances (namely in open syllables, although even here there are exceptions) this letter is used to denote a long vowel; if this is the case such a long vowel may have only the circumflex accent and will be pronounced exactly like *ą̃*, cf. section Ab. on long vowels.

Examples as a short vowel: *kadà* 'when', *àš* 'I', *Amèrika* 'America', *màno* 'my'.

Examples as a long vowel: *nãmas* 'house', *gãlas* 'end'.

e — this letter may denote a short stressed or unstressed vowel, not very tense, but rather close (not as close, however, as *ė*, see below). This sound is similar to the *e* in English *bet* or *nest*. Under certain circumstances (namely in open syllables, although even here there are exceptions) this letter is used to denote a long vowel; if this is the case such a long vowel may have only the circumflex accent and will be pronounced exactly like *ę̃*, cf. section Ab. on long vowels.

Examples as a short vowel: *kepì* 'you bake', *nešì* 'you carry', *nè* 'no', *namè* 'in the house'.

Examples as a long vowel: *kẽlias* 'road', *lẽdas* 'ice'.

i — this letter denotes a short, close, forward unrounded vowel (but not as close as the *y*, see below), somewhat more close than the *i* of English *sit*. It can be either stressed or unstressed.

Examples: *tikraĩ* 'for sure, surely', *tikì* 'you believe', *tìki* 'he believes', *tìk* 'only'.

4

o — this letter denotes a vowel which is somewhat closer and more rounded than the English *o* in *boat*, and without the English off-glide at the end. It can be stressed or unstressed. For its use to denote a long vowel see Ab below.
Examples: *poètika* 'poetics', *polìtika* 'politics; policy', *òpera* 'opera', *tòrtas* 'layer cake', *chòras* 'choir, chorus'.

u — this letter denotes a more or less tense, close *u* sound similar to the English *u* in *put*. It can be stressed or unstressed.
Examples: *pupà* 'bean', *turì* 'you have', *turìstas* 'tourist', *tù* 'you (familiar)' *sù* 'with', *mùdu* 'we two'.

Ab. Long Vowels

All long vowels and diphthongs may be either stressed or unstressed. If stressed they may have either the circumflex or the acute intonation.

ą — this letter denotes a long, open, central vowel somewhat similar to the *a* in English *father*.
Examples: *grąžìnti* 'to return', (acc. sing.) *výrą* 'man', (acc. sing.) *tą̃* 'that', *ą́žuolas* 'oak'.

On the right hand you see Fig. 1 which illustrates approximately the production of the Lithuanian *ą̃* (or *ā̃*).

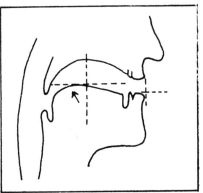

Fig. 1: A

ę — this letter denotes a rather open vowel, somewhat like the *a* in English *bad,* but more open and without the 'y' off-glide. It is produced with the mouth open and the tongue lax in a low frontal position. The lips are also lax, but pulled down slightly by the falling jaw, cf. Fig. 2.
Examples: *pėlę* (acc. sing.) 'mouse', *tęsinỹs* 'continuation', *sprę́sti* 'to decide', *kę̃sti* 'to suffer'.

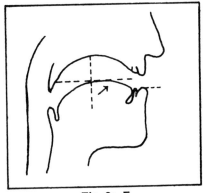

Fig. 2: E

5

ė — this letter denotes a vowel which differs considerably from the *ę*. *ė* is always long, rather close and forward and unrounded. It is rather like the *a* in English *made*, but without the 'y' off-glide. It is produced with the tongue tensely stretched in a mid-frontal position, a little lower than in the production of *i*. The tip of the tongue is behind the upper teeth. The muscles of the tongue

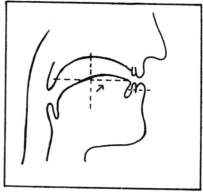

Fig. 3; ė

and of the jaw which is slightly lowered are tense. The lips are lax (See Fig. 3)

Examples: *dėdė* 'uncle', *dėti* 'to put', *raĩdė* 'letter (of the alphabet)', *mėgti* 'to like'.

y (also written *į*) — These two letters denote the same vowel sound which is a long, close, forward unrounded vowel similar to the *ee* in English *keel*, but without the characteristic English off-glide. This *y* (*į*) is produced with the tongue arched high in the front of the mouth towards the frontal part of the palate. The lips are lax and almost closed. (See Fig. 4) Examples: *yrà* 'is', *įvadas* 'intro-

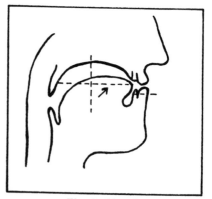

Fig. 4: Y or Į

duction', *įstrižas* 'diagonal', *tylà* 'silence', *ýrė* 'he rowed'.

6

o — this letter denotes a fairly close back rounded vowel; it is closer and more rounded than the English *o* in *boat*, but without the English off-glide at the end. It is somewhat similar to the *oo* in English *door*, but without the characteristic lowering before the *r*. It is produced with the tongue stretched in a mid-rear position. The lips are rounded and protruded, less than in the Lithu-

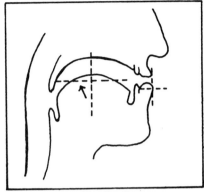

Fig. 5: O

anian *ū*, but more than in the *o* in English *core*. (See Fig. 5)

Examples: *óras* 'air, weather', *obelìs* 'apple-tree', *põnas* 'master, Mr.', *namõ* 'home' homeward', *nórs* 'although'.

ū (also written as *ų*) — these letters denote a close back rounded vowel. The *u* of English *truth* or orthographic *oo* in English *school*, *pool* represent a sound very similar to that of Lithuanian *ū*. The English vowel, however, is somewhat further back than the Lithuanian long *ū* (*ų*). It is produced with the tongue arched high in the back of the mouth and the tip of the tongue withdrawn in

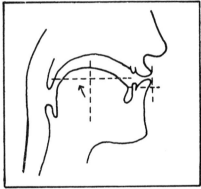

Fig. 6: U

back of the lower teeth. The lips are very protruded and rounded. (See Fig. 6)

Examples: *sūnùs* 'son', *jūsų* 'your, yours', *baltūjų* (gen. plur.) 'of the white (ones), *ūpas* 'mood', *pūsti* 'to blow', *lūpa* 'lip', *skųsti* 'to complain'.

Ac.

i used to indicate the palatalization of consonants (*ia, ią, io, iu, iū, ių*).

In syllables where the *i* stands before *a, ą, o, u, ū, ų*, this *i* is not pronounced at all; it merely denotes that the preceding consonant is palatalized, or soft, i.e. the middle of the tongue is raised towards the top of the mouth. Noteworthy in this connection is the fact that orthographic *ia, ią, iai, iau* etc. are merely ways of writing *e, ę, ei, eu* after soft consonants. Thus *kẽlias* 'road' is pronounced as though it were written **kẽles; kiaũlė* is pronounced as though it were written **keũlė*. In words like *brólio* 'brother's' the *i* is not pronounced at all, but merely shows that the preceding *l* is palatalized. In *liũtas* 'lion' the same thing is true. For further details on the palatalization of consonants see section B *Consonants*.

NB. In some foreign words which have been taken into Lithuanian recently the above does not hold true. In most of these words if the *i* occurs after a consonant and before a vowel it is pronounced as a short *i*: Thus *biològija* is syllabified *bi-o-lò-gi-ja, biològus* as *bi-o-lò-gas, sociològas* as *so-ci-o-lò-gas*, etc.

Ad. Diphthongs

The so-called 'pure diphthongs' consist of two vowels and are the following: *ai, au, ei, ie, ui, uo*. Each of these can be stressed or unstressed. As with the long vowels, if stressed they can have either the circumflex intonation (~) on the second vowel, or the acute intonation (′) on the first vowel. A diphthong with the acute intonation will have a heavier stress on the initial element and the initial element will be held longer than the second element. Just the reverse is true for a diphthong with the circumflex intonation.

ai — as *ái* it is somewhat similar to the *ai* of English *aisle*; *aĩ* is somewhat similar to the English *a* in *able*; in pronouncing it make the *a* very short and try to hold the *i* longer. Still the impression is that the *aĩ* is much shorter than *ái* and that even the *i* is shorter in *aĩ* than in *ái*. If *ai* is unstressed then it is pronounced more like a circumflex *aĩ* than an acute *ái*. Thus in *vaikaĩ* 'children' the first *ai* is pronounced much like the second *ai*, but with less amplitude.

Examples: *ái* 'ouch', *káimas* 'village', *áiškinti* 'to explain', *aĩ* 'oh', *laĩkas* 'time', *vaĩkas* 'child', *raidà* 'development', *gaivìnti* 'to revive'.

au — is somewhat similar to the *au* in American pronunciations of *Faust* or the *ou* of American-English *out*; with the acute stress, i.e. *áu* the initial element is longer than in such English words as *out*, *Faust*; *aū*, on the other hand, is somewhat similar to Canadian English *out*. *aū* appears to be shorter than *áu*. Unstressed *au* sounds like *aū* rather than *áu*, but the unstressed syllable has less amplitude than the stressed.

Examples: *áugti* 'to grow', *sáulė* 'sun', *láukti* 'to wait', *plaūkti* 'to swim', *šaūkti* 'to call', *raudónas* 'red', *laukè* (loc. sing.) 'outside'.

ei — as *éi* there is no such diphthong in English. It is somewhat similar to the North German *ei* in *beide*. It can be produced by saying the *a* in English *ban* and then adding a very quick 'y' off-glide at the end of the *a*. *eī* is quite similar to the *ei* in *weight*. An unstressed *ei* is more like *eī* (although, of course, with less amplitude) than *éi*.

Examples: *méilė* 'love', *léisti* 'to let', *véidas* 'face' *peīlis* 'knife', *eīti* 'to go', *keīsti* 'to change'.

ie — a kind of diphthong (or it may even be called a triphthong) which, beginning with *i* gradually becomes more open, i.e. tends to become *e*. There is no sharp break between the *i* and the *e* and the end of the diphthong is very open. When this diphthong occurs in initial position, there is a tendency in modern Lithuanian to pronounce it as though there were a *j* in front of it: *ieškóti* 'to hunt for' is pronounced as *jieškóti*, *ietis* 'spear' as *jietis* etc. Some Lithuanians write these words as *jieškóti*, *jietis*, etc.

Examples: *dienà* 'day', *riekė̃* 'slice', *píenas* 'milk', *píeva* 'meadow', *kíek* 'how much', *piẽtūs* 'South; dinner', *tiẽkti* 'to deliver', *piẽšti* 'to draw'.

ui — as *uī* there is nothing like this diphthong in English. As *ùi* (which, however, is relatively rare) it sounds something like a very rapidly pronounced *phooey* or *Louie*.

Examples: *puikùs* 'excellent', *buitìs* 'being', *puĩkiai* 'excellently', *muĩlas* 'soap', *muĩtas* 'custom, toll', *ùitena* 'man whom everybody dislikes', *mùistyti* 'to shake one's head'. In some foreign borrowings when the *i* is stressed the *u* and *i* are pronounced separately, i.e. they form the nuclei of two separate syllables: *jezuìtas* 'Jesuit' is syllabified as follows: *jė-zu-ì-tas*.

uo — this is a kind of diphthong (or triphthong) which, beginning with an *u*, gradually becomes more open and less rounded. There is no sharp break between the *u* and the *o* and the end of the diphthong is really a schwa vowel (usually written ə), i.e. one similar to the vowel of the second syllable in the English

9

words *above, Plymouth*, etc. This diphthong can perhaps be compared to the *uo* of Italian *buono*, etc.

Examples: *uogáuti* 'to pick berries', *uodegà* 'tail', *úoga* 'berry', *úostas* 'harbor', *sesuõ* 'sister', *ruduõ* 'autumn'.

Ae. Mixed Diphthongs

Diphthongs in which the possible initial elements *a, e, i* or *u* are followed by *l, m, n* or *r* are known as mixed diphthongs. The second element may be called a sonorant, continuant or semi-vowel.

In the mixed diphthongs as in the pure diphthongs either the first or the second element may be stressed. If the second element is stressed the ˜ will be written over the *l, m, n* or *r*. If the first element is stressed the ′ is written over the letters *a* and *e*, but is used over the letters *u* and *i*. If the second element is stressed it is held longer than the first element. If the first element is stressed it is pronounced with more amplitude and held longer than the second element. Thus, for example, in *ál* the *a* is louder and held longer than the *l*; in *aĺ* on the other hand the *l* is held longer than the *a*.

Examples: *válgyti* 'to eat', *kám* 'to whom', *ántis* 'duck', *kártis* 'pole'; *kaĺtas* 'guilty', *kam̃pas* 'corner', *añtis* 'bosom', *kar̃tis* 'bitterness'; *délnas* 'palm (of the hand)', *pémpė* 'peewit, lapwing', *sénti* 'to grow old', *pérduoti* 'to hand over'; *peĺnas* 'profit', *tem̃pia* 'he pulls', *studeñtas* 'student', *per̃* 'through'; *tìltas* 'bridge', *tìmptelėti* 'to pull', *tìnti* 'to swell', *tìrti* 'to investigate'; *tiĺpti* 'to fit into', *im̃ti* 'to take', *tiñkamas* 'fitting', *ir̃* 'and'; *pùlsas* 'pulse', *kùmštis* 'fist', *ùncija* 'ounce', *ùrna* 'urn'; *puĺkas* 'regiment', *trum̃pas* 'short', *tuñka* 'he is getting fat', *tur̃kas* 'Turk'.

B. CONSONANTS

One of the basic differences between English and Lithuanian consonants is that the unvoiced stops of Lithuanian (*p, t, k*) are not aspirated (i.e. there is no puff of breath after them) as in English in initial position.

Another important difference is that all Lithuanian consonants (except the *j* which is sometimes called a semi-vowel) exist in two varieties, palatalized (or soft) and unpalatalized (or hard). In the articulation of palatalized consonants the middle of the tongue is raised towards the top of the mouth. To the American ear the effect is that of a y-sound following the consonant, but this is not the case as far as the articulation is concerned. The y-sound must be made simultaneously with the consonant.

Consonants are always palatalized before the front vowels (*i, į, y, e, ę* and *ė*), also before the diphthong *ie*. Before the vowel letters *a, ą, o, u, ų* and *ū*, the *i* is used to denote palatalization of the preceding consonants. (See also Ac. of this Introductory Lesson).

Phonetically the palatalization of consonants before back vowels is stronger than that before front vowels. Thus in the word *niùrna* 'grumbler' the palatalization of the initial *n* is much more striking than the palatalization of the initial *n* in the word *ne* 'no, not'.

Ba. Voiced Stops b, d, g

b — strongly voiced unaspirated *b*; similar to the English *b*.

Unpalatalized:
bùtas 'apartment'
dárbas 'work'
labaĩ 'very'

Palatalized:
bèt 'but'
bìtė 'bee'
gabì 'gifted' (fem.)

d — this is a strongly voiced unaspirated *d*; the *d* is a true dental, i.e. pronounced with the tongue against the back of the upper teeth (not like the alveolar *d* in English). The best thing to remember about the articulation of the Lithuanian *d* is that the tip of the tongue touches the upper teeth, but not the gum as is the case with the English *d*.

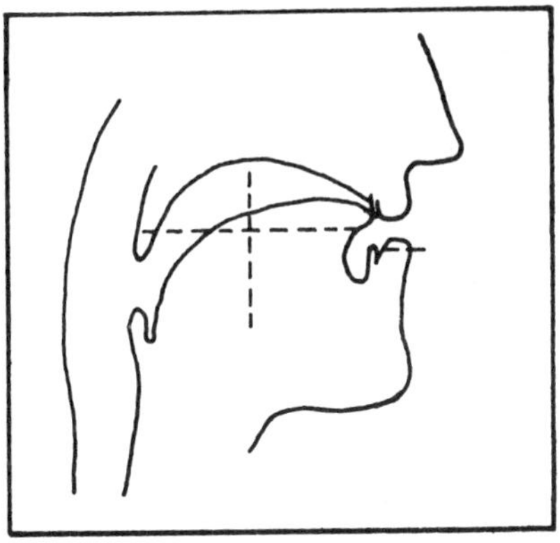

Fig. 7: D and T

Unpalatalized:
dantìs 'tooth'
dùrys 'door'
duktė̃ 'daughter'

Palatalized:
dìdelis 'large'
dègti 'to burn'
dė́mė̆ 'spot'

11

g — unaspirated voiced velar stop; English g as in *good* sounds like the unpalatalized Lithuanian g; English g as in *geese* sounds like Lithuanian palatalized g.

Unpalatalized:	Palatalized:
ganà 'enough'	*gì* (emphatic particle)
gar̃das 'pen, enclosure'	*gývas* 'alive'
gudrùs 'clever'	*gegùtė* 'cuckoo'

Bb. Voiceless Stops: p, t, k

p — voiceless, unaspirated p; similar to the English p, but without aspiration.

Unpalatalized:	Palatalized:
pãdas 'sole'	*per̃* 'through'
põ 'under'	*pirtìs* 'bath house'
púodas 'pot'	*pýpkė* 'pipe'

t — voiceless, unaspirated, dental t; similar in place of articulation to the (Lithuanian) d. It is rather different from the English t both in place of articulation and in that it is not aspirated.

Unpalatalized:	Palatalized:
tàs 'that' (masc.)	*teñ* 'there'
tà 'that' (fem.)	*tìk* 'only'
tõ 'of that' (masc.)	*tikraĩ* 'for sure, surely'

k — unaspirated voiceless velar stop; similar to the k-sound of English *cart*, but without aspiration. Palatalized k sounds like the k of English *keel*.

Unpalatalized:	Palatalized:
kàs 'who; what'	*kìtas* 'other; putty'
kadà 'when'	*keturì* 'four' (masc.)
tvarkà 'order'	*kiáušas* 'skull'

Bc. Labio-dental Fricatives: v and f

v — voiced labio-dental fricative like English v.

Unpalatalized:	Palatalized:
vaĩkas 'child'	*ver̃kti* 'to weep'
vóras 'spider'	*výras* 'man'
võs 'just; hardly'	*vìsas* 'whole'

ƒ — voiceless labio-dental fricative similar to the English *ƒ*.

Unpalatalized:	Palatalized:
fãbrikas 'factory'	*filològas* 'philologist'
fùtbolas 'soccer'	*filosòfas* 'philosopher'
fùnkcija 'function'	*fìzika* 'physics'

Bd. The Continuants: l, m, n, r

l — a lateral sound. The tongue tip touches the upper teeth and the central part of the tongue is lowered towards the bottom of the mouth in the unpalatalized variety. The *l* in English *elk* sounds like the unpalatalized Lithuanian *l*. English *l* as in *leaf* sounds somewhat like the Lithuanian palatalized *l*, although the palatalized Lithuanian *l* is a little more palatalized, or softer, somewhat like *l* in High German or in French.

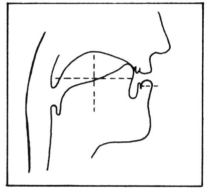

Fig. 8: Unpalatalized (hard) L

As we have already briefly mentioned above, in articulating the hard variety, the tip of the tongue touches the upper teeth and the central part of the tongue is lowered towards the bottom of the mouth. (See Fig. 8)

The palatalized (soft) *l* is produced by raising the rear part of the tongue to the rear part of the hard palate, by pressing the upper-front part of the tongue against the upper teeth, and allowing the breath stream through the sides of the blades of the tongue. (See Fig. 9)

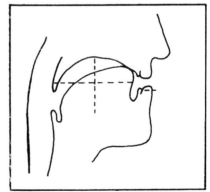

Fig. 9: Palatalized (soft) L

13

m — this is a voiced bilabial continuant like the English *m*.

Unpalatalized:
mamà 'mother; mom'
damà 'lady'
móteris 'woman'

Palatalized:
mẽs 'we'
mès 'he will throw'
miřti 'to die'

n — this is a voiced dental continuant, articulated in the same position as *d* and *t*. Before velar consonants the nasal is velar as in the English words *pink, bank,* etc., e.g. *brangùs* 'dear', *penkì* 'five', etc.

Unpalatalized:
nãmas 'house'
naũjas 'new'
nósis 'nose'

Palatalized:
nè 'no; not'
nès 'because'
septynì 'seven'

r — this is a tongue trilled *r*. As with the Italian *r* the tongue vibrates against the alveolar ridge. The palatalized *r* is difficult to pronounce for native Americans and great care must be taken to keep the tongue high at the same time that it vibrates against the alveolar ridge. The Lithuanian *r* is a clear voiced trilling without any admixture of guttural sounds. (See Fig. 10)

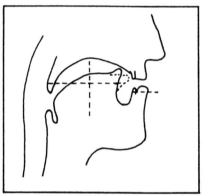
Fig. 10: R

Unpalatalized:
rãtas 'wheel'
ràsti 'to find'
rõgės 'sleigh'

Palatalized:
rẽtas 'rare'
rìsti 'to roll'
riešutas 'nut'

Be. The Sibilants : s, š, z, ž

s — this is a voiceless hissing alveolar spirant like the English *s*. English *s* before front vowels sounds palatalized to the Lithuanian ear. Thus, for example, *see* and *sit* seem to the Lithuanian to contain palatalized *s*.

Unpalatalized:
saũsas 'dry'
sakýti 'to say'
vìsas 'whole'

Palatalized:
siaũsti 'to rage'
sèkti 'to follow'
visì 'all'

14

š — this is a voiceless hushing spirant similar to the *sh* in English. The unpalatalized *š* is more retracted than the English *sh* is usually, but sounds somewhat like the *sh* in English *shirk* or the *sch* of German *schon*. The palatalized *š* sounds somewhat like the *sh* in English *sheep*, but the palatalization or 'y' sound is stronger in Lithuanian.

Unpalatalized:	Palatalized:
šáuti 'to shoot'	*šiáudas* 'straw'
šalìs 'country'	*šìs* 'this'
šókti 'to dance'	*šióks* 'such'

z — this is the voiced counterpart of *s* and is similar to the English *z* in *zoo* (unpalatalized) and *zeal* (palatalized).

Unpalatalized:	Palatalized:
Zarasaĩ (name of city)	*zenìtas* 'zenith'
zaũnyti 'to babble'	*zebrà* 'zebra'
zuĩkis 'hare'	*zigzãgas* 'zigzag'

ž — this is the voiced counterpart of *š*. In Lithuanian it occurs frequently in initial position, whereas in English only exceptionally in initial position, cf. Eng. *genre*, although it occurs in medial position or final, cf. Eng. *measure, rouge*, etc.

Unpalatalized:	Palatalized:
žalà 'damage'	*žìlas* 'gray'
žaltỹs 'adder'	*žélti* 'to grow (of beard, grass)'
žolė̃ 'grass'	*žioplỹs* 'dopey, joker'

Bf. Affricates: c and č

c — this is actually a combination of *t* plus *s*. It is similar to the *ts* of Eng. *pants*, but in Lithuanian it also appears at the beginning of a word.

Unpalatalized:	Palatalized:
cùkrus 'sugar'	*cìklas* 'cycle'
cukrainė 'confectionary'	*cỹpti* 'to squeal'
cukrúoti 'to sugar'	*civilizãcija* 'civilization'

NB. The voiced counterpart of *c* is *dz*, but it is a very rare combination. Unpalatalized: *dzū̃kas* 'speaker of an East Lithuanian dialect'. Palatalized: *dzim̃binti* 'to walk with one's head down', *dzinguliùkas* 'a type of bell'.

č — this is a combination of *t* plus *š*. It is somewhat like the *ch* of English *church*.

Unpalatalized:
čáižyti 'to whip'
čáižymas 'whipping'
čardāšas 'czardas'

Palatalized:
čià 'here'
čèkas 'Czech'
čiřkšti 'to crackle'

NB. The voiced counterpart of *č* is *dž*. The unpalatalized form of *dž* is very rare and even native Lithuanians tend to pronounce such words as *džāzas* with a palatalized *dž* so that it sounds like *džiãzas* 'jazz'. Palatalized *dž*, however, occurs quite frequently: *džiaũgtis* 'to be happy', *džiáuti* 'to hang up for drying', *džiovà* 'tuberculosis', etc.

Bg. The Fricatives h and ch

h — an aspirated sound; pronounced like English *h*, but only found in words of foreign origin. Unpalatalized: *harmònija* 'harmony', *homogèniškas* 'homogeneous'. Palatalized: *heròjus* 'hero', *hìmnas* 'national anthem', etc.

ch — unvoiced velar spirant. Unpalatalized *ch* is pronounced like the *ch* in German *Macht*, but the sound is only found in words of foreign origin.

Unpalatalized:
chárta 'charter'
chãosas 'chaos'
chòras 'choir'

The *ch* of German *ich* sounds like the palatalized Lithuanian *ch*:
chèmija 'chemistry'
chèmikas 'chemist'
chirùrgas 'surgeon'

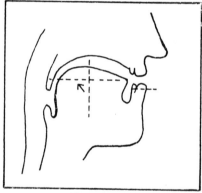
Fig. 11: CH

Bh. The j

j — this is a voiced palatal sound similar to the *y* in English *yes*, but the tongue is raised higher for the Lithuanian *j* and the impression for the English speaker is that of more emphasis or friction of the air as it is exhaled. It is the only consonant in

16

Lithuanian which occurs only in the palatalized variety: *jáunas* 'young', *jãvas* 'grain', *jáutis* 'ox', *jóti* 'to ride horseback'. In words borrowed from foreign languages the *j* is pronounced following the consonant: *barjèras* 'barrier', *objèktas* 'object', *adjùnktas* 'adjunct professor', etc.

The sequence of letters *bi* in Lithuanian denotes a palatalized *b* plus a *j* when it occurs before *au, o, u*. (The same holds true for the sequence of *pi* which denotes a palatalized *p* plus a *j* when it occurs before *au, o, u*). Thus in this case *i* is used instead of *j*. In the following examples the *b* and *p* are palatalized and followed by *j*: *biaurùs* 'ugly', *piáuti* 'to cut', *spiáuti* 'to spit'. Attempts have been made to institute the spellings *pj, bj* (and some Lithuanians use them); thus we sometimes find *bjaurùs* 'ugly', *pjáuti* 'to cut', *spjáuti* 'to spit', but these spellings have not been universally adopted.

Bi. Assimilation of Consonants

There is one basic rule for the consonant clusters of Lithuanian: *the second or last consonant in a sequence determines the character of the preceding one as regards palatalization, the lack thereof or voicing and the lack thereof, etc.*

If one consonant of a cluster is palatalized then the immediately preceding consonant will also be palatalized, e.g. in *nèščiau* 'I would carry' both the *č* and the preceding *š* are palatalized (soft).

In a consonant cluster a voiced consonant will cause an immediately preceding consonant to be voiced also, e.g. in *nèšdavau* 'I used to carry' the orthographic *š* is pronounced like *ž* (its voiced counterpart). On the other hand in *vèžti* 'to transport' the *ž* is pronounced like *š* (which is unvoiced) because of the following *t*. In *bėgti* 'to run' the *g* is pronounced like *k*, the unvoiced counterpart of *g*, because the *t* is, of course, unvoiced.

Before *č* the *s* is pronounced as *š*, e.g. in *pėsčias* 'on foot, pedestrian' the orthographic *s* is pronounced *š*. Likewise *z* is pronounced like *ž* when it occurs before *dž*, e.g. the gen. plur. of *vabzdỹs* 'insect' is *vabzdžių*, but it is pronounced *vabždžių*.

All final consonants are unvoiced (with the exception of *l, m, n, r*). Thus in final position *daũg* 'much, many' is pronounced *daũk*; *ùž* 'behind' is pronounced *ùš*, etc. *In final position all consonants are pronounced without palatalization*, i.e. they are hard, e.g. *vėl* 'again', *eik* 'come', *bėk* 'run', *dėl* 'for', etc.

C. SYLLABIFICATION

The number of syllables in a word is the same as the number of vocalic elements. By vocalic element we mean a single vowel or diphthong. Here it must be remembered that diphthongs in Lithuanian may have *m, n, l,* or *r* as the final element. Therefore, a word like *šim̃-tas* 'hundred' has two vocalic elements or syllables, *-im̃-* and *-a-*; *kasà* 'braid' has the two vocalic elements *-a-* and *-à-*; *rã-ša-las* 'ink' has three vocalic elements, viz. the three *-a-*'s; *lai-mìn-gas* 'lucky, fortunate' has three vocalic elements, *-ai-, -in-* and *-a-*. In the previous examples the hyphen marks the syllable division and it can be seen that in general a consonant between two vocalic elements is pronounced with the following vocalic element. If there is a group of two consonants between syllables, generally the first syllable is closed by the first consonant of the group and the second syllable begins with the second consonant of the group, e.g. *gañd-ras* 'stork', *pir̃š-tas* 'finger', *res-pùb-li-ka* 'republic'. However, the syllable division is found at the boundary of prefixes, certain suffixes and the component elements of compounds, e.g. *at-eĩ-ti* (*at* 'to', *eĩti* 'to come, to go'), *iš-im-tìs* 'exception' (*iš* 'out', *imtìs* 'that which is taken'), *pìkt-žolė* 'weed' (*pikt-* 'bad' *žolė* 'grass'). In writing and typing one follows the rules of syllable division when hyphenating words and transferring parts of words to another line.

TABLE OF VOWELS

	Front Vowels		Back Vowels	
High (close) vowels	y, į	i	u	ū, ų
Mid vowels	ė		o	o
Low-mid vowels	ę	e		
Low (open) vowels			a	ą
	Long	Short*	Short*	Long

* e and a are lengthened in most cases in open syllables: **gālas** 'end', **mēdis** 'tree' (But: **màno** 'my', etc.).

18

TABLE OF CONSONANTS

		labial	dental	retracted alveo-palatal	velar	glottal
stops	voiceless	p	t		k	
	voiced	b	d		g	
continuants	voiceless	f	s	š	ch	h
	voiced	v	z	ž		
	nasal	m	n			
affricates	voiced		dz	dž		
	voiceless		c	č		

apical trill: r
lateral: l
palatal spirant: j

IV. SOME COMMON EXPRESSIONS

GREETINGS.

1. *Lãbas rýtas!*	Good morning.
2. *Labà dienà!*	Good day.
3. *Lãbas vãkaras!*	Good evening.
4. *Lãbas!*	Hello! Hi!
5. *Sudiẽ(u).*	Goodbye.
6. *Iki pasimãtymo.*	So long.
7. *Ačiū.*	Thank you.
8. *Ačiū labaĩ.*	Thank you very much.
9. *Prašaũ.*	You're welcome.
10. *Labą̃nakt!*	Good night.

CLASSROOM EXPRESSIONS.

1. *Prašaũ skaitýti.*	Please read.
2. *Skaitýkite.*	Read(!)
3. *Prašaũ išveřsti.*	Please translate.

4. *Prašaũ rašýti.*	Please write.
5. *Prašaũ dėmesio!*	Attention, please.
6. *Prašaũ pakartóti.*	Repeat, please.
7. *Dár kar̃tą.*	Once more.
8. *Visì kartù.*	All together (please).
9. *Taĩ vìskas.*	That's all.
10. *Kàs nóri skaitýti?*	Who wants to read?

GETTING ACQUAINTED.

1. *Prašaũ susipažìnti.*	Please get acquainted.
2. *Čià põnas Smith (or Smitas)*	This is Mr. Smith.
3. *Aš esù Valỹs, Antãnas Valỹs.*	I am (Mr.) Valys, Anthony Valys.
4. *Ar̃ jũs ẽsate põnas Hood?*	Are you Mr. Hood?
5. *Taĩp, aš esù Gary Hood.*	Yes, I am Gary Hood.
6. *Nè, àš esù John Wilson.*	No, I am John Wilson.
7. *Kur̃ yrà profèsorius Mažéika?*	Where is Professor Mazeika?
8. *Profèsorius Mažéika yrà universitetè.*	Prof. Mazeika is at the university.
9. *Labaĩ malonù susipažìnti sù Jumìs.*	It is very nice to meet you.
10. *Labaĩ malonù.*	I am very glad...

ASKING FOR DIRECTIONS.

1. *Kur̃ yrà universitètas?*	Where is the university?
2. *Universitètas yrà kitojè miẽsto dalyjè.*	The university is in the other part of the city.
3. *Kur̃ yrà pãštas?*	Where is the post office?
4. *Pãštas yrà miẽsto centrè.*	The post office is in the center of the city.
5. *Kaĩp mán nuvažiúoti į̃ teãtrą?*	How do I get to the theatre?
6. *Važiúokite autobusù. Nùmeris peñktas.*	Go by bus. No. 5.
7. *O kaĩp važiúoti automobiliù?*	And how (do I go) by car?
8. *Kóks jũsų automobìlis?*	What kind of car do you have?
9. *Màno automobìlis naũjas...*	My car is new...
10. *Geraĩ, važiúokime jũsų automobìliù. Aš jùms paródysiu kẽlią.*	O.K., let's go by car (your car). I will show you the way.

Pirmoji pamoka

Lesson 1

MANO NAMAS

Aš esù studeñtas. Màno tẽvas yrà mókytojas. Màno brólis yrà taĩp pàt studeñtas. Aš iř brólis ẽsame studeñtai.

Màno nãmas yrà dìdelis iř gražùs. Kuř yrà màno nãmas? Màno nãmas yrà čià.

Kàs yrà màno tẽvas? Màno tẽvas yrà mókytojas. Kàs yrà màno brólis? Màno brólis yrà studeñtas. Kàs mẽs ẽsame? Mẽs ẽsame studeñtai.

Kuř mẽs eĩname vakarè? Mẽs eĩname namõ.

Kóks yrà màno nãmas? Màno nãmas yrà dìdelis. Màno nãmas yrà gražùs.

VOCABULARY

àš — I	taĩp pàt — also, too
esù — am	ẽsame — (we) are
studeñtas — student	studeñtai — students
nãmas — house	kuř — where
màno — my	čià — here
yrà — is	kàs — who, what
dìdelis — large	vakarè — in the evening
gražùs — beautiful	eĩname — (we) go
tẽvas — father	namõ — home, homeward
mókytojas — teacher	kóks — what kind
brólis — brother	iř — and

GRAMMAR

1.1 There are no articles in Lithuanian. Thus, *studeñtas* can mean: student, the student, a student.

1.2 There are only two genders in Lithuanian nouns: masculine and feminine. All nouns ending in *-as* are masculine.

1.3 The Present Tense of *bùti* 'to be' and *eĩti* 'to go'.

I am	*àš esù*	*àš einù*	I go, etc.
you are	*tù esì*	*tù einì*	
he, she is	*jìs, jì yrà*	*jìs, jì eĩna*	
we are	*mẽs ẽsame*	*mẽs eĩname*	
you are	*jũs ẽsate*	*jũs eĩnate*	
they are	*jiẽ, jõs yrà*	*jiẽ, jõs eĩna*	

The second person singular *tu* which corresponds to English *thou* is used to address children, real friends, members of the immediate family and God. It would correspond in use to German *du* or French *tu*. The second person plural is used for polite address:

Pẽtrai, kuř tù einì? — Peter, where are you going?
Põne Petráiti, kuř jũs eĩnate? — Mr. Petraitis, where are you going?

There is no progressive form in Lithuanian. Thus *àš einù* can mean: I go, I am going, I do go.

There is no auxiliary *to do* to help to form questions: you have to indicate the question by the tone of your voice, or by putting the little word *ař* in front of a question which has no other interrogative word in it. Thus:

Čià [yrà]* màno nãmas. — Here is my house.
Čià màno nãmas? — Is my house here?
Ař čià màno nãmas? — Is my house here?
Kuř màno nãmas? — Where is my house?

EXERCISES

A. Answer the following questions:

1. Kàs àš esù? 2. Kàs yrà màno tẽvas? 3. Kàs yrà màno brólis? 4. Kuř yrà mũsų nãmas? 5. Kóks yrà màno nãmas? 6. Kuř mẽs eĩname? 7. Kàs mẽs ẽsame?

---

* About leaving out **yra**, etc., see Lesson 6.

B. *Fill in:*

1. Màno (brother) .... yrà studeñtas. 2. Màno nãmas
yrà (large) .... 3. Mẽs eĩname namõ (in the evening)
.... 4. Mẽs eĩname (home) .... 5. Aš (am)
.... studeñtas.

C. *Complete:*

1. Mẽs ẽsame student......... 2. Màno brólis yrà student......... 3.
Màno tẽvas yrà mokytoj......... 4. Màno nãmas yrà didel......... iȓ
graž......... 5. Kàs yrà man......... tẽvas?

D. *Translate into Lithuanian:*

1. My brother is going home. 2. My father goes home. 3. My house
is large. 4. My brother and I are students. 5. I am going home. 6.
I go home. 7. My brother goes home.

CONVERSATION

GREETINGS, etc.

1. *Lãbas rýtas!* (Or: *Lãbą rýtą!*) — Good morning!
2. *Labà dienà!* (Or: *Lãbą diẽną!*) — Good day!
3. *Lãbas vãkaras!* (Or: *Lãbą vãkarą!*) — Good evening!
4. *Kaĩp gyvúojate?* — How are you? (Plural, politely)
5. *Kaĩp gyvúoji?* — How are you? (Familiar)
6. *Ačiū, geraĩ. O kaĩp jũs?* — Fine, thank you. And you?
7. *Aȓ jũs ẽsate põnas Valỹs?* — Are you Mr. Valys?
8. *Nè, àš esù Valáitis, Pẽtras Valáitis.* — No, I am Valaitis, Petras Valaitis.
9. *Jũs ẽsate studeñtas?* — Are you a student?
10. *Taĩp, àš esù studeñtas.* — Yes, I am a student.

NB. Learn these sentences by heart! Do not try to figure out what
the separate words mean: learn the whole phrase by heart.

NOTES: **Lãbas rýtas!** is used until about 10 AM. From then, until about 6 -
8 PM., depending on the time of the year: **Labà dienà!** After that:
Lãbas vãkaras! One never uses these expressions on taking leave.
Lãbas! alone can be used as a short 'Hello!', 'Hi!' at any time of
the day.

23

Antroji pamoka

Lesson 2

MANO ŠEIMA

Aš taĩp pàt turiù víeną sẽserį. Màno sesuõ yrà dár jaunà mergáitė. Jì dár nėrà studeñtė. Jì yrà mokinẽ. Jì eĩna į mokỹklą. Jái yrà dár tìk dẽšimt mẽtų.

Màno mamà yrà šeiminin̄kė. Jì dìrba namiẽ: vérda pùsryčius, pietùs, vakariẽnę, vãlo kam̄barius. Mẽs visì ją̃ labaĩ mýlime. Jì yrà labaĩ gerà mótina.

Vakarè mẽs visì ẽsame namiẽ. Mamà skaĩto laĩkraštį, tévas rãšo láišką, mẽs skaĩtome knygàs, mūsų sesùtė Rūtà ruõšia pãmokas. Mẽs ẽsame labaĩ laimìngi.

VOCABULARY

turiù — I have
šeimà — family
víeną — one (acc. sg. fem.)
sẽserį — sister (acc. sg.)
sesuõ — sister
dár — still, yet
jaunà (fem.) — young
mergáitė — girl
nėrà — is not
studeñtė — student girl (of a university)
mokinẽ — pupil (fem.) of an elementary, or secondary school
eĩna — (he, she) goes
į (prep. with acc.) — in, into, to
mokỹklą (acc. sg.) — school
jái (dat. sg.) — to her, her
tìk — only
dẽšimt — ten
mẽtų (gen. pl.) — of years, years

vérda — (he, she) cooks
pùsryčius (acc. pl.) — breakfast
pietùs (acc. pl.) — dinner
vakariẽnę (acc. sg.) — supper
vãlo — (he, she) cleans
kam̄barius (acc. pl.) — rooms
visì — everybody, all
ją̃ (acc. sg.) — her
labaĩ — very, very much
mýlime — we love
gerà (adj. fem.) — good
mótina — mother
skaĩto — (he, she) reads
laĩkraštį (acc. sg.) — newspaper
rãšo — (he, she) writes
láišką (acc. sg.) — letter
skaĩtome — we read
knygàs (acc. pl.) — books
sesùtė — sister (diminutive endearing form)

mamà — mother (popular)
šeimininkė — housewife, landlady, [hostess
jì dìrba — she works
namiė — at home

ruõšia — (he, she) prepares, does
pãmokas (acc. pl.) — lessons, home [work
laimìngi (nom. pl. masc.) — happy

GRAMMAR

2.1 The Present Tense of the Verbs.

Most of the verbs in Lithuanian are "regular". The verbs in Lithuanian are divided into 3 conjugations. The conjugation is determined by the ending of the third person, present tense.

1st Conjugation: 3rd person ends in -a. Infin.: *dìrbti* 'to work', *ruõšti* 'to prepare'

àš dìrbu	-u	àš ruošiù	-iu
tù dìrbi	-i	tù ruošì	-i
jìs dìrba	-a	jìs ruõšia	-ia
mẽs dìrbame	-ame	mẽs ruõšiame	-iame
jū̃s dìrbate	-ate	jū̃s ruõšiate	-iate
jiẽ dìrba	-a	jiẽ ruõšia	-ia

2nd Conjugation: -i — Infin.: *mylė́ti* 'to love'

àš mýliu	-iu	mẽs mýlime	-ime
tù mýli	-i	jū̃s mýlite	-ite
jìs mýli	-i	jiẽ mýli	-i

3rd Conjugation: -o — Infin.: *skaitýti* 'to read'

àš skaitaũ	-au	mẽs skaĩtome	-ome
tù skaitaĩ	-ai	jū̃s skaĩtote	-ote
jìs skaĩto	-o	jiẽ skaĩto	-o

NB.

1) The 3rd person singular and the 3rd person plural are always the same in all tenses in Lithuanian.

2) Plural forms can easily be formed by adding *-me* or *-te* respectively to the 3rd person form.

3) As one can see, the pattern of accentuation in Lithuanian is a complicated affair. For the present tense, the following general rules could be drawn:

26

a) The 3rd person singular and all the persons in the plural are stressed on the stem, never on the ending.

b) The 1st and the 2nd person singular will both be stressed alike: either both on the ending or both on the stem.
(From this lesson on, the forms of the 1st person singular and 3rd prs. will be given with the infinitive. Later, other forms will be added.)

c) For details, see Grammar Appendix; for individual verbs, see Lith.-English vocabulary.

2.2 Negation. The negative particle in Lithuanian is *ne*. It usually precedes that word which it negates. When it precedes a verbal form, then it is written together with the verb. *It is also written together with adjectives and adverbs.* It is usually not connected with nouns, unless the particle *ne* gives the noun the opposite meaning. *Nėrà* 'is not' is a contraction of *nè yrà*. With a negative verb the direct object must be *in the genitive, not in the accusative, as is the case after a positive verbal form.* More on negation: see 4.3.

2.3 Possessive Adjectives and Pronouns.

Possessive adjectives and pronouns are very easy to handle in Lithuanian: for each person there is only one form for both the possessive adjective and the possessive pronoun, and they are indeclinable!

Personal Pronoun	Possessive Adjective	Possessive Pronoun
àš — I	màno — my	màno — mine
tù — you, thou	tàvo — your, thy	tàvo — yours
jìs — he	jõ — his	jõ — his
jì — she	jõs — her	jõs — hers
mẽs — we	mū́sų — our	mū́sų — ours
jū̃s — you	jū́sų — your	jū́sų — yours
jiẽ — they (masc.)	jų̃ — their	jų̃ — theirs
jõs — they (fem.)	jų̃ — their	jų̃ — theirs

With the exception of *màno* and *tàvo*, the rest of these forms are actually the genitives of the personal pronouns. Examples:

màno tė́vas — my father
màno mamà — my mother
màno namaĩ — my houses
Šìtas nãmas yrà màno. — This house is mine.

EXERCISES

A. *Questions:*

1. Kàs yrà màno sesuõ? 2. Aȓ jì jaũ (already) yrà studeñtė? 3. Kíek jái mẽtų? (How old is she? Lit.: How many years to her?) 4. Kàs yrà màno mamà? 5. Kuȓ dìrba màno mamà? 6. Ką̃ jì dìrba? (ką̃—what) 7. Kuȓ mẽs ẽsame vakarè? 8. Kadà mẽs ẽsame namiẽ? (kadà—when) 9. Ką̃ skaĩto mamà? 10. Ką̃ rãšo màno tėvas?

B. *Give the present tense of:* turė́ti (turiù, tùri); valýti (valaũ, vãlo); rašýti (rašaũ, rãšo); vìrti (vérdu, vérda)*

C. *Complete:* 1. (My) .... sesuõ yrà jaunà mergáitė. 2. (My) .... tėvas yrà sẽnas. 3. (My) .... mamà yrà gerà šeiminin̄kė. 4. Mẽs ją̃ (very much) .... mýlime. 5. Vakarè mẽs ẽsame (at home) ....

D. *Translate into Lithuanian:* 1. My brother is a student. 2. My mother is a housekeeper. 3. Our sister goes to school. 4. She is a pupil. 5. Where are we in the evening?

CONVERSATION

ASKING FOR DIRECTIONS

1. *Kuȓ yrà pã̃štas?* — Where is the post office?
2. *Kuȓ yrà telefònas?* — Where is the telephone?
3. *Kuȓ yrà stotìs?* — Where is the station?
4. *Stotìs yrà miẽsto centrè.* — The station is in the center of the town.
5. *Į̃ dẽšinę. Į̃ kaĩrę.* — To the right. To the left.
6. *Antramè aukštè.* — On the second floor.
7. *Aȓ čià gyvẽna põnas Valỹs?* — Does Mr. Valys live here?
8. *Kaĩp mán nuvažiúoti į̃ stõtį?* — How do I get to the station?
9. *Aȓ jũs manè supran̄tate?* — Do you understand me?
10. *Prašaũ kalbė́ti pamažù.* — Please speak slowly.

NOTES:

3. **stotìs** actually means any kind of a station: RR, bus station; but it is used in the cities primarily for a RR station.
6. **antramè aukštè** is a locative case. See Lesson 3.

---

* There is a change of vowel in vìrti; the whole present tense will go like **vérda**: vérdu, vérdi, vérda, vérdame, vérdate, vérda.

Trečioji pamoka

Lesson 3

MŪSŲ MIESTAS

Mẽs gyvẽname dideliamè miestè. Jìs vadìnasi Vìlnius. Taĩ yrà Lietuvõs sóstinė. Miẽsto gãtvės yrà ìlgos iř siaũros. Į miẽstą atvažiúoja daũg studeñtų studijúoti jõ senamè universitetè.

Aš važiúoju į̃ universitètą autobusù. Autobùsui sunkù važiúoti senà gatvè, nès jì yrà labaĩ siaurà.

Universitètas yrà miẽsto centrè. Universitèto pastataĩ labaĩ senì.

Mán patiñka skaitýti senojè universitèto bibliotèkoje.

VOCABULARY

gyvénti (aš gyvenù, jis gyvẽna) — to live
dideliamè (loc. sg. of dìdelis 'large') — in the large
miestè (loc. sg.) — in the city
vadìnasi — is called
Vìlnius — Vilnius (Vilna)
taĩ — that (expletive)
Lietuvõs (gen. sg.) — Lithuania's, of
sóstinė — capital   [Lithuania
gãtvės (nom. pl.) — streets
ìlgos (nom. pl.) — long
siaũros (nom. pl.) — narrow
atvažiúoti (atvažiúoju, atvažiúoja) — to arrive
daũg — much, many
studeñtų (gen. pl.) — students
studijúoti (studijúoju, studijúoja) — to study at a university
senamè (loc. sg.) — in the old
autobùsas — bus
sunkù — difficult
gãtvė — street
nès — because
ceñtras — center
pãstatas — building
mán patiñka — I like
bibliotekà — library

29

GRAMMAR

3.1 The Cases.

There are *seven* declensional cases in Lithuanian:

1. Nominative   (Vardiniñkas)   who, what? — *kàs?**
2. Genitive   (Kilminiñkas)   whose, of what? — *kõ?*
3. Dative   (Naudiniñkas)   to whom? — *kám?*
4. Accusative   (Galiniñkas)   whom, what? — *ką̃?*
5. Instrumental (Įnagininkas)   with whom, with what? — *kuõ?*
6. Locative   (Viẽtininkas)   where, in what? — *kamè?, kur̃?*
7. Vocative   (Šauksminiñkas) (used for addressing, calling).

3.1.1 THE NOMINATIVE

The nominative case is the case of the subject of the sentence, or it may function as the case of the predicate in some copulative constructions.

1) *Màno brólis yrà studeñtas.* — My brother is a student.
   (Both the subject and the noun predicate are in the nominative case in the preceding example.)

2) *Màno nãmas yrà dìdelis.* — My house is big.
   (Both the subject and the predicate adjective are in the nominative case in the preceding example.)

3) *Mamà skaĩto laĩkraštį.* — Mother is reading a newspaper.
   (The subject is in the nominative case, but the object, *laĩkraštį* is in the accusative case; see below.)

3.1.2 THE GENITIVE

The genitive case may be used to show possession or some type of relationship which is commonly expressed in English by 'of' or 's. Examples:

1) *brólio stãlas* — the brother's desk

2) *miẽsto gãtvės* — the streets of the city

3) *Lietuvõs sóstinė* — the capital of Lithuania
   Certain prepositions require the genitive case. See Lesson 36.

---

* kas? means both who? and what?

3.1,3 THE DATIVE

The dative case is the case of the indirect object of the verb. Example:

Jìs dúoda bróliui knýgą. — He is giving [his] brother a book.

It may also function as the subject of an impersonal construction. Examples:

1) *Tėvui sunkù gyvénti čià.* — It is difficult for father to live here.

2) *Autobùsui sunkù važiúoti senà gatvè.* — It is difficult for the bus to travel on (along) the old street.

3.1,4 THE ACCUSATIVE

The accusative case functions as the case of the direct object of the verb. Examples:

1) *Mamà skaĩto laĩkraštį.* — Mother is reading the newspaper.
2) *Jì vérda pùsryčius.* — She is cooking breakfast.
3) *Tėvas rãšo láišką.* — Father is writing a letter.
4) *Àš turiù víeną sėserį.* — I have one sister.

The accusative case is also used in certain time expressions, see paragraphs 32.2-4, 32.6 and with certain prepositions, see paragraph 37.5.

3.1,5 THE INSTRUMENTAL

The instrumental case may denote the means by which, or the instrument with which, something is done. Examples:

1) *Jìs rãšo laĩšką pieštukù.* — He is writing a letter with a pencil. (Note that *pieštukù* is in the instrumental case to denote means, but that no preposition is used with it.)

2) *Àš važiúoju į̃ universitètą autobusù.* — I am going to the university by bus.

The instrumental case may denote the place along which or near something is moving. Example:

Jìs važiúoja senà gatvè. — He is driving along the old street.

Certain prepositions require the instrumental case, see Lesson 36.

3.1,6 THE LOCATIVE

The locative case denotes the place where something is. Examples:

1) *Mẽs gyvẽname miestè.* — We live in the city.
2) *Universitètas yrà miẽsto centrè.* — The university is in the center of the city.

3.2 The First Declension of Nouns.

To the first declension belong all nouns ending in -*as*, -*is* (gen. -*io*), -*ys*. They are all masculine nouns: *nãmas* 'house', *brólis* 'brother', *arklỹs* 'horse'.

N.	nãmas	-as	brólis	-is	arklỹs	-ys
G.	nãmo	-o	brólio	-io	árklio	-io
D.	nãmui	-ui	bróliui	-iui	árkliui	-iui
A.	nãmą	-ą	brólį	-į	árklį	-į
I.	namù	-u	bróliu	-iu	árkliu	-iu
L.	namè	-e	brólyje	-yje	arklyjè	-yje
V.	nãme!	-e	bróli!	-i	arklỹ!	-y

N B. The stress pattern varies: sometimes it remains on the same syllable throughout singular and plural, sometimes it varies greatly. For a brief explanation, see Lesson 5; for a full and detailed explanation see Appendix, paragraph 51.

3.3 Second Declension of Nouns.

To this declension belong feminine nouns which end in -*a*, -*ė* and -*i*: *dienà* 'day', *gãtvė* 'street', *martì* 'daughter-in-law'.*

N.	dienà	-a	gãtvė	-ė	martì	-i
G.	dienõs	-os	gãtvės	-ės	marčiõs	-ios
D.	diẽnai	-ai	gãtvei	-ei	mařčiai	-iai
A.	diẽną	-ą	gãtvę	-ę	mařčią	-ią
I.	dienà	-a	gatvè	-e	marčià	-ia
L.	dienojè	-oje	gãtvėje	-ėje	marčiojè	-ioje
V.	diẽna!	-a	gãtve!	-e	mařti!	-i

N.B. Whenever a combination of -*tia*, -*tią*, -*tio*, -*tiu*, -*tių* should occur, then t>č; tią>čią; -tio>čio; -tiu>čiu; -tių>čių.

---

* There are only two nouns in -i: **martì** 'daughter-in-law' and **patì** 'wife'.

3.3,1 A few second declension nouns such as *dėdė* 'uncle', *tėtė* 'father' (a term of endearment), *vaidilà* 'priest' (in pagan mythology) and some surnames are of the masculine gender. They are modified by masculine adjectives (cf. Lesson 11) and have masculine pronominal reference.

3.3,2 Some second declension nouns are of common gender, i.e. they can be either masculine or feminine depending upon the individual referred to: *nenúorama* 'mischief-maker', 'unruly child', *naktìbalda* 'one who roves about at night', *vėpla* 'gaping fool, gaper'.

3.4 The preposition *į* 'in, into, to' indicates destination, also direction, never location. It always governs the accusative.

į miẽstą — into the city, to the city
į universitètą — to the university

3.5 *Važiúoti* plus instrumental: 'to drive along'. . .
važiúoti gatvè — to drive along the street.

3.6 To express *I like*, Lithuanian uses the 3rd person of the verb *patìkti* 'to please' plus dative: *mán patiñka** (lit. it pleases to me) 'I like'.

Dative forms:

I — àš	mán	mán patiñka — I like
thou — tù	táu	táu patiñka — you like
he — jìs	jám	jám patiñka — he likes
she — jì	jái	jái patiñka — she likes
we — mẽs	mùms	mùms patiñka — we like
you — jū̃s	jùms	jùms patiñka — you like
they — jiẽ (masc.)	jíems	jíems patiñka — they like
they — jõs (fem.)	jóms	jóms patiñka — they like

Since *patiñka* is the third person for both singular and plural, it is used with singular, plural and infinitive subjects:

mán patiñka tàs nãmas — I like that house
mán patiñka tiẽ namaĩ — I like those houses
mán patiñka skaitýti bibliotèkoje** — I like to read in the library

---

* Irregular present tense: patinkù, patinkì, patiñka, patiñkame, patiñkate, patiñka

** More about 'I like', etc., see 6.4.

NB. In replacing the nouns with personal pronouns, one has to keep in mind that Lithuanian, just like many other European languages strictly adheres to grammatical gender:

E n g l i s h	L i t h u a n i a n
the city — it	miẽstas — jis (masc.)
the street — it	gãtvė — ji (fem.)

There is really no *it* as a personal pronoun. *Taĩ* is used for such cases of general reference as:

Taĩ labaĩ gražù. — That [it] is very beautiful.

EXERCISES

A. *Questions.* 1. Kuř mẽs gyvẽname? 2. Kuř jũs gyvẽnate? 3. Kaĩp vadìnasi mū́sų miẽstas? 4. Kàs yrà Lietuvõs sóstinė? 5. Ař miẽsto gãtvės yrà sẽnos? 6. Kuř atvažiúoja daũg studeñtų? 7. Kuř àš važiúoju? 8. Kuõ àš važiúoju į̃ universitètą? 9. Kuř yrà universitètas? 10. Kàs mán patiñka?

B. *Conjugate in the present tense:* gyvénti, važiúoti, atvažiúoti, studijúoti, patìkti.

C. *Decline in singular:* miẽstas, sóstinė, gãtvė, studeñtas, autobùsas, ceñtras, Lietuvà.

D. *Fill in:* 1. Jìs važiúoj.... senà gatvè. 2. Mẽs gyvẽname miest..... 3. Universitètas yrà miẽst.... centr...... 4. Į̃ miẽstą atvažiúoja student...... 5. Aš važiúoj.... nam......

E. *Translate into Lithuanian:* 1. He lives in a city. 2. He likes the city. 3. He likes the university. 4. We like the city. 5. We like the capital. 6. We go by bus. 7. The student goes by bus to the university. 8. The university is very old. 9. Vilnius is the capital of Lithuania. 10. We like to read in the library.

CONVERSATION

VALGYKLOJE

1. Kõ jũs nórite válgyti?
2. Prašaũ mán dúoti píeno iř dúonos.
3. Taĩp pàt iř puodùką kavõs.

4. Kõ nórs gérti?
5. Taĩp. Prašaũ mán atnèšti bùtelį alaũs.
6. Aȓ jũs taĩp pàt nórite sriubõs?
7. Ačiũ, nè. Aš niekuomèt neválgau sriubõs.
8. Prašaũ sąskaitą.
9. Prašaũ. Víenas dóleris.
10. Ačiũ. Sudiẽ(u).

IN A RESTAURANT

1. What do you wish to eat?
2. Please give me some milk and bread.
3. And a cup of coffee, too.
4. Something to drink?
5. Yes. Please bring me a bottle of beer.
6. Do you want [some] soup, too?
7. No, thank you. I never eat soup.
8. The bill, please.
9. Here you are. One dollar.
10. Thank you. Good bye.

NOTES:

1. kõ 'of what' is genitive.
2. píeno, kavõs — partitive genitive: 'some of ...'
3. puodùkas, actually diminutive of puõdas 'pot, kettle'.
7. With niekuomèt 'never', niẽko 'nothing', niẽkur 'nowhere' a double negative is used; sriubõs is also a genitive: the direct object of a negated verb must be in the genitive case, rather than the accusative.

35

Ketvirtoji pamoka

Lesson 4

UGNIS

Ugnìs yrà labaĩ reikalìnga. Bè ugniẽs žmogùs negãli gyvénti. Ugnìs padėjo sukùrti kultū̃rą iř civilizãciją.

Màno namè yrà krósnis. Krósnyje dė̃ga ugnìs iř šìldo nãmą. Bè krósnies àš negaliù gyvénti sàvo namè. Krósnis yrà taĩp pàt labaĩ reikalìnga. Màno krósnis yrà naujà iř gražì.

Akìs ùž ãkį, dantìs ùž dañtį! — An eye for an eye and a tooth for a tooth!

VOCABULARY

ugnìs — fire (cf. Latin 'ignis')
bè — (prep. with gen.) — without
žmogùs — man, human being
galė́ti (galiù, gãli) — to be able, can
reikalìnga (adj., fem.) — necessary
krósnis — stove, oven, range
dègti (degù, dė̃ga) — to burn
šìldyti (šìldau, šìldo) — to warm, to heat

ilgaĩ (adv.) — long, for a long time
padė́ti (pàdedu, pàdeda) — to help
sukùrti (sùkuriu, sùkuria) — to create
kultū̃rà — culture
civilizãcija — civilization
naujà (adj. *fem.*) — new
negaliù (ne+galiu) — I cannot
gražì (adj. *fem.*)—beautiful, pretty
ùž (prep. with acc.) — for, in return

GRAMMAR

4.1 The Third Declension of the Nouns.

akìs 'eye', *dantìs* 'tooth'

Singular

Feminine		Masculine	
N. akìs	-is	dantìs	-is
G. akiẽs	-ies	dantiẽs	-ies
D. ãkiai	-iai	dañčiui	-iui
A. ãkį	-į	dañtį	-į
I. akimì	-imi	dantimì	-imi
L. akyjè	-yje	dantyjè	-yje
V. akiẽ!	-ie	dantiẽ!	-ie

Most nouns of the third declension are of the feminine gender, but a few such as *dantis* 'tooth', *vagìs* 'thief' are masculine. In order to distinguish third declension nouns (all of which have the ending -*is* in the nominative singular) from those first declension nouns with the nominative singular ending -*is*, the genitive singular will be given also. For example:

peĩlis, -io — knife (first declension, masc.)

but

nósis, -ies — nose (fem.)

dantìs, -iẽs — tooth (masc.)

4.2 Cardinal numerals 1 - 10.

víenas, víenà	one (masc., fem.)
dù, dvì	two (masc., fem.)
trỹs	three (same for both genders)
keturì, kẽturios	four (masc., fem.)
penkì, peñkios	five ” ”
šešì, šẽšios	six ” ”
septynì, septýnios	seven ” ”
aštuonì, aštúonios	eight ” ”
devynì, devýnios	nine ” ”
dẽšimt	ten (same for both genders)

N B. All these numerals, with the exception of *dẽšimt*, are inflected, i.e. they are declined. *Víenas, víenà* are used with the nominative singular of nouns which they precede, 2 - 9 are used with the nominative plural. 10 is used with the genitive plural. For details, see Lesson 24.

4.3 Negation.

As we have already briefly mentioned, the negative particle in Lithuanian is *ne*. It always precedes the word which it negates. It is written together with following verbs, adjectives and adverbs. Examples:

1. *Krósnyje dẽga ugnìs.* — A fire is burning in the oven.
   Krósnyje nèdega ugnìs. — A fire is not burning in the oven.
2. *Ugnìs yrà labaĩ reikalìnga.* — The fire is very necessary.
   Ugnìs yrà labaĩ nereikalìnga. — The fire is very unnecessary.
3. *Ugnìs yrà labaĩ reikalìnga.* — The fire is very necessary.
   Ugnìs yrà nelabaĩ reikalìnga. — The fire is not very necessary.

Note that in the preceding examples it is the word which is negated which is immediately preceded by the negative particle *ne*. The negative particle is not written together with a following noun, unless the noun functions as a lexical compound, i.e. has a separate dictionary meaning:

Jìs yrà studeñtas. — He is a student.
Jìs yrà nè studeñtas, bèt profèsorius. — He is not a student, but a professor.

The negative particle *ne* with the verbal form *yra* 'is, are' makes a contraction *nèrà* 'is not, are not':

Ugnìs nèrà reikalìnga. — The fire is not necessary.
Jìs nèrà studeñtas. — He is not a student.

The direct object of a negated verb must be in the genitive rather than the accusative case:

Jìs tùri knỹgą. — He has a book.
Jìs netùri knỹgos. — He has no book.*

Contrary to English usage the negative must be repeated in each adverb of time or place occurring in a sentence:

Jìs niekadà nedìrba. — He never works.
(literally: He never doesn't work.)

---

* NB. All the verbs add **ne** to their positive form to form the negative. There are, however, two exceptions: **būti** 'to be' and **eiti** 'to go'; these add only n: **aš nesù, tu nesì, jis nèrà, mes nẽsame, jūs nẽsate, jie nèrà** — I am not, etc.; **aš neinù, tu neinì, jis neĩna, mes neĩname, jūs neĩnate, jie neĩna.** — 'I do not go', etc.

Jìs niēkur neĩna. — He doesn't go anywhere. (lit.: He doesn't go nowhere.)
Jìs niekadà niēkur niēko nedãro. — He doesn't ever do anything anywhere. (lit.: He doesn't do nothing nowhere never).

Likewise *niēko* 'nothing', the genitive case of *niēkas,* sometimes translates English 'anything' if it is in a negative sentence. Thus Lithuanian *jìs niēko nedãro* may be translated either as 'He does nothing' or 'He doesn't do anything'. Good English usage keeps us from using the literal translation 'He doesn't do nothing'.

N B. In Lithuanian, both *no* and *not* are expressed by the same negative particle *ne.* In the sense of *no, ne* is set off by a comma:

Nè, jìs nérà studeñtas. — No, he is not a student.

EXERCISES

A. *Questions.* 1. Bè kõ (without what) žmogùs negãli gyvénti? 2. Kuř dẽga ugnìs? 3. Ką̃ ugnìs šìldo? 4. Kàs padėjo sukùrti kultū̃rą iř civilizãciją? 5. Kuř yrà krósnis? 6. Kàs yrà labaĩ reikalìnga?

B. *Decline in the singular:* ausìs, nósis, krósnis, vagìs.

C. *Change all the pronouns and verbs to plural:* 1. Aš rašaũ láišką. 2. Jìs yrà namiẽ. 3. Jì skaĩto knỹgą. 4. Aš einù namõ. 5. Jì dìrba namiẽ. 6. Jì dẽga namè. 7. Jì šìldo nãmą. 8. Bè ugniẽs àš negaliù gyvénti.

D. *Translate into Lithuanian:* 1. I cannot live without fire. 2. Fire is very necessary. 3. He cannot live without fire. 4. In my house there is a new stove. 5. My stove is new. 6. Our stove is pretty. 7. A fire is burning in the stove. 8. We cannot live without a stove. 9. We cannot live without fire. 10. I like the new stove.

CONVERSATION

KAS TAI YRA?

1. Kàs taĩ yrà?
2. Taĩ yrà knygà.
3. Kuř yrà stãlas?
4. Stãlas yrà čià.

5. Nè, stãlas yrà teñ.
6. Kaĩp yrà "class" lietùviškai?
7. Kaĩp yrà "lángas" ángliškai?
8. Kaĩp pasakýti "Good morning!" lietùviškai?
9. Lietùvių kalbà yrà gražì kalbà.
10. Aš nesuprantù ángliškai; àš kalbù tìk lietùviškai.

WHAT IS THAT?

1. What is that?
2. That is a book.
3. Where is the table?
4. The table is here.
5. No, the table is there.
6. What is "class" in Lithuanian?
7. What is "langas" in English?
8. How does one say "Good morning!" in Lithuanian?
9. Lithuanian is a beautiful language.
10. I do not understand English; I speak only Lithuanian.

NOTES:

1. Lithuanian **tai** can be translated by either English **this** or **that** (or **these** or **those**, cf. below, also NB in 3.6). If you point to an object which is near you, then **Kàs taĩ yrà?** (or **Kàs yrà taĩ?**) can mean 'What is this?' **Taĩ** is undeclinable and can be used with singular and plural: **Kàs yrà taĩ? Taĩ yrà màno knỹgos.** 'What is that? These are my books'.
2. **lietùviškai, ángliškai** are adverbs, meaning: 'in Lithuanian, in the Lithuanian way, manner', etc.
3. **lietùvių kalbà** literally means "Lithuanians' language, the language of the Lithuanians." **lietùvių** is genitive plural of **lietùvis, lietùvė** "Lithuanian", (male and female; noun).

Penktoji pamoka
Lesson 5

REVIEW

VILNIUS

Màno tẽvas, mótina, brólis, sesuõ iř àš gyvẽname senamè miestè. Šìs miẽstas vadìnasi Vìlnius. Jìs yrà Lietuvõs sóstinė. Miẽsto centrè yrà sẽnas universitètas, kuriamè[1] studijúoja daũg studeñtų. Studeñtai suvažiúoja čià studijúoti iš vi̱sõs Lietuvõs.[2]

Mẽs visì gyvẽname sóstinėje. Mán vìskas[3] čià labaĩ patiñka: iř sẽnas universitètas, iř sẽnas miẽstas, iř[4] senà gãtvė, kurià[5] autobùsas važiúoja liñk[6] universitèto. Kiekvíeną rýtą[7] àš važiúoju tuõ[8] autobusù į̃ universitètą, kuř àš studijúoju.

Aš studijúoju medicìną. Aš nóriu bū́ti gýdytoju.[9] Màno brólis studijúoja ánglų kaĩbą[10] iř literatū́rą, nès jìs nóri važiúoti į̃ Amèriką, į̃ Angliją[11] iř į̃ Kanãdą. Jìs taĩp pat studijúoja amerikiẽčių literatū́rą iř Amèrikos istòriją.

Màno tẽvas dabař dìrba bibliotèkoje. Màno mamà yrà namiẽ vìsą diẽną.[12] Jì tùri labaĩ daũg dárbo. Vakarè mẽs eĩname į̃ teātrą arbà į̃ kìną.[13]

NOTES:

1) **kuriamè** — in which
2) **iš visõs Lietuvõs** — from all over Lithuania, lit. from the whole Lithuania
3) **vìskas** — everything
4) **iř ... iř ... iř ...** — both ... and; all these things
5) **kurià** — on which, along which
6) **liñk** — in the direction of, to
7) **kiekvíeną rýtą** — every morning, acc. of definite time
8) **tuõ** — on that, by that
9) **gýdytoju** — inst. of **gýdytojas** 'physician'. In popular speech: 'daktaras'

43

10) ángly kalbą — English, the English language, 'anglistics', see also Note 3, Conversation of Lesson 4.
11) **Anglija** — England
12) visą diēną — the whole day, the entire day. See Note 7.
13) kìnas — movie theater, 'movie'.

CONVERSATION

1.

Valáitis: Lãbas rýtas!
Žalỹs: Lãbas rýtas! Kaĩp gyvúojate?
Valaitis: Ačiū, geraĩ. O kaĩp jūs?*
Žalys: Geraĩ, tìk óras dabař blõgas.
Valaitis: Taĩp, perdaũg sniẽgo.
Žalys: Kuř jūs dabař eĩnate?
Valaitis: Aš einù namõ. O jūs?
Žalys: Iřgi namõ.

2.

A.: Ař jūsy brólis studeñtas?
B.: Nè. Jìs yrà mókytojas.
A.: Kuř jìs gyvẽna?
B.: Jìs gyvẽna Vìlniuje.
A.: Taĩ labaĩ sẽnas iř gražùs miẽstas.
B.: Taĩp. Vìlniaus universitètas įkùrtas 1579 (tūkstantis penkì šimtaĩ septýniasdešimt devintaĩs) mẽtais.

3.

Pẽtras: Kuř mamà?
Rūtà: Jì išvažiãvo į miẽstą.
Petras: O kuř tẽtis?
Rūta: Tẽtis namiẽ. Jìs skaĩto laĩkraštį.

4.

Brazỹs: Ař jūs nè põnas Kubìlius?
Kubìlius: Taĩp, taĩp. Aš esù Jõnas Kubìlius.
Brazys: Kuř jūs dabař gyvẽnate?
Kubilius: Aš dabař gyvenù Amèrikoje, Bòstone.
Brazys: Kuř dabař eĩnate?
Kubilius: Einù į bánką.

---

* In Lithuanian, àš 'I' is not capitalized. The polite form of 'you' **Jūs, Tù** 'thou, you' **Jūsy** 'your' and **Tàvo** 'your' are capitalized in letters.

44

5.

Antãnas: Sveĩkas, Jõnai! Kuř taĩp skubì?
Jõnas. Turiù greĩtai važiúoti namõ . . .
Antanas: Kàs gì atsitìko?
Jonas: Màno nãmas dẽga . . .
Antanas: Vistíek jaũ niẽko negalì padarýti.
Jonas: Nóriu nórs gaĩsro pasižiūrẽti . . . Sudiẽu! . . .

COMBINATION PRACTICE

1. *Combine to make sentences:*

   1. I like
   2. we like
   3. they like

   a. our house
   b. our city
   c. the capital
   d. the university
   e. her house

2. *Combine to make sentences:*

   1. I live
   2. they study
   3. we cannot live

   a. at home
   b. in a city
   c. in the city
   d. not at home
   e. at the university
   f. at a university

3. *Combine to make sentences:*

   1. I read
   2. we read
   3. she reads
   4. Mr. Valys reads
   5. Mr. Valys and Mr. Žukas read
   6. Petras and Jonas read
   7. They are reading

   a. a newspaper
   b. the newspaper
   c. a letter
   d. a book

THE ACCENT CLASSES OF THE LITHUANIAN NOUNS

1st ACCENT CLASS

Features:

1. In two-syllable nouns, the stress is always on the first syllable, i.e. on the root, and it is always an acute.

2. In polysyllabic nouns, one can have either the acute or the circumflex, not necessarily on the first syllable.

3. Finally, the most important feature: the stress always remains on the same syllable in all the cases in the singular and plural.

Basic pattern:

S i n g u l a r :

N.	výras (man)	ádata (needle)	bìtininkas (beekeeper)
G.	výro	ádatos	bìtininko
D.	výrui	ádatai	bìtininkui
A.	výrą	ádatą	bìtininką
I.	výru	ádata	bìtininku
L.	výre	ádatoje	bìtininke
V.	výre	ádata	bìtininke

P l u r a l :

N.	výrai	ádatos	bìtininkai
G.	výrų	ádatų	bìtininkų
D.	výrams	ádatoms	bìtininkams
A.	výrus	ádatas	bìtininkus
I.	výrais	ádatomis	bìtininkais
L.	výruose	ádatose	bìtininkuose
V.	výrai	ádatos	bìtininkai

Singular

Plural

1. All nouns of this class have the circumflex or the short intonation, mostly on the second syllable from the end.

2. The circumflex or the short stress remains constant, except:
   a) instrumental singular;
   b) accusative plural.

3. If the noun ends in -as, then in addition to the two cases above, the locative singular is also stressed on the ending.

4. If the noun has -a in nom. sing., then this -a is stressed.

Basic pattern:

S i n g u l a r :

N.	lãpė (fox)	rãtas (wheel)	rankà (arm)	lietùvis (Lithuanian)
G.	lãpės	rãto	rañkos	lietùvio
D.	lãpei	rãtui	rañkai	lietùviui
A.	lãpę	rãtą	rañką	lietùvį
I.	lapè	ratù	rankà	lietuviù
L.	lãpėje	ratè	rañkoje	lietùvyje
V.	lãpe!	rãte!	rañka!	lietùvi

P l u r a l :

N,V.	lãpės	rãtai	rañkos	lietùviai
G.	lãpių	rãtų	rañkų	lietùvių
D.	lãpėms	rãtams	rañkoms	lietùviams
A.	lapès	ratùs	rankàs	lietuviùs
I.	lãpėmis	rãtais	rañkomis	lietùviais
L.	lãpėse	rãtuose	rañkose	lietùviuose

S i n g u l a r

N.	~ _	~ _	_ `	_ ` _
G.	~ _	~ _	~ _	_ ` _
D.	~ _	~ _	~ _	_ ` _
A.	~ _	~ _	~ _	_ ` _
I.	_ `	_ `	_ `	_ _ `
L.	~ _ _	_ `	~ _ _	_ ` _
V.	~ _	~ _	~ _	_ ` _

47

Plural

N.	˜ _	˜ _	˜ _	_ ˋ _
G.	˜ _	˜ _	˜ _	_ ˋ _
D.	˜ _	˜ _	˜ _	_ ˋ _
A.	_ ˋ	_ ˋ	_ ˋ	_ _ ˋ
I.	˜ _ _	˜ _	˜ _ _	_ ˋ _
L.	˜ _ _	˜ _ _	˜ _ _	_ ˋ _ _

3rd ACCENT CLASS

1. All two-syllable nouns of this class have the acute intonation in most singular cases on the initial syllable.

2. The accusative singular and plural of the two-syllable nouns are always stressed with an acute on the first syllable:

3. In tri-syllabic and quadri-syllabic nouns the play of stress is between the initial syllable and the final syllable ordinarily. If the stress on the initial syllable is the acute these nouns are labeled 3ᵃ for tri-syllabic and 3⁴ᵃ for quadri-syllabic. If the stress on the initial syllable is circumflex they are labeled 3ᵇ and 3⁴ᵇ respectively.

Basic pattern:

Singular:

N. kélmas (stump)	sūnùs (son)	dóbilas (clover)	kãtilas (kettle)
G. kélmo	sūnaũs	dóbilo	kãtilo
D. kélmui	sŭnui	dóbilui	kãtilui
A. kélmą	sŭnų	dóbilą	kãtilą
I. kélmu	sūnumì	dóbilu	kãtilu
L. kelmè	sūnujè	dobilè	katilè
V. kélme!	sūnaũ!	dóbile!	kãtile!

Plural:

N. kelmaĩ	sŭnūs	dobilaĩ	katilaĩ
G. kelmų̃	sūnų̃	dobilų̃	katilų̃
D. kelmáms	sūnùms	dobiláms	katiláms
A. kélmus	sŭnus	dóbilus	kãtilus
I. kelmaĩs	sūnumìs	dobilaĩs	katilaĩs
L. kelmuosè	sūnuosè	dobiluosè	katiluosè
V. kelmaĩ!	sŭnūs!	dobilaĩ!	katilaĩ!

48

N.	´ _	_ `	´ _ _	~ _ _ _
G.	´ _	_ ~	´ _ _	~ _ _ _
D.	´ _	´ _	´ _ _	~ _ _ _
A.	´ _	´ _	´ _ _	~ _ _ _
I.	´ _	_ _ `	´ _ _	~ _ _ _
L.	_ `	_ _ `	_ _ `	_ _ _ `
V.	´ _	_ ~	´ _ _	~ _ _ _

Plural

N.	_ ~	´ _	_ _ ~	_ _ ~
G.	_ ~	_ ~	_ _ ~	_ _ ~
D.	_ ´	_ `	_ _ ´	_ _ ´
A.	´ _	´ _	´ _ _	~ _ _
I.	_ ~	_ _ `	_ _ ~	_ _ ~
L.	_ _ `	_ _ `	_ _ _ `	_ _ _ `
V.	_ ~	´ _	_ _ ~	_ _ ~

4th ACCENT CLASS

1. Nouns of the fourth accent class primarily have the circum-flex intonation on the root (first syllable), except:

   a) in the instrumental and locative singular;

   b) in all cases of the plural, except when nominative plural has -s, then the nom. pl. is stressed on the root, but all other plural cases—on the ending.

Basic pattern:

Singular:

N. vaĩkas (child)	šakà (branch)	~ _	_ `
G. vaĩko	šakõs	~ _	_ ~
D. vaĩkui	šãkai	~ _	~ _
A. vaĩką	šãką	~ _	~ _
I. vaikù	šakà	_ `	_ `
L. vaikè	šakojè	_ `	_ _ `
V. vaĩke!	šãka!	~ _	~ _

Plural:

N. vaikaĩ	šãkos	‿ ͠	͠ ‿
G. vaikų̃	šakų̃	‿ ͠	‿ ͠
D. vaikáms	šakóms	‿ ´	‿ ´
A. vaikùs	šakàs	‿ `	‿ `
I. vaikaĩs	šakomìs	‿ ͠	‿ ‿ `
L. vaikuosè	šakosè	‿ ‿ `	‿ ‿ `
V. vaikaĩ!	šãkos!	‿ ͠	͠ ‿

NB. There are no polysyllabic nouns in the 4th accent class. For further details see paragraph 51 of the Appendix.

Šeštoji pamoka

Lesson 6

GRAŽI DIENA

Šiandien yrà labaĩ gražì dienà. Dangùs grýnas — ně debesě-lio. Profèsorius Vìtkus eĩna pasiváikščioti. Profèsorius yrà jaũ sě-nas žmogùs. Jìs měgsta gérti arbãtą sù cùkrumi iř medumì. Jìs eĩna pàs sàvo sūnų, dãktarą Vìtkų. Dr. Vìtkus yrà gýdytojas, jáunas iř gabùs žmogùs.

Dr. Vìtkus gyvěna príemiestyje, kuř visuomèt gěras óras. Tě-vas iř sūnùs sědi laukè iř gěria arbãtą. Profèsorius Vìtkus ne-měgsta alaũs, jìs gěria tìk arbãtą iř mìdų. Midùs yrà sěnas gěri-mas. Senóvėje lietùviai darýdavo iř gérdavo mìdų.

— Gražùs dangùs, ař nè? — sāko profèsorius.

— Puikùs óras, tačiaũ ateĩna lietùs, — atsāko sūnùs.

— Iš kuř tù taĩ žinaĩ? — kláusia těvas.

— Tìk ką̃ prànešė peř rãdiją . . .

VOCABULARY

šiañdien — today

gražùs, -ì — beautiful, handsome, fine

dienà (4) — day

grýnas, -à — pure, clear

ně — [here] not a

debesělis, -io (2) — cloud (diminutive of debesìs)

profèsorius (1) — professor

pasiváikščioti (pasiváikščioju, pasi-váikščioja) — to take a walk

jaũ — already

měgti — to like; irreg.: aš měgstu, tu měgsti, jis měgsta, mes měgstame, jūs měgstate, jie měgsta

arbatà (2) — tea

alùs (4) — beer

midùs (4) — mead (a sweet drink made from honey)

gěrimas (1) — drink, beverage

senóvėje — in ancient times, a long time ago

lietùvis -io (2) — Lithuanian (noun, masc.)

darýdavo — used to make, see 12.4

gérdavo — used to drink, see 12.4

ař nè? — is it not?, see 6.3

sakýti (sakaũ, sãko) — to say

puikùs, -ì — fine, excellent

tačiaũ — but, in spite of that, never-theless; see 38.1

sù (prep. with instr.) — with
cùkrus (2) — sugar
medùs (4) — honey
pàs (prep. with acc.) — at, by, to, [with
sàvo — his (own)
sūnùs (3) — son
dáktaras (3b) — Doctor, Ph.D., M.D.
gýdytojas (1) — physician
jáunas, -à — young
gabùs, -ì — talented, gifted
príemiestis, -čio (1) — suburb
visuomèt — always
óras (3) — air, weather
sėdéti — to sit, to be seated; irreg.: aš
sėdžiu, tu sėdi, jis sėdi, mes sėdime,
jūs sėdite, jie sėdi
laukè — outside, outdoors

ateīti (ateinù, ateīna) — to come
lietùs (3) — rain
atsakýti (atsakaū, atsãko) — to answer
iš kuř — [here] how, (literally: out of [where
žinóti (žinaū, žìno) — to know (a
fact)
kláusti (kláusiu, kláusia) — to ask
(a question)
rãdijas (1) —radio
peř (prep. with acc.) — through
peř rãdiją — on the radio
tik ką — just now, a few moments ago
(lit. 'only what')
pranèšti (prànešu, pràneša) — to announce

NB. Starting with this lesson, we will indicate the accent class of
the nouns by putting a number in ( ) after each noun. See
also Lesson 5.

GRAMMAR

6.1 Nouns. The Fourth Declension.

All nouns ending in -us (also in -ius) belong to the fourth
declension. They are all masculine.

Singular

N.	sūnùs	-us (3) 'son'	profèsorius	-ius (1) 'professor'
G.	sūnaũs	-aus	profèsoriaus	-iaus
D.	sūnui	-ui	profèsoriui	-iui
A.	súnų	-ų	profèsorių	-ių
I.	sūnumì	-umi	profèsoriumi	-iumi
L.	sūnujè	-uje	profèsoriuje	-iuje
V.	sūnaũ!	-au	profèsoriau!	-iau

6.2 Present tense forms of the verb *būti* (to be) may be omitted;
a dash may be written between two nouns:
Màno tévas — mókytojas. My father is a teacher.

One may also say, however, *Màno tévas yrà mókytojas* 'My
father is a teacher.' Both sentence types can be used, but the sentence without the verb is a little less formal and more familiar.

The word *yrà* may mean 'there is' or 'there are'. Examples:
Màno namè yrà rãdijas. — There is a radio in my home.
Añt stãlo yrà stiklaĩ. — There are glasses on the table.

In subordinate clauses *yrà* with the meaning 'there is, there are' may be omitted. Example:

...*, kuř visuomèt gẽras óras.* — ..., where there is always nice weather.

This could also be expressed by:

...*, kuř visuomèt yrà gẽras óras.* — ..., where there is always nice weather.

6.3 The Tag Question.

The "tag question" is not as frequently used in Lithuanian as it is in English. There are several ways of expressing this 'do you, don't you, have you, haven't you, will you, won't you, aren't you', etc. in Lithuanian:

1) With a negative question *ař nè?*, after positive statements. Literally it means: 'is it not, was it not, will it not', etc. This is used most frequently.

Dr. Vìtkus yrà jáunas, ař nè? — Dr. Vitkus is young, isn't he?
Jìs puikùs žmogùs, ař nè? — He is a fine man, isn't he?

2) With a positive word-question *tiesà?* 'true, correct?'. This word can be used both after the positive statements and the negative statements.

Jõ nãmas gẽras, tiesà? — His house is nice (good), is it not?
Jìs niẽko nežìno, tiesà? — He knows nothing, does he?

3) With a negative question *ař nè tiesà?* 'is that not so?' Primarily, this is used after positive statements, but sometimes it occurs after negative sentences, or clauses.

Jìs yrà gẽras profèsorius, ař nè tiesà? — He is a good professor, isn't he?
Jìs yrà nekóks žmogùs, ař nè tiesà? — He is not a very fine man, is he?

6.4 *Mẽgti* versus *patìkti.*

In 3.6 we described the usage of *patìkti*. *Mẽgti* can also be used for the same purpose, expressing a little more 'permanent' liking, a more intimate relationship, but this difference is actually very slim, very idiomatic.

53

I like Professor Vitkus: 1) *Mán patiñka profèsorius Vìtkus.*
2) *Aš mĕgstu profèsorių Vìtkų.*

No. 1 would mean: I like him as a man, his appearance, etc.

No. 2 — I like him as a professor, his way of lecturing, etc.

Sometimes the choice of the word *mĕgti* or *patìkti* depends upon the object. Thus it is better to say *mán patiñka Amèrika* 'I like America', *mán patiñka šìtas nāmas* 'I like this house', *mán patiñka šìta mergáitė* 'I like this girl' than *mĕgstu Amèriką* 'I like America', *mĕgstu šìtą nāmą* 'I like this house', *mĕgstu šìtą mergáitę* 'I like this girl'.

But it is possible to say *mĕgstu júodą dúoną* 'I like black bread', *mĕgstu vaisiùs* 'I like fruit', *mĕgstu skaitýti* 'I like to read', *megstu keliáuti* 'I like to travel' or *mán patiñka juodà dúona* 'I like black bread', *mán patiñka vaĩsiai* 'I like fruit', *mán patiñka skaitýti* 'I like to read', *mán patiñka keliáuti* 'I like to travel'.

EXERCISES

A. *Questions.* 1. Kokià yrà šiañdien dienà? 2. Kóks yrà šiañdien dangùs? 3. Kuř eīna profèsorius Vìtkus? 4. Ką̃ jìs mĕgsta gérti? 5. Kàs yrà jõ sūnùs? 6. Kuř gyvĕna dãktaras Vìtkus? 7. Kuř jiẽ sédi? 8. Kàs yrà midùs? 9. Kàs darýdavo senóvėje mìdų? 10. Ką̃ sãko profèsorius sůnui?

B. Add *ař nè?, tiesà?, ař nè tiesà?*: 1. Dr. Vìtkus yrà gýdytojas, ... 2. Ateĩna lietùs, ... 3. Midùs yrà sénas gérimas, ... 4. Jìs eīna pàs sàvo brólį, ... 5. Jìs mĕgsta gérti ãlų, ...

C. *Decline in singular:* dangùs, midùs, cùkrus, alùs, lietùs, žmogùs.

D. *Fill in:* 1. Ateĩna (rain) .... 2. Aš geriù (beer) .... 3. Màno tĕvas gĕria tìk (tea) .... 4. Màno brólis nègeria (beer) .... 5. Mĕs gyvĕname (in a suburb) ....

E. *Translate into Lithuanian:* 1. I am going for a walk. 2. My brother is also going for a walk. 3. My father never goes for a walk. 4. I like to go for a walk. 5. My brother also likes to go for a walk. 6. We sit outside and drink beer. 7. She **never** drinks beer, she only drinks tea. 8. The rain is coming. 9. Dr. Vitkus is a young man. 10. His father is a professor.

54

CONVERSATION

AR JŪS NE PONAS ŠARKIS?

Valỹs: 1. Ař jŭs nè pōnas Šárkis? Aš čià jõ láukiu.
Rìmas: 2. Nè. Aš esù Antãnas Rìmas. O jŭs?
Valys: 3. Jõnas Valỹs. Aš esù advokãtas.
Rimas: 4. Aš esù pãšto valdiniñkas. Aš dìrbu paštè.
Valys: 5. Ař jŭs ēsate vēdęs? Tùrite šeĩmą?
Rimas: 6. Taĩp. Turiù víeną sũnų iř víeną dùkterį. Màno duktě yrà studeñtė.
Valys: 7. O jŭsų sūnùs?
Rimas: 8. Màno sūnùs yrà inžiniẽrius.
Valys: 9. Bùvo labaĩ malonù sù jumìs pasikalběti. Sudiẽu.
Rimas: 10. Sudiẽu.

ARE YOU NOT MR. ŠARKIS?

Valys: 1. Are you not Mr. Šarkis? I have been waiting for him here.
Rimas: 2. No. I am Antanas Rimas. And you?
Valys: 3. Jonas Valys. I am a lawyer.
Rimas: 4. I am a postal employee. I work at the post office.
Valys: 5. Are you married? Do you have a family?
Rimas: 6. Yes. I have a son and a daughter. My daughter is a student.
Valys: 7. And your son?
Rimas: 8. My son is an engineer.
Valys: 9. It was a pleasure to speak with you. Good-bye.
Rimas: 10. Good-bye.

NOTES:

1. **jõ láukiu**: **jo** is genitive of **jis** 'he'. **Láukti** requires the direct object in the genitive case.
4. **valdiniñkas** — official, employee, civil officer of the state, municipality.
5. **vēdęs** — married (of men only).
9. **pasikalběti** is a compound verb: **pa-si-kalběti**: **kalběti** 'to speak, to talk', **-si-** — reflexive particle, **pa-** — prefix which gives the verb the meaning of doing something for a short while, etc. See also 14.2,6 and Appendix: Verbal Prefixes.

Septintoji pamoka

Lesson 7

ŠUO IR VANDUO

Aš turiù grãžų šùnį. Jõ var̃das Márgis. Màno draũgas taĩp pàt mė́gsta Márgį. Mẽs susitiñkame priẽ ùpės. Márgis braĩdo vandenyjè, o mẽs juõkiamės.

Màno sesuõ taĩp pàt tùri mãžą šùnį. Jìs vadìnasi Rùdis. Visì mė́gsta Rùdį: jìs labaĩ gudrùs šuõ. Rùdis labaĩ mė́gsta žaĩsti gãtvėje, bèt jìs labaĩ bìjo vandeñs. Jìs niekuomèt nebė́ga priẽ ùpės.

Aš sakaũ sàvo sė́seriai:

— Kur̃ tù einì, Rū́ta?

— Einù namõ.

— Kur̃ tàvo Rùdis?

— Jìs yrà namiẽ, nès jìs bìjo vandeñs.

— Geraĩ. Dabar̃ eĩk namõ ir̃ vir̃k pietùs.

— Eĩkime kartù! Tù mán turì padė́ti!

PRIE VANDENS

Nórkus: Eĩkime máudytis, vanduõ šiañdien yrà labaĩ šil̃tas.

Jonáitis: Ateĩkite čià! Vandenyjè mãtosi dìdelis raudónas akmuõ.

Norkus: Jū̃s mãnote, kàd mẽs gãlime tą̃ ãkmenį pakélti?

Jonaitis: Dúokite mán tą̃ lãzdą! Dabar̃ àš pasilenkiù ir̃ galiù lazdà ãkmenį pasíekti.

Norkus: Ar̃ tikraĩ jū̃s jį̃ gãlite vandenyjè matýti?

Jonaitis: Jéi nórite, ir̃ pàts gãlite matýti.

Norkus: Dabar̃ mataũ ... Vanduõ šil̃tas, eĩkime máudytis!

VOCABULARY

šuõ (4) irreg. — dog
vaȓdas (4) — name (first name)
Márgis -io (1) — Margis (usually: black and white; 'Spotty')
draũgas (4) — friend
susitìkti (susitinkù, susitiñka) — to meet
priẽ (prep. with gen.) — at, by, by the side of, etc.
ùpė (2) — river
vanduõ (3a) — water
braidýti (braidaũ, braĩdo) — to wade
juõktis (juokiúosi, juõkiasi) — to laugh
taĩp pàt — also, too
mãžas, -à — little, small
vadìntis (vadinúosi, vadìnasi) — to call oneself, to be called
Rùdis -džio (4) — Rudis ('Brownie', a brown dog)
gudrùs, -ì — clever
žmogùs (4) — man, human being
žaĩsti — to play; irreg.: žaidžiù, žai-dì, žaĩdžia; žaĩdžiame, žaĩdžiate, žaĩdžia
gãtvė (2) — street
bijóti (bijaũ, bìjo) — to be afraid, to fear
niekuomèt — never
bėgti (bėgu, bėga) — to run

piẽtūs (plural only) — dinner
kartù — together
padėti — to help; irreg.: pàdedu, pà-dedi, pàdeda; pàdedame, pàdedate, pàdeda
máudytis (máudausi, máudosi) — to bathe, swim
šìltas, -à — warm
mãtosi — can be seen (lit.: it sees it-self)
raudónas, -a — red
manýti (manaũ, mãno) — to think, to believe, to mean
galėti (galiù, gãli) — to be able, can
pakélti (pàkeliu, pàkelia) — to lift up
dúoti — to give; irreg.: dúodu, dúodi, dúoda; dúodame, dúodate, dúoda
lazdà (4) — stick
dabaȓ — now
pasileñkti (pasilenkiù, pasileñkia) — to bow, to bend down
pasíekti (pasíekiu, pasíekia) — to reach
gãlima — possible
tikraĩ — for sure, indeed, surely, cer-tainly
jéi — if
Jūs — you
matýti (mataũ, mãto) — to see

GRAMMAR

7.1 The Fifth Declension of Nouns.

The number of nouns belonging to this declension is not very large, and some are irregular.

To this declension belong feminine nouns in -uo, -ė, (gen. -ers) and masculine nouns in -uo (gen. -ens). From now on, this book will always indicate the genitive form of these nouns, so that the student may know their gender and declensional pattern.

Masculine				Feminine		
N. akmuõ (3b)	-uo	sesuõ (3b)	-uo	duktė̃ (3b)	-ė	
G. akmeñs	-ens	seseȓs	-ers	dukteȓs	-ers	
D. ãkmeniui	-eniui	sẽseriai	-eriai	dùkteriai	-eriai	
A. ãkmenį	-enį	sẽserį	-erį	dùkterį	-erį	
I. ãkmeniu	-eniu	sẽseria	-eria	dùkteria	-eria	
L. akmenyjè	-enyje	seseryjè	-eryje	dukteryjè	-eryje	
V. akmeniẽ!	-enie	seseriẽ!	-erie	dukteriẽ!	-erie	

N B. *šuõ* (4) 'dog' is irregular: šuõ - šuñs - šùniui - šùnį - šuniù - šunyjè - šuniẽ!

Other irregular nouns will be given later on, especially in the Lith.-English Vocabulary.

7.2 Reflexive Verbs.

The reflexive verbs in Lithuanian can be divided into two groups:

1) simple reflexive verbs where the reflexive particle *si* or *s* is added at the end;

2) compound reflexive verbs where the reflexive particle *si* is inserted between the prefix and the verb proper. To this group also belong all reflexive verbs in their negative forms: the negative particle *ne* is treated in such cases as a prefix: *aš lenkiúosi* 'I bow', *aš nesilenkiù* 'I do not bow'.

In the latter group, the conjugation of the basic verb does not change at all, only the *si* is inserted:

susitìkti	— 'to meet each other'; it is derived from
sutìkti	— 'to meet [someone]'.
sutìkti,	in turn, is a compound of the simple verb
tìkti	— 'to fit, to agree, to happen' and the prefix
su-	which means 'with':
sutìkti	also means 'to agree'. . .

Present tense

àš sutinkù 'I meet, I agree'	àš susitinkù	'I meet with someone'
tù sutinkì	tù susitinkì	
jìs sutiñka	jìs susitiñka	

mẽs sutiñkame	mẽs susitiñkame
jũs sutiñkate	jũs susitiñkate
jiẽ sutiñka	jiẽ susitiñka

It is a little more difficult to learn the simple reflexive verbs. Certain changes occur both in the endings of these verbs and the reflexive particle *si*:

59

1st Conjugation

leñkti 'to bend'   leñktis 'to bow' orig.: 'to bend'

àš lenkiù	àš lenkiúosi	àš nesilenkiù
tù lenkì	tù lenkíesi	tù nesilenkì
jìs leñkia	jìs leñkiasi	jìs nesileñkia
mẽs leñkiame	mẽs leñkiamės	mẽs nesileñkiame
jũs leñkiate	jũs leñkiatės	jũs nesileñkiate
jiẽ leñkia	jiẽ leñkiasi	jiẽ nesileñkia

2nd Conjugation

tıkė́tı 'to believe'   tikė́tis 'to expect, to hope for'

àš tikiù	àš tikiúosi
tù tikì	tù tikíesi
jìs tìki	jìs tìkisi
mẽs tìkime	mẽstìkimės
jũs tìkite	jũs tìkitės
jiẽ tìki	jiẽ tìkisi

3rd Conjugation

matýti 'to see'   matýtis 'to see each other,
                            to meet,
                            to meet socially'

àš mataũ	àš mataũsi
tù mataĩ	tù mataĩsi
jìs mãto	jìs mãtosi
mẽs mãtome	mẽs mãtomės
jũs mãtote	jũs mãtotės
jiẽ mãto	jiẽ mãtosi

NB. The reflexive particle *si* is a short form of the full reflexive pronoun, acc. sg. and pl. *savè*. In plural forms which end in *e*, i.e. in the first and second plural, instead of *si*, only *s* is added, and the short final *e* of these forms is replaced by *ė* (long, very narrow *ė*, see Introd. Lesson).

The first person singular endings *-u* and *-iu* are replaced by *-uo* and *-iuo* respectively and the second person singular ending

-*i* is replaced by -*ie*. The reflexive particle -*si* is then added to these expanded forms giving (1st person) -*uosi, -iuosi* and (2nd person) -*iesi*. The stress pattern is the same as in the non-reflexive verbs.

7.3 Imperative.

There are three basic forms of imperative in Lithuanian: 2nd person singular, 2nd person plural and 1st person plural. The first is used in addressing close friends, members of the family, children and animals. The second is used to address a group of persons (or animals), or to address one person politely. The third form would render the English: *let us* . . .

The formation of these forms is not complicated:

2nd person singular: drop the -*ti* from the infinitive, add *k*: darýti > darý+k! 'do'; kalbĕti > kalbĕ+k! 'speak'.

2nd person plural: drop the -*ti* from the infinitive, add -*kite:* darýti > darý+kite!; kalbĕti > kalbĕ+kite!

1st person plural: drop the -*ti*, add -*kime*: darýti > darý+kime! "let's do'; kalbĕti > kalbĕ+kime! 'let's speak'.

In reflexives, it follows this pattern:

non-reflexive:	*reflexive:*
matýti 'to see'	matýtis 'to see each other,
matýk!	matýkis! to meet'
matýkite!	matýkitės!
matýkime!	matýkimės!

NB. If the infinitive stem, after dropping of -*ti*, ends in -*g* or -*k*, then these are dropped and a *k* is added:

bĕgti 'to run'	baĩgti 'to end'	šaũkti 'to shout'
bĕk!	baĩk!	šaũk!
bĕkite!	baĩkite!	šaũkite!
bĕkime!	baĩkime!	šaũkime!

The stress is the same as in the infinitive.

EXERCISES

A. *Questions.* 1. Kàs tùri šùnį? 2. Kóks jõ vařdas? 3. Kàs mẽgsta Márgį? 4. Kuř mẽs susitiñkame? 5. Kaĩp vadìnasi màno seseřs šuõ? 6. Kóks šuõ yrà Rùdis? 7. Kõ (what) Rùdis bìjo? 8. Kuř jìs niekuomèt nebẽga? 9. Ką̃ àš sakaũ Rūtai? 10. Ką̃ jì dãro namiẽ?

B. *Give the three imperative forms of the following verbs:* eĩti, matýti, žaĩsti, máudytis, susitìkti, turẽti, pasileñkti.

C. *Complete:* 1. Aš mataũ (a stone) .... 2. Akmuõ yrà (in the water) .... 3. Aš mýliu sàvo (sister) .... 4. Mẽs eĩname (into the water) .... 5. Màno brólis bìjo (water) ....,....... ... 6. Mẽs (meet) .... priẽ van- dens. 7. Jìs visuomèt (laughs) .... 8. Aš (am afraid) .... vandeñs. 9. Jìs (bathes, swims) .... ùpėje. 10. (Go) .... namõ!

D. *Translate into Lithuanian:* 1. My brother has a dog. 2. His dog is called Rudis. 3. He goes to the river. 4. He wants to swim in the river. 5. Mr. Sakaitis sees a stone in the river. 6. The water is very warm. 7. He likes to play in the street. 8. Go home and read! 9. Let us go home! 10. Jonai (voc. of Jonas), read the newspaper!

CONVERSATION

SUSIPAŽINIMAS

Vaĩtkus: Labà dienà, põne Podrỹ! Kaĩp gyvúojate?

Podrỹs: Ačiū, geraĩ. Léiskite supažìndinti jùs sù ponù Jonáičiu.

Vaitkus: Vaĩtkus (shaking hands with Jonaitis). Labaĩ malonù.

Jonáitis: Jonáitis. Labaĩ malonù susipažìnti... Ař jū̃sų brólis negyvẽna Kaunè?

Vaitkus: Taĩp, jìs gyvẽna Kaunè. O kuř jū̃s gyvẽnate?

Jonaitis: Aš gyvenù Vìlniuje. Aš esù žurnalìstas.

Podrys: Taĩp, taĩp... Põnas Jonáitis jaũ seniaĩ čià dìrba.

Vaitkus: Mán jaũ reĩkia eĩti. Bùvo labaĩ malonù susipažìnti. (Shakes hands with Jonaitis and Podrys).

Jonaitis: Mán taĩp pàt. Iki pasimãtymo.

Vaitkus: Iki pasimãtymo.

MEETING PEOPLE

Vaitkus: Good day, Mr. Podrys. How are you?

Podrys: Fine, thank you. Allow me to introduce Mr. Jonaitis to you.

Vaitkus: Vaitkus (shaking hands with Jonaitis). Very pleased.

Jonaitis: Jonaitis. It is very nice to meet you. Doesn't your brother live in Kaunas?

Vaitkus: Yes, he lives in Kaunas. And where do you live?

Jonaitis: I live in Vilnius. I am a journalist.

Podrys: Yes, yes ... Mr. Jonaitis has been working here for a long time.

Vaitkus: I have to go. It was very nice meeting you.

Jonaitis: For me, too ... So long.

Vaitkus: So long.

NOTES:

2. **supažìndinti Jùs sù ponù Jonáičiu**: make you acquainted with Mr. J.; 'with' governs the instrumental.

7. **Jaū seniaĩ čià dìrba**: is present tense. An action begun in the past, but continuing into the present is expressed by the present tense in Lithuanian, not by the perfect progressive as in English.

8. **Mán reĩkia**: see 9.5.

10. **Ikì pasimãtymo**: lit. 'until seeing each other again'.

Aštuntoji pamoka
Lesson 8

LAIŠKAS

Brangùs Antãnai,

Vãkar norė́jau rašýti Táu láišką, bèt neturė́jau laĩko. Turė́jau daũg dárbo. Bùvo gražì dienà, taĩ dìrbau laukè. Màno brólis dìrbo daržè. Jìs kãsė žė́mę, õ àš sodinaũ mė́dį.

Vakarè àš buvaũ teatrè, kuř mačiaũ naũją drãmą. Aš niekadõs nemė́gau komèdijos, todė́l šì naują dramà mán patìko. Màno brólis mė́gsta òperą, jám iřgi nepatiñka komèdija.

Mùms labaĩ patìko Tàvo láiškas. Pàs mùs óras dabař šiĩtas, mė̃s dažnaĩ eĩname máudytis į̃ ùpę. Jì yrà gilì, iř jojè gãlima plaũkti.

Vãkar bùvo labaĩ gražì naktìs. Põ teãtro mė̃s visì ė́jome pasiváikščioti. Sù mumìs taĩp pàt ė́jo mū́sų šuõ Márgis. Mė̃s jį̃ labaĩ mýlime, iř jìs mùs labaĩ mýli.

Prašaũ mán vė̃l greĩtai parašýti.

Tàvo

Pė̃tras

VOCABULARY

láiškas (3) — letter, epistle
brangùs, -ì — dear, expensive
vãkar — yesterday
norė́ti (nóriu, nóri) — to want, to wish
rašýti (rašaũ, rãšo) — to write
laĩkas (4) — time
dařžas (4) — vegetable garden
kàsti (kasù, kãsa) — to dig
žė́mė (2) — earth, soil
sodìnti (sodinù, sodìna) — to plant
mė́dis (gen. mė́džio) (2) — tree
teãtras (2) — theater (legitimate)

dramà (2) — drama, serious play
òpera (1) — opera
iřgi — also
niekadõs — never
komèdija (1) — comedy
todė́l — that's why, for that reason
dažnaĩ — often
gilì (adj. fem.) — deep
plaũkti (plaukiù, plaũkia) — to swim
naktìs (gen. naktiẽs) (4) — night
vė̃l — again
greĩtai — soon, fast, quickly

65

GRAMMAR

8.1 Past Tense.

In meaning the simple preterit in Lithuanian corresponds more or less to the simple past tense of English.

The past tense stem is formed by dropping the infinitive ending -ti; if a -y- precedes the -ti, then final -yti is dropped also. Thus for *dìrbti* 'to work' the past tense stem is *dirb-*; for *rašýti* 'to write' the past tense stem is *raš-*.

8.1,1 First Conjugation *dìrbti* 'to work'; *ruõšti* 'to prepare':

'I worked'

	Singular			*Plural*	
1)	àš dìrbau	-au		mẽs dìrbome	-ome
2)	tù dìrbai	-ai		jũs dìrbote	-ote
3)	jìs, jì dìrbo	-o		jiẽ, jõs dìrbo	-o

'I prepared'

1)	àš ruošiaũ	-iau		mẽs ruõšėme	-ėme
2)	tù ruošeĩ	-ei		jũs ruõšėte	-ėte
3)	jìs, jì ruõšė	-ė		jiẽ, jõs ruõšė	-ė

8.1,2 Second Conjugation (*mylḗti* 'to love')

'I loved'

	Singular			*Plural*	
1)	àš mylḗjau	-jau		mẽs mylḗjome	-jome
2)	tù mylḗjai	-jai		jũs mylḗjote	-jote
3)	jìs, jì mylḗjo	-jo		jiẽ, jõs mylḗjo	-jo

8.1,3 Third Conjugation (*žinóti* 'to know'; *rašýti* 'to write')

'I knew'

	Singular			*Plural*	
1)	àš žinójau	-jau		mẽs žinójome	-jome
2)	tù žinójai	-jai		jũs žinójote	-jote
3)	jìs, jì žinójo	-jo		jiẽ, jõs žinójo	-jo

'I wrote'

1)	àš rašiaũ	-iau	mẽs rãšėme	-ėme
2)	tù rašeĩ	-ei	jũs rãšėte	-ėte
3)	jìs, jì rãšė	-ė	jiẽ, jõs rãšė	-ė

(*skaitýti* 'to read')

'I read'

1)	àš skaičiaũ	-iau	mẽs skaĩtėme	-ėme
2)	tù skaiteĩ	-ei	jũs skaĩtėte	-ėte
3)	jìs, jì skaĩtė	-ė	jiẽ, jõs skaĩtė	-ė

8.1,4 Remarks on the conjugations:

A) There are essentially only two types of endings in the past tense (simple preterit):

(1) -au, -ai, -o, -ome, -ote
(2) -iau, -ei, -ė, -ėme, ėte

If a first conjugation verb has the present stem ending in (1st sing.) -iu, (3rd prs.) -ia, then it usually will have a type (2) past tense. Many verbs with a present stem (1st sing.) -u, (3rd prs.) -a have a type (1) past tense. But this is not always the case; e.g. *nèšti* 'to carry' and *vèsti* 'to lead' etc. have type (2) endings and are conjugated (1st sing.) *neš-iaũ, vedž-iaũ*; (2nd sing.) *neš-eĩ, ved-eĩ*; (3rd prs.) *nẽš-ė, vẽd-ė*, etc.

First conjugation verbs with an infinitive stem in -uo or -au replace final -uo or -au by -av and type (1) endings are added. Thus *dainúoti* 'to sing' and *dalyváuti* 'to participate' are conjugated (1st sing.) *dainav-aũ, dalyvav-aũ*, (2nd sing.) *dainav-aĩ, dalyvav-aĩ*, (3rd prs.) *daināv-o, dalyvãvo*, etc. There are, however, certain exceptions to the above mentioned rules. For example, *dúoti* 'to give' has the past tense *dav-iaũ, dav-eĩ, dãv-ė*, etc and *griáuti* 'to thunder' has the past tense *grióv-iau, grióv-ei, grióv-ė*, etc.

B) Second and third conjugation verbs with infinitive stems in -ė or -o drop the -ti, but a -j- is inserted between the stem and the ending, cf. paragraphs 8.1,2 and *žinóti* in 8.1,3.
Third conjugation verbs with the infinitive in -yti drop the -yti and type (2) endings are added, cf. 8.1,3 *rašýti* and *skaitýti*.

C) It is impossible to tell from the infinitive what the past tense conjugation will be. Therefore in the vocabulary following the infinitive the following four forms are listed: 1st sing. pres., 3rd prs. pres., 3rd prs. past tense (simple preterit) and 3rd prs. future. If the 3rd prs. past tense is in -o then all endings are of type (1); if the 3rd prs. past tense is in -ė then all endings are of type (2).

D) There is no distinction in the form of the third person singular and third person plural, the same form being used for both just as in the present tense. As in the present tense the endings -me and -te can be added directly to the third person in order to get the first and second plural forms respectively.

E) The stress is either on the end in the first and second singular and the stem elsewhere or constant on the stem syllable throughout the conjugation:
    rašiaũ, rašeĩ, rãšė, rãšėme, rãšėte
    kándau, kándai, kándo, kándome, kándote
    (from ką́sti 'to bite'). It usually follows the stress pattern of the present tense.

NOTE: There are many verbs in Lithuanian which have an irregular past tense. Always check the principal parts of the verbs in the Lith. - English Vocabulary. Some will be given in the vocabulary lists of the individual lessons.

8.2 Past tense of *bū́ti* 'to be' and *eĩti* 'to go'.

These are the past tenses of *bū́ti* and *eĩti*:

bū́ti 'to be'	*eĩti* 'to go'
àš buvaũ 'I was'	àš ėjaũ 'I went, I was going'
tù buvaĩ	tù ėjaĩ
jìs bùvo	jìs ė́jo
mẽs bùvome	mẽs ė́jome
jū̃s bùvote	jū̃s ė́jote
jiẽ bùvo	jiẽ ė́jo

NB. 1) In *bū́ti*, *ū* is long, but in *buvaũ*, the *u* is short, even under the stress.

2) In *eĩti, e* is replaced by *ė* and *i* by *j*.

8.3 Past Tense of the Reflexive Verbs.

The past tense of the reflexive verbs is formed like the past tense of the corresponding non-reflexives, and the reflexive particle is then added.*

1st Conjugation		*2nd Conjugation*		*3rd Conjugation*	
sùkti 'to turn'		*mylė́ti* 'to love'		*skaitýti* 'to read'	
sùktis 'to rotate'		*mylė́tis* 'to love each other'		*skaitýtis* 'to reckon with'	
sukaũ	sukaũsi	mylė́jau	mylė́jausi	skaičiaũ	skaičiaũsi
sukaĩ	sukaĩsi	mylė́jai	mylė́jaisi	skaiteĩ	skaiteĩsi
sùko	sùkosi	mylė́jo	mylė́josi	skaĩtė	skaĩtėsi
sùkome	sùkomės	mylė́jome	mylė́jomės	skaĩtėme	skaĩtėmės
sùkote	sùkotės	mylė́jote	mylė́jotės	skaĩtėte	skaĩtėtės
sùko	sùkosi	mylė́jo	mylė́josi	skaĩtė	skaĩtėsi

In compound reflexive verbs, where the reflexive particle is added between the main verb and the prefix, the past tense is just like that of a non-reflexive verb:

sutìkti 'to meet, to agree'	*susitìkti* 'to meet each other, (to meet with someone)'
sutikaũ	susitikaũ
sutikaĩ	susitikaĩ
sutìko	susitìko
sutìkome	susitìkome
sutìkote	susitìkote
sutìko	susitìko

NB. 1) Whenever the verb is in the negative, the negative particle *ne-* is added to the verb, and if the verb is reflexive, the particle *si* is inserted between the *ne-* and the verb:

sukaũsi	b u t :	nesisukaũ
sukaĩsi		nesisukaĩ
sùkosi		nesisùko
sùkomės		nesisùkome
sùkotės		nesisùkote
sùkosi		nesisùko

---

* See also Lesson 7.

2) In the 1st and 2nd person plural, whenever the reflexive
-s is added, the e is replaced by ė: mylėjome, but: mylė-
jomės; sùkote, but: sùkotės, etc.

8.4 The Declension of the Personal Pronouns.

Singular

I	(thou), you	he	she
N. àš	tù	jìs	jì
G. manę̃s	tavę̃s	jõ	jõs
D. mán	táu	jám	jái
A. manè	tavè	jį̃	ją̃
I. manimì	tavimì	juõ	jà
L. manyjè	tavyjè	jamè	jojè

Plural

we	you	they (masc.)	they (fem.)
N. mẽs	jū̃s	jiẽ	jõs
G. mū́sų	jū́sų	jų̃	jų̃
D. mùms	jùms	jíems	jóms
A. mùs	jùs	juõs	jàs
I. mumìs	jumìs	jaĩs	jomìs
L. mumysè	jumysè	juosè	josè

8.5 The Use of the Personal Pronouns.

The use of the personal pronouns is similar to that of English.
One must remember, however, that the 3rd person agrees with
the word it refers to in number and gender. The case of the pronoun is determined by its use in the clause in which it occurs.

Examples:

1) *Šìs stãlas yrà naũjas. Jìs yrà màno kambaryjè.* 'This table
is new. It is in my room.' Note that *jis,* the masc. nom. sing. pronoun is translated by *it.* In Lithuanian the form *jìs* agrees in
gender and number with *stãlas.* It is in the nominative case because it is the subject of the sentence.

2) *Aš nusipirkaũ naũją lémpą. Bè jõs negaliù dìrbti.* 'I bought
[for myself] a new lamp. Without it I cannot work.' The pronoun

jos is feminine singular because it refers to *lempa*. It is in the genitive case because it is the object of the preposition *be* 'without' which requires the genitive case.

8.6 *Tu* and *jūs*.

Tu 'thou', the 2nd singular pronoun is a familiar form which is to be used only with close friends, the closest members of the family, children and animals. *Jūs* has to be used whenever one addresses one or several persons who are not members of the above mentioned groups. *Jūs* is, of course, used when addressing more than one person familiarly. This usage is practically identical with the use of *tu* and *vous* in French or *du* and *Sie*, (*ihr*) in German.

NB. Whenever *tù* or *jū̃s*, or any possessive pronouns derived from them, i.e., *tàvo, jū́sų* are used in a letter or describing conversation or direct speech referring to the person, or persons, to whom the letter is addressed, then all of these words are capitalized: *Tù, Jū̃s, Tàvo, Jū́sų*.

Other forms of address used in Lithuanian: *Támsta* 'you', *Pàts* 'thou' (lit. 'you yourself'), *Sveĩkas* 'thou' (lit. 'healthy').

EXERCISES

A. *Questions*. 1. Kadà Pétras norė́jo rašýti láišką? 2. Kokià bùvo dienà? 3. Kuř̃ Pétras dìrbo? 4. Ką̃ jìs dìrbo? 5. Kuř̃ jìs bùvo vakarè? 6. Kàs jám teñ patìko? 7. Ką̃ mė́gsta jõ brólis? 8. Kóks yrà óras dabař̃? 9. Kokià yrà mū́sų ùpė? 10. Kokià bùvo naktìs, kaĩ Pétras ė́jo pasiváikščioti?

B. *Give the full past tense of the following verbs:*

norė̆ti (nóriu, nóri)   plaũkti (plaukiù, plaũkia)
kàsti (kasù, kãsa)   parašýti (parašaũ, parãšo)
sodìnti (sodinù, sodìna)

C. *Replace words in parentheses with personal pronouns:* 1. (Màno tė̃vas) yrà sẽnas. 2. (Jõ brólis) dìrbo laukè. 3. (Naktìs) bùvo labaĩ gražì. 4. (Rýtas) bùvo labaĩ šáltas. 5. Àš ė́jau sù (bróliu). 6. (Màno bróliui) nepatìko komèdija. 7. Bè (naũjo stãlo) àš negaliù dìrbti.

D. *Turn all the verbs into the past tense:* 1. Aš einù namõ. 2. Tù esì studeñtas. 3. Jũs ẽsate màno profèsorius. 4. Mẽs dìrbame laukè. 5. Jìs visuomèt tùri laĩko. 6. Jìs gyvẽna priẽ ùpės. 7. Mẽs eĩname pasiváikščioti. 8. Põnas Žalỹs skaĩto láišką. 9. Vìlnius yrà gražùs miẽstas.

E. *Translate into Lithuanian:* 1. I am reading a letter. 2. I read (past tense) the letter. 3. I read (past tense) it. 4. My brother went home. 5. He was going home. 6. Our river is pretty. 7. It (the river) is pretty. 8. Please (I ask) write me again soon. 9. They were at the theatre last night (lit. yesterday evening). 10. We were going home.

CONVERSATION

ŽUKIENĖ IR RIMIENĖ

Žukíenė:	1.	Lãbas rýtas!
Rimíenė:	2.	Lãbas rýtas! Labaĩ malonù, kàd užėjote pàs manè.
Žukíenė:	3.	Seniaĩ norėjau užeĩti pàs jùs, bèt vìs neturėjau laĩko.
Rimíenė:	4.	Kuř jũsų výras?
Žukíenė:	5.	Jìs dìrba. Vãkar jìs bùvo namiẽ.
Rimíenė:	6.	Išgérkime puodùką kavõs!
Žukíenė:	7.	Ačiū labaĩ. Mielaĩ.
Rimíenė:	8.	Ař girdėjote ką́ nórs naũjo?
Žukíenė:	9.	Niẽko ypatìngo. Vãkar vìsą diẽną buvaũ namiẽ.
Rimíenė:	10.	Bèt àš girdėjau, kàd ...

MRS. ŽUKAS AND MRS. RIMAS

Mrs. Žukas:	1.	Good morning.
Mrs. Rimas:	2.	Good morning. It is very nice of you to drop in.
Mrs. Žukas:	3.	I have been wanting to drop in for a long time, but I simply did not have time.
Mrs. Rimas:	4.	Where is your husband?
Mrs. Žukas:	5.	He is working. He was at home yesterday.
Mrs. Rimas:	6.	Let's have a cup of coffee.

Mrs. Žukas:	7.	Thank you. I'll be glad to . . .
Mrs. Rimas:	8.	Have you heard anything new?
Mrs. Žukas:	9.	Nothing special. I was at home all day yesterday.
Mrs. Rimas:	10.	But I have heard that . . .

NOTES:

1. **Žukíenė, Rimíenė** — Mrs. Žukas, Mrs. Rimas. See 11.3.
2. **užėjote pàs manè** — 'dropped in on me, stopped by, came to see me'
7. **mielaĩ** — lit. 'gladly'.
8. **naũjo** (gen. of **naũjas**) — 'new'; **Kàs nórs naũjo** 'something new', acc. **ką̃ nórs naũjo** — only **kàs** is inflected.
9. **Niẽko ypatìngo** — lit. 'of nothing special'. It is used in the genitive form.
10. **vìsą diẽną** — acc. of definite time.

73

Devintoji pamoka

Lesson 9

SEKMADIENIS

Rytój sekmãdienis. Mán nereikẽs eĩti į̃ universitètą. Rytój mẽs visì eĩsime į̃ bažnýčią, kuř̃ mẽs meĩsimės iř̃ giedósime. Jéigu bùs gražùs óras, taĩ mẽs põ pamaldų̃ važiúosime į̃ káimą. Káime gyvẽna mũsų senēlis iř̃ senēlė. Jiẽ tùri grãžų̃ ū̃kį̃ priẽ Nēmuno. Mẽs juõs aplankýsime iř̃ sù jaĩs pasikalbēsime. Jiẽ mùms duõs mãžą̃ kačiùką, kurį̃ mẽs parsivẽšime į̃ miẽstą.

Rytój vakarè mẽs eĩsime į̃ miẽsto párką, kuř̃ bùs gražùs kon-cèrtas. Mẽs sėdēsime párke iř̃ klausýsimės mùzikos. Bùs gražì naktìs, dangujè plaũks mēnùlis, mẽs bũsime labaĩ laimìngi.

Nãktį̃, kaĩ sēnas Vìlnius miegõs, mẽs eĩsime namõ senà gatvè prõ universitètą, prõ kãtedrą, prõ Gedimìno kálną.

VOCABULARY

rytój — tomorrow
sekmãdienis -io (1) — Sunday
mán nereikẽs — I won't have to
bažnýčia (1) — church
meĩstis (meldžiúosi, meĩdžiasi, meĩdė-si) — to pray
giedóti (gíedu, gíeda, giedójo) — to sing (hymns)
jéigu — if
taĩ (conjunction) — so then
põ (prep. with gen.) — after
pamaldų̃ (gen. plur.) — (religious) service
káimas (1) — village
senēlis -io (2) — grandfather
senēlė (2) — grandmother

kačiùkas (diminutive of katẽ) — kitten
parsivèžti (parsìvežu, parsìveža, par-sìvežė) — to bring along (in a ve-hicle)
rytój vakarè — tomorrow evening
párkas (1) — park
koncèrtas (2) — concert
sėdēti (sėdžiu, sėdi, sėdējo) — to sit (i.e. to be in the sitting position)
klausýti (klausaũ, klaũso, klaũsė) — to listen to
klausýtis (klausaũsi, klaũsosi, klaũ-sėsi) — to listen to
dangùs (4) — sky, heaven
mēnùlis -io (2) — moon

75

ūkis -io (1) — farm
prič (prep. with gen.) — on, by, at
Nėmunas (3b) — Nemunas (Niemen, Memel), a river in Lithuania
aplankýti (aplankaũ, aplañko, aplañ-kė) — to visit
pasikalbėti (pasìkalbu, pasìkalba, pa-sikalbėjo) — to have a talk, chat

laimìngi (nom. plur. masc.) — happy
nãktį — at night, during the night
miegóti (míegu, míega, miegójo) — to sleep
prõ (prep. with acc.) — past
kãtedra (1) — cathedral
Gedimìnas — Gediminas, grand duke (king) of Lithuania (1311-1341)

GRAMMAR

9.1 The Future Tense.

Examples of the future tense are given below:
dìrbti 'to work' (1st conjugation)

Singular			Plural	
1)	àš dìrbsiu	-siu	mẽs dìrbsime	-sime
2)	tù dìrbsi	-si	jũs dìrbsite	-site
3)	jìs, jì dir̃bs	-s	jiẽ, jõs dir̃bs	-s

mylẽti 'to love' (2nd conjugation)

Singular			Plural	
1)	àš mylẽsiu	-siu	mẽs mylẽsime	-sime
2)	tù mylẽsi	-si	jũs mylẽsite	-site
3)	jìs, jì mylẽs	-s	jiẽ, jõs mylẽs	-s

skaitýti 'to read' (3rd conjugation)

Singular			Plural	
1)	àš skaitýsiu	-siu	mẽs skaitýsime	-sime
2)	tù skaitýsi	-si	jũs skaitýsite	-site
3)	jìs, jì skaitỹs	-s	jiẽ, jõs skaitỹs	-s

A) As can be seen from the above examples the future tense is formed by dropping the -ti from the infinitive and adding the appropriate future tense endings.

B) The stress is always on the same syllable as in the infinitive. In the 3rd person an acute (in case of u and i, it is ù and ì) is replaced by a circumflex stress.

C) Some verbs with a monosyllabic stem shorten the root vowel in the 3rd person, e.g. bùti 'to be' which has the future conjugation *bū́siu, bū́si, bùs*, etc. or *dýgti* 'to germinate' which has the future conjugation *dýgsiu, dýgsi, dìgs*, etc.

D) Certain consonantal contractions are characteristic of the future tense: s+s=s; š+s=š; z+s=s; ž+s=š.

Examples:

mèsti 'to throw'		*nèšti* 'to carry'	
Singular	*Plural*	*Singular*	*Plural*
1 mèsiu < mes+siu	mèsime	1 nèšiu < neš+siu	nèšime
2 mèsi < mes+si	mèsite	2 nèši < neš+si	nèšite
3 mès < mes+s		3 nèš < neš+s	

ziřzti 'to whine'		*vèžti* 'to transport'	
Singular	*Plural*	*Singular*	*Plural*
1 ziřsiu < zirz+siu	ziřsime	1 vèšiu < vež+siu	vèšime
2 ziřsi < zirz+si	ziřsite	2 vèši < vež+si	vèšite
3 ziřs < zirz+s		3 vèš < vež+s	

9.2 The Future of the Reflexive Verbs.

An example of the reflexive future conjugation is given below: *skaitýtis* 'to reckon with':

	Singular		*Plural*	
1)	àš skaitýsiuos(i)	-siuosi	mẽs skaitýsimės	-simės
2)	tù skaitýsies(i)	-siesi	jū̃s skaitýsitės	-sitės
3)	jìs, jì skaitýsis	-sis	jiẽ, jõs skaitýsis	

The reflexive endings of the future are very similar to those of the present tense (see Lesson 7). The 3rd person is different.

9.2,1 Just as in the past tense (see 8.3) in compound and negated reflexive verbs the reflexive particle -*si*- is inserted between the prefix (or negative particle) and the verbal stem:

	susitìkti 'to meet'	
	Singular	*Plural*
1)	àš su-si-tìksiu	mẽs su-si-tìksime
2)	tù su-si-tìksi	jū̃s su-si-tìksite
3)	jìs, jì su-si-tìks	jiẽ, jõs su-si-tìks

77

nesisùkti 'not to turn (around)'

1) àš ne-si-sùksiu   mẽs ne-si-sùksime
2) tù ne-si-sùksi   jũs ne-si-sùksite
3) jìs, jì ne-si-sùks   jiẽ, jõs ne-si-sùks

In ordinary orthography the hyphen is not written between the elements of the verb. Here we have put it in so that the student may more clearly see the formation of the reflexive.

9.3 Principal Parts of the Verb.

From now on the vocabulary will list after each verb the so-called principal parts from which all the other verbal forms can be derived.

Examples:

Infinitive		1st present	3rd present	3rd past	3rd future
dìrbti	'to work'	dìrbu	dìrba	dìrbo	dìŕbs
ruõšti	'to prepare'	ruošiù	ruõšia	ruõšė	ruõš
mylė́ti	'to love'	mýliu	mýli	mylė́jo	mylė́s
rašýti	'to write'	rašaũ	rãšo	rãšė	rašу̃s
skaitýti	'to read'	skaitaũ	skaĩto	skaĩtė	skaitу̃s
bū́ti	'to be'	esù	yrà	bùvo	bùs
eĩti	'to go'	einù	eĩna	ė́jo	eĩs

In Lithuanian grammars intended for Lithuanians, usually only the infinitive, the 3rd present and the 3rd past are listed.

9.4 Word Order.

The common word order in Lithuanian is: subject, verb, direct or indirect object, adverb, infinitive and then the other parts of the sentence. Examples:

Aš rašaũ láišką bróliui. — I am writing a letter to my brother.
or
Aš rašaũ jám láišką. — I am writing him a letter.

However, such a word order is not by any means necessary, because in Lithuanian the word order is free. Therefore it is possible to say:

(1) *Àš turiù jám šiañdien rašýti láišką.*
or
(2) *Àš turiù rašýti jám láišką šiañdien.*
or
(3) *Àš turiù jám láišką šiañdien rašýti.*
or
(4) *Àš turiù jám šiañdien láišką rašýti.*
— 'I must write him a letter today.'

The word in any position may receive the logical emphasis of the sentence.

9.4,1 In Lithuanian an *interrogative sentence* is indicated by the sentence intonation or else by the particle *ar̃* in sentence initial position:

1) *Tù buvaĩ vãkar miestè?* — Were you in the city yesterday?
2) *Ar̃ tù buvaĩ vãkar miestè?* —   (" ")

An interrogative adverb of some sort may also introduce an interrogative sentence. Examples:

1) *Kadà tù buvaĩ miestè?* — When were you in the city?
2) *Kur̃ gyvẽna tàvo tẽvas?* — Where does your father live?
3) *Kàs gãli mán pasakýti, kur̃ yrà viẽšbutis "Euròpa"?* — Who can tell me where the hotel "Europe" is?

9.4,2 *In dependent clauses* the word order is very similar to that of the main clause. Examples:

1) *Àš žinaũ, kàd tù vãkar buvaĩ miestè.*
I know that you were in the city yesterday.

2) *Àš žinaũ, kàd vãkar tù buvaĩ miestè.*
I know that yesterday you were in the city.

3) *Àš žinaũ, kàd tù buvaĩ vãkar miestè.*
I know that you were in the city yesterday.

9.5 *'I need, I have to', etc.*

To express obligation one can use the verb *turḗti* 'to have, to have to'. Examples:

1) *Àš turiù eĩti namõ.* — I have to (must) go home.
2) *Àš turḗjau eĩti namõ.* — I had to go home.
3) *Àš turḗsiu eĩti namõ.* — I shall have to go home.

79

To express need or necessity the verb *reikěti* 'to be necessary' is used. The logical subject is in the dative case. Examples:

1) *Mán reĩkia eĩti namõ.* — I have to (need to) go home.
2. *Mán reikějo eĩti namõ.* — I had to (needed to) go home.
3. *Mán reikės eĩti namõ.* — I shall have to (shall need to) go home.
4) *Màno bróliui reikės eĩti namõ.* — My brother shall have to go home.

EXERCISES

A. *Questions.* 1. Kadà mán reikės eĩti į universitètą? 2. Kuř mẽs rytój eĩsime? 3. Kàs gyvẽna káime? 4. Ką jiẽ tùri namiẽ? 5. Kuř yrà jų ūkis? 6. Ką jiẽ mùms duõs rytój? 7. Kuř mẽs eĩsime rytój vakarè? 8. Ką mẽs darýsime párke? 9. Kokià bùs naktis? 10. Kuř bùs mėnùlis?

B. *Give the future conjugation of the following verbs:* norěti, rašýti, kàsti (kas+siu=kàsiu), sodìnti, plaũkti, parašýti.

C. *Put all of the italicized forms in the future tense:* 1. Aš turějau eĩti namõ. 2. Màno brólis *yrà* studeñtas. 3. Mẽs *ẽsame* labaĩ laimìngi. 4. Mẽs *eĩname* prõ Gedimìno kálną. 5. Aš *rašaũ* láišką.

D. *Fill in the blanks:* 1. Aš (have to) .... eĩti namõ. 2. Mán (have to) .... skaitýti láišką. 3. Mẽs (have to) .... važiúoti namõ. 4. Mùms (have to) .... važiúoti namõ. 5. Aš (must) .... kalbėti lietùviškai.

E. *Translate into Lithuanian:* 1. I will go to school tomorrow. 2. We will read the letter. 3. We will live in the city. 4. He will work the whole day (vìsą diẽną). 5. I will read a book. 6. They will visit grandmother and grandfather. 7. There will be a concert in the park. 8. I have to go home. 9. We will have to go home. 10. We must read a book.

CONVERSATION

AR JŪS KALBATE LIETUVIŠKAI?

Mókytojas: 1. Ař jūs [ẽsate] lietùvis ař amerikiẽtis?
Mokinỹs: 2. Aš esù amerikiẽtis, bèt nóriu išmókti lietùviškai.
Mokytojas: 3. Ař jūs jaũ geraĩ kaĺbate lietùviškai?
Mokinys: 4. Dabař dár geraĩ negaliù kalbėti lietùviškai.

Mokytojas: 5. Taĭp, mēs dabař kalbėsime klãsėje tìk lietùviškai. Rašýsime iř skaitýsime taĭp pàt tìk lietùviškai.

Mokinys: 6. Labaĭ geraĭ. Tókiu būdù mēs geraĭ išmóksime lietùviškai.

Mokytojas: 7. O kaĭp jŭs kaĺbate namiē?

Mokinys: 8. Namiē mēs kaĺbame ángliškai, nès màno tėvaĭ lietùviškai nemóka.

Mokytojas: 9. Gaĭla. Jŭs negalėsite namiē kalbĕti lietùviškai...

Mokinys: 10. Bèt gál iř jiē išmõks lietùviškai kalbĕti. Aš juõs išmókysiu!

DO YOU SPEAK LITHUANIAN?

Teacher: 1. Are you a Lithuanian or an American?

Pupil: 2. I am an American, but I want to learn Lithuanian.

Teacher: 3. Do you already speak Lithuanian well?

Pupil: 4. Now I still cannot speak Lithuanian well...

Teacher: 5. Yes, from now on we shall speak only Lithuanian in class. We will read and write only in Lithuanian, too.

Pupil: 6. Very well. In this way we will learn Lithuanian well!

Teacher: 7. [And] what language (literally: how) do you speak at home?

Pupil: 8. At home we speak English because my parents don't know Lithuanian.

Teacher: 9. That's too bad. You will not be able to speak Lithuanian at home.

Pupil: 10. But perhaps they will learn Lithuanian too. I will teach them!

NOTES:

2. **išmókti** — to learn (well, thoroughly)

6. **tókiu būdù** — in such a way, such a manner, thus.
   išmóksime lietùviškai — we shall learn (to speak) Lithuanian.

8. **tėvaĭ** — parents (also, fathers).

9. **gaĭla** — it is too bad, it's a pity.

10. **iř jiē** — ir in this phrase means 'also, too'.
    mókyti — to teach; **išmókyti** 'to teach thoroughly, fully' cf. the related words: **mokinỹs** 'pupil', **mókytojas** 'teacher'.

Dešimtoji pamoka
Lesson 10

I.

LIETUVA

Pažiūrėkime į žemėlapį. Čià yrà Amèrika, arbà Jungtìnės Amèrikos Valstýbės — JAV.* Amèrika yrà dìdelė šalìs taȓp Atlánto vandenýno iȓ Rãmiojo vandenýno, taȓp Kanãdos iȓ Mèksikos. Lietuvà yrà nedìdelė šalìs. Jì yrà priẽ Báltijos júros. Senóvėje[1] Lietuvà bùvo labaĩ dìdelė valstýbė. Jõs pirmàsis karãlius bùvo Mìndaugas (ca. 1200-1263). Į šiáurę[2] nuõ Lietuvõs yrà Lãtvija, į rýtus — Gudijà, į pietùs — Lénkija. Vakaruosè[3] yrà Báltijos júra.[4]

Báltijos júroje yrà daũg giñtaro.[5] Lietuvõs pajúryje taĩp pàt gãlima ràsti daũg giñtaro. Jaũ labaĩ senaĩs laikaĩs[6] Lietuvà prekiãvo giñtaru[7] sù kitomìs Euròpos valstýbėmis,[8] nèt sù senóvės graikaĩs iȓ romėnais.[9] Lietuváitės mėgsta puõštis giñtaro papuošalaĩs.[10]

Didžiáusias[11] Lietuvõs miẽstas yrà jõs sóstinė Vìlnius. Toliaũ eĩna[12] Kaũnas, Klaĩpėda, Šiauliaĩ. Klaĩpėda yrà Lietuvõs úostas priẽ Báltijos júros.

NOTES ON 'LIETUVA':
1. **Senóvėje** — in ancient times.
2. **Į šiáurę** — to the North.
3. **Vakaruosè** — loc. plural of **Vakaraĩ** 'West': in the West.
4. **Báltijos júra** — Baltic Sea.

* JAV — in Lithuanian, this abbreviation is read in full: 'Jungtìnės Amèrikos Valstýbės'.

5. **daũg giñtaro** — gintaro is genitive. After words and expressions of quantity, the genitive case is used. For more details see 16.2.
6. **senaĩs laikaĩs** — senóvėje (see Note 1 above). Instrumental case is used in certain cases to express time. See Lesson 23.
7. **prekiãvo giñtaru** — 'traded in amber'; prekiáuti plus instr. case.
8. **sù kitomìs Euròpos valstýbėmis** — 'with other states of Europe'.
9. **sù senóvės graikaĩs iȓ romėnais** — 'with ancient Greeks and Romans'.
10. **puõštis giñtaro papuošalaĩs** — 'to wear jewelry (ornaments) made from amber'.
11. **didžiáusias** — 'the largest'.
12. **toliaũ eĩna** — 'there follows'.

II.

PEIZAŽAS[1]

By Jonas Aistis[2]

Laũkas, kẽlias, píeva, kȓýžius,
Šìlo júosta mėlyna,[3]
Debesėlių tánkus ìžas[4]
Iȓ graudì graudì dainà.

Bėga kẽlias, iȓ beržėliai
Liñksta vėjo pučiamì;[5]
Samanótas stógas žãlias
Iȓ šuñs baĺsas prietemỹ.[6]

O toliaũ — paskeñdęs káimas,[7]
Tìk žirgėliai[8] taȓp klevų̃ —
Šlãma líepos tókia láime,[9]
Tókiu liũdesiu savù.

Tìk sukȓýkš, lýg gérvė, svìrtis,[10]
Sušlamės dainà klevuõs . . .[11]
Gẽra[12] čià gyvént[13] iȓ miȓti!
Gẽra vaȓgt[14] čià, Lietuvõj! . . .[15]

NOTES ON 'PEIŽAŽAS':

1. **Peizãžas** — 'landscape' (here: a landscape, or a view of an old-fashioned Lithuanian village, countryside).
2. **Jonas Aistis** — Born 1904. One of the leading Lithuanian lyric poets.
3. **júosta** — sash, ribbon'; šìlo júosta mėlyna: a blue ribbon of (pine) forest, a bluish strip of woods.
4. **debesėlių tánkus ìžas** — ižas: ice-floe on rivers; ice-floe like little clouds.
5. **vėjo pučiamì** — 'blown by the wind'.
6. **prietemỹ** — 'at dusk'.
7. **paskeñdęs káimas** — lit. 'sunken village', i.e., almost hidden in the foliage of groves, orchards and trees.

84

8. **žirgẽliai** — lit. 'little horses' (=dim. of **žìrgas** 'steed'). Here **žirgẽliai** refers to ancient Lithuanian roof ornaments, at the high point of the gable, in a stylized shape of horse heads.
9. **tókia láime** — 'with such happiness', Instrumental case. Same for **tókiu liūdesiu savù**: 'with such intimate sadness'.
10. **svìrtis** — 'water pully, water lift', a device by which water is raised from a well. Almost each farm in Lithuania used to have a **svìrtis**.
11. **klevuõs** — 'in the *maple* trees', an abbreviation of **klevuosè** (see Lesson 14). In poetry and also in rapid speech, this happens fairly often.
12. **gẽra** — 'It is good', neuter form of the adjective **gẽras, gerà** 'good' (See 12.3).
13. **gyvént** — an abbreviation of the infinitive **gyvénti** 'to live'. See also Note 11 above).
14. **vaȓgt** — abbr. of **vaȓgti** 'to suffer, to eke out a living', (cf. Notes 13 & 11).
15. **Lietuvõj** — abbr. of **Lietuvojè** 'in Lithuania' (see 3.3).

CONVERSATIONS

1.

Valiùlis: Kuȓ jũs rytój važiúosite?

Gudẽlis: Dár nežinaũ. Màno sesuõ nóri važiúoti į̃ káimą, bèt àš nenóriu.

Valiulis: Gál rytój bùs blõgas óras, iȓ mẽs visì turẽsime bũti namiẽ.

Gudelis: Porỹt mán reikẽs važiúoti į̃ Vìlnių.

Valiulis: Ką̃ jũs teñ darýsite?

Gudelis: Aš teñ aplankýsiu sàvo senẽlį.

2.

Pètkus: Kuȓ jũs bùvote vakarè?

Karnỹs: Buvaũ namiẽ. Niẽkur negalẽjau eĩti.

Petkus: Kodẽl?

Karnys: Mán reikẽjo daũg dìrbti.

Petkus: O ką̃ jũs vakarè dìrbate?

Karnys: Aš rašaũ knỹgą ...

COMBINATION PRACTICE

A.

1.	I live	a.	in the city
2.	they live	b.	in the suburb
3.	Dr. Vitkus lives	c.	in Vilnius
4.	we live	d.	in Kaunas
5.	my sister lives	e.	in Lithuania
6.	the student lives	f.	in America*

---

* America=**Amerika**, 2nd declension (see 3.3), in popular speech **Amerika**= U. S. A.

7. she lives
8. Professor Kubilius lives
9. My father and mother live
10. Mr. Vainoras lives

B.

1. I like to drink   a. coffee
2. Professor likes to drink   b. tea
3. They like to drink   c. water
                            d. tea with sugar

VARIATION PRACTICE

A.

Màno brólis gyvēna miestè.
1. My brother lives in the city.
2. My sister lives in the city.
3. My father lives in Vilnius.
4. My father and my mother lived in Vilnius.
5. My brother and my sister will live in the city.
6. Dr. Vitkus lived in the village.
7. Professor Valys will live in Kaunas.
8. The student (male) lives in the suburb.
9. The student (female) will live at home.
10. My professor lives in America.

B.

a. *Mán patiñka gyvénti miestè.*
b. *Aš mĕgstu gyvénti miestè.*
1. They like to live in the city.
2. She likes to live in Lithuania.
3. We like to live in America.
4. He likes to read a newspaper.
5. Dr. Vitkus likes to drink tea with honey.
6. My brother likes to go by bus.
7. He likes to go by bus to the university.
8. We like to read a book.
9. Professor Petraitis likes to work at home.
10. Professor Valys likes to work at the university.*

---

* at the university=unìversitetè (regular Locative of **universitètas**).

86

Vienuoliktoji pamoka
Lesson 11

MANO KAMBARYS

Màno kambarỹs yrà mãžas, bèt mán jìs labaĩ patiñka. Kambaryjè yrà tìk víenas lángas, priẽ lángo stóvi màno sẽnas stãlas. Añt stãlo gùli raudónas pieštùkas iȓ mẽlyna knygà. Màno sesùtė Rūtà įeĩna į kaṁbarį iȓ sãko:

— Výtai, kuȓ tàvo naũjas pieštùkas? Mán jõ reĩkia.

— Tù rašýk gerà plùnksna, nè pieštukù.

— Aš nenóriu rašýti, àš nóriu piẽšti. Mán reĩkia tàvo raudóno pieštùko.

— Geraĩ. Galì iṁti. Jìs gùli añt stãlo.

— Ačiū. O kuȓ tàvo geltónas põpierius?

— Vìskas añt stãlo. Iṁk vìską: raudóną pieštùką, geltóną põpierių, tìk palìk manè ramýbėje. Aš skaitaũ naũją romãną.

— Geraĩ, geraĩ. Tìk nebúk jaũ tóks pìktas!

— Aš nepìktas. Tìk tù búk gerà iȓ manẹ̃s netrukdýk!

— Aš tuojaũ išeĩsiu. Aš eĩsiu pàs mū́sų kaimýnę, põnią Matulíenę.

— Eĩk, kuȓ nóri — pàs Matulíenę, Matulýtę ar Matùlį, — mán vistíek!

— Ačiū, màno míelas brolẽli. Iki pasimãtymo.

VOCABULARY

kambarỹs -io (3b) — room
mãžas, -à (4) — small, little
bèt — but
lángas (3) — window
priẽ (prep. with gen.) — by, near, at, at the side of

piẽšti (piešiù, piẽšia, piẽšė, piẽš) — to draw, to draw pictures
iṁti (imù, ìma, ẽmė, iṁs)* — to take, to pick up
ãčiū — thanks, thank you
geltónas, -a — yellow

stovéti (stóviu, stóvi, stovéjo, stověs)
— to stand (i.e. to be in a standing
position)
sěnas, -à (4) — old
stãlas (4) — table
guléti (guliù, gùli, guléjo, gulěs) —
— to lie (i.e. to be in a lying or
horizontal position)
raudónas (1) — red
pieštùkas (2) — pencil
mělynas, -a (1) — blue
jeĩti (įeinù, įeĩna, įějo, įeĩs) — to enter, to come in, to step in
sakýti (sakaũ, sãko, sãkė, sakýs) —
to say
Výtai (voc. sg.) — Vytas (first name,
shortened form of Výtautas)
naũjas, -à (4) — new
reikěti (reĩkia, reikějo, reikěs) — to
need (only used in 3rd person)
mán jõ reĩkia — I need it
gěras, -à (4) — good
plùnksna (1) — pen; feather

pŏpierius (1) — paper
palìkti (paliekù, paliěka, palìko, pa-
lìks)* — to leave (behind)
ramýbė (1) — quiet, peace
romãnas (2) — novel
geraĩ (adverb) — well, O.K.
jaũ — already, just
tóks — such, such a
pìktas, -à (4) — angry
trukdýti (trukdaũ, trùkdo, trùkdė,
trukdýs) — to disturb, to pester
tuojaũ — right away, soon
pàs (prep. with acc.) — by, to, at
(the place of)
kaimýnė (1) — neighbor (fem.)
ponià (4) — lady, Mrs.
vistíek — all the same
broléli (voc. sing.) — dear brother,
brother dear
iki (prep. with the gen.) — until, till,
up to
pasimãtymas (1) — meeting, seeing
(one another), 'date', rendezvous

Idioms

mán jõ reĩkia — I need it (him)

mán reĩkia raudóno pieštùko — I need a (the) red pencil

netrukdýk manęs — leave me in peace; let me be

iki pasimãtymo — so long (literally: until we see each other)

NB. *daũg* 'much, many' is used with the genitive case: *daũg cùk-
raus* 'much sugar', etc.

GRAMMAR

11.1 First Declension of Adjectives.

All adjectives ending in *-as* in the masculine nominative singular belong to the first declension. The singular is listed below
and the plural cases are given in Lesson 21.

Masculine			Feminine	
N.,V.	báltas (3)	-as 'white'	baltà	-a
G.	bálto	-o	baltõs	-os
D.	baltám	-am	báltai	-ai
A.	báltą	-ą	báltą	-ą
I.	báltu	-u	bálta	-a
L.	baltamè	-ame	baltojè	-oje

* Irregular verbs. See Lith.-English Vocabulary.

Masculine			Feminine	
N.,V.	raudónas (1)	-as 'red'	raudóna	-a
G.	raudóno	-o	raudónos	-os
D.	raudónam	-am	raudónai	-ai
A.	raudóną	-ą	raudóną	-ą
I.	raudónu	-u	raudóna	-a
L.	raudóname	-ame	raudónoje	-oje

The numbers in parentheses refer to the accent classes which are almost the same as for the nouns. They were briefly discussed in Lesson 5 and in the Appendix, paragraph 51.

The declension of the adjective of the first declension should be compared with that of the first and second declension noun. The declension of the masculine adjective differs in the dative, locative and vocative cases from that of the first declension noun.

Only the masculine and feminine forms of the adjective are declined. The residual neuter form is limited to the nominative case; it is formed by dropping the -s from the nominative singular masculine.

11.2 The use of *reikěti* 'to be necessary' and *reikalingas* 'necessary':

The logical subject of the verb *reikěti* is in the dative case and the logical object is in the genitive case. Examples:

1. *Mán reĩkia kaṁbario.* — I need a room (literally: To me is necessary a room.)
2. *Mán reikějo kaṁbario.* — I needed a room.
3. *Mán reikěs kaṁbario.* — I shall need a room.
4. *Tévui reĩkia pieštùko.* — Father needs the pencil.
5. *Tévui reikějo pieštùko.* — Father needed the pencil.
6. *Tévui reikěs pieštùko.* — Father will need the pencil.
7. *Jõ bróliui reĩkia ramýbės.* — His brother needs rest.
8. *Jõ bróliui reikějo ramýbės.* — His brother needed rest.
9. *Jõ bróliui reikěs ramýbės.* — His brother will need rest.

11.2,1 As an inflected adjective *reikalingas* agrees in case, number and gender with the noun it modifies. Examples:

1. *Mán [yrà] reikalingas stãlas.* — I need a table (literally: To me is necessary a table.)

2. *Jùms [yrà] reikalinga naujà knygà.* — You need a new book (literally: to you is necessary a new book.)

3. *Màno šeĩmai [yrà] reikalìngas dìdelis nãmas.* — My family needs a large house (lit.: To my family is necessary a large house.)

4. *Mán bùvo reikalìngas stãlas.* — I needed a table (literally: To me was necessary a table.)

5. *Mán bùs reikalìngas stãlas.* — I shall need a table (literally: To me will be necessary a table.)

11.3 Names in Lithuanian.

In Lithuanian the suffixes *-as, -is, -ys, -us, -ė, -a* can be added to the root to form the family name for a male. The suffix *-ienė* (sometimes *-uvienė*) denotes a married woman; the suffixes *-aitė, -ytė, -utė* and *-iūtė* denote unmarried women. Examples:

Mr. = *põnas*:	Mrs. = *ponià*:	Miss = *panėlė*:
Šãpal*as*,	Šãpal*ienė*	Šapal*áitė*
Gaĩgal*as*	Gaĩgal*ienė*	Gaigal*áitė*
Mìškìn*is*	Mìškin*íenė*	Mìškin*ýtė*
Valáit*is*	Valáit*ienė*	Valait*ýtė*
Rainỹs	Rain*íenė*	Rain*ýtė*
Ruzgỹs	Ruzg*íenė*	Ruzg*ýtė*
Rìmk*us*	Rìmk*uvienė*	Rimk*ùtė*
Stánk*us*	Stánk*uvienė*	Stank*ùtė*
Peldž*ius*	Peldž*iuvienė*	Peldž*iūtė*
Katėl*ė*	Katel*íenė*	Katel*ýtė*
Razm*à*	Razm*íenė*	Razm*áitė*

The words *põnas, ponià* and *panėlė* are of Polish origin. They originally meant 'lord, master', but now are used only with the meaning of 'Mr., Mrs., and Miss' respectively.

The suffix *-ienė* (or *-uvienė*) is added directly to the root after the suffix *-as, is, -ys, -ė* or *-a* is dropped. The suffix *-aitė* is added to the root after the suffix *-as* or *-a* is dropped, the suffix *-utė* (*-iūtė*) after the *-us* is dropped and the suffix *-ytė* after the suffix *-is, -ys* or *-ė* is dropped.

The only names having the suffix *-uvienė* are those formed from disyllabic masculine names with the ending *-us* or *-ius*. But even in this case the suffix *-ienė* is used, so that beside *Star̃kuvienė* we also find *Starkíenė*.

Names with the suffix *-uvienė* have the stress in the same position as the corresponding masculine names, thus *Stánkus — Stánkuvienė*.

Names with the suffix -*ienė* have the stress in the same place as the corresponding masculine name, if the latter has the acute intonation (and belongs to the first accent class) or the circumflex intonation (and belongs to the third accent class) on the third syllable from the end, e.g. *Jonáitis - Jonáitienė, Gaĩgalas - Gaĩgalienė.*

In all the other cases feminine names have the stress on the suffix, e.g. *Kaũnas - Kauníenė, Daukšà - Daukšíenė.*

Names with the suffix -*aitė* have the stress on this suffix except for those which are formed from masculine names with the suffixes -*ūnas, -ėnas, -ýnas* (of the first accent class). Thus we have *Armináitė, Burbáitė,* but *Bradū́naitė, Bražė́naitė, Tamulý̃naitė.*

Names with the suffixes, -*ytė, -utė* and -*iūtė* always have the stress on the suffix, e.g. *Rainýtė, Senkùtė, Peldžiū̃tė.*

11.4 The Vocative of Proper Names.

In general the vocative of the proper nouns or names are the same as the vocative forms of the corresponding declension of common nouns. Examples:

Name (nom. sing.)	Vocative	Declension	Lesson
Rainỹs	Rainỹ	1	3
Miškìnis	Miškìni	1	3
Katėlė	Katėle	2	3
Rìmkus	Rìmkau	4	6
Rìmkuvienė	Rìmkuviene	2	3
Rimkùtė	Rimkùte	2	3

Names ending in -*as* in the nominative singular form an exception to this rule. The vocative of such nouns ends in -*ai*, e.g. *Antãnas* has the vocative *Antãnai, Kòstas* has the vocative *Kòstai, Čė̃pas,* voc. *Čė̃pai, Rìmas,* voc. *Rìmai,* etc.

EXERCISES

A. *Questions.* 1. Kóks yrà màno kambarỹs? 2. Kàs stóvi priẽ lángo màno kambaryjè? 3. Kàs gùli añt stãlo? 4. Kàs įeĩna į̃ màno kam̃barį? 5. Ką̃ jì sãko? 6. Kõ màno sesùtei reĩkia? 7. Ar̃ jì nóri rašýti? 8. Ką̃ àš skaitaũ? 9. Kur̃ eĩs Rūtà? 10. Ar̃ àš esù gẽras brólis?

B. *Decline in the singular:* báltas nãmas, sẽnas pieštùkas, naujà krósnis (-ies, etc. 3rd declension), sẽnas arklỹs, gerà plùnksna, mė̃lynas dangùs, raudónas akmuõ.

C. *Fill in the blanks:* 1. Aš turiù (small) .... kaṁbarį.
2. Màno (in [my] small) .... kambaryjè stóvi (a new)
.... stãlas. 3. Mán patiñka màno (old) ....
plùnksna. 4. Màno sesuõ Rūtà rãšo (with the yellow) ....
pieštukù. 5. Aš rašaũ (with the red) .... pieštukù.

D. *Fill in the blanks:* 1. Mán reĩkia nauj........ knyg........ 2. Jám
reik........ (pres. tense) eĩti namõ. 3. Màno bróliui reĩkia mélyn........
pieštuk........ 4. Mùms reik........ (past tense) eĩti namõ. 5. Jíems
reik........ (future) eĩti namõ. 6. Mùms [yrà] reikaling........ naũjas
stãlas. 7. Màno sẽseriai bùvo reikaling........ senà knygà. 8. Mán
reikaling........ naũjas pieštùkas. 9. Mán nereĩkia eĩti nam........ 10.
Aš esù nam........

E. *Complete:*

1. Põnas Žilỹs,   ponià ...., panẽlė ....
2. Põnas Kalãdė,   ponià ...., panẽlė ....
3. Põnas Stùkas,   ponià ...., panẽlė ....
4. Põnas Gudẽlis, ponià ...., panẽlė ....
5. Põnas Stóškus, ponià ...., panẽlė ....
6. Põnas Švẽdas,   ponià ...., panẽlė ....

F. Put all the forms of Exercise E into the *vocative case:* e.g.:
Põne Žilỹ, põnia Žilíene, panẽle Žilýte, etc.

G. *Translate into Lithuanian:* 1. I have an old table. 2. My old
table stands in my small room. 3. I like my little room. 4. I need
a new pencil. 5. You need a new pen. 6. You had to have (=needed
to have) a new table. 7. Mrs. Rugys is at home. 8. Miss Klimas
goes home. 9. I like Miss Žukas. 10.We need a large room.

CONVERSATION

MIESTE: KUR YRA ...?

Valáitis: 1. Atsiprašaũ. Aȓ gãlite mán pasakýti, kuȓ yrà viẽšbutis 'Amèrika'?

Policininkas: 2. Viẽšbutis 'Amèrika' yrà netolì. Eĩkite tiesióg dvì
minutès, tadà kairėjè gãtvės pùsėje pamatýsite
raudóną nãmą ...

Valaitis: 3. Labaĩ ãčiū. Aš dár tìk neseniaĩ esù júsų miestè.
Kuȓ čià yrà gẽras restorãnas?

Policininkas: 4. Restorãnas 'Nidà' yrà labaĩ gẽras. Jìs yrà kitojè
gãtvės pùsėje.

Valaitis:	5.	O kuř yrà òperos teãtras?
Policininkas:	6.	Operos teãtras yrà miẽsto centrè. Jùms reikẽs važiúoti autobusù. Autobùsas Nr. (= nùmeris) 5 (peñktas).
Valaitis:	7.	Mán taĩp pàt reĩkia nusipiřkti naũją iř gẽrą miẽsto plãną. Kuř àš jį galiù ràsti?
Policininkas:	8.	Jũs gãlite gáuti miẽsto plãną knygýne. Knygýnas yrà pirmojè gãtvėje dešinėjè.
Valaitis:	9.	Ačiũ labaĩ. Dabař àš jaũ susiràsiu, kõ mán reĩkia. Sudiẽu.
Policininkas:	10.	Sudiẽu, sudiẽu. Laimìngai.

IN THE CITY: ASKING DIRECTIONS

Valaitis:	1.	Pardon me please. Can you tell me where the hotel 'America' is?
Policeman:	2.	The hotel 'Amerika' is not too far. Go straight ahead for two minutes, then you will see a red house on the left side of the street ...
Valaitis:	3.	Thank you very much. I have been in your city only a short time. Where is there a good restaurant around here?
Policeman:	4.	The 'Nida' restaurant is a good restaurant. It is on the other side of the street.
Valaitis:	5.	And where is the opera theater?
Policeman:	6.	The opera theater is in the center of the city. You will have to go by bus. Bus No. 5.
Valaitis:	7.	I also have to buy a new and a good city map. Where can I find it?
Policeman:	8.	You can get a city map in the bookstore. The bookstore is on the first street on the right.
Valaitis:	9.	Thank you very much. Now, I will be able to find what I need. Good-by.
Policeman:	10.	Good-by, good-by. Good luck!

NOTES:

3. **dár tìk neseniaĩ esù** — lit. 'still only not long am'.
Note the use of the present tense in Lithuanian to express a condition which has begun in the past and continues into the present. In English we use a perfect tense to express such an action.

6. **Nr. 5** — nùmeris peñktas: lit. 'the fifth number'.

9. **susiràsiu** — lit. 'I will find for myself'.

10. **Laimìngai** — lit. 'luckily'.

Dvyliktoji pamoka
Lesson 12

MANO GIMTASIS KAIMAS

Vãkar àš aplankiaũ sàvo gìmtąjį káimą. Màno gimtàsis káimas sẽnas iř gražùs. Jìs yrà priẽ Nẽmuno. Nẽmunas yrà platì ùpė. Aš mačiaũ taṁsų mìšką, kuriamè mẽs žaĩsdavome. Ėjaũ plačiù keliù, kuriuõ eĩdavau į mokỹklą, kaĩ dár buvaũ vaĩkas. Aš aplankiaũ sẽną kaimýną, kurìs pãsakodavo mùms gražių̃ pãsakų, kadà jìs tìk turẽdavo laĩko.

Kaĩ mẽs dár gyvẽnome káime, mẽs dìrbdavome nuõ rýto lìgi vãkaro, bèt dárbas bũdavo mùms visuomèt labaĩ malonùs.

Dabař àš miestè dìrbu suñkiai iř skubiaĩ, nès reĩkia vìską greĩtai padarýti. Káime visuomèt bũdavo gražù iř smagù.

VOCABULARY

vãkar — yesterday
aplankýti (aplankaũ, aplañko, aplañkė, aplankỹs) — to visit
gimtàsis — native
káimas (1) — village
gražùs, -ì (4) — beautiful
priẽ (prep. with gen.)—at, by, near, on
platùs, -ì (4) — wide
tamsùs, -ì (4) — dark
mìškas (4) — forest, woods
kuriamè (loc. sing.) — in which
žaĩsti (irreg.: žaidžiù, žaĩdžia, žaĩdė, žaĩs) — to play
kẽlias (4) — way, road
kuriuõ (inst. sing.) — [here] along which
kaimýnas (1) — neighbor
kurìs (nom. sing.) — who, which
pãsakoti (pãsakoju, pãsakoja, pãsakojo, pãsakos) — to tell, to narrate

pãsaka (1) — fairy tale, folk tale
kadà — when
kadà tìk — whenever
kaĩ (conjunction) — when
nuõ (prep. with gen.) — from, starting from
rýtas (3) — morning
lìgi (prep. with gen.) — till, until
dárbas (3) — work
malonùs, -ì (4) — pleasant
sunkùs, -ì (4) heavy, difficult
suñkiai (adverb) — heavily, hard (in the adverbial sense)
skubùs, -ì (4) — hurried
skubiaĩ (adverb) — hurriedly
greĩtai — fast, right away, soon
padarýti (padaraũ, padãro, padãrė, padarỹs) — to do, to accomplish
õ — but, and
smagùs, -ì (4) — cheerful

GRAMMAR

12.1 Second Declension of Adjectives.

Adjectives belonging to this declension are characterized by the ending -us in the masculine nominative singular and the ending -i in the feminine nominative singular. The singular is listed below and the plural cases are given in Lesson 22.

Masculine			Feminine	
N.,V.	sunkùs	-us (4) 'heavy'	sunkì	-i
G.	sunkaũs	-aus	sunkiõs	-ios
D.	sunkiám	-iam	suñkiai	-iai
A.	suñkų	-ų	suñkią	-ią
I.	sunkiù	-iu	sunkià	-ia
L.	sunkiamè	-iame	sunkiojè	-ioje

Masculine			Feminine	
N.,V.	platùs	-us (4) 'wide'	platì	-i
G.	plataũs	-aus	plačiõs	-ios
D.	plačiám	-iam	plãčiai	-iai
A.	plãtų	-ų	plãčią	-ią
I.	plačiù	-iu	plačià	-ia
L.	plačiamè	-iame	plačiojè	-ioje

The endings of the nouns of the fourth declension (Lesson 6) should be carefully compared with the masculine endings above. The endings of feminine nouns in -i of the second declension should be carefully compared with the feminine endings above (Lesson 3). Some of the endings are different (e.g. the masculine dat. sing.), but enough of them are similar to aid in memorization.

-ti- (and -di-) are replaced by -či- (and -dži- respectively) in position before the vowels -a-, -o-, -u- in the second declension of adjectives. In this position -či- and -dži- merely denote a soft or palatalized -č- or -dž- sound; the letter -i- here does not denote a vowel, but merely the softening or palatalization of the preceding consonant. (Cf. also 3.3 and the Introductory Lesson.)

12.2 Formation of Adverbs.

Adverbs can be formed from adjectives of the first declension (-as, -a) by dropping the -as of the nominative singular masculine and adding -ai. Adverbs can be formed from second declension adjectives by dropping the -*us* of the nominative singular masculine and adding -*iai* (with the appropriate changes discussed above if the stem ends in -*t* or -*d*). Examples:

1) *gẽras* 'good'   *geraĩ* 'well'
2) *báltas* 'white'   *baltaĩ* 'white, whitish'
3) *sunkùs* 'heavy, hard'   *suñkiai* 'heavily, hard (of work)'
4) *platùs* 'wide'   *plačiaĩ* 'widely'
5) *gražùs* 'beautiful'   *gražiaĩ* 'beautifully'

12.3 The Neuter Form of the Adjectives.

From the adjectives of the first and second declension a neuter form can be derived by dropping the -*s* from the masculine nominative singular, cf. Examples:

M a s c u l i n e   N e u t e r
1) *gẽras* 'good'   *gẽra* 'the good, that which is good'
2) *báltas* 'white'   *bálta* 'that which is white'
3) *gražùs* 'beautiful'   *gražù* 'that which is beautiful'
4) *sunkùs* 'difficult'   *sunkù* 'difficult, hard, heavy'

These neuter forms occur only in the nominative singular, and mostly as parts of the predicate. They are commonly used with the verb 'to be' in certain impersonal constructions. Examples:

1) *Mán čià labaĩ gẽra.* — I feel fine (good) here (literally: To me here it is very good).
2) *Jám vìskas čià bùvo gražù.* — He found everything beautiful here (literally: To him everything here was beautiful).
3) *Čià [yrà] labaĩ gražù.* — Here it is very beautiful.
4) *Čià bùvo labaĩ gražù.* — Here it was very beautiful.
5) *Čià bùs labaĩ gražù.* — Here it will be very beautiful.
6) *Mán šálta.* — I am cold (literally: To me it is cold).

Note that this is the correct way to express the idea of feeling heat, cold, etc. The sentence *àš esù šáltas* would mean 'I am cold' in the sense 'my body is cold when you touch it' or 'my body is exuding cold'. The dative case of the noun or pronoun is used with the adjective in the neuter:

7) *Táu šálta.* — You (sg.) are cold.
8) *Jám šálta.* — He is cold.
9) *Jái šálta.* — She is cold.

97

10) *Mùms šálta.* — We are cold.
11) *Jùms bùs šálta.* — You will be cold.
12) *Jíems bùvo šálta.* — They (masculine) were cold.
13) *Jóms bùvo šálta.* — They (feminine) were cold.

NB. It is very important to remember that these neuter adjectives cannot be used as adverbs.

Neuter Adjectives	Adverbs
Čià labaĩ gražù. —	*Jìs rãšo gražiaĩ.* —
'It is very beautiful here'	'He writes beautifully'
Táu šìlta,	*nès tù šiltaĩ apsireñgęs.*
'You are warm	because you are dressed warmly'
Mán bùvo labaĩ malonù. —	*Jìs maloniaĩ kalbėjo.* —
'I was very pleased;	'He spoke pleasantly'
it was very pleasant for me.'	

12.4 The Frequentative Past Tense. *(būtàsis dažnìnis laĩkas)*

In addition to the simple past tense (or preterit) discussed in Lesson 8 there is another past tense, the frequentative past, which denotes an action which took place several times, frequently, at repeated intervals in the past. It can be translated by such English expressions as: *I used to...; I kept...; I would...* To obtain the stem for this tense, drop the infinitive ending *-ti* and add the following endings: 1st sing. *-davau*, 2nd sg. *-davai*, 3rd person *-davo*, 1st plur. *-davome*, 2nd plur. *-davote*. Note that this tense consists essentially of *-dav-* plus the preterit endings *-au, -ai, -o*, etc.

1st Conjugation: *dìrbti* 'to work'

Singular		Plural	
1) dìrbdavau 'I used to work'	-dav-au	dìrbdavome	-dav-ome
2) dìrbdavai	-dav-ai	dìrbdavote	-dav-ote
3) dìrbdavo	-dav-o	dìrbdavo	-dav-o

2nd Conjugation: *mylė́ti* 'to love'

Singular		Plural	
1) mylė́davau 'I used to love'	-dav-au	mylė́davome	-dav-ome
2) mylė́davai	-dav-ai	mylė́davote	-dav-ote
3) mylė́davo	-dav-o	mylė́davo	-dav-o

3rd Conjugation: *skaitýti* 'to read'

Singular			Plural	
1)	skaitýdavau 'I used to read'	-dav-au	skaitýdavome	-dav-ome
2)	skaitýdavai	-dav-ai	skaitýdavote	-dav-ote
3)	skaitýdavo	-dav-o	skaitýdavo	-dav-o

As is evident from the examples above the method of formation is the same for all three conjugations. The stress is *always* on the stem, *never* on the ending.

EXERCISES

A. *Questions.* 1. Ką àš vãkar aplankiaũ? 2. Kóks yrà màno gimtàsis káimas? 3. Kuř jìs yrà? 4. Kokià ùpė yrà Nėmunas? 5. Kuř àš eĩdavau plačiù keliù, kaĩ àš buvaũ vaĩkas? 6. Ką mùms pãsakodavo sėnas kaimýnas? 7. Kóks bùvo dárbas káime? 8. Kaĩp reĩkia dìrbti miestè? 9. Kuř júsų gimtàsis káimas? 10. Kuř [yrà] geriaũ gyvénti — káime ař miestè?

B. *Decline in the singular:* gražùs, tamsùs, skubùs, malonùs, smagùs.

C. *Form adverbs from the following adjectives:* raudónas, mėlynas, báltas, jáunas, platùs, smagùs, malonùs, skubùs, tamsùs, gražùs.

D. Using the examples of 12.3 substitute: *šilta* 'warm' and *káršta* 'hot' for *šálta* 'cold', e.g. *mán yrà šilta* 'I am warm', etc.

E. *Translate into Lithuanian:* 1. In the village I used to work hard. 2. In the city I do not work so hard. 3. He always used to be (bū́davo) cold. 4. I have a beautiful dog. 6. My father used to live in the village, but now he lives in Vìlnius. 7. She writes very beautifully. 8. She used to write very beautifully. 9. I don't want to work hard, I only want to live nicely. 10. When he was a student, he used to read much, but (=õ) now he does not read anything.

CONVERSATION

KUŘ SKANIAU VALGYTI

Kilmónis: 1. Ką jūs válgote pùsryčių?

Skìnkis: 2. Aš válgau dúoną sù svíestu iř geriù sáldžią kãvą sù píenu.

99

Kilmonis: 3. O ką jūs válgote pietų?

Skinkis: 4. Pietùms àš válgau lėkštę sriubõs, mėsõs iř kõ nórs saldaūs.

Kilmonis: 5. Aš nemėgstu sriubõs. Aš jõs niekuomèt neválgau.

Skinkis: 6. Aš iřgi anksčiaū neválgydavau sriubõs, bèt dākta-ras (gýdytojas) mán pàtarė válgyti.

Kilmonis: 7. O àš anksčiaū válgydavau daūg sriubõs, bèt dabař negaliù.

Skinkis: 8. Kuř jūs válgote — namiē ař restoranè?

Kilmonis: 9. Aš visuomèt válgau restoranè, nès àš gyvenù víe-nas iř nemėgstu vìrti.

Skinkis: 10. Gaīla. Namiē gālima geraī, skaniaī iř pigiaī pavál-gyti, õ restoranè vìskas yrà brangù iř nè taīp skanù.

WHERE IT IS BETTER (TASTIER) TO EAT

Kilmonis: 1. What do you eat for breakfast?

Skinkis: 2. I eat bread and (with) butter and I drink sweet coffee with milk.

Kilmonis: 3. And what do you eat for dinner?

Skinkis: 4. For dinner I eat a plate of soup, meat and a des-sert (literally: something sweet).

Kilmonis: 5. I don't like soup. I never eat it.

Skinkis: 6. I, too never used to eat it before, but the doctor (physician) advised me to do it.

Kilmonis: 7. I used to eat a lot of soup before, but now I can't.

Skinkis: 8. Where do you eat—at home or in a restaurant?

Kilmonis: 9. I always eat in a restaurant because I live alone and I don't like to cook.

Skinkis: 10. That's too bad. At home one can eat well, have good tasting food, and eat inexpensively, but in a restaurant everything is expensive and not very tasty.

NOTES:

1. pùsryčių — gen. plural: 'for breakfast'.
2. saldì kavà — kavà sù cùkrumi: 'sweet coffee, coffee with sugar, sweeten-ed coffee'.
4. kõ nórs saldaūs — partitive genitive. Lit. 'of something sweet'.
6. Both gýdytojas 'physician' and dāktaras 'doctor' are used when one speaks of an MD. However, it is usual to address an MD only as dāktaras: Dāk-tare Petráiti: (vocative) Dr. Petraitis.
9. víenas — 'one', here: 'alone'.
10. geraī, skaniaī, pigiaī — are adverbs; brangù, skanù — are neuter adjec-tives.

100

Tryliktoji pamoka

Lesson 13

MIESTE

Výtautas: Labà dienà, Antãnai. Kur̃ taĩp skubì?
Antãnas: Lãbas, lãbas, Výtautai. Einù apžiūrẽti naũjo nãmo.
Vytautas: Taĩ ką̃ gì, nóri pir̃kti naũją nãmą?
Antanas: Taĩp. Mataĩ, mẽs turẽjome tą̃ sẽną medìnį, bèt dabar̃ nórime pir̃kti mūrìnį.
Vytautas: Bèt sãko, kàd medìniame namè sveikiaũ gyvénti.
Antanas: Gál ir̃ taĩp, bèt mūrìnis nãmas vistíek mán dabar̃ daugiaũ patiñka.
Vytautas: Taĩp, taĩp. Sidabrìnis laĩkrodis geraĩ eĩna, bèt visì nóri auksìnio...
Antanas: Aš esù turẽjęs ir̃ auksìnį laĩkrodį, bèt par̃daviau, nès sugẽdo.
Vytautas: Ar̃ esì jaũ apžiūrẽjęs vìsą miẽstą?
Antanas: Visur̃ jaũ bevéik esù bùvęs, bèt tuõ tárpu dár jókio gẽro mūrìnio nãmo nesù rãdęs.
Vytautas: Taĩ žinaĩ ką̃ padarýk: pir̃k geležìnį ar̃ plienìnį nãmą. Arbà dár geriaũ aliumìninį — neĩ supùs neĩ surūdỹs.
Antanas: Nà, žinaĩ, bičiùli, tù jaũ pràdedi juokáuti. Mán jaũ laĩkas eĩti. Iki pasimãtymo.
Vytautas: Iki. Linkiù táu sẽkmẽs!

VOCABULARY

skubẽti (skubù, skùba, skubẽjo, skubẽs) — to hurry, to be in a hurry
apžiūrẽti (apžiūriù, apžiũri, apžiūrẽjo, apžiūrẽs) examine carefully
jaũ — already
bevéik — almost
tuõ tárpu — so far, in the meantime
jókio (gen. case of **jóks**) — no, none

101

taĩ ką̃ gi (idiom) — well, well; well, now

piřkti (perkù, peřka, piřko, piřks) — to buy

medìnis, -ė (2) — wooden

mūrìnis, -ė (2) — brick, stone (house)

sveikiaũ (comparative adjective neuter) — healthier, better

gál iř taĩp (idiom) — perhaps it is so, it may be so

vistíek — inspite of, nevertheless

sidabrìnis, -ė (2) — silver, made of silver

laĩkrodis -džio (1) — watch, clock

iř — and, too, also

pardúoti (pardúodu, pardúoda, pařda-vė, parduõs) — to sell

nès — because

sugèsti (sugeñda, sugẽdo, sugès) — to break down, to go bad

visuř — everywhere

ràsti (irreg.: randù, rañda, rãdo, ràs) —to find

padarýti (padaraũ, padãro, padãrė, padarỹs) — to do, to perform, to make (perfective)

gelèžinis, -ė — iron, made of iron

plienìnis, -ė — steel, made of steel

geriaũ (compar. adverb) — better

dár geriaũ — even better

aliuminìnis — aluminum

supúti (supúva, supùvo, supùs) — to rot, putrefy

surūdýti (surūdìja, surūdìjo, surūdỹs) — to rust

neĩ... neĩ... — neither... nor...

bičiùlis -io — friend

juokáuti (juokáuju, juokáuja, juokã-vo, juokaũs) — to joke

linkėti (linkiù, liñki, linkėjo, linkės) — to wish (good luck, etc.)

sėkmė̃ (4) — good luck

GRAMMAR

13.1 Third Declension Adjectives.

The nominative singular of all adjectives in this declension is in -*is* for the masculine and -*ė* for the feminine. They are usually derived from nouns:

NOUN	ADJECTIVE
áuksas 'gold'	*auksìnis* 'gold, golden'
mẽdis 'tree'	*medìnis* 'wood, wooden'
vãsara 'summer'	*vasarìnis* 'summer, summer-like'
nãmas 'house'	*namìnis* 'domestic (animals)'
dárbas 'work'	*darbìnis* 'work (clothes, etc.)'

There are also some adjectives of this declension which are derived from:
a) other adjectives,
b) past passive participles.

Examples:
a) Derived from adjectives:

saldùs 'sweet'   *saldìnis* 'of sweet kind'
                 (*saldìnis obuolỹs* 'sweet apple')

beñdras 'common'   *bendrìnis* 'belonging to all'
             (*bendrìnė kalbà* 'common language, standard language')

b) Derived from past passive participles:*

leñktas 'bent'　　　　　　lenktìnis 'which can be bent, closed'
　　　　　　　　　　　　　(lenktìnis peīlis 'pocket knife')
sudétas 'put together'　　　sudétinis 'compound'
　　　　　　　　　　　　　(sudétinis sakinỹs 'compound sentence')

13.2 Singular of Third Declension Adjectives.

M a s c u l i n e

	'wooden'	'gold'	'artificial'	
N.,V.	medìnis (2)	auksìnis (2)	dirbtìnis (2)	-is
G.	medìnio	auksìnio	dirbtìnio	-io
D.	medìniam	auksìniam	dirbtìniam	-iam
A.	medìnį	auksìnį	dirbtìnį	-į
I.	mediniù	auksiniù	dirbtiniù	-iu
L.	medìniame	auksìniame	dirbtìniame	-iame

F e m i n i n e

	'wooden'	'gold'	'artificial'	
N.,V.	medìnė (2)	auksìnė (2)	dirbtìnė (2)	-ė
G.	medìnės	auksìnės	dirbtìnės	-ės
D.	medìnei	auksìnei	dirbtìnei	-ei
A.	medìnę	auksìnę	dirbtìnę	-ę
I.	medinè	auksinè	dirbtinè	-e
L.	medìnėje	auksìnėje	dirbtìnėje	-ėje

13.3 The Formation of the Past Active Participle.

Of all of the participles in Lithuanian the most important is
the past active participle because it is used in the formation of
compound tenses. To form the past active participle take the past
tense stem and add the ending -ęs for the masculine nominative
singular and the ending -usi for the feminine nominative singular,
-iusi if the verb belongs to the 3ʳᵈ conjugation.　　　For
plural: add -ę for masculine, -usios (-iusios) for feminine.

Examples:

　　1st conjugation: dìrb-o '(he) worked'

Masculine singular		Feminine singular	
dìrbęs 'having worked'	-ęs	dìrbusi	-usi

---

* For past passive participles, see Lesson 33.

$$ruõš\dot{e}\ \text{'(he) prepared'}$$

ruõš\k{e}s 'having prepared'   -\k{e}s   ruõšiusi   -iusi

2nd conjugation: myl\dot{e}j-o '(he) loved'

myl\dot{e}j\k{e}s 'having loved'   -\k{e}s   myl\dot{e}jusi   -usi

3rd conjugation: žinój-o '(he) knew'

žinój\k{e}s 'having known'   -\k{e}s   žinójusi   -usi

$$r\~{a}š\dot{e}\ \text{'(he) wrote'}$$

r\~{a}š\k{e}s 'having written'   -\k{e}s   r\~{a}šiusi   -iusi

$$ska\~{i}t\dot{e}\ \text{'(he) read'}$$

ska\~{i}t\k{e}s 'having read'   -\k{e}s   ska\~{i}čiusi   -iusi

Note that -ti- and -di- are replaced by -či- and -dži- respectively in position before -usi.

The full declension of the participle is given in Lesson 26.

13.4 The Present Perfect Tense — (būtàsis kartìnis atliktìnis laĩkas).

Up to this point we have discussed only simple tenses:
the present tense (esamàsis laĩkas),
the past tense or simple preterit (būtàsis kartìnis laĩkas),
the frequentative past (būtàsis dažnìnis laĩkas),
and the future tense (būsimàsis laĩkas).

As in English the present perfect tense denotes the present state which is the result of a past action. (It may not, however, denote a past action continuing into the present as does the English perfect tense.) Thus, for example, the sentence: 'I have been living here three years' would be translated into Lithuanian by: Aš čià gyvenù jaũ trejì mētai with a Lithuanian present tense.

The perfect tense is formed with the present conjugation of the verb bùti 'to be' and that form of the past active participle which agrees in gender and number with the subject. Examples:

Masculine

àš esù dìrb\k{e}s 'I have worked'; ruõš\k{e}s 'prepared'; žinój\k{e}s 'known'
tù esì dìrb\k{e}s 'you (sg.) have worked', etc.
jìs yrà dìrb\k{e}s 'he has worked', etc.
mẽs ẽsame dìrb\k{e} 'we have worked', etc.
jũs ẽsate dìrb\k{e} 'you (pl.) have worked', etc.
jiẽ yrà dìrb\k{e} 'they have worked', etc.

Feminine

àš esù dìrbusi 'I have worked'; *ruõšiusi* 'prepared'; *žinójusi* 'known'
tù esì dìrbusi 'you (sg.) have worked', etc.
jì yrà dìrbusi 'she has worked', etc.
mẽs ẽsame dìrbusios 'we have worked', etc.
jũs ẽsate dìrbusios 'you have worked', etc.
jõs yrà dìrbusios 'they have worked', etc.

The past active participle stem of *bùti* 'to be' is *buv-* (cf. *bùvo* '(he) was').

1) *Aš jaũ kelìs kartùs esù bùvęs New Yorke. —*
   I have already been in New York several times.
2) *Aš tìk víeną kar̃tą esù bùvęs New Yorke. —*
   I have been in New York only once.
3) *Mẽs dár niẽkad nẽsame bùvę Kalifòrnijoje. —*
   We haven't been in California yet.

EXERCISES

A. *Questions.* 1. Kur̃ taĩp skubėjo Antãnas? 2. Ką̃ jìs nóri pir̃kti? 3. Kókį nãmą jìs nóri pir̃kti? 4. Kokiamè (in which kind of) namè sveikiaũ gyvénti? 5. Kóks nãmas Antãnui geriaũ patiñka? 6. Kodėl Antãnas par̃davė auksìnį laĩkrodį? 7. Ar̃ jũs ẽsate apžiūrėję vìsą miẽstą? 8. Kóks nãmas niekuomèt nesupùs? 9. Kàs pradėjo juokáuti? 10. Ar̃ mùms jaũ laĩkas eĩti namõ?

B. *Decline in the singular:* mūrìnis nãmas, medìnis nãmas, auksìnis laĩkrodis, namìnis gyvulỹs.

C. *Conjugate in the present perfect tense* (in both genders): turė́ti, bùti, dìrbti, rašýti, matýti.

D. *Change from the simple past (preterit) to the present perfect:* 1. Aš dìrbau namiė̃. 2. Jìs turėjo medìnį nãmą. 3. Mẽs pir̃kome naũją nãmą. 4. Mẽs niekuomèt nebùvome Vìlniuje. 5. Jõs neskaĩtė tõs naujõs knỹgos. (Use *nèrà* for the negative form*).

E. *Translate into Lithuanian:* 1. I have been in Vilnius. 2. I still haven't found a good house. 3. It is better (more healthy) to live in a wooden house than in a brick house. 4. He has had a gold watch. 5. We want to buy a brick house, but mama wants a wood house. 6. She wants to buy a silver watch. 7. Have you (sg.) already been in the city? 8. I still haven't been [there] because

---

* In the negative: àš nesù, tù nesì, jìs nèrà; mẽs nẽsame, jũs nẽsate, jie nèrà (ne+esù=nesù, etc.).

I have too much work. 9. Let's go and buy a new wood house.
10. He lives in a wood house, but we live in a brick (one).

CONVERSATION

NAUJAS FILMAS

Kazỹs: 1. Ar̃ jaũ esì bùvęs kadà nórs tamè naujamè kìno teatrè? (or *kinè,* popularly)

Paũlius: 2. Dár nesù bùvęs, bèt nóriu šiañdien vakarè pamatýti
tą̃ naũją lietùvišką fìlmą.

Kazys: 3. Aš jaũ esù tą̃ fìlmą mãtęs. Labaĩ gẽras fìlmas.

Paulius: 4. Taĩ tù nenóri sù manimì eĩti?

Kazys: 5. Šiañdien neturiù laĩko. Mán reĩkia parašýti tẽvui
láišką.

Paulius: 6. Rytój parašýsi. Šiañdien eĩsime į̃ kìną!

Kazys: 7. Ką̃ gi àš teñ darýsiu? Aš gi táu jaũ sakiaũ: àš jaũ
esù mãtęs tą̃ fìlmą.

Paulius: 8. O àš víenas nenóriu eĩti.

Kazys: 9. Paskam̃bink Stãsei, gál jì galẽs sù tavimì eĩti.

Paulius: 10. Gẽras patarìmas! Taĩp ir̃ padarýsiu.

A NEW FILM

Kazys: 1. Have you ever been in that new movie theater?

Paulius: 2. I have not been there yet, but I want to see that
new Lithuanian movie this evening.

Kazys: 3. I have already seen that movie. It is a good movie.

Paulius: 4. So, you don't want to go with me?

Kazys: 5. I have no time today. I have to write a letter to
[my] father.

Paulius: 6. You will (can) write it tomorrow. Today we shall
go to the movies.

Kazys: 7. And what shall I do there? I already told you that
I had seen that movie.

Paulius: 8. But I don't want to go alone.

Kazys: 9. Call up Stase. Maybe she will be able to go with you.

Paulius: 10. A good bit of advice! I'll do that.

NOTES:
1. **Kazỹs** — an abbreviated form of Kazìmieras 'Casimir'.
   kìno teãtras — 'movie theatre'. In colloquial Lithuanian: **kìnas** 'movies'.
2. **Paũlius** — cf. Latin 'Paulus'.
7. **gi** — an emphatic particle. Cf. German 'schon, doch, ja'; Russian 'zhe'.
9. **paskam̃bink** — lit. 'ring, ring up'.
   Stãsei — dative singular of **Stãsė,** a feminine name.
10. **taĩp** — lit. 'yes, so'. Translate it here as 'that'.

106

Keturioliktoji pamoka

Lesson 14

LAIŠKAS
A LETTER

Vytautas Vìtkus
Trakų g. 15
Vilnius

Jonas Vilutis
Birutės g. 193
Kaunas

Vìlnius, 1961. 10. 27

Miẽlas Jõnai,

Táu jaũ esù parãšęs trìs láiškus, õ Tù mán dár vìs neatsakaĩ. Kàs gi įvỹko? Ař Tàvo draugaĩ iřgi tokiẽ tinginiaĩ, kaĩp Tù? Ař Tù taĩp esì užsiẽmęs darbaĩs, kàd nèt užmirštì sàvo gerùs bičiuliùs?

Pàs mùs dabař jaũ ruduõ: mẽdžių lãpai geltóni, rudì, miškaĩ pasipuõšę kaĩp karãliai. Universitetè studeñtai nenóri mókytis, õ

107

tìk eĩna į príemiesčius, į párkus, į miškùs pasiváikščioti. Aš iřgi dažnaĩ išeinù iš miẽsto į laukùs, kuř dabař yrà taĩp gražù.

Dabař àš jaũ baĩgsiu iř láuksiu laiškų̃ iš Tavę̃s: Tù jaũ esì mán kelìs skolìngas. Svéikink Birùtę iř tėveliùs.

Výtautas

VOCABULARY

láiškas (3) — letter
įvỹkti (įvỹksta, įvỹko, įvỹks) — to happen, to take place, to occur (used only in the 3rd person)
tinginỹs (3a) — lazy-bones
užsiim̃ti (užsìimu, užsìima, užsìėmė, užsiim̃s) — to be busy, occupied
nèt — even
bičiùlis -io (2) — friend, 'buddy'
ruduõ — fall, autumn
mẽdis (gen. mẽdžio) (2) — tree
lãpas (2) — leaf (of a tree), sheet (of paper)
geltóni (nom. pl.) — yellow
rudì (nom. pl.) — brown
mìškas (4) — forest, wood
pasipuõšti (pasipuošiù, pasipuõšia, pasìpuošė, pasìpuoš) — to be adorned, to 'spruce up'

karãlius (4th declension noun, nom. pl. karãliai) (2) — king
príemiestis (gen. príemiesčio) (1) — suburb
laũkas (4) — field
kelìs (acc. pl.) — some, a few
skolìngas — indebted
tėveliùs (acc. pl.) — parents
Birùtė — a girl's name

IDIOMS

àš esù užsiė̃męs — I am busy, occupied
pàs mùs — at our place, here with us (cf. German 'bei uns')
tù esì mán skolìngas — you owe me
àš esù táu skolìngas — I owe you

GRAMMAR

14.1 The Plural of the First Declension Nouns.

The plural cases for the first declension nouns are as follows:

	'home, houses'		'brothers'		'horses'	
N.,V.	namaĩ	-ai (4)	bróliai	-iai (1)	arkliaĩ	-iai (3)
G.	namų̃	-ų	brólių	-ių	arklių̃	-ių
D.	namáms	-ams	bróliams	-iams	arkliáms	-iams
A.	namùs	-us	brólius	-ius	árklius	-ius
I.	namaĩs	-ais	bróliais	-iais	arkliaĩs	-iais
L.	namuosè	-uose	bróliuose	-iuose	arkliuosè	-iuose

The final -s of the dative plural ending and the final -e of the locative plural ending (of all declensions of nouns) are frequently dropped in colloquial speech.

The vocative plural is always like the nominative plural.

The numbers in parentheses denote the accentuation class. Cf. Lesson 5 and Appendix, paragraph 51.

14.2 In Lithuanian there are many prefixes which may change or modify the meaning of the verb. Several examples of common prefixes with a few of the ordinary meanings are given below:

14.2,1 The prefix *at-* (*ata-, ati-, ato-*) may denote:

a) motion towards the speaker,

b) motion to a certain place, or that the action is reversed from its ordinary direction; (the hyphen separates the prefix from the main verb, but it would not be written in standard Lithuanian).

at-nèšti 'to bring'
at-eĩti 'to arrive, to come'
ati-dúoti 'to give back, to return'
ati-darýti 'to open'

14.2,2 *į-* may denote motion into something:

į-eĩti 'to enter'
į-nèšti 'to bring in'
į-tráukti 'to drag into'

14.2,3 *nu-* may denote:

a) motion away from the speaker,

b) separation from something, or

c) direction down from somewhere:

nu-eĩti 'to go away'
nu-piáuti 'to cut off'
nu-lìpti 'to climb down'

14.2,4 *iš-* may denote motion out from the inside of something:

iš-eĩti 'to come out'
iš-nèšti 'to carry out'
iš-lìpti 'to climb out, to get out'

14.2,5 *per-* may mean 'across, over' or contain some general idea of division:

pér-eiti 'to cross'
pér-lipti 'to climb over'
pér-laužti 'to break into pieces'

14.2,6 *pa-* may denote:

  a) the completion of an action,
  b) a short duration of an action, or
  c) lack of intensity of the action (cf. the Appendix, section on aspect):

   pa-sakýti 'to say'
   pa-skaitýti 'to read for a while'
   pa-dirbĕti 'to work a little bit'

14.2,7 *pra-* may denote motion through or past something, the beginning of an action or the fact that a certain amount of time is spent performing an action:

   pra-mùšti 'to beat through'
   pra-eĩti 'to pass by'
   pra-kalbĕti 'to begin to speak'
   pra-búti 'to stay for a certain length of time'

14.2,8 *su-* may denote gathering together or a coming-together:

   su-eĩti 'to come together, to meet'
   su-darýti 'to form, to constitute'
   su-dĕti 'to put together'

14.2,9 *už-* may denote motion behind something or motion going up (like climbing up):

   už-eĩti 'to go behind'
   už-lìpti (añt stógo) 'to climb up (on the roof)'

14.2,10 The prefixes listed above have other meanings in addition to those given. The student should not try to create words on the basis of his knowledge of the prefixes and the verbal roots. On the other hand he may more easily understand the formation of many of the verbs if he keeps this principle of word formation (prefix plus root) in mind. For more detailed and more complete listing of verbal prefixes see Appendix, paragraph on Verbal Prefixes. Consult the vocabulary every time you are in doubt.

EXERCISES

A. *Questions.* 1. Kíek Výtautas yrà jaũ parãšęs laiškų̃ Jõnui? 2. Ar̃ Jõno draugaĩ yrà tinginiaĩ? 3. Kàs yrà dabar̃ labaĩ užsiě̃męs? 4. Kàs užmir̃šta sàvo gerùs bičiuliùs? 5. Kóks mẽtų laĩkas (season) yrà dabar̃? 6. Kokiẽ yrà mẽdžių lãpai? 7. Kokiẽ yrà miškaĩ? 8. Ką̃ dãro studeñtai universitetè? 9. Kur̃ jiẽ eĩna? 10. Kur̃ dabar̃ yrà taĩp labaĩ gražù?

B. *Give the plural declension of the following nouns:* tė́vas, studeñtas, láiškas, laĩkraštis (gen. laĩkraščio), miẽstas, universitẽtas, rýtas, teãtras.

C. *Change all the words in italics into the plural:* 1. Aš jám rašaũ *láišką.* 2. Màno *brólis* gyvẽna Vìlniuje. 3. Màno *senẽlis* gyvẽna priẽ Nẽmuno. 4. *Mẽdžio* lãpai yrà rudì. 5. *Studeñtas* skaĩto *láišką.* 6. Màno *mókytojas* gyvẽna Vìlniuje. 7. Màno *draũgas* yrà taĩp pàt *studeñtas.* 8. Mẽs rãšome *pieštukù.* 9. Màno *namè* yrà daũg kambariũ. 10. Mū́sų *miestè* áuga daũg mẽdžių.

D. *Translate into Lithuanian:* 1. The students study at (in) the university. 2. We go (travel) to the university by buses. 3. The university buildings are in the center of the city. 4. My friends live in the suburbs. 5. My brother reads many newspapers. 6. Our gardens are in the suburbs. 7. He already wrote me many letters. 8. In our city there are two theaters. 9. In the summer in our beautiful park there will be many concerts. 10. My parents live in an old house near the university.

CONVERSATION

AUTOBUSŲ STOTYJE

Putvỹs: 1. Kadà išeĩna autobùsas į̃ Kaũną?

Tarnáutojas: 2. Sẽkantis autobùsas išeĩna ùž pùsės valandõs.

Putvys: 3. Taĩ réiškia, dešim̃tą vãlandą.

Tarnautojas: 4. Taĩp. Iš Vìlniaus į̃ Kaũną eĩna daũg autobùsų: dù autobùsai kiekvíeną vãlandą.

Putvys: 5. Ar̃ aš galiù dár gáuti 5 (penkìs) bìletus? Màno tėvaĩ ir̃ màno dù bróliai taĩp pàt važiuõs sù manimì.

Tarnautojas: 6. Dár gãlima. Dabař nedaũg keleĩvių važiúoja dešimtõs valandõs autobusù.

Putvys: 7. Kíek kainúoja 5 (penkì) bìletai?

Tarnautojas: 8. Penkì bìletai kainúoja 10 (dẽšimt) lìtų iř 10 ceñtų.

Putvys: 9. Prašaũ. (Putvys gives the money to the official
and takes the tickets and change). Kuř yrà stotiẽs restorãnas?

Tarnautojas: 10. Restorãno šìtoje stotyjè nėrà, bèt yrà gẽras restorãnas kitojè gãtvės pùsėje.

AT THE BUS STATION

Putvys: 1. When does the bus leave for Kaunas?

Official: 2. The next bus leaves in half an hour.

Putvys: 3. That means at ten o'clock.

Official: 4. Yes. There are many buses running between Vilnius
and Kaunas: two buses every hour.

Putvys: 5. Can I still get 5 tickets? My parents and my two
brothers are also going with me.

Official: 6. Yes. It is still possible. Not too many travelers take
the 10 o'clock bus now.

Putvys: 7. How much do 5 tickets cost?

Official: 8. Five tickets cost 10 litas and 10 cents.

Putvys: 9. Here you are. Where is the station restaurant?

Official: 10. There is no restaurant in this station, but there is
a good restaurant on the other side of the street.

NOTES:
1. **išeĩna** — 'goes out', here: 'leaves'.
   Į̃ Kaũną — 'to Kaunas' (here: leaves for Kaunas).
2. **ùž** — (preposition with gen. and acc.) used with time expressions (with
   gen.) to denote 'in', i.e. 'at the end of a certain period of time'.
3. **dešim̃tą vãlandą** — (acc.) 'at ten o'clock'. For time expressions see Lesson 32.
4. **iš Vìlniaus** — 'from Vilnius'.
   kiekvíeną vãlandą — (acc. of definite time) 'every hour'.
5. **penkìs** — (acc. of penkì 'five'). Numerals are declined in Lithuanian, see
   Lesson 24.
6. **dešimtõs valandõs autobusù** — 'by the 10 o'clock bus'.
   autobusù — is in the instrumental case to denote means.
8. **lìtas** — The lìtas was the monetary unit of Lithuania; it was worth about
   twenty cents. For the use of the genitive case here see 24.4,1.

112

Penkioliktoji pamoka
Lesson 15

REVIEW

1.

NEMUNAS

Nẽmunas yrà didžiáusia iř ilgiáusia[1] Lietuvõs ùpė. Jì tẽka bevéik peř vìsą Líetuvą iř įteka[2] į Báltijos jūrą netolì Klaĩpėdos.[3] Priẽ Nẽmuno yrà daũg senų̃ miẽstų, miestēlių[4] iř káimų. Nẽmunas tẽka peř laukùs iř miškùs. Kaũnas, kurìs yrà antràsis[5] Lietuvõs miẽstas, yrà iřgi priẽ Nẽmuno. Priẽ Kaũno į Nẽmuną įteka Nerìs,[6] antróji Lietuvõs ùpė, kurì tẽka prõ Vìlnių, Lietuvõs sóstinę.

Kaunè, tařp Nẽmuno iř Neriẽs, yrà senõs piliẽs griuvẽsiai. Tą̃ mūrìnę pìlį pastãtė didỹsis Lietuvõs kunigáikštis[7] Kęstùtis, nórs iř anksčiaũ teñ yrà jaũ bùvusi medìnė pilìs.[8]

Nẽmunu plaũkia gárlaiviai. Gãlima nuplaũkti nuõ Klaĩpėdos lìgi Alytaũs.[9]

NOTES:

1. **didžiáusia iř ilgiáusia** — the largest and longest (see Lesson 27). Nemunas is 650 miles long.
2. **įteka** — flows into
3. **Klaĩpėda** — Klaipėda, Lithuanian harbor on the Baltic Sea (ca. 80,000 inhabitants).
4. **miestēlių** — miestēlis is diminutive of **miẽstas** 'city': town smaller than **miẽstas**.
5. **antràsis** — second (see Lesson 28); second largest.
6. **Nerìs** — River Neris, ca. 450 miles long.
7. **didỹsis Lietuvõs kunigáikštis** — Grand Duke (king) of Lithuania. Kęstutis ruled 1345-1377.
8. **medìnė pilìs** — 'wooden castle, castle built of wood'. (The oldest Lithuanian castles were built on hills, primarily of hard oak timber.)
9. **Alytùs** — a city in picturesque south-east Lithuania. It is the county seat of Alytus county (ca. 20,000 inhabitants).

Nemunas

The Nemunas River

2.

PASAKA APIE LAIMINGĄ ŪKININKĄ

Víenas neturtìngas ūkininkas vìsą diēną suñkiai dìrbo laukè.[1]
Kaĩ labaĩ pavaȓgo, jìs atsìgulė añt píevos pasilsĕti iȓ užmìgo.

Jìs sapnãvo, kàd jám pasiródė ángelas, jį̃ pasvéikino iȓ tãrė:
— Vargìngas žmogaũ, prašýk, kõ[2] tàvo širdìs trókšta — vìsa gáusi.

Ūkininkas išsigañdo, bèt šiaĩp taĩp[3] pràtarė:
— Dangaũs pasiuntinỹ, jéi tàvo tokià valià,[4] taĩ padarýk taĩp, kàd vìsa[5], ką̃ àš rankà paliẽsiu, paviȓstų[6] į̃ áuksą.

Angelas nusišypsójo iȓ tãrė:
— Tù galĕjai kõ nórs gerèsnio[7] paprašýti, bèt bùs taĩp, kaĩp tù nóri.

Iȓ ángelas išnýko.
— Dĕkui Diẽvui[8], — tãrė ūkininkas, — dabaȓ àš bū́siu turtingas.

Iȓ tikraĩ! Võs tìk jìs pàlietė šą̃ką mẽdžio, põ kuriuõ jìs miegójo, tuojaũ jì paviȓto į̃ auksìnę šą̃ką iȓ nuliñko žemỹn.

Põ tõ ūkininkas parėjo namõ iȓ pirmiáusia[9] norėjo geraĩ užválgyti.[10] Bèt kai tìk jìs pàlietė dúonos kẽpalą, tuojaũ tàs paviȓto į̃ áuksą. Auksìnis dúonos kẽpalas bùvo tóks sunkùs, kàd vaȓgšas[11] žmogùs võs galėjo jį̃ pakélti.

Ūkininkas dabaȓ norėjo nórs vandeñs atsigérti, bèt iȓ vanduõ paviȓto į̃ áuksą.

— Ką̃ àš dabaȓ darýsiu? Kám[12] mán auksìnė dúona, kám mán auksìnis nãmas, kám mán auksìnis vanduõ, jéigu àš pàts badù miȓsiu![13] Tegù dabaȓ mán viẽtoj šiõ áukso kàs pàdeda[14] juodõs dúonos iȓ vandeñs[15] — daugiaũ niẽko àš nebenorėsiu.[16]

Iš tõs báimės[17] vargdiẽnis[18] ūkininkas nèt iš miẽgo[19] pabùdo. Jìs dabaȓ labaĩ džiaũgėsi, kàd taĩ bùvo tìk sãpnas. Jìs dabaȓ žinójo, kàd víen[20] áuksas nepadãro žmogaũs laimìngo.

NOTES:

1. **laukè** — lit. 'in the field'; here: 'in the fields, outside'.
2. **kõ** — genitive case, **trókšti** 'to desire' takes the genitive.
3. **šiaĩp taĩp** — lit. 'this way - that way'; real meaning: 'with great effort, barely'.
4. **jéi tàvo tokià valià** — lit. 'if your will is such; if you wish'.
5. **vìsa** — neuter adj. of **vìsas, visà**: 'the whole, all, total, everything'.
6. **paviȓstų** — would turn [into].

7. **kŏ nórs gerèsnio** — 'something better'; (genitive case, because **prašýti, paprašýti** requires the genitive case).

8. **dėkui Diẽvui** — 'thank God' (Dėkui is derived from the verb **dėkóti** 'to thank', Diẽvui is dative: **dėkóti** requires a dative case).

9. **pirmiáusia** — 'first of all' (See Lesson 27).

10. **užválgyti** — 'to have a bite, a snack'; **geraĩ užválgyti** — 'to have a good meal'.

11. **vaȓgšas** — 'poor'. This is a noun, but when it is used with another noun, it precedes that noun and agrees with that noun in gender, number and case.

12. **kám** — lit. 'to what'. **Kám mán**: 'what do I need [something] for'.

13. **badù miȓti** — 'to die of hunger'.

14. **tegù ... kàs pàdeda** — 'let someone place [before me]; if someone only placed'.

15. **dúonos iȓ vandeñs** — partitive genitive (See Lesson 19).

16. **nebenorėsiu** — 'I will (never) want'.

17. **ìš ... báimės** — 'from fear'.

18. **vargdiẽnis** — **vaȓgšas**. See Note 11 above.

19. **pabùdo** — 'woke up'; **ìš miẽgo pabùsti**: 'to wake up (from sleep)'.

20. **víenas** — here: 'alone'.

3.

KAMBARYS

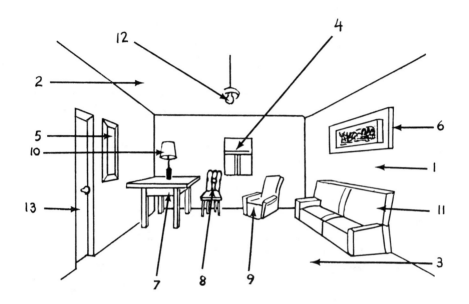

	English	Lithuanian	Examples
1.	wall	síena	Šì síena yrà baltà.
2.	ceiling	lùbos*	Màno kam̃bario lùbos yrà báltos
3.	floor	griñdys*	Griñdys yrà rùdos.
4.	window	lángas	Aš turiù tìk víeną lángą.
5.	mirror	véidrodis	Jì žiū̃ri į̃ véidrodį.
6.	picture	pavéikslas	Aš nóriu pir̃kti pavéikslą.
7.	table	stãlas	Knygà gùli añt stãlo.
8.	chair	kėdė̃	Kėdė̃ stóvi priẽ stãlo.
9.	easy chair	fòtelis	Fòtelis stóvi kampè.
10.	lamp	lémpa	Uždèk lémpą!
11.	sofa	sofà	Sė̃skite añt sòfos!
12.	bulb	elèktros lempùtė	Dúok mán naū̃ją lempùtę!
13.	door	dùrys*	Prašaũ uždarýti durìs!

---

* All these three nouns are used in plural only, although the meaning is singular: cf. English 'scissors, trousers', etc. See also Lesson 23.

CONVERSATION

1.

Turìstas: Atsiprašaũ. Gál gãlite mán pasakýti, kuř yrà zoolò-gijos sõdas?

Polìcininkas: Zoològijos sõdas yrà kitojè miẽsto pùsėje. Jùms rei-kẽs važiúoti autobusù.

Turìstas: Kuř yrà autobùsų sustojìmo vietà?

Policininkas: Eĩkite šià gatvè lìgi kaṁpo, tadà pasùkite kairẽn. Te-naĩ tuojaũ pamatýsite autobùsų sustojìmo viẽtą.

Turìstas: Kuriuõ autobusù mán reĩkia važiúoti?

Policininkas: Nùmeriu 5 (penkì). Jìs jùs nuvẽš priẽ pàt zoològijos sõdo.

Turìstas: Labaĩ ãčiū.

2.

Padavėja: Prašaũ meniù.

Žvigáitis: Ačiū. Aš norėčiau (I would like) tìk puodùką kavõs.

Padavėja: Sù píenu iř cùkrumi?

Žvigaitis: Nè, juodõs.

Padavėja: Tuojaũ.

3.

Irenà: Marýte, táu patiñka šìs fìlmas?

Marýtė: Nelabaĩ. Peř daũg kaľba. Iř nėrà méilės ...

Irena: Taĩ eĩkime į̃ kìtą kìną. Tenaĩ gál bùs méilės fìlmas.

Marytė: Geraĩ, eĩname!

4.

Keleĩvis: Prašaũ dù bìletus į̃ Klaĩpėdą.

Tarnáutojas: 5 (penkì) lìtai.

Keleivis: Prašaũ. Kadà išeĩna sẽkantis autobùsas į̃ Klaĩpėdą?

Tarnautojas: Ačiū. Sẽkantis autobùsas išeĩna ùž dẽšimt (10) mi-nùčių.

Keleivis: Ačiū.

5.

Mókytojas: Kuř yrà Lietuvà?

Mokinỹs: Lietuvà yrà Euròpoje.

Mokytojas: Kàs yrà Lietuvõs sóstinė?

Mokinys: Lietuvõs sóstinė yrà Vìlnius.

Mokytojas: Kurì yrà didžiáusia Lietuvõs ùpė?

Mokinys: Didžiáusia Lietuvõs ùpė yrà Nẽmunas.

COMBINATION PRACTICES

Combine to make sentences:

A.

a.	We need	1.	a red pencil
b.	they need	2.	a good room
c.	my father needed	3.	a good neighbor
d.	his brother needed	4.	pleasant work
e.	I will need	5.	a white house
f.	you will need	6.	a new house
g.	we will need	7.	a beautiful house
h.	they will need	8.	an old house
		9.	a new book
		10.	a new table

B.

a.	we are	1.	cold (šálta)
b.	they are	2.	warm (šilta)
c.	my father is	3.	hot (káršta)
d.	her brother is		
e.	our sister is		

C.

a.	We will go	1.	home
b.	Her mother will go	2.	to the university
c.	She will go	3.	to Vilnius
d.	Your brother will go	4.	to Lithuania
e.	My sister will go	5.	to America
		6.	to Klaipėda
		7.	to school
		8.	to the station
		9.	to the city
		10.	to the village

VARIATION PRACTICE

A.

a) *Mán reĩkia naũjo pieštùko.*

b) *Mán reikalìngas naũjas pieštùkas.*

1. I need a new pencil. 2. I needed a new pencil. 3. I will need a new pencil. 4. My teacher needs a new pencil. 5. My teacher needed a new red pencil.

B.

Mán labaĩ šálta (šìlta, káršta)

1. I am very cold. 2. I was very cold. 3. They are very cold. 4. They were very cold. 5. My new teacher is very cold.

C.

Aš dár niēkad nesù bùvęs (bùvusi) Lietuvojè.

1. I have never yet been in Lithuania.
2. I have never yet been in Europe.
3. I have never yet been in Canada.
4. My father has never yet been in Europe.
5. His sister has never yet been in a university.
6. Her young daughter has never yet been in school.
7. My new teacher has never yet been in Vilnius.
8. Our little sister has never yet been in the church.
9. Their young teacher has never yet been in Lithuania.
10. Your old father has never yet been in England.

Šešioliktoji pamoka

Lesson 16

PELĖDOS IR VARNOS

Priēš daũg mētų, kaĩ àš dár tìk pradējau mókytis raĩdžių, mẽs gyvēnome màno senēlių ūkyje. Apliñk namùs áugo ēglės iř líepos. Líepose bùvo pelēdų lìzdas. Dienomìs mẽs pelēdų nematýdavome: pelēdos išskrìsdavo ìš líepų tìk nãktį.

Víeną rudeñs rýtą mẽs išgiřdome laukè dìdelį triùkšmą. Añt líepų šakų̃ tupējo daũg várnų. Várnos gařsiai kranksējo iř tókiu būdù kēlė dìdelį triùkšmą.

Kaĩ jaũ galējome geraĩ matýti, pamãtėme mū́sų pelēdas. Jõs tupējo añt líepų šakų̃ iř gýnėsi nuõ várnų. Matýt, várnoms patìko tõs líepos, iř jõs norējo pelēdas ìš líepų išvarýti. Taĩ bùvo paũkščių kãras.

Praējo trỹs vãlandos. Várnos pagaliaũ nugalējo pelēdas, kuriõs ìš líepų nuskrìdo į̃ mìšką iř daugiaũ į̃ mū́sų líepas nesugrį̃žo. Nuõ tõ laĩko pelēdos neturējo lizdų̃ mū́sų líepose, iř líepas iř eglès užvaĺdė várnos.

Mẽs várnų nemēgome, nès jõs visuomèt kēlė dìdelį triùkšmą, bèt jõs mēgo mū́sų líepas iř eglès iř josè apsigyvēno.

VOCABULARY

kaĩ — when, as
dár — still
tìk — only
dár tìk — only
pradēti (pràdedu, pràdeda, pradējo, pradēs) — to begin
mókytis (mókausi, mókosi, mókėsi, mókysis; with gen.) — to learn
raĩdė (2) — letter (of the alphabet)

apliñk (prep. with acc.) — around
áugti (áugu, áuga, áugo, aũgs) — to grow
ēglė (2) — spruce
líepa (1) — linden tree
pelēda (1) — owl
lìzdas (4) — nest
dienà (4) — day

dienomìs (inst. pl.) — by day , during the day

išskrìsti (ìšskrendu, ìšskrenda, išskrìdo, išskrìs) — to fly out

nãktį — at night

išgiřsti (išgirstù, išgiřsta, išgiřdo, išgiřs) — to hear, to catch the sound of

triùkšmas (4) — noise

šakà (4) — branch

tupėti (tupiù, tùpi, tupėjo, tupės) — to perch, to sit (of birds, animals)

várna (1) — crow

gařsiai — loudly

kranksėti (kránksiu, kránksi, kranksėjo, kranksės) — to cackle, to caw

tókiu būdù — in this manner, in such a way that

kélti (keliù, kẽlia, kẽlė, keĺs) — to raise, to lift up

kélti triùkšmą — to make a lot of noise, to raise a ruckus

pamatýti (pamataũ, pamãto, pamãtė, pamatỹs) — to see, to notice

gìntis (ginúosi, gìnasi, gýnėsi, gìñsis) — to defend oneself

nuõ (prep. with gen.) — from, away from

matýt (abbreviation of matýti) — apparently, seemingly

išvarýti (išvaraũ, išvãro, išvãrė, išvarỹs) — to chase out, away

paũkštis -čio (2) — bird

kãras (4) — war

praeĩti (praeinù, praeĩna, praẽjo, praeĩs, cf. eĩti) — to pass

valandà (3b) — hour

pagaliaũ — finally

nugalėti (nùgaliu, nùgali, nugalėjo, nugalės, cf. galėti) — to conquer, to vanquish

nuskrìsti (nùskrendu, nùskrenda, nuskrìdo, nuskrìs) — to fly away to

daugiaũ — more

daugiaũ ne — no more, no longer

sugrį̃žti (sugrį̃žtù, sugrį̃žta, sugrį̃žo, sugrį̃š) — to return

laĩkas (4) — timė

nuõ tõ laĩko — since that time, since then

nès — because

užvaldýti (užvaldaũ, užvaĺdo, užvaĺdė, užvaĺdỹs) — to take over, to occupy

apsigyvénti (apsigyvenù, apsigyvẽna, apsigyvẽno, apsigyveñs) — to take up residence, to move in

GRAMMAR

16.1 Plural of the Nouns of the 2nd Declension.

Examples are given below:

	'days'		'streets'		'daughters-in-law'	
N.V.	diẽnos	-os (4)	gãtvės	-ės (2)	mařčios	-ios (4)
G.	dienų̃	-ų̃	gãtvių	-ių	marčių̃	-ių
D.	dienóms	-oms	gãtvėms	-ėms	marčióms	-ioms
A.	dienàs	-as	gatvès	-es	marčiàs	-ias
I.	dienomìs	-omis	gãtvėmis	-ėmis	marčiomìs	-iomis
L.	dienosè	-ose	gãtvėse	-ėse	marčiosè	-iose

In the plural the vocative is like the nominative most of the time.

16.2 The Use of the Genitive Case.

a) When the genitive case is used to show possession the noun in the genitive case is usually placed directly before the object possessed, e.g. *výro stãlas* 'the man's desk' or 'the desk of the man'.

b) The genitive is used as the direct object of a negated verb, e.g. *jìs nedìrba stãlo* 'he isn't making a desk'.

c) The object of an infinitive which is in turn the object of a negated verb may be in the genitive case, e.g. *jìs nenóri dìrbti stãlo* 'he doesn't want to make a desk'. Note that the word *stãlo* 'desk' is in the genitive case although it is the direct object of *dìrbti*, not *nóri*.

d) The genitive case is used with adverbs of quantity, e.g. *daũg miẽstų* 'many cities', *kíek stalų?* 'how many tables?', *mažaĩ brólių* 'few brothers'.

e) Many prepositions require the genitive case. Those listed below are used only with the genitive case. Cf. also 37.2.

    1) *bè* — without
        Aš esù bè dárbo. — I am without work (i.e. out of work)

    2) *añt* — on
        Pieštùkas (yrà) añt stãlo. — The pencil is on the desk.

    3) *ìš* — out of, away from
        Jìs bẽga ìš kiẽmo. — He runs out of the yard.

    4) *priẽ* — by, at, at the side of, in the presence of
        Mẽs gyvẽname priẽ ùpės. — We live by the river.
        Kẽdẽ stóvi priẽ síenos. — The chair stands by the wall.

    5) *nuõ* — from, away from
        Katẽ nušóko nuõ stãlo. — The cat jumped from the table.
        Nuõ penkių valandų ìki šešių (valandų). — From five o' clock to six (o'clock).

    6) *ìki* — to, up to, until
        Iki pasimãtymo. — So long. Lit.: until we see each other.
        Eĩk ìki mẽdžio. — Go as far as that tree.

    7) *lìgi* — up to, until
        Lìgi vãkar. — Until yesterday.
        Eĩk lìgi stãlo. — Go up to the table.

    8) *tar̃p* — between
        Kẽdẽ stóvi tar̃p síenos ir̃ stãlo. — The chair stands between the wall and the table.

f) Certain verbs require the direct object in the genitive case rather than the accusative. The case required by each verb will be pointed out in the vocabularies from now on.

Examples:

1) *norĕti* — to wish, to want
Aš nóriu dúonos. — I want [some] bread.

2) *láukti* — to expect, to wait for
Jìs láukia manę̃s. — He is waiting for me.
Mẽs láukiame brólio. — We are waiting for (expecting) [our] brother.

3) *mókytis* — to learn
Jìs mókosi lietùvių kalbõs.* — He is learning Lithuanian.

4) *ieškóti* — to look for, to seek
Jìs manę̃s visu̇̃r ieškójo. — He looked everywhere for me.

16.3 Numerals 11 - 20.

Differently from the numerals 1 - 9 there is no gender distinction here, but the noun quantified by the numeral is in the genitive plural.

11 — vienúolika	(namų̃, várnų) '11 houses, crows'		
12 — dvýlika		″	″
13 — trýlika		″	″
14 — keturiólika		″	″
15 — penkiólika		″	″
16 — šešiólika		″	″
17 — septyniólika		″	″
18 — aštuoniólika		″	″
19 — devyniólika		″	″
20 — dvìdešimt		″	″

The numbers *dvýlika, trýlika* and *dvìdešimt* are stressed on the initial syllable whereas the others are stressed on the third syllable from the end. The numbers 11-19 are formed by adding *-lika* to the stems of the numbers 1 - 9. Compare the numbers 1 - 9 with the numbers 11 - 19 and note the various changes in the stem of the initial element.

16.4 The 'Progressive' Tenses.

The past or future tense of the verb *būti* 'to be' may be compounded with the appropriate form of the present active parti-

---

* This has a different meaning from the sentence: **Jìs studijúoja lietùvių kaĺbą.** — 'He is studying Lithuanian'. This latter sentence implies a thorough, methodical study with the aim of learning the language completely.

ciple (prefixed with *be-*) to express an action which is not, or could not be completed. These forms are somewhat similar in meaning to the various progressive tenses of English with the exception that they are not used in the present tense.* The formation of the participle is discussed in Lesson 26. The number and gender of the participle are always the same as the number and gender of the subject. The participle is always in the nominative case to agree with the subject of the verb which, of course, is also in the nominative case. A sample paradigm with the past tense is given below:

Singular

Masculine	Feminine
1) buvaũ beateiną̃s	(beateĩnanti)
2) buvaĩ beateiną̃s	(beateĩnanti)
3) bùvo beateiną̃s	(beateĩnanti)

Plural

Masculine	Feminine
1) bùvome beateiną̃	(beateĩnančios)
2) bùvote beateiną̃	(beateĩnančios)
3) bùvo beateiną̃	(beateĩnančios)

1) *Aš buvaũ beeiną̃s iš namų̃, bèt pradėjo smar̃kiai lýti iř turėjau lìkti namiẽ.* — I was just leaving the house, but it began to rain hard and I had to stay home.

2) *Bùvome besėją̃, bèt lietùs tuõ tárpu sutrùkdė.* — We were sowing, but the rain stopped [us].

3) *Jìs bùvo besirengią̃s eĩti pàs mùs, kaĩ àš pàs jį̃ užėjaũ.* — He was getting ready to come to our place when I dropped in on him.

EXERCISES

A. *Questions.* 1. Kuř mẽs gyvẽnome priẽš daũg mẽtų? 2. Kàs áugo apliñk mū́sų namùs? 3. Kuř bùvo pelė́dų lìzdas? 4. Kadà pelė́dos išskrìsdavo iš líepų? 5. Ką̃ mẽs išgir̃dome viéną rudeñs rýtą? 6. Kuř tupė́jo várnos? 7. Ką̃ várnos dãrė? 8. Kóks taĩ bùvo kãras? 9. Kàs nugalė́jo? 10. Kàs užvaĺdė mū́sų líepas iř eglès?

---

* In some Lithuanian grammars, some examples are cited for the present tense also. In reality, the 'progressive' present tense is not used in modern Lithuanian.

125

B. *Decline in the singular and plural:* mergáitė, studeñtė, mokinė, mokyklà, mótina, knygà, pamokà, sóstinė, ùpė, òpera.

C. *Put the italicized nouns into the plural:* 1. Mū́sų *miestè* yrà *mokyklà.* 2. Jõ *mókytoja* geraĩ kaĺba lietùviškai. 3. *Gatvè* važiúo-ja daũg automobìlių. 4. *Jõs martì* gyvēna *káime.* 5. *Katè* miẽga põ *stalù.* 6. *Studeñtè* skaĩto *knỹgą.* 7. *Várna* tùpi *líepoje.* 8. *Várna* kranksėjo vìsą rýtą. 9. *Upė* tēka (flows) tỹliai (silently). 10. Aš nóriu pamatýti *òperą.*

D. *Translate into Lithuanian:* 1. Many trees grew around my house. 2. They lived on my parents' farm. 3. The crows in the linden trees raised a great ruckus. 4. Yesterday we saw many crows. 5. We like lindens and spruces. 6. Seven hours passed. 7. Fifteen minutes passed. 8. The owls don't have nests in our linden trees. 9. Only the crows caw in our trees. 10. They don't like crows.

CONVERSATION

KRAUTUVĖJE

Pardavėja: 1.   Labà dienà. Kuõ galiù patarnáuti?

Jasáitis: 2.   Prašaũ mán dúoti dvì dėžutès cigarèčių "Pirmỹn" iř degtùkų.

Pardavėja: 3.   Prašaũ. Taĩ bùs 60 (šēšiasdešimt) ceñtų. Gál dár kõ nórs?

Jasaitis: 4.   Ař jūs tùrite laiškáms põpieriaus iř vokų̃?

Pardavėja: 5.   Taĩp, tùrime. Štaĩ čià dėžùtė sù 20 (dvìdešimt) lãpų põpieriaus iř 10 (dēšimt) vokų̃.

Jasaitis: 6.   Kíek taĩ kainúoja?

Pardavėja: 7.   50 (peñkiasdešimt) ceñtų. Bèt mēs tùrime iř ge-resnių̃ vokų̃ ...

Jasaitis: 8.   Bùs gerì iř šìtie. Prašaũ mán dúoti dvì dėžutès.

Pardavėja: 9.   Taĩ bùs víenas lìtas.

Jasaitis: 10.   Prašaũ. (Giving her the money and taking the packages.) Ačiū. Sudiẽu.

AT THE STORE

Clerk:* 1.   Hello (good day). What can I do for you?

Jasaitis: 2.   Please give me two packs of 'Pirmyn' ('Forward') cigarettes and [some] matches.

---

* (feminine)

Clerk:	3.	Here you are. That will be 60 cents. Anything else?
Jasaitis:	4.	Do you have any stationery (letter-paper and envelopes)?
Clerk:	5.	Yes, we do. Here is a box with 20 sheets of paper and 10 envelopes.
Jasaitis:	6.	How much does it cost?
Clerk:	7.	50 cents. But we also have better envelopes.
Jasaitis:	8.	These will be all right. Give me two boxes, please.
Clerk:	9.	That will be one *litas*.
Jasaitis:	10.	Here you are. (Giving her the money and taking the packages.) Thanks. Good-by.

NOTES:

1. **Kuõ galiù patarnáuti?** — lit. 'with what can I help (serve) you?
2. **cigarètè** — 'cigarette'. For local cigarettes, with long mouthpieces, Lithuanians also use: **papiròsas**.
4. **laiškáms põpieriaus** — lit. '[some of] paper for letters'; laiškáms is dative plural, põpieriaus is partitive genitive; **vokų** — partitive genitive plural '(of some) envelopes'.
8. **Bùs gerì iř šìtie** — lit. 'these here also will be good', an idiom: 'these here will do, will be OK'.
10. **Prašaũ** — this verb is used with several meanings:
   a) **prašaũ tavęs píeno** — 'I am asking you for milk';
   b) **prašaũ** — (handing something over): 'here you are';
   c) **prašaũ** — after receiving thanks: 'don't mention it, that's OK, you are welcome'.

Family Members and Relatives

parents — *tėvai; gimdytojai*
father — *tėvas (tėvelis, tėtė, tėtis, tėtukas)*
mother — *motina (mama, mamytė, mamutė)*
son — *sūnus*
daughter — *duktė*
grandfather — *senelis*
grandmother — *senelė*
grandparents — *seneliai*
grandson — *vaikaitis*
granddaughter — *vaikaitė*
cousin (male) — *pusbrolis*
cousin (female) — *pusseserė*
uncle — *dėdė*
aunt — *teta*
father-in-law — *uošvis*
mother-in-law — *uošvė*
son-in-law — *žentas*
daughter-in-law — *marti*
brother-in-law — *svainis*
sister-in-law — *svainė*
relative (male) — *giminaitis*
relative (female) — *giminaitė*
relatives — *giminės*

Septynioliktoji pamoka

Lesson 17

KLASĖJE

Mókytoja: Kàs mán gãli pasakýti, kíek žmogùs tùri akiũ?

Jonùkas: Kiekvíenas žmogùs tùri dvì akìs, dvì ausìs, bèt tìk víeną nósį.

Mókytoja: Labaĩ geraĩ. O tù, Petriùk, gál galì mùms pasakýti, kuõ mēs giřdime?

Petriùkas: Mēs giřdime ausimìs, bèt nevisì gãlime geraĩ girdĕti. Aldonà niekuomèt negiřdi, kaĩ mókytoja áiškina pãmoką...

Aldonà: Màno aũsys taĩp pàt gēros, kaĩp iř Petriùko, bèt jõ ãkys blõgos: jìs nemãto, kaĩ mókytoja rãšo lentojè.

Mókytoja: Vaikaĩ, vaikaĩ, negražù taĩp kalbĕti! Kaĩ kàs tùri geràs akìs, kaĩ kàs — geràs ausìs, kaĩ kàs — gērą nósį.

Jonùkas: Põnia mókytoja, àš žinaũ, kíek žmogùs tùri akiũ, kíek ausũ, kíek nósių, bèt àš nežinaũ, kíek žmogaũs burnojè yrà dantũ.

Mókytoja: Burnojè yrà daũg dantũ. Mēs dár visũ dantũ nemókame suskaitýti. Taĩgi, sakýkime, kàd žmogùs tùri daũg dantũ. Ausimìs mēs giřdime, akimìs mãtome, nósimi úostome, õ ką mēs dãrome dantimìs?

Aldonà: Aš žinaũ, ką mēs dãrome dantimìs: mēs dantimìs kramtome saldainiùs, šokolãdą, kramtomąją gùmą...

Mókytoja: O dúoną, daržóves?

Aldonà: Taĩp, taĩp, iř jas; bèt mán geriaũ patiñka saldaĩniai, šokolãdas.

Mókytoja: Tìk neválgykite per daũg saldaĩnių iř šokolãdo: taĩ keñkia dantìms.

VOCABULARY

kiekvíenas, -a — every, each
akìs -iễs (4) — eye
ausìs -iễs (4) — ear
nósis -ies (1) — nose
gál — perhaps
girdéti (girdžiù, gìrdi, girdėjo, girdės)
— to hear
nevisì — not all, not everybody
Aldonà — Aldona (a girl's name)
niekuomèt — never
kaĩ — when
mókytoja (1) — teacher (fem.)
áiškinti (áiškinu, áiškina, áiškino,
áiškins) — to explain
taĩp pàt... kaĩp — just as ... as
Petriùkas, dim. of Pė́tras — Peter,
Pete
lentà (4) — blackboard, board
kaĩ kàs — some (people)

burnà (3) — mouth
suskaitýti (suskaitaũ, suskaĩto, suskaĩtė, suskaitỹs) — to count
úostyti (úostau, úosto, úostė, úostys)
— to smell (transitive)
kramtýti (kramtaũ, kraĩto, kraĩtė,
kramtỹs) — to chew
saldaĩnis -io (2) — candy
šokolãdas (2) — chocolate
gumà (4) — rubber, gum
kraĩtomąją gùmą (acc. singular) —
— chewing gum
dúona (1) — bread
mėsà (4) — meat
daržóvė (1) — vegetable
iĩ — and, too, also
per daũg — too much, too many
keñkti (keñkiù, keñkia, keñkė, keñks)
— to harm (with dat.)

GRAMMAR

17.1 The Plural of Third Declension Nouns:

Feminine			Masculine		
N.	ãkys	-ys (4) 'eyes'	dañtys	-ys (4) 'teeth'
G.	akiū̃	-iū̃	dantū̃	-ū̃
D.	akìms	-ims	dantìms	-ims
A.	akìs	-is	dantìs	-is
I.	akimìs	-imis	dantimìs	-imis
L.	akysè	-yse	dantysè	-yse

There is no general rule allowing the student to determine which third declension nouns have the genitive plural in -ių and which have -ų. A list of the most important nouns in -ių is given below. Unless specified to the contrary the student may assume that the rest of the nouns of this category take the genitive plural in -ų.

Feminine
akìs - akiū̃   'eye'
vilnìs - vilniū̃   'wave'
pirtìs - pirčiū̃   'bath-house'
ántis - ánčių   'duck'
ugnìs - ugniū̃   'fire'
nósis - nósių   'nose'
króshis -ių̃ ~   'oven'
vínis -viniū̃   'nail'

Masculine

vagìs - vagiū̃   'thief'

130

17.2 *The Optative Mood.* The optative (or permissive) may be formed by prefixing *-te* to the third person form of the verb, e.g. *te-sãko* 'may he say, let him say', *tè-perka* 'may he buy, let him buy'. Sometimes these forms are created by a synthetic combination of *teguĺ* or *tegù* with the third person of the verb, e.g. *teguĺ sãko* 'may he say', etc. *teguĺ peřka* 'may he buy', etc.

17.3 An alternative formation* is furnished by adding the endings *-ai* (for verbs with the first singular *-au*) or *-ie* for other verbs to the present stem. Thus the forms given above may be replaced by *te-sãkai* and *te-perkiẽ* respectively. Examples:
1) *Tesãkai tiẽsą.* — May he tell the truth.
2) *Teateiniẽ tàvo karalỹstė.* — Thy kingdom come.
3) *Tebūniẽ tàvo valià kaĩp dangujè, taĩp iř žẽmėje.* — Thy will be done on earth as it is in heaven.

17.4 Frequently the first person plural of the present tense is used without a pronoun with hortative meaning. Examples:
1) *Eĩname (eĩnam)!* — Let's go.
2) *Rãšome (rãšom)!* — Let's write.

EXERCISES

A. *Questions.* 1. Kuõ mẽs mãtome? 2. Kuõ mẽs giřdime? 3. Kuõ mẽs kramtome? 4. Kuõ mẽs rãšome? 5. Kuõ mẽs úostome? 6. Kàs tùri geràs akìs? 7. Kuř mókytoja rãšo? 8. Kàs mẽgsta kramtýti? 9. Ař yrà sveĩka válgyti daũg saldaĩnių? 10. Kàs keñkia dantìms?

B. *Decline in the singular and plural:* ausìs, nósis, akìs, krósnis, dantìs.

C. *Fill in the blanks:* 1. Žmogùs tùri daũg dant......... 2. Mẽs dant .... kramtome maĩstą. 3. Jìs nemãto víena ak......... 4. Šìtame namè yrà daũg krósn......... 5. Jõs aus......... yrà labaĩ gėros.

D. *Translate into Lithuanian:* 1. A man has only one nose, but many teeth. 2. My teacher has very good eyes. 3. My grandfather cannot see well. 4. In a man's mouth there are many teeth. 5. With (our) teeth we chew food. 6. With (our) ears we can hear, but we cannot smell anything with them. 7. With (our) nose we can smell, but we cannot hear anything with it. 8. Peter is writing on the board. 9. I never hear anything if I don't want to. 10. Chocolate and candy (use plural) hurts the teeth.

---

* The 'alternative formations' are older optative forms. The student will find them in older Lithuanian writings. Today, usually the ones given in 17.2 are used.

CONVERSATION

PAS KIRPĖJĄ

Rainỹs: 1. Lãbas rýtas. Aš norė̃čiau pasikiȓpti pláukus. Aȓ ilgaĩ reikė̃s láukti?

Kirpėjas: 2. Prašaũ sė̃sti. Jùms nereikė̃s ilgaĩ láukti.

Rainys: 3. Aȓ tùrite šiõs dienõs laĩkraštį?

Kirpėjas: 4. Taĩp, tenaĩ añt kėdė̃s.

Rainys: 5. Ačiū. Aš paláuksiu.

Kirpėjas: 6. Dabaȓ prašaũ. Kaĩp jùms pakiȓpti?

Rainys: 7. Trumpaĩ užpakalyje, bèt per daũg nesutrum̃pinkite
apiẽ ausìs!

Kirpėjas: 8. Geraĩ, taĩp iȓ padarýsime. Šiañdien karštà dienà,
tiesà?

Rainys: 9. Taĩp, šiañdien jaũ tikrà vãsara.

Kirpėjas: 10. Mán patiñka vãsara: tadà žmónės dažniaũ keȓpasi
pláukus!

AT THE BARBER'S

Rainys: 1. Good morning. I would like to have a haircut. Shall
I have to wait long?

Barber: 2. Please take a seat. You won't have to wait long.

Rainys: 3. Do you have today's newspaper?

Barber: 4. Yes, over there on the chair.

Rainys: 5. Thanks. I will wait.

Barber: 6. It's your turn now. How would you like your hair
cut?

Rainys: 7. Short in the back, but not too short around the ears.

Barber: 8. All right, we'll do that. It's a hot day today, isn't it?

Rainys: 9. Yes, it's really summer, today.

Barber: 10. I like summer. Then people get haircuts more often.

NOTES:

1. **norė̃čiau** — 'I would like to' (See Lesson 31).
   pasikiȓpti pláukus — 'to get one's hair cut'.
3. **šiõs dienõs** — gen. of **šì dienà** lit. 'this day'.
6. **Kaĩp jùms pakiȓpti?** — lit. 'how to you to cut'; to be translated: 'How
   shall I cut your hair?'
7. **užpakalyje** — loc. of **užpakalis** 'the back'.
8. **taĩp iȓ** — 'so'; the **ir** is for emphasis.
10. **žmónės** — irregular nom. plur. of **žmogùs** 'man'. See 18.1.
    keȓpasi — 'have their hair cut'.
    pláukas is one hair; the plural **plaukaĩ** translates English 'hair' in the
    collective sense.

132

Aštuonioliktoji pamoka
Lesson 18

TRYS SŪNŪS

Víeną kaȓtą gyvẽno ū́kininkas iȓ turė́jo devýnis sū́nus. Trỹs sū́nūs bùvo tinginiaĩ, trỹs bùvo vãgys, trỹs bùvo gerì sū́nūs. Tinginiaĩ niẽko nedìrbo, tìk gulė́jo iȓ žiūrė́jo į̃ dañgų. Vãgys vìską võgdavo iš žmonių̃, iȓ žmónės jų̃ labaĩ nemė́go. Trỹs gerì sū́nūs dìrbo tė́vo ū̃kyje, iȓ juõs visì žmónės mylė́jo.

Kaĩ tė́vas pasẽno, jìs pasãkė sàvo sūnùms:

— Màno sū́nūs, àš jaũ esù sẽnas, mán laĩkas miȓti. Jùms, màno gerì sū́nūs, palìksiu vìsą ū̃kį, nès jū̃s jamè dìrbote. Jùms, màno tinginiaĩ sū́nūs, palìksiu dañgų, į̃ kurį̃ jū̃s žiūrė́jote. Jùms, vãgys, nepalìksiu niẽko, nès jū̃s niẽko nedìrbote, õ tìk võgėte.

Taĩp padalìno sàvo tuȓtą tė́vas sàvo sūnùms iȓ nùmirė.

VOCABULARY

vìeną kaȓtą — once (one time), once upon a time

ū́kininkas (1) — farmer

devýnis (accus. masc.) — nine

tinginỹs (3a) — lazy bone

vagìs -ìẽs (masc.) (4) — thief

gerì (masc. nom. pl.) — good

võgti (vagiù, vãgia, võgė, võgs) irreg.: vagiù, vagì, vãgia; vãgiame, vãgiate, vãgia — to steal

žmónės (irreg. pl. of **žmogùs**) — men, people, human beings

ū́kis -io (1) — farm

pasénti (pasénstu, pasénsta, pasẽno, paseñs) irreg.: pasénstu, pasénsti, pasénsta; pasénstame, pasénstate, pasénsta — to get old, to grow old

pasakýti (pasakaũ, pasãko, pasãkė, pasakỹs) — to say, to tell (perfective)

palìkti (paliekù, paliẽka, palìko, palìks); irreg.: paliekù, paliekì, paliẽka; paliẽkame, paliẽkate, paliẽka — to leave, to leave behind, to bequest

mán laĩkas miȓti — it is time for me to die

kuriẽ (pl. masc. nom., relat. pronoun) — who, which

padalìnti (padalinù, padalìna, padalìno, padalìns) — to divide up

numiȓti (numìrštu, numìršta, nùmirė, numìrs); irreg.: numìrštu, numìršti, numìršta; numìrštame, numìrštate, numìršta — to die (perfective)

GRAMMAR

18.1 The Plural of the Fourth Declension.

The plural cases for the fourth declension are as follows:

	'sons'		'professors'	
N.V.	sū́nūs	-ūs (3)	profèsoriai	-iai (1)
G.	sūnų̃	-ų	profèsorių	-ių
D.	sūnùms	-ums	profèsoriams	-iams
A.	sū́nus	-us	profèsorius	-ius
I.	sūnumìs	-umis	profèsoriais	-iais
L.	sūnuosè	-uose	profèsoriuose	-iuose

Note that those nouns which have the nominative singular in -ius have the plural declension exactly like the first declension.

The noun *žmogùs* 'man, human being' has the following declension:

Singular			Plural	
'man'			'men, people'	
N.	žmogùs	-us (4)	žmónės	-ės (3)
G.	žmogaũs	-aus	žmonių̃	-ių
D.	žmõgui	-ui	žmonėms	-ėms
A.	žmõgų	-ų	žmónes	-es
I.	žmogumì	-umi	žmonėmìs	-ėmis
L.	žmogujè	-uje	žmonėsè	-ėse
V.	žmogaũ	-au	žmónės	-ės

18.2 Certain Impersonal Constructions with the Neuter Adjective.

The neuter form of the adjective may be used with an infinitive of a verb occuring as subject of certain constructions. Examples:

1) *Mė́są sveĩka válgyti.* — (It is) good (healthy) to eat meat.
2) *Knỹgą sunkù skaitýti.* — (It is) difficult to read the book.
3) *Taisyklès gãlima mokéti atmintinaĩ.* — (One can) know the rules by heart.
4) *Šáltą ãlų malonù gérti.* — (It is) pleasant to drink cold beer.
5) *Tuõs dalykùs sunkù supràsti.* — (It is) difficult to understand these things.

Another type of such a construction is also possible with the neuter adjective, although such a construction is to be considered an exception rather than the general rule. In such constructions the logical object of the infinitive is in the nominative case. Examples:

1) *Mėsà sveĩka válgyti.* — Meat is good (healthy) to eat.

In this example the word *mėsà* 'meat' may be considered the subject and *sveĩka válgyti* 'good to eat' may be considered the predicate.

2) *Knygà sunkù skaitýti.* — The book is difficult to read.

3) *Taisýklės gālima mokěti atmintinaĩ.* — The rules can be known by heart.

4) *Šáltas alùs malonù gérti.* — Cold beer is pleasant to drink.

5) *Tiẽ dalýkai sunkù supràsti.* — These things are difficult to understand.

18.3 The nominative case is used with all of the various tenses of the verb *bũti* 'to be', cf. 3.1,1, but also 23.3,5 for the possible instrumental case in such constructions. Examples:

1) *Jìs bùvo gýdytojas.* — He was a doctor.

2) *Jìs mán bùvo labaĩ gẽras.* — He was very good to me.

3) *Aš bũsiu mókytojas.* — I shall be a teacher.

EXERCISES

A. *Questions.* 1. Kíek sūnų̃ turḗjo ū́kininkas? 2. Kokiẽ bùvo jõ sū́nūs? 3. Ką̃ dãrė tinginiaĩ? 4. Ką̃ dãrė vãgys? 5. Kuř dìrbo gerì sū́nūs? 6. Ką̃ visì žmónės mḗgo? 7. Kõ visì žmónės labaĩ nemḗgo? 8. Ką̃ palìko ū́kininkas tinginiáms? 9. Ką̃ palìko sẽnas tẽvas vagìms? 10. Kadà sẽnas ū́kininkas nùmirė?

B. *Decline in singular and plural:* sūnùs, žmogùs, lietùs, profèsorius, dangùs (pl. only poetically).

C. *Change the italicized nouns into plural:* 1. Mano *sūnùs* gyvẽna miestè. 2. *Žmogùs* tùri daũg dìrbti. 3. Aš palìksiu sàvo *sũnui* ū́kį. 4. *Tẽvas* mýli *sũnų*. 5. Tàs (pl. tiẽ) *tẽvas* nemýli sàvo *sūnaũs*. 6. Jìs ṇepalìko sàvo *sũnui* ū́kio. 7. *Tinginỹs* niẽko nedìrba. 8. *Vagìs* vìską vãgia. 9. Mẽs nemḗgstame *tiñginio* iř *vagiẽs*. 10. *Ū́kininkui* nepatiñka *tinginỹs*.

D. *Translate into Lithuanian:* 1. The old farmer has nine sons. 2. All the people like his sons. 3. Three sons do not do anything: they are lazy-bones. 4. Three sons are good sons: they work on their father's farm. 5. Three sons are thieves. 6. My sons are lazy-bones. 7. His sons work on the farm. 8. I have only one son. 9. Other people liked him. 10. I do not like lazy-bones.

CONVERSATION

GATVĖJE

Grìgas: 1. Kodėl čià tíek daũg žmonių̃?

Spãlis: 2. Kažkàs atsitìko. Ródos, automobìliai susidū́rė.

Čiurlỹs: 3. Taĩp, taĩp. Vienamè automobìlyje važiãvo tėvas sù sàvo sūnumìs. Kìtą vairãvo senà móteris ...

Grigas: 4. Taĩ vìs tõs móterys! Geriaũ jóms bū́tų namiẽ sėdė́ti.

Spalis: 5. Sãko, kàd móterys geriaũ vairúoja automobìlį ...

Grigas: 6. Aš nètikiu: kuř̃ tìk automobìliai susìduria, visuř̃ móterys ...

Čiurlys: 7. Visókių yrà žmonių̃: vienì sãko taĩp, kitì kitaĩp.

Spalis: 8. Žiūrė́kite, žiūrė́kite — dár daugiaũ žmonių̃ susiriñko.

Čiurlys: 9. Žmónės yrà labaĩ smalsū̃s — nóri vìską matýti.

Grigas: 10. Aš jaũ turiù eĩti namõ. Sudiču.

ON THE STREET

Grigas: 1. Why are there so many people here?

Spalis: 2. Something has happened. It seems, two cars collided.

Ciurlys. 3. Yes, yes. In one car there was a father with his sons. Another one was driven by an old woman.

Grigas: 4: Here we go again: women. It would be better if they stayed at home.

Spalis: 5. Well, they say, women are better drivers ...

Grigas: 6. I do not believe it: wherever there is a car collision, there are always women ...

Ciurlys: 7. There are all kinds of people: some say this, some that.

Spalis: 8. Look, look—more people have gathered.

Ciurlys: 9. People are very curious—they want to see everything.

Grigas: 10. I have to go home now. Good bye.

NOTES:

2. **ródos** — abbreviation of **ródosi** 'it seems'.
   susidū́rė — lit. 'hit each other, struck each other, met with force'.
3. **važiãvo** — 'drove, were in the car'.
   kìtą vairãvo senà móteris — lit. 'an old woman drove (steered) the other one'.
4. **taĩ vìs tõs móterys** — lit. 'this [is] always those women'.
5. **vairúoja** — lit. 'steer', but here: 'drive'.
6. **visókių** — gen. pl. of **visóks**: 'all kinds'. See Lesson 34.
7. **taĩp ... kitaĩp** — lit. 'so ... otherwise'.
8. **susiriñko** — this is a reflexive verb in Lithuanian.

136

Devynioliktoji pamoka
Lesson 19

ŠEIMA

Mókytojas: Kàs mán gãli pasakýti, kàs yrà šeimà?

Výtautas: Aš žinaũ, kàs yrà šeimà: tévaĩ iř vaikaĩ yrà šeimà.

Mokytojas: Labaĩ geraĩ.

Kęstùtis: Mū́sų šeimojè dár yrà iř senẽliai: màno tévẽlio tẽvas iř mamà gyvẽna kartù sù mumìs. Jiẽ yrà màno senẽlis iř senẽlė.

Mokytojas: Taĩp, jéigu senẽliai gyvẽna kartù, taĩ jiẽ iřgi priklaũso šeĩmai.

Vytautas: Mū́sų šeimà yrà labaĩ dìdelė: àš turiù dù brólius iř penkiàs sẽseris.

Antãnas: Taĩ tàvo šeimà, Výtautai, yrà dár mažà: àš turiù tìk trìs sẽseris, bèt penkìs brólius.

Mokytojas: O tù, Aldònà, kíek turì seserų̃ iř brólių?

Aldonà: Aš neturiù neĩ seserų̃, neĩ brólių, àš esù vienà.

Jõnas: Aš iřgi neturiù seserų̃: àš turiù tìk trìs brólius.

Mokytojas: Taĩgi tévaĩ iř vaikaĩ, senẽliai, bróliai iř sẽserys sudã́ro šeĩmą. Kaĩ kuriẽ iš jū́sų tùri brólius iř sẽseris, kaĩ kuriẽ netùri brólių, õ tìk sẽseris, kaĩ kuriẽ tùri tìk sẽseris, õ netùri brólių. Aldònos šeimà yrà labaĩ mažà: jì netùri neĩ brólių neĩ seserų̃.

VOCABULARY

šeimà (4) — family

vaĩkas (2) — child

tėvẽlis (2) (diminutive of tẽvas) —
— father, dad, daddy

senẽlis (2) — grandfather

senẽlė (2) — grandmother

senẽliai (2) — grandparents

kartù — together

priklausýti (priklausaũ, priklaũso,

priklaũsė, priklausỹs) — to belong
to (with dative)

penkiàs (fem. acc.) — five

penkìs (masc. acc.) — five

neĩ ... neĩ — neither ... nor

sudarýti (sudaraũ, sudãro, sudãrė,
sudarỹs) — to compose, to make up

kaĩ kuriẽ — some

kaĩ kuriẽ ìš jũsų — some of you

GRAMMAR

19.1 The Fifth Declension of Nouns.

The plural cases for the fifth declension are as follows:

Feminine

N.	sẽserys (sẽsers)	-ys (3[b]) 'sisters
G.	seserų̃	-ų̃
D.	seserìms	-ims
A.	sẽseris	-is
I.	seserimìs	-imis
L.	seserysè	-yse

Masculine

N.	ãkmenys (ãkmens)	-ys (3[b]) 'stones'
G.	akmenų̃	-ų̃
D.	akmenìms	-ims
A.	ãkmenis	-is
I.	akmenimìs	-imìs
L.	akmenysè	-ysè

N.B. šuõ 'dog' has the regular form nom. pl. šùnys, but an older
form šùnes is sometimes used.

19.1,2 The Dual of Nouns.

The dual is hardly ever used in today's modern literary Lithuanian, however, it is still used in some dialects, and the student
will see it frequently in older Lithuanian writings. We are giving
here the synopsis of those dual cases which differ from the regular
plural cases. For this, we will take all the nouns the plurals of
which were given in Lessons 14, 16, 17, 18, and 19.

Nominative:

du: namù,	bróliu,	árkliu	— 1st declension
dvi: dienì,	gatvì,	martì	— 2nd declension
dvi: akì,	du: dañčiu		— 3rd declension
du: sũnu,	profèsoriu		— 4th declension
dvi: sẽseri,	du: ákmeniu		— 5th declension

Dative:

dvíem:	namám,	bróliam,	arkliám
	dienóm,	gãtvėm,	marčióm
	akìm,	dantìm,	
	sūnùm,	profèsoriam	
	seserìm,	akmenìm	

Instrumental:

dviẽm:	namaĩs,	bróliais,	arkliaĩs
	dienom̃,	gãtvėm,	marčiom̃
	akim̃,	dantim̃	
	sūnum̃,	profèsoriais	
	seserim̃,	akmenim̃	

The dual forms can only be used with the preceding numeral *du, dvi* (in the appropriate case).

The dative and instrumental dual of the second, third, fourth and fifth declension differ only in that in accent classes 3 and 4 the instrumental case has the circumflex accent (as opposed to the short or acute in the dative). The accusative is like the nominative and the other cases are the same as the corresponding plural forms. The instrumental dual of the first declension is usually the same as that of the plural.

N.B. The student should only note this for the eventual reading of Lithuanian literature. For practical purposes he can always use only the plural forms, even when he uses the numeral **du** before nouns.

19.2 The Use of the Genitive Case.

The genitive case may be used to denote some quality of the object or individual described. Examples:

1) *Jìs yrà gerõs širdiẽs.* — He is good-hearted (lit.: of a good heart).

2) *Antãnas yrà menkõs sveikãtos.* — Anthony has poor health (lit.: of poor health).

19.3 The genitive is used with certain adverbs of quantity. (Cf. also 16.2, section d). Examples:

1) *Kíek žmonių̃ dìrba fabrikè?* — How many men work in the factory?

2) *Atėjo daũg žmonių̃.* — Many people arrived (came).

3) *Mūsų bibliotèkoje peř mãža knỹgų.* — In our library there are too few books.

19.4 The genitive can be used as the complement of certain verbs meaning 'to fill', 'to stuff', etc. Examples:

1) *Jìs prikimšo pýpkę tabāko.* — He stuffed tobacco into his pipe.
2) *Pripýlė stìklą vandeñs.* — He poured water into the glass. (He filled the glass with water.)

19.5 In order to express an indefinite amount or quantity the genitive may be used where either the nominative or the accusative would otherwise be required. Examples:

1) *Ar̃ esì mãtęs lietùvių?* — Have you seen any Lithuanians?
2) *Svečių̃ atvažiúoja.* — Some guests are coming.
3) *Taleñto jìs tùri.* — He has some talent.
4) *Ar̃ tù turì prõto?* — Do you have any sense?

19.6 The genitive may be used as a nominal object of an infinitive which follows a verb of motion. Examples:

1) *Jìs atėjo kárvės pir̃kti.* — He came to buy a cow.
2) *Aš atėjaũ gėlių̃ suriñkti.* — I came to gather flowers.

The verbs *pir̃kti* 'to buy' and *suriñkti* 'to gather' are transitive verbs and must take a direct object in the accusative case in most other occurences.

1) *Jìs pir̃ko kárvę.* — He bought a cow.
2) *Jìs suriñko gėlès.* — He gathered flowers.

19.6,1 The Supine.

In the older literature a verbal form called the supine was commonly used as the object of a verb of motion. (The supine is just like the infinitive except that the -ti of the infinitive is removed and -tų, the ending of the supine is added.) Thus *pir̃kti* and *suriñkti* in the examples above could have been replaced by *pir̃ktų* and *suriñktų* respectively, giving the rather archaic sounding sentences: (1) *Jìs atėjo kárvės pir̃ktų.* — He came to buy a cow; (2) *Aš atėjaũ gėlių̃ suriñktų.* — I came to gather flowers.

19.6,2 The supine could in general be used as the object of a verb of motion in the older literature. Examples:

1) *Aš einù guĺtų.* — I am going (some place) to sleep.
2) *Jì eĩna válgytų.* — She is going (some place) to eat.

140

In modern Lithuanian such constructions are not used. The infinitive is used in its place:

1) *Aš einù guĺti.* — I am going (some place) to sleep.
2) *Jì eĩna válgyti.* — She is going (some place) to eat.

19.7 The genitive case is used as the object of certain verbs. Examples:

1) *Kõ jũs íeškote?* — What are you hunting (looking) for?
2) *Ligónis jaũ kùnigo prãšo.* — The sick man is already asking for a priest.

19.7,1 Sometimes it is used as a kind of goal of the action of certain intransitive verbs. Examples:

1) *Lìkit pietũ.* — Stay for lunch.
2) *Eĩkit pietũ.* — Go to lunch.
3) *Važiúojam namõ Kalė́dų.* — Let's go home for Christmas.

19.8 The genitive is sometimes used with the meaning 'from the point of view of' or 'as far as ... is concerned'. Examples:

1) *Gerùmo jìs gė́ras, bèt visái negudrùs.* — From the point of view of goodness he is good, but he is not clever.
2) *Vaĩsiai, didùmo sulìg gálva, kreñta iš mė́džio.* — The pieces of fruit, as big as a [human] head, fall from the tree.
3) *Skaĩčiaus jų̃ bùvo penkì šimtaĩ.* — In number, there were five hundred of them.
4) *Ař iš tõlo ė́sate kilìmo?* — Do you come from a distant place? (lit.: Are you from a distance in origin?)

EXERCISES

A. *Questions.* Kíek jũs tùrite brólių iř seserų̃? 2. Ař Aldonà tùri daũg brólių? 3. Kàs yrà senēlis? 4. Kàs yrà senēlė? 5. Kàs sudãro šeĩmą? 6. Kienõ (whose) šeimà yrà mažà? 7. Ař jũs nórite turḗti dìdelę šeĩmą? 8. Kuř gyvēna jū́sų šeimà? 9. Kàs netùri neĩ seserų̃ neĩ brólių? 10. Kíek brólių iř seserų̃ tùri Výtautas?

B. *Decline in singular and plural:* sesuõ, akmuõ, šuõ, vanduõ (the plural of vanduõ is used only in poetic language).

C. *Change all the italicized nouns into the plural forms:* 1. Jìs netùri *seser̃s.* 2. Màno *šuõ* yrà namiẽ. 3. Mẽs dabar̃ netùrime *šuñs.* 4. Jõ *sesuõ* gyvẽna *káime.* 5. *Brólis* ir̃ *sesuõ* ẽjo į́ mokȳklą. 6. Jõs *sesuõ* skaĩto laĩkraštį̃. 7. *Akmuõ* kriñta į̃ vándenį. 8. Jìs važiãvo sù *seserimì.* 9. Mán patiñka jõ *sesuõ.* 10. Màno *sẽseriai* patiñka jõ *brólis.*

D. *Translate into Lithuanian.* 1. I like only big dogs. 2. He doesn't like dogs. 3. He has many brothers and sisters. 4. He has neither brothers nor sisters. 5. She is an only child (lit.: she is one [alone] in the family). 6. He is an only child. 7. His grandparents live together with him. 8. The children like the grandparents very much. 9. The grandparents love the children very much. 10. The grandparents, parents and children make up the family.

CONVERSATION

GELEŽINKELIO STOTYJE

Dabùlis:	1.	Kadà išeĩna traukiniaĩ į̃ Vìlnių?
Tarnáutojas:	2.	Víenas išeĩna 5-tą (peñktą) vãlandą rýto, víenas 6:30 (šẽšios trìsdešimt) vakarè.
Dabulis:	3.	Prašaũ mán dúoti 2 (dù) biłetus į̃ Vìlnių.
Tarnautojas:	4.	Prašaũ. 25 (dvìdešimt penkì) lìtai, 60 (šẽšiasdešimt) ceñtų.
Dabulis:	5.	Ačiū. (After having noticed his friend Jonas Žȳgas). Lãbas, Jõnai, kur̃ tù nóri važiúoti?
Žȳgas:	6.	Nóriu važiúoti į̃ Pãlangą pailsẽti ir̃ sveikãtos pataisýti.
Dabulis:	7.	Taĩ ką̃, per daũg dìrbai?
Žygas:	8.	Nè, bèt smar̃kiai sirgaũ, nèt ligóninėje gulẽjau.
Dabulis:	9.	Taĩp, taĩp. Dabar̃ mataũ, kàd esì pavar̃gęs. Taĩ linkiù táu greĩto pagijìmo ir̃ gerų̃ atóstogų!
Žygas:	10.	Ačiū, ãčiū. Dabar̃ jaũ turiù eĩti į̃ tráukinį. Sudiẽu.

AT THE RAILROAD STATION

Dabulis:	1.	When do the trains leave for Vilnius?
Official:	2.	One leaves at 5 a.m., the other one at 6:30 p.m.
Dabulis:	3.	Please give me two tickets for Vilnius.
Official:	4.	Here you are. 25 litas and 60 cents.

Dabulis:	5.	Thank you. (After having noticed his friend Jonas Žygas). Hello, Jonas, where do you want to go?
Žygas:	6.	I want to go to Palanga to rest and to recuperate.
Dabulis:	7.	What happened, did you work too much?
Žygas:	8.	No, but I was very ill and I was even in the hospital.
Dabulis:	9.	So that's what happened. Now I see that you are tired. Well, I wish you a speedy recovery and a good vacation.
Žygas:	10.	Thanks. Now I have to get on my train. Good bye.

NOTES:

2. For more details on the expression of time, see Lesson 32.
6. **Palangà** (3b) — Lithuanian resort on the Baltic Sea.
8. **smar̃kiai** — lit. 'powerfully, heavily'.
8. **sir̃gti** (sergù, ser̃ga, sir̃go, sir̃gs) — 'to be sick, ill'.
8. **gulė́ti ligóninėje** — lit. 'to lie in a hospital'.
9. **linkė́ti** — 'to wish' takes the dative case of the person ('to whom') and the genitive case of the thing wished ('of what').
   atóstogas — acc. of **atóstogos** 'vacation' is used only in plural, (feminine, 2nd declension).

Various Expressions of Time

today — *šiandien*
tomorrow — *rytoj*
yesterday — *vakar*
day before yesterday — *užvakar*
day after tomorrow — *poryt*
in the morning — *rytą (ryte)*
in the evening — *vakare*
at night — *naktį, nakčia*
during the day — *dieną*
tomorrow morning — *rytoj rytą*
tomorrow evening — *rytoj vakare*
yesterday morning — *vakar rytą*
yesterday evening — *vakar vakare*
last night — *vakar naktį* or *vakar vakare* (in the sense of
    'the previous evening')
in five days — *už penkių dienų*
in five weeks — *už penkių savaičių*
early — *anksti*
late — *vėlai*
too early — *per anksti*
too late — *per vėlai*
long (for a long time) — *ilgai*
too long — *per ilgai*

Dvidešimtoji pamoka

Lesson 20

A.

COUNTRIES, INHABITANTS AND THEIR LANGUAGES

a) Europa — Europe

English	Country	Inhabitant (male, female)	Language	Adjective*
Albania	Albãnija	albãnas, albãnė	albãnų kalbà	albãniškas
Austria	Austrìa	áustras, áustrė	vókiečių kalbà	áustriškas
Belgium	Bel̃gija	bel̃gas, bel̃gė	prancūzų kalbà valònų kalbà flãmų kalbà	bel̃giškas
Bulgaria	Bulgãrija	bulgãras, bulgãrė	bulgãrų kalbà	bulgãriškas
Czechoslovakia	Čekoslovãkija Čèkija Slovãkija	čekoslovãkas, -vãkė čèkas, čèkė slovãkas, slovãkė	čèkų kalbà slovãkų kalbà	čekoslovãkiškas čèkiškas slovãkiškas
Denmark	Dãnija	dãnas, dãnė	dãnų kalbà	dãniškas
England	Anglìja	ánglas, ánglė	ánglų kalbà	ángliškas
Estonia	Estìja	èstas, èstė	èstų kalbà	èstiškas
Finland	Súomija	súomis, súomė	súomių kalbà	súomiškas
France	Prancūzìjà	prancūzas, prancūzė	prancūzų kalbà	prancūziškas
Germany	Vokietìjà	vókietis, vókietė	vókiečių kalbà	vókiškas
Greece	Graikìjà	graĩkas, graĩkė	graikų̃ kalbà	graĩkiškas
Holland	Olándija	olándas, olándė	olándų kalbà	olándiškas
Hungary	Veñgrija	veñgras, veñgrė	veñgrų kalbà	veñgriškas
Ireland	Aĩrija	aĩris, aĩrė	aĩrių kalbà	aĩriškas
Italy	Itãlija	itãlas, itãlė	itãlų kalbà	itãliškas
Latvia	Lãtvija	lãtvis, lãtvė	lãtvių kalbà	lãtviškas
Lithuania	Lietuvà	lietùvis, lietùvė	lietùvių kalbà	lietùviškas

* Only the masc. nom. sg. is given. The student should be able to derive all other forms: masc. **albãniškas**, fem. **albãniška**, adverb **albãniškai**: **Jìs kaĺ-ba albãniškai** 'He speaks Albanian' etc. etc.

145

Norway	Norvėgija	norvėgas, norvėgė	norvėgų kalbà	norvėgiškas
Poland	Lénkija	lénkas, lénkė	lénkų kalbà	lénkiškas
Rumania	Rumùnija	rumùnas, rumùnė	rumùnų kalbà	rumùniškas
Russia	Rùsija	rùsas, rùsė	rùsų kalbà	rùsiškas
Spain	Ispãnija	ispãnas, ispãnė	ispãnų kalbà	ispãniškas
Sweden	Švėdija	švėdas, švėdė	švėdų kalbà	švėdiškas
Switzerland	Šveicãrija	šveicãras, šveicãrė	kalbos: vókiečių prancūzų itãlų rėto-romãnų	šveicãriškas
Yugoslavia	Jugoslãvija	jugoslãvas, -slãvė	kalbos: seŕbo-kroãtų slovėnų makedoniėčių	jugoslãviškas

b) Azija — Asia

Afghanistan	Afganistãnas	afganistaniėtis, -ė	afgãnų kalbà (pūštu kalbà)	afgãniškas
Burma	Bùrma	burmiėtis, -ė	burmiėčių kalbà	bùrmiškas
Cambodia	Kambòdija	kambodiėtis, -ė	kmèr kalbà tão kalbà	kambodiėtiškas
China	Kìnija	kìnas, -ė	kìnų kalbà	kìniškas
India	Indija	ìndas, -ė	ìndų kalbà	ìndiškas*
Indonesia	Indonėzija	indonėzas, -ė (indoneziėtis, -ė)	indonėzų kalbà	indonėziškas
Iran	Irãnas (Peŕsija)	iraniėtis, -ė (peŕsas, -ė)	peŕsų kalbà	irãniškas (peŕsiškas)
Iraq	Irãkas	irakiėtis, -ė	arãbų kalbà	irãkiškas
Israel	Izraèlis	žỹdas, -ė (izraelìtas, -ė)	hebrãjų kalbà	izraèliškas (žỹdiškas)
Japan	Japònija	japònas, -ė	japònų kalbà	japòniškas
Jordan	Jordãnas	jordaniėtis, -ė	arãbų kalbà	jordãniškas
Korea	Korėja	korėjiėtis, -ė	korėjiėčių kalbà	korėjiškas
Laos	Lãosas	laosiėtis, -ė	kmèr* kalbà (lão* kalba)	laòsiškas
Lebanon	Libãnas	libaniėtis, -ė	arãbų kalbà	libãniškas
Mongolia	Mongòlija	mongòlas, -ė	mongòlų kalbà	mongòliškas
Pakistan	Pakistãnas	pakistaniėtis, -ė	pakistaniėčių k.	pakistãniškas**
Phillippines	Filipìnai	filipiniėtis, -ė	filipiniėčių kalbà	filipìniškas**
Saudi Arabia	Arãbija	arãbas, -ė	arãbų kalbà	arãbiškas
Syria	Sìrija	sìras, -ė	arãbų kalbà	sìriškas
Thailand	Tailándas (Siãmas)	tailandiėtis, -ė (siamiėtis, -ė)	siamiėčių kalbà	tailandiškas (siãmiškas)
Tibet	Tibėtas	tibetiėtis, -ė	tibetiėčių kalbà	tibėtiškas
Turkey	Tuŕkija	tuŕkas, -ė	tuŕkų kalbà	tùrkiškas
Vietnam	Vietnãmas	vietnamiėtis, -ė	vietnamiėčių k. (kmèr, lão kalbos)	vietnãmiškas
Yemen	Jemènas	jemeniėtis, -ė	arãbų kalbà	jemèniškas

---

* Other languages of As ia such as **hindi, gujarati, telugu, kmer, lao** — are indeclinable.

** These adjectives are rarely used in practice. Very often, Lithuanian will replace them by the genitive case of name of the country, e.g.: the Yemen(i) deserts — **Jemèno dỹkumos**; the Tibetan mountains — **Tibèto kalnaĩ**.

146

c) Šiaurės Amerika — North America

Canada	Kanadà	kanadiẽtis, -ė	ánglų kalbà prancūzų kalbà	kanãdiškas
Costa Rica	Kostarikà	kostarikiẽtis, -ė	ispãnų kalbà	kostarìkiškas
Cuba	Kubà	kubiẽtis, -ė	ispãnų kalbà	kùbiškas
Dominican Republic	Domininkõnų Respùblika	domininkiẽtis	ispãnų kalbà	Domininkõnų Respùblikos*
Guatemala	Gvatemalà	gvatemaliẽtis, -ė	ispãnų kalbà	gvatemãliškas
Haiti	Haĩtis	haitiẽtis, -ė	prancūzų kalbà (kreõlų kalbà)	haĩtiškas
Honduras	Hondùras	honduriẽtis, -ė	ispãnų kalbà	hondùriškas
Mexico	Mèksika	meksikiẽtis, -ė	ispãnų kalbà	mèksikiškas
Nicaragua	Nikarãgua	nikaragujiẽtis	ispãnų kalbà	nikarãgujiškas
Panama	Panamà	panamiẽtis, -ė	ispãnų kalbà	panãmiškas
Salvador	Salvadòras	salvadoriẽtis, -ė	ispãnų kalbà	salvadòriškas
U.S.A.	Jungtìnės Amèrikos Valstýbės (Amèrika)	amerikiẽtis, -ė	ánglų kalbà	amerikìnis (amerikiẽtiškas)

d) Pietų Amerika — South America

Argentina	Argentinà	argentiniẽtis, -ė	ispãnų kalbà	argentìniškas
Bolivia	Bolìvija	bolivijiẽtis, -ė	ispãnų kalbà	bolìviškas
Brazil	Brazìlija	brazìlas, -ė	portugãlų kalbà	brazìliškas
Chile	Čìlė	čiliẽtis, -ė	ispãnų kalbà	čìliškas
Colombia	Kolùmbija	kolumbiẽtis, -ė	ispãnų kalbà	kolùmbiškas
Ecuador	Ekvadòras	ekvadoriẽtis, -ė	ispãnų kalbà	ekvadòriškas
Guiana	Gvijanà	gvijaniẽtis, -ė	kalbos: ánglų prancūzų olándų	gvijãniškas
Paraguay	Paragvãjus	paragvajiẽtis, -ė	ispãnų kalbà	paragvãjiškas
Peru	Perù*	perujiẽtis, -ė	ispãnų kalbà	perùjiškas
Uruguay	Urugvãjus	urugvajiẽtis, -ė	ispãnų kalbà	urugvãjiškas
Venezuela	Venecuèla	venecualiẽtis, -ė	ispãnų kalbà	venecuèliškas

e) Afrika — Africa

Algeria	Alžìrija	alžiriẽtis, -ė	arãbų kalbà	alžìriškas
Congo	Kòngas	kongiẽtis, -ė	Kòngo kaĩbos	kòngiškas
Egypt	Egìptas	egiptiẽtis, -ė	egiptiẽčių kalbà	egìptiškas
Ethiopia	Etijòpija	etijòpas, -ė	etijòpų kalbà	etijòpiškas
Liberia	Libèrija	liber(ij)iẽtis, -ė	ánglų kalbà (liberiẽčių k.)	libèriškas
Libya	Lìbija	libiẽtis, -ė	arãbų kalbà	lìbiškas
Morocco	Maròkas	marokiẽtis, -ė	arãbų kalbà	maròkiškas
Nigeria	Nigèrija	nigeriẽtis, -ė	nigeriẽčių kalbà	nigèriškas
Tunisia	Tunìsija	tunisiẽtis, -ė	arãbų kalbà	tunìsiškas
Union of South Africa	Pietų Afrika	Pietų Afrikos gyvéntojas*	kaĩbos: ánglų afrikãnų kilčių (tribal)	Pietų Afrikos**

---

* Kostarìkos, Domininkõnų Respùblikos, Nikarãguos, Salvadòro: see footnote for pakistãniškas.
* Peru is undeclinable.
* Pietų Afrikos gyvéntojas — the inhabitant of South Africa'. Afrikiẽtis means a native of Africa.
** See the footnote for pakistãniškas.

B.

NAMO DALYS

The Parts of the House

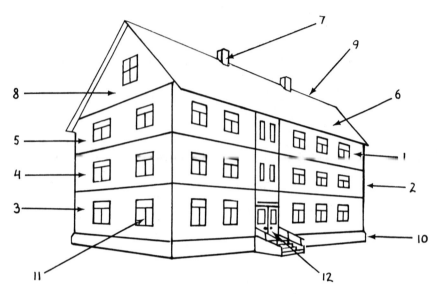

English	Lithuanian	Examples
1. wall	síena (1)	Šią́ síeną reĩkia dažýti.
2. corner	kam̃pas (4)	Stovė̃k priẽ nãmo kam̃po!
3. first floor	pìrmas aũkštas (2)	Aš gyvenù pirmamè aukštè.
4. second floor	añtras aũkštas (2)	Jìs gyvẽna antramè aukštè.
5. third floor	trẽčias aũkštas (2)	Aš gyvenù trečiamè aukštè.
6. roof	stógas (3)	Katė̃ tùpi añt stógo.
7. chimney	kãminas (3ᵇ)	Iš kãmino rū̃ksta dū́mai.
8. garret, attic	pastógė (1)	Jìs gyvẽna pastógėje.
9. roof top	kraĩgas	Karvẽlis tùpi añt kraĩgo.
10. foundation	pamataĩ*	Padė̃k nãmui gerùs pãma-
11. window	lángas (3)	Atidarýk lángą! [tus!
12. door	dùrys* (2)	Jìs nudãžė durìs mė́lynaĩ.

---

* **pamataĩ** used usually only in plural, although occasionally **pãmatas** (3b) is used.

dùrys plural only. See Lesson 23.

JUOKAI

"Jokes"

1.

Kùnigas: Pasakýk mán, vaikēli, ař yrà Diēvas kambaryjè?
Juozùkas: Taĩp, yrà.
Kunigas: O laukè?
Juozukas: Teñ jõ dabař nėrà.
Kunigas: Kodėl?
Juozukas: Laukè šiañdien labaĩ šálta.

2.

A.: Aš atėjaũ pataisýti jūsų pianìno.
B.: Bèt jūsų niēkas nėkvietė.
A.: O taĩp! Jūsų abù kaimýnai.

3.

Petriùkas: Māma, ką̃ žmónės turėjo, kaĩ nebùvo neĩ rādijo, neĩ televìzijos?
Mótina: Ramýbę.

4.

Mótina: Ką̃ veikeĩ šiañdien mokýkloje, Vytùk?*
Vytùkas: Láukiau, lìgi pasibaĩgs pāmokos.

5.

Sūnùs: Tėvēli,** šiañdien visojè klāsėje tìk àš víenas galėjau atsakýti į̃ kláusimą.
Tėvas: O kõgi tavę̃s kláusė?
Sūnùs: Kàs ìšmušė klāsės lángą ...

6.

Mókytojas: Kóks bùs būsimàsis laĩkas veiksmāžodžio 'võgti'?
Mokinỹs: Sėdėti kalėjime, põne mókytojau.***

---

* Vytùk is an abbreviation of Vytùkai, a diminutive of Výtautas, or Vỹtas, a man's first name, after the Lithuanian Grand Duke Vytautas the Great (1392-1430).
** tėvēli — Daddy; tėvēlis is a diminutive of tėvas.
*** mókytojau is an irregular vocative of mókytojas. See Appendix.

D.

COMBINATION PRACTICE

I.

1. I have	a. one nose
2. the child has	b. two eyes
3. the teacher has	c. two ears
4. my father has	d. two houses
5. man has	e. two cars

II.*

a.	b.	c.
1. I have	1. here	1. two houses
2. we had	2. in the city	2. two cars
3. she will have	3. in the village	3. two dogs

III.

(125 possible sentences!)

a.	b.	c.
1. I am	1. always	1. a good student
2. you are	2. today	2. a good son (daughter)
3. he is	3. at home	3. a good father (mother)
4. my sister is	4. here	4. a good neighbor
5. my brother is	5. there	5. a good man (woman)

IV.

a.	b.	c.
1. My teacher will teach	the whole day	the Lithuanian language
2. His sister will study	tomorrow	to write Lithuanian

---

* This is a somewhat more complicated combination practice: combine Nos. a,1 with b,1 and c,1, c,2 and c,3. Then: a,1 with b,2 and c,1; c,2 and c,3, etc. (27 combinations in all here).

E.

VARIATION PRACTICE

I.

*Use two versions:**

a) Màno bróliams patiñka važiúoti naujù automobiliù.

b) Màno bróliai mēgsta važiúoti naujù automobiliù.

1. My brothers like to ride in a new car.
2. My sisters like to ride in a new car.
3. My parents like to ride in a new car.
4. My students like to ride in a new car.
5. My teachers like to ride in a new car.
6. My professors like to ride in new cars.
7. My brothers like to drive (vairúoti!) new cars.
8. Your sisters like to go to movies (a movie).
9. His students like to go to Lithuania.
10. Our teachers like to drink coffee.

II.

*Use two versions:***

a) Màno brólis tùri važiúoti į Líetuvą. (— ... has to)

b) Màno bróliui reĩkia važiúoti į Líetuvą (— ... needs to; ... it
    is necessary)

1. My brother has to (needs to) go to Lithuania.
2. My brothers have to go to Lithuania.
3. My brothers had to go to Lithuania.
4. My brothers will have to go to Lithuania.
5. His sister has to go to the (į) university.
6. His sister had to go home.
7. His sisters will have to go to school.
8. Our students have to go to Canada.
9. Our students had to go down town (į miestą).
10. Our students will have to go home.

---

* Review 6.4.
** Review 11.2.

Dvidešimt pirmoji pamoka
Lesson 21

Klaipėda, 1932. VI. 20

Míelas Aĺgirdai,

Šiañdien mḗs àtplaukėme į̃ Klaĩpė̃dą̃. Klaĩpėda yrà Lietuvṍs úostas priḗ Báltijos jū́ros. Į̃ úostą atplaũkia dideli laivaĩ iš tolimų̃ kraštų̃: iš Amèrikos, Anglijos, Vokietìjos, Ispãnijos, Japònijos iř̃ nèt iš Austrālijos.

Uoste mùs sutìko Dr. Vìtkus iř̃ jõ sū́nùs. Dr. Vìtkus yrà màno dḗdė. Jõ sū́nùs Gedimìnas yrà màno pùsbrolis. Aš dár niēkad nebuvaũ mãtę̃s Lietuvṍs, taĩ mán vìskas bùvo labaĩ į̃domù. Dr. Vìtkus iř̃ Gedimìnas taĩp pàt nebùvo mãtę̃ manę̃s jaũ trejì mētai, taĩ jiẽ iř̃gi bùvo labaĩ paténkinti.

Tù atsìmeni, kaĩp àš visuomèt norḗjau pamatýti Líetuvą̃. O dabař̃ àš jaũ tikraĩ Lietuvojè! Visì lietùviai, kuriuõs tìk sutikaũ, labaĩ draũgiški. Jiẽ stēbisi, kàd àš taĩp geraĩ kalbù lietùviškai, nórs Lietuvṍs nebuvaũ niēkad mãtę̃s. Dabař̃ mán dár neleñgva greĩtai kalbė́ti, bèt põ porõs dienų̃ àš jaũ kalbė́siu labaĩ geraĩ iř̃ greĩtai.

Netolì Klaĩpėdos yrà Kuřšių̃ Neringà, kuř̃ mḗs aplañkėme báltas kopàs. Kuřšių̃ Neringojè labaĩ gražù: čià daũg mažų̃ kuròrtų sù mažaĩs vasárnamiais. Mḗs čià pasilìksime põrą̃ dienų̃, tadà plaũksime gárlaiviu Némunu į̃ Kaũną̃. Taĩ bùs labaĩ gražì keliõnė: Némunas tēka peř̃ žaliùs laukùs, dìdelius miškùs, prõ senùs pìliakalnius, prõ senùs miestùs iř̃ káimus. Girdė́jau, kàd gãlima bùs pamatýti iř̃ senų̃ pilių̃.

Kaĩp Jū̃s visì gyvúojate? Prašaũ pérduoti nuõ manę̃s linkė́jimus Tàvo tėvẽliams iř̃ Rū́tai.

Tàvo Pētras

P. S. Iř̃ neužmiř̃šk mán tuojaũ parašýti!

Žvejų uostas

The Fishermen's Harbor

VOCABULARY

atplaũkti (atplaukiù, atplaũkia, àtplaukė, atplaũks) — to arrive (on
board ship)

tõlimas, -à (3a) — far away, distant

Vokietijà (2) — Germany

Ispãnija (1) — Spain

Japònija (1) — Japan

Austrãlija (1) — Australia

pùsbrolis -io (1) — cousin (male)

vìskas — everything

įdomùs, -i (4) — interesting

paténkintas, -a — satisfied

atsimiñti (atsìminė, atsimiñs) irreg.:
atsìmenu, atsìmeni, atsìmena; atsì-
mename, atsìmenate, atsìmena —
to remember

pamatýti (pamataũ, pamãto, pamãtė,
pamatýs) — to see, to catch sight;
to visit

tikraĩ — really, for sure

draũgiškas, -a (1) — friendly

stebėtis (stebiúosi, stẽbisi, stebė̃josi,
stebė̃sis) — to wonder, to be sur-
prised

põ (prep. with gen.) — in (with time)
NB. põ with instr. — 'under', see
Lesson 37

porà (4) — a few, a couple (Noun!)

põ porõs dienų̃ — in a few days

netolì (adverb and prep. with gen.)
— not far (from)

Kuřšių Neringà — Couronian Isthmus
(A narrow isthmus on the Baltic
Sea)

kopà (2) — dune

kuròrtas (1) — spa, resort place

vasárnamis -io (1) — summer house,
cottage, villa

pasilìkti (pasilìko, pasilìks) irreg.:
pasiliekù, pasiliekì, pasilíeka; pasi-
líekame, pasilíekate, pasilíeka —
to remain

gárlaivis -io (1) — steamer

keliõnė (2) — trip, voyage

laũkas (4) — field

pìliakalnis -io (1) — 'castle hill' (hills
and mountains in Lithuania where
in ancient times stood castles, fortifications or warning towers)

pilìs -iẽs, fem. (4) — castle

pérduoti (pérdavė, pérduos) irreg.:
pérduodu, pérduodi, pérduoda; pér-
duodame, pérduodate, pérduoda –

linkė́jimas (1) — wish, regard *to give*

pérduoti linkė́jimus — to give regards

nuõ (prep. with gen.) — from

GRAMMAR

21.1 The Plural of the Adjectives — First Declension.

The plural cases for the first declension adjectives are:

	Masculine	Feminine
N.	baltì (3) 'white'	báltos
G.	baltų̃	baltų̃
D.	baltíems	baltóms
A.	báltus	báltas
I.	baltaĩs	baltomìs
L.	baltuosè	baltosè

The final -s of the dative plural (even the -is of the instrumental plural) and the final -e of the locative plural are sometimes dropped in conversational speech. This is true for second
and third declension adjectives also.

21.2 The declension of the adjective *dìdelis* 'big' is given below:

Singular

	Masculine	Feminine
N.	dìdelis (3ᵇ)	dìdelė
G.	dìdelio	didelės
D.	dideliám	dìdelei
A.	dìdelį	dìdelę
I.	dìdeliu	dìdele
L.	dideliamè	didelėjè

Plural

N.	didelì	dìdelės
G.	dìdelių	dìdelių
D.	didelíems	didelėms
A.	dìdelius	dìdeles
I.	dideliaĩs	didelėmìs
L.	dideliuosè	didelėsè

21.3 The Pluperfect Tense.

The pluperfect tense is a compound tense formed with the preterit of the verb *búti* plus the past active participle. The gender and number of the participle depend upon the gender and number of the subject.

Cf. Lesson 26 for the declension of the participles.

A sample paradigm with *buvaũ atėjęs* 'I had come' is given:

	Singular		Plural	
	Masc.	Fem.	Masc.	Fem.
1)	buvaũ atėjęs	(atėjusi)	bùvome atėję	(atėjusios)
2)	buvaĩ atėjęs	(atėjusi)	bùvote atėję	(atėjusios)
3)	bùvo atėjęs	(atėjusı)	bùvo atėję	(atėjusios)

This tense denotes a state which had been attained in the past. It may have been completed either during the time when another action took place or prior to the time another action took place:

1) *Ligónis jaũ bùvo mìręs, kaĩ mẽs nuėjome.* —
The patient had already died (was dead), when we arrived.

2) *Kaĩ jìs mùms àtnešė knỹgą, mẽs jaũ bùvome išėję.* —
When he brought us the book we had already gone out.

3) *Kaĩ jì gyvẽno Lietuvojè, jì niẽkad nebùvo mãčiusi liũto.* —
When she lived in Lithuania she had never seen a lion.

21.4 The Frequentative Perfect Tense.

The frequentative perfect tense is a compound tense formed
with the frequentative past of the verb *bùti* plus the past active
participle.

Singular   Plural

	Masc.	Fem.	Masc.	Fem.
1)	bùdavau atėjęs	(atėjusi)	bùdavome atėję	(atėjusios)
2)	bùdavai atėjęs	(atėjusi)	bùdavote atėję	(atėjusios)
3)	bùdavo atėjęs	(atėjusi)	bùdavo atėję	(atėjusios)

This tense denotes a state which was attaired at different
times in the past. Example:

1) *Màno žmonà, kaĩ bùdavo pavar̃gusi, niẽkur neĩdavo.* —
Whenever my wife was tired, she wouldn't go anywhere.

2) *Jõ tėvaĩ, kaĩ bùdavo susir̃gę, niẽko nedarýdavo.* —
His parents did nothing when(ever) they were sick.

For further information on these tenses see the section on
aspect in the appendix.

21.5 The Use of the Dative Case.

a)

The primary function of the dative case (as in all Indo-
European languages) is that of the indirect object:

1) *Tévas dãvė vaĩkui óbuolį.* — Father gave (to) the child an
apple.
(*To whom* did father give an apple? — *to the child: vaĩkui*).

2) *Jìs mán niẽko nèdavė.* — He did not give (to) me anything.
(*To whom* he did not give anything? — *to me: man*).

b)

In many cases, Lithuanian uses the indirect object (i.e. dative
case without any prepositions) where in English one uses expressions such as: *for, for the sake of,* etc.:

1) *Jìs vìską aukója sàvo šeĩmai.* — He sacrifices everything for (for the sake of) his family.
2) *Jìs mán vìską nùperka.* — He buys everything for me. (Or: He buys me everything).

c)

There are a number of verbs in Lithuanian which require the dative case. Some examples are given below:
atléisti 'to forgive':
1) *Iř atléisk mùms mūsų kaltès.* — And forgive us our trespasses.
atsakýti 'to answer':
2) *Atsakýk mán į kláusimą.* — Answer me my question.
dovanóti 'to give as a gift':
3) *Jìs mán dovanójo knỹgą.* — He gave me a book (as a gift).
dúoti 'to give':
4) *Dúok vaĩkui válgyti.* — Give the child (something) to eat.
léisti 'to allow':
5) *Léisk jám namõ eĩti.* — Allow him to go home.
padė́ti 'to help':
6) *Jìs mán niekadõs nepàdeda.* — He never helps me.

d)

The dative case is also used as the object of an infinitive to express purpose. In English we would have a direct object in a corresponding construction.
1) *Jìs sam̃do manè dárbui dìrbti.* — He is hiring me to do work.
2) *Jìs nusipiřko naũją plùnksną tám svarbiám láiškui rašýti.* — He bought (himself) a new pen to write that important letter.

Note that in the examples given above the words *dárbui* and *tám svarbiám láiškui* are in the dative case.

21.6 The relative pronoun *kurìs* 'which, who' is declined like *jìs*, cf. below:

Singular

	Masculine	Feminine
N.	kurìs	kurì
G.	kuriõ	kuriõs
D.	kuriám	kuriái
A.	kurį̃	kurią̃
I.	kuriuõ	kurià
L.	kuriamè	kuriojè

158

Plural

N.	kuriė	kuriõs
G.	kurių	kurių
D.	kuríems	kurióms
A.	kuriuõs	kuriàs
I.	kuriaĩs	kuriomìs
L.	kuriuosè	kuriosè

21.6,1 The relative pronoun agrees in number and gender with the word to which it refers, but its case is determined by its function in its own clause. Examples:

1) *Aš mataũ stãlą, añt kuriõ gùli knygà.* — I see a table on which lies a book.

The relative pronoun *kuriõ* is masculine and singular because it refers to *stãlą* which is masculine singular; it is in the genitive case as the object of the preposition *añt* which requires an object in the genitive case.

2) *Stãlas, kurį̃ jìs dãžo, yrà labaĩ dìdelis.* — The table which he is painting is very big.

Here *kurį̃* is masculine singular because it refers to *stãlas* which is masculine singular; it is in the accusative case as the object of *dãžo*.

3) *Mergáitė, kuriái àš daviaũ knỹgą, yrà màno duktė̃.* — The girl to whom I gave the book is my daughter.

kuriái is in the dative case as the indirect object of *daviaũ*. It is feminine singular because it refers to *Mergáitė*. Further information on relative pronouns is found in 36.3.

EXERCISES

A. *Questions.* 1. Kàs yrà Klaĩpėda? 2. Iš kokių̃ kraštų̃ atplaũkia laivaĩ į̃ Klaĩpėdą? 3. Kàs dár niekadõs nebùvo mãtęs Lietuvõs? 4. Ar̃ dãktaras Vìtkus bùvo mãtęs Pėtrą? 5. Kokiė vasárnamiai yrà Kuršių̃ Neringojè? 6. Kur̃ yrà báltos kõpos? 7. Per̃ kókius laukùs tėka Nėmunas? 8. Kokiė yrà pìliakalniai priė Nėmuno? 9. Ar̃ jūs ėsate kadà bùvęs Lietuvojè? 10. Ar̃ jūs žìnote, kàs yrà pìliəkalniai?

B. *Decline in the singular and plural:* báltas nãmas, baltà kopà, žãlias laũkas, dìdelis mìškas, sėnas úostas.

C. *Change all the italicized nouns and adjectives into the plural:* 1.
Mán patiñka *sēnas nāmas.* 2. Aš mēgstu *sēną nāmą.* 3. Nēmunas
tēka peř *žãlią píevą.* 4. Jiē gyvēna *dideliamè miškè.* 5. Jì piřko *gērą knỹgą.* 6. Jõ *automobìlis* yrà *raudónas.* 7. *Naujù gárlaiviu* mēs
plaūksime į̃ Kaūną. 8. Jìs mán bùvo parãšęs *ìlgą láišką.* 9. Jiē
gyvēna *senamè miestè.* 10. Mēs važiúosime į̃ Vìlnių *naujù automobiliù.*

D. *Conjugate in the pluperfect and in the frequentative perfect
tense the following verbs. Form sentences with them:* plaūkti,
atplaūkti, sutìkti, matýti, bū̃ti, atsimiñti, norḗti, kalbḗti, aplankýti, pérduoti, parašýti.

E. *Translate into Lithuanian:* 1. He had never been in Lithuania.
2. Big ships come ('arrive swimming') to the harbor. 3. Large forests lie (are) near the Nemunas. 4. They had never studied at the
University of Vilnius. 5. We like old houses. 6. Our old parents
(tēvaĩ) had never been in America. 7. They like old forests. 8.
Our cities are large. 9. Their villages are small. 10. I like new
automobiles.

CONVERSATION

UOSTE

Pētras:	1.	Kienõ yrà tàs báltas laĩvas sù žaliaĩs kaminaĩs?
Gedìminas:	2.	Taĩ yrà Anglijos laĩvas.
Petras:	3.	Ař tù jaũ esì bùvęs šìtame úoste?
Gedìminas:	4.	Taĩp. Aš labaĩ mēgstu jū́rą iř úostus. Čià àš visa- dõs galiù matýti dìdelius laivùs.
Petras:	5.	Mán atródo, kàd aniē dù pilkì laivaĩ yrà iš Ka- nãdos.
Gedìminas:	6.	Tõ taĩ àš tikraĩ nežinaũ, nès aš tokių̃ pilkų̃ laivų̃ ligšiõl dár nebuvaũ mãtęs.
Petras:	7.	Kuř yrà žvejų̃ úostas? Aš manaũ, kàd teñ yrà daũg mažų̃, senų̃ žvejų̃ laivų̃.
Gedìminas:	8.	Žvejų̃ úostas yrà už̃ tõ iškyšulio.
Petras:	9.	Mēs turḗsime tenaĩ nueĩti iř pažiūrḗti tų̃ senų̃ žvejų̃ laivų̃.
Gedìminas:	10.	Važiúokime dvìračiais! Aš iřgi norḗčiau dár kař- tą pamatýti žvejų̃ úostą.

AT THE HARBOR

Petras:	1.	Whose is that white ship with green smokestacks?
Gediminas:	2.	That is an English (England's) ship.
Petras:	3.	Have you (already) been at this harbor (before)?
Gediminas:	4.	Yes. I like the sea and the harbors very much. Here I can always see big ships.
Petras:	5.	It seems to me that those two gray ships are from Canada.
Gediminas:	6.	That I don't know for sure because I had never seen such gray ships.
Petras:	7.	Where is the fishermen's harbor? I suppose there are many small old fishermen's ships.
Gediminas:	8.	The fishermen's harbor is behind that point of land.
Petras:	9.	We'll have to go there and take a look at those old fishermen's ships.
Gediminas:	10.	Let's ride on the bicycles! I would also like to see the fishermen's harbor once more.

NOTES:

2. **Anglijos laĩvas** — lit. 'England's ship'.
5. **iš Kanãdos** — lit. 'out of Canada, from Canada'.
6. **tõ** — Genitive of **tàs** 'that', after negative.
   ligšiõl — lit. 'until now'.
9. **pažiūrẽti** — 'to look at' takes the genitive case.
10. **norẽčiau** — 'I would like to', a subjunctive form. See Lesson 31.

Dvidešimt antroji pamoka
Lesson 22

GARLAIVIU IŠ KLAIPĖDOS Į KAUNĄ

Dù pùsbroliai, Gedimìnas Vìtkus iř Pẽtras Žùkas, plaũkė gár-laiviu iš Klaĩpėdos į Kaũną. Jiẽ plaũkė Nẽmunu. Jiẽ stovẽjo añt gárlaivio dẽnio. Pẽtrui Žùkui, kurìs Lietuvojè bùvo pìrmą kařtą, vìskas bùvo labaĩ įdomù. Jìs nuõlat klausinẽjo sàvo pùsbrolį Ge-dimìną. Gedimìnas jám sténgėsi į visùs kláusimus áiškiai atsakýti.

— Gedimìnai, žiūrẽk, kokiẽ grãžūs miškaĩ: áukštos, grãžios ẽglės, puĩkios pùšys.

— Teñ taĩ tikraĩ grãžios ẽglės, bèt tiẽ ('those') puĩkūs mẽdžiai taĩ nè pùšys: taĩ senì ąžuolaĩ.

— Taĩp, taĩp, mán tiẽ žõdžiai dár vìs maĩšosi.

— Tù iř taĩp geraĩ kalbì lietùviškai — iř bevéik bè ángliško akceñto!... Aš niekadõs taĩp geraĩ ángliškai nekalbẽsiu...

— Tù, Gedimìnai, atvažiúosi pàs mùs į Amèriką iř tenaĩ iš-mõksi geraĩ ángliškai kalbẽti... Žiūrẽk, žiūrẽk, kokiẽ čià grãžūs Nẽmuno krantaĩ! Aš juõs labaĩ mýliu!

— Pẽtrai, geriaũ sak\ỹk: "Mán tiẽ grãžūs krantaĩ patiñka, la-baĩ patiñka." Lietùviškai "mylẽti" réiškia maždaũg "to love, to be in love"...

— Ačiū, prašaũ manè visuomèt pataisýti, kaĩ aš ką́ nórs ne-taisyklìngai pasakaũ. Aš nóriu taĩp geraĩ kalbẽti lietùviškai, kaĩp iř jũs visì, kuriẽ ẽsate gìmę iř užáugę Lietuvojè.

— Nesirūpink: Vìlniuje àš tavè supažìndinsiu sù jaunomìs, gražiomìs studeñtėmis, iř jõs tavè tuojaũ išmókys.

— Taĩ bùs puikù!

163

Piliakalnis
A Castle-Hill

VOCABULARY

gárlaivis -io (1) — steamer
pùsbrolis -io (1) — cousin (male)
dėnis -io (2) — deck (of a ship)
nuõlat — all the time, continually
klausinėti (klausinėju, klausinėja, klausinėjo, klausinės) — to ask questions, to question
sténgtis (sténgiuosi, sténgiasi, sténgėsi, sténgsis) — to try, to make an effort
áiškiai — clearly
áiškus, -i (3) — clear
ẽglė (2) — spruce
pušìs -iẽs (fem.) (4) — pine
puikùs, -ì (4) — fine, excellent
ą́žuolas (3a) — oak
maišýtis (maišaũsi, maĩšosi, maĩšėsi, maišýsis) — to get mixed up (with dative)
iř taĩp — (here) as it is
bevéik — almost
akceñtas (2) — accent
krañtas (4) — bank, shore

maždaũg — approximately
pataisýti (pataisaũ, pataĩso, pataĩsė, pataisỹs) — to correct (perfective)
kaĩ — when
ką̃ nórs — something
netaisyklìngai — incorrectly
gìmti (gìmė, gìms) irreg.: gimstù, gimstì, gìmsta; gìmstame, gìmstate, gìmsta — to be born
užáugti (užáugu, užáuga, užáugo, užáugs) — to grow up
rūpintis (rū́pinuosi, rū́pinasi, rū́pinosi, rū́pinsis) — to worry, care, be worried
nesirū́pink — do not worry (familiar)
supažìndinti (with the prep. sù and instrumental) (supažìndinu, supažìndina, supažìndino, supažìndins) — to introduce to
išmókyti (išmókau, išmóko, išmókė, išmókys) — to teach (perfective: 'to teach with some results')

GRAMMAR

22.1 The Plural of the Second Declension Adjectives.

The plural cases of the second declension adjectives are as follows:

	Masculine	Feminine
N.	suñkūs (4) 'heavy, difficult'	suñkios
G.	sunkių̃	sunkių̃
D.	sunkíems	sunkióms
A.	sunkiùs	sunkiàs
I.	sunkiaĩs	sunkiomìs
L.	sunkiuosè	sunkiosè

22.2 The Future Perfect Tense.

The future perfect tense is formed with the future tense of the verb *būti* plus the appropriate form of the past active participle. The gender and number of the participle depend upon the gender and the number of the subject. Cf. Lesson 26 for the full declension of the active participles.

165

A sample *conjugation* of the future perfect is given below:

'I shall have come'

Singular		Plural	
Masc.	Fem.	Masc.	Fem.
1) bū́siu atė̃jęs	(atė̃jusi)	bū́sime atė̃ję	(atė̃jusios)
2) bū́si atė̃jęs	(atė̃jusi)	bū́site atė̃ję	(atė̃jusios)
3) bùs atė̃jęs	(atė̃jusi)	bùs atė̃ję	(atė̃jusios)

The future perfect tense may express an action which will have taken place before another future action takes place. It may also express a condition or state which will last some time in the future as the result of a future action. Sometimes it expresses the probability that an event has taken place. Examples:

1) *Kaĩ jìs ateĩs, àš bū́siu baĩgęs dárbą.* — When he arrives, I shall have finished the work. (Note that in English we must use the present tense after w h e n, even if a future time is implied. Since this rule does not apply to Lithuanian the future tense must be used when a future time is specified.)

2) *Kaĩ jìs sugrį̃š, jū̃s bū́site rãdę knỹgą.* — When he returns, you will have found the book.

3) *Neateĩk tuomèt, kadà àš bū́siu atsigùlęs.* — Don't come when I (shall) have gone to bed.

4) *Netrùkus jì bùs važiãvusi tráukiniu.* — Soon she will have traveled by train.

5) *Jõs nėrà. Jì bùs nuė́jusi namõ.* — She isn't here. She must have gone home.

22.3 The Use of the Accusative Case.

a)

The accusative case is primarily the case of the direct object: all regular transitive verbs require the accusative case.

Àš mė́gstu òperą. — I like opera.

Màno brólis pir̃ko naũją nãmą. — My brother bought a new house.

NB. The student is reminded again that, with the verb in the negative, the direct object is expressed in Lithuanian in the genitive case:

Àš nemė́gstu òperos. — I do not like opera.

Màno brólis nepiřko naũjo nãmo. — My brother did not buy a new house.

See also 2.2 and 4.3.

b)

The accusative is also used to express definite time, limited time, duration of time, and certain periods of time, such as the day of the week, the week, the month, the season, etc.*

Jìs dìrbo vìsą diė́ną. — He worked all day.

Autobùsas išeĩna pìrmą vãlandą. — The bus leaves at one o'clock.

Àš važiúosiu namõ kìtą saváitę. — I will go home next week.
Saũsio mė́nesį yrà labaĩ šálta. — In the month of January it is very cold.

Pavãsarį žýdi gė́lės. — In spring, the flowers bloom.

c)

Many prepositions govern the accusative case. Here we shall list the most frequent ones. (For a full list of prepositions, see Lesson 37).

apiẽ — around, close by, about, concerning, of...
apliñk — around, in a circle
į̃ — in, into, to
peř — through (over the top), over
prõ — through (straight through)
ùž — for, for the sake of*

Examples:

Jiẽ kalbė́jo apiẽ naũją knỹgą.
Apliñk nãmą áuga daũg mẽdžių.
Jìs važiúoja į̃ miẽstą.
Mergáitė žiūrė́jo prõ lángą.
Jiẽ mìrė ùž tėvỹnę.

(Translate these sentences. Make other sentences with the prepositions given.)

---

* More about the expressions of time: Lesson 32.
* **ùž** with the meaning **behind** is used with the genetive case. See Lesson 37.

EXERCISES

A. *Questions.* 1. Kàs plaŭkė gárlaiviu iš Klaĩpėdos į̃ Kaŭną? 2. Kám vìskas bùvo labaĩ įdomù? 3. Kàs nuõlat klausinėjo Gedimìną? 4. Kokiẽ yrà mìškaĩ priẽ Nẽmuno? 5. Kaĩp vadìnasi tiẽ puĩkūs žalì mẽdžiai? 6. Kàs geraĩ kaĩba lietùviškai? 7. Kadà Gedimìnas išmóks geraĩ ángliškai kalbéti? 8. Sù kuõ Gedimìnas supažìndins Pétrą Vìlniuje? 9. Ar̃ jũs geraĩ kaĩbate lietùviškai? 10. Ką̃ réiškia 'myléti'?

β. *Decline in the singular and plural:* gražùs nãmas, puikùs mẽdis, platì ùpė, skanùs obuolỹs, ramì naktìs.

C. *Change all the italicized adjectives and nouns into plural:* 1. Màno *brólis* gyvēna priẽ *gražaũs mìško.* 2. Mán patìnka *platì gãtvė.* 3. *Autobùsas* važiúoja *plačià gatvè.* 4. *Studeñtė* mãtė *grãžų filmą.* 5. *Upė* yrà *platì.*

D. *Translate into Lithuanian:* 1. I like wide rivers. 2. We will have arrived, when he wakes up (will wake up). 3. He will have written the letter, when his cousin arrives (will arrive). 4. The steamers travel ('swim') in the wide rivers. 5. The old books are very heavy. 6. The Nemunas flows through beautiful forests and wide fields. 7. Our cities are beautiful. 8. Yesterday we saw an excellent film. 9. Not all (*nè visì*) films are excellent. 10. My uncles and my cousins live by the beautiful forests.

CONVERSATION

KNYGYNE

Nórkus: 1. Labà dienà. Ar̃ jaũ ẽsate gãvę naujų̃ knỹgų iš Amèrikos?

Pardavéja: 2. Taĩp. Tìk vãkar gãvome kelìs knỹgų siuñtinius iš Niujórko.*

Norkus: 3. Prašaũ mán paródyti naũją amerikiẽčių novèlių riñkinį.

Pardavéja: 4. Prašaũ. Štaĩ čià yrà vìsos naũjos knỹgos, kuriàs gãvome vãkar.

Norkus: 5. Ačiū. Aš paim̃siu šį̃ modernių̃ amerikiẽčių novèlių riñkinį.

---

* Concerning the spelling and pronounciation of foreign proper names, see Lesson 30.

Pardavėja:	6.	Mẽs taĩp pàt tùrime iř kaĩ kurių amerikiẽčių ra- šýtojų vertimùs į lietùvių, vókiečių iř prancũzų kalbàs.
Norkus:	7.	Aš skaitaũ tìk originalùs. Mãtote, àš esù gyvẽnęs Amèrikoje. Aš geraĩ móku ánglų kal̃bą.
Pardavėja:	8.	Aš dabař taĩp pàt mókausi ánglų kalbõs, bèt skai- týti ángliškai dár negaliù.
Norkus:	9.	Kiẽk kainúoja šìs ánglų - lietùvių kalbų̃ žodýnas? Aš jį̃ nóriu nupiřkti sàvo bróliui.
Pardavėja:	10.	Taĩ yrà labaĩ gẽras žodýnas. Jìs kainúoja dẽšimt lìtų.

AT THE BOOKSTORE

Norkus:	1.	Hello. (Good day). Did you get the new books from America?
Salesgirl:	2.	Yes. Only yesterday we received several book shipments from New York.
Norkus:	3.	Please show me the new collection of the Ameri- can short stories.
Salesgirl:	4.	Here you are. Here are all the books we received yesterday.
Norkus:	5.	Thanks. I'll take this collection of modern Amer- ican short stories.
Salesgirl:	6.	We also have (some) translations of some Ameri- can writers into Lithuanian, German and French.
Norkus:	7.	I read only the originals. You see, I have lived in America. I know the English language well.
Salesgirl:	8.	I also study English now. But I cannot read English yet.
Norkus:	9.	How much is this English-Lithuanian dictionary? I want to buy it for my brother.
Salesgirl:	10.	It is a very good dictionary. It costs ten *litas*.

NOTES:

1. **naujų̃ knýgų** — gen. pl.: partitive genitive: 'some of the new books'. books'.
2. **Niujórko** — N. Y. See Lesson 30.
3. **novèlių** — NB: **novèlė** 'short story' (from German 'Novelle'); **romãnas** 'novel' (from German 'Roman').
4. **kaĩ kurių̃** — only **kurių̃** is inflected. See Lesson 36.
5. **sàvo bróliui** — dative of interest: 'for my brother', see also 21.5.
10. **lìtų** — gen. plural: after **dẽšimt** 'ten'; see 24.4,1 also 4.2.

169

Dvidešimt trečioji pamoka

Lesson 23

KAUNE

Pètras iř Gedimìnas pasíekė Kaũną vakarè. Kadángi jiẽ bùvo labaĩ pavařgę, taĩ tuojaũ nuvỹko į viẽšbutį, paválgė vakariẽnę iř nuėjo miegóti.

Ankstì rýtą jiẽ pradėjo apžiūrinėti Kaũną. Kaũnas yrà sẽnas miẽstas, jõ namaĩ bevéik visì mūrìniai, jamè daũg senų̃ mūrìnių bažnýčių. Žmónės eĩna pėstì cementìniais šalìgatviais arbà važiúoja autobùsais. Mū́sų pùsbroliai pirmiáusia apžiūrėjo istòrinius pãstatus: Kaũno piliẽs griuvėsiùs Nẽmuno iř Neriẽs sántakoje, paskuĩ vadinamúosius Perkū́no namùs, kuriẽ bùvo pastatýti priẽš daũg šimtų̃ mẽtų.

Netolì nuõ piliẽs griuvėsių jiẽ aplañkė dìdžiojo Lietuvõs poèto Mairónio namùs, kuriuosè jìs gyvẽno. Dabař tuosè dideliuosè mūrìniuose namuosè yrà Mairónio muziẽjus.

Pietùs Pètras iř Gedimìnas paválgė studeñtų valgỹkloje priẽ universitèto. Iš teñ jiẽ autobusù nuvažiãvo į Výtauto Dìdžiojo Kultūros Muziẽjų, kuriamè kãbo Láisvės Vařpas. Jį̃ padovanójo Líetuvai Amèrikos lietùviai. Varpè yrà įrašas:

> *O skařbink peř ámžius*
> *Vaikáms Lietuvõs,*
> *Kàd láisvės neveřtas,*
> *Kàs nègina jõs.*

Iš teñ jiẽ autobusù nuvažiãvo į Čiurliónio Dailẽs Muziẽjų, kuriamè Pètras pìrmą kařtą pamãtė Čiurliónio pavéikslus. Jám jiẽ padãrė gìlų įspūdį.

Vytauto Didžiojo Kultūros Muziejus
The Vytautas The Great Museum of Culture

Vakarè Pḗtras iř̃ Gedimìnas bùvo teatrè. Teatrè jiẽ mãtė lietùvišką òperą. Nórs Pḗtras iř̃ Čikãgoje bùvo mãtęs keliàs òperas, bèt šì lietùviška òpera jám labaĩ patìko.

VOCABULARY

pasíekti (pasíekiu, pasíekia, pasíekė, pasiẽks) — to reach

vakarè — in the evening

kadángi — because

pavař̃gę — tired (see Lesson 26; infinitive **pavař̃gti** 'to get tired')

taĩ — (here) so

tuojaũ — right away

nuvýkti (nuvýko, nuvýks) irreg.: nuvykstù, nuvykstì, nuvýksta; nuvýkstame, nuvýkstate, nuvýksta — to get (somewhere)

viẽšbutis -čio (1) — hotel

nuėjo miegóti — went to sleep

ankstì — early

rýtą — in the morning

pradéti (prãdedu, prãdeda, pradėjo, pradẽs) irreg.: (see **dėti**, Lith.-English Vocab.) — to begin

pėsčias, -čia (plural: pėstì, pėsčios) (3) — on foot

jìs eĩna pėsčias — he goes on foot, etc.

cementìnis, -ė (2) — concrete, made of cement

šaligatvis -io (1) — sidewalk

pirmiáusia — in the first place, first

istòrinis, -ė (1) — historic

pãstatas (3b) — building

griuvėsiai (2) (plural only) — ruins

sántaka (1) — confluence

vadinamúosius — so called

Perkúno namaĩ — the Perkúnas house (**Perkúnas** 'Thunder' was one of the chief gods of the pagan Lithuanians. Perkúno namaĩ is considered to be one of the oldest buildings preserved in Kaunas)

bùvo pastatýti — were built (see Lesson 33)

priẽš (prep. with accusative) — before, in front of; with time expressions: ...ago (Cf. German: 'vor zwei Wochen')

priẽš daũg šimtų̃ mẽtų — many hundreds of years ago

dìdžiojo — (of the) great (see Lesson 28)

poètas (2) — poet

Mairónis -io — Mairónis (Rt. Rev. Jónas Mačiùlis, pseudonym Mairónis, 1862-1932, the national poet laureate of Lithuania)

rūmai (1) (usually plural only) — big house; palace, chamber

muziẽjus (2) — museum

valgyklà (2) — restaurant, 'diner'

nuvažiúoti (nuvažiúoju, nuvažiúoja, nuvažiãvo, nuvažiuõs) — to go, to get, to betake oneself (somewhere, in a vehicle)

Výtauto Dìdžiojo Kultū̃ros Muziẽjus —The Vytautas the Great Museum of Culture

kuriamè — in which (see Lesson 21 and 36)

kabóti (kabaũ, kãbo, kabójo, kabõs) — to hang (intransitive)

Láisvės Vař̃pas — Liberty Bell

į̃rašas (1) — inscription

skaṁbinti (skaṁbinu, skaṁbina, skaṁbino, skaṁbins) — to ring, toll

peř̃ ámžius — for ever (lit.: through ages)

nevertas (with gen.) — not worth

láisvė (1) — freedom, liberty

kàs — (here) he who, whoever (see Lesson 36)

gìnti (ginù, gìna, gýnė*, gìns) — to defend

čiurliónio Dailė̃s Muziẽjus — Ciurlionis Art Museum (**Čiurliónis**: Mikalojus Konstantinas Čiurlionis, 1887-1911, the foremost Lithuanian painter. He started symbolism and abstractionism in painting even before Kandinsky. Also a noted composer.)

pìrmą kař̃tą — (for) the first time

pavéikslas (1) — picture, painting

gilùs, -ì (4) — deep

įspū̃dis -džio (1) — impression

nórs — although

---

* For the change of i⁼y see the Lith.-English Vocabulary.

GRAMMAR

23.1 The Plural of the Third Declension Adjectives.

Masculine

	'golden'	'wooden'	'artificial'	
N.	auksìniai	medìniai	dirbtìniai	-iai
G.	auksìnių	medìnių	dirbtìnių	-ių
D.	auksìniams	medìniams	dirbtìniams	-iams
A.	auksiniùs	mediniùs	dirbtiniùs	-ius
I.	auksìniais	medìniais	dirbtìniais	-iais
L.	auksìniuose	medìniuose	dirbtìniuose	-iuose

Feminine

	'golden'	'wooden'	'artificial'	
N.	auksìnės	medìnės	dìrbtìnės	-ės
G.	auksìnių	medìnių	dirbtìnių	-ių
D.	auksìnėms	medìnėms	dirbtìnėms	-ėms
A.	auksìnès	medìnės	dirbtinès	-ès
I.	auksìnėmis	medìnėmis	dirbtìnėmis	-ėmis
L.	auksìnėse	medìnėse	dirbtìnėse	-ėse

23.2 The adjectives belong to any one of four different stress patterns just as the nouns. All of the adjectives listed above belong to stress pattern No. 2. Illustrations of adjectival stress patterns are given in the appendix. The short sketch of nominal stress classes is in Lesson 5.

23.3 Use of the Instrumental Case.

23.3,1 The instrumental case may denote the means with which something is done. Examples:

1) *Aš važiúoju į universitètą autobusù.* — I ride to the university by bus.
2) *Jìs rãšo pieštukù.* — He writes with a pencil.
3) *Jìs pakélė ãkmenį lazdà.* — He lifted up the stone with a stick.
    In place of the instrumental case by itself, one may also use the preposition *su* with the instrumental.
4) *Jìs pakélė ãkmenį sù lazdà.* — He lifted up the stone with a stick.

23.3,2 The instrumental may be used to indicate the place along which or through which something (or somebody) is moving.

Examples:

1) *Autobùsas važiúoja gatvè.* — The bus goes along the street.
2) *Jìs eĩna keliù.* — He walks along the road.
3) *Jì palydėjo brólį laukù.* — She accompanied (her) brother through the field.

23.3,3 It may also be used in certain expressions of time, cf. 32.7.

Examples:

1) *Jaũ senaĩs laikaĩs Lietuvà prekiãvo giñtaru.* — Already in ancient times Lithuania traded in amber.
2) *Vakaraĩs jiē visuomèt dainúoja.* — In the evenings they always sing.

Many fossilized expressions of time are actually old instrumental case forms:

1) *šiuõ metù* — this time, at this time, nowadays (from *šìs mētas* — this time)
2) *tuõ tárpu* — at this moment (from *tàs tárpas* — that span of time)

Frequently these expressions were shortened into adverbs of time:

1) *kaĩtais* — sometimes (from *kaĩtas* — time, occurence)
2) *kuomèt* — when (from *kuõ metù* — at what time)
3) *tuomèt* — then, at that time (from *tuõ metù* — at that time)
4) *anuomèt* — once, formerly (from *anu[õ] metù* — at that time)
5) *visuomèt* — always (from *visu[õ] metù* — at all times)

23.3,4 Certain verbs require a direct object or an indirect complement in the instrumental case. Examples:

1) *Lietuvà prekiãvo giñtaru.* — Lithuania traded in amber.
2) *Jìs bùvo išrinktas prezidentù.* — He was elected president.
3) *Àš jį̃ paskýriau kúopos vadù.* — I appointed him company commander.
4) *Jìs bùvo paskìrtas kúopos vadù.* — He was appointed company commander.
5) *Jiē jį̃ àpšauké kvailiù.* — They called him a fool.
6) *Studeñtai jį̃ vadìna tiñginiu.* — The students call him a lazybones.

7) *Jìs manè išvadìno kvailiù.* — He called me a fool.
8) *Jiẽ išsiriñko Jõną prezidentù.* — They chose John as their president.

23.3,5 The instrumental case may denote the condition or profession of an individual. Such constructions might be found with the verbs *viřsti* 'to turn into, to become', *dẽtis* 'to pretend to be', *laikýti* 'to consider ... as', *skìrti* 'to name, to appoint', *gìmti* 'to be born', *áugti* 'to grow (into)', *tarnáuti* 'to serve (as)', *mókytis* 'to study (to be)', *tàpti* 'to become'. Examples:

1) *Ūkininkas tãpo karãliumi.* — The farmer became a king.
2) *Bróliai paviřto júodvarniais.* — The brothers turned into ravens.
3) *Mẽs jį̃ laĩkome vadù.* — We consider him as (our) leader.
4) *Jõną paskýrė mókytoju.* — They appointed John (Jonas) a teacher.

As a predicate the instrumental may be used with the verb *bũti* 'to be', especially when it is close in meaning to *tàpti* 'to become'. Generally the nominative denotes a constant, (sometimes immutable) characteristic of the subject, whereas the instrumental denotes an accidental or temporary condition. The nominative is used to denote something which is always true of the noun, whereas the instrumental is used for an accidental attribute. In the sentence: *Várna yrà paũkštis* — 'The crow is a bird', the nominative is used because the crow is always a bird and will never be anything else. But in the sentence: *Bróliai diẽną lãkstė júodvarniais* — 'During the day the brothers flew about as ravens', the instrumental *júodvarniais* 'like ravens' is used because the brothers were ravens for only a certain length of time.

Therefore, as predicate of the verb *bũti* 'to be' the nominative is most common, whereas with the other verbs mentioned above the predicate is in the instrumental. But the instrumental may be used as the predicate of *bũti* when it means approximately the same as *tàpti* 'to become'. Examples:

1) *Jìs bùvo prezidentù* or *Jìs bùvo prezideñtas.* — He was president.
2) *Jìs bùs viřšininku* or *Jìs bùs viřšininkas.* — He will be the boss.
3) *Jìs norẽjo bũti gýdytoju* or *Jìs norẽjo bũti gýdytojas.* — He wanted to be a physician.

23.3,6 The instrumental case may be used as the object of certain prepositions, e.g. *sù* 'with', *sulìg* 'up to, as far as', *tiẽs* 'opposite'. Examples:

1) *Tẽvas sù sūnumì išvažiãvo.* — The father departed with (his) son.

2) *Válgo dúoną sù svíestu.* — (He) eats bread and (with) butter.

3) *Mẽdis bùvo sulìg namù aukštùmo.* — The tree was as high as a house (literally: up to a house in height).

4) *Jìs stovẽjo tiẽs lángu.* — He stood opposite the window.

23.4 Nouns Used Only in Plural.

Certain nouns used in the plural denote objects which speakers of English generally consider to be singular. Examples:

kélnės (1) '(pair of) trousers'
lašiniaĩ (3ᵇ) 'bacon'
akiniaĩ (3ᵇ) 'glasses, spectacles'
mẽtai (2) 'year'
vartaĩ (2) 'gate'
žìrklės (1) 'pair of scissors'
marškiniaĩ (3ᵃ) 'shirt'
baltiniaĩ (3ᵃ) 'underwear'
pùsryčiai (1) 'breakfast' (although the singular *pùsrytis* is also used sometimes)

akẽčios (1) 'harrow'
pãmaldos (3ᵇ) '(religious) service'
pabaigtùvės (1) 'feast (celebrating the completion of some task)'
piẽtūs (4) 'dinner'
vestùvės (2) 'wedding'
sukaktùvės (2) 'anniversary'

Special numerals which are used with these nouns are listed in 24.5.

EXERCISES

A. *Questions.* 1. Kadà Pẽtras iř Gedimìnas pasíekė Kaũną? 2. Kodėl jiē tuojaũ nuėjo miegóti? 3. Kokiē namaĩ yrà Kaunè? 4. Kuõ važiúoja žmónės Kaunè? 5. Kuř yrà Kaũno pilìs? 6. Kàs yrà Mairónis? 7. Kàs padovanójo Líetuvai Láisvės Vařpą? 8. Kuõ abù (both) pùsbroliai nuvažiãvo į Čiurliónio Dailės Muziẽjų? 9. Kókį įspūdį padãrė Čiurliónio pavéikslai Pẽtrui? 10. Kókią òperą jiē mãtė teatrè?

B. *Decline in the singular and in plural:* medìnis nãmas, mūrìnis nãmas, auksìnis laĩkrodis, istòrinis pãstatas.

C. *Use the instrumental case:* 1. Aš rašaŭ láiška (with a pencil). 2. Studeñtai važiúoja į universitètą (by bus). 3'. Jiẽ plaŭkė (by a steamer). 4. Jìs atėjo sù sàvo (cousin). 5. Miestè mẽs eĩname (on the side-walks). 6. Autobùsai važiúoja (on the wide streets). 7. Jìs nóri bū́ti (a teacher). 8. Aš nenóriu bū́ti (a teacher). 9. Aš buvaŭ teatrè (with students). 10. Aš jùs supažìndinsiu sù (Dr. Vitkus).

D. *Translate into Lithuanian:* 1. The new buses run along the new streets. 2. I like only old brick houses. 3. My brother has many (*daŭg* plus genitive) golden watches. 4. Wooden houses are not as (*nè tókie*) good as brick houses. 5. The historical buildings in Kaunas are very old. 6. Petras and Gediminas will see many (see No. 3 above) historical buildings in Vilnius. 7. In Kaunas, there are many brick churches. 8. She lives in a large brick palace. 9. She went to the theatre with her (own—*sàvo*) parents. 10. Our teacher likes to talk about the old historical buildings.

CONVERSATION

DU PUSBROLIAI

Gediminas: 1. Kaĩp tù žinaĩ, àš esù bùvęs Amèrikoje, bèt labaĩ trũmpą laĩką. Sakýk, ãr visì namaĩ teñ mūrìniai?

Pẽtras: 2. Nè visì. Dideliuosè miẽstuose visì namaĩ yrà mūrìniai miẽsto centrè, bèt príemiesčiuose yrà daŭg medìnių namū̃.

Gediminas: 3. O kaĩp Čikãgoje?

Petras: 4. Čikãgoje, ýpač príemiesčiuose, yrà daŭg medìnių namū̃.

Gediminas: 5. O kóks jū̃sų nãmas Čikãgoje?

Petras: 6. Mū̃sų nãmas yrà mūrìnis. Mẽs gyvẽname, kaĩp tù jaŭ žinaĩ, príemiestyje.

Gediminas: 7. Taĩ táu reĩkia tolì važiúoti į universitètą.

Petras: 8. Aš turiù važiúoti tráukiniu, paskuĩ autobusù arbà tramvãjumi.

Gediminas: 9. Ãr tù galì nuvažiúoti automobiliù?

Petras: 10. Taĩp, galiù. Tėtis manè kaȓtais nùveža automobiliù, bèt mán dár nedúoda automobìlio į universitètą važinėti, nórs àš iȓ geraĩ móku vairúoti.

THE TWO COUSINS

Gediminas: 1. As you know, I have been in America, but only for a very short time. Tell me, are all houses there brick homes?

Petras: 2. Not all. In the big cities, all the houses are brick houses in the center of the city, but there are many wooden houses in the suburbs.

Gediminas: 3. And how is it in Chicago?

Petras: 4. In Chicago, especially in the suburbs, there are many wooden houses.

Gediminas: 5. And what kind of a house is your house in Chicago?

Petras: 6. Our house is of brick. We live, as you already know, in a suburb.

Gediminas: 7. Thus, you have a long way to travel to the university.

Petras: 8. I have to go by train, then by bus, or streetcar.

Gediminas: 9. Can you go by car to the university?

Petras: 10. Yes, I can. My father sometimes takes me by car, but he does not give me the car to commute to the university, although I am a good driver.

NOTES:

1. **ar̃** — untranslatable particle which begins a question without an interrogative word. If it begins an indirect question, then it can be rendered into English as 'if' or 'whether'.

5. **nãmas** — means both 'house' and 'home'. For the latter meaning, however, **namaĩ**, plural of **nãmas** is normally used with the meaning 'home': **Jis netùri namų̃** — 'He has no home (He is homeless)'.

7. **taĩ** — here it means 'thus, so, and so'.

8. **tramvãjus** — a borrowing from English 'tramway'.

9. **àš geraĩ móku vairúoti (automobìlį)** — literal meaning: 'I know well (how) to drive (a car)'.

Dvidešimt ketvirtoji pamoka
Lesson 24

KELIONĖ IŠ KAUNO Į VILNIŲ

Iš Kaŭno į Vìlnių Pėtras iř Gedimìnas važiãvo tráukiniu. Traukinỹs bùvo ìlgas: penkiólika keleĩvinių vagònų. Kiekvienamè vagonè bùvo dvėjos dùrys iř daŭg langų̃. Kiekvienamè vagonè taĩp pàt bùvo šešì skyrėliai, arbà kupė. Tamè skyrėlyje, kuriamè sėdėjo Pėtras iř Gedimìnas, bùvo dár penkì keleĩviai: dù senì výrai iř trỹs jáunos mergáitės.

Traukinỹs sustójo Petrošiūnuose, tìk dėšimt kilomètrų nuõ Kaŭno. Į tráukinį čià įlìpo penkiólika keleĩvių: šešì výrai, peñkios móterys iř keturì vaikaĩ.

Traukinỹs greĩtai važiãvo peř žaliùs laukùs, prõ tamsiùs miškùs, prõ senùs, gražiùs káimus. Vienà iš mergáičių užkálbino Pėtrą:

— Atsiprašaŭ, jū̃s, tur bū́t, ìš Amèrikos?

— Kaĩp jū̃s taĩ gãlite žinóti? — pakláusė Pėtras.

— Aš mačiaŭ añt jū́sų lagamìno priklijúotą kortėlę "Chicago, Illinois". Be tõ, taĩ gãlima matýti iř ìš jū́sų drabùžių...

— Taĩp, taĩp... Aš esù ìš Čikãgos. Aš dár tik peñkios diẽnos esù Lietuvojè. Bèt aš bū́siu Vìlniuje kėturias saváites...

— Mẽs vìsos trỹs ėsame studeñtės iř taĩp pàt važiúojame į Vìlnių. Mẽs studijúojame Vìlniaus universitetè. Bèt sakýkite, kuř jū̃s taĩp geraĩ išmókote kalbėti lietùviškai?

— Amèrikoje, Čikãgoje. Mẽs namiẽ kaĩbame tìk lietùviškai, tókiu būdù mẽs geraĩ išmókome iř ángliškai iř lietùviškai. Ař jū̃s nėsate bùvusios Amèrikoje?

— Nè, dár nẽsame teñ bùvusios . . . Aš nóriu nuvažiúoti į Amèriką, kaĩ baĩgsiu universitètą. Čikãgoje gyvẽna màno dẽdė . . .

— Kaĩp jõ pavardė?

— Jõ pavardė yrà Šiṁkus, Jõnas Šiṁkus.

— Aš jõ nepažį́stu, bèt gál màno tėvaĩ jį̃ pažį̃sta.

— Jìs gyvẽna Cìcero príemiestyje.

— Mẽs gyvẽname priẽ ẽžero, gál dvìdešimt mýlių nuõ Cìcero. Traukinỹs sustójo Trãkų stotyjè. Visì norẽjo pamatýti šį̃ sẽną miẽstą. Pẽtras i̇̃r Gedimìnas susipažìno sù šiomìs trimìs studeñtėmis i̇̃r susìtarė susitìkti kìtą diẽną Vìlniuje.

— Nórs Vìlniaus àš dár nesù mãtęs, bèt jìs mán jaũ labaĩ patiñka, — pasãkė Pẽtras Gedimìnui.

— Ȧ̃r àš táu nesakiaũ? — atsãkė jám Gedimìnas. — Vìlnius yrà labaĩ sẽnas i̇̃r gražùs miẽstas. Pamatýsi!

— Aš tuõ tikiù . . . Mergáitės Vìlniuje, atródo, taĩp pàt grã žios . . .

VOCABULARY

penkiólika — fifteen

keleĩvis -io (2) — passenger (noun)

keleĩvinis, -ė (1) — passenger (adj.)

vagònas (2) — wagon, (railway) car

kiekvienamè — in each (see Lesson 11)

dvẽjos — two (see Lesson 24.5)

skyrẽlis -io — a little chapter; (here) compartment

kupė̃ — coupé; train compartment

tamè — in that (see Lesson 36)

dár — (here) more

sustóti (sustóju, sustója, sustójo, sustõs) — to stop, to halt

Petrošiúnai (pl. 1st decl.) — Petrošiūnai, a town near Kaunas

kilomètras (2) — kilometer

nuõ (prep. with genitive) — from, away from, down, etc.

įlìpti (į̃lipu, į̃lipa, į̃lipo, į̃lips) — to get in, to climb in, to climb up

užkálbinti (užkálbinu, užkálbina, užkálbino, užkálbins) — to start talking to

atsiprašýti (atsiprašaũ, atsiprãšo, atsiprãšė, atsiprašýs) — to excuse oneself, to ask for forgiveness

atsiprašaũ — pardon me, excuse me

tur bū̃t — perhaps

pakláusti (pakláusiu, pakláusia, pakláusė, paklaũs) — to ask (one a question)

lagamìnas (2) — suitcase

priklijúota (fem. acc. sg. past passive participle; see Lesson 26) — attached, (stuck to)

kortẽlė (2) — a little card, sticker

be tõ — besides

taĩ gãlima matýti — one can see that

i̇̃r — (here) also

drabùžis -io (2) — (a piece of) clothing, clothes

drabùžiai (in plural) — clothes

baĩgti (baigiù, baĩgia, baĩgė, baĩgs) — to finish

baĩgti universitètą — to finish studies at a university; to be graduated from a university

pavardė (3b) — last name, family name

pažìnti (pažį̃no, pažìns) irreg.: pažį́stu, pažį̃sti, pažį̃sta; pažį̃state, pažį̃sta; — to know (to be acquainted)

ẽžeras (3b) — lake

mylià (2) — mile

Cìceras (or Cìcero) — Cicero (a suburb of Chicago)

stotìs -iẽs (fem.) (4) — station

susipažìnti (susipažį́stu, susipažį̃sta, susipažìno, susipažìnęs, see pažìnti, above) — to get acquainted

šiomìs (fem. instr. pl.; see Lesson 36) — these

susitar̃ti (susìtariu, susìtaria, susìtarė, susitar̃s) — to agree
susitìkti (susitìko, susitìks) irreg.:
susitinkù, susitinkì, susitiñka; susitiñkame, susitiñkate, susitiñka —
to meet (one another)

kìtą dìeną — (here) the next day;
some other day
pamatýsi! — you will see!
tikė́ti (tikiù, tìki, tikė́jo, tikė́s) — to
believe, to trust (with instr.)
atródo — it seems

GRAMMAR

24.1 The Cardinal Numbers.

The cardinal numerals are listed below (in the nominative
case if the numeral is declined). If there is no difference between
the masculine and feminine forms, only one form is listed:

		feminine
0	nùlis (2)	
1	víenas	vienà (3)
2	dù	dvì
3	trỹs (4)	
4	keturì	kẽturios (3[b])
5	penkì	peñkios (4)
6	šešì	šẽšios (4)
7	septynì	septýnios (3)
8	aštuonì	aštúonios(3)
9	devynì	devýnios (3)
10	dẽšimt (dešimtìs) (3[b])	
11	vienúolika (1)	
12	dvýlika (1)	
13	trýlika (1)	
14	keturiólika (1)	
15	penkiólika (1)	
16	šešiólika (1)	
17	septyniólika (1)	
18	aštuoniólika (1)	
19	devyniólika (1)	
20	dvìdešimt, (dvì dẽšimtys)	
21	dvìdešimt víenas	
22	dvìdešimt dù, etc.	
30	trìsdešimt, (trỹs dẽšimtys)	
40	kẽturiasdešimt (kẽturios dẽšimtys)	
50	peñkiasdešimt, (peñkios dẽšimtys)	
60	šẽšiasdešimt, (šẽšios dẽšimtys)	
70	septýniasdešimt, (septýnios dẽšimtys)	
80	aštúoniasdešimt, (aštúonios dẽšimtys)	

183

90	devýniasdešimt, (devýnios dẽšimtys)
100	šim̃tas (4)
200	dù šimtaĩ
300	trỹs šimtaĩ
400	keturì šimtaĩ
500	penkì šimtaĩ, etc.
1,000	tū́kstantis, -čio (1)
2,000	dù tū́kstančiai
3,000	trỹs tū́kstančiai
1,000,000	milijõnas (2), tū́kstantis tū́kstančių
1,000,000,000	milijárdas (1)

Other examples:

484	keturì šimtaĩ aštúoniasdešimt keturì
5,673	penki tūkstančiai šeši šimtaĩ septýniasdešimt trỹs

24.2 The number *vienas* (3) is declined like a regular first declension adjective and agrees in case, number and gender with the noun which it modifies, e.g. *àš turiù víeną sū́nų* — 'I have one son'.

24.3 The declensions of the numbers 2, 3, 4, 5, and 7 below:
(—— means that the form is the same in both genders)

	Masc.	Fem.	Masc.	Fem.
N.	dù 'two'	dvì	trỹs (4) 'three'	——
G.	dviejų̃	——	trijų̃	——
D.	dvíem	——	trìms	——
A.	dù	dvì	trìs	——
I.	dviẽm	——	trimìs	——
L.	dviejuosè	dviejosè	trijuosè	trijosè

	Masc.	Fem.	Masc.	Fem.
N.	keturì (3b) 'four'	kẽturios	penkì (4) 'five'	peñkios
G.	keturių̃	——	penkių̃	——
D.	keturíems	keturíoms	penkíems	penkíoms
A.	kẽturis	kẽturias	penkìs	penkiàs
I.	keturiaĩs	keturiomìs	penkiaĩs	penkiomìs
L.	keturiuosè	keturiosè	penkiuosè	penkiosè

	Masc.	Fem.
N.	septynì (3) 'seven'	septýnios
G.	septynių̃	——
D.	septyníems	septynióms
A.	septýnis	septýnias
I.	septyniaĩs	septyniomìs
L.	septyniuosè	septyniosè

In colloquial Lithuanian and sometimes even in its written form, the dative and instrumental cases are abbreviated by skipping -s in the dative and -is, in the instrumental, if it is preceded by -m. Thus: trìms—trìm; trimìs—trim̃; keturíems—keturíem; keturiomìs—keturiom̃, etc.

Note that the declension of penkì and septynì differ from keturì only by virtue of the fact that they belong to different accent classes. Šešì is declined and accented like penkì, and aštuonì and devynì like septynì.

24.3,1 The numerals from 2 - 9 agree with the word they modify in case and gender, e.g. Jìs dãvė pinigų̃ trìms studeñtams. — He gave (some) money to three students.

24.4 dešimtìs* 'ten' is declined like a regular third declension noun (cf. Lesson 4) of accent class 3ᵇ; vienúolika 'eleven' (and the following numbers up to and including devyniólika 'nineteen') is declined like a regular second declension noun of the first accent class, except that the accusative is like the nominative: vienúolika (not: vienúoliką!); šim̃tas 'hundred' is declined like a regular first declension noun of the fourth accent class; tū́kstantis 'thousand' is declined like a regular first declension noun of the first accent class; milijõnas 'million' is declined like a regular first declension noun of the second class.

24.4,1 Those numbers the last digit of which is zero, i.e. 10, 20, 30, etc.; 100, 200, 300, etc.; 1,000, 2,000, 3,000, etc.; 1,000,000, etc.; 1,000,000,000, etc. and those ending in -lika (11-19) require that the noun quantified be in the genitive plural. These forms are treated as nouns and are known as nominal numbers: Examples:

---

* dešimtìs, etc. is rather rarely used; instead, use the indeclinable form — dẽšimt, etc.

1) *dēšimt stalū̃* — ten tables
2) *šiṁtas dienū̃* — one hundred days
3) *Jiẽ tùri vienúolika vaikū̃.* — They have eleven children.
4) *Milijõnui knỹgų reĩkia didelės bibliotèkos.* — For a million books a big library is necessary.
5) *Milijárdą sudãro túkstantis milijõnų.* — In a billion there are a thousand millions. (Lit.: A thousand million makes a billion)

Note that in example (3) *vienúolika* is in the accusative case —because it is the direct object of the verb *tùri*; *vaikū̃* is in the genitive plural because it is governed in turn by *vienúolika*. In example (4) *milijõnui* is in the dative singular with the meaning 'for a million', but the word *knỹgų* is in the genitive plural since it is governed by *milijõnui*.

24.4,2 If the numeral is not one of those mentioned in 24.4,1 then the entire number will agree in case and gender with the word modified. Examples:
1) *Mẽtai tùri trìs šimtùs šẽšiasdešimt penkiàs arbà šešiàs dienàs.* — A year has three hundred sixty-five or six days.
2) *Visuosè tuosè penkiuosè túkstančiuose dviejuosè šimtuosè trìsdešimt šešiuosè mìestuose gyvẽna daugiaũ negù dẽšimt túkstančių gyvéntojų.* — In all those five thousand two hundred thirty six cities live more than ten thousand inhabitants.
3) *Tõ maĩsto keturíems túkstančiams trìms šimtáms šẽšiasdešimt dvíem vaikáms neužtèks.* — That food will not be sufficient for the four thousand three hundred and sixty-two children.

24.5 Those numerals which are reserved for use with nouns which have a plural form but a singular meaning are as follows: (the masculine nom. plur. is listed first, then the feminine nom. plur.)

1.	vienerì	(3ᵃ)	víenerios
2.	dvejì	(3ᵃ)	dvẽjos
3.	trejì	(3ᵃ)	trẽjos
4.	ketverì	(3ᵃ)	kẽtverios
5.	penkerì	(4)	peñkerios
6.	šešerì	(4)	šẽšerios
7.	septynerì	(3ᵇ)	septýnerios
8.	aštuonerì	(3ᵇ)	aštúonerios
9.	devynerì	(3ᵇ)	devýnerios

N.B. (There are no special forms for 10-20, 30, 40, etc.; 100, etc.)

But: 21. dvìdešimt vienerì, víenerios
     22. dvìdešimt dvejì, dvẽjos, etc.
     31. trìsdešimt vienerì, víenerios
     32. trìsdešimt dvejì, dvẽjos, etc., etc.

	Masculine	Feminine	Masculine	Feminine
N.	vienerì (3ª)	víenerios	dvejì (4)	dvẽjos
G.	vienerių̃	——	dvejų̃	——
D.	vieneríems	vienerióms	dvejíems	dvejóms
A.	víenerius	víenerias	dvejùs	dvejàs
I.	vieneriaĩs	vieneriomìs	dvejaĩs	dvejomìs
L.	vieneriuosè	vieneriosè	dvejuosè	dvejosè

All the rest of these numerals are declined like *vienerì* except that in those of accent class 3^b the root is stressed with the circumflex instead of the acute. Examples of the use:

1) *Àš turiù tìk víenerius márškinius.* — I have only one shirt.

2) *Jaũ penkerì mẽtai, kaĩ jìs mìrė.* — It is already five years since he died.

3) *Jìs pir̃ko dvejàs žìrkles.* — He bought two pairs of scissors.

24.6 The collective numbers (all belonging to accent class one and declined like regular first declension nouns) are as follows:

2.	dvẽjetas	6.	šẽšetas
3.	trẽjetas	7.	septýnetas
4.	kẽtvertas	8.	aštúonetas
5.	peñketas	9.	devýnetas

These show that the objects in consideration are to be taken as a group. Examples:

1) *Jìs važiúoja trẽjetu arklių̃.* — He is driving (a team of) three horses.

2) *Jìs tùri šẽšetą vištų̃.* — He has (a flock of) six hens.

Note that the noun quantified by these collective numbers is always in the genitive plural.

24.7 The fractions are as follows:

pùsė	half
trẽčdalis	one third
ketviřtis, ketvirtãdalis	one fourth
penktãdalis	one fifth
šeštãdalis	one sixth
septintãdalis	one seventh
aštuntãdalis	one eighth
devintãdalis	one ninth
dešimtãdalis	one tenth

N.B. All these words (one third—one tenth) are masculine nouns, declined like *peĩlis*.

In mathematical terminology we find such forms as *vienà antróji* 'one-half', *vienà trečióji* 'one-third', *dvì peñktosios* 'two-fifths', etc. The numerator is the cardinal number and the denominator is the feminine form of the ordinal number (originally to agree with *dalìs* 'part', although the word *dalìs* does not appear in any fraction). The cases are determined according to the syntactic rules of 24.4,1 and 24.4,2. For forms such as *antróji*, etc., see Lessons 28 and 29. Examples:

1) *ìš vienõs trečiõsios* — from one-third
2) *sù dviẽm penktõsiomis* — with two-fifths
3) *šešiólikoje dvìdešimt penktū̃jų* — in sixteen twenty-fifths
4) *Dúok jám pùsę dòlerio.* — Give him half a dollar.
5) *Taĩ atsitìko priẽš ketviřtį valandõs.* — That happened a quarter of an hour ago.

In example (1) the entire expression is in the feminine genitive singular because it is the object of the preposition *ìš* 'from' which requires the genitive case, cf. Lesson 37. In example (2) both *dviẽm* and *penktõsiomis* are in the instrumental case as the object of the preposition *sù* 'with'. In example (3) the word *šešiólikoje* is in the locative case, *dvìdešimt* is indeclinable, but *penktū̃jų* is in the genitive plural since it is quantified by *šešiólikoje* (one of the numbers which requires the quantified noun and, of course, the modifying adjective, be in the genitive plural). In examples (4) and (5) the genitive case is used with the words *pùsė* 'half' and *ketviřtis* 'a quarter'.

24.7,1 A group of whole numbers plus the fraction one-half which are found only in the genitive case are listed below, masculine first, feminine second and plural last:

1½	pusañtro, pusantrõs, pusantrų̃
2½	pustrẽčio, pustrečiõs, pustrečių̃
3½	pusketvir̃to, pusketvirtõs, pusketvirtų̃
4½	puspeñkto, puspenktõs, puspenktų̃
5½	pusšẽšto, pusšeštõs, pusšeštų̃
6½	pusseptiñto, pusseptintõs, pusseptintų̃
7½	pusaštuñto, pusaštuntõs, pusaštuntų̃
8½	pusdeviñto, pusdevintõs, pusdevintų̃, etc.

Examples:

1) *Màno draũgas mán dãvė pusañtro dòlerio.* — My friend gave me a dollar and a half.
2) *Jìs teñ gyvẽno pustrečių̃ mẽtų.* — He lived there two and a half years.
3) *Àš būsiu čià pusantrõs dienõs.* — I will be here a day and a half.

Note that the genitive case of the noun is used with the fractions listed in this paragraph.

The concept 1½ etc. may be rendered also by Lith.:

a) *víenas ir̃ pùsė* — lit. 'one and one half'
b) *víenas sù pusè* — lit. 'one with a half'
   2½:
a) *dù (dvì) ir̃ pùsė* — lit. 'two and a half'
b) *dù (dvì) sù pusè* — lit. 'two with a half', etc.

24.8 Expressing One's Age.

In expressing age the name of the individual is put in the dative case and the age is put in the nominative case. Examples:

1) *Mán yrà penkiólika mẽtų.* — I am fifteen years old. (Lit.: To me are fifteen years)
2) *Pérnai mán bùvo keturiólika mẽtų.* — Last year I was fourteen years old.
3) *Ùž trejų̃ mẽtų mán bùs aštuoniólika mẽtų.* — In three years I will be 18 years old.

4) *Màno bróliui jaũ peñkiasdešimt vienerì mētai.* * — My brother is already 51 years old.

5) *Profèsoriui Jõnui Vāliui jaũ peñkiasdešimt aštuonerì mētai.* * — Professor Jonas Valys is already 58 years old.

NB. There is another way of expressing age: with the nominative case of the person, with the genitive of the age:

1) *Aš esù penkiólikos mētų (ámžiaus).* — Lit.: I am of fifteen years (of age).
2) *Pérnai àš buvaũ keturiólikos mētų.*
3) *Už trejų̃ mētų àš būsiu aštuoniólikos mētų.*
4) *Màno brólis jaũ peñkiasdešimt vienerių̃ mētų.*
5) *Profèsorius Jõnas Valỹs jaũ peñkiasdešimt aštuonerių̃ mētų.*

The first way is used more frequently, however the second way can also be used.

24.9 Addition, Subtraction, Multiplication, Division.
(sudėtìs, atimtìs, daugýba, dalýba)

In everyday use		*In mathematics, statistics, etc.*
2+2=4	Dù iř dù yrà keturì	Dù pliùs dù yrà keturì
5+7=12	Penkì iř septynì yrà dvýlika	Penkì pliùs septynì yrà dvýlika
7—3=4	Septynì bè trijų̃ yrà keturì	Septynì mìnus trỹs yrà keturì
18—9=9	Aštuoniólika bè devynių̃ yrà devynì.	Aštuoniólika mìnus devynì yrà devynì
9×3=27	Devynì padáuginti iš trijų̃ yrà dvìdešimt septynì	
5×7=35	Penkì padáuginti iš septynių̃ yrà trìsdešimt penkì	
33:3=11	Trìsdešimt trỹs padalìnti iš trijų̃ yrà vienúolika	
35:7=5	Trìsdešimt penkì padalìnti iš septynių̃ yrà penkì	

24.10 Writing Differences.

a) In Lithuanian numbers are written as in other countries of continental Europe: 1, 2, 3, 4, 5, 6, 7, 8, 9, 10, 11, etc.

---

* **mētai** is used with the meaning **year**, (**years**) only in plural. Thus special numerals must be used with it. Cf. 23.4 and 24.5.

NB. Lithuanians living in the English-speaking countries tend to use the local system: 1, 7, etc.

b) Wherever we use a comma, Lithuanians use a period and vice-versa:

English	Lithuanian
1.5	1,5 — 1½
15.75	15,75 — $15^{75}/_{100}$
5,000,000	5.000.000 — 5 million
	or:
	5 000 000, etc.

NB. However, in Lithuanian newspapers and books published in the U.S.A., England, and the other English-speaking countries, the local (i.e. the English) way is used.

24.11 The Use of the Locative Case.

a) The locative case is used primarily to indicate location, and answers the question *kuř, kamè* 'where'. Examples:

Jìs gyvéna dìdeliamè miestè. — He lives in a large city.

Lietuvà yrà Euròpoje. — Lithuania is in Europe.

b) It is also used in certain expressions of time:

vakarè — in the evening*

senóvėje — in ancient times

darbýmety(je) — during harvest (time); during busy season

vidùdieny(je) — in the middle of the day; at noon

viduřnakty(je) — at midnight

viduřvasary(je) — in the middle of the summer

pavakarȳ(je) — in the early evening; toward evening

dabartyjè — in the present (time)

praeityjè — in the past

ateityjè — in the future

jaunȳstéje — in (one's) youth

senãtvéje — in old age

saũsio ménesyje — in (the month of) January

or: *saũsyje* — in January

For the usage with *rytaĩs, vakaraĩs* (instrumental plural) 'in the mornings, in the evenings', see 23.3,3 and Lesson 32.

---

* But accusative of definite time: **šį vãkarą** 'this evening, tonight'; **anã vã-karą** 'that evening', etc. Also **vãsarą, pavãsarį** 'in the summer, in the spring', etc. Cf. 22.3b and Lesson 32.

EXERCISES

A. *Questions.* 1. Kuõ važiãvo Pẽtras iř Gedimìnas į̃ Vìlnių? 2. Kíek bùvo skyrẽlių (kupė̃) kiekvienamè vagonè? 3. Kíek bùvo keleĩvių tamè tráukinio skyrėlyje, kuriamè sė́dėjo Pẽtras iř Gedimìnas? 4. Kíek keleĩvių į̃lipo į̃ tráukinį Petrošiū́nuose? 5. Kuř gyvẽna Gedimìnas? 6. Kuř gyvẽna Pẽtras? 7. Ař jū̃s ẽsate bùvęs Vìlniuje? 8. Kàs yrà bùvęs Lietuvojè? 9. Kuř yrà Lietuvà? 10. Kuř yrà Vìlnius?

B. *Combine:* a) From *one* to *101* with: gražùs nãmas, jaunà studeñtė, sẽnas profèsorius, gerà knygà.

b) *He is one year old:* Two ways: Jám vienerì mẽtai
Jìs yrà vienerių̃ mẽtų (ámžiaus)

From one (vienerì) to 100 (šim̃tas).

C. *Read aloud and write out in full:* 11, 13, 27, 35, 67, 131, 476, 800, 1116, 1222, 1492, 1776, 1914, 1918, 1964, 1984;
3½ (trỹs iř pùsė; *or* pusketvir̃to, *or* trỹs sù pusè);
$4^3/_4$, $7^2/_5$, $8^3/_8$, $10^5/_7$, $11^2/_3$.

D. *Use the locative case.* 1. Mẽs gyvẽname (in a large city). 2. At the University of Vilnius) studijúoja daũg studeñtų. 3 (In Lithuania) yrà daũg pilių̃ griuvė̃sių. 4. Màno dė̃dė gyvẽna (in Chicago). 5. (In a new house) malonù gyvénti. 6. (In America) yrà daũg didelių̃ miẽstų. 7. (In the big cities) yrà daũg mūrìnių namų̃. 8. (In our school) mẽs mókomės ánglų kalbõs. 9. (In America) gyvẽna apiẽ* víenas milijõnas lietùvių.

E. *Translate into Lithuanian:* 1. My father is fifty five years old. 2. I have three sisters and five brothers. 3. In three years, my brother will be eighteen years old. 4. His grandfather was seventy years old three years ago (*priẽš trejùs metùs*). 5. I live fifteen kilometers (or: miles) from (*nuõ* with gen.) Vilnius. 6. Two hundred twenty five students study the Lithuanian language at our university. 7. Five hundred seventy three students study English (the English language) at the University of Vilnius. 8. Thirteen and five is eighteen. 9. Twenty minus eleven is nine. 10. Fifty divided by five is ten.

---

* **apiẽ** here means 'approximately'.

CONVERSATION

DRABUŽIŲ KRAUTUVĖJE

Pėtras: 1. Aš norė́čiau nusipiȓkti dvì vasarinės eilutės: víeną pìlką iȓ víeną rùdą. Kíek kainúoja šì rudà
eilùtė?

Pardavėjas: 2. Šì eilùtė kainúoja trìsdešimt devýnis dòlerius iȓ
devýniasdešimt aštúonis centùs.

Petras: 3. Kitaȋp sãkant, kė́turiasdešimt dòlerių... O kíek
kainúoja šì pilkà eilùtė sù baltaȋs taškė́liais? O
štaȋ čià yrà káina: kė́turiasdešimt devynì dòleriai
iȓ devýniasdešimt aštuonì ceñtai.

Pardavėjas: 4. Dár neužmiȓškite pridė́ti miẽsto mókesčio: trỹs
proceñtai...

Petras: 5. Geraȋ. Aš paiȓsiu abì šiàs eilutès. Kíek taȋ bùs
vìso lãbo?

Pardavėjas: 6. Tuojaũ... Kė́turiasdešimt devynì iȓ devýniasdešimt aštuonì pliùs pusañtro dòlerio miẽsto mókesčio yrà peñkiasdešimt víenas dòleris iȓ kė́tu-
riasdešimt aštuonì ceñtai. O čià trìsdešimt devynì
iȓ devýniasdešimt aštuonì pliùs dòleris dvìdešimt
yrà kė́turiasdešimt víenas iȓ aštuoniólika. Vìso:
devýniasdešimt dù dòleriai iȓ šė́šiasdešimt šešì
ceñtai.

Petras: 7. Geraȋ. Aš dúosiu jùms čèkį...

Pardavėjas: 8. Labaȋ atsiprašaũ, bèt mẽs čèkių nepriȋmame. Vìsos káinos — grynaȋs pinigaȋs.

Petras: 9. Jũs čèkių nepriȋmate? Aš turiù tìk dvìdešimt penkìs dòlerius kišėnėje... Taȋ peȓ mãža. Aš eȋsiu
teñ, kuȓ priìma čekiùs. Ačiū.

Pardavėjas: 10. Prašaũ, prašaũ. Mãtote, mẽs pardúodame tìk ùž
grýnus pìnigus.

IN A CLOTHES STORE

Petras: 1. I would like to buy two summer suits for myself:
one gray one and one brown. How much is this
brown suit?

Clerk: 2. This suit costs $39.98.

Petras: 3. In other words, forty dollars... And how much is
this gray suit with (little) white dots. Oh, here is
the price: $49.98.

Clerk:	4.	Do not forget to add the city tax: three percent.
Petras:	5.	All right. I will take both these suits. How much will that be all together?
Clerk:	6.	Right away ... 49.98 plus one dollar and fifty cents tax makes 51.48. And here — 39.98 plus one dollar and twenty makes 41.18. All told: 92.66.
Petras:	7.	All right. I will give you a check ...
Clerk:	8.	I am very sorry, but we do not accept checks. All prices—cash ...
Petras:	9.	You do not accept checks? I have only 25 dollars in my pocket ... That is not enough. I will go somewhere where they accept checks. Thanks.
Clerk:	10.	You are welcome, I am sure. You see, we sell only for cash.

NOTES:

1. **nusipiȓkti** — reflexive: 'to buy for oneself'.
3. **kitaȋp sākant** — lit.: 'saying it differetntly'.
5. **abȉ** — 'both' (feminine).
6. **vȉso** — genitive of **vȉsas** 'all, total, whole'.
7. **vȉso lãbo** — Render into English 'altogether, all-told'.
8. **grynaȋs piniɡaȋs** — Instrumental plural of **grýnas pȉnigas** 'pure money, cash'. Instr. is used because it actually depends on the verb **mokẽti** 'to pay' which requires the instr.: **Mokẽti grynaȋs pinigaȋs** 'to pay cash'.

194

Dvidešimt penktoji pamoka
Lesson 25

A. THE HUMAN BODY — ŽMOGAUS KŪNAS

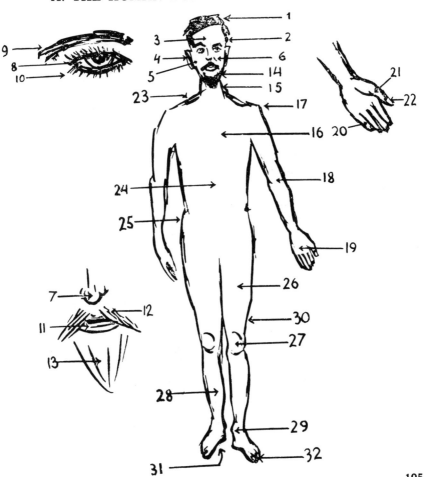

English	Lithuanian	Pattern Sentences
1. hair(s)	pláukas, plaukaĩ — *Jõs plaukaĩ yrà labaĩ gråžūs.*	
2. head	galvà — *Jìs tùri gẽrą gálvą.*	
3. forehead	kaktà — *Jõ kaktojè yrà daũg raukšlių̃.*	
4. ear	ausìs (-iẽs, fem.) — *Jõ aũsys yrà labaĩ dìdelės.* (gen. pl. ausų̃)	
5. face	véidas — *Aš nemataũ jõ véido.*	
6. cheek	skrúostas — *Jõ skrúostai paraũdo nũo šalčio.*	
7. nose	nósis (-ies, fem.) — *Jìs nušãlo nósį.* (gen. pl. nósių)	
8. eye	akìs (-iẽs, fem.) — *Jì víena akimì nemãto.* (gen. pl. akių̃)	
9. eyebrow	añtakis (-io) — *Jõ žmonà išsipešiójo añtakius.*	
10. eyelashes	blakstíenos — *Jám nũo miẽgo nèt blakstíenos*	
11. mouth	burnà — *Jì tùri grãžią bùrną.*	[sulìpo.
12. moustache	ūsai (pl.) — *Senélis raĩtė såvo žilùs ūsùs.*	
13. beard	barzdà — *Jìs glóstė såvo bar̃zdą.*	
14. chin	smãkras — *Barzdà áuga añt smãkro.*	
15. neck	kãklas — *Jì negražì: jõs kãklas per ìlgas.*	
16. chest	krūtìnė — *Jì glaũdė vaĩką priẽ krūtìnės.*	
17. shoulder	petỹs (-iẽs, masc. 1st decl. — *Jõ dešinỹsis petỹs* (gen. pl. pečių̃)* [yrà aukštèsnis.	
18. arm	rankà — *Jõ labaĩ ìlgos rañkos.*	
19. hand	rankà (plåštaka) — *Aš rañkoje laikaũ pieštùką.*	
20. finger	pir̃štas — *Jìs mán pirštù paródė, kur̃ eĩti.*	
21. thumb	nykštỹs** — *Jám reikėjo nupiáuti nýkštį.*	
22. nail	nãgas — *Jõs nagaĩ labaĩ ìlgi ir̃ raudónai nudažýti.*	
23. back	nùgara — *Jìs nẽša dìdelį maĩšą añt nùgaros.*	
24. belly	pìlvas — *Jõ tóks dìdelis pìlvas, kàd jìs vòs gãli*	
25. hip	klùbas — *Jõ klùbai atsikìšę.*	[eĩti.
26. thigh	šlaunìs (-iẽs, fem.) — *Màno brólis susìžeidė šlaũ-* (gen. pl. šlaunų̃) [nį.	
27. knee	kẽlis (-io) — *Iš báimės mán nèt kẽliai drebėjo.*	
28. shin	blauzdà — *Vanduõ jám siekė lìgi pùsės blauzdų̃.*	
29. ankle	kulkšnìs (kulnélis) — *Vaĩkas apsidaũžė kulkšnìs*	
30. leg	kója — *Jõnas nusiláužė kóją.* [(kulneliùs).	
31. foot	pėdà — *Aš susìžeidžiau pėdą.*	
32. toe	(kójos) pir̃štas — *Naũjas bãtas mán (kójos) pirš-* [tùs spáudžia.	

---

* petỹs is a noun of the 1st declension, i.e. it is declined like **gaidỹs** 'rooster', except for the genitive singular which is **petiẽs** (3rd decl.).
** Other fingers in consecutive order: **smalìžius, didžiùlis, bevar̃dis, mažẽlis.**

B. MEN'S CLOTHES — VYRIŠKI DRABUŽIAI

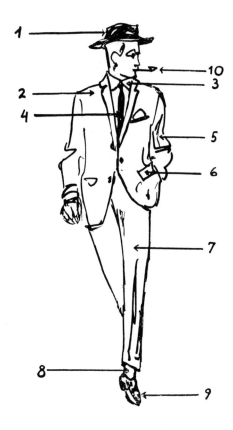

1. hat   skrybėlė — *Aš nóriu piřkti naũją skrýbėlę.*
2. jacket   švařkas — *Taĩ jõ naũjas švařkas.*
3. shirt   marškiniaĩ (pl. only) — *Jõ marškiniaĩ švãrūs.*
4. tie   kaklãraištis (-čio) — *Mán nepatiñka šìs raudónas*
                                         [kaklãraištis.
5. sleeve   rankóvė — *Jõ švařko rankóvės yrà per ìlgos.*
6. pocket   kišēnė — *Aš turiù tìk víeną dólerį kišēnėje.*
7. trousers   kēlnės (pl. only) — *Jõ kēlnės per trum̃pos.*
8. sock   kójinė — *Jìs mēgsta báltas kójines.*
9. shoe   bãtas — *Rytõj àš piřksiu naujùs batùs.*
10. pipe   pýpkė — *Jìs rūko pýpkę.*

C. WOMEN'S CLOTHES — MOTERIŠKI DRABUŽIAI

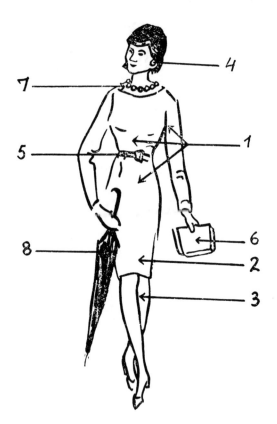

1. dress   suknėlė — *Jì kasdiēn peřka naũją suknėlę.*
2. skirt   sijõnas — *Kíek kainúoja šìs rùdas sijõnas?*
3. stocking   kójinė — *Nupiřk mán dvì poràs kójinių.*
4. earring   aũskaras — *Jìs žmónai nupiřko gintariniùs aũs-*
                                            [karus.
5. belt   diřžas — *Vãkar àš pàmečiau žaliõs suknėlės diřžą.*
6. handbag   rankinùkas — *Mán reĩkia naũjo rankinùko.*
7. necklace   karõliai — *Jì tùri puikiùs gintariniùs karoliùs.*
8. umbrella   skĕtis — *Mán reĩkia skĕčio, nès laukè lŷja.*
9. wallet(purse) piniginė — *Nusipirkaũ naũją piniginę.*

NB. Some of these items are the same for men and women: **hat, belt, umbrella**, just like in English. Also note that in Lithuanian for both 'sock' and 'stocking' **kójinė** is used. If one wants to be specific, one can always add **výriškas, -a** 'man's, masculine' or **móteriškas, -a** 'woman's, feminine' — **výriškos kójinės** 'socks', **móteriškos kójinės** 'stockings', etc.

D. ŽYNĖ IR MERGAITĖ

Viduryjè mìško áugo sēnas ą́žuolas. Põ tuõ ą́žuolu bùvo dìdelis akmuõ. Añt tõ akmeñs dažnaĩ ilsḗdavos žynė,[1] kurì gyvēno tamè mìškè.

Kar̃tą žynė sėdėjo añt akmeñs põ ą́žuolu ir̃ pamãtė mergáitę, kurì riñko[2] žolès.

— Prieĩk priè manę̃s, mergáite, — tãrė[3] žynė. Mergáitė priėjo.

— Kám renkì[4] tàs žolès? — pakláusė žynė.

— Iš šìtų žolių̃ àš vìrsiu māmai váistų.[5] Màno mamà jaũ seniaĩ ser̃ga.

— Kókia ligà ser̃ga tàvo mamà? — vė̃l pakláusė žynė.

— Aš nežinaũ, — atsãkė mergáitė.

— Bèt àš žinaũ, — tãrė žynė. Aš taĩp pàt galiù táu dúoti váistų, kuriẽ pagýdys tàvo mãmą. Bèt ùž taĩ tù mán turḗsi padarýti trìs dárbus.

— Aš vìską padarýsiu, — sušùko mergáitė.

— Tù turḗsi mán atidúoti sàvo báltą karvēlį, kur̃į tù labaĩ mýli. Paskuĩ atidúosi mán sàvo kárvę, kurì táu kasdiẽn dúoda píeno. O kaĩ tàvo mamà pasveĩks, tù turḗsi ateĩti pàs manè ir̃ čià turḗsi víenerius metùs dìrbti . . .

— Aš vìską padarýsiu, — atsãkė mergáitė. — Aš ir̃ dvejùs metùs galė́siu táu dìrbti, tìk pagýdyk màno mãmą.

— Mataũ, kàd tù esì gerà mergáitė ir̃ labaĩ mýli sàvo mãmą. Aš tìk norė́jau tavè išbandýti. Štaĩ táu trỹs raudónos kruopēlės.[6] Kàs rýtas[7] mamà teguĩ suválgo[8] víeną kruopēlę. Jì tuojaũ pasveĩks. Dabar̃ skubė́k namõ ir̃ gýdyk sàvo mãmą.

Praė́jo kḗturios díenos. Ligónė pasveĩko. Mergáitė nuėjo padėkóti žỹnei ùž váistus. Bèt žynė̃s nesurãdo.

NOTES:

1. **žynė** — a fairy, a (good) sorceress.
2. & 4. **riñko, renkì** — see under **riñkti** 'to gather' in the Lithuanian-English Vocabulary.
3. **tãrė** — said.
5. **váistų** — partitive gen. pl. of **váistai** (sg. **váistas**) 'medicine'. (**Váistai** is usually used only in plural.)
6. **kruopēlė** — 'little flake, little pill'.
7. **kàs rýtas** — this is a nominative of time, used here instead of accus., (of definite time) **kiekvíeną rýtą** 'every morning'.
8. **teguĩ suválgo** — 'let her eat'.

E. ŠIMTAS VILKŲ

Víeną kar̃tą vaĩkas parė́jo iš mìško iř̃ sãko tė́vui:

— Žinaĩ, tė́vẽli, miškè mačiaũ šim̃tą vilkų̃.

— Negãli bū́ti, — atsãkė tė́vas. — Čià tiẽk daũg vilkų̃ nėrà.

— Nà, taĩ vìs dė́ltõ[1] bùvo apiẽ peñkiasdešimt.

— Negãli bū́ti.

— Trìsdešimt taĩ jaũ[2] tikraĩ bùvo.

— Negãli bū́ti.

— Dė́šimt taĩ jaũ tikraĩ bùvo.

— Negãli bū́ti.

— Nà, taĩ kàs teñ lãpuose čežė́jo?

NOTES:
1. vìs dė́ltõ — 'nevertheless, in spite of that'.
2. taĩ jaũ — (here) 'at least'.

F. COMBINATION PRACTICE

Combine to make sentences:

I.

1. I am	a. 15 years old
2. Two years ago I was	b. 20 years old
3. His son is	c. 18 years old
4. My sister is	d. 23 years old
5. My daughter will be	e. 35 years old

Use either: *Màn penkerì mė́tai*
   or: *Àš esù penkerių̃ mė́tų* 'I am 5 years old' (See Lesson 24.)

II.

1. I am writing a letter	a. to him
2. I will write a letter	b. to her
3. His sister writes a letter	c. to my brother
	d. to my mother
	e. to them

III.

1. Every day	a. I work in the city
2. Every week	b. I read a book
3. Every month	c. He goes to New York
4. Every year	
5. Every winter	
6. Every summer	

IV.

1. He wanted to be	a. a student
2. I wanted to be	b. a teacher
	c. the president
	d. a professor
	e. a farmer

V.

1. My brother wants to live	a. in a new house
2. I don't want to live	b. in new houses
3. I will live	c. in large new houses
	d. in the village
	e. in large cities

G. VARIATION PRACTICE

a) *Màno brólis yrà penkiólikos mẽtų.*
b) *Màno bróliui yrà penkiólika mẽtų.*

1. My brother is 15 years old.
2. My sister is 5 years old.
3. My father is 51 years old.
4. My grandmother is 74 years old.
5. Tomorrow, she will be 16 years old.
6. Yesterday, he was 29 years old.
7. This university is 200 years old.
8. Our university is only 150 years old.
9. This castle is 800 years old.
10. Vilnius is 1000 years old.

Dvidešimt šeštoji pamoka

Lesson 26

VILNIUJE

Tìk ką atvỹkę į Vìlnių, abù pùsbroliai tuojaū skùbinosi iš-lìpti ìš tráukinio. Priē stóvinčio tráukinio jiē pamãtė daūg láu-kiančių žmonių. Taĩ bùvo Gedimìno šeimà, pažìstami iř draugaĩ, kuriē bùvo atėję sutìkti sàvo gimináičio ìš Amèrikos. Pasisvéikinę iř susipažìnę sù visaĩs láukiančiais giminėmìs iř pažįstamais, Ge-dimìnas iř Pêtras sudėjo sàvo lagaminùs į automobìlį iř važiãvo į Gedimìno namùs.

Važiúodami jiē kalbėjosi sù Gedimìno mótina, kurì taĩp pàt niekuomèt nebùvo mãčiusi Pêtro. Jì stebėjosi, kàd Pêtras, nórs iř gìmęs Amèrikoje iř niekuomèt nebùvęs Lietuvojè, taĩp geraĩ kaĺba lietùviškai. Važiúodami prõ Gedimìno kálną, jiē mãtė sēną Vìl-niaus kãtedrą, taĩp pàt Gedimìno piliēs bókštą.

Paválgę pietùs, abù pùsbroliai tuojaū išėjo pasiváikščioti miēsto gãtvėmis. Jiē pirmiáusia įlìpo į Gedimìno kálną, ìš kuř bùvo gãlima matýti bevéik vìsą sēną miēstą. Stovėdami Gedimìno bókšto viršujè, jiē mãtė põ jū kójomis gùlintį Vìlnių. Senãmiesčio gãtvės atródė labaĩ siaūros, ìš susiglaūdusių namų visuř kýšojo senų bažnýčių bókštai.

Jíems taĩp bežiūrint iř besìkalbant, atėjo vãkaras. Jiē sugrį̃žo namõ iř, susėdę Gedimìno namų sodėlyje, ilgaĩ kalbėjosi apiē se-nùs Vìlniaus pãstatus iř apiē taĩ, ką jiē darỹs rytój. Pêtras turėjo Gedimìno tėváms papãsakoti apiē sàvo tėvus, pasilìkusius Čikã-goje, apiē Čikãgą, apiē Amèriką, apiē sàvo ateitiēs planùs...

VOCABULARY

atvỹkti (atvykstù, atvỹksta, atvỹko, atvỹks) — to arrive
tuojaũ — right away
skùbintis (skùbinuosi, skùbinasi, skù-binosi, skùbinsis) — to hurry
išlìpti (išlipu, ìšlipa, išlìpo, išlìps) — to get off, to climb out
stovėti (stóviu, stóvi, stovėjo, stovės) — to stand
pažįstamas, -a (1) — acquaintance
sutìkti (sutinkù, sutiñka, sutìko, sutìks — (here) to meet
pasisvéikinti (pasisvéikinu, pasisvéi-kina, pasisvéikino, pasisvéikins) — to greet
sudėti (sùdedu, sùdeda, sudėjo, sudės) — to put in, to load in
kãtedra (1) cathedral
bókštas (1) — tower
paválgyti (paválgau, paválgo, pavál-gė, paválgys) — to eat (perfective)
pirmiáusia — first of all; in the first place

bevéik — almost
viršùs (4) — the top
senãmiestis -čio (1) — old city; the old part of the city
susiglaũsti* (susiglaudžiù, susiglaũ-džia, susìglaudė, susiglaũs) — to press together; to be very close to another
visuř — everywhere
kýšoti (kýšoja, kýšojo, kýšos) — to stick out
susėsti (susėdu, susėda, susėdo, su-sės) — to sit down, to sit together
sodėlis -io (2) — dim. of sõdas 'or-chard'; (here) garden, back yard
papãsakoti (papãsakoju, papãsakoja, papãsakojo, papãsakos) — to tell, to narrate
pasilìkti (pasiliekù, pasiliẽka, pasilì-ko, pasilìks) — to remain, to stay (behind)
sugrįžti (sugrįžtù, sugrįžta, sugrįžo, sugrįš) — to return

GRAMMAR

26.1 The Participles.

Participles in Lithuanian are similar to participles in English and other languages. They are a variety of adjectives derived from verbs. In Lithuanian they are inflected (declined) just like adjectives and they can denote, like adjectives, the characteristic of an object. But, since they are formed from verbs, they also have verbal characteristics, i.e. they can denote action and are inflected for tense and can be active and passive. In general, participles and special gerunds can be used in the following four cases: (1) as modifiers [adjectival use], (2) in compound tenses, (3) in separate participial phrases and (4) in indirect discourse in place of a verb.

The passive participles will be discussed in Lesson 33.

First we shall discuss the formation and then the meaning. Discussion of compound tenses is omitted from this lesson, except for the reflexives cf. 26.9,1.

---

* Several of the verbs in this lesson are irregular. The student should be able to spot these now and look them up in the Lith.-English Vocabulary.

26.2 The Present Active Participle

The present active participle is formed by replacing the 3rd person endings -*a*, -*i*, -*o* with the (masculine nominative singular) endings -*ąs*, -*įs*, -*ąs* or the (feminine nominative singular) endings -*anti*, -*inti*, -*anti*. Thus *nẽša* 'he carries' furnishes *neš-ąs*, *nẽš-anti* 'carrying'; *dìrba* 'he works' furnishes *dìrb-ąs*, *dìrb-anti* 'working'; *stóvi* 'he stands' furnishes *stov-įs*, *stóv-inti* 'standing'; *rãšo* 'he writes' furnishes *raš-ąs*, *rãš-anti* 'writing'. For the plural endings, see 26.2,1.

26.2,1 An example of the declension of the present active participle (*dìrbti* 'to work'):

Singular

	Masculine	Feminine
N.	dirbą̃s (or dìrbantis)	dìrbanti
G.	dìrbančio	dìrbančios
D.	dìrbančiam	dìrbančiai
A.	dìrbantį	dìrbančią
I.	dìrbančiu	dìrbančia
L.	dìrbančiame	dìrbančioje

Plural

	Masculine	Feminine
N.	dirbą̃ (or dìrbantys)	dìrbančios
G.	dìrbančių	dìrbančių
D.	dìrbantiems	dìrbančioms
A.	dìrbančius	dìrbančias
I.	dìrbančiais	dìrbančiomis
L.	dìrbančiuose	dìrbančiose

The forms in parentheses are used only when the participle is used in its simple adjectival function: *dìrbantis žmogùs* 'working man', *dìrbantys žmónės* 'working people', etc.

26.2,2 The present active participle may be used with a simple adjectival function. Examples:

1) *bėgantis (bėgą̃s) vanduõ* — running water
2) *skam̃bantis (skambą̃s) var̃pas* — ringing bell

26.2,3 The present active participle may be used in separate participial phrases. Examples:

1) *Profèsorius, skaitą̃s knỹgą, tuojaũ eĩs į̃ bibliotèką.* — The professor reading the book will go to the library immediately.

2) *Àš mačiaũ žmõgų, nẽšantį dìdelį maĩšą bùlvių.* — I saw a man carrying a big sack of potatoes.

Note that in example 1 the word *knỹgą* 'book' is in the accusative case because it is the direct object of the participle *skaitą̃s*. Likewise in example 2 *maĩšą* 'sack' is in the accusative case as the direct object of *nẽšantį*. The case, number and gender of the participle are determined by the case of the word modified. In the first sentence the word modified (*profèsorius*) by the participle is nominative singular masculine, but in the second sentence the word modified (*žmõgų*) is accusative singular masculine.

26.3 The Past Active Participle

The past active participle is formed by replacing the 3rd person simple preterit endings -*o* and -*ė* with the (masculine nominative singular) -*ęs* and the (feminine nominative singular) ending -*usi* (-*iusi* for all 3rd conjugation verbs). Thus, *dìrbo* 'he worked' furnishes *dìrbęs, dìrbusi* '(the one who has) worked'; *stovéjo* 'he stood' furnishes *stovéjęs, stovéjusi* '(the one who has) stood'; *rãšė* 'he wrote' furnishes *rãšęs, rãšiusi* '(the one who has) written'. For the plural endings, see 26.3,1.

26.3,1 An example of the declension of the past active participle (*dìrbti* 'to work'):

Singular

	Masculine	Feminine
N.	dìrbęs	dìrbusi
G.	dìrbusio	dìrbusios
D.	dìrbusiam	dìrbusiai
A.	dìrbusį	dìrbusią
I.	dìrbusiu	dìrbusia
L.	dìrbusiame	dìrbusioje

Plural

Masculine	Feminine
N. dìrbę	dìrbusios
G. dìrbusių	dìrbusių
D. dìrbusiems	dìrbusioms
A. dìrbusius	dìrbusias
I. dìrbusiais	dìrbusiomis
L. dìrbusiuose	dìrbusiose

26.3,2 The past active participle may be used with simple adjectival function. Example:

Mìrusio žmogaũs kū́nas negãli kéltis. — 'The body of a dead (literally: having died) man cannot arise.' This could have been expressed with a relative pronoun and a subordinate clause as follows: *Kū́nas žmogaũs, kurìs mìrė, negãli kéltis.* 'The body of a man who died cannot arise'.

26.3,3 The past active participle may be used in separate participial phrases. Examples:

1) *Àš mačiaũ žmõgų, atnẽšusį* (i.e. *kurìs àtnešė*) *jám tą̃ naũją knỹgą.* — I saw the man who brought him that new book.

2) *Kaimýnas atė́jo sù draugù, jaũ seniaĩ skaĩčiusiu tą̃ knỹgą.* — The neighbor arrived with a friend who had already read that book a long time ago.

26.3.4 The Frequentative Past Active Participle.

The frequentative past active participle is formed by removing the third person ending and adding the same endings as those used for the past active participle (see the preceding paragraph), e.g. *dìrbdavo* '(he) used to work' gives us the stem *dirbdav-* to which the (masculine nominative singular) ending *-ęs*, (feminine nominative singular) ending *-usi* can be added. Thus we find *dìrbdavęs, dìrbdavusi* etc. It is declined like the past active participle. It can be used in the same ways as the past active participle. An example of its use in place of a subordinate clause is given below:

Àš pažį́stu žmõgų, dìrbdavusį (i.e. *kurìs dìrbdavo*) *stovỹkloje vãsarą.* — I know a man who used to work in a camp during the summer.

26.3,5 The Future Active Participle

The future active participle is formed by adding the same endings as those used for the present active participle to the future stem (2nd person singular) -si. (Since all of the present active participle endings begin with a vowel, the orthographic -si- stands merely for palatalized -s-.) The endings (masc. nom. sing.) -ęs, (fem. nom. sing.) -anti etc. added to the stem dìrbsi—furnish the forms (masc. nom. sing.) dìrbsiąs, (fem. nom. sing.) dìrbsianti, etc. It is declined like the present active participle.

26.4 The Special Adverbial Active Participle.

There is a special adverbial active participle which is formed by dropping the infinitive ending -ti and adding the (masculine nominative singular) ending -damas, (feminine nominative singular) -dama. Since this only modifies the subject of the sentence it can only occur in the nominative case. The plural endings are (masculine) -dami, (feminine) -damos. From rašýti 'to write', nèšti 'to carry' we have the adverbial participles rašýdamas, nèšdamas, etc.

26.5 The adverbial participle always denotes an action which is performed by the subject and occurs simultaneously with the action of the main verb of the sentence. If the concomitant action is not performed by the subject of the main verb, then the special gerund (26.7) is used. Examples:

1) *Žmogùs miegódamas niẽko negiȓdi.* — The man hears nothing while sleeping.
2) *Žmogùs miegódamas niẽko negirdėjo.* — The man heard nothing while sleeping.
3) *Mergáitės dainúodamos grẽbė šiẽną.* — The girls raked hay as they sang.

This differs from the present active participle in that it cannot occur in any case but the nominative and in that the present active participle is adjectival in meaning, whereas the adverbial active participle has an adverbial meaning. Thus the sentence *miegą̃s žmogùs niẽko negiȓdi* means 'a sleeping man hears nothing', i.e. 'a man who is sleeping'. The adverbial active participle, on the other hand, merely denotes an action simultaneous with that of the main verb. It does not identify the man as does the participle.

26.6 The Neuter Forms of the Participles.

The neuter form of the active participle is the same as the nominative plural masculine. It may be used in impersonal sentences: *Ar̃ jaũ nustójo lìję?* 'Did it stop raining?'

26.7 The Special Gerunds.

A special gerund is formed from the active participles by dropping the final *-i* of the feminine nominative singular form, e.g. from *dìrbanti* we have the form *dìrbant*; from *dìrbusi* we have *dìrbus*; from *dìrbdavusi* we have *dìrbdavus*; from *dìrbsianti* we have *dìrbsiant*. This gerund denotes an action or situation which is accessory or incidental to the action of the main verb; such forms are used rather than the adverbial participle or the past active participle to show that the subject of the concomitant action is not the same as that of the main verb. Examples:

1) *Lȳjant mẽs ėjome namõ.* — (While it was) raining we went home.

2) *Baĩgus dárbą, reikė̃s pasilsė́ti.* — When the work is finished, it will be necessary to rest. (Lit.: Having finished the work, it will be necessary to rest.)

3) *Parãšius láišką, reĩkia nunèšti į̃ pãštą.* — Having written the letter, one must (lit.: it is necessary to) take it to the post-office.

4) *Tiẽsą sãkant, jìs kvailỹs.* — To tell the truth, he is a fool.

The gerund can have not only an object, but a subject too. Such a subject is put in the dative case and then we have what is known as a dative absolute construction. Examples:

5) *Jám kal̃bant, vìsi klaũso.* — When he is talking, everyone listens (lit.: him talking . . .)

6) *Sáulei tẽkant, jìs atsikė́lė.* — When the sun rose, he got up. (lit.: the sun rising . . .)

7) *Jìs išvažiãvo líetui lȳjant.* — While it was raining (lit.: the rain raining), he drove away.

Sometimes the gerund is used in such constructions as the following:

8) *Láukiu sūnaũs grį̃žtant.* — I am waiting for (my) son's return. One could have said also: *Láukiu sūnaũs grį̃žtančio.* — I am waiting for (my) son's return. There is no difference in meaning between the two sentences.

9) *Aš jį̃ palikaũ begùlint* (or) *Aš jį̃ palikaũ begùlintį.* — I left him lying down.

Since the participial phrase occupies a position between that of a part of a sentence and a complete sentence it can frequently be reduced to a simple adverb of circumstance, e.g. *tiẽsą sãkant* 'strictly speaking, to tell the truth'; *bendraĩ kal̃bant* 'generally speaking'; *ìmant dė́mesiñ* 'taking into consideration'; *išskýrus šį̃ dalỹką* 'except for this', etc.

26.8 The Active Participles and Gerunds of *bū́ti* and *eĩti*:

Infinitive	*bū́ti*	*eĩti*
Pres. Act. Partcpl.:	esą̃s, ė̃santi	einą̃s, eĩnanti
Past Act. Partcpl.:	bùvęs, bùvusi	ė̃jęs, ė̃jusi
Freq. Past Act. Partcpl.:	bū́davęs, bū́davusi	eĩdavęs, eĩdavusi
Future Act. Partcpl.:	bū́siąs, bū́sianti	eĩsiąs, eĩsianti
Adverbial Participle:	bū́damas, būdamà	eĩdamas, eidamà

Gerunds:

	Present:	ė̃sant	eĩnant
	Past:	bùvus	ė̃jus
	Future:	bū́siant	eĩsiant

26.9 The Reflexive Participle.

The participles can also be reflexive. The reflexive particle -*s* is added to the end of the simple participle in the singular and -*si* to the plural. In the masculine singular there is an -*i*- inserted between the particle and the final -*s* of the participial ending, so that two *s*'s will not come together.

Present Active Participle

gìrtis 'to brag'

Nominative Singular		*Nominative Plural*
Masculine	Feminine	Masculine
girią̃s-is	gìrianti-s	girią̃-si

Past Active Participle

sùktis 'to revolve'

Nominative Singular		*Nominative Plural*
Masculine	Feminine	Masculine
sùkęs-is	sùkusi-s	sùkę-si

These participles are used only in the masculine and feminine singular and the masculine plural.

26.9.1 If the verb is prefixed, then the reflexive particle -*si*- is inserted after the prefix, but before the root of the verb. Then all of the cases of the participle may be used, e.g. masc. nom. sing. *be-si-sukąs*, masc. gen. sing. *be-si-sùkančio*, masc. dat. sing. *be-si-sùkančiam* 'turning', etc.

Past active participle, masc. nom. sing. *pa-si-sùkęs*, masc. gen. sing. *pa-si-sùkusio*, masc. dat. sing. *pa-si-sùkusiam* 'having turned', etc.

26.9.2 A table illustrating the usage of the participles and gerunds is given below:

	The actions take place at the same time	The action of the participle or gerund precedes that of the main verb
Subject of main verb same as subject of participle	Adverbial participle -*damas* *Eĩdamas namõ, sutikaũ draũgą.* — Going home I met a friend.	Past active participle -*ęs, usi* *Parėjęs [parėjusi] namõ, radaũ svečiũ.* — Having arrived home, I found some guests.
Subject of main verb different from subject of participle	Present gerund -*ant* *Mán eĩnant namõ, draũgui neláimė atsitìko.* — While I was going home (my) friend had an accident.	Past gerund -*us* *Mótinai parėjus, vaikaĩ apsìdžiaugė.* — (Their) mother having arrived, the children rejoiced.

EXERCISES

A. *Questions.* 1. Ką̃ dãrė abù pùsbroliai, atvỹkę į̃ Vìlnių? 2. Ką̃ jiē pamãtė priẽ stóvinčio tráukinio? 3. Kõ bùvo atėję sutìkti Gedimìno gìminės iř pažį̃stami? 4. Sù kuõ jiē kalbėjosi, važiúodami pàs Gedimìną? 5. Ką̃ jiē mãtė, važiúodami prõ Gedimìno kálną? 6. Ką̃ jiē mãtė, stovėdami añt Gedimìno bókšto? 7. Apiẽ ką̃ jiē kalbėjo, susėdę sodėlyje? 8. Ař gãlima išlìpti ìš eĩnančio tráukinio? 9. Ař sveĩka skaitýti gùlint lóvoje? 10. Ař sveikiaũ válgyti sėdint ař stóvint?

B. *Form all four active participles, also the special adverbial active participle and the three special gerunds from the following verbs:* matýti, girdėti, skaitýti, piřkti, važiúoti,* válgyti, dúoti,* im̃ti,* kélti,* supràsti.*

Examples:

Infinitives and principal parts:

dìrbti (dìrba, dìrbo, diřbs — 1st conjugation)
mylėti (mýli, mylėjo, mylės — 2nd conjugation)
rašýti (rãšo, rãšė, rašỹs — 3rd conjugation)

Present active participles:

dirbą̃s, dìrbanti
mylį̃s, mýlinti
rašą̃s, rãšanti

Past active participles:

dìrbęs, dìrbusi
mylėjęs, mylėjusi
rãšęs, rãšiusi

Frequentative past active participles:

dìrbdavęs, dìrbdavusi
mylėdavęs, mylėdavusi
rašýdavęs, rašýdavusi

---

* Irregular verbs; look up their principal parts in the Lithuanian-English Vocabulary.

Future active participles:
dìrbsiąs, dìrbsianti
mylḗsiąs, mylḗsianti
rašýsiąs, rašýsianti

Special adverbial active participles:
dìrbdamas, dirbdamà
mylḗdamas, mylḗdama
rašýdamas, rašýdama

Special present tense gerund:	dìrbant
	mýlint
	rãšant
Special past tense gerund:	dìrbus
	mylḗjus
	rãšius
Special future tense gerund:	dìrbsiant
	mylḗsiant
	rašýsiant

C. *Decline in the singular and plural:* dirbą̃s žmogùs, bùvęs studeñtas (a former student), bḗgą̃s vaĩkas, skaĩtanti studeñtė, rãšanti mergáitė.

D. *Translate into Lithuanian:* 1. I saw a man standing on the street. 2. While driving we saw the old church. 3. Standing on the top of the tower. 4. I like my former (bùvęs) teacher. 5. (While) lying in bed, he was reading a book.

E. *Re-write the reading passage of this lesson replacing all participles and gerunds by relative clauses. Examples:* 1) Tìk ką̃ atvýkę į̃ Vìlnių, . . . Kaĩ jiē tìk atvýko į̃ Vìlnių, . . . 2) Priē stóvinčio tráukinio jiē pamãtė daũg žmonių̃. Priē tráukinio, kurìs stovḗjo, jiē pamãtė daũg žmonių̃, kuriē láukė. 3) Važiúodami prõ Gedimìno kálną, . . . Kaĩ (kadà) jiē važiãvo prõ Gedimìno kálną, . . . 4) Stovḗdami añt Gedimìno bókšto . . . Kaĩ (kadà) jiē stovḗjo añt Gedimìno bókšto, . . . etc. . . ., etc. . . .

CONVERSATION

ORAS

Paũlius: 1. Lãbas rýtas, Tãdai, kaĩp išmiegójai?

Tãdas: 2. Lãbas, lãbas. Sušalaũ bemiegódamas: kaĩp žinaĩ, bùvo labaĩ šaltà naktìs, õ àš palikaũ lángą̃ ãtvirą . . .

213

Paulius: 3. Aš nežinaū, kàs čià pasidārė, kàd šiẽmet tóks šáltas pavāsaris.
Tadas: 4. Turbū̃t, Kanadà supýko añt Amèrikos, taĩ pùčia sàvo šáltą órą į̃ pietùs . . .
Paulius: 5. Mẽs jaũ norėjome gėlių̃ pasodiñti, bèt bìjome, nès dár gãli bū́ti šalnà
Tadas: 6. Aš vākar skaičiaū laĩkraštyje, kàd dár tókio šálto pavāsario čià niekuomèt nėrà bùvę.
Paulius: 7. Važiúokime į̃ Flòridą: teñ vākar bùvo 85 láipsniai, õ pàs mùs — 34. Brrrr . . .
Tadas: 8. Aš pérnai buvaū nuvažiāvęs į̃ Flòridą, bèt teñ mán bùvo peř̃ kár̃šta.
Paulius: 9. Nuvažiāvęs į̃ Flòridą, àš nórs sušìlti galė́čiau . . .
Tadas: 10. Nesiskùbink: peř̃ rādiją prànešė, kàd rytõj iř̃ pàs mùs bùs 75 láipsniai . . .

THE WEATHER

Paul: 1. Good morning, Tadas. Did you sleep well?
Tadas: 2. Hello, hello! I got frozen while sleeping: as you know the night was very cold, and I left the window open.
Paul: 3. I don't know what happened here that we are having such cold weather.
Tadas: 4. Perhaps Canada got mad at America, and so they blow their cold weather down to the south . . .
Paul: 5. We already wanted to plant some flowers, but we are afraid because there still may be frost.
Tadas: 6. I read in the paper yesterday that there had never been such a cold spring hereabouts.
Paul: 7. Let us go to Florida: they had 85 down there yesterday, and here we had 34. Brrrr . . .
Tadas: 8. I went down to Florida last year, but it was too hot for me down there.
Paul: 9. Getting to Florida at least would make me warm . . .
Tadas: 10. Do not hurry: it was announced on the radio that we will have 75 degrees here tomorrow . . .

NOTES:

9. **Nuvažiāvęs į̃ Flòridą, àš nórs sušìlti galė́čiau:** Lit.: 'After having gone to Florida, I at least could get warm'.

Dvidešimt septintoji pamoka

Lesson 27

TRAKAI

Pavãsaris yrà gražiáusias mẽtų laĩkas: diẽnos dabař yrà il-gèsnės, õ nãktys trumpèsnės. Aukščiaũ iř aukščiaũ kỹla sáulė, iř visì žmónės dãrosi linksmesnì. Vìs daugiaũ iř daugiaũ paũkščių čiuĺba mẽdžiuose iř sõduose. Màno mãmai labiaũ patiñka ruduõ negù pavãsaris, Rūtà sãko, kàd jái linksmiáusia yrà žiẽmą, màno tẽvui labiáusiai patiñka vãsara, bèt mán iř bróliui gražiáusia iř linksmiáusia yrà pavãsarį.

Víeną sekmãdienio rýtą mẽs sù bróliu atsikẽlėme anksčiaũ negù paprastaĩ, greičiaũ nusìprausėme iř paválgėme pùsryčius. Mẽs norẽjome tą rýtą nuvažiúoti dvìračiais į Trakùs, kuř ketì-nome aplankýti senùs piliẽs griuvėsiùs. Trãkų apýlinkės pavãsarį dár gražèsnės iř įdomèsnės negù žiẽmą: ẽžero vanduõ atródo gi-lèsnis iř skaidrèsnis, žmónės judresnì iř draugiškesnì.

Màno brólis Výtautas yrà stiprèsnis ùž manè, todẽl jìs gãli greičiaũ važiúoti dvìračiu negù àš. Tačiaũ àš jám nenóriu pasi-dúoti, nórs àš jaunèsnis iř silpnèsnis. Taĩp belenktyniáudami mẽs greĩtai pasíekiame Trakùs, kuř žmónės dár tìk kẽliasi.

Trãkų ẽžero salojè stóvi vienõs iš seniáusių iř garsiáusių Lie-tuvõs pilių griuvėsiai. Čià jaũ seniáusiais laikaĩs bùvo vienà iš svarbiáusių Lietuvõs tvirtóvių. Čià gyvẽno didỹsis Lietuvõs kuni-gáikštis Gediminas, kurìs vẽliau pastãtė dár didèsnę pìlį Vìlniuje, į kuř jìs pérkėlė Lietuvõs sóstinę. Vìlnius nuõ tõ laĩko tãpo di-džiáusiu iř gražiáusiu Lietuvõs miestù.

Trakai

pavãsaris -io (1) — spring
mẽtų laĩkas — season
kìlti (kylù, kỹla, kìlo, kiĩs) — to rise
darýtis (daraũsi, dãrosi, dãrėsi, darý-
    sis) — to become
liñksmas (4) — gay, happy, cheerful
vìs + comparative adj. or adverb —
    more and more...
paũkštis -čio (2) — bird
čiulbẽti (čiùlbu, čiùĩba, čiulbẽjo, čiul-
    bẽs) — to sing (of a bird)
ruduõ (3b) — fall, autumn
žiemà (4) — winter
vãsara (1) — summer
sekmãdienis -io (1) — Sunday
atsikẽlti (atsìkeliu, atsìkelia, atsìkẽ-
    lė, atsikeĩs) — to get up
ankstì — early
negù — than
paprastaĩ — usually
nusipraũsti (nusiprausiù, nusipraũsia,
    nusìvrausė, nusipraũs) — to wash
    up
paválgyti (paválgau, paválgo, pavál-
    gė, paválgys) — to eat, to have a
    meal
nuvažiúoti (nuvažiúoju, nuvažiúoja,
    nuvažiãvo, nuvažiuõs) — to go, to
    drive, to get somewhere (with a
    vehicle)
Trãkai (2) — Trakai (city)
ketìnti (ketinù, ketìna, ketìno, ketiñs)
    — to intend
aplankýti (aplankaũ, aplañko, aplañ-
    kė, aplankỹs) — to visit
pilìs -iẽs (fem.) (4) — castle

griuvẽsiai (usually only pl.) (2) —
    — ruins
apýlinkė (1) — surroundings, area,
    district
įdomùs, -ì (4) — interesting
dár — (here) even
ẽžeras (3b) — lake
gilùs, -ì (4) — deep
skaidrùs, -ì (3) — clear, transparent,
    clean
judrùs, -ì (4) — agile, active
draũgiškas, -a (1) — friendly
ùž — (here) than
pasidúoti (pasidúodu, pasidúoda, pa-
    sìdavė, pasiduõs) — to give in, to
    give up
sìlpnas, -à (4) — weak
tačiaũ — but, nevertheless
belenktyniáudami — racing, trying to
    outdo each other
pasíekti (pasíekiu, pasíekia, pasíekė,
    pasíẽks) — to reach
kẽltis (keliúosi, kẽliasi, kẽlėsi, keĩsis)
    — to get up, to be getting up
salà (4) — island
garsùs, -ì (4) — famous
svarbùs, -ì (4) — important
tvirtóvė (1) — fortified castle
didỹsis kunigáikštis — Grand Duke
pastatýti (pastataũ, pastãto, pastãtė,
    pastatỹs) — to build
pérkelti (pérkeliu, pérkelia, pérkėlė,
    pérkels) — to move to, to transfer
tàpti (tampù, tam̃pa, tãpo, tàps) —
    to become (with instrumental)

GRAMMAR

27.1 Comparison of Adjectives.

There are three basic degrees of comparison in Lithuanian just as in English: the positive, the comparative and the superlative.

27.2 The Positive Degree.

This degree has already been discussed in Lesson 11 - 14; it merely denotes a characteristic or quality, e.g. *báltas* 'white', *saũsas* 'dry'.

27.3 The Comparative Degree.

The comparative degree is formed by dropping the -as, -ias, -us or -is* of the masculine nominative singular of the adjective and adding -esnis (-esnė for feminine) which is then declined like an adjective of the first declension:

Masculine

Singular		Plural	
N.	gerèsnis (2) 'better'	geresnì	
G.	gerèsnio	gerèsnių (geresnių̃)	
D.	gerèsniam (geresniám)	gerèsniems (geresníems)	
A.	gerèsnį	geresniùs	
I.	geresniù	gerèsniais (geresniaĩs)	
L.	gerèsniame (geresniamè)	gerèsniuose (geresniuosè)	

Feminine

	Singular	Plural	
N.	gerèsnė	gerèsnės	
G.	gerèsnės (geresnė̃s)	gerèsnių (geresnių̃)	
D.	gerèsnei	gerèsnėms (geresnė̃ms)	
A.	gerèsnę	geresnès	
I.	geresnè	gerèsnėmis (geresnėmìs)	
L.	gerèsnėje (geresnėjè)	gerèsnėse (geresnėsè)	

(The forms in parentheses show the alternate class 4 accentuation which is characteristic of conversational style.)

The comparative degree denotes that there is a greater degree of the quality in question in one object than in another. The concept "than" is expressed by nekaĩp or more often by negù with the following noun in the nominative case or ùž with the accusative case. Examples:

1) *Tàvo rankà baltèsnė negù màno rankà.* — Your hand is whiter than my hand.

2) *Jõ knygà yrà gerèsnė negù tàvo knygà.* — His book is better than your book.

3) *Màno žmonà gražèsnė negù tàvo.* — My wife is more beautiful than yours.

---

* With the adjectives of the third declension in -is and -ė, there is practically no comparison. Cf. English: wooden, iron, etc.

4) *Šìs obuolỹs minkštèsnis nekaĩp tàs.* — This apple is softer than that one.
5) *Béržas aukštèsnis ùž klẽvą.* — A birch is taller than a maple.

27.4 The Superlative Degree.

The superlative degree is formed by dropping the *-as, -ias, -us (-is*)* of the masculine nominative singular of the adjective and adding *-iáusias (-iáusia* for fem.); if the stem ends in *-d* or *-t* these are replaced by *-dž* and *-č* respectively.

The superlative degree denotes the highest or greatest existing degree of the quality expressed by the adjective. Examples:

1) *Taĩ yrà minkščiáusias obuolỹs.* — That is the softest apple.
2) *Àš mataũ gražiáusią mergáitę.* — I see the most beautiful girl.
3) *Mūsų ármija yrà galingiáusia iš visų ármijų.* — Our army is the strongest of all the armies.

27.5 In the adjective *dìdelis* 'big' the ending *-elis* is dropped before the addition of the comparative or superlative endings. Thus we find *didèsnis* 'bigger', *didžiáusias* 'biggest'. The declension of *didžiáusias* 'biggest' is given below:

Masculine

	Singular	Plural
N.	didžiáusias (1)	didžiáusi
G.	didžiáusio	didžiáusių
D.	didžiáusiam	didžiáusiems
A.	didžiáusią	didžiáusius
I.	didžiáusiu	didžiáusiais
L.	didžiáusiame	didžiáusiuose

Feminine

	Singular	Plural
N.	didžiáusia	didžiáusios
G.	didžiáusios	didžiáusių
D.	didžiáusiai	didžiáusioms
A.	didžiáusią	didžiáusias
I.	didžiáusia	didžiáusiomis
L.	didžiáusioje	didžiáusiose

---

* See footnote for 27.3.

27.6 There is a degree which is somewhat stronger than the positive and weaker than the comparative which is formed with the suffix (masculine) *-ėlèsnis*, (feminine *-ėlèsnė*), thus from *gēras* 'good' we have *gerėlèsnis -ė* 'a little better', 'somewhat better.' Some other transitional stages are expressed by the prefixes *apy-* and *po-* or the suffix *-okas*, (feminine *-oka*), e. g. *apýgeris* 'pretty good', *pójuodis* 'pretty black', *mažókas* 'rather small'.

27.7 The Comparison of Neuter Adjectives.

The neuter adjective* also has a comparative *-iau*, superlative *-iausia*. Examples:

1) *Šiañdien gražiaũ nekaĩp vãkar.* — Today it is more beautiful than yesterday.
2) *Mán lengviáusia mókytis lietùvių kalbõs.* — It is easiest for me to study Lithuanian.

One should be careful not to confuse the superlative of the neuter adjective such as the form *lengviáusia* with the superlative of the corresponding adverb such as *lengviáusiai*, discussed in paragraph 27.8.

27.8 The Comparison of Adverbs*

The comparative degree of the adverbs ends in *-iau*. Thus the comparatives of *geraĩ* 'well', *lengvaĩ* 'easily', *gražiaĩ* 'beautifully' are respectively *geriaũ, lengviaũ, gražiaũ*. The superlative degree of the adverb ends in *-iáusiai* if the positive degree ends in *-ai*. The superlative degree of the preceding three adverbs is *geriáusiai, lengviáusiai, gražiáusiai*. For the adverbs which do not end in *-ai* in the positive degree, the superlative ending is *-iáusia*, e.g. positive *daũg* 'much, many', comparative *daugiaũ* 'more', superlative *daugiáusia* 'most'; positive *artì* 'near', comparative *arčiaũ*, superlative *arčiáusia*. (Note that in the adverb as in the adjective *-d* and *-t* are replaced by *-dž* and *-č* before the ending *-iau*.) Examples:

1) *Jìs tùri daugiaũ knýgų negù àš.* — He has more books than I.
2) *Aš lengviáusiai mókausi lietùvių kalbõs.* — I study Lithuanian most easily.
3) *Jìs gyvẽna arčiáusia.* — He lives the closest.

---

* For the positive of the neuter adjective, see 12.3.
* For the formation of adverbs, see 12.2.

EXERCISES

A. *Questions.* 1. Kurìs yrà gražiáusias mẽtų laĩkas? 2. Kám labiaũ patiñka ruduõ negù pavãsaris? 3. Kadà mẽs atsikẽlẽme ankščiaũ negù paprastaĩ? 4. Kuř yrà Trãkai? 5. Kurìs miẽstas yrà didèsnis: Vìlnius ař Trãkai? 6. Kaĩp mẽs ketìname važiúoti į̃ Trakùs? 7. Kuř stóvi Trãkų pilìs? 8. Kàs gyvẽno Trãkuose? 9. Kàs pastãtẽ didèsnę pìlį Vìlniuje? 10. Kurìs yrà didžiáusias iř gražiáusias Lietuvõs miẽstas?

B. *Give comparatives and superlatives of the following adjectives. Then decline them in the singular and plural, combining with nouns given below:*
dìdelis, mãžas, gẽras, blõgas, áukštas, žẽmas, puikùs, baisùs, báltas, jáunas, sẽnas, tólimas, platùs, siaũras, sunkùs, leñgvas.
nãmas, miẽstas, mergáitė, brólis, knygà, gãtvė, lietùs, ùpė, akmuõ, nósis, arklỹs, studeñtas.

C. *Using examples given before, make* **30** *sentences, following the patterns:*

a) Màno nãmas yrà senèsnis negù jū́sų nãmas.

b) Màno nãmas yrà senèsnis ùž jū́sų nãmą.

c) Màno nãmas yrà seniáusias.

D. *Translate into Lithuanian:* 1. I want to buy a larger house. 2. My father is much older than her father. 3. They live in a much larger, older and more beautiful city than we (do). 4. My sister is the most beautiful girl in our whole city. (In Lithuanian reverse the position of *our* and *whole*). 5. My brother can run much faster than yours. 6. Our house is the most beautiful in the whole area. 7. His automobile is much more expensive than mine. 8. He wants to move to a smaller and quieter town. 9. This lesson is more difficult than that one. But the following (sẽkanti) lesson is the most difficult in the whole book. 10. My younger brother speaks Lithuanian much better than I (do).

CONVERSATION

PERSIKĖLIMAS

Pẽtras: 1. Kodẽl tù nóri pardúoti sàvo nãmą?
Jõnas: 2. Mataĩ, àš nóriu pérsikelti į̃ didèsnį iř švarèsnį miẽstą.

Petras: 3. Bèt jùk Filadèlfija* yrà víenas iš didžiáusių miẽstų Amèrikoje!

Jonas: 4. Taĩp. Teisýbė, bèt Los Angeles yrà iř didèsnis iř gražèsnis.

Petras: 5. Bèt lietùvių teñ yrà daũg mažiaũ negù Filadèlfijoje.

Jonas: 6. Aš tõ tikraĩ nežinaũ. Girdėjau, kàd vìs daugiaũ iř daugiaũ lietùvių pérsikelia į Los Angeles.

Petras: 7. O kaĩp tàvo žmonà iř vaikaĩ: ař jiẽ iřgi nóri išvažiúoti iš Pensilvãnijos*?

Jonas: 8. Taĩp. Jíems čià jaũ nusibódo.

Petras: 9. Ką̃ gi padarýsi. Laimìngos keliõnės!

Jonas: 10. Ačiū. Jéigu mùms teñ nepatìks, taĩ vėl sugrį̃šime.

MOVING

Peter: 1. Why do you want to sell your house?

John: 2. Well, you see, I want to move to a larger and cleaner city.

Peter: 3. But Philadelphia is one of the largest cities in America, is it not?

John: 4. Yes. That's right, but Los Angeles is larger and more beautiful.

Peter: 5. But there are far fewer Lithuanians there than in Philadelphia.

John: 6. I do not know that for sure. I heard that more and more Lithuanians are moving to Los Angeles.

Peter: 7. What about your wife and the children? Do they also want to leave Pennsylvania?

John: 8. Yes. They are getting bored (tired of it) here.

Peter: 9. Well, what can you do. Bon voyage!

John: 10. Thanks. If we do not like it there, then we will come back.

NOTES:

2. **pérsikelti** — 'to move'; **per-si-kelti: per-** — through, over; **-si-** — reflexive particle; **kélti** — lift, lift up. (Literal translation: 'to lift oneself up to another place)'

4. **Teisýbė** — lit. 'the truth', here: 'that's right'.

---

* For the forms and usage of proper names, see Lesson 30.

5. **lietùvių** — gen. pl. because of **mažiaū** — 'less, fewer'; **daūg mažiaū lietù-vių** — 'far fewer (of the) Lithuanians', **lietùvių** is used right after **bèt** for emphasis. Same applies for **lietùvių** in 6: **Vìs daugiaū iř daugiaū lietùvių** — 'more and more (of the) Lithuanians'.

8. **nusibósti (nusibósta, nusibódo, nusibõs)** — irreg., primarily used only impersonally, with dative:

   mán nusibósta, nusibódo — I am tired of, was tired of ...
   táu nusibósta, nusibódo — (thou) are tired of, were tired of ...
   jám nusibósta, nusibódo — he is tired, was tired, etc.

9. **Ką̃ gì padarýsi.** — lit. 'What will you do' (future).

   Laimìngos keliónės. — Genitive because it implies the verb **linkéti** which governs that case: (I wish you) a good trip: (**Aš linkiù táu) laimìngos keliónės.**

Dvidešimt aštuntoji pamoka
Lesson 28

GRAŽIOJI VASARA

Visì mẽtų laikaĩ yrà grãžūs: šaltóji žiemà, žaliàsis pavãsaris, spalvingàsis ruduõ, tačiaũ vãsara yrà gražiáusias mẽtų laĩkas. Vãsarą diẽnos yrà ìlgos, nãktys — truĩpos. Vãsarą didíeji miškaĩ yrà pilnì raudonū̃jų úogų i̇̃ skaniū̃jų grỹbų. Plačiuõsiuose laukuosè žaliúoja javaĩ i̇̃ daržaĩ.

Žìnoma, kaĩ kàs mẽgsta taĩp pàt ilgą́sias žiemõs naktìs, lietìngą́sias rudeñs dienàs, bèt mán labiáusiai patiñka grãžiosios vãsaros diẽnos, kaĩ ū́kininkai vìsą diẽną dìrba sàvo žaliuõsiuose laukuosè.

Pirmóji vãsaros dienà yrà 22 (dvìdešimt antróji) birželio. Tą̀ diẽną prasìdeda vãsara. Nè tìk pradžiõs mokỹklose, bèt taĩp pàt i̇̃ aukštõsiose mokỹklose prasìdeda vãsaros ìlgosios atóstogos.

Tìk labaĩ gaĩla, kàd tõs ìlgosios atóstogos taĩp greĩtai praeĩna . . .

VOCABULARY

mẽtų laĩkas — season (of the year)
spalvìngas, -a (1) — colorful
didỹsis, didžióji — great, the big one
pìlnas, -à (3) — full
úoga (1) — berry
grỹbas (2) — mushroom
žaliúoti (žaliúoju, žaliúoja, žaliãvo, žaliuõs) — to be green
jãvas (4) — crop
daržas (4) — vegetable garden
žìnoma — to be sure, of course
kaĩ kàs — some (people)
lietìngas, -a (1) — rainy (cf. lietùs 'rain')
pirmàsis, pirmóji — the first

birželis -io (2) — June
prasidéti (prasìdeda, prasidėjo, prasidė̃s) — to begin (intransitively, primarily in 3rd person only)
pradžiõs mokyklà — elementary school
aukštóji mokyklà — university; college; institution of higher learning
ìlgosios atóstogos — the long vacation (summer vacation)
gaĩla — (here) it is too bad
greĩtai — fast
praeĩti (praeinù, praeĩna, praẽjo, praeĩs) — to pass, to go by, to go past. Cf. eĩti

225

GRAMMAR

28.1 The Definitive Adjective.

In general the forms of the definite adjective are obtained by adding the appropriate case of the 3rd person pronoun to the indefinite adjective:

báltas - jìs ('white - he') — baltàsis

baltà - jì ('white - she') — baltóji

But there are certain changes in the vowels in their declension which the student should note.

Masculine

Singular	Plural
N. baltàsis (3) 'white'	baltíeji
G. báltojo	baltū́jų
D. baltájam	baltíesiems
A. báltąjį	baltúosius
I. baltúoju	baltaĩsiais
L. baltãjame (-jam)*	baltuõsiuose (-iuos)

Feminine

Singular	Plural
N. baltóji	báltosios
G. baltõsios	baltū́jų
D. báltajai	baltósioms
A. báltąją	baltą́sias
I. baltą́ja	baltõsiomis
L. baltõjoje (-oj)	baltõsiose (-ios)

Masculine

Singular	Plural
N. sausàsis (4) 'dry'	sausíeji
G. saũsojo	sausū́jų
D. sausájam	sausíesiems
A. saũsąjį	sausúosius
I. sausúoju	sausaĩsiais
L. sausãjame (-jam)	sausuõsiuose (-iuos)

---

* The alternate endings given in parentheses are shorter endings used mainly in spoken language, also in poetry whenever handy and needed.

Feminine

Singular		Plural
N.	sausóji	saũsosios
G.	sausõsios	sausũjų
D.	saũsajai	sausósioms
A.	saũsąją	sausą́sias
I.	sausą́ja	sausõsiomis
L.	sausõjoje (-oj)	sausõsiose (-ios)

28.2 Although it is not necessary to have an active knowledge of the dual declension, for recognition knowledge a sample is given below:

N. & A.	dù baltúoju lángu	dvì baltíeji rankì
	'the two white windows'	'the two white hands'
D.	dvíem baltíe(m)jiem langám	dvíem baltójom rañkom
I.	dviẽm baltiẽ(m)jiem langam̃	dviẽm baltõjom rañkom

The stress pattern of the dual of *sausàsis* 'dry' is the same as that of *baltàsis*. The rest of the forms of the dual are the same as those of the corresponding plural form. One m a y use plural forms in all cases instead of dual forms, e.g. nom. *dù baltíeji langaĭ*, acc. *dù baltúosius lángus*, etc.

The definite form of the adjective *dìdis* 'great'

Masculine

Singular		Plural
N.	didỹsis (4)	didíeji
G.	dìdžiojo	didžiũjų
D.	didžiájam	didíesiems
A.	dìdįjį	didžiúosius
I.	didžiúoju	didžiaĩsiais
L.	didžiájame	didžiũosiuose

Feminine

Singular		Plural
N.	didžióji	dìdžiosios
G.	didžiõsios	didžiũjų
D.	dìdžiajai	didžiósioms
A.	dìdžiąją	didžią́sias
I.	didžią́ja	didžiõsiomis
L.	didžiõjoje	didžiõsiose

28.3 If we wish to point out some particular object in a group of similar objects we can use the definite form of the adjective. Example: *Krautùvéje yrà daũg lémpų — geltónų, raudónų, baltų. Mán daugiaũ patiñka tà baltóji.* 'In the store are many lamps, yellow, red, white. I prefer the (that) white one.'

NB. In most cases the English *Adjective+one* construction could be best rendered by the definite adjective in Lithuanian.

28.4 An adjective can be definite also in its comparative and superlative degree. Examples:

gēras 'good' *gerèsnis* 'better', def. form: *geresnýsis, geresnióji*
              geriáusias 'best', def. form: *geriáusiasis, geriáusioji*

More about this, especially declension, see *Appendix: Adjectives.*

Many participles (both active and passive) also have definite forms. See *Appendix: Participles* (under: *Verbs*).

28.5 The definite form of the adjective may also impart a generic meaning to the noun, because of the fact it denotes a permanent characteristic. Thus *júodas gañdras* merely means 'a black stork', i.e. a stork which happens to be black, whereas *juodàsis gañdras* is the variety 'black stork' (Latin *Ciconia nigra*). Likewise *pirmà pamokà* means 'a first lesson' or the first lesson in a series of lessons without implying anything about the content of the lessons. On the other hand, *pirmóji pamokà* means 'the first lesson' and implies that there is something in the lesson itself which makes it the first one, i.e. that there is some inherent firstness in the lesson. This is the reason why the definite adjectives are used in proper names: *Baltíeji Rūmai* 'The White House', *Výtautas Didỹsis* 'Vytautas the Great', *Naujóji Zelándija* 'New Zealand', etc.

In many cases the definite adjectives differ very little from the simple adjectives. The definite adjectives merely emphasize more the attributive characteristics of the noun. Thus, their use is often subjective.

EXERCISES

A. *Questions.* 1. Kurìs yrà gražiáusias mētų laĩkas? 2. Kadà dídieji miškaĩ yrà pilnì úogų? 3. Kàs žaliúoja vãsarą plačiuõsiuose laukuosè? 4. Kókios diēnos yrà žiēmą? 5. Kókios diēnos yrà rùdenį? 6. Kuř dìrba ūkininkai vãsarą? 7. Kadà prasìdeda vãsara?

8. Kuriuõ mẽtų laikù yrà ìlgosios atóstogos? 9. Kàs greĩtai praeĩna? 10. Kurìs mẽtų laĩkas júms labiáusiai patiñka?

B. *Decline in the singular and plural:* žaliàsis mìškas, geràsis studeñtas, gražióji vãsara.

C. *Form sentences with the following expressions:* aukštà mokyklà, aukštóji mokyklà; pirmà pamokà, pirmóji pamokà; gẽras tẽvas,
geràsis tẽvas; brangì knygà, brangióji knygà.

D. *Translate into Lithuanian:* 1. The forests of Lithuania are
beautiful. 2. In the beautiful forests of Lithuania there are many
old trees. 3. It was my first lesson in the new school. 4. The new
school is in the center of the city. 5. I always like new teachers.
6. Our teacher is a Lithuanian. 7. New cars are very expensive.
8. All the new cars are very beautiful. 9. He bought a new house.
10. He already lives in his new house.

CONVERSATION

ATOSTOGOS

Tãdas: 1. Klausýkite, mẽs tùrime nutar̃ti, kur̃ šią̃ vãsarą pra-
léisime atóstogas.

Rūtà: 2. Aš taĩ nóriu važiúoti kur̃ nórs į̃ káimą, nès àš labaĩ
mẽgstu árklius . . .

Paũlius: 3. O àš nóriu važiúoti tiktaĩ priẽ Atlánto. Teñ taĩ gãlima tikraĩ pasimáudyti!

Tadas: 4. Aš nóriu važiúoti į̃ Kanãdą, į̃ tólimąją šiáurę — teñ
taĩ tikraĩ nekár̃šta.

Rūta: 5. Geraĩ: tù, Tãdai, važiúok į̃ Kanãdą, tù, Paũliau, važiúok priẽ Atlánto, o àš važiúosiu pàs kókį ūkininką.

Paulius: 6. Kaĩpgi mẽs gãlime taĩp važiúoti: mẽs tùrime tìk víeną automobìlį.

Tadas: 7. Aš jaũ galiù víenas nuvažiúoti autobusù arbà tráukiniu į̃ Kanãdą.

Paulius: 8. Aš taĩ skrìsiu lėktuvù: taĩp daũg greičiaũ . . .

Rūta: 9. Jūs tìk víeną dalỹką užmir̃štate: tokióms ilgóms ke-
liónėms reĩkia daũg pinigų̃, õ pinigų̃ jūs nè víenas
netùrite.

Tadas: 10. Teisýbė . . . Reikės, turbū́t, kartù sù tėvẽliais važiúoti atóstogų . . .

VACATIONS

Tadas: 1. Listen, we have to decide where we are going to spend our vacation this summer.

Ruta: 2. I want to go to the village (countryside) somewhere because I like horses so much...

Paul: 3. And I, I want to go only to the Atlantic. There one can really swim!

Tadas: 4. I want to go to Canada, to the far North: there certainly it will not be hot.

Ruta: 5. All right: you, Tadas, you go to Canada; you Paul, you go to the Atlantic, and I am going to go to some farmer's.

Paul: 6. How can we really go this way: we have only one car.

Tadas: 7. I can go alone by bus or by train to Canada.

Paul: 8. I will fly by plane: it is faster this way...

Ruta: 9. You are forgetting one thing: for such long trips one has to have much money, and you have no money.

Tadas: 10. That is true... Most probably, we will have to go together with our parents on vacation.

NB: These are three children of the same family planning their vacation...

Dvidešimt devintoji pamoka

Lesson 29

KLASĖJE

Mókytojas: Kàs nóri šiandien pìrmas skaitýti pāmoką?

Jõnas: Kurią pāmoką mēs šiandien skaitýsime?

Mókytojas: Šiandien mēs skaitýsime peñktąją pāmoką.

Jõnas: O aš maniaũ, kàd mēs skaitýsime ketviřtąją pāmoką, nès àš penktõsios pamokõs dár geraĩ neišmókau...

Mókytojas: Peñktąją pāmoką mēs pàbaigėme vākar. Daugiaũ jõs jaũ klāsėje nekartósime. Jũs tùrite ją išmókti namiẽ, nès jì nėrà sunkì.

Antānas: Aš vākar namiẽ buvaũ pradėjęs skaitýti šēštąją pāmoką, bèt àš jõs nesuprantù. Pìrmą pùslapį pérskaičiau trìs kartùs iř, tìk trēčią kařtą skaitýdamas, kaĩ ką pradėjau supràsti.

Mókytojas: Geraĩ. Pirmiáusia mēs pérskaitysime peñktąją pāmoką, o põ tõ àš jùms paáiškinsiu šēštąją pāmoką.

VOCABULARY

kurìs, kurì — which

manýti (manaũ, māno, mānė, manỹs) —to think

išmókti (išmókstu, išmóksta, išmóko, išmõks) — to learn (well)

pabaĩgti (pabaigiù, pabaĩgia, pàbaigė, pabaĩgs) — to finish (perfective)

daugiaũ — more

daugiaũ nè... — no more, no longer

kartóti (kartóju, kartója, kartójo, kartõs) — to repeat, to review

pùslapis -io (1) — page

pradėti (pràdedu, pràdeda pradėjo, pradės) — to begin

supràsti (suprantù, supranñta, suprãto, supràs) — to understand

pirmiáusia — in the first place

pérskaityti (pérskaitau, pérskaito, pérskaitė, pérskaitys) — to read (through)

paáiškinti (paáiškinu, paáiškina, paáiškino, paáiškins) — to explain (perfective)

29.1 The Ordinal Numerals.

The ordinal numbers denote place in a series. They are declined like regular adjectives and agree with the word they modify in case, number and gender. Some are listed below:

Masculine Nom. Sing.	Feminine Nom. Sing.	
pìrmas (3)	pirmà	first
añtras (4)	antrà	second
trẽčias (4)	trečià	third
ketviřtas (4)	ketvirtà	fourth
peñktas (4)	penktà	fifth
šẽštas (4)	šeštà	sixth
septiñtas (4)	septintà	seventh
aštuñtas (4)	aštuntà	eighth
deviñtas (4)	devintà	ninth
dešim̃tas (4)	dešimtà	tenth
vienúoliktas (1)	vienúolikta	eleventh
dvýliktas (1)	dvýlikta	twelfth
trýliktas (1)	trýlikta	thirteenth
keturióliktas (1)	keturiólikta	fourteenth
penkióliktas (1)	penkiólikta	fifteenth
šešióliktas (1)	šešiólikta	sixteenth
septynióliktas (1)	septyniólikta	seventeenth
aštuonióliktas (1)	aštuoniólikta	eighteenth
devynióliktas (1)	devyniólikta	nineteenth
dvidešim̃tas (4)	dvidešimtà	twentieth
trisdešim̃tas (4)	trisdešimtà	thirtieth
keturiasdešim̃tas (4)	keturiasdešimtà	fortieth
penkiasdešim̃tas (4)	penkiasdešimtà	fiftieth
šešiasdešim̃tas (4)	šešiasdešimtà	sixtieth
septyniasdešim̃tas (4)	septyniasdešimtà	seventieth
aštuoniasdešim̃tas (4)	aštuoniasdešimtà	eightieth
devyniasdešim̃tas (4)	devyniasdešimtà	ninetieth
šim̃tas (4)	šimtà	hundredth
dušim̃tas	dušimtà	two hundredth
túkstantas (1)	túkstanta	thousandth

Examples:

1) *Aš esù pìrmą kar̃tą Amèrikoje.* — This is my first time in America.
2) *Trẽčią diẽną jìs jaũ išvỹko namõ.* — (On) the third day he left for home.

29.2 The Definite Ordinal Numerals.

Every ordinal numeral can also be used, like any other adjective, in its definite form. The definite forms are made like the adjectives of the 1st declension (-as, -a). Examples:

1) *Žvìlgterėk į trẽčiąją klãsę.* — Look into the third class (room).
2) *Jų̃ pirmàsis vaĩkas mažėsnis ùž añtrąjį.* — Their first child is smaller than (their) second.

29.3 In a compound ordinal number only the final element has the form of an ordinal and is declined. The other elements remain in the nominative case.

N.   Keturì šimtaĩ peñkiasdešimt aštuñtas vaĩkas —
      the four hundred fifty eighth child'
G.   Keturì šimtaĩ peñkiasdešimt aštuñto vaĩko
D.   Keturì šimtaĩ peñkiasdešimt aštuntám vaĩkui
A.   Keturì šimtaĩ peñkiasdešimt aštuñtą vaĩką
      etc.

29.4 The Reflexive Pronoun *savę̃s*

Reflexive (all numbers)
(No nominative)

G. savę̃s (sàvo)
D. sáu
A. savè
I. savimì, saviñ
L. savyjè, -ỹj, -ỹ

The reflexive pronoun *savę̃s*, etc. generally refers to the subject of the sentence, whatever person the subject may be. Therefore in English it may be translated as 'myself, yourself, himself, ourselves, yourselves, themselves' depending upon whether the subject is 1st, 2nd or 3rd person and whether it is singular or plural. Examples:

1) *Àš negailiù savę̃s.* — I am not sorry for myself.
2) *Dìrbame sáu, nè sàvo žmonóms.* — We are working for ourselves, not (our) wives.
3) *Tù stataĩ savè į pavõjų.* — You are putting yourself in danger.
4) *Jìs pasiìm̃s knýgą sù savimì.* — He will take the book with him.

233

29.5 The Emphatic Pronoun *pàts* 'oneself'

The emphatic pronoun *pàts* 'oneself' is declined as follows:

Masculine

Singular		Plural
N.	pàts (4)	pãtys
G.	patiẽs	pačiũ
D.	pačiám	patíems
A.	pãtį	pačiùs
I.	pačiù	pačiaĩs
L.	pačiamè	pačiuosè

Feminine

	Singular	Plural
N.	patì (4)	pãčios
G.	pačiõs	pačiũ
D.	pãčiai	pačióms
A.	pãčią	pačiàs
I.	pačià	pačiomìs
L.	pačiojè	pačiosè

The emphatic pronoun emphasizes or sets off the noun or the pronoun to which it refers. Examples:

1) *Jìs pàts taĩ žìno.* — He himself knows that.
2) *Vaikaĩ jaũ pãtys paválgo.* — The children already (know how to) eat by themselves.
3) *Jì patì vienà atẽjo.* — She came all by herself.

EXERCISES

A. *Questions.* 1. Kàs nóri pìrmas skaitýti pãmoką? 2. Kurì yrà pirmóji alfabèto raĩdė? 3. Kàs pirmàsis atrãdo (discovered) Amèriką? 4. Kaĩp vadìnasi penktóji saváitės dienà? 5. Kurią pãmoką mókytojas nóri skaitýti? 6. Kurì yrà lengviáusia pamokà šiojè (in this) gramãtikoje? 7. Kurì yrà sunkiáusia pamokà? 8. Kurią pãmoką mẽs pàbaigėme vãkar? 9. Kuriõs pamokõs mẽs daugiaũ nekartósime? 10. Kurią pãmoką mókytojas paáiškins?

B. *Decline in the singular and plural:* pìrmas pùslapis, pirmàsis pùslapis; pirmà pamokà, pirmóji pamokà; pirmà gãtvė, pirmóji gãtvė; trečià knygà, trečióji knygà.

C. *Translate into Lithuanian:* 1. I am the second son. 2. He is already reading the fifth book. 3. Only the first five days are difficult. 4. We are going to read the twenty-fifth lesson. 5. They are repeating the eighteenth lesson.

CONVERSATION

VASARA

Výras: 1. Lãbas vãkaras, Onùte. Kodėl šiandien atródai tokià pavar̃gusi?

Žmonà: 2. Ar̃ tù užmiršai̇̃, kàd šiandien pirmà vãsaros dienà?

Vyras: 3. Tikrai̇̃ buvaũ užmir̃šęs. Bèt...

Žmona: 4. Matai̇̃, pavãsaris bùvo šáltas, o šiandien bùvo kár̃šta: vãsara pagaliaũ atėjo.

Vyras: 5. Tai̇̃ ką̃ tù šiandien dìrbai? Gėlès láistei?

Žmona: 6. Nè, niėko ypatìngo nedariaũ, tìk sù kaimýnėmis laukè kalbėjausi...

Vyras: 7. Štai̇̃ kai̇̃p... Tai̇̃ todėl tai̇̃p pavargai̇̃ ir̃ pietùms niėko negalėjai paruõšti...

Žmona: 8. Galì pàts pasiim̃ti ką̃ nõrs iš šaldytùvo. Mán galvà skaũda.

Vyras: 9. Gerai̇̃, gerai̇̃, tìk nepradėk pýkti.

Žmona: 10. Aš nepykstù. Aš nekaltà, kàd tai̇̃p kár̃šta. O, žinai̇̃, Žukiėnė mán pásakojo, kàd...

SUMMER

Husband: 1. Good evening, Anne dear. Why do you look so tired today?

Wife: 2. Did you forget that today is the first day of summer?

Husband: 3. I had really forgotten (all about it). But...

Wife: 4. You see, spring was cold, and today was very warm: summer finally arrived.

Husband: 5. Well, what did you do today? Did you water the flowers?

Wife: 6. No, I did not do anything special, only chatted with the neighbors outside...

Husband: 7. That's what it is... That's why you got tired and did not prepare anything for dinner...

Wife: 8. You yourself can get something from the refrigerator. I have a headache.

Husband: 9. All-right, all-right, don't get angry.

Wife: 10. I am not angry: I cannot help it, that it is so hot. You know, Mrs. Žukas told me that...

NOTES:

7. **Pietùms** — 'for dinner', (dative plural).

9. **tìk nepradėk pýkti** — lit. 'only do not start to get angry'.

10. **aš nekaltà, kàd tai̇̃p kár̃šta** — lit. 'I am not guilty (responsible) that it is so hot'.

Animals and Their Young-Ones

DOMESTIC ANIMALS:

horse, mare, stallion, colt — *arklys, kumelė, eržilas, kumeliu-*
cow, bull, calf — *karvė, bulius, veršis*   [*kas*
ewe, ram, lamb — *avis, avinas, ėriukas*
sow, boar, piglet — *kiaulė, kuilys, paršas*
hen, rooster, chicken — *višta, gaidys, viščiukas*

WILD ANIMALS:

Wolf, she-wolf, wolf-cub — *vilkas, vilkė, vilkiukas*
lion, lioness, lion-cub — *liūtas, liūtė, liūtukas*
elephant, elephant (cow), elephant-cub — *dramblys, "dramb-
lienė", drambliukas*

Trisdešimtoji pamoka
Lesson 30

A. NON-LITHUANIAN PROPER NAMES
IN LITHUANIAN

Just like other nouns, most of the proper names in Lithuanian are also inflected, i.e. supplied with endings. These endings can be attached to the name which is otherwise unchanged, e.g. *Bòs-tonas*, or the name may be adapted somewhat to Lithuanian spelling, e.g. *Berlýnas* 'Berlin', *Stòkholmas* 'Stockholm'. Some proper names are used without Lithuanian endings. Thus we have three basic ways of rendering foreign names in Lithuanian.

a) Names ending in -*a* are not changed at all, whereas other names require the ending -*as* or -*is*. Ending -*a*: Romà, Manilà, Barcelonà, Lisabonà, Pizà; ending -*as*: Bòstonas, Detròitas, Bèrnas, Hártfordas, Leningrãdas, Lòndonas, Madrìdas, Hámburgas, Tehe-rãnas; ending -*is* Brìstolis, Dènveris, Hèlsinkis.

b) A rather large number of proper names have Lithuanian endings, but the spelling is somewhat changed. Ending -*as*: Niu-jòrkas, Vãšingtonas, Berlýnas, Miùnchenas, Toròntas, Kaìras, Pè-kinas, Budapèštas, Bukarèštas, Kìjevas, Strãsburgas, Stòkholmas; ending -*is* (gen. -*io*): Montreãlis, Versãlis, Bãzelis, Lìverpulis, Mar-sèlis; ending -*us*: Parýžius, Šanchãjus, Altãjus; ending -*a*: Čikagà, Kalkutà, Maskvà, Váršuva, Víena, Filadelfija, Hirošimà, Venèci-ja, Floreñcija, Ženevà; ending -*ė*: Báltimorė, Adeláidė.

The proper names of groups a) and b) are usually names which have been used in Lithaunian for a long time, i.e. they are familiar to most Lithuanians. However in Lithuanian newspapers in foreign countries, proper names are also used in their original spelling with Lithuanian endings, e.g. New Yorkas, Washingtonas, Chicaga, etc.

c) Certain names are usually used without any attempt to adapt them to Lithuanian patterns: Atlantic City, Salt Lake City, Los Angeles, Milwaukee, Bordeaux, Rio de Janeiro, etc. Such names are usually not inflected, but if one has to use, let us say, the locative case, one usually says 'in the city of Rio de Janeiro' — *Rio de Janeiro miestè, Salt Lake City miestè*, etc.

Above we have given only names of cities, but what we have said for cities holds true, of course, for all proper names. Examples:

a) States: Oregònas, Màrylandas, but New Jersey, Ohio, etc.
b) Family names: Adamsas, Mādisonas, Garibáldis, Eisenhoweris, Wèbsteris, but Kennedy, McKinley, Lodge, etc.
    A few names have been adapted:
    Vāšingtonas, Liñkolnas, Šekspýras ('Shakespeare'), Moljèras, Voltèras, Dantė, Heinė, Goethė, even Gėtė, etc.

It is suggested that the student should note the usage of proper names as he reads Lithuanian texts. Some Lithuanian newspapers use an apostrophe after the foreign name, inflecting it as may be required. Examples:

Dean Rusk — (1) Dean Rusk or (2) Dean'as Rusk'as
                                 (Dean'o Rusk'o, etc.)
De Gaulle — (1) De Gaulle or (2) De Gaulle'is
                            (gen. De Gaulle'io, etc.)

Some Lithuanian dictionaries also give usage in regard to proper names.

In Soviet occupied Lithuania, following the practice of Russian, all foreign names are spelled and pronounced in a more or less Lithuanian form: *Churchill* becomes *Čiorčilis*, *Massachusetts* becomes *Masačiusetsas*, etc.

B. COMBINATION PRACTICE

I.

a. we live	1. in large houses
b. we lived	2. in big cities
c. we will live	3. by the large rivers
	4. near the dark forests
	5. near the beautiful harbors

238

II.

a. I am	1. 30 years old*
b. I was	2. 42 years old
c. I will be	3. 55 years old
d. My father is	4. 33 years old
e. My sister is	5. 91 years old

III.

a. dúok mán	1. a new book
b. dúokite mán	2. a new pencil
c. kodėl mán nedúodate	3. her interesting letter

C. VARIATION PRACTICE

I.

a) *Màno brólis yrà trìsdešimt penkerių̃ mẽtų (ámžiaus).*

b) *Màno bróliui (yrà) trìsdešimt penkerì mẽtai.*

1. My brother is 35 years old.
2. My sister is 15 years old.
3. Professor Žukas is 62 years old.
4. His wife is 35 years old.
5. My son is 7 years old.

II.

Aš rašaũ profèsoriui Jonýnui láišką.

1. I am writing a letter to professor Jonynas.
2. She is writing a letter to the president.
3. He wrote a long letter to his parents.
4. I will write a letter to my mother tomorrow.
5. Why didn't you write* me a letter yet?

---

* Give two versions: a) Mán trìsdešimt mẽtų.
    b) Aš esù trisdešimtiẽs mẽtų (ámžiaus).
* did ... not write — **neparašeĩ** (perfective).

Foods

A. MEATS:

beef — *jautiena* (from *jautis* 'ox')
pork — *kiauliena* (from *kiaulė* 'pig)
veal — *veršiena* (from *veršis* 'calf')
mutton (lamb) — *aviena* (from *avis* 'sheep')
ham — *kumpis*
bacon — *lašiniai* (plural only)
sausage — *dešra*

B. OTHER FOODS:

potato — *bulvė*
flour — *miltai* (plural only)
sugar — *cukrus*
salt — *druska*
milk — *pienas*
butter — *sviestas*
cheese — *sūris*
cream — *grietinė*
cottage cheese — *varškė*
coffee — *kava*
tea — *arbata*
honey — *medus*

Trisdešimt pirmoji pamoka

Lesson 31

LAIŠKAS IŠ VILNIAUS

Vìlnius, 1940. II. 17.

Brángūs tėvėliai,

Aš tìk vãkar vakarè atvažiavaũ į̃ Vìlnių. Jéigu bū́čiau žinójęs, kàd Vìlnius tóks gražùs miẽstas, taĩ bū́čiau daũg anksčiaũ atvažiãvęs. Bè tõ, vãkar Vìlniuje iř visojè Lietuvojè bùvo švenčiamà Nepriklausomýbės Šveñtė — Vasãrio 16-ji (šešióliktoji), taĩ vìskas bùvo labaĩ įdomù. Vasãrio šešióliktoji yrà Lietuvojè maždaũg kaĩp Líepos 4-ji (ketvirtóji) Amèrikoje. Vìlniuje bùvo daũg parãdų, koncèrtų, visuř plevėsãvo vė̃liavos: geltóna, žalià, raudóna . . .

Kàd aš žinóčiau, kàs Jùms įdomù, taĩ daũg parašýčiau. Bèt kadángi aš esù labaĩ pavařgęs, o visókių įspūdžių turiù daugýbę, taĩ tìk norė́čiau Jùms pranèšti, kàd esù kelionè labaĩ paténkintas. Norė́čiau Vìlniuje ilgiaũ pabū́ti, jéigu Jū̃s mán galė́tute atsių̃sti daugiaũ pinigų̃ . . .

Prašaũ mán parašýti, kàs Jùms įdomù, taĩ tadà daugiaũ parašýsiu. Iř gál mán rytój pasių̃stute kókius penkìs šimtùs dólerių . . .

Jùs mylį̃s sūnùs

J ù r g i s .

VOCABULARY

jéigu — if
tóks, tokià (3) — such
anksčiaū — earlier
bè tõ — in addition to that, moreover
švę̃sti (šveñčia, šveñtė, švę̃s) Irreg.: švenčiù, šventì, šveñčia; šveñčiame, šveñčiate, šveñčia — to celebrate
taĩ — (here) so, thus, then
maždaūg — approximately
parãdas (2) — parade
plevėsúoti (plevėsúoja, plevėsãvo, plevėsuõs) — to flutter (in the wind), to sway
vėliava (1) — flag

kadángi — because
visóks, visókia (1) — of all kinds, various
daugýbė (1) — multitude, mass
pranèšti (prànešu, pràneša, pranèš) — to inform, to let know, to announce
atsių̃sti (atsiunčiù, atsiuñčia, àtsiuntė, atsių̃s) Irreg.: atsiunčiù, atsiuntì, atsiuñčia; atsiuñčiame, atsiuñčiate, atsiuñčia — to send
kóks, kokià (3) — what kind, how
kókius penkìs šimtùs — about 500 dollars (or so)

GRAMMAR

31.1 The Subjunctive Mood.

The subjunctive is formed by removing the infinitive ending -*ti* and adding the endings listed below:

	Singular	Plural
1.	rašý-čiau	rašý-tume*
2.	rašý-tum	rašý-tute
3.	rašý-tų	rašý-tų

31.2 The subjunctive mood may be used in both the main clause and the if-clause of a sentence which contains a contrary-to-fact condition. Examples:

1) *Jéigu àš bū́čiau turtìngas, àš nusipìrkčiau batùs.* — If I were rich, I would buy (some) shoes.

2) *Jéigu jìs bū́tų protìngas, taĩp nedarýtų.* — If he were wise, he would not do (it).

3) *Jéigu jìs parašýtų jùms láišką, jūs apsidžiaū́gtute.* — If he would write you a letter, you would rejoice.

4) *Jéi tù padė́tum, àš tuõj baĩgčiau.* — If you would help, I would finish immediately.

5) *Jéi prašýtum, gáutum.* — If you would ask, you would receive.

6) *Jéi paieškótum, ràstum.* — If you would seek, you would find.

---

* Next to **mēs rašýtume** and **jūs rašýtute**, longer forms are used in various writings: **mēs rašýtumėm(e)**, **jūs rašýtumėt(e)**.

242

Note, however, that if there is no contrary-to-fact condition, then the subjunctive mood is not required, e.g. *Jéi galė́siu, ateĩsiu.* — If I can, I shall come. (The future tense—not the present, as in English—is used with *jéi* 'if', when a future time is implied.) An example with the present tense: *Jéi nežinaĩ, nekalbė́k.* — If you don't know, don't say (anything).

31.3 The subjunctive mood is also used to express purpose, generally with the subordinating conjunction *kàd* 'that', in order that'. Examples:

1) *Jìs nóri, kàd àš dìrbčiau.* — He wants me to work. (Lit.: He wants that I should work.)
   Note that in Lithuanian you cannot use the object of a verb of wishing or saying as the subject of an infinitive as you can in English.

2) *Màno draũgas prãšo, kàd àš taĩ padarýčiau.* — My friend asks me to do it.

3) *Kàd tù prasmègtum!* — May you fall through. (Expression equivalent to English 'May the deuce take you.')

4) *Kàd iř kaĩp prašýtum, negáusi.* — No matter how much you may (would) beg, you'll not get (it).

31.4 The Subjunctive Progressive Tense.

The subjunctive progressive is a compound of the subjunctive of the verb *bū́ti* plus the present active participle of the verb in question (with the prefix *be-*).

rašýti 'to write'

	Singular		Plural	
	Masculine	Feminine	Masculine	Feminine
1.	bū́čiau berašą̃s,	berãšanti	bū́tume berašą̃,	berãšančios
2.	bū́tum berašą̃s,	berãšanti	bū́tute berašą̃,	berãšančios
3.	bū́tų berašą̃s,	berãšanti	bū́tų berašą̃,	berãšančios

Examples:

1) *Dabař àš jaũ bū́čiau bemiegą̃s, jéigu nè tàs triùkšmas.* — I would be asleep (sleeping) now, if it weren't for that noise.

2) *Jì bū́tų jaũ bedìrbanti, jéigu nè lietùs.* — She would be working already, if it weren't for the rain.

31.5 The Subjunctive Preterit.

The subjunctive preterit is a compound of the subjunctive of the verb *bū́ti* plus the past active participle of the verb in question.

rašýti 'to write'

Singular		Plural	
Masculine	Feminine	Masculine	Feminine
1. bū́čiau rãšęs,	rãšiusi	bū́tume rãšę,	rãšiusios
2. bū́tum rãšęs,	rãšiusi	bū́tute rãšę,	rãšiusios
3. bū́tų rãšęs,	rãšiusi	bū́tų rãšę,	rãšiusios

31.6 Examples of the use of the subjunctive progressive and the subjunctive preterit:

1) *Bū́tum berašą̃s láišką, jéigu nebū́čiau sutrùkdęs.* — You would (still) be writing the letter, if I had not disturbed (you).

2) *Kàd bū́tume tiesiõg važiãvę, dabar̃ jaũ bū́tume bùvę miestè.* — If we had come directly, then we would already have been in the city.

3) *Jéigu bū́tum strõpiai mókęsis, taĩ bū́tum geriaũ baĩgęs pradìnę mokỹklą.* — If you had studied diligently, then you would have finished primary school better.

4) *Kaĩp gardžiaĩ jìs bū́tų iš savę̃s júokęsis, jéigu bū́tų pàts savè iš šaliẽs mãtęs.* — How heartily he would have laughed at himself, if he could have seen himself from outside.

EXERCISES

A. *Questions.* 1. Kám Jùrgis rãšo láišką? 2. Ką̃ jìs bū́tų dãręs, jéigu jìs bū́tų žinójęs, kàd Vìlnius yrà tóks gražùs miẽstas? 3. Kokià šveñtė bùvo švenčiamà Lietuvojè? 4. Kur̃ bùvo daũg koncèrtų, parãdų? 5. Kokià yrà Lietuvõs vėliava? 6. Ar̃ Jùrgis yrà paténkintas kelionè? 7. Kur̃ jìs norė́tų ilgiaũ pabū́ti. 8. Kodė́l jìs prãšo sàvo tėvų̃ atsių̃sti jám daugiaũ pinigų̃? 9. Kadà jìs daugiaũ parašỹs sàvo tėváms? 10. Kíek jám reĩkia pinigų̃?

B. *Give the subjunctive present and subjunctive preterit tenses of the following verbs:* bū́ti, eĩti, važiúoti, matýti, rašýti, skaitýti.

C. *Change the following real if-clauses into the contrary-to-fact statements, referring to the present time and to the past: Example:* (Real if-clause): Jéigu àš turė́siu laĩko, taĩ àš ateĩsiu. (Contrary-to-fact if-clause referring to the present time): Jéigu àš turė́čiau laĩko, taĩ àš ateĩčiau. (Contrary-to-fact if-clause referring to the past time): Jéigu àš bū́čiau turė́jęs laĩko, taĩ àš bū́čiau atė́jęs. 1. Jéigu àš važiúosiu į̃ Líetuvą, taĩ àš gyvénsiu Vìlniuje. 2. Jéigu jū̃s nórite geraĩ išmókti lietùviškai, taĩ tùrite važiúoti į̃ Líetuvą. 3. Jéigu àš turė́siu automobìlį, taĩ àš važiúosiu į̃ Kanãdą. 4. Jéigu laukè lýja, taĩ mẽs negãlime eĩti į̃ mokýklą. 5. Jéigu jìs bùs gḗras studeñtas, taĩ jìs išmóks geraĩ lietùviškai kalbė́ti, skaitýti iř rašýti.

D. *Translate into Lithuanian:* 1. If I were rich, I would give you a thousand dollars. 2. If I had been rich, I would have given you a hundred dollars. 3. If I lived in Lithuania, I would know Lithuanian very well. 4. If I had lived in Lithuania, I would have known Lithuanian very well. 5. I would go to Canada if I had a new car. 6. I would have gone (važiúoti) to Canada, if I had had a new car. 7. If I had more time, I would help you. 8. I would have helped you, if I had had more time. 9. Our teacher would buy this expensive book, if he had money. 10. Her teacher would have bought this fine book, if she had had the money. (For *money* use *pinigų̃*, a partitive genitive plural.)

CONVERSATION

JEIGU AŠ TURĖ́ČIAU MILIJONĄ DOLERIŲ...

Aldonà: 1. Jéigu àš turė́čiau milijõną dólerių, taĩ àš tuojaũ važiúočiau į̃ Itãliją...

Jõnas: 2. Į̃ Itãliją?! O ką̃ gì tù teñ darýtum?

Aldona: 3. Aš vìsiškai niẽko nedarýčiau, õ tìk gyvénčiau gražiáusioje vìloje kuř nórs Ròmos príemiestyje, kasdiẽn eĩčiau į̃ La Scala òperą...

Jonas: 4. Pirmiaũ táu reikė́tų geriaũ susipažìnti sù geogrãfija: La Scala yrà nè Ròmoje, õ Milanè!

Aldona: 5. Taĩ kàs? Tù taĩ jaũ labaĩ gudrùs! O ką̃ gì tù darýtum, jéigu tù turė́tum milijõną dólerių?

Jonas: 6. Aš... hm... Pirmiáusia padė́čiau pìnigus į̃ bánką, õ paskuĩ jaũ sugalvóčiau, ką̃ darýti... Bèt taĩ tìk tàvo tùščios svajõnės. Geriaũ pagalvótum, ką̃ mẽs šiañdien darýsime.

Aldona: 7. Eĩkime į̃ kìną!

Jonas: 8. Iř àš norė́čiau eĩti, bèt neturiù pinigų̃...

245

Aldona: 9. Jéigu bū́tum vãsarą ilgiaũ dìrbęs fabrikè, taĩ dabař turė́tum pinigų̃. Aš táu paskólinčiau, jéigu žinóčiau, kàd mán greĩtai grąžìnsi.

Jonas: 10. Taĩgi, bū́tų geraĩ, kàd àš turė́čiau nórs penkìs dólerius . . .

IF I HAD A MILLION DOLLARS . . .

Aldona: 1. If I had a million dollars, I would go to Italy right away . . .

Jonas: 2. To Italy?! And what would you do there?

Aldona: 3. I would not do anything at all. I would just live in the most beautiful villa somewhere in a suburb of Rome. I would go to La Scala every day . . .

Jonas: 4. First, you should get better acquainted with geography: La Scala is not in Rome, but in Milan!

Aldona: 5. So what? You are really a clever one! And what would you do, if you had a million dollars?

Jonas: 6. I . . . hm . . . First of all, I would deposit the money in a bank, and then I would figure out what to do (with it) all right . . . But these are only your empty dreams. You had better think over what we are going to do today.

Aldona: 7. Let's go to the movies!

Jonas: 8. I would like to go, too, but I have no money . . .

Aldona: 9. If you had worked longer at the factory in the summer, you would now have (some) money. I would lend it to you, if I knew that you would return (it) soon (to me).

Jonas: 10. Gee, it would be nice, if I had at least five dolars . . .

NOTES:

3. **vìsiškai niẽko** — lit. 'completely nothing'.
4. **taĩ jaũ** — lit. 'so already'; idiomatically: 'really, indeed'.
5. **svajõnės** — lit. 'day-dreams, reveries, imaginings'.
8. **iř** — here it means 'too, also'.
9. **pinigų̃** — gen. plural of **pinigaĩ** 'money'. Sing. **pìnigas** is used only to indicate a single individual coin.
10. **nórs** — it means 'although' as a conjunction, but here as an adverb it means 'only, at least'.

246

Trisdešimt antroji pamoka

Lesson 32

RYTĄ

Jõnas: Algirdai, kélkis! Jaũ aštúonios, õ mēs deviñtą vãlandą jaũ tùrime būti universitetè. Profèsorius Valáitis labaĩ nemēgsta, kaĩ studeñtai vėlúoja į jõ pãskaitas.

Algirdas: Geraĩ, geraĩ. Pagaĺ màno laĩkrodį dár tìk pùsė aštuoniǫ. Matýt, màno laĩkrodis vėlúoja.

Jonas: Praėjusią savãitę tù pramiegójai dvì pãskaitas. Iř vìs tàvo laĩkrodis bùvo kaĺtas. Nèšk sàvo laĩkrodį pàs laĩkrodininką pataisýti, nès kitaĩp tù vìsą semèstrą vėlúosi į profèsoriaus Valáičio pãskaitas.

Algirdas: Šį mēnesį àš dár negaliù ... Neturiù pinigǫ. Ateĩnantį mēnesį àš gál turėsiu daugiaũ pinigǫ. Sakýk, kadà prasìdeda Kalėdǫ atóstogos?

Jonas: Paláuk, àš pažiūrėsiu į kalendõrių. Kalėdǫ atóstogos prasidės devynióliktą grúodžio, trečiãdienį. Vadìnas, ùž trijǫ savãičių. Bèt àš nóriu važiúoti namõ anksčiaũ, gál pirmãdienį, septyniólikтą grúodžio, õ gál dár anksčiaũ.

Algirdas: Kíek dabař laĩko? Jaũ mán tikraĩ reĩkia kéltis!

Jonas: Dabař jaũ dēšimt (minùčių) põ aštuoniǫ. Tù pasiskùbink apsireñgti, õ àš jaũ baigiù ruõšti pùsryčius. Pùsė devyniǫ mēs jaũ tùrime išeĩti iš namǫ.

Algirdas: Geraĩ, geraĩ. Peř dēšimt minùčių àš būsiu pasiruõšęs.

VOCABULARY

kéltis (keliúosi, kēliasi, kélėsi, keĺsis) — to get up, to rise

vėlúoti (vėlúoju, vėlúoja, vėlãvo, vėluõs) — to be late

paskaità (3b) — lecture

pagaĺ (prep. with acc.) — according to; along

laĭkrodis -džio (1) — watch, clock

praėjęs, praėjusi (past active participle of **praeĭti** 'to pass') — last, the last (referring to time); past

saváitė (1) — week

pramiegóti (pramiegù, pramiēga, pramiegójo, pramiegõs) — to oversleep

iĭ vìs — (here) and for all this, all the time

kaĺtas, -à (4) — guilty, responsible

nèšti (nesù, nesa, nėšė, nėš) — to carry, to take to

pàs (prep. with acc.) — by, near, at the house of; (here) to

laĭkrodininkas (1) — watchmaker

pataisýti (pataisaũ, pataĭso, pataĭsė, pataisỹs) — to repair

nès — because

kitaĭp — otherwise

semèstras (2) — semester

pasivėlúoti (pasivėlúoju, pasivėlúoja, pasivėlãvo, pasivėluõs) — to be late; to get (somewhat late) somewhere

mėnuo (gen. mėnesio, see Appendix) — month

Kalėdos (plural only) — Christmas

atóstogos (plural only, fem., 2nd decl.) — vacation

kalendõrius (2) — calendar

grúodis -džio (1) — December

trečiãdienis -io (1) — Wednesday

vadìntis (vadinúosi, vadìnasi, vadìnosi, vadìnsis) — to call oneself; to mean; to express

vadìnas — it means; thus

ùž (preposition with gen. and acc.) — (here) in

anksčiaũ — earlier (from **ankstì** 'early')

gál — perhaps

pirmãdienis -io (1) — Monday

tikraĭ — indeed, for sure

pasiskùbinti (pasiskùbinu, pasiskùbina, pasiskùbino, pasiskùbins) — to hurry up

apsireñgti (apsirengiù, apsireñgia, apsìrengė, apsireñgs)—to get dressed

baĭgti (baigiù, baĭgia, baĭgė, baĭgs) — to finish, to be finishing

ruõšti (ruošiù, ruõšia, ruõšė, ruõš) — to prepare

išeĭti (išeinù, išeĭna, išėjo, išeĭs) — to go out, to leave

peĭ (prep. with acc.) — through, across; (here) in, in the course of

pasiruõšti (pasiruošiù, pasiruõšia, pasìruošė, pasiruõš) — to get prepared, to get ready, to get finished

GRAMMAR

32.1 The Hour of the Day.

32.1,1 'What time is it?' may be expressed by:

1) *Kíek laĭko?* (lit.: 'How much time?')

2) *Kurì dabaĭ valandà?* (lit.: 'Which hour is it now?')

3) *Kelintà dabaĭ valandà?* (lit.: 'Which hour is it now?')

The student may use any one of these expressions, but (1) is preferred because of its brevity.

32.1,2 To answer the question 'What time is it?' one generally uses the cardinal number with the hours: Examples:

1) *Dabaĭ septýnios.* — It is now seven o'clock.

2) *Dabař trỹs válandos (rýto).* — It is now three o'clock (A.M.; in the morning)
3) *Dabař dvýlika (valandũ) naktiẽs.* — It is now twelve midnight.
4) *Dabař (lýgiai) dvýlika.* — It is now (exactly) twelve noon.
5) *Dabař vienà.* — It is now one o'clock.
6) *Dabař dẽšimt.* — It is now ten o'clock.

In examples (5) and (6) the cardinals may be replaced by ordinals in popular speech: (5a) *Dabař pirmà.* — It is now one PM; (6a) *Dabař dešimtà.* — It is now ten PM.
7) *Dabař peñkios (minùtės) põ dvýlikos.* — It is now five after twelve.
7a) *Dabař peñkios (minùtės) põ dvýliktos.* — It is now five minutes after twelve.

32.1,2 (cont.) The half hours are as follows:

8) *Dabař pùsė pirmõs.* — It is now half past twelve. (Note that the ordinal is used here.)
9) *Dabař pùsė dviejũ.* — It is now half past one.
Contrary to example (8) above the cardinal is commonly used rather than the ordinal here. But it should be pointed out that the construction: *Dabař pùsė antrõs.* — 'It is now half past one', is also possible.
10) *Dabař pùsė trijũ.* — It is now half past two.
11) *Dabař pùsė keturiũ.* — It is now half past three.
12) *Dabař pùsė penkiũ.* — It is now half past four. Etc.

Note that in this usage (with *pùsė*) the ordinal number refers to the preceding hour; in other words the first hour is that between twelve and one o'clock, the second hour is that between one and two, etc.

32.1,3 *The Hour plus Minutes.* There are two ways of expressing the hour plus the minutes: one is an 'official' way, e.g. for radio programs, time-tables, etc. and the other way is the popular way. Examples:

        a) official time
        b) popular expression

1:05   a) vienà (valandà) (iř) peñkios (minùtės)
       b) peñkios (minùtės) põ vienõs (valandõs)

1:10	a)	vienà (valandà) (iř) dẽšimt (minùčių)
	b)	dẽšimt (minùčių) põ vienõs (valandõs)
1:15	a)	vienà (valandà) (iř) penkiólika (minùčių)
	b)	penkiólika (minùčių) põ vienõs (valandõs)
1:25	a)	vienà (valandà) (iř) dvìdešimt peñkios
	b)	dvìdešimt peñkios (minùtės) põ vienõs
1:30	a)	vienà (valandà) (iř) trìsdešimt (or, of course, pùsė dviejų̃, see 32.1,2)
	b)	trìsdešimt põ vienõs
1:35	a)	vienà (valandà) trìsdešimt peñkios (minùtės)
	b)	peñkios (minùtės) põ pùsės dviejų̃
1:40	a)	vienà (valandà) kẽturiasdešimt (minùčių)
	b)	bè dvìdešimt (minùčių) dvì (vãlandos)
1:45	a)	vienà (valandà) kẽturiasdešimt peñkios (minùtės)
	b)	bè penkiólikos (minùčių) dvì (vãlandos)
1:55	a)	vienà (valandà) peñkiasdešimt peñkios (minùtės)
	b)	bè penkių̃ (minùčių) dvì (vãlandos)

Thus one may say either (1) *Dabař vienà peñkios* or (2) *Dabař peñkios põ vienõs* (or *põ pirmõs*) for 'Now it is five minutes past one.'

32.1,4 *P. M. and A. M. are expressed as follows:*

A.M. — *rýto* (lit.: of the morning)

P.M. — *vãkaro* (lit.: of the evening)

However, a third expression is used in Lithuanian for the afternoon hours, somewhere between 1:00 P. M. and 6:00 P. M.: *põ pietų̃* 'after dinner, after the mid-day meal'. A fourth expression: *naktiẽs* 'of the night' refers to the early morning hours.

2:00 A. M. — *antrà valandà rýto* (lit.: the second hour of the morning), or:

2:00 A. M. — *antrà valandà naktiẽs* (lit.: the second hour of night)

4:00 A. M. — *ketvirtà valandà rýto* (or: *naktiẽs*)

6:00 A. M. — *šeštà valandà rýto* (or: *naktiẽs*)

1:00 P. M. — *pirmà valandà põ pietų̃* (lit.: the first hour after the mid-day meal)

10:00 A. M. — *dešimtà valandà rýto*

5:00 P. M. — *penktà valandà põ pietų̃*

7:00 P. M. — *septintà valandà vãkaro*

11:00 P. M. — *vienúolikta valandà vãkaro*

To express the difference between 12 noon and midnight the following expressions are used:

12:00 P. M. — *dvýlikta valandà naktiẽs* (lit.: the twelfth hour of the night)

vidur̃naktis (or *vidùnaktis)* means 'midnight' and *vidùrdienis* (or *vidùdienis*) means 'noon'.

32.1.5 *'At what time?'* may be expressed by: (1) *kadà* 'when', (2) *kurią̃ vãlandą* 'what hour' or (3) *keliñtą vãlandą* 'what hour.' Note that the second and third expressions above are in the accusative case.

To answer this question, i.e. to express the concept 'at a certain hour', generally the ordinal with the accusative case is used for even hours.

1) *Mẽs ateĩsime dvỹliktą vãlandą.* — We shall come at twelve o'clock.
2) *trẽčią vãlandą (rýto)* — at three o'clock in the morning.
3) *pìrmą vãlandą (põ pietų̃)* — at one o'clock in the afternoon.
4) *dešiñtą vãlandą (vãkaro* or *vakarè)* — at ten o'clock in the evening.

To express the concept 'at a certain half-hour' *pùsė* is used with the cardinal or ordinal. But note carefully that the word *pùsė* 'half' remains in the nominative case. Note that the accusative case to denote 'at a certain time' is limited to the ordinal number. With the cardinal numbers the nominative case is used.

5) *Mẽs ateĩsime pùsė pirmõs.* — We shall arrive at twelve thirty.
6) *pùsė dviejų̃* (or) *pùsė antrõs* — at 1:30
7) *pùsė trijų̃* (or) *pùsė trečiõs* — at 2:30
8) *pùsė keturių̃* — at 3:30 (never use the ordinal here)
9) *pùsė penkių̃* — at 4:30 (never use the ordinal here)
10) *pùsė septynių̃* — at 6:30 (never use the ordinal here)

To express the concept 'at a certain time' when minutes occur in the expression all cardinal numerals not governed by prepositions are in the nominative case.

11) *Mẽs ateĩsime peñkios põ vienõs.* — We shall arrive at five after one.
12) *Mẽs ateĩsime penkiólika põ vienõs.* — We shall arrive at 1:15.
13) *Mẽs ateĩsime bè penkiólikos aštúonios.* — We shall arrive at a quarter to eight.

251

14) *Mẽs ateĩsime bè penkiólikos kẽturios.* — We shall arrive at a quarter to four.
15) *Koncèrtas prasìdeda bè penkių̃ šẽšios.* — The concert begins at five minutes to six.
16) *peñkios põ dvýlikos* — at five after twelve
17) *dvìdešimt peñkios põ dvýlikos* — at twenty-five after twelve.

32.1,6 *The twenty-four hour system* is used in official Lithuanian. It was used in independent Lithuania to announce radio programs, theater performances, etc. Example:

12:55 — Žìnios (News)
13:00 — Simfonìnis koncèrtas (Symphony concert)
14:00 — Pranešìmas ū́kininkams (Report to the farmers)
14:30 — Profèsorius X : Į̃vadas į̃ kalbótyrą (or: kalbótyros į̃vadas) (Introduction to linguistics)

32.2 The Days of the Week.

pirmãdienis — Monday	penktãdienis — Friday
antrãdienis — Tuesday	šeštãdienis — Saturday
trečiãdienis — Wednesday	sekmãdienis — Sunday
ketvirtãdienis — Thursday	

Note the use of the accusative with the names of the days:
1) *Àš ateĩsiu pàs tavè (šį̃) pirmãdienį.* — I shall come to your place (this) Monday. Forms in parentheses may be omitted.
2) *Jìs bùvo namiẽ praėjusį antrãdienį.* — He was at home last Tuesday.
3) *Mẽs eĩsime teñ kìtą trečiãdienį.* — We shall go there next Wednesday.

The student should note that the days of the week are merely compounds: *pirmà* 'first' plus *dienà* 'day' gives *pirmã-dienis* 'Monday'; *antrà* 'second' plus *dienà* 'day' gives *antrã-dienis* 'Tuesday', etc. etc.

32.3 Other Uses of the Accusative in Time Expressions.

1) *šią̃ saváitę* — this week
2) *kìtą saváitę* — next week
3) *šį̃ mė́nesį* — this month
4) *šį̃ rýtą* — this morning

5) *vãkar rýtą* — yesterday morning

6) *šį vãkarą* — this evening

7) *Víeną kar̃tą teñ buvaũ.* — I was there once.

8) *Jìs manè mùšė trìs kartùs.* — He hit me three times.
See also 22.3 part b.

32.4 The accusative case is also used with *kàs* to denote 'each, every':

1) *Kàs diẽną rašaũ láišką.* — Every day I write a letter.

2) *Kàs savái̇tę važinėju namõ.* — Every week I drive home.

32.5 The Nominative Case in Time Expressions.

The nominative case is used in certain time expressions.

Examples:

1) *Jaũ kẽlios diẽnos, kaĩ smar̃kiai lỹja.* — It has been raining hard several days already. (lit.: Already several days since it has been raining hard.) Note also the use of the present tense to denote an action which began in the past, but continues into the present.

2) *Jaũ septynerì mẽtai, kaĩ jìs studijúoja lietùvių kal̃bą.* — It is already seven years that he has been studying Lithuanian.

3) *Jõnas: Sakýk, Kazìmierai, kur̃ tàvo draũgas Pẽtras? Jaũ penkì mẽnesiai nesù jõ mãtęs.* — John: Say, Casimir, where is your friend Peter? I haven't seen him for five months.
Kazìmieras: Jìs sẽdi kalėjime. Ir̃ nè penkì mẽnesiai, õ jaũ aštuonì mẽnesiai, kaĩ jìs sẽdi . . . — Casimir: He is (sitting) in prison. And it isn't five months, it is already eight months that he has been (there). . .

4) *Jaũ penkì mẽnesiai, kaĩ jìs mán nerãšo.* — It is already five months that he hasn't written to me.

5) *Jaũ peñkios diẽnos nuõ prezideñto Kenedžio nužùdymo.* — It is already five days since President Kennedy's assassination.

32.6 The Accusative: Extent of Time.

The accusative case may denote extent of time:

1) *Àš tą knýgą rašaũ jaũ kẽturias savái̇tes* (or: *kẽturios savái̇tės*). — I have been writing this book for four weeks already.

2) *Teñ gyvénsiu kìtą žiẽmą.* — I shall live there next winter.

3) *Praėjusią vãsarą tikraĩ suñkiai dìrbau.* — Last summer I really worked hard.

4) *Atvažiúok rùdenį.* — Come in the fall. (See also 22.3)

32.7 The Instrumental in Expressions of Time.

The instrumental case is used in certain expressions of time:

1) *šiaĩs mẽtais* — this year
2) *praėjusiais mẽtais* — last year
3) *kitaĩs mẽtais* — next year
4) *saváitėmis* — for weeks
5) *birželio, líepos iř rugpiúčio mẽnesiais* — during the months of June, July and August
6) *šiomìs dienomìs* — these days

The instrumental plural may imply that something happens repeatedly or regularly at a certain time:

7) *Jìs atsìkelia rytaĩs.* — He gets up in the morning(s).
8) *vakaraĩs* — in the evening(s), evenings
9) *Dienomìs žmónės dìrba, õ naktimìs miẽga.* — People work (during the) days, but sleep (during the) nights. See also 23.3.

32.8 The Locative in Expressions of Time.

The locative case is used in certain expressions of time:

1) *vãkar vakarè* — last night (lit.: 'yesterday evening')
2) *rytój vakarè* — tomorrow night (lit.: 'tomorrow evening') See also 24.11b.

32.9 Year, etc.

In Lithuanian the word *mẽtai* 'year' is declined like a masculine plural noun, although it is to be translated by the singular 'year' in English.* The instrumental case of the ordinal (cf. Lesson 29) may be used to denote the date. Examples:

1) *Jõ sūnùs gìmė túkstantis devynì šimtaĩ šẽšiasdešimt pirmaĩs mẽtais.* — His son was born in 1961.

2) *Jõ tẽvas mìrė túkstantis devynì šimtaĩ keturiasdešimtaĩs mẽtais.* — His father died in 1940. (See also paragraph 32.7)

---

* **mẽtas** — (sing.)=time (for something); it is time (to do something).

32.10 The Months.

The months in Lithuanian are as follows:

saũsis (2) — January
vasãris (2) — February
kóvas (1) — March
balañdis (2) — April
gegužė (3b) — May
biržẽlis (2) — June

líepa (1) — July
rugpiũtis* (1) — August
rugsėjis (1) — September
spãlis (2) — October
lãpkritis (1) — November
grúodis (1) — December**

Generally these are used in the expressions *saũsio mẽnuo* 'the month of January', *vasãrio mẽnuo* 'the month of February', etc. To express 'In January', etc.: *saũsio mẽnesį* (genitive of the name of the month, accusative of *mẽnuo*).

32.11 The Dates.

The date is expressed with the ordinal number referring to the year (in the genitive plural), the genitive singular of the month and the ordinal number denoting the day (in whatever case the construction requires). Examples:

1) *tūkstantis devynì šimtaĩ šẽšiasdešimt pirmų̃ mẽtų kóvo (mẽnesio) septyniólikta (dienà)* — the 17th of March, 1961. (Abbr. *1961 m. kovo 17*, or *1961.3.17*, or *1961.III.17*)

2) *tūkstantis devynì šimtaĩ trisdešimtų̃ mẽtų spãlio (mẽnesio) dvìdešimt trečià (dienà)* — the 23rd of October, 1930. (Abbr. *1930 m. spalio 23*, or *1930.10.23*, or *1930.X.23*).

The accusative case of the ordinal referring to the day is used to denote 'on a certain date', e.g. *Jõ duktė̃ gìmė tūkstantis devynì šimtaĩ peñkiasdešimt ketvirtų̃ mẽtų* (or *ketvir̃tais mẽtais*) *vasãrio (mẽnesio) trýliktą (dieną)* (or *1954 m. vasãrio 13*, or *1954.2.13*, or *1954.II.13*). — His daughter was born on the 13th of February, 1954. Forms in parentheses may be omitted.

---

* Also spelled **rugpjū́tis** (pronounced rugpjū́tis = **rugiaĩ** 'rye' + **pjáuti** (piáuti) 'to cut' — to reap, harvest).

** **saũsis** = **saũsas** 'dry'; **vasãris** = **vãsara** 'summer'; **kóvas** = **kóvas** 'a raven'; **balañdis** = **balañdis** 'pigeon'; **gegužė** = **gegùtė** 'cuckoo'; **biržẽlis** = **bér̃žas** 'birch'; **líepa**=**líepa** 'linden tree'; **rugpiũtis** — see footnote (*); **rugsėjis**= **rugiaĩ** 'rye' + **sė́ti** 'sow'; **spãlis** = **spãlis** 'chaff'; **lãpkritis** = **lãpas** 'leaf' + **krìsti** 'to fall'; **grúodis** = **grúodas** 'frost'.

32.12 Prepositions with Expressions of Time.

1) į — in (with acc.):
   Jì važiúoja tráukiniu trìs kartùs į saváitę.* — She travels by
   train three times a week.
2) peř — during (with acc.):
   a. Peř vìsą nãktį dìrbau. — I worked (during) the whole night.
   b. Peř visùs metùs jìs niẽko nedãrė. — During the entire year
   he did nothing.
3) põ — after (with gen.):
   a. Põ valandõs jìs ateĩs. — In (after) an hour he will come.
   b. Põ dviejų saváičių baĩgsiu dárbą. — In (after) two weeks
   I will finish the work.
4) ùž — after (with gen.):
   Ùž kelių dienų baĩgsiu dárbą. — In (after) a few days I will
   finish the work.
5) priẽš — ago (with acc.):
   Priẽš mẽnesį buvaũ ligóninėje. — A month ago I was in the
   hospital.**

EXERCISES

A. *Questions.* 1. Kurią vãlandą jũs válgote pùsryčius? 2. Kadà
jìs eĩna miegóti? 3. Kuriaĩs mẽtais jũs atvýkote į Amèriką? 4. Kadà yrà jũsų gimìmo dienà (birthday)? 5. Kadà jũs eĩnate namõ ìš
dárbo? 6. Kurią vãlandą prasìdeda koncèrtas? 7. Kíek mẽtų jũs
gyvẽnote Anglijoje? 8. Kaĩp ilgaĩ jũs studijúojate lietùvių kaĩbą?
9. Kadà Kolùmbas atrãdo (discovered) Amèriką? 10. Kíek dabař
laĩko?

B. *Express the following in writing in full:* 7:05 AM; 10:29 PM;
11:14 AM; 3:30 AM; 3:30 PM; at noon; at midnight; in the afternoon.

C. *Practice giving dates (in full):* 1776.VII.4; 1942; 1914; 1918;
1939; 1945; 1918.II.16.

D. *Translate into Lithuanian:* 1. She travels to Boston three times
a week. 2. In a few days he will be here. 3. A month ago he was
in the hospital. 4. We have been studying Lithuanian for four
months. 5. On Monday he will go home. 6. After ten hours he
will be in Europe. 7. We worked the whole night. 8. The whole
day he did nothing. 9. In a few months we will speak Lithuanian
very well. 10. I could not sleep all night.

---

* Also: peř saváitę, saváitėje.
** See also Lesson 37.

CONVERSATION

PRIEŠ KONCERTĄ

Výras: 1. Klausýk, brangióji, pasiskùbink! Mḗs pavėlúosime į koncèrtą. Dabař jaũ pùsė septynių!

Žmonà: 2. Nesinèrvink, suspḗsime. Pagaľ màno laĩkrodį dár tìk penkiólika põ šešių.

Vyras: 3. Tàvo laĩkrodis amžinaĩ vėlúoja. Neužmiřšk, kàd koncèrtas prasìdeda septiñtą vālandą.

Žmona: 4. Geraĩ, geraĩ, àš jaũ baigiù. Aš maniaũ, kàd koncèrtas prasìdeda penkiólika põ septynių.

Vyras: 5. Nè, koncèrtas prasìdeda lýgiai septiñtą. Kaĩp nórs jaũ paskubḗk, nès autobùsas mū́sų tikraĩ nelaũks.

Žmona: 6. Taĩ važiúokime automobiliù! Aš nemḗgstu autobusù važiúoti.

Vyras: 7. Jùk tù žinaĩ, kàd mū́sų automobìlis sugḗdęs. Jaũ trỹs diḗnos, kaĩ nùvežiau pataisýti, iř vìs dár nepataĩsė.

Žmona: 8. Galḗjai iř anksčiaũ nuvèžti, taĩ dabař nereikḗtų autobusù trankýtis.

Vyras: 9. Dabař jaũ bè dvìdešimt (minùčių) septýnios. Autobùsas išeĩna ùž trijų̃ minùčių.

Žmona: 10. Geraĩ, geraĩ, tìk nešaũk! Aš jaũ pasiruõšusi. Gālime eĩti.

BEFORE A CONCERT

Husband: 1. Listen, dear, hurry up. We will be late to the concert. It is already half past six.

Wife: 2. Don't get nervous, we will get there in time. According to my watch, it is only a quarter past six.

Husband: 3. Your watch is always (eternally) late. Don't forget the concert starts at seven.

Wife: 4. All right, all right, I am almost ready. I thought the concert starts at a quarter after seven ...

Husband: 5. No, the concert starts at seven sharp. Hurry it up somehow because the bus certainly is not going to wait for us.

Wife: 6. Then let's go by car. I don't like to go by bus.

Husband: 7. You know, don't you, that our car is broken down. Three days ago I took it to be repaired, and they have not repaired it yet.

Wife:	8.	You could have taken it there earlier, so now we would not have to go (on a rough ride) by bus.
Husband:	9.	It is already twenty to seven. The bus is leaving in three minutes.
Wife:	10.	All right, all right. Don't shout. I am ready. We can go.

NOTES:

8. **Trankýtis autobusù** — **trankýtis** 'to shake, to jolt'; **trankýtis autobusù** 'to have a bumpy, uncomfortable ride'.

Trisdešimt trečioji pamoka

Lesson 33

KLASĖJE

Mókytoja: Kàs mán gãli pasakýti, kadà bùvo įkùrtas Vìlnius?

Mokinỹs: Vìlnius bùvo įkùrtas Gedimìno trýliktame šim̃tmetyje.

Mokytoja: Taĩp, nórs tojè viẽtoje, kur̃ dabar̃ stóvi Vìlnius, jaũ seniaĩ bùvo gyvẽnama lietùvių. Tìk pirmóji didèsnė pilìs bùvo pastatýta teñ Gedimìno.

Mokinys: Kaĩp bùvo stãtomos sẽnosios lietùvių pìlys?

Mokytoja: Pãčios seniáusios pìlys Lietuvojè bùvo stãtomos iš mẽdžio. Vėliaũ pradėta statýti mūrìnės pìlys, tókios, kurių̃ griuvėsiùs visì mẽs jaũ ẽsame mãtę Trãkuose, Vìlniuje, Kaunè ir̃ kitur̃.

Mokinys: Ar̃ pìlys tuomèt bùvo taĩp stãtomos, kaĩp dabar̃ yrà stãtomi didelì mūrìniai namaĩ, pãvyzdžiui mū́sų mokyklà?

Mokytoja: Nevisái taĩp. Senóvėje pìlys bùvo stãtomos pirmiáusia apsigìnti nuõ príešų. Jų̃ síenos bùvo dãromos stóros, jõs bùvo apjúostos vandeñs groviù. Dabar̃ naujì namaĩ (yrà) stãtomi kitíems reikaláms; jų̃ síenos (yrà) daũg plonèsnės, langaĩ (yrà) dãromi daũg didesnì.

Mokinys: O kaĩp bùs stãtomi namaĩ ateityjè?

Mokytoja: Niẽkas tikraĩ negãli pasakýti, kokiẽ ir̃ kaĩp bùs stãtomi namaĩ ateityjè. Tìk tíek gãlima tikraĩ nuródyti: ateityjè namaĩ bùs dár geresnì ir̃ modernesnì negù šiañdien.

VOCABULARY

įkùrti (įkuriu, įkuria, įkūrė, įkuřs) —
  to found, to establish
šiṁtmetis -čio (1) — century
vietà (2) — place, location, space
pastatýti (pastataũ, pastãto, pastãtė,
  pastatýs) — to build (perfective)
statýti (stataũ, stãto, stãtė, statýs)
  — to build
kituř — elsewhere
tuomèt — at that time, then
pavyzdỹs -džio (3b) — sample, example
pãvyzdžiui — for example
nevisái — not wholly, not exactly

apsigìnti (apsìginu, apsìgina, apsigý-
  nė, apsigiñs) — to defend oneself
príešas (1) — enemy
apjúosti (apjúosiu, apjúosia, apjúosė,
  apjuõs) — to surround, to encircle
griovỹs (4) — ditch, moat
iř taĩp toliaũ — etc., and so on, and
  so forth (Abbr.: ir t.t.)
reĩkalas (3b) — purpose, matter,
  'business'
ateitìs -tiẽs (fem.) (3b) — future
ateityjè — in the future
nuródyti (nuródau, nuródo, nuródė,
  nuródys) — indicate, to point out
modernùs, -ì (4) — modern

GRAMMAR

33.1 The Passive Participles.

In Lithuanian the present passive participle and the past passive participle are more common than the other passive participles.
The future passive participle is relatively rare. Mention should
also be made of the so-called 'participle of necessity' which is also
passive. The present and past passive participles may be used
either to form the passive voice of various tenses or they may be
used attributively like adjectives.

33.2 The Present Passive Participle.

The present passive participle is formed by adding the endings (nom. sg. masc.) -mas, (nom. sg. fem.) -ma to the 3rd person
present of the finite verb, e.g. from dìrba '(he) works' we have
the forms dìrbamas, dirbamà, etc., cf. the declension below:

	Singular Masculine	Feminine		Plural Masculine	Feminine
N.	dìrbamas	dirbamà	N.	dirbamì	dìrbamos
G.	dìrbamo	dirbamõs	G.	dirbamų̃	dirbamų̃
D.	dirbamám	dìrbamai	D.	dirbamíems	dirbamóms
A.	dìrbamą	dìrbamą	A.	dìrbamus	dìrbamas
I.	dìrbamu	dìrbama	I.	dirbamaĩs	dirbamomìs
L.	dirbamamè	dirbamojè	L.	dirbamuosè	dirbamosè

33.3 The Passive Voice with Present Passive Participles.

Various tenses of the passive voice can be formed* with the verb *bū́ti* 'to be' plus the present passive participle. The tense of the verbal form of *bū́ti* is the same as the tense of the whole compound. Examples:

1) *Jì yrà giriamà.* — She is being praised. (Note that the form *yrà* 'is' denotes that the entire compound *yrà giriamà* 'is being praised' is in the present tense.)

2) *Jìs bùvo visų̃ žmonių̃ mýlimas.* — He was (being) loved by all the people. (Note that the tense of the compound *bùvo ... mýlimas* 'was (being) loved' is the same as that of *bùvo*.)

The logical subject, i. e. the performer of the action of a Lithuanian passive construction is in the genitive case. Thus in example (2) above *visų̃ žmonių̃* '(by) all men' is in the genitive case.

Frequently the participle is used as a simple adjective without regard to tense. Examples:

3) *Jì netéko mylimõs mótinos.* — She lost her beloved mother.

4) *Jìs nusipiřko siùvamą mašìną.* — He bought himself a sewing machine.

5) *miegamàsis kambarỹs* — bedroom (lit.: room for sleeping)

6) *valgomàsis šáukštas* — spoon for eating

7) *rašomàsis stãlas* — writing table**

When formed from a prefixed verb this participle may denote possibility (or with a negative, impossibility), e.g. *nepagý-doma lìgà* 'incurable illness', *nepakeliamà naštà* 'a burden which cannot be lifted', etc. In this case the meaning of possibility derives from the fact that both verbs are perfective, cf. the Appendix.

33.4 The Past Passive Participle.

The past passive participle is formed by removing the infinitive ending -*ti* and adding the (masc. nom. sg.) ending -*tas* or (fem. nom. sg.) -*ta*.

---

* See also Lesson 34.

** Sometimes there are passive forms which are almost synonomous with active forms, e.g. **tiñkamas** or **tiñkantis** (**tiñkąs**) 'suitable' from **tìkti** 'to suit'), **priklaũsomas** or **priklaũsantis** (**priklaũsąs**) 'dependent' (from **pri-klausýti** 'to depend').

	Singular		Plural	
	Masculine	Feminine	Masculine	Feminine
N.	dìrbtas (3)	dirbtà	N. dirbtì	dìrbtos
G.	dìrbto	dirbtõs	G. dirbtų̃	dirbtų̃
D.	dirbtám	dìrbtai	D. dirbtiéms	dirbtóms
A.	dìrbtą	dìrbtą	A. dìrbtus	dìrbtas
I.	dìrbtu	dìrbta	I. dirbtaĩs	dirbtomìs
L.	dirbtamè	dirbtojè	L. dirbtuosè	dirbtosè

33.5 The Passive Voice with Past Passive Participles.

Various tenses of the passive voice are formed* with the appropriate tense of the verb *bùti* 'to be' plus the past passive participle. The present tense of *bùti* plus the past passive participle forms the present perfect tense; the simple past (or preterite) tense of *bùti* plus the past passive participle forms the pluperfect (or past perfect) tense; the future tense of *bùti* plus the past passive participle forms the future perfect tense. (One can compare this with the corresponding Latin forms *laudatus sum* 'I have been praised', *laudatus eram* 'I had been praised', *laudatus ero* 'I shall have been praised'). Examples:

1) *Tà knygà jaū bùvo brólio pérskaityta, kaĩ tù atėjaĩ.* — That book had already been read through by brother when you arrived.

   (Note that *bùvo ... pérskaityta* 'had been read through' is in the pluperfect tense; *brólio* '(by) brother' is in the genitive case as the logical subject of the participle.)

2) *Tàs dárbas jaū yrà màno àtliktas.* — That work has already been completed by me. (Note that *yrà ... àtliktas* 'has been completed' is in the present perfect tense.)

The past passive participle can be used as a simple adjective too. Examples:

1) *Tõ raudónu rãšalu parašýto láiško niẽkas nemãtė.* — Nobody saw the letter which had been written with red ink. (Note that *parašýto* 'written' is in the genitive case modifying *láiško* which is in the genitive case as the direct object of a negated verb.)

2) *Pérskaitytą knỹgą padėjau į̃ lentýną.* — I put the book, which had been read, on the shelf (*pérskaitytą* 'read' is in the accusative case because it modifies *knỹgą* the direct object of *padėjau*.)

---

* See also Lesson 34.

33.6 The Neuter Passive Participle.

The passive voice can be formed also with the neuter form of the passive participle by dropping the -s from the masculine nominative singular form. The subject of the neuter passive participle is in the genitive case. Such participles may be created from intransitive as well as transitive verbs. Examples:

1) *Čià žmonių dìrbama iř nórima dìrbti.* — Here people work and want to work. (Note that the logical subject *žmonių* 'people' is in the genitive plural and the present passive participles *dìrbama* and *nórima* do not modify any word.) A literal translation of the preceding sentence would be: Here by people (it is) worked and (it is) wanted to work.

2) *Kienõ čià bûta?* — Who was here? The Lithuanian expression: *Kàs čià bùvo?* can also be translated by "Who was here?', but this has a more general meaning while the former expression implies the surprise caused by the facts which only now were perceived.

3) *Kienõ čià gyvénta?* — Who lived here?

4) *Čià jų bûta iř išeita.* — They were here (but) they went out. The pronoun *jų* in the genitive plural functions as the logical subject of the construction.

5) *Žiūrẽk — jõ teñ ẽsama.* — Look, there he is. *ẽsama* is the neuter present passive participle of *bûti* 'to be'.

33.7 The Future Passive Participle.

The future passive participle is formed by adding the endings (mas. nom. sg.) -mas or the (fem. nom. sg.) -ma to the 2nd person sg. of the future tense, e.g. from *dìrbsi* 'you (sg.) will work' we have *dìrbsimas, dìrbsimà,* etc. This form is only used in certain special cases.

	Singular			Plural	
	Masculine	Feminine		Masculine	Feminine
N.	dìrbsimas	dirbsimà	N.	dìrbsimì	dìrbsimos
G.	dìrbsimo	dirbsimõs	G.	dirbsimų	dirbsimų
D.	dirbsimám	dìrbsimai	D.	dìrbsimíems	dirbsimóms
A.	dìrbsimą	dìrbsimą	A.	dìrbsimus	dìrbsimas
I.	dìrbsimu	dìrbsima	I.	dìrbsimaĩs	dirbsimomìs
L.	dirbsimamè	dirbsimojè	L.	dirbsimuosè	dirbsimosè

The future passive participle denotes future action or condition. It may even be formed from intransitive verbs, e.g. *būsimas* 'future' (from *būti* 'to be'). Example:

Jìs mãtė sàvo bū́simą mókytoją. — He saw his future teacher (teacher to be).

33.8 The Participle of Necessity.

The participle of necessity is formed by adding the endings (masc. nom. sg.) *-nas* or (fem. nom. sg.) *-na* to the verbal infinitive, e.g. from *dìrbti* we have *dìrbtinas, dirbtinà,* etc. The declension is adjectival like that of the future participle. The participle of necessity denotes an action which should be performed or is worthy of being performed. Examples:

1) *Jìs yrà gìrtinas.* — He is to be praised (worthy of being praised, should be praised).

2) *Čià yrà víenas minė́tinas dalýkas.* — Here is an affair that should be mentioned.

3) *Jóks dárbas nėrà atidė́tinas.* — No work should be postponed.

An example of the neuter form of the participle of necessity:

4) *Jéi važiúotina — važiúok.* — If (one should) go, then go.

EXERCISES

A. *Questions.* 1. Kadà bùvo įkùrtas Vìlnius? 2. Kienõ bùvo įkùrtas Vìlnius. 3. Iš kõ (out of what) bùvo stãtomos pãčios seniáusios pìlys Lietuvojè? 4. Iš kõ yrà dabar̃ stãtomi modeřnūs namaĩ? 5. Kàs parãšė šią knỹgą? 6. Kienõ yrà parašýta šì knygà? 7. Iš kõ yrà stãtomi mūriniai namaĩ? 8. Iš kõ bùs stãtomi medìniai namaĩ? 9. Ar̃ šì knygà yrà visų̃ studeñtų skaĩtoma? 10. Iš kõ yrà padarýta šì lentà?

B. *Change the following sentences to the passive voice:* Example: Màno brólis stãto šį̃ nãmą. Šìs nãmas yrà stãtomas màno brólio. 1. Visì studeñtai skaĩto šią knỹgą. 2. Visì studeñtai skaĩtė šią knỹgą. 3. Visì studeñtai skaitỹs šią knỹgą. 4. Tė́vas bãra sàvo sū́nų. 5. Vãkar jìs parãšė ìlgą láišką.

C. *Translate into Lithuanian:* 1. Yesterday this letter was written by the president. 2. These new books are (being) read by all my students. 3. This book was written by my old friend. 4. These cars are made in Detroit. 5. Many new houses are (being) built in the suburbs.

CONVERSATION

BIBLIOTEKOJE

Valỹs:	1.	Kodėl àš negaliù gáuti šių naujų knỹgų?
Tarnáutojas:	2.	Mãtote, šiõs knỹgos yrà tìk ką̃ išléistos...
Valys:	3.	Àš žinaũ, kàd jõs tìk ką̃ išléistos, bèt àš nóriu jàs tuojaũ gáuti.
Tarnautojas:	4.	Jõs yrà labaĩ visų̃ skaĩtomos. Ypač jàs skaĩto jaunìmas.
Valys:	5.	Geraĩ, àš suprantù. Bèt, sakýkite, kodėl jũs nenùperkate kiekvienõs knỹgos beñt põ penkìs egzempliorius?
Tarnautojas:	6.	Šių̃ naujų̃ knỹgų bùvo nùpirkta põ trìs, bèt, kaĩp pãtys mãtote, jõs vìsos yrà pàimtos skaitýtojų.
Valys:	7.	Kadà gì àš galėsiu jàs gáuti?
Tarnautojas:	8.	Kaĩ tìk knỹgos bùs sugrąžìntos, mēs jùms tuojaũ pranèšime.
Valys:	9.	Geraĩ, àš turėsiu paláukti. Ačiū.
Tarnautojas:	10.	Prašaũ. Àš tikiúosi, kàd põ porõs dienų̃ knỹgos bùs jaũ sugrąžìntos.

AT THE LIBRARY

Valys:	1.	Why can't I get these new books?
Employee:	2.	You see, these books have just been published...
Valys:	3.	I know that they have been published just recently, but I would like to get them right away.
Employee:	4.	They are being read by everybody. Especially the young people read them.
Valys:	5.	All right, I understand. But tell me, please, why don't you buy at least (about) five copies of each book?
Employee:	6.	Three copies were bought of each of these new books, but, as you yourself can see, they have all been taken out (by the readers).

265

Valys: 7. When will I be able to get them?

Employee: 8. As soon as these books are returned (will have been returned), we shall let you know.

Valys: 9. All right, I will have to wait. Thanks.

Employee: 10. You are welcome. I hope the books will be returned in a couple of days.

NOTES:

2. tìk ką̃ išléistos — lit. 'only that (just) released, published'.
4. jaunìmas — 'youth, young people'.
5. põ penkìs egzemplioriùs — 'five copies each, of each'.
8. Kaĩ tìk — lit. 'when only', here: 'as soon as'.

Trisdešimt ketvirtoji pamoka
Lesson 34

GINTARAS

Giñtaras — taĩ lýg kóks Lietuvõs áuksas. Iš jõ yrà dãromi karõliai, apýrankės iř kitókie daiktaĩ. Jaũ giliojè senóvėje lietùvių bùvo prekiáujama giñtaru sù graikaĩs iř roménais. Gintariniùs karoliùs labaĩ mė́gsta nešióti lietuváitės.

Giñtaras yrà kietì sakaĩ spygliuõčių mẽdžių, kuriẽ priẽš ledų́ gadýnę áugo Pabaltijỹ(je). Tiẽ mẽdžiai bùvo labaĩ sakúoti. Kař- tais suvarvė́davo didelì gabalaĩ sakų́, kuriẽ greĩt sukietė́davo.

Suvarvė́ję sakaĩ ùpių vandeñs bùvo nunešamì į̃ jū́rą iř teñ suklóstomi. Teñ jiẽ maĩšėsi sù kitomìs núosėdomis, bùvo suslėgtì iř viřto giñtaru.

Kàd giñtaras yrà nè akmuõ, nè stìklas, õ sakaĩ, ródo iř taĩ, jóg jìs dẽga iř malõniai kvėpia.

Kařtais į̃ giñtaro gãbalus patèkdavo iř sustìngdavo įvairių̃ vabzdžių̃, mùsių, skruzdžių̃, skorpiònų. Yrà gintarè iř mẽdžių lã- pų, žiedų̃, šakėlių. Iš vìsa tõ mókslininkų bùvo išáiškinta, kokiẽ tadà mẽdžiai áugo iř kokiẽ vabzdžiaĩ veĩsėsi.

Daũg giñtaro yrà rañdama Lietuvõs pajū́ryje, kuř jìs yrà vandeñs išpláunamas į̃ krañtą.

VOCABULARY

giñtaras (3b) — amber
taĩ lýg kóks — that is something like, it is like
áuksas (1) — gold
karõliai (plural only) (2) — neklace, beads
apýrankė (1) — bracelet

dáiktas (3) — thing, object
gilùs, -ì (4) — deep
giliojè senóvėje — in ancient times
prekiáuti (prekiáuju, prekiáuja, pre- kiãvo, prekiaũs) — to trade
graĩkas (4) — Greek (noun)
roménas (1) — Roman (noun)

gintarìnis, -ė (2) — amber (adjective)
nešióti (nešióju, nešiója, nešiójo, nešiõs) — to wear
lietuváitė (1) — Lithuanian (a girl; especially a young girl)
sakaĩ (plural only) (4) — resin
spygliuõtas mēdis, spygliuõtis mēdis — coniferous tree
gadýnė (1) — era, epoch, age
ledų̃ gadýnė — ice age
Pabaltìjỹs (3b) — Baltic area, Baltic shores
sakúotas, -a (1) — resinous
kar̃tais — sometimes
suvarvėti (sùvarva, suvarvėjo, suvarvė̃s) to gather by dripping
gãbalas (3b) — piece, hunk, chunk
sukietėti (sukietėja, sukietėjo, sukietės) — to get hard, harden
suklóstyti (suklóstau, suklósto, suklóstė, suklóstys) — to fold, to lay in layers
maišýtis (maĩšosi, maĩšėsi, maišýsis) — to get mixed together with
núosėdos (plural only, 2nd decl. fem.) (1) — residue
suslėgti (sùslegiu, sùslegia, sùslėgė, suslėgs) — to press together
vìrsti (virstù, vir̃sta, vir̃to, vir̃s) — to become, to turn into

stìklas (4) — glass
kvepėti (kvepiù, kvẽpia, kvepėjo, kvepės) — to smell (good); to give out fragrance
patèkti (patenkù, pateñka, patèko, patèks) — to get to, to get into
sustìngti (sustìngstu, sustìngsta, sustìngo, sustiñgs) — to get hard; to harden
įvairùs, -ì (4) — various, different
vabzdỹs -džio (4) — insect
mùsė (2) — fly
skruzdė̃ (4) — ant
skorpiònas (2) — scorpion
lãpas (2) — leaf
žíedas (3) — blossom
šakēlė (2) — twig, little branch
móksliniñkas (1) — scientist
išáiškinti (išáiškinu, išáiškina, išáiškino, išáiškins) —to explain (perfective)
áugti (áugu, áuga, áugo, aũgs) — to grow
veĩstis (veĩsiasi, veĩsėsi, veĩsis) — to multiply, to proliferate, to live
pajū́ris -io (1) — sea shore
išpláuti (išpláunu, išpláuna, išplóvė, išplaũs) — to wash out, to deposit on shore (of seas, lakes, rivers)
krañtas (4) — shore

GRAMMAR

34.1 The Tenses of the Passive Voice.

As was mentioned in Lesson 33, the passive voice is formed in Lithuanian with the auxiliary verb 'to be' *bū́ti*. This means that there are as many tenses in the passive voice as there are tenses in the conjugation of the verb *bū́ti*.

But, since both the present passive participle and the past passive participle can be used to form the passive voice, there are actually always two tenses possible: one with the present passive participle, the other with the past passive participle. The difference in meaning is that, in the tenses where the present passive participle is used, one can render these tenses into English as a regular passive, but with the word *being* because the action is still being done (present tense), was being done (past tense), used to be being done (frequentative past), or will be being done (future). On the other hand, the passive tenses with the past passive participle will express the action as already complete, or completed, in any tense. The former is sometimes called the *actional passive,* and the latter the *statal passive.*

34.2 *The Paradigms of the Passive Voice. Their Meaning.*

Present Tense

(ACTIONAL PASSIVE)		(STATAL PASSIVE)	
àš esù mùšamas, -à	'I am being beaten', etc.	àš esù mùštas, -à	'I am beaten' (I have been beaten)
tù esì mùšamas, -à		tù esì mùštas, -à	
jìs yrà mùšamas		jìs yrà mùštas	
jì yrà mušamà		jì yrà muštà	
mẽs ẽsame mušamì, -os		mẽs ẽsame muštì, -os	
jũs ẽsate mušamì, -os		jũs ẽsate muštì, -os	
jiẽ yrà mušamì		jiẽ yrà muštì	
jõs yrà mùšamos		jõs yrà mùštos	

Past Tense

àš buvaũ mùšamas, -à 'I was being beaten'		àš buvaũ mùštas, -à	'I was beaten ('I had been beaten')
tù buvaĩ mùšamas, -à		tù buvaĩ mùštas, -à	
jìs bùvo mùšamas		jìs bùvo mùštas	
jì bùvo mušamà		jì bùvo muštà	
mẽs bùvome mušamì		mẽs bùvome muštì, -os	
jũs bùvote mušamì, -os		jũs bùvote muštì, -os	
jiẽ bùvo mušamì		jiẽ bùvo muštì	
jõs bùvo mùšamos		jõs bùvo mùštos	

Frequentative Past

àš bū́davau mùšamas, -à 'I used to be (being) beaten' etc.

àš bū́davau mùštas, -à ' I used to be beaten, I would be beaten' etc.

Future

àš bū́siu mùšamas, -à 'I will be (being) beaten' etc.

àš bū́siu mùštas, -à 'I will be beaten' ('I will have been beaten') etc.

There is a possibility, and some individual writers have used it, to even form the passive forms with the compound tenses of *bùti: àš esù bùvęs mùšamas* 'I have been beaten' , but this occurs infrequently and the student should be able to figure this out in case he runs into such usage in reading Lithuanian. For full treatment of this, see Appendix: Verbs.

34.3 The Subjunctive of the Passive Voice.

To form the subjunctive of the passive voice, one has to combine the two subjunctive tenses of the verb to be (*bùti*) and the appropriate passive participle.

Present Tense Subjunctive, Passive Voice: (Actional Passive)

àš bùčiau mùšamas, -à	'I would be (being) beaten', etc.

tù bùtum mùšamas, -à
jìs bùtų mùšamas
jì bùtų mušamà

mẽs bùtume mušamì, -os
jũs bùtute mušamì, -os
jiẽ bùtų mušamì
jõs bùtų mùšamos

Present Tense Subjunctive, Passive Voice (Statal Passive)

àš bùčiau mùštas, -à	'I would be beaten', etc.
etc.	('I would have been beaten')

Present Perfect Subjunctive, Passive Voice (Actional Passive)

àš bùčiau bùvęs mùšamas, -à	'I would have been (being) beaten'
etc.	etc.

Present Perfect Subjunctive, Passive Voice (Statal Passive):

àš bùčiau bùvęs mùštas, -à	'I would have been beaten (up)'

Examples for passive subjunctive:

1) Nãmas jaũ *bùtų* dabař *stãtomas*, jéigu jìs *bùtų sumokėjęs* vìsą káiną. — The house would be (being) built now, if he had paid (in full) the entire price.
2) Vìskas jaũ *bùtų padarýta*, jéigu àš taĩ *bùčiau žinójęs*.* — Everything would be done (already), if I had known that.

---

* padarýta is a neuter adjective. In the passive it can be used only with the third person singular, primarily in impersonal expressions, with such words as vìskas 'everything', all things', taĩ 'that, this', etc.

3) Šì gramãtika jaũ seniaĩ *bū̃tų bùvusi parašýta*, jéigu jõs áutorius *nebū̃tų susiȓgęs*. — This grammar would have been written a long time ago, if its author had not fallen ill.

34.4 The Passive Imperative.

The passive imperative is formed with the imperative forms
of the verb *bū̃ti* and the appropriate passive participle:

bū̃k gìriamas	be praised (referring to *tù* 'thou', masculine)
bū̃k giriamà	be praised (referring to *tù* 'thou', feminine)
bū̃kite giriamì	be praised (referring to *jū̃s* 'ye', masculine)
bū̃kite gìriamos	be praised (referring to *jū̃s* 'ye', feminine)
bū̃kime giriamì	be praised (referring to *mẽs* 'we', masculine)
bū̃kime gìriamos	be praised (referring to *mẽs* 'we', feminine)

The imperative with the past passive participle is as follows:

bū̃k pasvéikintas, -a	'be greeted; welcome!'
bū̃kite pasvéikinti	
bū̃k pagárbintas	'be adored, be praised' (primarily of God).
bū̃k paténkintas	'be satisfied'

34.5 The Passive Infinitive.

The passive infinitive is formed by putting together the infinitive of the verb *bū̃ti* and the appropriate passive participle in
the dative case:

(Actional Passive Infinitive)

bū̃ti mušamám	to be (being) beaten (masculine, singular)
bū̃ti mùšamai	to be beaten (feminine, singular)
bū̃ti mušamíems	to be (being) beaten (masculine, plural)
bū̃ti mušamóms	to be (being) beaten (feminine, plural)

(Statal Passive Infinitive)

suiȓti — 'to arrest'

bū̃ti suimtám	to be arrested (masculine, singular)
bū̃ti sùimtai	to be arrested (feminine, singular)
bū̃ti suimtíems	to be arrested (masculine, plural)
bū̃ti suimtóms	to be arrested (feminine, plural)

271

Examples for the use of the passive infinitives:

1) *Bū́ti polìcijos suimtám ùž vagỹstę yrà dìdelė gė́da.* — To be arrested (by the police) for theft is a great shame.
2) *Mókytojui labaĩ patiñka bū́ti visų̃ mokinių̃ mylimám.* — The teacher likes very much to be loved by all the pupils.

NB. This usage, with the passive participle in the dative case is restricted to cases where the passive infinitive is also the subject of the (impersonal) sentence. Where the passive infinitive is not the subject of the sentence, the passive participle has to be used in the nominative case*:

Jìs nóri bū́ti (visų̃) mė́gstamas. — He wants to be liked by everybody.
Jì nóri bū́ti (visų̃) mėgotamà. — She wants to be liked...
Jiẽ nóri bū́ti (visų̃) mė́gstamì. — They want to be liked...
Jõs nóri bū́ti (visų̃) mė́gstamos. — They want to be liked...

EXERCISES

A. *Questions.* 1. Kuř yrà rañdamas giñtaras? 2. Kàs yrà dãroma iš giñtaro? 3. Kuõ bùvo lietùvių prekiáujama sù graikaĩs iř romė́nais? 4. Kuř bùvo nunešamì mẽdžių sakaĩ? 5. Kaĩp sakaĩ viřto giñtaru? 6. Kàs ródo, kàd giñtaras nėrà stìklas? 7. Kaĩp bùvo mókslininkų išáiškinta, kokiẽ mẽdžiai senóvėje áugo Pabaltijỹ(je)? 8. Kodė́l daugiáusia giñtaro yrà rañdama pajúryje? 9. Ař yrà rañdama giñtaro Amèrikoje? 10. Ař jũs ėsate kadà nórs rãdę giñtaro?

B. *Give all the tenses of the passive voice of the following verbs:* gìrti, gárbinti, peĩkti

C. *Change the following sentences into the passive voice:* Example: Màno brólis skaĩto šìą įdõmią knỹgą. — Šì įdomì knygà yrà màno brólio skaĩtoma.
1. Màno tėvas stãto šį̃ dìdelį nãmą. 2. Màno tėvas stãtė šį̃ dìdelį nãmą. 3. Màno tėvas statỹs šį̃ dìdelį nãmą. 4. Mótina bãra sàvo vaikùs. 5. Mótina bãrė sàvo dukrẽlę. 6. Mótina baŕs mùs visùs...

D. *Translate into Lithuanian:* 1. This book is (being) written by five professors. 2. This house was built by my uncle 30 years ago. 3. Only modern houses are being built now. 4. He is liked by everyone. 5. This letter was written many years ago.

---

* In other words, the participle is used here as an adjective, i.e. **Jìs nóri bū́ti gė́ras** 'He wants to be good'.

CONVERSATION

PRIEMIESTYJE

Šaulỹs: 1. Šìs príemiestis yrà labaĩ išáugęs. Kaĩ àš čià buvaũ priẽš trejùs metùs, taĩ čià namaĩ bùvo dár tìk stãtomi.

Genỹs: 2. Taĩp, peř paskutiniùs trejùs metùs čià bùvo pastatýta keliasdẽšimt naujų̃ namų̃.

Šaulys: 3. Kokiẽ namaĩ čià yrà daugiáusia stãtomi?

Genys: 4. Daugiáusia yrà stãtomi medìniai víeno aũkšto namaĩ.

Šaulys: 5. Kàs juõs čià stãto: privãtūs statýbininkai ař miẽstas?

Genys: 6. Miẽstas niẽkur naujų̃ namų̃ nestãto: vìskas yrà stãtoma privačių̃ statýbininkų.

Šaulys: 7. O kàs daugiáusia peřka tókius namùs?

Genys: 8. Šiẽ namaĩ nėrà perdaũg brángūs, taĩ juõs daugiáusia peřka mókytojai, profèsoriai iř fabrikų̃ darbiniñkai.

Šaulys: 9. O kuř yrà stãtomi mūrìniai, brángūs namaĩ?

Genys: 10. Už dviejų̃ mỹlių nuõ čià yrà stãtomi labaĩ brángūs namaĩ: mūrìniai, akmenìniai,... bèt juõs gãli piřkti tiktaĩ labaĩ turtìngi žmónės...

IN A SUBURB

Saulys: 1. This suburb has grown very much. When I was here three years ago, houses were only being built here.

Genys: 2. That's right. In the course of the last (few) years, there were quite a few houses built here.

Saulys: 3. What kind of houses are (being) built here mostly.

Genys: 4. Mostly one-story wooden houses are built here.

Saulys: 5. Who builds them here: (private) builders, or the city?

Genys: 6. The city does not build new houses anywhere. Everything is done (built) by (private) builders.

Saulys: 7. And who buys such houses mostly?

Genys: 8. These houses are not too (overly) expensive; thus mostly teachers and professors, and factory workers buy them.

Saulys: 9. And where are there expensive brick homes (being) built?

Genys: 10. Two miles from here there are built very expensive houses: stone and brick houses,... but only very rich people can (afford to) buy them...

NOTES:

2. **keliasdẽšimt** — lit. 'several tens'. The real value of this phrase: somewhere betwen 20 and 100.

8. **perdaũg** — lit. 'too much'.

Fruits and Vegetables

A. FRUITS:

apple — *obuolys*

pear — *kriaušė*

cherry — *vyšnia*

plum — *slyva*

peach — *persikas*

orange — *apelsinas*

banana — *bananas*

apricot — *aprikosas*

B. VEGETABLES:

cabbage — *kopūstas*

cucumber — *agurkas*

tomato — *pamidoras*

radish — *ridikėlis*

spinach — *špinatas*

onion — *svogūnas*

carrot — *morka*

pea — *žirnis*

Trisdešimt penktoji pamoka

Lesson 35

BALTŲ TAUTOS

Báltų taũtos taĩ indoeuropiẽčiams priklaũsanti tautų̃ grùpė Báltijos jū́ros pietų̃ rytų̃ atkraštyjè, kuriái priskiriamì dabartìniai lietùviai, lãtviai, XVIII a.[1] pradžiojè suvókietinti prū́sai, XVI a.[2] sulatvė́ję beĩ sulietuvė́ję kuřšiai iř žiemgãliai, taĩp pàt sė́liai, iš-nŷkę jaũ XIV a.[3] Šìs kúopinis báltų tautų̃ vařdas kalbótyroje var-tójamas siauresnè prasmè néi geogrãfijoje, kuř juõ vadìnamos vìsos Pãbaltijo taũtos, taĩgi iř lietùviams - lãtviams kraujù beĩ kalbà visái svetimì èstai iř súomiai. Vařdas pasidarýtas ìš Báltijos jū́ros, kuriõs etimològinė reikšmė̃ bètgi niẽko beñdra netùri sù mū́sų bū́dvardžiu báltas. Iš istòrijos šaltìnių áiškų báltų tautų̃ su-siskìrstymo iř jų̃ gyvénamų̃jų plótų váizdą gáuname võs XIII a.[4] pradžiojè.

Vakaruosè nuõ Nė́muno ìki Výslos gyvéna prū́sai, susiskìrstę nèt dẽšimčia atskirų̃ kilčių̃. Prū́sams Dùsburgas[5] prìskiria iř Kùl-mo[6] iř Liubãvo[7] sritìs, kuriõs dár priẽš Ordino atsikráustymą bù-vusios (lénkų) išteriótos. Čià, matýti, lénkų iř põ tõ įsikùrta. Šiaĩp Ordino laikaĩs prū́sų-lénkų síena laĩkoma Osos[8] ùpė. Toliaũ į̃ rý-tus galìndų kiltiẽs (išnaikìntos taĩp pàt priẽš Ordino laikùs) pie-tìnės sodýbos síekė ìki Nãrevo,[9] nórs Vìznos[10] pilìs jaũ XII a.[11] pradžiojè priklaũso lénkams. Šì ùpė atribója nuõ mozùrų iř rùsų taĩp pàt iř sū́duviùs, arbà jótvingiùs, kuriẽ, spréndžiant iř ìš trū́k-tinų̃ kalbõs liēkanų, laikýtini prū́sais. Panemunėjè pleištù tařp sū́dùvių iř lietùvių įsikerta rùsai: jų̃ (báltų žẽmėje) įkùrto Gař-dino (Gorodeń) kunigáikščiai pažį́stami jaũ XII a.[11] pirmõjoje pù-sėje. Tautų̃ trijùlė: kuřšiai, žiemgãliai iř sė́liai yrà gyvénusi da-bař lãtvių iř lietùvių gyvénamoje teritòrijoje. Kuřšiams XIII a.[12]

šaltìnių liùdijimu teñka vakarìnė Kuřžemė tařp Báltijos jū́ros iř Rygõs į̃lankos, išskýrus tìk šiaurìnę jõs dãlį, gyvĕnamą lýbių, iř bè tõ didókas Žemaĩčių šiáurės vakarų̃ kaĩpas — Cēklio[13] sritìs — sù Klaĩpėdos apýlinke. Sù kalbiniñkų téigiamu Cēklio kuršiškumù nesutiñka dalìs istòrikų iř šią̃ srìtį prìskiria lietùviams. Nuõ Rygõs į̃lankos pietų̃ liñk mažnè visamè Líelupės-Mūšõs[14] upýne bùvo ištìsęs žiemgãlių krãštas, kurìs ribójasi sù lietùviškomis Šiaulių̃ iř Upýtės sritimìs. Į̃ rýtus nuõ žiemgãlių kairiúoju Dauguvõs pãkraščiu gyvĕno sė́liai; Lietuvojè jų̃ sodýbos síekė ìki Taurãgnų iř Svedasų̃. Tikrų́jų lãtvių tadà gyvénta tìk dabartìnėje Lãtgaloje[15] iř rytìnėje Vìdžemės [16] dalyjè, maždaũg ìki Aĩzkrauklės (priē Dauguvõs) - Bùrtniekų[17] ēžero lìnijos. Vìsas rytìnis Rygõs į̃lankos pakraštỹs sù artimája Rygõs apýlinke priklaũsė lýbiams.*

NOTES:

1) aštuonióliktojo ámžiaus.
2) šešióliktajame ámžiuje.
3) keturióliktajame ámžiuje.
4) trýliktojo ámžiaus.
5) Petri de Dusburg Chronicon terrae Prussiae, ed. by M. Toeppen in **Scriptores Rerum Prussicarum**, Vol. 2.
6) terra Culmensis, Culmerland; today the city of Kulm (Polish Chełmno) on the right bank of the Vistula river.
7) Löbau (Polish Lubów, Lubowo).
8) Ossa, the right tributary of the Vistula.
9) Narew, a tributary of the Bug river in Poland.
10) Wizna, a little town in Poland.
11) dvýliktojo ámžiaus.
12) trýliktojo amžiaus.
13) Ceclis
14) In the Lithuanian area, this river is called **Mūšà**, in the Latvian area, however: **Lielupe**.
15) Lãtgala: area inhabited by Latgalians: Latgallian area, Latgallia.
16) Vìdžemė: Livland, western part of Latvia.
17) The nominative (in Latvian): Burtnieki, in Lithuanian: Bùrtniekai.

* Taken from: Antanas Salys, Lietuviškoji Enciklopedija Vol. II (Kaunas 1934), p. 999-1004.

REVIEW AND SUMMARY OF THE PARTICIPLES AND GERUNDS

A. The Active Participles (dìrbti 'to work'; mylė́ti 'to love'; skaitýti 'to read')*

Tense	Formed from	(dropped)	added	Examples	English	Lesson
Present	3rd person present tense	(-a)+-ąs (-i)+-įs (-o)+-ąs	-anti -inti -anti	dirb(-a)+-ąs, -anti : dirbąs, dirbanti mýl(-i)+-įs, -inti : mylįs, mýlinti skait(-o)+-ąs, -anti : skaitąs, skaitanti	'(the one who is) working', etc.	26.2 Appendix
Past	3rd person past tense	(-o, -ė)+-ęs, -usi		dirb(-o)+-ęs, -usi : dirbęs, dirbusi mylėj(-o)+-ęs, -usi : mylėjęs, mylėjusi skait(-ė)+-ęs, -(i)usi : skaitęs, skaičiusi	'(the one who has) worked', etc.	26.3 Appendix
Frequent. Past	3rd person freq. past	(-o)+-ęs, -usi		dirbdav(-o)+-ęs, -usi : dirbdavęs, dirbdavusi mylėdav(-o)+-ęs, -usi : mylėdavęs, mylėdavusi skaitydav(-o)+-ęs, -usi : skaitydavęs, skaitydavusi	'the one who used to have worked'	26.3,4 Appendix
Future	2nd person sg. future	+-ąs, -anti		dirbsi+-ąs, -anti : dirbsiąs, dirbsianti mylėsi+-ąs, -anti : mylėsiąs, mylėsianti skaitýsi+-ąs, -anti : skaitýsiąs, skaitýsianti	'the one who is going to be working', etc.	26.3,5 Appendix

* dìrbti (dìrba) — 1st conjugation; mylė́ti (mýli) — 2nd conj.; skaitýti (skaĩto) 3rd conj. For the participles of **bū́ti** 'to be' and **eĩti** 'to go', see 26.8.

B. The Passive Participles (mùšti 'to beat', mylėti 'to love', skaitýti 'to read')

Tense	Formed from	(dropped)	added	Examples	English	Lesson
Present	3rd person Present T.		+-mas, -ma	mùša+-mas, -ma : mùšamas, mùšamà mýli+-mas, -ma : mýlimas, mýlimà skaĩto+-mas, -ma : skaĩtomas, skaĩtoma	'the one (or thing) which is being beaten', etc.	33.2 Appendix
Past	Infinitive	(-i)	+-tas, -ta	mùšt(-i)+-tas, -ta : mùštas, mùštà mylėt(-i)+-tas, -ta : mylėtas, mylėta skaitýt(-i)+-tas, -ta : skaitýtas, skaitýta	'the one (or thing) which was beaten, which has been beaten', etc.	33.4 Appendix
Future	2nd person sg. future		+-mas, -ma	mùši+-mas, -ma : mùšimas, mùšimà mylėsi+-mas, -ma : mylėsimas, mylėsima skaitýsi+-mas, -ma : skaitýsimas, skaitýsima	'the one (or thing) which is to be beaten, which ought to be beaten', etc.	33.7 Appendix

N.B. There is no passive participle of the frequentative past. The student of course should keep in mind that only transitive verbs can have a **passive voice**.

C. The Gerunds (the Adverbial Participles or the Participial Adverbs) (*mùšti* 'to beat', *mylė́ti* 'to love', *skaitýti* 'to read')

Tense	Formed from (dropped)	Examples		English	Lesson
Present	Present Active Participle, Feminine Nom. Sg. (-i)	mùšant (-i) mýlint (-i) skaĩtant (-i)	: mùšant : mýlint : skaĩtant	'while beating, beating', etc.	26.7 Appendix
Past	Past Active Participle, Fem. Nom. Sg. (-i)	mùšus (-i) mylė́jus (-i) skaĩčius (-i)	: mùšus : mylė́jus : skaĩčius	'after having beaten', etc.	26.7 Appendix
Frequent. Past	Freq. past Active Part. Fem. Nom. Sg. (-i)	mùšdavus (-i) mylė́davus (-i) skaitýdavus (-i)	: mùšdavus : mylė́davus : skaitýdavus	'after having beaten several times', etc.	26.7 Appendix
Future	Future Active Participle, Fem. Nom. Sg. (-i)	mùšiant (-i) mylė́siant (-i) skaitýsiant (-i)	: mùšiant : mylė́siant : skaitýsiant	(Used in special phrases to express future action)*	26.7 Appendix

* As in: Jis mãnė juõs važiúosiant į Niujòrką 'He thought they were going (to go) to New York'.

D. The Special Adverbial Active Participle.

Formed from	(dropped) added	Examples	English	Lesson
Infinitive	(-ti)+-*damas*, -*dama*	mùš(-ti)+-*damas*, -*dama* : mùšdamas, mušdamà mylė(-ti)+-*damas*, -*dama* : mylėdamas, mylėdama skaitý(-ti)+-*damas*, -*dama* : skaitýdamas, skaitýdama	'while beating', etc.	26.4 Appendix

E. The Special Participle of Necessity.

Formed from	(dropped) added	Examples	English	Lesson
Infinitive	+-*nas*, -*na*	mùšti+-*nas*, -*na* : mùštinas, muštinà mylėti+-*nas*, -*na* : mylėtinas, mylėtina skaitýti+-*nas*, -*na* : skaitýtinas, skaitýtina	'the one (or: thing) which is to be beaten', etc.	33.8 Appendix

Trisdešimt šeštoji pamoka

Lesson 36

MINDAUGAS
(1200? - 1263)

Mìndaugas yrà pirmàsis suviēnytos Lietuvõs karãlius. Priēš jõ laikùs Lietuvà bùvo vaĨdoma daũgelio atskirū̃ kunigáikščių. Iš istòrijos šaltìnių nežìnome, kuriaĩs mētais Mìndaugas baĩgė viēnyti Líetuvą. Tačiaũ mēs jaũ tikraĩ žìnome, kàd 1236 mētais Lietuvà bùvo vaĨdoma víeno valdõvo — Mìndaugo. Màt, taĩs mētais lietùviai, vadováujami Mìndaugo, sùmušė kalavijuočiùs didelėsè iř labaĩ svarbiosè kautỹnėse priē Šiauliū̃. Nuõ tõ smũgio vókiečių kalavijuõčių òrdinas niekuomèt daugiaũ neatsigãvo iř kíek vėliaũ susijùngė sù kryžiuõčių òrdinu, kurìs tuõ metù atsikėlė į̃ Prũsus.

1251 mētais pópiežius Inoceñtas IV (ketvirtàsis) àtsiuntė Mìndaugui karãlišką vainìką. Mìndaugas sù sàvo šeimà iř dìdeliu Lietuvõs didìkų būriù prìėmė krìkštą iř bùvo pópiežiaus atstõvo vainikúotas Lietuvõs karãliumi. Tókiu būdù Lietuvà tãpo krikščióniška valstýbe, pasiriñkusi Vakarū̃ kultũros kēlią.

Nórs Mìndaugui iř bùvo pasisēkę tvirtaĩ suviēnyti Líetuvą, tačiaũ daũgelis bùvusių kunigáikščių jám pavydėjo. 1263 mētais Mìndaugas bùvo nužudýtas, kartù iř jõ dù sūnūs.

Žùvus Mìndaugui, Lietuvà atsidūrė pavõjuje:kaimýnai rùsai, lénkai, kryžiuõčiai galėjo pùlti bè valdõvo lìkusią valstýbę. Galējo taĩp pàt sukìlti bùvę sritìniai kunigáikščiai iř išsidalìnti Mìndaugo sukùrtą Lietuvõs valstýbę.

Kàd taĩp neatsitìko, yrà karãliaus Mìndaugo núopelnas. Nórs jìs pàts iř jõ dù jaunesníeji sūnūs žùvo, bèt suviēnytoji Lietuvõs valstýbė išlìko. Lietùviai jaũ bùvo suprãtę, kàd vienà stiprì valstýbė yrà reikalìnga. Taĩ suprãto iř pãtys Mìndaugo žudìkai.

Taĩgi Mìndaugas sàvo darbaĩs įvedė Líetuvą į krikščióniškų-jų Euròpos valstýbių tárpą, ùžmezgė ryšiùs sù Vakarų̃ Euròpos tautomìs iř padãrė sàvo taũtą iř valstýbę žìnomą tolimuosè pasáulio kraštuosè.

Narsùs, apdairùs iř ryžtìngas Mìndaugas priēš 700 mētų sukū̃rė Lietuvõs karalýstę iř tuõ žygiù dãvė prãdžią naujám polìtiniam Lietuvõs gyvēnimui.

VOCABULARY

suviēnyti (suviēniju, suviēnija, suviēnijo, suviēnys) — to unify, to unite
karãlius (2) — king
valdýti (valdaũ, vaĩdo, vaĩdė, valdỹs) — to rule
daũgelis -io (noun with gen. pl.) — many, several (quite a few)
kuriaĩs mētais — which year, which years, in which year
baĩgti (baigiù, baĩgia, baĩgė, baĩgs) — to finish; to complete
tikraĩ — for sure, surely; factually, really
valdõvas (2) — ruler
màt (matýti) — to be sure; indeed; because; since
vadováuti (vadováuju, vadováuja, vadovãvo, vadovaũs) — to lead
vadováujami — under the leadership; under...
sumùšti (sùmušu, sùmuša, sùmušė, sumùš) — to beat (and win); to crush (in war); to win (a battle); to smash
kalavijuõtis -čio (2) — the knight of the Order of "Sword Bearers" (1201-1236 in Livonia)
šiauliaĩ — a city in Northern Lithuania
niekuomèt — never
daugiaũ — more
niekuomèt daugiaũ — no more; never more
atsigáuti (atsigáunu, atsigáuna, atsigãvo, atsigaũs) — to recover (oneself), to recuperate, to rise again
kíek vėliaũ — a little later
susijùngti (susijùngiu, susijùngia, susijùngė, susijùngs) — to get oneself united with (sù plus instrumental)
dìdelis, -ė (3) — large, big
kautýnės (fem., plural only) (2) — battle, engagement (mil.)
smūgis -io (2) — hit, blow

atsikélti (atsìkeliu, atsìkelia, atsikėlė, atsikeĩs) — to rise, to get up; to move into, to arrive (after moving)
pópiežius (1) — pope
atsiųsti (atsiunčiù, atsiuñčia, àtsiuntė, atsiųs) — to send (to)
karãliškas, a (1) — royal
vainìkas (2) — wreath; crown
didìkas (2) — nobleman, noble
būrỹs -io (4) — group, gang; platoon
priiñti (prìimu, prìima, prìėmė, priiñs) — to accept, to receive
krìkštas (4) — baptism
atstõvas (2) — representative; legate
vainikúoti (vainikúoju, vainikúoja, vainikãvo, vainikuõs) — to crown
tókiu būdù — in such a way; so, this way
tàpti (tampù, tam̃pa, tãpo, tàps) — to become
krikščióniškas, -a (1) — Christian (Adjective)
valstýbė (1) — state
pasiriñkti (pasìrenku, pasìrenka, pasiriñko, pasiriñks) —to choose, to elect (for oneself)
kēlias (4) — way, road
pasisèkti (only 3rd person used: pasìseka, pasìsekė, pasìsèks, with dative) — to succeed (in)
pavydėti (pavýdžiu, pavýdi, pavydė-jo, pavydės) — to envy, to be jealous
nužudýti (nužudaũ, nužùdo, nužùdė, nužudỹs) — to assassinate
kartù — together
kartù sù — together with
žū̃ti (žū̃stu, žū̃sta, žùvo, žùs) — to perish; to die; to be killed
atsidùrti (atsìduriu, atsìduria, atsidū̃rė, atsidùrs) — to be exposed to, to get (into), to run (into)
pavõjus (2) — danger

atsidùrti pavõjuje — to be exposed to danger, to be endangered

kaimýnas (1) — neighbor

kryžiuõtis -čio (2) — a knight of the Teutonic Order

sukìlti (sukylù, sukỹla, sukìlo, sukìls) — to rise (against)

sritìnis, -ė (2) — regional, area, divisional

išsidalìnti (išsidalinù, išsidalìna, išsidalìno, išsidalìñs) — to divide up

sukùrti (sùkuriu, sùkuria, sukū́rė, sukùrs) — to create, to found

atsitìkti (3rd person only: atsitiñka, atsitìko, atsitìks) — to happen, to occur, to take place

núopelnas (1) — merit; achievement; deed

išlìkti (išliekù, išliẽka, išlìko, išlìks) — to remain, to be saved (with instrumental)

būtinaĩ — absolutely, indeed

žudìkas (2) assassin

įvèsti (įvedù, įvedà, įvedė̃, įvès) — to lead into

užmègzti (ùžmezgu, ùžmezga, ùžmezgė, ùžmegs) — to tie

užmègzti ryšiùs — to get connected with

ryšỹs -io (4) — connection, contact

narsùs, -ì (4) — brave, courageous, bold

apdairùs, -ì (4) — cautious, clever

ryžtìngas, -a (1) — determined

žỹgis -io (2) — campaign, deed

dúoti prãdžią — to start, to begin

GRAMMAR

36.1 The Demonstrative Pronouns *šìs, šìtas, tóks, anóks*

The declension of the demonstrative pronouns *šìs* 'this', *tàs* 'that' and *anàs* 'that (one over yonder)' is given below:

	Masculine		Feminine	
	Singular	Plural	Singular	Plural
N.	šìs 'this'	šiẽ	šì	šiõs
G.	šiõ	šių̃	šiõs	šių̃
D.	šiám	šíems	šiái	šióms
A.	šį̃	šiuõs	šią̃	šiàs
I.	šiuõ	šiaĩs	šià	šiomìs
L.	šiamè	šiuosè	šiojè	šiosè

N.	tàs 'that'	tiẽ	tà	tõs
G.	tõ	tų̃	tõs	tų̃
D.	tám	tíems	tái	tóms
A.	tą̃	tuõs	tą̃	tàs
I.	tuõ	taĩs	tà	tomìs
L.	tamè	tuosè	tojè	tosè

N.	anàs 'that'	aniẽ	anà	anõs
G.	anõ	anų̃	anõs	anų̃
D.	anám	aníems	anái	anóms
A.	aną̃	anuõs	aną̃	anàs
I.	anuõ	anaĩs	anà	anomìs
L.	anamè	anuosè	anojè	anosè

36.1 The Demonstrative Pronouns

One can compare the declension of *šìs* with that of *jìs* in paragraph 8.4. The declension of *tàs* and *anàs* is just like that of a first declension adjective, except for the instrumental singular and the nominative and accusative plural (*tuõ*; *tiẽ, tuõs*; *anuõ*; *aniẽ, anuõs*). The declension of *šìtas* 'this, that' is exactly like that of *tàs*, except that the stress remains constant on the initial syllable.

The demonstrative *šìs* 'this' contrasts with *tàs* 'that'. Both *šìs* and *tàs* contrast with *anàs* 'that' which denotes a third object which is farther away than *tàs*. Examples:

1) *Šì lémpa yrà màno, tà lémpa yrà tàvo, õ anà lémpa yrà jõ.* — This lamp is mine, that lamp is yours, but the one over there is his.

2) *Šì knygà yrà gerèsnė ùž tą̃.* — This book is better than that.

3) *Mán patiñka šìs stãlas, bèt nè tàs.* — I like this table, but not that one.

The form *šìtas* is perhaps more emphatic than *šìs* e.g. *šìtas žmogùs ùžmušė màno tėvą* 'that man killed my father'.

36.1,2 The declension of *tóks* 'such (a)' is given below:

	Masculine		Feminine	
	Singular	Plural	Singular	Plural
N.	tóks (3)	tokiẽ	tokià	tókios
G.	tókio	tokių̃	tokiõs	tokių̃
D.	tokiám	tokíems	tókiai	tokióms
A.	tókį	tókius	tókią	tókias
I.	tókiu	tokiaĩs	tókia	tokiomìs
L.	tokiamè	tokiuosè	tokiojè	tokiosè

anóks (1) 'that kind of', *šìtoks* (1) 'this kind of' have the same endings, but the stress pattern is different. (Always on the same syllable). Examples:

1) *Tóks žmogùs niẽko nepadarỹs.* — Such a man will do nothing.

2) *Àš jaũ gavaũ šìtokį láišką, bèt anókio niekadà negavaũ.* — I already received this kind of letter, but I never got that kind.

36.2 The Interrogative *kàs*.

The interrogative pronoun-adjective *kàs* 'who, what' is declined as follows: N. kàs, G. kõ, kienõ, D. kám, A. ką̃, I. kuõ, L. kamè. It has no plural declension and it may refer to either masculine or feminine nouns or pronouns.

36.2,1 *Kelì* 'how many' is used only in the plural.

	Masculine	Feminine
N.	kelì (4)	kḗlios
G.	kelių̃	kelių̃
D.	kelíems	kelióms
A.	kelìs	keliàs
I.	keliaĩs	keliomìs
L.	keliuosè	keliosè

36.2,2 *Kóks, tóks, kurìs, katràs, kelerì, keliñtas, keleriópas, kienõ.*

kóks (3) 'which' is declined like *tóks*; *kurìs* (4) 'which' is declined like *jìs*; *katràs* (4) 'which' (only said of two objects in standard Lithuanian) is declined like *tàs*; *kelerì* (3b) 'how many' is declined like *kelì* (cf. 36.2,1); *keliñtas* (4) 'which' and *keleriópas* (1) 'of how many kinds' are declined like regular adjectives.

Examples:

1) *Kàs atsitìko?* — What happened?
2) *Kõ jìs nóri?* — What does he want?
3) *Kienõ tà knygà?* — Whose is that book?
   kienõ 'whose, of whom, by whom' is used to denote possession or as the subject of a passive verbal construction (cf. Lesson 34), whereas *kõ* is reserved for other genitive uses.
4) *Kám tù daveĩ knýgą?* — To whom did you give the book?
5) *Ką̃ jìs mãto?* — What does he see?
6) *Sù kuõ tù einì?* — With whom are you going?
   kóks may mean 'which' in the sense of 'which kind of' or 'to what extent'.
7) *Kóks dabar̃ óras?* — What is the weather like now?
8) *Kelì žmónės atẽjo?* — How many men came?
9) *Keliàs dienàs jìs čià bùvo?* — How many days was he here?
10) *Kurìs mėnuo šilčiáusias Lietuvojè?* — What month is the warmest in Lithuania?
11) *Kurì knygà táu patiñka?* — Which book do you like?

285

12) *Kurìs ìš jūsų taĩ padãrė? —* Which of you did it?
13) *Katràs sūnùs ateĩs? —* Which son (of two) will come?
   kelerì is used with nouns which in the plural form may have a singular meaning, e.g. *marškiniaĩ* 'shirt', etc.
14) *Kēleris márškinius tù turì? —* How many shirts do you have?
15) *Keleriópas prekès jìs tùri? —* How many kinds of wares does he have?

36.3 Relative Pronouns *kurìs, kàs, kóks.*

kàs, kurìs and *kóks* can also be used as relative pronouns. The number and the gender of the relative pronoun are determined by the word to which it refers, but the case of the relative pronoun is determined by its use in the clause of which it is a part. Examples:

1) *Mán patiñku tà knygà, kurią̃ tù mán daveĩ. —* I like the book which you gave me.
   Notice that *kurią̃* is feminine and singular because it refers to *knygà* which is feminine and singular; it is in the accusative case because it is the object of the verb *daveĩ.*

2) *Àš pažį̃stu tą̃ žmógų, sù kuriuõ jū̃s kal̃bate. —* I know that man with whom you are speaking.
   Note that *kuriuõ* is masculine singular because *žmógų* is masculine singular; it is the instrumental case because it is the object of the preposition *sù* which requires the instrumental case.

3) *Kàs geraĩ dìrba, tàs daũg pinigų̃ gáuna. —* Whoever works well (that one=*tàs*) gets much money.

4) *Kokià sėjà, tokià iर̃ piūtìs. —* You reap what you sow. (lit.: whatever the sowing is, such also is the harvest.)

5) *Kóks kláusimas, tóks iर̃ atsãkymas. —* Whatever the question is (like), thus also is the answer.

N.B. To render the English relative pronouns 'who', 'that', 'which' (and their various forms), use *kurìs.* See also 21.6.

36.4 *Kažkàs, bet kàs, kas-ne-kàs.*

kàs may be used as an indefinite pronoun by itself; it may be used in conjunction with *nórs*, thus *kàs nórs* 'anybody, somebody or other; anything, something or other'. The form *kažkàs* (*kažìn kas*) 'somebody, something' differs in meaning from the preceding in that it refers to somebody or something definite, but either the speaker doesn't know exactly what this thing is, who the person is, or else the speaker does not consider it necessary to reveal it.

The forms *bet kàs*, (*by kàs*, *bile kàs*) '(just) anybody, somebody'; *kai kàs* 'many a', some; *kas-ne-kàs* 'a few, not many' are also used. In these forms the element *kàs* is declined. Examples:

1) *Ař kàs (kas nórs) atėjo?* — Did anyone come?
2) *Kažkàs atėjo.* — Someone came.
3) *Bet kàs taĩ gãli padarýti.* — Anyone can do that.
4) *Nè bet kàs jį̃ suprañta.* — Not everyone understands him.
5) *Kai kám tà knygà nepatiñka.* — Some people don't like this book.
6) *Turiù dár ką̃-ne-ką̃ nusipiřkti.* — I still have to buy a few (things).

36.5 Special Uses of *kóks* and *kurìs* (as Pronoun-Adjectives).

The pronoun-adjectives *kóks* and *kurìs* are used in many constructions similar to those given above.

1) *Gál ateĩs kóks nórs svéčias.* — Perhaps some guest (or other) will come.
2) *Skaitýk kókią nórs knỹgą.* — Read any book (some book or other).
3) *Kažkóks svẽčias atėjo.* — Some guest came.
4) *Sù bet kókiu žmogumì nekalbẽk.* — Don't talk with any man.
5) *Kaĩ kuriẽ mokiniaĩ tojè klãsėje yrà labaĩ gãbūs.* — Some pupils in that class are very talented (gifted).

The expression *šióks tóks* denotes poor or mediocre quality of the word modified; *ne-kóks* means 'rather poor, bad' (colloquially 'lousy').

7) *Nusipirkaũ šiókį tókį apsiaũstą.* — I bought an ordinary (a coat of rather poor quality) coat.
8) *Jìs gãvo nekókį dárbą.* — He got a 'lousy' job.
9) *Jìs mán duõs kurį̃ nórs apsiaũstą.* — He will give me some coat.
10) *Ateĩk kurią̃ diẽną.* — Come some day.
11) *Kažkuriẽ ìš jų̃ taĩ padãrė.* — Some of them did that.
12) *Teateĩna bèt kurìs ìš júsų.* — Come, any of you.
13) *Kaĩ kuriẽ žmónės taĩ dãro.* — Some people do that.
14) *Kuriẽ-ne-kuriẽ taĩ sãko.* — Certain ones say that.

36.6 *Kelì, kelerì* 'several' are also used as indefinite pronoun-adjectives. Examples:

1) *Aš nusipirkaũ šią knỹgą priẽš kẽlerius metùs.* — I bought this book a few years ago.
2) *Aš norė́čiau pasakýti kelìs žodžiùs.* — I would like to say a few words.

36.7 *Víenas kìtas* means 'a few', e.g. *víenas kìtas atė́jo* — a few came.

36.8 To express the idea 'each other' *víenas* (not declined) is used plus some case of *kìtas* (not the nom. or the voc.) depending upon the syntactic construction involved. Examples.

1) *Šiẽ žmónės víenas kìto nepažį̃sta.* — These men don't know each other.
2) *Šiẽ žmónės víenas kitám pàdeda.* — These men help each other.
2) *Šiẽ žmónės víenas kìtą gìria.* — These men praise each other.
4) *Šiẽ žmónės víenas kitù pasìtiki.* — These men have confidence in each other.
5) *Šiẽ žmónės víenas kitamè mãto gènijų.* — These men see a genius in each other.

36.8.1 'Each other' with prepositions:

6) *Eĩna víenas põ kìto.* — They go one after another.
7) *Stóvi víenas priẽš kìtą.* — They stand in front of each other.

36.9 *Niẽkas* and *jóks*. The declension of the negative pronoun *niẽkas* 'no-one, nothing' is as follows: N. niẽkas, G. niẽko (niẽkieno), D. niẽkam, A. niẽką, I. niekù, L. niekamè. There is no distinction for gender or number.

The negative pronoun-adjective *jóks* (3) 'none, not any' is declined like *tóks*. Examples:

1) *Jìs niẽko nežìno.* — He knows nothing.
2) *Niẽkas nemė́gsta tõs knỹgos.* — No one likes that book.
3) *Jìs netùri jokių̃ knỹgų.* — He has no books.
4) *Jóks žmogùs negãli taĩ padarýti.* — No man can do that.

Note that *ne* must be used with the verb in a negated sentence with *jóks* or *niẽkas*. The resulting meaning is not that of a double negative as it would be in standard English. The correct usage in Lithuanian (as in many other languages) is translatable by the substandard English usage. Compare the substandard English 'he don't know nothin'' with Lith. *jìs niẽko nežìno.*

EXERCISES

A. *Questions.* 1. Kàs suviẽnijo Líetuvą? 2. Kienõ bùvo vaĺdoma Lietuvà priẽš Mìndaugą? 3. Kuriaĩs mētais Mìndaugas sùmušė kalavijuočiùs priẽ Šiaulių̃? 4. Kókį kẽlią pasirìñko Lietuvà? 5. Kàs Mìndaugui pavydėjo? 6. Kuriaĩs mētais Mìndaugas bùvo nužudýtas? 7. Aŕ jùms patìñka šì knygà? 8. Aŕ jũs jaũ skaĩtėte aną̃ knỹgą, kurì gùli añt stãlo? 9. Aŕ kàs nórs jį̃ mãtė? 10. Kuŕ àš galiù piŕkti víeną kìtą knỹgą?

B. *Decline in the singular and plural:* šìs gẽras studeñtas, jóks turtìngas žmogùs, tóks gražùs rýtas, tà gražì mergáitė, tokià tamsì naktìs.

C. *Fill in with the relative pronoun* k u r ì s *in appropriate forms:*
1. Žmogùs, (whom) .... àš vãkar mačiaũ teatrè, yrà jõ sẽnas draũgas. 2. Tiẽ studeñtai, su (whom) .... profèsorius Valáitis kaĺba, studijúoja lietùvių kaĺbą. 3. Nãmas, (in which) .... jiẽ gyvẽna, yrà labaĩ sẽnas. 4. Knỹgos, (which) .... àš vãkar pirkaũ knygýne, yrà labaĩ bráñgios. 5. Mẽdžiai, (which) .... áuga mìško vidurjyè, yrà gražiáusi. 6. Žmónės, (who) .... mėgsta dainúoti, yrà laimìngi.

CONVERSATION

PABAUDA UŽ PER GREITĄ VAŽIAVIMĄ

Polìcininkas: 1. Prašaũ paródyti vairúotojo liùdijimą.

Naujókas: 2. Tuojaũ suràsiu. (Padúoda polìcininkui sàvo vairúotojo liùdijimą). Kodėl manè sustãbdėte?

P. 3. Jũs per greĩtai važiãvote.

N. 4. Kaĩp taĩ per greĩtai? Aš važiavaũ tìk 35 (trìsdešimt penkiàs) myliàs į̃ vãlandą (or: peŕ vãlandą).*

P. 5. Aŕ jũs nemãtėte eĩsmo žénklo:* šià gatvè gãlima važiúoti tìk 25 (dvìdešimt penkiàs) myliàs* į̃ vãlandą.

N. 6. Aš labaĩ atsiprašaũ. Tikraĩ tõ žénklo nepastebėjau.

P. 7. Jũs nèkreipéte démesio į eĩsmo žénklus. Tèks sumokéti pãbaudą: 25 (dvìdešimt penkìs) dólerius.

N. 8. Bèt ... bèt àš jùk pamažù važiavaũ ...

P. 9. Jũs iš tikrũjų važiãvote 40 (kéturiasdešimt) mỹlių į vãlandą. Anksčiaũ iř jũs pàts sãkéte, kàd važiãvote 35 myliàs į vãlandą. Taĩgi ...

N. 10. Geraĩ, geraĩ ... Turésiu sumokéti pãbaudą. Ką̃ gì padarýsi ... Ateityjè turésiu atidžiaũ sèkti eĩsmo žénklus.

TICKET FOR SPEEDING

Policeman: 1. Please show me (your) driver's license.

Naujokas: 2. Right away (I will find it). [Hands over his driver's license to the policeman] Why did you stop me?

P. 3. You were driving too fast.

N. 4. What do you mean (how come) too fast? I was driving only 35 miles per hour.

P. 5. Didn't you see the traffic (speed) sign? On this street you are allowed to drive only 25 miles an hour. (The speed limit is ...)

N. 6. I am very sorry. I really did not notice that sign.

P. 7. You were not paying attention to the traffic signs. You will have to pay the fine: 25 dollars.

N. 8. But ... but I was actually driving slowly ...

P. 9. Really, you were driving 40 miles per hour. You yourself just said you were driving 35 miles per hour. Thus, ...

N. 10. All right, all right. I will have to pay the fine. What can one do about it? In the future, I will have to watch the road signs more carefully.

NOTES:

4. į vãlandą — also: peř vãlandą 'per hour'.
5. eĩsmo žénklas — traffic (road, speed) sign.
   dvìdešimt penkiàs myliàs — this expression of speed measurement has to be in the accusative case.

Trisdešimt septintoji pamoka

Lesson 37

VYTAUTAS DIDYSIS

Põ Mìndaugo nužùdymo Lietuvà kíek susilpnėjo, nès dažnaĩ keĩtėsi valdõvai. Bèt nuõ Vytėnio (1295-1316) iř ýpač nuõ Gedimìno (1316-1341) laikų̃ Lietuvõs valstýbė nuõlat stiprėjo ir áugo užimdamà vìs didesniùs plótus į̃ rýtus iř į̃ pietų̃ rýtus. Gedimìno pālikuonys, istòrijoje vadìnami Gedimináičiais (Gedimináičių dinãstija), Líetuvą išùgdė į̃ pirmaeĩlę valstýbę.

Gedimìno sūnūs, Aľgirdas (1345-1377) ir Kęstùtis (1345-1382), kuriẽ bendraĩ vaĩdė Líetuvą, ìšplėtė Lietuvõs ribàs lìgi Maskvõs apýlinkių, õ pietuosè jaũ pasíekė Júodąją jū́rą.

Bèt labiáusiai Lietuvà sustiprėjo Kęstùčio sūnaũs Výtauto Dìdžiojo viešpatāvimo metù (1392-1430). Jìs sutvaŕkė valstýbės administrāciją, galutinaĩ pràplėtė Lietuvõs ribàs lìgi Juodõsios jū́ros. Jìs stãtė pilìs, tiẽsė keliùs, laĩkė geraĩ apmókytą nuolatìnę kariúomenę. Výtauto viešpatāvimo metù Lietuvà šalià Anglijos, Vokietijos iř Prancūzìjos bùvo vienà iš keturių̃ didžiáusių Euròpos valstýbių. Tuõ metù bevéik visà Rùsija bùvo pavergtà totõrių, õ patì Maskvà bùvo tìk nedìdelės kunigaikštìjos sóstinė.

1410 mẽtais Lietuvõs kariúomenė išsìrengė dideliám žỹgiui į̃ Prū́siją, į̃ Kryžiuõčių òrdino žemès. Jaũ bevéik pusañtro šim̃to mẽtų Lietuvà nuõlat kariãvo sù kryžiuõčiais. Bùvo įvỹkę daũg kãro žỹgių iř mūšių iš abiejų̃ pùsių, tačiaũ nė vienà pùsė nebùvo galutinaĩ laimėjusi.

Výtautas, susitãręs sù Lénkijos karãliumi Jogáila, kurìs bùvo jõ pùsbrolis, nùtarė galutinaĩ sunaikìnti kryžiuočiùs. Lemiamàsis mũšis įvỹko 1410 mẽtų líepos 10 diẽną priẽ Tànnenbergo káimo. Jungtìnės lietùvių iř lénkų pãjėgos, vadováujamos Vỹtauto, vìsiškai sùmušė kryžiuočiùs iř jų̃ talkininkùs ìš daũgelio Euròpos kraštų̃. Šiuõ laimėjimu bùvo galutinaĩ sustabdýtas vókiečių veržìmasis į̃ rýtus.

Põ šiõ labaĩ svarbaũs laimėjimo Vỹtautas daũg nebekariãvo, bèt tvařkė sàvo valstýbę iř sàvo sumanumù bùvo jái užtìkrinęs taikìngą gyvẽnimą, kuriõ Lietuvà nebùvo turėjusi peř paskutiniùs dù šimtùs mẽtų.

VOCABULARY

susilpnẽti (susilpnẽju, susilpnẽja, susilpnẽjo, susilpnẽs) — to grow weaker, to weaken
keĩstis (keičiúosi, keĩčiasi, keĩtėsi, keĩsis) — to turn over, to exchange, to succeed (in power)
ýpač — especially
nuõlat — all the time, by and by, continually
užiřmti (ùžimu, ùžima, ùžėmė, užiřms) — (here) to occupy
plótas (1) — area, region
į̃ rýtus — to the east
į̃ pietų̃ rýtus — to the south-east
palikuonìs -ỹẽs (3b) — descendent
išugdýti (išugdaũ, išùgdo, išùgdė, išugdỹs) — to raise, to nurture, to expand
pirmaeĩlis, -ė (2) — first class (adj.)
bendraĩ — together, commonly
išplė̃sti (išplečiu, išplẽčia, išplė̃tė, išplė̃s) — to expand, to extend
ribà (4) — boundary
pietuosè — in the South
Juodóji jū́ra — Black Sea
viešpatãvimas (1) — reign
sutvarkýti (sutvarkaũ, sutvařko, sutvařkė, sutvarkỹs) — to put in order, to straighten out, to arrange
galutinaĩ — finally, for good
praplė̃sti (pràplečiu, pràplečia, pràplėtė, praplė̃s) — to extend, to widen
apmókyti (apmókau, apmóko, apmókė, apmókys) — to train
nuolatìnis, -ė (2) — permanent
kariúomenė (1) — army

pavergti (pavergiù, pavergia, pàvergė, pàvergs) — to subjugate
totõrius (2) Tatar (noun)
kunigaikštijà (2) — dukedom, principality
išsireñgti (išsirengiù, išsireñgia, išsìrengė, išsireñgs) — to get ready, to set out
žỹgis -io (2) — campaign
ìš abiejų̃ pùsių — from both sides, on both sides
susitařti (susìtariu, susìtaria, susìtarė, susitařs) — to make an agreement, to conclude an agreement
karãlius (2) — king
sunaikìnti (sunaikinù, sunaikìna, sunaikìno, sunaikiñs) — to destroy
lēmiamas, -à (3) — decisive
įvỹkti (impers.: įvỹksta, įvỹko, įvỹks) — to take place, to occur, to happen
pãjėgos (3b) — (here) forces
vadováuti (vadováuju, vadováuja, vadovãvo, vadovaũs) — to lead, to command
talkiniñkas (2) — helper, supporter
laimėjimas (1) — victory
sustabdýti (sustabdaũ, sustãbdo, sustãbdė, sustabdỹs) — to stop
veržìmasis (1) (refl. noun) — push, drive
sumanùmas (2) — cleverness, wisdom, shrewdness
užtìkrinti (užtìkrinu, užtìkrina, užtìkrino, užtìkrins) — to assure
taikìngas, -a (1) — peaceful
paskutìnis, -ė (2) — last

GRAMMAR

37.1 Prepositions.

The object of each preposition must be in the case which the preposition requires, e.g. genitive, accusative, instrumental.

37.2 Prepositions with the Genitive Case.

Some examples of prepositions which require the genitive case are listed below:

1) *abìpus* — on both sides of.
   Kaũnas yrà abìpus Nẽmuno (ùpės). — Kaunas is on both sides of the Nemunas (River).

2) *anàpus* — on the other side of.
   St. Paul miẽstas yrà anàpus Mississìpi ùpės. — (The city of) St. Paul is on the other side of the Mississippi River.

3) *anót* — according to (repeating someone's words exactly).
   Jìs, anót tẽvo, gẽras žmogùs. — He, according to (my) father, is a good man.

4) *añt* — on; expresses feelings towards (someone).
   Knygà gùli añt stãlo. — The book is (lying) on the table.
   Jìs pỹksta añt sàvo brólio. — He is angry at his brother.

5) *artì* — close to.
   Jìs bùvo artì namṹ. — He was close to his home.

6) *aukščiaũ* — above; (really an adverb 'higher').
   Tojè ùpėje vandeñs bùvo aukščiaũ kẽliṵ. — In that river, the water stood above the knees.

7) *bè* — without; in addition to.
   Sunkù gyvénti bè pinigṵ. — It is difficult to live without money.
   Bè knỹgṵ, teñ yrà dár i͠r rañkrasčiṵ. — In addition to the books, there are manuscripts there, too.
   bè ãbejo, bè abejónės — without a doubt, doubtless, doubtlessly
   bè gãlo — without end, endless, endlessly
   bè reĩkalo — without any need, needless, needlessly, etc.

8) *dėkà* — thanks to, owing to.
   Tẽvo dėkà àš šiañdien dár dìrbu. — Thanks to father I am still working today.

9) *dėl (dėlei)* — for, for the sake of, because of.
   Dėl kõ neišmókote pamokõs? — Why (lit.: because of what) didn't you study (learn) your lesson?

293

10) *gretà* — near, beside.
   Jìs stóvi gretà manę̃s. — He stands beside me.

11) *iki* — until, up to; as far as (may be used with dative case in certain fixed expressions, cf. 37.4).
   Iki pasimãtymo. — So long (lit.: until we see each other).
   Aš nuėjaũ iki ùpės. — I went up to the river.

12) *įstrižaĩ* — diagonally across.
   Jìs atsìgulė įstrižaĩ lóvos. — He lay down diagonally across the bed.

13) *iš* — out of; from; since.
   Jìs išeĩna iš namų̃. — He is going out of his house (home).
   Jìs gãvo iš manę̃s láišką. — He got a letter from me.
   Jìs iš jaunų̃ dienų̃ tóks. — He has been that way since youth.

14) *išilgaĩ* — along.
   Kẽlias eĩna išilgaĩ ùpės. — The road runs along the river.

15) *lìg, lìgi* — until; as far as. (*Lìg, lìgi* is synonymous with *iki*, cf. 11)
   Aš skaičiaũ lìgi vãkaro. — I read (was reading) until evening.
   Aš nuėjaũ lìgi jõ namų̃. — I went up to his home.

16) *liñk (liñkui)* — toward, to.
   Jìs bė́ga liñk mìško. — He runs (is running) toward the forest.

17) *netolì* — not far from, near; approximately.
   Universitètas yrà netolì miẽsto ceñtro. — The university is not far away from the center of the city.
   Teñ bùvo netolì šim̃to žmonių̃. — About a hundred people were there.

18) *nuõ* — from, off; (guarding) against; since, from; by reason of, because of.
   Vanduõ bė́ga nuõ stõgo. — Water runs off the roof.
   Váistai nuõ galvõs skaudė́jimo. — Medicine for (against) a headache.
   Jìs dìrba nuõ rýto lìgi vãkaro. — He works from morning 'til night.
   Jìs keñčia nuõ kar̃ščio. — He is suffering from the heat.

19) *pasàk* — according to (relating someone else's words, or opinion; *pasàk* is synonymous with *anót*, cf. 3)
   Ir̃ Pẽtras, pasàk jõ, niẽko netùri. — And Peter, according to him, does not have anything.

20) *pir̃m (pirmà)* — before; in front of.
   Niẽko nedarýk pir̃m laĩko. — Don't do anything ahead of time.
   Jìs eĩna pirmà manę̃s. — He is going in front of me.

21) *põ* — after.

Põ koncèrto àš parėjaũ namõ. — After the concert I went home.

NB. This preposition can also be used with other cases with different meanings, cf. below.

22) *priẽ* — at, near, in the vicinity of; in the presence of; in the time of.

Šìs autobùsas sustója priẽ bibliotèkos. — This bus stops near the library.

Vaikaĩ užáugo priẽ tėvũ. — The children grew up with their parents.

Priẽ sẽno karãliaus visì geraĩ gyvẽno. — In the time of the old king everybody lived well.

23) *pusiáu* — half way up, half way along.

Pasitikaũ jã pusiáu kẽlio. — I met her half way along the road.

24) *skersaĩ* — across, athwart.

Jìs gùli skersaĩ lóvos. — He is lying across the bed.

NB. This preposition can be used with the accusative case also with no difference in meaning:
Jìs pérėjo skersaĩ kẽlią. — He went across the road.

25) *šalià* — beside.

Jìs atsisẽdo šalià manę̃s. — He sat down beside me.

26) *šiàpus* — on this side of.

Universitètas yrà šiàpus ùpės. — The university is on this side of the river.

27) *tar̃p* — between, among.

Tar̃p Jõno ir̃ Pètro yrà dìdelis skìrtumas. — There is a big difference between John and Peter.

Kėdė̃ stóvi tar̃p stãlo ir̃ síenos. — The chair stands between the table and the wall.

28) *ùž* — behind; at a distance of; in, after (in expressions of time).

Vaĩkas stovėjo ùž mótinos ir̃ ver̃kė. — The child stood behind (his) mother and cried.

Ùž trijũ mètrų pasiródė vanduõ. — At the depth of three meters water appeared.

Jìs baĩgs dárbą ùž (vieneriũ) mė̃tų. — He will finish the work in a year.

Jì pàėmė manè ùž rañkos. — She took me by the hand.

NB. This preposition can also be used with the accusative case, cf. below.

29) *vidùj* — within, inside of (This is really an abbreviated form
of *vidujè*, which is the locative sg. of *vidùs*, 'the inside, the
inner side').
Vidùj mìško bùvo daũg šilčiaũ. — It was much warmer within the forest.
30) *Vir̃š, viršùj, viršuñ* — over, beyond; above.
Taĩ vir̃š màno jė́gų. — That is beyond my strength.
Vir̃š mẽdžių skraĩdė dideli paũkščiai. — Above the trees large
birds were flying.
31) *žemiaũ* — below.
Upėje vandeñs bùvo žemiaũ kẽlių. — Water in the river was
below the knees.

37.3 Compound prepositions with *iš* as the initial element require
the genitive case also.
a) *Iš anàpus mìško pakìlo lėktùvas.* — An airplane rose from the
other side of the forest. (... from behind ...)
b) *Katė̃ išbė́go ìš põ stãlo.* — A cat ran out from under the table.

37.4 Prepositions in Certain Fixed Expressions.

(Prepositions with the Dative Case.)
A few prepositions are used with the dative case in certain
fixed expressions. Otherwise there are no prepositions in Lithuanian which regularly require the dative case.
1) *põ šiái diẽnai* — up to the present time
2) *põ senóvei* — as it was; 'nothing new'; 'things are the same'
(lit.: according to the past).
3) *põ kám* — how much (obsolete).
4) *põ dẽšinei* — to the right
5) *põ kaĩrei* — to the left
6) *ìki šiái diẽnai* — up to the present time (but also possible: *ìki
šiõs dienõs*, same meaning).
7) *ìki šiám laĩkui* — up to this time (also: *ìki šiõ laĩko*).

37.5 Prepositions with the Accusative Case.

Some examples of prepositions which require the accusative
case are listed below:
1) *apiẽ* — round about, near; approximately; concerning.
Apiẽ sõdą áuga mẽdžiai. — Round about the orchard, trees
grow.

Jìs kalba apiẽ manè. — He is talking about me.

Ateĩk apiẽ dvýliktą vãlandą. — Come at about (around) 12 o'clock.

2) *apliñk (apliñkui)* — around, by.

Apliñk manè stovėjo daũg jaunų̃ žmoniṹ. — Many young people stood around me.

3) *į̃* — in, into, to.

Vaĩkas eĩna į̃ kam̃barį. — The child is going into the room (The child is entering the room).

Màno visì vaikaĩ jaũ eĩna į̃ mokỹklą. — All my children (already) go to school (attend school).

Kaimýnas važiúoja į̃ miẽstą, į̃ tur̃gų. — The neighbor is going to the city, to the market.

Berniùkas lìpa į̃ mẽdį. — The boy is climbing a tree.

Mokinỹs atsãko į̃ kláusimus. — The pupil answers the questions.

Jìs niekuomèt neatsãko į̃ màno láiškus. — He never replies to my letters.

Jìs labaĩ panašùs į̃ sàvo tẽvą. — He is very similar to his father (He looks very much like his father).

4) *pagal* — along, beside; according to.

Jìs bẽga pagal tvõrą. — He runs along the fence.

Jiẽ visuomèt dìrba pagal plãną. — They always work according to plan.

5) *paleĩ* — along, by the side of, beside.

Jìs stovėjo paleĩ síeną. — He stood beside the wall.

6) *pàs* — at, at the home of, at the house of, to.

Ateĩkite pàs manè. — Come to my place.

Jìs gyvẽna pàs manè. — He is living at my place.

7) *paskuĩ* — right after, close behind.

Eĩk paskuĩ manè. — Follow (right) behind me.

8) *per̃* — through, across; during, throughout.

Jiẽ bẽgo per̃ laukùs. — They ran across the fields.

Per̃ kãrą mẽs daũg mãtėme. — During the war we saw a lot.

9) *põ* — round about, here and there.

Jìs váikščiojo põ miẽstą. — He was walking in (about) the town.

NB. This preposition may also have a distributive meaning which cannot be translated by any single English expression: *Jìs dúoda vaikáms põ gãbalą sṹrio.* — He gives the children each a piece of cheese. Note also that it can be used with other cases.

10) *priẽš* — before, in the presence of; ago; against.

Priẽš jõ namùs áugo dìdelė líepa. — In front of his house grew a large linden tree.

Priẽš dẽšimt mẽtų jìs dár čià gyvẽno. — Ten years ago he still lived here.

Jìs kovójo priẽš manè. — He fought against me.

11) *prõ* — by, past; through.

Mẽs pravažiãvome prõ sẽną pìlį. — We drove past the old castle.

Jì žiūri prõ lángą. — She is looking through the window.

12) *skersaĩ* — across, cf. example 24, §37.2.

13) *už* — than; for, in return for.

Už dárbą gavaũ pinigų. — I received some money for the work.

Mẽs kovójame ùž láisvę. — We are fighting for freedom.

Padirbĕk ùž manè. — Work for me (Take over my work for a while).

37.6 Prepositions with the Instrumental Case.

Some examples of prepositions which require the instrumental case are listed below:

1) *põ* — under.

Šuõ gùli põ stalù. — A dog is lying under the table.

2) *sù* — with; approximately the size of.

Eĩk sù manimì. — Go with me.

Jìs sù medžiù lýgus. — He is about the size of a tree.

3) *sulìg* — up to, as far as.

Vandeñs bùvo sulìg krantaĩs. — The water was up to the banks.

4) *tiẽs* — opposite, in front of.

Jìs stóvi tiẽs lángu. — He is standing in front of the window.

Lietùvių pulkaĩ tiẽs Kaunù plaŭkė peř Nẽmuną. — The Lithuanian troops (regiments) swam across the Nemunas (river) opposite Kaunas.

37.7 Prepositions Used with Several Cases.

Note that *põ* can be used with the genitive case (when it means 'after'), with the dative case (in certain fixed expressions), with the accusative case (when it means 'here and there, round about' or when it has distributive meaning) or with the instrumental case (when it means 'under').

The preposition *ùž* can be used with the genitive case (when it means 'in, after') or with the accusative case (when it means 'for').

The preposition *skersaĩ* 'across, athwart' can be used with either the genitive or the accusative case with no difference in meaning.

The preposition *ìki* ordinarily is used with the genitive case, but in certain fixed expressions it is used with the dative case.

37.8 A review list of prepositions used with various cases:

GENITIVE — *abìpus, anàpus, anót, añt, artì, aukščiaũ, bè, dėkà, dėl, gretà, ìki, įstrižaĩ, ìš, išilgaĩ, lìgi, liñk, netolì, nuõ, pasàk, piřm, põ, priẽ, pusiáu, skersaĩ, šalià, šiàpus, tařp, ùž, vidùj, viřš, viršùj, viršuř, žemiaũ, iš anãpus, iš põ,* etc.

DATIVE — *ìki, põ* (only in certain fixed expressions).

ACCUSATIVE — *apiẽ, apliñk, į̃, pagaĩ, paleĩ, pàs, paskuĩ, peř, põ, priẽš, prõ, skersaĩ, ùž*

INSTRUMENTAL — *põ, sù, sulìg, tiẽs*

37.9 Prepositions and Adverbs.

Some prepositions in Lithuanian are derived from adverbs. These prepositions, in most cases, may still be used as adverbs. Examples:

a) *Berniùkas stovėjo gretà, õ mergáitė kiẽk toliaũ.* — The boy was standing close by, and the girl was a little farther (from there).

b) *Víenas studeñtas ėjo pirmà, kìtas paskuĩ.* — One student walked in front (first), the other one—after (him).

37.10 Expressions with Prepositions and without them.

In some special cases one may either use a preposition with a certain case, or the noun can be used without a preposition, but in such a case which has the same meaning as the preposition together with the noun. One can say . . .

e i t h e r :
Jì paviřto į̃ pẽlę. — She turned into a mouse.

o r :
Jì paviřto pelè. — She turned . . . (*pelè*—instrumental)

either:

Jiẽ mìrė ìš (nuõ) bãdo. — They died from hunger (famine).

o r :

Jiẽ mìrė badù. — They died ... (*badù*—instrumental)

either:

Jìs gùli añt lóvos. — He is lying on the bed.

o r :

Jìs gùli lóvoje. — He is lying ... (*lóvoje*—locative)

EXERCISES

A. *Questions.* 1. Kadà Lietuvà susilpnėjo? 2. Kaĩp yrà istòrijoje vadìnami Gedimìno pãlikuonys? 3. Lìgi kuriõs jūros Výtautas iš-plėtė Lietuvõs ribàs? 4. Kàs įvýko 1410-siais mētais líepos 10 diē-ną? 5. Ką̃ dãrė Výtautas põ Tannenbergo mūšio? 6. Priẽ kokiõs ùpės yrà Vìlnius? 7. Priẽ kokiõs ùpės yrà Kaũnas? 8. Priẽ kokiõs ùpės yrà Niujòrkas? 9. Kàs gyvēna pàs jùs? 10. Iš kuriõs knỹgos jū̃s taĩ nusirãšėte (copied)?

B. *Form sentences with the following prepositions:* añt, põ, ùž, pàs, priẽ, peř, prõ.

C. *Copy sentences from reading selections of lessons 31-35 where prepositions occur. Translate the prepositions.*

D. *Translate into Lithuanian:* 1. His children still live at his place (home). 2. We are going with our old friends to take a walk in the park. 3. They live near us (not far away from us). 4. His house stands near the river. 5. Five new books are lying on the table. 6. She is looking through that window. 7. I walked along the fence. 8. He is going to Europe. 9. I am going home. 10. She is always at home (sits at home).

CONVERSATION

VASARA

Výras: 1. Šiañdien šeštãdienis. Tìk ką̃ prànešė peř rãdiją, kàd bùs labaĩ káršta. Važiúokime kuř nórs pasimáudyti.

Žmonà: 2. Bū́tų geraĩ nuvažiúoti priẽ jūros, bèt tolóka ...

Vyras: 3. Gál važiúokime į̃ miẽsto baseĩną.

Žmona: 4. Teñ šiañdien bùs labaĩ daũg žmonių̃ ...

Vyras:	5.	Taĩ gál važiúokime kuř nórs į párką; vaikaĩ galĕs pabĕgióti, õ mĕs pasĕdĕsime põ mĕdžiais.
Žmona:	6.	Kaĩ tìk tù nuvažiúoji į párką, tuojaũ užmingì, pavĕsyje patõgiai iššitiĕsęs!
Vyras:	7.	O ką̃ gì teñ párke darýti?
Žmona:	8.	Tù visái nemataĩ gamtõs grõžio, vãsaros žalùmo, mĕdžių šlamĕjimo. Visì výrai tokiẽ ...
Vyras:	9.	Geraĩ jaũ geraĩ: važiúosime teñ, kuř tù nóri.
Žmona:	10.	Eĩk, suràsk visùs máudymosi kostiumùs, sukráuk vìską į automobìlį. Tùrime skubĕti, nès vĕliaũ bùs labaĩ káršta.

SUMMER

Husband:	1.	Today is Saturday. It was announced on the radio that it will be very hot. Let's go swimming somewhere.
Wife:	2.	It would be nice to go to the sea shore, but it is rather far . . .
Husband:	3.	Well then, let's go to the public (city) swimming pool.
Wife:	4.	There will be a lot of people down there today.
Husband:	5.	Then perhaps we should go to some park somewhere; the children will be able to run around, and we will be able to sit under the trees.
Wife:	6.	As soon as you get to the park, you fall asleep right away, after having stretched out comfortably in the shade.
Husband:	7.	And what can one do in a park?
Wife:	8.	You do not see the beauty of nature, the green of the summer, the rustling of the trees. All men are like that.
Husband:	9.	All right, all right. We will go wherever you want to go.
Wife:	10.	Well, get a move on, gather all the bathing suits, put them in the car. We must hurry because it is going to get hot later on.

Useful Expressions and Idioms

How are you? — a) *Kaip gyvuojate?*

b) *Kaip einasi?*

c) *Kaip laikotės?*

d) *Kaip sekasi?*

I like this book. — *Man patinka ši knyga.*

You like this book, etc. — *Jums (Tau) patinka ši knyga, ir t.t.*

I am cold. — *Man (yra) šalta.*

You are cold. — *Jums (Tau) šalta.*

I was cold, etc. — *Man buvo šalta, ir t.t.*

There is nothing one (you) can do about it — *Nieko nepadarysi.*

Thank you very much — *Labai ačiū.*

You're welcome — *Prašau.*

Don't mention it — *Nėr už ką. (Prašau).*

Trisdešimt aštuntoji pamoka
Lesson 38

KRISTIJONAS DONELAITIS
(1714 - 1780)

Víenas iš didžiáusių lietùvių poètų yrà Kristijõnas Doneláitis. Jìs gìmė, mókėsi iȓ vìsą gyvẽnimą praléido Mažõjoje Lietuvojè. Ilgiáusiai jìs išgyvẽno Tolmìnkiemyje (1743-1780), kuȓ jìs bùvo liuterõnų parãpijos klebõnas. Teñ jìs iȓ parãšė sàvo svarbiáusią kūrinį — poèmą "Mẽtai".

Pàts Doneláitis niekuomèt nemãtė sàvo poèmos išspausdìntos — visùs sàvo raštùs palìko rañkraščiuose. Jiẽ bùvo išspausdìnti põ jõ mirtiẽs 1818 mẽtais.

"Mẽtai" yrà parašýti hegzãmetru. Šiojè poèmoje Doneláitis aprãšo Mažõsios Lietuvõs ūkininkų gyvẽnimą. Gražiaĩs vaizdaĩs jìs piẽšia jū̃ dárbus, vargùs iȓ rūpesčius. Blogùs ūkininkus jìs papeĩkia, gerúosius pàgiria.

"Mẽtai" yrà svarbiáusias lietùvių literatū̃ros veĩkalas, parašýtas 18-me (aštuonióliktajame) ámžiuje. Jìs išverstas į̃ keliàs kalbàs.

Doneláičio kalbà yrà kíek senóviška, bèt turtìnga iȓ vaizdìnga. Jõ "Mẽtai" laĩkomi labaĩ svarbiù lietùvių kalbõs paminklù. Štaĩ kẽletas eilùčių iš Doneláičio "Mẽtų" kartù sù ánglišku vertimù:

PAVASARIO LINKSMYBĖS

Jaũ saulẽlė vẽl atkópdama bùdino svíetą
Iȓ žiemõs šaltõs triūsùs pargriáudama juõkės.
Šalčių prãmonės sù ledaĩs sugaĩšti pagãvo,

Iř putódams sniẽgs visuř į niẽką paviřto.
Tuõ laukùs oraĩ drungnì gaivìndami glóstė
Iř žolelès visàs iš numìrusių šaũkė.
Krúmai sù šilaĩs visaĩs issibùdino kéltis,
O laukų̃ kalnaĩ sù klóniais pàmetė skrándas.

THE SPRING'S JOYS

Now the sun rose again to rouse the world
and laughed to topple down chill winter's labors.
And cold's creations, with the ice, diminished
as foam of snow changed everywhere to nothing.
Soon the bland weather stroked and woke the fields,
called up herbs of all species from the dead.
Thickets and very heath bestirred themselves;
hill, meadow, dale threw down their sheepskin jackets.*

VOCABULARY

poètas (2) — poet
Mažóji Lietuvà — Lithuania Minor
liuterõnas (2) — Lutheran (noun)
parãpija (1) — parish
klebõnas (2) — pastor
svarbùs (4) — important
kūrinỹs (3a) — creation, work
išspausdìnti (išspausdinù, išspausdì-na, išspausdìno, išspausdìns) — to print
rãštas (2) — writing, (written) work, (poetical) work
palìkti (paliekù, paliẽka, palìko, pa-lìks) — to leave
rañkraštis -čio (1) — manuscript
mirtìs -iẽs (4) fem. — death
hegzãmetras (1) — hexameter
poemà (2) — poem, (epic) poem
aprašýti (aprašaũ, aprãšo, aprãšė, aprašỹs) — to describe
vaízdas (4) — view, picture, portrayal
vařgas (4) — care, worry, suffering, hardship
rūpestis -čio (1) — care, worry

papeĩkti (papeikiù, papeĩkia, pàpeikė, papeĩks) — to scold, to admonish
pagìrti (pàgiriu, pàgiria, pagýrė, pa-giřs) — to praise
veĩkalas (3b) — work, (poetical) work
senóviškas (1) — archaic
vaizdìngas (1) — full of beautiful images, poetical, expressive
pamiñklas (2) — monument
šaltìnis -io (2) — source, well
výstytis (výstausi, výstosi, výstėsi, výstysis) — to develop
besivýstant — in the process of development
bendrìnis, -ė — common
bendrìnė kalbà — common language, standard language (both spoken and written)
pacitúoti (pacitúoju, pacitúoja, paci-tãvo, pacituõs) to cite, to quote
eilùtė (diminutive of eilẽ 'row') — line (of a poem, a page)
kartù — together with
vertìmas (2) — translation

* Translated by Clark Mills. Taken from: **The Green Oak**. Selected Lithuanian Poetry. Ed. by Algirdas Landsbergis and Clark Mills, Voyages Press, New York, 1962.

NB. No vocabulary is given for this passage of "Metai".

GRAMMAR

38.1 Co-ordinating Conjunctions (*iř̃*, *tačiaũ*, *õ*, *bèt*, etc.)

The words *iř̃* 'and', *tačiaũ* 'but, nevertheless, however' *ař̃*
'whether', *arbà ... arbà* 'either ... or', *neĩ ... neĩ* 'neither ... nor',
õ 'and, but', *bèt* 'but' are co-ordinating conjunctions and can connect either clauses, phrases or single words. Examples:

1) *Miẽsto gãtvės yrà ìlgos iř̃ siaũros.* — The streets of the city
   are long and narrow.
2) *Jìs atẽjo, tačiaũ nedìř̃bs.* — He came, but he won't work.
3) *Ař̃ diř̃bs, ař̃ nediř̃bs, vis tíek jìs gaũs pinigų̃.* — Whether he
   works or not, he will still get some money.
4) *Ateĩkite arbà šiañdien, arbà rytój.* — Come either today or
   tomorrow.
5) *Neĩ mokinỹs, neĩ mokinė̃ nedìrba.* — Neither the boy nor the
   girl pupil works.
   The conjunction *õ* 'but' is used to contrast two ideas.
6) *Jìs turtuõlis, õ àš vař̃gšas žmogėlis.* — He is a rich man, but
   I am just a poor little fellow.
7) *Jìs tùri daũg laĩko, õ atvažiúoti pàs mùs nenóri.* — He has
   lots of time, but he doesn't want to come to see us.
8) *Jìs gãli, õ àš negaliù.* — He can, but I can't.
   It may also be used following a negative clause.
9) *Jìs negãli, õ àš galiù.* — He can't, but I can.
10) *Àš nesù daĩlininkas, õ jìs yrà.* — I am not an artist (painter)
    but he is.

In each of the preceding examples *õ* could have been replaced
by *bèt*, which is more emphatic than *õ*. For example in sentence
6, the word *bèt* would have stressed the fact that it is *I* (not another) who is the ordinary little fellow, whereas *õ* merely contrasts the two clauses. Likewise in sentence 9 the *õ* merely contrasts the two clauses, whereas *bèt* would have stressed the ability
of the speaker.

The clause introduced by *bèt* also denotes in some clauses
something which is unexpected in view of the meaning of the
main clause.

11) *Jìs visái sìlpnas, bèt vìs (dár) dìrba iř̃ dìrba.* — He is very
    weak, but (even so) he works and works.
12) *Nórs iř̃ neturiù pinigų̃, bèt kaĩp nórs atvažiúosiu.* — Although
    I don't have any money, I shall come somehow or other.
13) *Jìs nedìdelis výras, bèt stiprùs kaĩp liũtas.* — He is a small
    man, but strong as a lion.

In examples 11, 12 and 13, *tačiaũ* 'nevertheless' might have been used, but *tačiaũ* is generally limited to formal discourse, whereas *bèt* is common in every day conversation. *Tačiaũ* is perhaps more common after a negative clause.

õ may introduce an interrogative sentence and/or one expressing mild surprise.

14) *O kàs gi čià?* — (Well,) what's this here? (or 'What's going on?')

15) *O kàs gi čià?!* — (Well,) what do you know?! (or 'My oh my!') in a conversation.

16) *O kaĩp tàvo bróliui Jõnui (sẽkasi)? Aȓ jìs jaũ išẽjo ìš ligóninės?* — And how about your brother John? Did he get out of the hospital yet?

17) *O ìš kuȓ tù taĩ žinaĩ?* — And how do you know that? (or: How come you know that?)

18) *O kaĩp gi jūs taĩ padarýsite?* — And how are you going to manage (to do) that?

19) *Bèt ką̃ gi jūs dabaȓ darýsite?* — But what (on earth) will you do now?

In general one might say that *õ* and *bèt* are similar in usage, but *bèt* is more emphatic; *bèt* may be replaced by *tačiaũ* especially after negative clauses. One also finds such expressions as *õ vìsgi, bèt vìsgi, o vìs déltõ* 'but, nevertheless', *õ vis tíek, bèt vis tíek* 'but even so' or *o tačiaũ* 'however'; (*tačiaũ* is never used in combination with *bèt*).

The conjunction *beĩ* 'and' can only unite two closely related words or phrases, not two clauses:

20) *Tévas beĩ mótina gyvẽna miestè.* — Father and mother live in the city.

38.2 The common conjunctions *kàd* 'that', *jóg* 'that', *idañt* (rarely used and a bit archaic) 'in order that', *kadángi* 'because, for' (generally *kadángi* is found as the first word of a sentence), *nès* 'because' (not used in sentence initial position), *jéigu* 'if', *nórs* 'although', *kad ĩr* 'although' are subordinating conjunctions. Examples:

1) *Aš nežinójau, kàd (jóg) jìs čià.* — I didn't know that he is here.

2) *Jìs taĩp dãro, idañt visì matýtų.* — He does this so that everybody would (could) see.

3) *Kadángi (lietùs) lìjo, àš likaũ namiẽ.* — Since it was raining I remained at home.

4) *Mẽs ẽsame gerì studeñtai, nès mẽs daũg mókomės.* — We are good students because we study a lot.
   See paragraph 31.2 for the uses of *jéigu.*
5) *Nórs jìs yrà gẽras kaimỹnas, mẽs jõ vistíek nemẽgstame.* — Although he is a good neighbor, we don't like him even so.
6) *Niẽko nemačiaũ, kàd ir̃ (nórs ir̃) labaĩ sténgiausi.* — I didn't see anything, although I tried very hard.

38.3 List of Common Conjunctions.

A list of common conjunctions follows:

ar̃ — whether	*negù, nekaĩp* — than
arbà . . . arbà — either . . . or	*néi* (rarely used) — than
bèt — but	*neĩ . . . neĩ* — neither . . . nor
bètgi — but (emphatic)	*nebeñt* — except that, save that
ir̃ — and	*nès* — because
idañt — in order that	*nórs* — although
jéi, jéigu — if	*õ* — but (and)
jóg, jógei —that	*tačiaũ* — nevertheless, but
kàd — that	*tàd* — therefore
kadángi — since, because	*taĩ* — then, so
kaĩ — when, whenever	

NB. One must keep in mind that not only conjunctions are used to connect clauses: pronouns and adverbs are also used.

Examples: *kàs, kóks, kurìs, kadà, kaĩp, kodėl, kõl, kíek . . .* are used in the dependent clauses. (See also Lesson 21 and Lesson 36 for relative pronouns). *tàs, tóks, tadà, taĩp, tôdėl, tõl, tíek . . .* are used in the main clauses.
1) *Kàs dìrba, tàs tùri.* — He who works, has (something; is not a pauper).
2) *Kadà prašýsi, tadà gáusi.* — When you ask (for something), you will get (it), etc.
   See also Appendix and various lessons where these questions are explained.

38.4 Interjections.

For a list of common Lithuanian interjections, see Appendix. The use of the interjections is similar to that of English. Examples:
1) *à* — oh; *A, kaĩp šálta!* — Oh, how cold it is!
2) *nà* — well, there now; *Nà, pāsakok vìską iš prādžios.* — Well, tell us everything from the beginning.
3) *štaĩ* — here, look here; *Štaĩ jìs!* — Here he is.

38.5 The Particles.

Some common Lithuanian particles (dalelýtès) are listed below:

1) -aĩ — emphatic particle which serves to reinforce the preceding word. Thus one could say either tàs mẽdis 'that tree' or tasaĩ mẽdis 'that tree'. In the second case the meaning of tàs 'that' is reinforced.

2) aȓ (aȓgi) — interrogative particle. As an interrogative particle aȓ appears as the first word of a sentence, e.g. Aȓ jìs žìno? — Does he know?

3) bè — may function as an interrogative particle; Bè nežinaĩ? Don't you know?

4) benè — interrogative particle with the meaning 'is it possible that?, can it really be that?'; Benè tù vaĩkus? — Is it possible that you are a child?; Benè jìs ką̃ žìno? — Does he really know something?

5) gì — a particle serving for accentuation or emphasis; Ką̃ gì àš turiù darýti? — What on earth am I supposed to do?; Àš gì nè vagìs! — I am not a thief.

6) jaũ — particle of emphasis; Kàs jaũ táu atsitìko? — What on earth happened to you?; Tóks jaũ jìs iš mažeñs — That's the way he has been since childhood.

7) jùk — why, well, but; Bèt jùk jõ teñ nebùvo. — But he wasn't there anyway; Jùk tù pàts žinaĩ. — But you yourself know.

8) Kažìñ, kažì <(kàs žìno) — who knows, it's hard to say; Kažìñ aȓ jìs ateĩs. — Who knows whether he will come.

9) laĩ — may one, let one; Laĩ gyvúoja! — May he live ... (Long live ...)

10) màt — let one ..., may one ... (used only in special expressions); Màt jį̃ gãlas! — Let's forget him; Màt tavè dievaĩ! — All right, have it your way.

11) nèt — even; Nèt Jõnas tõ nežinójo. — Even John did not know that.

12) te- (usually attached to the following verb) — only; Kaȓtą̃ teñ tebuvaũ. — I was there only once.

13) tè, teguĺ — may, let ...; Tedìrba. Teguĺ dìrba. — Let him work; may he work.

14) tè and šè — particle with the meaning of (familiar) 'take'; Tè, pasiìmk sàvo knýgą. — Here, take your book.

38.6 Special Adverbs.

Frequently special adverbs ending with the letter *n* denote the object of motion whereas the same root with the locative ending denotes location. Cf.

laukañ — out of doors, outside (as the object of motion); *Àš einù laukañ.* — I am going outside.

laukè — outside (not as the object of motion); *Àš esù laukè.* — I am outside.

1) *aukštỹn* — upwards; *aukštaĩ* — up, in a high place.
2) *žemỹn* — downwards; *žemaĩ* — down, in a low place.
3) *tolỹn* — farther on; into the distance; *tolì* — far; at a distance.

The adverb *namõ* has no final *n*, yet it denotes the object of motion. Example: *namõ* — home, homewards, to one's home; *namiẽ* — at home; at one's home.

EXERCISES

A. *Questions.* 1. Kuř gìmė Kristijõnas Doneláitis? 2. Kàs jìs bùvo? 3. Kuř jìs parãšė poèmą "Mėtai"? 4. Kadà bùvo išspausdìnti Doneláičio rãštai? 5. Ką̃ jìs aprãšo sàvo poèmoje? 6. Kokià yrà Doneláičio kalbà? 7. Kuř yrà Mažóji Lietuvà? 8. Ař jũs jaũ skaĩtėte Doneláičio "Metùs"? 9. Kókias knygàs jũs mėgstate skaitýti? 10. Kaĩp vadìnasi pirmóji "Mėtų" dalìs?

B. In lessons 31-35, write out all the sentences where *bèt* or *õ* is used. Compare them, paying particular attention to the meaning of *bèt* and *õ*.

C. *Translate into Lithuanian.* 1. He can speak Lithuanian, but his wife cannot (speak it). 2. Because it was raining, I remained at home. 3. They are good students because they have studied a lot. 4. I cannot go home, because the weather is bad. 5. He is a bad student, because he always sleeps in class.

CONVERSATION

PAMOKŲ RUOŠIMAS*

Prãnas: 1. Jokūbai, ař jaũ pérskaitei Doneláičio "Metùs"?

Jokūbas: 2. Dár nèt nepradėjau, nės ne tìk neturėjau laĩko, bèt iř knýgos dár nesù nusipiřkęs.

Pranas: 3. Aš jaũ pradėjau skaitýti, bèt nekaĩp sėkasi: kíek senóviška kalbà, õ be tõ, tàs hegzãmetras!

309

Jokūbas: 4. Mataĩ, reĩkia pirmiáusia geraĩ išstudijúoti pãtį lai-kótarpį, taĩp pàt patiẽs Doneláičio gyvẽnimą.

Pranas: 5. Kuř čià žmogùs galì vìską pérskaityti! Tíek daũg yrà prirašýta apiẽ Doneláitį, kàd neįmãnoma nẽ da-lẽlės pérskaityti.

Jokūbas: 6. Žinaĩ kã: àš turiù gẽrą sumãnymą. Eĩkime pàs Juõ-zą; jìs vìską jaũ yrà pérskaitęs, jìs mùms padẽs.

Pranas: 7. Geraĩ, tàvo sumãnymas neblõgas, bèt reikẽtų iř mùms patíems kã́ nórs paskaitýti.

Jokūbas: 8. Nebúk tù tóks jaũ sãžinìngas. Verčiaũ eĩkime gòlfo pažaĩsti.

Pranas: 9. O kaĩp sù Doneláičiu?

Jokūbas: 10. Doneláitis nepabẽgs. Rytój nueĩsime pàs Juõzą, iř bùs vìskas áišku kaĩp añt délno.* (or: kaĩp diẽną*)

HOMEWORK:

Pranas: 1. Jokubas (James), did you read Donelaitis' Metai? (The Seasons).

Jokubas: 2. Didn't even start it because it was not only that I did not have time, but I have not bought the book yet.

Pranas: 3. I did start to read it already, but it is not going too well: the language is somewhat archaic, and (in addition to that)—that hexameter.

Jokubas: 4. You see, one has first to study the era itself well, then the life of Donelaitis himself.

Pranas: 5. How can a body read all that! There has been so much written about Donelaitis; it is nigh impossible.

Jokubas: 6. You know what, I have a good idea. Let us go over to Joe's. He has read everything, he will help us.

Pranas: 7. O.K., your idea is not too bad, but we should also do something ourselves.

Jokubas: 8. Do not be so conscientious. We'd better go and play some golf.

Pranas: 9. And what about Donelaitis?

Jokubas: 10. Donelaitis will not run away. Tomorrow we will go to (see) Joe, and everything will be as clear as day.

NOTES:

 pamokų ruošìmas — lit. 'preparation of lessons'.
10. añt délno — lit. 'on the palm of one's hand'.
 diẽną — (acc. of def. time) 'during the day, at daytime'.

310

Trisdešimt devintoji pamoka
Lesson 39

LIETUVIŲ KALBA

Lietùvių kalbà kartù sù lãtvių iř išmìrusiomis prūsų, kuřšių, žiemgãlių ir sélių kalbomìs sudãro báltų kalbų grùpę indoeuropièčių kalbų šeimojè. Indoeuropiěčių kalbų šeimà yrà skìrstoma į 15 (penkiólika) kalbų grùpių:

1. tochãrų (kalbà)	9. albãnų
2. indo-iraněnų	10. ilìrų
3. arměnų	11. itãlikų (arbà romãnų)
4. hitìtų	12. keĩtų
5. Anatòlijos kaĩbos	13. slãvų
6. frìgų	14. germãnų
7. trãkų	15. báltų (kaĩbos).
8. graikų	

Taĩgi, kaĩp gãlima matýti iš šiõ sąrašo, lietùvių kalbà yrà báltų kalbų grùpės narỹs. Báltų kalbų grùpė išsivýstė iš indoeuropiěčių prókalbės, ìš kuriõs taĩp pàt išsivýstė iř 14 (keturiólika) kitų indoeuropiěčių kalbų grùpių. Tuõ būdù lietùvių kalbà tùri panašùmų sù kiekvienà indoeuropiěčių kalbà. Žìnoma, laĩkui bégant iř visóms kalbóms keĩčiantis, susidãrė iř daũg skìrtumų visosè kalbų grùpėse iř paskirosè kalbosè.

Báltų prókalbė atsiskýrė iš indoeuropiěčių prókalbės maždaũg apiē 3000-2500 metùs pr. Kr. (priēš Krìstų). Véliaũ báltų prókalbė suskìlo į dvì dalìs — rytìnę iř vakarìnę (apiē 500 pr. Kr.). Iš vakarìnių báltų išsivýstė prūsų kalbà, iš rytìnės báltų grùpės — lietùvių, lãtvių, žiemgãlių iř sélių kaĩbos. Kuřšių kalbà tùri panašùmo sù rytìnėmis iř vakarìnėmis grùpėmis. Kuřšiai, žiemgãliai iř sélai sulietuvėjo arbà sulatvėjo priēš maždaũg 500 (penkìs šimtùs) mẽtų. Prūsai ìšmirė XVII-me (septynióliktame) ámžiuje. Tìk dvì báltų kaĺbos išlìko gývos: lãtvių iř lietùvių.

Lietùvių kalbà yrà svarbì lýginamajai indoeuropiẽčių kalbótyrai, nès jì yrà išlaĩkiusi daũg senóviškų kalbìnių brúožų. Kaĩ kuriẽ lietùvių kalbõs žõdžiai iř kaĩ kuriõs lýtys (fòrmos) yrà išlìkusios senoviškèsnės nèt ùž senũjų iñdų (sanskrìto), graikų iř lotýnų kalbų žodžiùs iř fòrmas. Bèt daũg dalýkų lietùvių kalbojè taĩp pàt gerókai pasìkeitė, nórs gál nè tíek, kíek kitosè dár gyvosè indoeuropiẽčių kalbosè.

VOCABULARY

prūsas (1) — Prussian, Old Prussian
kuřšis -io (2) — Couronian
žiemgãlis -io (2) — Zemgallian (Semigallian)
sėlis -io (1) —Selian (Selonian)
sudarýti (sudaraũ, sudaŕo, sudãrė, sudarýs) — to compose, to form
indoeuropiẽtis -čio (2) — Indo-European (noun)
skìrstyti (skìrstau, skìrsto, skìrstė, skìrstys) — to divide, to apportion, to classify
tochãras (2) — Tokharian
indo-iranėnas (1) — Indo-Iranian (noun)
armėnas (1) — Armenian (noun)
hitìtas (2) — Hittite (noun)
Anatòlija — Anatolia
frìgas (2) — Phrygian (noun)
trãkas (2) — Thracian (noun)
graĩkas (4) — Greek (noun)
albãnas (2) — Albanian (noun)
ilìras (2) — Illyrian (noun)
itãlikas (1) — speaker of the Italic languages
romãnas (2) — speaker of the Romance languages
keĩtas (2) — Celt
slãvas (2) — Slav
germãnas (2) — Teuton, member of the (old) Germanic tribes
báltas (1) — Balt
taĩgi — so, thus, therefore
sąrašas (3a) — list
narỹs (4) — member
išsivýstyti (išsivýstau, išsivýsto, išsivýstė, išsivýstys) — to develop (oneself)
prókalbė (1) — proto-language
panašùmas (2) — similarity
laĩkui bėgant — in the course of time

keĩstis (keičiúosi, keĩčiasi, keĩtėsi, keĩsis) — to change (oneself)
skìrtumas (1) — difference
pãskiras, -à (3b) — individual, separate, single
atsiskìrti (atsìskiriu, atsìskiria, atsiskýrė, atsiskìřs) — to separate (oneself from)
maždaũg — approximately
priẽš Krìstų (abr. pr. Kr.) — B.C.
suskìlti (suskylù, suskỹla, suskìlo, suskìls) — to branch out, to split (intransitive)
sulietuvėti (sulietuvėju, sulietuvėja, sulietuvėjo, sulietuvės) — to become Lithuanian
sulatvėti (sulatvėju, sulatvėja, sulatvėjo, sulatvės) — to become Latvian
išlìkti (išliekù, išliẽka, išlìko, išlìks) — to remain (extant)
lyginamàsis, -móji — comparative
lyginamóji kalbótyra — comparative linguistics
išlaikýti (išlaikaũ, išlaĩko, išlaĩkė, išlaikỹs) — to preserve
senóviškas, -a (1) — archaic
kalbìnis, -ė (2) — language (adjective), linguistic, pertaining to language
brúožas (1) — trait, characteristic
lytìs -iẽs, fem. (4) — form
seníeji iñdai — Old Indic people
sanskrìtas (2) — Sanskrit (noun)
lotýnas (2) — Latin (noun)
gerókai — considerably
pasikeĩsti (pasikeičiù, pasikeĩčia, pasìkeitė, pasikeĩs) — to change (oneself)
nórs — although
gál — perhaps
gývas, -à (3) — alive

312

GRAMMAR

39. Participial Phrases.

Adjectival participles, adverbial participles and special gerunds can function in a fashion similar to the participial phrases in English. The phrases have a meaning similar to that of subordinate clauses. (For form, cf. Lessons 26 & 35, also Appendix).

39.1 If the subject of the participial phrase and the main clause is the same and the action of the participle and the action of the main verb are simultaneous, then a special adverbial active participle will be used in the participial phrase. Examples:

1) *Vìsą diẽną dìrbdamas, Jõnas labaĩ pavar̃go.* — Working all day, John became very tired.
2) *Dár vaĩkas bū́damas, Jõnas mė̃go knygàs.* — While still (being) a child, John liked books.
3) *Žmogùs miegódamas niẽko negir̃di.* — The man hears nothing while sleeping.

39.2 If the subject of the participial phrase and the main clause is the same, but the action of the participial phrase is prior to the action of the verb of the main clause, then a past active participle is used in the participial phrase. Examples:

1) *Sugrį̃žęs namõ, tuõj atsìgulė.* — Having returned home, he immediately lay down.
2) *Nuė́jęs pàs jį̃, jõ jaũ neradaũ namiẽ.* — Having arrived at his place, I didn't find him at home.
3) *Pažvel̃gęs prõ lángą, Jõnas pamãtė žmógų.* — Having looked through the window, John saw a man.
4) *Pagalvójęs, kàd kaimýnas jaũ sugrį̃žo, Pẽtras nuė́jo jõ aplankýti.* — Thinking (having thought) that the neighbor had already returned, Peter went to visit him.

39.3 If the subject of the participial phrase and that of the main clause are different, but the action of the participial phrase is simultaneous with that of the main clause, then the special gerund derived from the present active participle (cf. 26.7) is used in the participial phrase. The subject of the participial phrase (if expressed) is in the dative case.

1) *Sáulei tẽkant, darbiniñkai atsikė́lė.* — (While) the sun was rising, the workers got up.

2) *Jám kal̃bant, visì klaũso.* — When he talks (lit.: him **talking**), everybody listens.
3) *Eĩnant namõ, laukuosè giedójo paũkščiai.* — (While we were) going home, in the fields the birds were singing.
4) *Gãlima bū́tų̃ važiúoti peř mìšką, žìnant, kàd teñ yrà kóks nórs kẽlias.* — It would be possible to ride through the forest, knowing (if one knew) that there is some kind of road there.

39.4 If the subject of the participial phrase and that of the main clause are different, and the action of the participial phrase precedes that of the verb of the main clause, then the special gerund derived from the past active participle (cf. 26.7) is used in the participial phrase. The subject of the participial phrase (if expressed) is in the dative case

1) *Rãsai nukrìtus, visì stójo į̃ dárbą.* — The dew having fallen, everybody joined in the work.
2) *Jónui atė́jus pàs manè, àš jám daviaũ knỹgą.* — John having come to my place, I gave him a book.
3) *Jùrgiui baĩgus dárbą, Jónas jám dãvė pinigų̃.* — George having finished the work, John gave him some money.

39.5 Participles and Gerunds in Indirect Discourse.

In indirect discourse participles may be used instead of verbs. We have to do with indirect discourse when the writer (or the speaker) transmits the conversation or narrative of another person or persons in his own (i.e. the writer's or the speaker's) words. This may occur in simple or compound sentences. Examples:
(Simple sentences)
1) *Jónas sãkosi daũg žìnąs.* — John says that he knows a lot.
2) *Jìs gýrėsi vãkar miestè bùvęs.* — He boasted that he was in the city yesterday.
3) *Jiẽ dabař̃ gìnasi niẽko nežinóję.* — They defend themselves now (by saying that) they knew nothing.
(Compound sentences)
4) *Jonáitis gìriasi, kàd dabař̃ gyvẽnąs labaĩ gražiojè viẽtoje.* — Jonaitis boasts that now he is living in a very pretty place.
5) *Pẽtras pãsakojo, kuř̃ iř̃ kíek piř̃kęs mìško.* — Peter told where and how much lumber he bought.
6) *Kaimýnas prànešė, kàd rytój važiúosiąs į̃ miẽstą.* — (Our) neighbor announced that tomorrow he will go to the city.

The writer uses the participles *gyvenąs, pìrkęs, važiúosiąs* in sentences 4, 5 and 6 to show that the words are not his, but those of Jonaitis, Petras and the neighbor respectively which he heard in the simple verbal forms (i.e. not the participles).

Sometimes the writer relates the speech of some unknown person and then the statement(s) of this unknown person are accompanied by the word *sãko* 'says' (*kàžkas* 'someone'). Example:

7) *Jõnas, sãko, vãkar miestè bùvęs.* — John (someone says) was in the city yesterday.

On occasion the person whose speech the writer is relating may not be expressly identified, e.g. the author of some story. Then the story is begun in indirect discourse without mentioning the name of the author. Example:

8) *Víenas pirklỹs bùvęs labaĩ šykštùs. Kañtą jám bevažiúojant sù pinigaĩs, ėmę témti. Tadà jìs privažiãvęs ūkininką, užsùkęs į̃ kiẽmą iñ apsinakvójęs.* — A certain merchant was very miserly. Once when he was traveling with (a considerable amount of) money it started to become dark. Then he approached a farmer, turned into the farmyard and spent the night (there).

But not only participles are used in indirect discourse. Finite verbs sometimes figure in indirect discourse also. Thus in stories it is possible to say either *kañtą gyvẽnęs karãlius* or *kañtą gyvẽno karãlius* 'there once lived a king'.

In indirect discourse in place of the participle the special gerund can be used in sentences with the verb *sakýti* 'to say'. Examples:

9) *Sãko jį̃ daũg žìnant* (=*Sãko, kàd jìs daũg žìnąs*) — They say, he knows a lot.

10) *Sãko jį̃ vãkar miestè bùvus* (=*Sãko, jìs vãkar miestè bùvęs*) — They say, he was in the city yesterday.

See also the table in 26.9,2.

EXERCISES

A. *Questions.* 1. Kókiai kalbų̃ šeĩmai priklaũso lietùvių kalbà? 2. Kuriái indoeuropiẽčių kalbų̃ grùpei priklaũso lietùvių kalbà 3. Kíek kalbų̃ grùpių sudãro indoeuropiẽčių kalbų̃ šeĩmą? 4. Sù kuriomìs kalbomìs lietùvių kalbà tùri panašùmų? 5. Kuriõs báltų kal̃bos yrà dár gývos? 6. Kuriõs báltų kal̃bos yrà jaũ išmìrusios?

7. Kodėl lietùvių kalbà yrà svarbì lýginamajai indoeuropiẽčių kalbótyrai? 8. Kàs atsitìko sù kuȓšiais, žiemgãliais iȓ sėliais? 9. Kuȓ gyvẽno prūsai? 10. Kuȓ gyvẽna graikaĩ?

B. *Turn the participial phrases into dependent clauses:* (Sample: Sugrį̃žęs namõ, àš tuojaũ jám parašiaũ láišką = Kaĩ àš sugrį̃žaũ namõ, àš jám tuojaũ parašiaũ láišką)
1. Nuėjęs pàs jį̃, àš jõ neradaũ namiẽ. 2. Miegódamas žmogùs niẽko negiȓdi. 3. Pabaĩgę dárbą, visì studeñtai nuėjo į̃ restorãną paválgyti vakariẽnės. 4. Mán bestóvint priẽ stotiẽs, pradėjo smaȓkiai lýti. 5. Darbiniñkai pradėjo dìrbti sáulei tẽkant.

C. *In Lessons 31-35, write out all participial phrases and change them into dependent clauses.*

CONVERSATION

RUDUO

Tévas: 1. Šiañdien labaĩ gražì dienà. Mẽs turėtume pasinaudóti tókiu gražiù óru iȓ važiúoti kuȓ nórs į̃ káimą.
Vytùkas: 2. Aš labaĩ norėčiau nuvažiúoti pàs dėdę Jõną. Dabaȓ teñ labaĩ gražù: sõdas pìlnas obuolių̃, õ apliñkui — gražiáusi mẽdžiai sù geltónais, rudaĩs iȓ raudónais lãpais . . .
Rūtà: 3. Tėvėli, iȓ àš norėčiau nuvažiúoti pàs dėdę Jõną.
Tévas: 4. Geraĩ, važiúosime pàs dėdę Jõną. Bèt kuȓ yrà mamà?
Vytukas: 5. Aš tikraĩ nežinaũ, bèt priẽš keliàs minutès àš ją̃ mačiaũ kaĩbant sù kaimýne.
Tévas: 6. Rūta, nueĩk pàs kaimýnę iȓ pasakýk mãmai, kàd mẽs visì norėtume nuvažiúoti į̃ káimą.
Rūta: 7. Geraĩ, tėvėli. Aš tuojaũ sugrį̃šiu.
(Pakeliuĩ į̃ káimą)
Vytukas: 8. Žiūrėkite, žiūrėkite: kokiẽ grãžūs ẽžero krantaĩ, pilnì visokiáusių spalvų̃.
Rūta: 9. Aš taĩp norėčiau pasiváikščioti põ tuõs krantùs.
Tévas: 10. Geraĩ, kaĩ nuvažiúosime pàs dėdę, jū̃s sù Vytukù galėsite eĩti pasiváikščioti jõ miškè.

AUTUMN

Father: 1. It's a beautiful day today. We should take advantage of such beautiful weather and go somewhere into the country (village).

316

Vytukas:	2.	I would like very much to go to Uncle John's. It is very beautiful out there now: (his) orchard is full of apples, and all around (there are) most beautiful trees with yellow, brown and red leaves ...
Ruta:	3.	Daddy, I, too, would like to go to Uncle John's.
Father:	4.	All right, we will go to Uncle John's. But where is (your) Mother?
Vytukas:	5.	I am not sure, but a few minutes ago I saw her talking to (our) neighbor.
Father:	6.	Ruta, go over to the neighbor's and tell Mother, that we all want to take a trip to the country.
Ruta:	7.	O.K., Daddy. I will be back shortly.
		(On the way to the country)
Vytukas:	8.	Just look at this! Such beautiful shores of (this) lake; they are full of all kinds of colors.
Ruta:	9.	I would like so much to go walking along those shores.
Father:	10.	Very well. When we get to Uncle John's, Vytukas and you can go for a walk in his forest.

The Lithuanian National Anthem

LIETUVOS HIMNAS

Lietuva, tėvyne mūsų,
Tu didvyrių žeme,
Iš praeities Tavo sūnūs
Te stiprybę semia.

Tegul Tavo vaikai eina
Vien takais dorybės,
Tegul dirba Tavo naudai
Ir žmonių gėrybei.

Tegul saulė Lietuvos
Tamsumus prašalina,
Ir šviesa ir tiesa
Mūs žingsnius telydi.

Tegul meilė Lietuvos
Dega mūsų širdyse,
Vardan tos Lietuvos
Vienybė težydi.

Words and music by Dr. Vincas Kudirka

Keturiasdešimtoji pamoka

Lesson 40

R E V I E W
Translate into Lithuanian*

Review Lesson 1

1. My brother is a student.
2. I am also a student.
3. My father is a teacher.
4. Is my father a student?
5. Is my house large and beautiful?

Review Lesson 2

1. My sister is a good housekeeper.
2. She is not a good housekeeper.
3. My brother and my sister are reading a newspaper.
4. We are writing a letter.
5. Is my mother writing a letter?

Review Lesson 3

1. We are working at home.
2. My sister and my brother are also doing their homework
   (=preparing lessons).
3. I love my family.
4. Do you love your family?
5. He does not read this letter.

---

* There are 200 sentences in this Review Lesson, 5 for each lesson. Each
"group" of five sentences illustrates some of the main grammatical points
covered in a particular lesson. Vocabulary items are not necessarily from
that one particular lesson: they are drawn, more or less, from the entire
book.

Review Lesson 4

1. Man cannot live without the fire.
2. Man cannot live without a home (house).
3. A tooth for a tooth and an eye for an eye.
4. We cannot live without fire.
5. She does not go to school yet; she works at home.

Review Lessons 1 - 5

1. We live in Vilnius.
2. They live in Boston.
3. I am not a student. I am a teacher.
4. In the evening I am at home. I read a newspaper.
5. I cannot live in Boston, I can only live in Vilnius.

Review Lesson 6

1. My sister likes his son.
2. The professor does not like to live in the city.
3. We like our new home (house).
4. They do not like our new home.
5. Her son likes to read.

Review Lesson 7

1. Go home and read a newspaper!
2. Let us go to school and prepare our lessons.
3. She likes to go for a walk with her dog.
4. I see a stone in the water.
5. There is a lot of (much) water in the river.

Review Lesson 8

1. She wanted to write you a letter yesterday.
2. In the evening, we were at the theater where we saw a drama.
3. She likes his letter very much.
4. We went for a walk: the day was very beautiful.
5. We did not go to the theater; we went home.

Review Lesson 9

1. Tomorrow I will read a book; then I will work.
2. If the weather is (will be!) nice, we will go to the village.
3. He will give us a book.
4. The night will be very beautiful, and she will be very happy.
5. Tomorrow we will visit the university, the cathedral and a church.

320

Review Lessons 6-10

1. The student likes to drink coffee.
2. I like her, but she does not like me.
3. She likes him, but he does not like her.
4. I like Vilnius very much, but I cannot live in it.
5. Professor Valys likes to drink tea with sugar and honey.

Review Lesson 11

1. I like a yellow house, but my sister likes a white house.
2. I have a red pencil, but I need (some) yellow paper.
3. Our family needs a large house.
4. My father needs a new red pencil.
5. The professor needs a new book.

Review Lesson 12

1. I am cold; let's go home!
2. He is a very pleasant man, and he always speaks pleasantly.
3. Lesson 12 is a difficult lesson.
4. I do not like this difficult lesson.
5. I used to read a newspaper, when(ever) I used to sit in this chair.

Review Lesson 13

1. She has worked in that brick house.
2. We have been in New York only once.
3. I have never been in Vilnius.
4. They (fem.) have never worked in this new factory.
5. I have written him a letter, but he did not answer yet.

Review Lesson 14

1. I have five houses; my friends live in them.
2. My brothers are students at the University of Vilnius.
3. Many students live in the cities; they like to live in the cities.
4. I have received two letters yesterday; tomorrow, I will receive no letters.
5. I go into the fields where it is so beautiful.

Review Lessons 11-15

1. The students do not like to study now: they go to walk in the suburbs.
2. I have not yet read the newspapers.

3. They do not like our newspapers.
4. We do not like their universities.
5. They need many books and pencils.

Review Lesson 16
1. He is a rich man: he has twelve houses.
2. Fifteen owls are sitting in the linden trees.
3. The spruces and the linden are trees.
4. My father likes the linden trees very much.
5. His friend likes only the spruces.

Review Lesson 17
1. I have two eyes and two ears.
2. Each man has two hands and two legs.
3. May he write my friend a letter?
4. Thy kingdom come.
5. Thy will be done on earth as it is in heaven.

Review Lesson 18
1. That farmer had five sons.
2. Many people live in the city.
3. Cold beer is pleasant to drink.
4. Our old professors like us, but we do not like our young professors.
5. He always worked with his sons.

Review Lesson 19
1. I have five sisters and two brothers.
2. She has two brothers and two sisters.
3. Grandparents also live with them; they also belong to the family.
4. I do not have a brother.
5. She is the only daughter in her family; she has no sister.

Review Lessons 16 - 20
1. He is a German, but he can also speak English.
2. He is not a Lithuanian, but he speaks Lithuanian very well.
3. She is a Lithuanian, and she also speaks German very well.
4. Many Lithuanians live in the USA (Jungtinėse Amerikos Valstybėse).
5. Many Americans want to learn (to speak) Lithuanian.

Review Lesson 21
1. I am going to give him this book.
2. He had written me many long letters, but I had not answered those letters yet.
3. Sit down and write him a letter!
4. Let him go home.
5. He buys everything for his family.

Review Lesson 22
1. I will never speak English so well as you (do).
2. The river flows through the beautiful forests and wide fields.
3. She saw an excellent film yesterday.
4. I will go to Europe next week.
5. We worked all day yesterday.

Review Lesson 23
1. All the houses in the big cities are brick houses.
2. I like these golden watches.
3. In the evening we always read many newspapers.
4. I go (ride) to the university by car.
5. I write everything with this red pencil.

Review Lesson 24
1. Last year I was fifty-two years old.
2. How old is she? She is only eleven years old.
3. My grandfather is very old: last year he was 90.
4. In five years, she will be twenty years old.
5. I am not old yet! I am only 61 years old!
NB. Use two possible versions for all these sentences.

Review Lessons 21 - 25
1. Her eyes are very big (She has big eyes).
2. In (my) hand I hold a book.
3. My brother broke his leg yesterday.
4. This man had very large ears.
5. She buys a new hat every day.

Review Lesson 26
1. I saw them standing near the train.
2. Driving past the cathedral they saw the castle.

3. After having greeted each other, they drove to the university.
4. While they were speaking (talking), I was writing a letter.
5. After having eaten dinner, they went for a walk.

Review Lesson 27
1. I am much older than my brother.
2. Canada is much larger than Lithuania.
3. Your house is much more beautiful than their house.
4. These books are much better than those.
5. Our university is the best university in America.

Review Lesson 28
1. The third lesson is the easiest lesson in this book.
2. I like the long beautiful nights of the summer (summer nights).
3. I like all these lamps; but I like this yellow lamp best.
4. He is a student at an institution of higher learning.
5. The new school is in the center of our city.

Review Lesson 29
1. Today, we are going to read the ninth lesson.
2. She was reading the fifth page of her new book.
3. I cannot understand the fifth lesson.
4. (On) the third day he left (for) home.
5. Their second child is more clever than their first child.

Review Lessons 26 - 30
1. My mother is sixty years old; she is younger than your mother.
2. Mr. Jonaitis is the richest man in our city; but he does not know that I am richer than he is.
3. Our school is much larger than your school; our school is the largest in Lithuania.
4. He can speak Lithuanian better than I, although (nors) he is much younger than I.
5. Better late (Lith.=later) than never.

Review Lesson 31
1. If I were rich, I would give you this new car.
2. If you had come yesterday, I would have shown you our new house.
3. If he were sick, he would not talk so much.

4. If you had studied Lithuanian, you would have been able to read this letter.
5. I would like to stay longer in Vilnius, if you could send me some money . . .

Review Lesson 32
1. Every morning I get up at six o'clock.
2. It is already ten o'clock. Let's go home.
3. Every day he goes to the university. He returns home at five.
4. On Tuesday we will all go to the museum. Next week we will go to Boston.
5. He comes (will come) in five hours.

Review Lesson 33
1. This house was built last year. It was built by my father.
2. When this book was (being) written, I had to help him.
3. The first castle was built by Mindaugas.
4. In the cities, many new homes are (being) built.
5. Many new homes are (being) built in the suburb by rich people.

Review Lesson 34
1. In the olden days, many things (thing=dalykas!) were made from amber.
2. Amber is washed up on the shore by the water.
3. These new houses will be built on the hill (hill=kalvà).
4. Those new houses will be built by these young men near (prie) the lake.
5. Where are brick homes (being) built?

Review Lessons 31 - 35
1. I do not want to be beaten.
2. After having read this book, I went for a walk.
3. The book which was written by him last year, is already sold out (išparduoti=to sell out).
4. If this book had not been written, we would not have known anything about his life.
5. If this could be done, (then) it would be very nice.

Review Lesson 36
1. I don't like this house; I want to buy that one.
2. She does not like such people who never read anything.

3. Whose is that book? That is her book.
4. How many letters did you write yesterday? I wrote only a few letters.
5. Someone is at (prie) the door. Go and ask him what he wants.

Review Lesson 37
1. I cannot live without these good friends.
2. In his room there are a lot of old newspapers: they are lying on the table, under the chairs, by the walls.
3. They read (past) until evening; in the evening they went to movies.
4. These young students must work from morning until evening.
5. This bus stops near the library.

Review Lesson 38
1. Because I had no money, I could not go to the concert.
2. Although he is still a young man, he can speak five languages.
3. Neither my parents nor my relatives knew anything about this.
4. I cannot speak Lithuanian yet because I did not study hard enough.
5. If I had studied harder, I would have learned this language.

Review Lesson 39
1. While it was raining, we went to school.
2. Working all day, we got very tired.
3. Having returned home, she started to read this new book.
4. While the sun was rising, all the birds began to sing.
5. John having finished the work, his father gave him some money.

Review Lessons 36 - 40
1. For the past two years we have been learning Lithuanian.
2. We have never yet been in Lithuania, but we will go as soon as we learn to speak Lithuanian.
3. Lithuanian is an old language: it has many endings and forms.
4. After having learned Lithuanian, we will be able to read Lithuanian newspapers, journals and books.
5. Freedom is the most precious thing in the world.

Grammatical Appendix

41. NOUNS

41.10 First declension nouns in -as: výras (1) 'man'

	Singular	Plural
Nominative	výras	výrai
Genitive	výro	výrų
Dative	výrui	výrams
Accusative	výrą	výrus
Instrumental	výru	výrais
Locative	výre	výruose, -uos
Vocative	výre	výrai

41.11 First declension nouns in -is: brólis (1) 'brother'

	Singular	Plural
Nominative	brólis	bróliai
Genitive	brólio	brólių
Dative	bróliui	bróliams
Accusative	brólį	brólius
Instrumental	bróliu	bróliais
Locative	brólyje, -yj, -y	bróliuose
Vocative	bróli	bróliai

41.12 First declension nouns in -ỹs: arklỹs (3) 'horse'

	Singular	Plural
Nominative	arklỹs	arkliaĩ
Genitive	árklio	arklių̃
Dative	árkliui	arkliáms
Accusative	árklį	árklius
Instrumental	árkliu	arkliaĩs
Locative	arklyjè, -ỹj, -ỹ	arkliuosè ,-uõs
Vocative	arklỹ	arkliaĩ

41.13 First declension nouns in -ias: svẽčias (4) 'guest'

	Singular	Plural
Nominative	svẽčias	svečiaĩ
Genitive	svẽčio	svečių̃
Dative	svẽčiui	svečiáms
Accusative	svẽčią	svečiùs
Instrumental	svečiù	svečiaĩs
Locative	svetyjè, -ỹj, -ỹ	svečiuosè, -uõs
Vocative	svetỹ	svečiaĩ

327

41.131 The vocative of *vélnias* 'devil' is *vélne*.

41.14 First declension noun in *-is* showing alternation of *-d-* and
-dž- in declension: *mēdis* (2) 'tree'; *-t-* and *-č-* alternate in
the same way.

	Singular	Plural
Nominative	mēdis	mēdžiai
Genitive	mēdžio	mēdžių
Dative	mēdžiui	mēdžiams
Accusative	mēdį	medžiùs
Instrumental	medžiù	mēdžiais
Locative	mēdyje, -yj, -y	mēdžiuose, -uos
Vocative	mēdi	mēdžiai

41.15 First declension noun in *-ỹs* showing alternation of *-d-* and
-dž-: *gaidỹs* (4) 'rooster'

	Singular	Plural
Nominative	gaidỹs	gaidžiaĩ
Genitive	gaĩdžio	gaidžių̃
Dative	gaĩdžiui	gaidžiáms
Accusative	gaĩdį	gaidžiùs
Instrumental	gaidžiù	gaidžiaĩs
Locative	gaidyjè, -ỹj, -ỹ	gaidžiuosè, -uõs
Vocative	gaidỹ	gaidžiaĩ

41.20 Second declension nouns in *-a*: *várna* (1) 'crow'

	Singular	Plural
Nominative	várna	várnos
Genitive	várnos	várnų
Dative	várnai	várnoms
Accusative	várną	várnas
Instrumental	várna	várnomis
Locative	várnoje	várnose
Vocative	várna	várnos

41.21 Second declension nouns in *-ė*: *gérvė* (1) 'crane'

	Singular	Plural
Nominative	gérvė	gérvės
Genitive	gérvės	gérvių
Dative	gérvei	gérvėms
Accusative	gérvę	gérves
Instrumental	gérve	gérvėmis
Locative	gérvėje	gérvėse
Vocative	gérve	gérvės

41.22 Second declension nouns in *-i*: *martì* (4) 'daughter-in-law'

	Singular	Plural
Nominative	martì	marčios
Genitive	marčiŏs	marčių̃
Dative	marčiai	marčióms
Accusative	marčią	marčiàs
Instrumental	marčià	marčiomìs
Locative	marčiojè	marčiosè
Vocative	marti	marčios

41.23 Second declension nouns in *-ia*: *valdžià* (4) 'government, power'

	Singular	Plural
Nominative	valdžià	valdžios
Genitive	valdžiŏs	valdžių̃
Dative	valdžiai	valdžióms
Accusative	valdžią	valdžiàs
Instrumental	valdžià	valdžiomìs
Locative	valdžiojè	valdžiosè
Vocative	valdžia	valdžios

41.30 Third declension nouns may be either masculine or feminine: *akìs* (4) 'eye' (feminine).

	Singular	Plural
Nominative	akìs	ãkys
Genitive	akiẽs	akių̃
Dative	ãkiai	akìms
Accusative	ãkį	akìs
Instrumental	akià, akimì	akimìs
Locative	akyjè, akýj, aký	akysè,
Vocative	akiẽ	ãkys

41.31 *dantìs* (4) 'tooth' is a third declension noun of masculine gender.

	Singular	Plural
Nominative	dantìs	dañtys
Genitive	dantiẽs	dantų̃
Dative	dañčiui	dantìms
Accusative	dañtį	dantìs
Instrumental	dančiù, dantimì	dantimìs
Locative	dantyjè	dantysè
Vocative	dantiẽ	dañtys

41.40 Fourth declension nouns in -us: sūnùs (3) 'son'

	Singular	Plural
Nominative	sūnùs	sûnūs
Genitive	sūnaũs	sūnų̃
Dative	sûnui	sūnùms
Accusative	sûnų	sûnus
Instrumental	sūnumì, -um̃	sūnumìs
Locative	sūnujè, -ùj	sūnuosè
Vocative	sūnaũ	sûnūs

41.41 Fourth declension nouns in -ius: skaĩčius (2) 'number'

	Singular	Plural
Nominative	skaĩčius	skaĩčiai
Genitive	skaĩčiaus	skaĩčių
Dative	skaĩčiui	skaĩčiams
Accusative	skaĩčių	skaičiùs
Instrumental	skaĩčiumi	skaĩčiais
Locative	skaĩčiuje	skaĩčiuose
Vocative	skaĩčiau	skaĩčiai

41.42 The noun žmogùs (4) 'man' is declined in the singular like a fourth declension noun, but in the plural like a second declension noun:

	Singular	Plural
Nominative	žmogùs	žmónės
Genitive	žmogaũs	žmonių̃
Dative	žmógui	žmonėms
Accusative	žmógų	žmónes
Instrumental	žmogumì, žmogum̃	žmonėmìs
Locative	žmogujè	žmonėsè
Vocative	žmogaũ	žmónės

41.50 Fifth declension nouns in -uo: šuõ (4) 'dog' (masculine)

	Singular	Plural
Nominative	šuõ	šùnys, šùnes
Genitive	šuñs, šùnio, šuniẽs	šunų̃
Dative	šùniui	šunìms
Accusative	šùnį	šunìs
Instrumental	šuniù, šunimì, šunim̃	šunimìs
Locative	šunyjè	šunysè
Vocative	šuniẽ	šùnys

41.51 vanduõ (3a) 'water' (masculine):

	Singular	Plural
Nominative	vanduõ	vándenys, -ens
Genitive	vandeñs, vándenio	vandenų̃
Dative	vándeniui	vandenìms
Accusative	vándenį	vándenis
Instrumental	vándeniu, -enimì, -enim̃	vandenimìs
Locative	vandenyjè, -ȳj, -ȳ	vandenysè
Vocative	vandeniẽ	vándenys

41.52 *sesuõ* (3b) 'sister' (feminine):

	Singular	Plural
Nominative	sesuõ	sẽserys, -ers
Genitive	seseřs	seserų̃
Dative	sẽseriai	seserìms
Accusative	sẽserį	sẽseris
Instrumental	sẽseria, -erimì, -eriñ	seserimìs
Locative	seseryjè	seserysè
Vocative	seseriẽ	sẽserys

41.53 *mė́nuo* (1) 'moon, month' (masculine):

	Singular	Plural
Nominative	mė́nuo	mė́nesiai
Genitive	mė́nesio	mė́nesių
Dative	mė́nesiui	mė́nesiams
Accusative	mė́nesį	mė́nesius
Instrumental	mė́nesiu	mė́nesiais
Locative	mė́nesyje	mė́nesiuose
Vocative	mė́nesi	mė́nesiai

41.54 Fifth declension nouns in *-ė*: *duktė̃* (3b) 'daughter' (fem.)

	Singular	Plural
Nominative	duktė̃	dùkterys, -ers
Genitive	dukteřs	dukterų̃
Dative	dùkteriai	dukterìms
Accusative	dùkterį	dùkteris
Instrumental	dùkteria, -erimì, -eriñ	dukterimìs
Locative	dukteryjè	dukterysè
Vocative	dukteriẽ	dùkterys

41.55 The noun *sė́menys* (3) 'linseed' is commonly only used in the plural. The plural declension is: N. *sė́menys*, G. *sė́menų*, D. *sė́menìms*, A. *sė́menis*, I. *sė́menimìs*, L. *sė́menysè*, V. *sė́menys*.

41.6 In the modern standard language the dual is no longer used. In older texts it is met for the most part in the nominative and accusative case. Examples of dual forms of certain of the nouns in this section are given below.

Masculine

N. - A. - V. — dù výru, bróliu, árkliu, svečiù, medžiù, skaičiù
D. — dvíem výram, bróliam, arkliám, svečiám, mė́džiam, skaĩčiam
I. — dvíem výram, bróliam, arkliañ, svečiañ, mė́džiam, skaĩčiam

Feminine

N. - A. - V. - — dvì várni, gérvi, martì, valdì, akì, sẽseri
D. — dvíem várnom, gérvėm, marčióm, valdžióm, akìm, seserìm
I. — dviẽm várnom, gérvėm, marčiõm, valdžiõm, akiÞ̃, seseriÞ̃
    The other cases are the same as those of the plural.

42. ADJECTIVES

42.1   First declension adjectives: *báltas* (3) 'white'

	Singular		Plural	
	Masculine	Feminine	Masculine	Feminine
N.	báltas	baltà	baltì	báltos
G.	bálto	baltõs	baltŨ	baltŨ
D.	baltám	báltai	baltíems	baltóms
A.	báltą	báltą	báltus	báltas
I.	báltu	bálta	baltaĩs	baltomìs
L.	baltamè	baltojè	baltuosè	baltosè

saũsas (4) 'dry'

	Singular		Plural	
N.	saũsas	sausà	sausì	saũsos
G.	saũso	sausõs	sausŨ	sausŨ
D.	sausám	saũsai	sausíems	sausóms
A.	saũsą	saũsą	sausùs	sausàs
I.	sausù	sausà	sausaĩs	sausomìs
L.	sausamè	sausojè	sausuosè	sausosè

dìdis (4) 'large'

	Singular		Plural	
N.	dìdis	didì	didì	dìdžios
G.	dìdžio	didžiõs	didžiŨ	didžiŨ
D.	didžiám	didžiai	didíems	didžióms
A.	dìdį	dìdžią	didžiùs	didžiàs
I.	didžiù	didžià	didžiaĩs	didžiomìs
L.	dìdžiamè	didžiojè	didžiuosè	didžiosè

42.11   Comparative degree: *gerèsnis* (2) 'better' (sometimes found in accent class 4)

	Singular		Plural	
	Masculine	Feminine	Masculine	Feminine
N.	gerèsnis	gerèsnė	geresnì	gerèsnės
G.	gerèsnio	gerèsnės	gerèsnių	gerèsnių
D.	gerèsniam	gerèsnei	gerèsniems	gerèsnėms
A.	gerèsnį	gerèsnę	geresniùs	gerèsnès
I.	geresniù	gerèsnè	gerèsniais	gerèsnėmis
L.	geresniamè	gerèsnėje	gerèsniuose	gerèsnėse

puikùsis (4) 'splendid'

Singular		Plural	
N.	puikùsis	puikióji	puikíeji	puĭkiosios
G.	puĭkiojo	puikiõsios	puikiũjų	puikiũjų
D.	puikiájam	puĭkiajai	puikíesiems	puikiósioms
A.	puĭkųjį	puĭkiąją	puikiúosius	puikiąsias
I.	puikiúoju	puikiąja	puikiaĩsiais	puikiõsiomis
L.	puikiãjame	puikiõjoje	puikiuõsiuose	puikiõsiose

42.43 Definite adjectives of the third declension: *paskutinỹsis* (2) 'last'

Singular		Plural	
Masculine	Feminine	Masculine	Feminine
N.	paskutinỹsis	paskutinióji	paskutiníeji	paskutìniosios
G.	paskutìniojo	paskutiniõsios	paskutiniũjų	paskutiniũjų
D.	paskutiniájam	paskutìniajai	paskutiníesiems	paskutiniósioms
A.	paskutìnįjį	paskutìniąją	paskutiniúosius	paskutiniąsias
I.	paskutiniúoju	paskutiniąja	paskutiniaĩsiais	paskutiniõsiomis
L.	paskutiniãjame	paskutiniõjoje	paskutiniuõsiuose	paskutiniõsiose

The definite adjective forms of the third declension are rarely used.

42.44 The comparative degree of the definite adjective: *geresnỹsis* (4) 'better'

Singular		Plural	
Masculine	Feminine	Masculine	Feminine
N.	geresnỹsis	geresnióji	geresníeji	gerèsniosios
G.	gerèsniojo	geresniõsios	geresniũjų	geresniũjų
D.	geresniájam	gerèsniajai	geresníesiems	geresniósioms
A.	gerèsnįjį	gerèsniąją	geresniúosius	geresniąsias
I.	geresniúoju	geresniąja	geresniaĩsiais	geresniõsiomis
L.	geresniãjame	geresniõjoje	geresniuõsiuose	geresniõsiose

42.45 The superlative degree of the definite adjective: *geriáusiasis* (1) 'best'

Singular		Plural	
Masculine	Feminine	Masculine	Feminine
N.	geriáusiasis	geriáusioji	geriáusieji	geriáusiosios
G.	geriáusiojo	geriáusiosios	geriáusiųjų	geriáusiųjų
D.	geriáusiajam	geriáusiajai	geriáusiesiems	geriáusiosioms
A.	geriáusiąjį	geriáusiąją	geriáusiuosius	geriáusiąsias
I.	geriáusiuoju	geriáusiąja	geriáusiaisiais	geriáusiosiomis
L.	geriáusiajame	geriáusiojoje	geriáusiuosiuose	geriáusiosiose

42.5 *Dual forms of adjectives.* Dual forms of certain of the adjectives listed in this section are given below.

Masculine

N.-A.-V.: dù báltu, áiškiu, sausù, didžiù, puikiù, geresniù, geriáusiu
D.: dvíem baltíem, aiškíem, sausíem, puikíem, gerèsniem, geriáusiem
I.: dviẽm baltiẽm, aiškiẽm, sausiẽm, puikiẽm, gerèsniem, geriáusiem

Feminine

N.-A.-V.: dvì bálti, áiški, sausì, didì, puikì, geresnì, geriáusi
D.: dvíem baltóm, aiškióm, sausóm, didžióm, puikióm, gerèsnem, geriáusiom
I.: dviẽm baltõm, aiškiõm, sausõm, didžiõm, puikiõm, gerèsnem, geriáusiom

42.51 The nominative-accusative-vocative has the same stress as the accusative plural. The dative dual is stressed like the dative plural. In the instrumental dual disyllabic nouns have the circumflex stress on the end; nouns with more than two syllables have the same stress in the instrumental dual as they do in the instrumental plural.

43. VERBS

In simple verbs the third person singular and plural (and dual) are not distinguished, the same form being used with both singular and plural (and dual) subjects.

43.1 INDICATIVE MOOD. ACTIVE VOICE

43.11 *Present tense.*

1st conjugation

dìrbti 'to work'		sùkti 'to turn'		jaũsti 'to feel'	
		Singular			
1) dìrbu	'I work,	sukù	'I turn,	jaučiù	'I feel,
2) dìrbi	am working,	sukì	am turning,	jautì	am feeling,
3) dìrba	etc.'	sùka	etc.'	jaũčia	etc.'

336

	Plural		
1)	dìrbame	sùkame	jaũčiame
2)	dìrbate	sùkate	jaũčiate
3)	dìrba	sùka	jaũčia

1st conjugation (reflexive)

	dìrbtis	'to make for oneself'	sùktis	'to turn, to be turned'	jaũstis	'to feel'
			Singular			
1)	dìrbuos(i)		sukúos(i)		jaučiúos(i)	
2)	dìrbiesi(i).		sukíes(i)		jautíes(i)	
3)	dìrbas(i)		sùkas(i)		jaũčias(i)	

	Plural		
1)	dìrbamės	sùkamės	jaũčiamės
2)	dìrbatės	sùkatės	jaũčiatės
3)	dìrbas(i)	sùkas(i)	jaũčias(i)

2nd conjugation

mylėti 'to love'　　　　**tikėti 'to believe'**

	Singular					Plural	
1)	mýliu	'I love,	tikiù	'I believe,	1)	mýlime	tìkime
2)	mýli	am loving,	tikì	am believing,	2)	mýlite	tìkite
3)	mýli	etc.'	tìki	etc.'	3)	mýli	tìki

2nd conjugation (reflexive)

mylėtis 'to love oneself, to love each other'　　　**tikėtis 'to hope'**

	Singular					Plural	
1)	mýliuos(i)	'I love myself'	tikiúos(i)	'I hope'	1)	mýlimės	tìkimės
2)	mýlies(i)		tikíes(i)		2)	mýlitės	tìkitės
3)	mýlis(i)		tìkis(i)		3)	mýlis(i)	tikis(i)

3rd conjugation

mókyti 'to teach'　　　　**matýti 'to see'**

	Singular					Plural	
1)	mókau	'I teach,	mataũ	'I see, am	1)	mókome	mãtome
2)	mókai	am teaching,	mataĩ	seeing,	2)	mókote	mãtote
3)	móko	etc.'	mãto	etc.	3)	móko	mãto

3rd conjugation (reflexive)

mókytis 'to learn'　　　　**matýtis 'to see each other'**

	Singular				Plural	
1)	mókaus(i)	mataũs(i)	1)	mókomės	mãtomės
2)	mókais(i)	mataĩs(i)	2)	mókotės	mãtotės
3)	mókos(i)	mãtos(i)	3)	mókos(i)	mãtos(i)

43.12 *Simple preterit.*

1st conjugation

dìrbti 'to work'		sùkti 'to turn'		jaũsti 'to feel'	

Singular

1)	dìrbau	'I worked,	sukaũ	'I turned,	jaučiaũ	'I felt,
2)	dìrbai	did work'	sukaĩ	did turn'	jauteĩ	did feel'
3)	dìrbo		sùko		jaũtė	

Plural

1)	dìrbome	sùkome	jaũtėme
2)	dìrbote	sùkote	jaũtėte
3)	dìrbo	sùko	jaũtė

1st conjugation (reflexive)

dìrbtis	'to make for oneself'	sùktis	'to turn, to be turned'	jaũstis	'to feel'

Singular

1)	dìrbaus(i)	sukaũs(i)	jaučiaũs(i)
2)	dìrbais(i)	sukaĩs(i)	jauteĩs(i)
3)	dìrbos(i)	sùkos(i)	jaũtės(i)

Plural

1)	dìrbomės	sùkomės	jaũtėmės
2)	dìrbotės	sùkotės	jaũtėtės
3)	dìrbos(i)	sùkos(i)	jaũtės(i)

2nd conjugation

mylėti 'to love'		tikėti 'to believe'	

		Singular				Plural	
1)	mylėjau	'I loved,	tikėjau	'I believed,	1)	mylėjome	tikėjome
2)	mylėjai	did love,	tikėjai	did believe,	2)	mylėjote	tikėjote
3)	mylėjo	etc.'	tikėjo	etc.'	3)	mylėjo	tikėjo

3rd conjugation

mókyti 'to teach'		matýti 'to see'	

		Singular				Plural	
1)	mókiau	'I taught,	mačiaũ	'I saw,	1)	mókėme	mãtėme
2)	mókei	did teach,	mateĩ	did see,	2)	mókėte	mãtėte
3)	mókė	etc.'	mãtė	etc.'	3)	mókė	mãtė

The reflexive forms of the simple preterit of the 2nd and 3rd conjugations are omitted; the endings are precisely the same as those of the 1st conjugation.

43.13 *Frequentative past tense.*

1st conjugation

dìrbti 'to work'	sùkti 'to turn'	jaũsti 'to feel'

Singular

1)	dìrbdavau	'I used to	sùkdavau	'I used to	jaũsdavau	'I used to
2)	dìrbdavai	work'	sùkdavai	turn'	jaũsdavai	feel'
3)	dìrbdavo		sùkdavo		jaũsdavo	

Plural

1)	dìrbdavome	sùkdavome	jaũsdavome
2)	dìrbdavote	sùkdavote	jaũsdavote
3)	dìrbdavo	sùkdavo	jaũsdavo

1st conjugation (reflexive)

dìrbtis 'to make for oneself'	sùktis 'to turn oneself'	jaũstis 'to feel'

Singular

1)	dìrbdavaus(i)	sùkdavaus(i)	jaũsdavaus(i)
2)	dìrbdavais(i)	sùkdavais(i)	jaũsdavais(i)
3)	dìrbdavos(i)	sùkdavos(i)	jaũsdavos(i)

Plural

1)	dìrbdavomės	sùkdavomės	jaũsdavomės
2)	dìrbdavotės	sùkdavotės	jaũsdavotės
3)	dìrbdavos(i)	sùkdavos(i)	jaũsdavos(i)

The 2nd and 3rd conjugations are conjugated just like the 1st conjugation, e.g. *mylĕdavau* 'I used to love', *mylĕdavaus(i)* 'I used to love myself' and *mókydavau* 'I used to teach', *mókydavaus(i)* 'I used to learn', etc. This tense is formed on the infinitive stem.

43.14 *Future tense.*

1st conjugation

dìrbti 'to work'	sùkti 'to turn'	jaũsti 'to feel'

Singular

1)	dìrbsiu	'I shall	sùksiu	'I shall turn'	jaũsiu	'I shall feel'
2)	dìrbsi	work'	sùksi		jaũsi	
3)	diřbs		sùks		jaũs	

Plural

1)	dìrbsime	sùksime	jaũsime
2)	dìrbsite	sùksite	jaũsite
3)	diřbs	sùks	jaũs

1st conjugation (reflexive)

dìrbtis 'to make for oneself'	**sùktis** 'to turn oneself'	**jaũstis** 'to feel'
	Singular	
1) dìrbsiuos(i)	sùksiuos(i)	jaũsiuos(i)
2) dìrbsies(i)	sùksies(i)	jaũsies(i)
3) dìr̃bsis	sùksis	jaũsis
	Plural	
1) dìrbsimės	sùksimės	jaũsimės
2) dìrbsitės	sùksitės	jaũsitės
3) dìr̃bsis	sùksis	jaũsis

The 2nd and 3rd conjugations are conjugated just like the 1st conjugation, e.g. *mylė́siu* 'I shall love', reflexive *mylė́siuos(i)* 'I shall love myself', and *mókysiu* 'I shall teach', reflexive *mókysiuos(i)* 'I shall learn', etc. This tense is formed on the infinitive stem.

43.14,5 In old texts and in dialects where the dual is still used, it is formed by replacing the plural endings -*me*, -*te* by the endings -*va*, -*ta* and the reflexive endings -*mės*, -*tės* by the endings -*vos*, -*tos*. The dual forms of the verb are used with the dual forms of the pronoun (masculine)*mùdu* 'we two (males)', (feminine) *mùdvi* 'we two (females)'; (masculine)*jùdu* 'you two (males)', (feminine) *jùdvi* 'you two (females)'. The 3rd person dual pronouns (masculine) *juõdu* 'they two, the two of them' and (feminine) *jiẽdvi* 'they two, the two of them' are used with the 3rd person form of the verb which is the same for the singular, plural and dual.

1st conjugation
Dual

1) *mùdu, mùdvi* (present tense) *dìrbava*, (simple preterit) *dìrbova*, (frequentative past tense) *dìrbdavova*, (future tense) *dìrbsiva*
2) *jùdu, jùdvi* (present tense) *dìrbata*, (simple preterit) *dìrbota*, (frequentative past tense) *dìrbdavota*, (future tense) *dìrbsita*

1st conjugation (reflexive)
Dual

1) *mùdu, mùdvi* (present tense) *dìrbavos*, (simple preterit) *dìrbovos*, (frequentative past tense) *dìrbdavovos*, (future tense) *dìrbsivos*

2) *jùdu, jùdvi* (present tense) *dìrbatos,* (simple preterit) *dìrbo-tos,* (frequentative past tense) *dìrbdavotos,* (future tense) *dìrbsitos*

43.15 *Indicative mood. Active Voice. Perfect tense.* The present tense of *bùti* is used with the past active participle. Since the principle of formation is the same for all conjugations, the examples are all from first conjugation verbs.

dìrbti 'to work'

	Singular		Plural	
1)	esù dìrbęs, -usi	'I have worked'	ẽsame dìrbę, -usios	
2)	esì	"	ẽsate	"
3)	yrà	"	yrà	"

sùktis 'to turn' (reflexive)

1)	esù sùkęsis, -usis	'I have turned'	ẽsame sùkęsi, -usios	
2)	esì	"	ẽsate	"
3)	yrà	"	yrà	"

43.16 *Pluperfect tense.* The simple preterit of *bùti* is used with the past active participle.

dìrbti 'to work'

	Singular		Plural	
1)	buvaũ dìrbęs, -usi	'I had worked'	bùvome dìrbę, -usios	
2)	buvaĩ	"	bùvote	"
3)	bùvo	"	bùvo	"

43.17 *Frequentative perfect tense.* The frequentative past tense of *bùti* is used with the past active participle.

dìrbti 'to work'

	Singular		Plural	
1)	bũdavau dìrbęs, -usi	'I had worked	bũdavome dìrbę, -usios	
2)	bũdavai	"	(at intervals)'	bũdavote	"
3)	bũdavo	"		bũdavo	"

43.18 *Future perfect tense.* The future perfect tense is formed by using the future tense of *bùti* with the past active participle.

dìrbti 'to work'

	Singular		Plural	
1)	bũsiu dìrbęs, -usi	'I shall have	bũsime dìrbę, -usios	
2)	bũsi	"	worked'	bũsite	"
3)	bùs	"		bùs	"

43.2 *Indicative mood. Active voice. Progressive tenses.* In these tenses various forms of the auxiliary verb *bū́ti* 'to be' are combined with the appropriate form of the present active participle which is then prefixed with *be-*. The participle agrees in gender and number with the subject. Since the principle of formation is the same for all conjugations, the examples are all given with *dìrbti* 'to work'.

43.21 The present progressive tense which would be conjugated *esù bedirbą̃s*, etc. is not used because it would have the same meaning as the simple present *dìrbu* etc., i.e. 'I am working'.

43.22 *Progressive preterit tense.*

	Singular			Plural		
1)	buvaũ bedirbą̃s, -anti		'I was (still)	bùvome bedirbą̃, -ančios		
2)	buvaĩ	"	working'	bùvote	"	
3)	bùvo	"		bùvo	"	

43.23 *Progressive frequentative past tense.*

	Singular			Plural		
1)	bū́davau bedirbą̃s, -anti		'I used to be	bū́davome bedirbą̃, -ančios		
2)	bū́davai	"	(still)	bū́davote	"	
3)	bū́davo	"	working'	bū́davo	"	

43.24 *Progressive future tense.*

	Singular			Plural		
1)	bū́siu bedirbą̃s, -anti		'I shall be	bū́sime bedirbą̃, -ančios		
2)	bū́si	"	(still) workıng'	bū́site	"	
3)	bùs	"		bùs	"	

43.3 *Indicative mood. Passive voice.* In forming the passive either the present passive or the past passive participle is used with some form of the auxiliary verb *bū́ti* 'to be'.

43.31 *Present tense* (with present passive participle). The verb *mùšti* 'to beat', a 1st conjugation verb, is chosen for the examples, but the principle of formation is the same for all conjugations.

	Singular			Plural		
1)	esù mùšamas,-à		'I am being	ẽsame mušamì, mùšamos		
2)	esì	"	beaten'	ẽsate	"	"
3)	yrà	"		yrà	"	"

342

Simple preterit (with present passive participle)

	Singular			Plural	
1)	buvaũ mùšamas, -à	'I was being	bùvome	mušamì, mùšamos	
2)	buvaĩ	"	beaten'	bùvote	"	"
3)	bùvo	"		bùvo	"	"

Frequentative past tense (with present passive participle)

	Singular			Plural	
1)	bū́davau mùšamas, -à	'I used to be	bū́davome	mušamì, mùšamos	
2)	bū́davai	"	beaten'	bū́davote	"	"
3)	bū́davo	"		bū́davo	"	"

Future tense (with present passive participle)

	Singular			Plural	
1)	bū́siu mùšamas, -à	'I shall be	bū́sime	mušamì, mùšamos	
2)	bū́si	"	beaten'	bū́site	"	"
3)	bùs	"		bùs	"	"

Perfect tense (with masculine present passive participle)

	Singular			Plural	
1)	esù bùvęs mùšamas	'I have been	ẽsame	bùvę mušamì	
2)	esì	"	"	beaten'	ẽsate	"	"
3)	yrà	"	"		yrà	"	"

Perfect tense (with feminine present passive participle)

	Singular		Plural	
1)	esù bùvusi mušamà		ẽsame bùvusios mùšamos	
2)	esì	"	"	ẽsate	"	"
3)	yrà	"	"	yrà	"	"

Pluperfect tense (with masculine present passive participle)

	Singular			Plural	
1)	buvaũ bùvęs mùšamas	'I had been	bùvome	bùvę mušamì	
2)	buvaĩ	"	"	beaten'	bùvote	"	"
3)	bùvo	"	"		bùvo	"	"

Pluperfect tense (with feminine present passive participle)

	Singular			Plural	
1)	buvaũ bùvusi mušamà		bùvome	bùvusios mùšamos	
2)	buvaĩ	"	"	bùvote	"	"
3)	bùvo	"	"	bùvo	"	"

Future perfect tense (with masculine present passive participle)

	Singular			Plural	
1)	bū́siu bùvęs mùšamas	'I shall have	bū́sime bùvę mušamì		
2)	bū́si	"	"	been beaten'	bū́site	"	"
3)	bùs	"	"		bùs	"	"

Future perfect tense (with feminine present passive participle)

	Singular			Plural	
1)	bū́siu bùvusi mušamà		bū́sime bùvusios mùšamos	
2)	bū́si	"	"	bū́site	"	"
3)	bùs	"	"	bùs	"	""

43.32 *Present tense* (with past passive participle)

	Singular		Plural	
1)	esù mùštas, -à	'I am beaten'	ė̃same mùštì, -os	
2)	esì	"	ė̃sate	"
3)	yrà	"	yrà	"

Simple preterit (with past passive participle)

	Singular		Plural	
1)	buvaũ mùštas, -à	'I was beaten'	bùvome mùštì, -os	
2)	buvaĩ	"	bùvote	"
3)	bùvo	"	bùvo	"

Frequentative past tense (with past passive participle)

	Singular			Plural	
1)	bū́davau mùštas, -à	'I used to be	bū́davome mùštì, -os	
2)	bū́davai	"	beaten'	bū́davote	"
3)	bū́davo	"		bū́davo	"

Future tense (with past passive participle)

	Singular			Plural	
1)	bū́siu mùštas, -à	'I shall be	bū́sime mùštì, -os	
2)	bū́si	"	beaten'	bū́site	"
3)	bùs	"		bùs	"

Perfect tense (with masculine past passive participle)

	Singular			Plural	
1)	esù bùvęs mùštas	'I have been	ė̃same bùvę mùštì	
2)	esì	"	"	beaten'	ė̃sate	"	"
3)	yrà	"	"		yrà	"	"

Perfect tense (with feminine past passive participle)

	Singular			Plural	
1)	esù bùvusi mùštà		ė̃same bùvusios mùštos	
2)	esì	"	"	ė̃sate	"	"
3)	yrà	"	"	yrà	"	"

344

Pluperfect tense (with masculine past passive participle)

	Singular			Plural		
1)	buvaũ	bùvęs mùštas	'I had been	bùvome	bùvę muštì	
2)	buvaĩ	"	"	beaten'	bùvote	"	"
3)	bùvo	"	"		bùvo	"	"

Pluperfect tense (with feminine past passive participle)

	Singular			Plural		
1)	buvaũ	bùvusi muštà	bùvome	bùvusios mùštos
2)	buvaĩ	"	"	bùvote	"	"
3)	bùvo	"	"	bùvo	"	"

Future perfect tense (with masculine past passive participle)

	Singular			Plural		
1)	bū́siu	bùvęs mùštas	'I shall have	bū́sime	bùvę muštì	
2)	bū́si	"	"	been beaten'	bū́site	"	"
3)	bùs	"	"		bùs	"	"

Future perfect tense (with feminine past passive participle)

	Singular			Plural		
1)	bū́siu	bùvusi muštà	bū́sime	bùvusios mùštos
2)	bū́si	"	"	bū́site	"	"
3)	bùs	"	"	bùs	"	"

43.4 *Subjunctive.* Since all verbs form the subjunctive in the same way, that is, by adding the subjunctive endings to the infinitive stem, all the examples are given with verbs of the first conjugation.

43.41 *Active voice*

Present tense

	Singular		Plural
1)	dìrbčiau 'I would work'	dìrbtume
2)	dìrbtum.	dìrbtute
3)	dìrbtų	dìrbtų

Present tense (reflexive)

	Singular		Plural
1)	sùkčiaus(i) 'I would turn'	sùktumės
2)	sùktumeis(i)	sùktutės
3)	sùktųs(i)	sùktųs(i)

345

Perfect tense

	Singular			Plural	
1)	bū́čiau dìrbęs, -usi	'I would have		bū́tume dìrbę, -usios	
2)	bū́tum	"	worked'	bū́tute	"
3)	bū́tų	"		bū́tų	"

Perfect tense (reflexive)

	Singular			Plural	
1)	bū́čiau sùkęsis, -usis	'I would have		bū́tume sùkęsi, -usios	
2)	bū́tum	"	turned'	bū́tute	"
3)	bū́tų	"		bū́tų	"

43.42 *Passive voice*

Present tense (with present passive participle)

	Singular			Plural	
1)	bū́čiau mùšamas, -à	'I would be		bū́tume mušamì, -os	
2)	bū́tum	"	beaten'	bū́tute	"
3)	bū́tų	"		bū́tų	"

Perfect tense (with masculine present passive participle)

	Singular			Plural		
1)	bū́čiau bùvęs mùšamas	'I would have		bū́tume bùvę mušamì		
2)	bū́tum	"	"	been beaten'	bū́tute	"	"
3)	bū́tų	"	"		bū́tų	"	"

Perfect tense (with feminine present passive participle)

	Singular			Plural		
1)	bū́čiau bùvusi mušamà			bū́tume bùvusios mùšamos		
2)	bū́tum	"	"	bū́tute	"	"
3)	bū́tų	"	"	bū́tų	"	"

Present tense (with past passive participle)

	Singular			Plural	
1)	bū́čiau mùštas, -à	'I would be		bū́tume muštì, -os	
2)	bū́tum	"	beaten'	bū́tute	"
3)	bū́tų	"		bū́tų	"

Perfect tense (with masculine past passive participle)

	Singular			Plural		
1)	bū́čiau bùvęs mùštas	'I would have		bū́tume bùvę muštì		
2)	bū́tum	"	"	been beaten'	bū́tute	"	"
3)	bū́tų	"	"		bū́tų	"	"

Perfect tense (with feminine past passive participle)

	Singular			Plural		
1)	bū́čiau bùvusi muštà			bū́tume bùvusios mùštos		
2)	bū́tum	"	"	bū́tute	"	"
3)	bū́tų	"	"	bū́tų	"	"

43.43 *Progressive subjunctive. Active voice.*

	Singular		Plural	
1)	bûčiau bedirbą̃s, -anti	'I would (still)	bûtume bedirbą̃, -ančios	
2)	bûtum	"	be working'	bûtute	"
3)	bûtu̧	"		bûtu̧	"

43.5 *Imperative mood.*

1st conjugation: *dìrbti* 'to work'

	Singular	Plural
1)	——	dìrbkime 'let us work'
2)	dìrbk 'work!'	dìrbkite 'work!'
3)	tedirbiẽ, tedìrba, tegù(l) dìrba 'may he (she) work'	tedirbiẽ, tedìrba, tegù(l) dìrba

1st conjugation (reflexive): *dìrbtis* 'to make for oneself'

	Singular	Plural
1)	——	dìrbkimės
2)	dìrbkis	dìrbkitės
3)	tesidirbiẽ, tesidìrba, tegù(l) dìrbasi	tesidirbiẽ, tesidìrba, tegù(l) dìrbasi

2nd conjugation: *mylĕti* 'to love'

	Singular	Plural
1)	——	mylĕkime 'let us love'
2)	mylĕk 'love!'	mylĕkite 'love!'
3)	temyliẽ, tegù(l) mýli 'may he (she) love'	temyliẽ, tegù(l) mýli

2nd conjugation (reflexive): *mylĕtis* 'to love each other'

	Singular	Plural
1)	——	mylĕkimės 'let us love one another'
2)	mylĕkis	mylĕkitės 'love one another'
3)	tesimyliẽ, tegù(l) mýlisi	tesimyliẽ, tegù(l) mýlisi

3rd conjugation: *mókyti* 'to teach'

	Singular	Plural
1)	——	mókykime 'let us teach'
2)	mókyk 'teach!'	mókykite 'teach!'
3)	temókai, tegù(l) móko 'may he (she) teach'	temókai, tegù(l) móko

3rd conjugation (reflexive): *mókytis* 'to learn'

	Singular	Plural
1)	——	mókykimės 'let us learn'
2)	mókykis 'learn!'	mókykitės 'learn!'
3)	tesimókai, tegù(l) mókosi 'may he (she) learn'	tesimókai, tegù(l) mókosi

347

43.6 PARTICIPLES

43.61 *Present active participle.*

1st conjugation: *dìrbti* 'to work'

	Singular		Plural	
	Masculine	Feminine	Masculine	Feminine
N.	dirbąs 'working' (dìrbantis)	dìrbanti	dirbą (dìrbantys)	dìrbančios
G.	dìrbančio	dìrbančios	dìrbančių	dìrbančių
D.	dìrbančiam	dìrbančiai	dìrbantiems	dìrbančioms
A.	dìrbantį	dìrbančią	dìrbančius	dìrbančias
I.	dìrbančiu	dìrbančia	dìrbančiais	dìrbančiomis
L.	dìrbančiame	dìrbančioje	dìrbančiuose	dìrbančiose

2nd conjugation: *mylė́ti* 'to love'

	Singular		Plural	
	Masculine	Feminine	Masculine	Feminine
N.	mylį̃s (mýlintis)	mýlinti	mylį̃ (mýlintys)	mýlinčios
G.	mýlinčio	mýlinčios	mýlinčių	mýlinčių
D.	mýlinčiam	mýlinčiai	mýlintiems	mýlinčioms
A.	mýlintį	mýlinčią	mýlinčius	mýlinčias
I.	mýlinčiu	mýlinčia	mýlinčiais	mýlinčiomis
L.	mýlinčiame	mýlinčioje	mýlinčiuose	mýlinčiose

3rd conjugation: *matýti* 'to see'

	Singular		Plural	
	Masculine	Feminine	Masculine	Feminine
N.	matą̃s (mãtantis)	mãtanti	matą̃ (mãtantys)	mãtančios
G.	mãtančio	mãtančios	mãtančių	mãtančių
D.	mãtančiam	mãtančiai	mãtantiems	mãtančioms
A.	mãtantį	mãtančią	mãtančius	mãtančias
I.	mãtančiu	mãtančia	matančiais	mãtančiomis
L.	mãtančiame	mãtančioje	mãtančiuose	mãtančiose

43.62 *Present active participle* (definite form).

1st conjugation: *dìrbti* 'to work'

	Singular		Plural	
	Masculine	Feminine	Masculine	Feminine
N.	dirbantýsis	dìrbančioji	dìrbantieji	dìrbančiosios
G.	dìrbančiojo	dìrbančiosios	dìrbančiųjų	dìrbančiųjų
D.	dìrbančiajam	dìrbančiajai	dìrbantiesiems	dìrbančiosioms
A.	dìrbantįjį	dìrbančiąją	dìrbančiuosius	dìrbančiąsias
I.	dìrbančiuoju	dìrbančiąja	dìrbančiaisiais	dìrbančiosiomis
L.	dìrbančiajame	dìrbančiojoje	dìrbančiuosiuose	dìrbančiosiose

The definite participle is declined just like the definite adjective. The method of formation from the verb is the same as for the corresponding indefinite participle. The declension is the same for all conjugations.

43.63 *Past active participle.*

1st conjugation: *dìrbti* 'to work'

	Singular		Plural	
	Masculine	Feminine	Masculine	Feminine
N.	dìrbęs	dìrbusi	dìrbę	dìrbusios
G.	dìrbusio	dìrbusios	dìrbusių	dìrbusių
D.	dìrbusiam	dìrbusiai	dìrbusiems	dìrbusioms
A.	dìrbusį	dìrbusią	dìrbusius	dìrbusias
I.	dìrbusiu	dìrbusia	dìrbusiais	dìrbusiomis
L.	dìrbusiame	dìrbusioje	dìrbusiuose	dìrbusiose

2nd conjugation *mylėti* 'to love'

	Singular		Plural	
	Masculine	Feminine	Masculine	Feminine
N.	mylėjęs	mylėjusi	mylėję	mylėjusios
G.	mylėjusio	mylėjusios	mylėjusių	mylėjusių
D.	mylėjusiam	mylėjusiai	mylėjusiems	mylėjusioms
A.	mylėjusį	mylėjusią	mylėjusius	mylėjusias
I.	mylėjusiu	mylėjusia	mylėjusiais	mylėjusiomis
L.	mylėjusiame	mylėjusioje	mylėjusiuose	mylėjusiose

3rd conjugation: *matýti* 'to see'

	Singular		Plural	
	Masculine	Feminine	Masculine	Feminine
N.	mãtęs	mãčiusi	mãtę	mãčiusios
G.	mãčiusio	mãčiusios	mãčiusių	mãčiusių
D.	mãčiusiam	mãčiusiai	mãčiusiems	mãčiusioms
A.	mãčiusį	mãčiusią	mãčiusius	mãčiusias
I.	mãčiusiu	mãčiusia	mãčiusiais	mãčiusiomis
L.	mãčiusiame	mãčiusioje	mãčiusiuose	mãčiusiose

43.64 *Past active participle* (definite form).

1st conjugation: *dìrbti* 'to work'

	Singular		Plural	
	Masculine	Feminine	Masculine	Feminine
N.	dirbusýsis	dìrbusioji	dìrbusieji	dìrbusiosios
G.	dìrbusiojo	dìrbusiosios	dìrbusiųjų	dìrbusiųjų
D.	dìrbusiajam	dìrbusiajai	dirbusiesiems	dìrbusiosioms
A.	dìrbusįjį	dìrbusiąją	dìrbusiuosius	dìrbusiąsias
I.	dìrbusiuoju	dìrbusiąja	dìrbusiaisiais	dìrbusiosiomis
L.	dìrbusiajame	dìrbusiojoje	dìrbusiuosiuose	dìrbusiosiose

The definite participle is declined just like the definite adjective. The method of formation from the verb is the same as for the corresponding indefinite participle. The declension is the same for all conjugations.

43.65 *Frequentative past active participle.*

1st conjugation: *dìrbti* 'to work'

	Singular		Plural	
	Masculine	Feminine	Masculine	Feminine
N.	dìrbdavęs	dìrbdavusi	dìrbdavę	dìrbdavusios
G.	dìrbdavusio	dìrbdavusios	dìrbdavusių	dìrbdavusių
D.	dìrbdavusiam	dìrbdavusiai	dìrbdavusiems	dìrbdavusioms
A.	dìrbdavusį	dìrbdavusią	dìrbdavusius	dìrbdavusias
I.	dìrbdavusiu	dìrbdavusia	dìrbdavusiais	dìrbdavusiomis
L.	dìrbdavusiame	dìrbdavusioje	dìrbdavusiuose	dìrbdavusiose

The declension is the same for the 2nd and 3rd conjugations, the endings -*davęs*, -*davusi*, etc. being added directly to the infinitive stem, e.g. (2nd conjugation) nom. sing. masc. *mylẽdavęs*, nom. sing. fem. *mylẽdavusi*, etc. or (3rd conjugation) nom. sing. masc. *matýdavęs*, nom. sing. fem. *matýdavusi*.

43.66 *Frequentative past active participle* (definite form).

1st conjugation: *dìrbti* 'to work'

	Singular		Plural	
	Masculine	Feminine	Masculine	Feminine
N.	dirbdavusỹsis	dìrbdavusioji	dìrbdavusieji	dìrbdavusiosios
G.	dìrbdavusiojo	dìrbdavusiosios	dìrbdavusiųjų	dìrbdavusiųjų
D.	dìrbdavusiajam	dìrbdavusiajai	dìrbdavusiesiems	dìrbdavusiosioms
A.	dìrbdavusįjį	dìrbdavusiąją	dìrbdavusiuosius	dìrbdavusiąsias
I.	dìrbdavusiuoju	dìrbdavusiąja	dìrbdavusiaisiais	dìrbdavusiosiomis
L.	dìrbdavusiajame	dìrbdavusiojoje	dìrbdavusiuosiuose	dìrbdavusiosiose

The definite participle is declined just like the definite adjective. The method of formation from the verb is the same as for the corresponding indefinite participle. The declension is the same for all conjugations.

43.67 *Future active participle.*

1st conjugation: *dìrbti* 'to work'

	Singular		Plural	
	Masculine	Feminine	Masculine	Feminine
N.	dìrbsiąs	dìrbsianti	dìrbsią	dìrbsiančios
G.	dìrbsiančio	dìrbsiančios	dìrbsiančių	dìrbsiančių
D.	dìrbsiančiam	dìrbsiančiai	dìrbsiantiems	dìrbsiančioms
A.	dìrbsiantį	dìrbsiančią	dìrbsiančius	dìrbsiančias
I.	dìrbsiančiu	dìrbsiančia	dìrbsiančiais	dìrbsiančiomis
L.	dìrbsiančiame	dìrbsiančioje	dìrbsiančiuose	dìrbsiančiose

The declension is the same for the 2nd and 3rd conjugations, the endings -siąs, -sianti, etc. being added directly to the infinitive stem, e.g. (2nd conjugation) nom. sing. masc. *mylḗsiąs*, nom. sing. fem. *mylḗsianti*, etc. or (3rd conjugation) nom. sing. masc. *matýsiąs*, nom. sing. fem. *matýsianti*, etc.

43.68 *Future active participle* (definite form).

1st conjugation: *dìrbti* 'to work'

	Singular		Plural	
	Masculine	Feminine	Masculine	Feminine
N.	dirbsiantýsis	dìrbsiančioji	dìrbsiantieji	dìrbsiančiosios
G.	dìrbsiančiojo	dìrbsiančiosios	dìrbsiančiųjų	dìrbsiančiųjų
D.	dìrbsiančiajam	dìrbsiančiajai	dìrbsiantiesiems	dìrbsiančiosioms
A.	dìrbsiantįjį	dìrbsiančiąją	dìrbsiančiuosius	dìrbsiančiąsias
I.	dìrbsiančiuoju	dìrbsiančiąja	dìrbsiančiaisiais	dìrbsiančiosiomis
L.	dìrbsiančiajame	dìrbsiančiojoje	dìrbsiančiuosiuose	dìrbsiančiosiose

The definite participle is declined just like the definite adjective. The method of formation from the verb is the same as for the corresponding indefinite participle. The declension is the same for all conjugations.

43.69 *Present passive participle.*

1st conjugation: *dìrbti* 'to work'

	Singular		Plural	
	Masculine	Feminine	Masculine	Feminine
N.	dìrbamas	dirbamà	dirbamì	dìrbamos
G.	dìrbamo	dirbamõs	dirbamų̃	dirbamų̃
D.	dirbamám	dìrbamai	dirbamíems	dirbamóms
A.	dìrbamą	dìrbamą	dìrbamus	dìrbamas
I.	dìrbamu	dìrbama	dirbamaĩs	dirbamomìs
L.	dirbamamè	dirbamojè	dirbamuosè	dirbamosè

2nd conjugation: *mylḗti* 'to love'

	Singular		Plural	
	Masculine	Feminine	Masculine	Feminine
N.	mýlimas	mylimà	mylimì	mýlimos
G.	mýlimo	mylimõs	mylimų̃	mylimų̃
D.	mylimám	mýlimai	mylimíems	mylimóms
A.	mýlimą	mýlimą	mýlimus	mýlimas
I.	mýlimu	mýlima	mylimaĩs	mylimomìs
L.	mylimamè	mylimojè	mylimuosè	mylimosè

3rd conjugation: *matýti* 'to see'

| | Singular | | Plural | |
---	Masculine	Feminine	Masculine	Feminine
N.	mãtomas	mãtoma	mãtomi	mãtomos
G.	mãtomo	mãtomos	mãtomų	mãtomų
D.	mãtomam	mãtomai	mãtomiems	mãtomoms
A.	mãtomą	mãtomą	mãtomus	mãtomas
I.	mãtomu	mãtoma	mãtomais	mãtomomis
L.	mãtomame	mãtomoje	mãtomuose	mãtomose

43.70 *Present passive participle* (definite form).

1st conjugation: *dìrbti* 'to work'

| | Singular | | Plural | |
---	Masculine	Feminine	Masculine	Feminine
N.	dirbamàsis	dirbamóji	dirbamíeji	dìrbamosios
G.	dìrbamojo	dirbamõsios	dirbamũjų	dirbamũjų
D.	dìrbamájam	dìrbamajai	dirbamíesiems	dirbamósioms
A.	dìrbamąjį	dìrbamąją	dirbamúosius	dirbamą́sias
I.	dirbamúoju	dirbamą́ja	dirbamaĩsiais	dirbamõsiomis
L.	dirbamãjame	dirbamõjoje	dirbamuõsiuose	dirbamõsiose

The definite participle is declined just like the definite adjective. The method of formation from the verb is the same as for the corresponding indefinite participle. The declension is the same for all conjugations.

43.71 *Past passive participle.*

1st conjugation: *dìrbti* 'to work'

| | Singular | | Plural | |
---	Masculine	Feminine	Masculine	Feminine
N.	dìrbtas	dirbtà	dirbtì	dìrbtos
G.	dìrbto	dirbtõs	dirbtũ	dìrbtũ
D.	dirbtám	dìrbtai	dirbtíems	dirbtóms
A.	dìrbtą	dìrbtą	dìrbtus	dìrbtas
I.	dìrbtu	dìrbta	dirbtaĩs	dirbtomìs
L.	dìrbtamè	dirbtojè	dirbtuosè	dirbtosè

2nd conjugation: *mylḗti* 'to love'

| | Singular | | Plural | |
---	Masculine	Feminine	Masculine	Feminine
N.	mylḗtas	mylḗta	mylḗti	mylḗtos
G.	mylḗto	mylḗtos	mylḗtų	mylḗtų
D.	mylḗtam	mylḗtai	mylḗtiems	mylḗtoms
A.	mylḗtą	mylḗtą	mylḗtus	mylḗtas
I.	mylḗtu	mylḗta	mylḗtais	mylḗtomis
L.	mylḗtame	mylḗtoje	mylḗtuose	mylḗtose

352

3rd conjugation: *matýti* 'to see'

	Singular		Plural	
	Masculine	Feminine	Masculine	Feminine
N.	matýtas	matýta	matýti	matýtos
G.	matýto	matýtos	matýtų	matýtų
D.	matýtam	matýtai	matýtiems	matýtoms
A.	matýtą	matýtą	matýtus	matýtas
I.	matýtu	matýta	matýtais	matýtomis
L.	matýtame	matýtoje	matýtuose	matýtose

43.72 *Past passive participle* (definite form).

1st conjugation: *dìrbti* 'to work'

	Singular		Plural	
	Masculine	Feminine	Masculine	Feminine
N.	dirbtàsis	dirbtóji	dirbtíeji	dìrbtosios
G.	dìrbtojo	dirbtõsios	dirbtūjų	dirbtūjų
D.	dirbtájam	dìrbtajai	dirbtíesiems	dirbtósioms
A.	dìrbtąjį	dìrbtąją	dirbtúosius	dirbtą́sias
I.	dirbtúoju	dirbtą́ja	dirbtaĩsiais	dirbtõsiomis
L.	dirbtãjame	dirbtõjoje	dirbtuõsiuose	dirbtõsiose

The definite participle is declined just like the definite adjective. The method of formation from the verb is the same as for the corresponding indefinite participle. The declension is the same for all conjugations.

43.73 *Future passive participle.*

1st conjugation: *dìrbti* 'to work'

	Singular		Plural	
	Masculine	Feminine	Masculine	Feminine
N.	dìrbsimas	dirbsimà	dirbsimì	dìrbsimos
G.	dìrbsimo	dirbsimõs	dirbsimū̃	dirbsimū̃
D.	dirbsimám	dìrbsimai	dirbsimíems	dirbsimóms
A.	dìrbsimą	dìrbsimą	dìrbsimus	dìrbsimas
I.	dìrbsimu	dìrbsima	dirbsimaĩs	dirbsimomìs
L.	dìrbsimamè	dirbsimojè	dirbsimuosè	dirbsimosè

The declension is the same for the 2nd and 3rd conjugations, the endings -*mas*, -*ma*, etc. being added directly to the 2nd singular of the future tense, e.g. (2nd conjugation) nom. sing. masc. *mylḗsimas*, nom. sing. fem. *mylḗsima*, etc. or (3rd conjugation) nom. sing. masc. *matýsimas*, nom. sing. fem. *matýsima*, etc.

43.74 *Future passive participle* (definite form).

1st conjugation: *dìrbti* 'to work'

	Singular		Plural	
	Masculine	Feminine	Masculine	Feminine
N.	dirbsimàsis	dirbsimóji	dirbsimíeji	dìrbsimosios
G.	dìrbsimojo	dirbsimõsios	dìrbsimūjų	dirbsimūjų
D.	dìrbsimájam	dìrbsimajai	dirbsimíesiems	dirbsimósioms
A.	dìrbsimąjį	dìrbsimąją	dirbsimúosius	dirbsimą́sias
I.	dirbsimúoju	dirbsimą́ja	dirbsimaĩsiais	dirbsimõsiomis
L.	dirbsimãjame	dirbsimõjoje	dirbsimuõsiuose	dirbsimõsiose

The definite participle is declined just like the definite adjective. The method of formation from the verb is the same as for the corresponding indefinite participle. The declension is the same for all conjugations.

43.75 *Participle of necessity.*

1st conjugation: *dìrbti* 'to work'

	Singular		Plural	
	Masculine	Feminine	Masculine	Feminine
N.	dìrbtinas	dirbtinà	dirbtinì	dìrbtinos
G.	dìrbtino	dirbtinõs	dirbtinų̃	dirbtinų̃
D.	dirbtinám	dìrbtinai	dirbtiníems	dirbtinóms
A.	dìrbtiną	dìrbtiną	dìrbtinus	dìrbtinas
I.	dìrbtinu	dìrbtina	dirbtinaĩs	dirbtinomìs
L.	dirbtinamè	dirbtinojè	dirbtinuosè	dirbtinosè

The declension is the same for the 2nd and 3rd conjugations, the endings -*nas*, -*na*, etc. being added directly to the infinitive, e.g. (2nd conjugation) nom. sing. masc. *mylĕtinas*, nom. sing. fem. *mylĕtina* or (3rd conjugation) nom. sing. masc. *matýtinas*, nom. sing. fem. *matýtina*, etc.

43.76 *Participle of necessity* (definite form).

1st conjugation *dìrbti* 'to work'

	Singular		Plural	
	Masculine	Feminine	Masculine	Feminine
N.	dirbtinàsis	dirbtinóji	dirbtiníeji	dìrbtinosios
G.	dìrbtinojo	dirbtinõsios	dirbtinų̃jų	dirbtinų̃jų
D.	dirbtinájam	dìrbtinajai	dirbtiníesiems	dirbtinósioms
A.	dìrbtinąjį	dìrbtinąją	dirbtinúosius	dirbtiną́sias
I.	dirbtinúoju	dirbtiną́ja	dirbtinaĩsiais	dirbtinõsiomis
L.	dirbtinájame	dirbtinõjoje	dirbtinuõsiuose	dirbtinõsiose

The definite participle is declined just like the definite adjective. The method of formation from the verb is the same as for the corresponding indefinite participle. The declension is the same for all conjugations.

43.8 *Reflexive participles.* Generally only the nominative of reflexive participles is still used; in the singular we find both the masculine and the feminine, but in the plural only the masculine. The other cases are rarely found nowadays. Examples are given of the 1st conjugation verb *sùktis* 'to turn, to be turned', the 2nd conjugation verb *mylėtis* 'to be in love', *matýtis* 'to meet with'.

43.81 *Present active participle (reflexive).*

Singular

Masculine

N. sùkąsis, mýlįsis, mãtąsis

Feminine

sùkantis, mýlintis, mãtantis

Plural

N. sùkąsi, mýlįsi, mãtąsi

43.82 *Past active participle (reflexive).*

Singular

Masculine

N. sùkęsis, mylėjęsis, mãtęsis

Feminine

sùkusis, mylėjusis, mãčiusis

Plural

Masculine

N. sùkęsi, mylėjęsi, mãtęsi

43.83 It is possible also to find other tenses of the reflexive participles, cf. the frequentative past active participle of *sùktis*: (masc. nom. sing.) *sùkdavęsis*, (fem. nom. sing.) *sùkdavusis*, (masc. nom. plural) *sùkdavęsi*. Likewise a reflexive future active participle is found, cf. (masc. nom. sing.) *sùksiąsis*, (fem. nom. sing.) *sùksiantis*, (masc. nom. plural) *sùksiąsi*.

43.9 *The Supine (Siekinỹs).* The supine is formed by dropping the infinitive ending *-ti* and adding *-tų*, e.g. from *nèšti* we have *nèštų*. The supine denotes an action which is accomplished by means of another action. The supine is commonly used with verbs which denote some motion or movement from one place to another and it becomes the goal of the action of the main verb.

Examples:

1) *Jìs eĩna gùlt̨ų.* — He goes to bed (to lie down).

2) *Jõnas nùėjo kir̃vio parsinèšt̨ų.* — John went to bring the axe home.

3) *Jìs išvažiãvo málk̨ų kir̃st̨ų.* — He went out to cut firewood.

Note that the object of the supine is always in the genitive case.

The stress of the supine is the same as that of the infinitive. It is used only in older texts. The infinitive is used instead of the supine in the modern standard language.

43.91 *The Second Infinitive (Būdinỹs).*

The second infinitive *(būdinỹs)* is formed by removing the infinitive ending *-ti* and adding either *-te* or *-tinai*. Second infinitives with the ending *-te* are used without prefixes and without the reflexive particle *-si*. For example from *bė̆gti* 'to run' the second infinitive would be either *bė̆g-tè* or *bė̆g-tinai* 'running, in a running manner'. The meaning is difficult to render in English. Roughly the idea is that of intensification of the action or a description of the manner in which an action takes place. Examples:

1) *Jìs bė̆gtè bė̆go.* — He ran as fast as he could.

2) *Jìs rė̆ktè rė̆kė.* — He shouted at the top of his lungs.

3) *Jį̃ mirtinaĩ sùžeidė.* — He was mortally wounded.

If the second infinitive ends in *-te*, two stress patterns are possible. Those formed on a monosyllabic stem are stressed on the end, cf. *bė̆g-tè, rė̆k-tè.* Those formed on polysyllabic stems have the same stress and intonation as the infinitive. The same patterns are observed for the second infinitive in *-tinai*, but the existence of a prefix or reflexive has no effect on the stress, e.g. *nusikélti - nusikéltinai.*

44. PRONOUNS

44.1 *Personal pronouns.*

Singular

	1st	2nd	3rd Masculine	Feminine
N.	àš	tù	jìs	jì
G.	manę̃s	tavę̃s	jõ	jõs
D.	mán	táu	jám	jái
A.	manè	tavè	jį̃	ją̃
I.	manimì	tavimì	juõ	jà
L.	manyjè	tavyjè	jamè	jojè

Plural

	1st	2nd	3rd Masculine	Feminine
N.	mẽs	jū̃s	jiẽ	jõs
G.	mū́sų	jū́sų	jų̃	jų̃
D.	mùms	jùms	jíems	jóms
A.	mùs	jùs	juõs	jàs
I.	mumìs	jumìs	jaĩs	jomìs
L.	mumysè	jumysè	juosè	josè

Dual

	Masc.	Fem.	Masc.	Fem.	Masculine	Feminine
N.	mùdu,	mùdvi	jùdu,	jùdvi	juõdu (jiẽdu)	jiẽdvi
G.	mùdviejų		jùdviejų		jùdviejų	jùdviejų
D.	mùdviem		jùdviem		jíedviem	jódviem
A.	mùdu,	mùdvi	jùdu,	jùdvi	juõdu	jiẽdvi
I.	mùdviem		jùdviem		jiẽmdviem	jõdviem
L.	mùdviese		jùdviese		juõdviese	jiẽdviese

44.12 The reflexive pronoun *savę̃s* cannot be used in the nominative case because it always refers to the subject of the sentence which, of course, is in the nominative case. The same form is used for both singular and plural.

Genitive	savę̃s
Dative	sáu
Accusative	savè
Instrumental	savimì
Locative	savyjè

44.2 *Possessive pronouns.*

44.21 The possessive pronouns *màno* 'my, mine', *tàvo* 'yours (sg.); thy, thine', *sàvo* 'one's own', *jõ* 'his', *jõs* 'her, hers', *mū́sų* 'our, ours', *jū́sų* 'your, yours', *jų̃* 'their, theirs' are undeclined. The forms *jõ, jõs, mū́sų, jū́sų, jų̃* are merely the genitive case form of the corresponding personal pronoun.

357

44.22 The rarer forms *mànas* 'my, mine', *tàvas* 'yours (sg.); thy, thine', *sãvas* 'one's own' are declined like the adjective *saũsas, sausà*. The definite forms *manàsis, tavàsis*, etc. are declined like *sausàsis, sausóji*, etc.

44.23 The rarer forms *manìškis* 'my, mine', *tavìškis* 'yours (sg.); thy, thine', *savìškis* 'one's own', *mūsìškis* 'our, ours', *jūsìš-kis* 'your, yours' are declined like *geležìnis, geležìnė*.

44.3 *Demonstrative pronouns.*

'this'

	Singular		Plural	
	Masculine	Feminine	Masculine	Feminine
N.	šìs	šì	šiẽ	šiõs
G.	šiõ	šiõs	šiũ	šiũ
D.	šiám	šiái	šíems	šíoms
A.	šį̃	šią̃	šiuõs	šiàs
I.	šiuõ	šià	šiaĩs	šiomìs
L.	šiamè	šiojè	šiuosè	šiosè

'this (one here)'

	Singular		Plural	
	Masculine	Feminine	Masculine	Feminine
N.	šìtas	šìta	šìtie	šìtos
G.	šìto	šìtos	šìtų	šìtų
D.	šìtam	šìtai	šìtiems	šìtoms
A.	šìtą	šìtą	šìtuos	šìtas
I.	šìtuo	šìta	šìtais	šìtomis
L.	šìtame	šìtoje	šìtuose	šìtose

'that'

	Singular		Plural	
	Masculine	Feminine	Masculine	Feminine
N.	tàs	tà	tiẽ	tõs
G.	tõ	tõs	tũ	tũ
D.	tám	tái	tíems	tóms
A.	tą̃	tą̃	tuõs	tàs
I.	tuõ	tà	taĩs	tomìs
L.	tamè	tojè	tuosè	tosè

'that (one over there)'

	Singular		Plural	
	Masculine	Feminine	Masculine	Feminine
N.	anàs	anà	aniẽ	anõs
G.	anõ	anõs	anũ	anũ
D.	anám	anái	aníems	anóms
A.	aną̃	aną̃	anuõs	anàs
I.	anuõ	anà	anaĩs	anomìs
L.	anamè	anojè	anuosè	anosè

'such a . . . as that'

	Singular		Plural	
	Masculine	Feminine	Masculine	Feminine
N.	anóks (1)	anókia	anókie	anókios
G.	anókio	anókios	anókių	anókių
D.	anókiam	anókiai	anókiems	anókioms
A.	anókį	anókią	anókius	anókias
I.	anókiu	anókia	anókiais	anókiomis
L.	anókiame	anókioje	anókiuose	anókiose

'such a . . .'

	Singular		Plural	
	Masculine	Feminine	Masculine	Feminine
N.	tóks (3)	tokià	tokiě	tókios
G.	tókio	tokiõs	tokių	tokių
D.	tokiám	tókiai	tokíems	tokióms
A.	tókį	tókią	tókius	tókias
I.	tókiu	tókia	tokiaĩs	tokiomìs
L.	tokiamè	tokiojè	tokiuosè	tokiosè

'such (a)'

	Singular		Plural	
	Masculine	Feminine	Masculine	Feminine
N.	šìtoks (1)	šìtokia	šìtokie	šìtokios
G.	šìtokio	šìtokios	šìtokių	šìtokių
D.	šìtokiam	šìtokiai	šìtokiems	šìtokioms
A.	šìtokį	šìtokią	šìtokius	šìtokias
I.	šìtokiu	šìtokia	šìtokiais	šìtokiomis
L.	šìtokiame	šìtokioje	šìtokiuose	šìtokiose

šióks 'such (a)' is declined like *tóks*.

'oneself'

	Singular		Plural	
	Masculine	Feminine	Masculine	Feminine
N.	pàts	patì	pãtys	pãčios
G.	patiěs	pačiõs	pačių	pačių
D.	pačiám	pãčiai	patíems	pačióms
A.	pãtį	pãčią	pačiùs	pačiàs
I.	pačiù	pačià	pačiaĩs	pačiomìs
L.	pačiamè	pačiojè	pačiuosè	pačiosè

jóks 'no, not one, not a', *kóks* 'what a', are declined like *tóks*; *kitóks* 'another kind of', *vienóks* 'the same kind of, identical', *visóks* 'all kinds of, diverse' are declined like *anóks*. *niēkas* 'no-one, nothing' and *vìskas* 'everything' are not distinguished as to number and gender.

N.	niĕkas 'nothing'	vìskas 'everything'	
G.	niĕko (niĕkieno)	vìsko	
D.	niĕkam	vìskam	
A.	niĕką	viską	
I.	niekù	vìskuo	
L.	niekamè	viskamè	

44.4 Interrogative pronouns.

kàs 'who, what' does not distinguish gender or number.

Nominative	kàs
Genitive	kŏ (kienŏ)
Dative	kám
Accusative	ką̃
Instrumental	kuŏ
Locative	kamè

kurìs is declined like jìs. kóks 'which, which kind of, what kind of' is declined like tóks. kelì 'how many', kelerì 'how many' are declined like penkì 'five', ketverì 'four'.

katràs 'which of two' is declined as given below:

	Singular		Plural	
	Masculine	Feminine	Masculine	Feminine
Nominative	katràs	katrà	katriĕ	katrŏs
Genitive	katrŏ	katrŏs	katrų̃	katrų̃
Dative	katrám	katrái	katríems	katróms
Accusative	katrą̃	katrą̃	katruŏs	katràs
Instrumental	katruŏ	katrà	katraĩs	katromìs
Locative	katramè	katrojè	katruosè	katrosè

44.5 The relative pronouns kàs 'who, which', kurìs (kur̃s) 'which, who' and kóks 'which' are declined like the corresponding interrogatives.

44.6 The indefinite pronoun kas-ne-kàs 'perhaps someone' is declined below. There is no distinction of gender or number.

Nominative	kas-ne-kàs
Genitive	ko-ne-kŏ
Dative	kam-ne-kám
Accusative.	ką-ne-ką̃
Instrumental	kuo-ne-kuŏ
Locative	kame-ne-kamè

44.7 *Definite pronouns.*

	Singular		Plural	
	Masculine	Feminine	Masculine	Feminine
N.	jisaĩ	jinaĩ (jĩji)	jiẽji	jõsios
G.	jõjo	jõsios	jũjŲ	jũjŲ
D.	jájam	jájai	jíesiems	jósioms
A.	jĩjĮ	jãjĄ	júosius	jĄsias
I.	júoju	jĄja	jaĩsiais	jõsiomis
L.	jãjame	jójoje	juõsiuose	jõsiose

šisaĩ 'this', *tasaĩ* 'that', *šìtasai* 'this', *anasaĩ* (*anàsis*) 'that', *kursaĩ* 'which' are declined like *jisaĩ*. The forms *patsaĩ, toksaĩ, anoksaĩ* and *koksaĩ* are generally only used in the masculine nominative singular.

45. NUMERALS

45.1 *Cardinal numbers:*

0. nùlis (2)
1. (masc.) víenas, (fem.) vienà (3)
2. (masc.) dù, (fem.) dvì
3. trỹs (4)
4. (masc.) keturì, (fem.) kẽturios (3[b])
5. (masc.) penkì, (fem.) peñkios (4)
6. (masc.) šešì, (fem.) šẽšios (4)
7. (masc.) septynì, (fem.) septýnios (3)
8. (masc.) aštuonì, (fem.) aštúonios (3)
9. (masc.) devynì, (fem.) devýnios (3)
10. dẽšimt (dešimtìs) (3[b])
11. vienúolika (1)
12. dvýlika (1)
13. trýlika (1)
14. keturiólika (1)
15. penkiólika (1)
16. šešiólika (1)
17. septyniólika (1)
18. aštuoniólika (1)
19. devyniólika (1)
20. dvìdešimt, (dvì dẽšimtys)
21. dvìdešimt víenas
22. dvìdešimt dù, etc.
30. trìsdešimt, (trỹs dẽšimtys)
40. kẽturiasdešimt, (kẽturios dẽšimtys)

361

50. peñkiasdešimt, (peñkios dẽšimtys)
60. šẽšiasdešimt, (šẽšios dẽšimtys)
70. septýniasdešimt, (septýnios dẽšimtys)
80. aštúoniasdešimt, (aštúonios dẽšimtys)
90. devýniasdešimt, (devýnios dẽšimtys)
100. šim̃tas (4)
200. dù šimtaĩ
300. trỹs šimtaĩ
400. keturì šimtaĩ
500. penkì šimtaĩ, etc.
1,000. tū́kstantis (1)
2,000. dù tū́kstančiai
3,000. trỹs tū́kstančiai
1,000,000. milijõnas (2), tū́kstantis tū́kstančių
1,000,000,000. milijárdas (1)

Other examples:

484. keturì šimtaĩ aštúoniasdešimt keturì
5,673. penkì tū́kstančiai šešì šimtaĩ septýniasdešimt (septýnios dẽšimtys) trỹs

45.2 *Declension of the cardinal numbers 2, 3, 4, 5 and 7:*

	Masc.	Fem.	Masc.	Fem.	Masc.	Fem.
N.	dù	dvì	trỹs (4)	——	keturì (3b)	kẽturios
G.	dviejų̃	——	trijų̃	——	keturių̃	——
D.	dvíem	——	trìms	——	keturíems	keturióms
A.	dù	dvì	trìs	——	kẽturis	kẽturias
I.	dviẽm	——	trimìs	——	keturiaĩs	keturiomìs
L.	dviejuosè	dviejosè	trijuosè	trijosè	keturiuosè	keturiosè

	Masc.	Fem.	Masc.	Fem.
N.	penkì	peñkios	septynì (3)	septýnios
G.	penkių̃	——	septynių̃	——
D.	penkíems	penkióms	septyníems	septynióms
A.	penkìs	penkiàs	septýnis	septýnias
I.	penkiaĩs	penkiomìs	septyniaĩs	septyniomìs
L.	penkiuosè	penkiosè	septyniuosè	septyniosè

45.3* *Numerals used with nouns which have only plural form* (pluralia tantum).

1. vienerì (3a), víenerios
2. dvejì (4), dvẽjos
3. trejì (4), trẽjos
4. ketverì (3b), kẽtverios

5. penkerì (3b), peñkerios
6. šešerì (3b), šẽšerios
7. septynerì (3a), septýnerios
8. aštuonerì (3a), aštúonerios
9. devynerì (3a), devýnerios

	Masc.	Fem.	Masc.	Feminine
N.	vienerì (3a)	víenerios	dvejì (4)	dvẽjos
G.	vienerių̃	——	dvejų̃	——
D.	vieneríems	vienerióms	dvejíems	dvejóms
A.	víenerius	víenerias	dvejùs	dvejàs
I.	vieneriaĩs	vieneriomìs	dvejaĩs	dvejomìs
L.	vieneriuosè	vieneriosè	dvejuosè	dvejosè

45.4 *Fractions:* $^1/_2$ — pùsė; $^1/_3$ — trẽčdalis; $^1/_4$ — ketvir̃tis, ketvirtãdalis; $^1/_5$ — penktãdalis; $^1/_6$ — šeštãdalis; $^1/_7$ — septintãdalis; $^1/_8$ — aštuntãdalis; $^1/_9$ — devintãdalis; $^1/_{10}$ — dešimtãdalis. Or: $^1/_2$ — vienà antróji, $^1/_3$ — vienà trečióji, $^1/_4$ — vienà ketvirtóji, $^1/_5$ — vienà penktóji, $^1/_6$ — vienà šeštóji, $^1/_7$ — vienà septintóji, $^1/_8$ — vienà aštuntóji, $^1/_9$ — vienà devintóji, $^1/_{10}$ — vienà dešimtóji. These latter forms are used in mathematics, bookkeeping, accounting, etc.

45.5 *Collective numerals:* 2 — dvẽjetas, 3 — trẽjetas, 4 — kẽtvertas, 5 — peñketas, 6 — šẽšetas, 7 — septýnetas, 8 — aštúonetas, 9 — devýnetas.

45.6 *Whole numbers plus one-half:*

1½. pusañtro, pusantrõs, pusantrų̃
2½. pustrẽčio, pustrečiõs, pustrečių̃
3½. pusketvir̃to, pusketvirtõs, pusketvirtų̃
4½. puspeñkto, puspenktõs, puspenktų̃
5½. pusšẽšto, pusšeštõs, pusšeštų̃
6½. pusseptiñto, pusseptintõs, pusseptintų̃
7½. pusaštuñto, pusaštuntõs, pusaštuntų̃
8½. pusdeviñto, pusdevintõs, pusdevintų̃, etc.

45.7 *Ordinal numbers:*

Masculine Nom. Sing.	Feminine Nom. Sing.	
pìrmas (3)	pirmà	first
añtras (4)	antrà	second
trẽčias (4)	trečià	third
ketvir̃tas (4)	ketvirtà	fourth

peñktas (4)	penktà	fifth
šẽštas (4)	šeštà	sixth
septiñtas (4)	septintà	seventh
aštuñtas (4)	aštuntà	eighth
deviñtas (4)	devintà	ninth
dešiɱtas (4)	dešimtà	tenth
vienúoliktas (1)	vienúolikta	eleventh
dvýliktas (1)	dvýlikta	twelfth
trýliktas (1)	trýlikta	thirteenth
keturióliktas (1)	keturiólikta	fourteenth
penkióliktas (1)	penkiólikta	fifteenth
šešióliktas (1)	šešiólikta	sixteenth
septynióliktas (1)	septyniólikta	seventeenth
aštuonióliktas (1)	aštuoniólikta	eighteenth
devynióliktas (1)	devyniólikta	nineteenth
dvidočiɱtas (4)	dvìdešimta	twentieth
trisdešiɱtas (4)	trisdešimtà	thirtieth
keturiasdešiɱtas (4)	keturiasdešimtà	fortieth
penkiasdešiɱtas (4)	penkiasdešimtà	fiftieth
šešiasdešiɱtas (4)	šešiasdešimtà	sixtieth
septyniasdešiɱtas (4)	septyniasdešimtà	seventieth
aštuoniasdešiɱtas (4)	aštuoniasdešimtà	eightieth
devyniasdešiɱtas (4)	devyniasdešimtà	ninetieth
šiɱtas (4)	šimtà	hundredth
dušiɱtas (4)	dušimtà	two hundredth
tū́kstantas (1)	tū́kstanta	thousandth

46. PREPOSITIONS

The prepositions may be used with the genitive, accusative or instrumental case; a few may be used with the dative case.

46.1 The following prepositions are used with the genitive case:
abìpus 'on both sides of'; anàpus 'on the other side, beyond, across'; anót 'according to (repeating someone's words exactly)'; añt 'on'; artì 'near, close by'; aukščiaũ 'above'; bè 'without'; dėkà 'thanks to, owing to'; dėl, dėlei 'for, for the sake of, because of'; gretà 'side by side, near, by the side of'; iki 'until, up to, as far as'; lìg, lìgi 'until, as far as'; iš 'out of, from, since'; iš with other prepositions takes the genitive case also, e.g. iš anàpus 'from the other side of'; iš põ 'from under'; išilgaĩ 'along'; įstrižaĩ 'diagonally across'; liñk, liñkui 'to, towards'; netolì 'not far from, near'; nuõ

'from, off, (guarding against), since, from, by reason of, because of'; *pasàk* 'according to (someone else)'; *pirmà* 'in front of, before'; *priẽ* 'at, near, in the vicinity of, to, in the time of'; *pusiáu* 'half way up, half way along'; *šalià* 'near, by, at the side of'; *šiàpus* 'on this side of'; *taȓp* 'between, among'; *vidùj* 'within, inside of'; *viȓš*, *viršùj*, *viršuñ* 'over, beyond, above'; *žemiaũ* 'below, farther down than, under'.

46.2 The following prepositions are used with the accusative case: *apiẽ* 'round about, about'; *apliñk* 'round'; *į̃* 'into, to'; *pagaĩ* 'along, beside, according to'; *paleĩ* 'along, by the side of, beside'; *pàs* 'at, with, at the home of, to'; *paskuĩ* 'after, behind'; *peȓ* 'through, across, during, throughout'; *priẽš* 'before, in the presence of, ago, against, contrary to'; *prõ* 'by, past, through'.

46.3 The following prepositions are used with the instrumental case: *sù* 'with'; *sulìg* 'according to, up to, until'; *tiẽs* 'opposite to, in front of, near, by, at'.

46.4 Some prepositions have different meanings depending upon the case with which they are used:

a.) *põ* (with the genitive) 'after, past'; (with the dative in certain idiomatic expressions) *põ šiái diẽnai* 'up to the present time'; *põ senóvei* 'as it was (lit.: according to the past)'; *po kám* 'how much (does it cost)?'; (with the accusative) 'in, through, all about'; (with the instrumental) 'under'.

b.) *skersaĩ* (with either the genitive or the accusative, but with no difference in meaning) 'across, athwart'.

c.) *ùž* (with the genitive) 'behind, across, at'; (with the accusative) 'for, in return for, than'.

d.) In certain fixed expressions *ìki* is used with the dative: *ìki šiái diẽnai* 'up to today'; *ìki šiám laĩkui* 'up to this time'.

47. ADVERBS

Most adverbs are formed from other parts of speech, e.g. nouns, adjectives, numerals, pronouns and various verbal forms.

47.1 *Adverbs formed from nouns.*

47.11 Truncated and fossilized case forms of nouns: *namõ* 'home', *namiẽ* 'at home', *rytój* 'tomorrow', *porýt* 'the day after tomorrow', *šiañdien* 'today', *vãkar* 'yesterday', etc.

47.12 Prepositions plus nouns: *be gãlo* 'without end, endlessly', *iš tikrũjų* 'really, indeed', *iš lė́to* 'slowly'.

47.13 Prepositions derived from fossilized instrumental case forms: *gretà* 'beside, near'; *nakčià* 'by night'; *staigà* 'suddenly'; *kar̃tais* 'sometimes'; *viẽtomis* 'here and there, in places'; *tárpais* 'at times, intermittently'.

47.2 *Adverbs formed from adjectives.*

47.21 Adverbs formed by adding -*ai* to the adjective stem: *bendraĩ* 'commonly, in common'; *ilgaĩ* 'a long time, a long while'; *griežtaĩ* 'strictly, severely'; *lietùviškai* 'in Lithuanian'; *trumpaĩ* 'briefly'. This is a particularly common and productive adverbial suffix in modern Lithuanian.

47.22 Adverbs formed by adding the suffix -*yn* denote a change into the condition denoted by the root adjective: *aukštỹn* 'up, upwards' (derived from the adjective *áukštas* 'high'); *baltỹn* '(turning, becoming) white' (derived from *báltas* 'white'); *pirmỹn* 'forward, onward, on' (derived from *pìrmas* 'first').

47.3 *Adverbs derived from numerals.* Examples: *dviese* 'two by two, in twos'; *trisè* 'in a group of three'; *keturíese* 'in a group of four'; *penkíese* 'in a group of five'; *dvėja* 'twice'; *trėja* 'three times'; *dùsyk* 'twice'; *trìssyk* 'three times'; *vienaĩp* 'in one way, in one manner'; *antraĩp* 'in another way, in a contrary manner'; *trečiaĩp* 'in a third way, in a third manner'.

47.4 *Adverbs derived from pronouns.* Examples: *kamè* 'where, somewhere'; *kuř* 'where'; *kaĩp* 'how'; *kíek* 'how much, how many'; *čià* 'here'; *teñ* 'there'; *visadà* 'always'; *kitaĩp* 'otherwise'; *tadà* 'then'.

47.5 *Adverbs derived from participles.*

47.51 Adverbs derived from present active participles: *prìderančiai* 'in a proper manner' (derived from *prìderąs*, the present active participle of *priderė́ti* 'to be proper').

47.52 Adverbs derived from past active participles: *nevỹkusiai* 'unsuccessfully, badly' (derived from *nevỹkęs*, the past active participle *nevỹkti* 'not to go on well; not to succeed').

366

47.53 Adverbs derived from present passive participles: *suprañ-tamai* 'understandably' (derived from *suprañtamas* the present passive participle of *supràsti* 'to understand').

47.54 Adverbs derived from past passive participles: *nelauktaĩ* 'unexpectedly' (derived from *láuktas*, the past passive participle of *láukti* 'to wait for').

48. CONJUNCTIONS

Co-ordinating conjunctions	*Subordinating conjunctions*
ař — whether, or	idañt — so that, in order that
arbà — or	jéi — if, in the case that
arbà ... arbà — either ... or	jéigu — if, in the case that
beĩ — and (can only be used to unite two words, not phrases or clauses)	jóg — that
	kàd — that, so that; since, be-
bètgi — but, however	kàd iř — although [cause
iř — and	kadañgi — since, because, as
neĩ ... neĩ — neither ... nor	nès — because
õ — but, and; whereas, while	nórs — although, though
	tačiaũ — but, nevertheless, still, however

49. INTERJECTIONS (*Jaustùkai*)

Some common Lithuanian interjections are listed below:

à, ã — oh, ah, I see (to express surprise, understanding)

ahà — ah, so

ái — oh, alas, dear me (to express pain, fear, surprise)

aimán — unfortunately, what a pity

ajè — alas, dear me

àk — alas, oh (moan)

antaĩ — there now (to bring the action closer to the speaker, to make it more vivid)

dejà — unfortunately, what a shame, what a pity

dievažì, dievàž — surely, by God, God knows (to express certainty)

ẽ, è, ě — hey (to call, to express surprise)

nà — well, there, now (to express encouragement, threat, surprise)

nù — now then (to express surprise, a threat)

õ — o, alas, ah (to express surprise, displeasure)

ohõ — my goodness (to express surprise)

ói — ah, oh (to express pain, difficulty)

ojè — oh (to express surprise, to call)
štaĩ — here, look here
ùi — oh, ouch (to express surprise, fear, pain)
và — look here, (to express the command to look at something)
vajè — oh, good heavens, ah (to express surprise, exclamation)
vái — oh, ah, here (to express vividness, to bring the action closer
    to the speaker)
valiõ — hurray, hurrah (to express approval)

50.   INTERJECTIONS (*Ištiktùkai*)

Certain interjections are commonly formed from a truncated verbal stem. They generally denote a sudden momentary action and in some cases may be used instead of a form of the finite
verb with momentary meaning. Some of these interjections are
listed below:

bàkst, bàst — denotes a sudden light piercing action
bárkšt — expresses the idea of rattling, clinking
blìnkt — expresses the idea of throwing something
bràkšt — crash, bang (expresses the concept of breaking, smashing)
cínkt — crash (expresses the sound of breaking)
čiũkšt — denotes a sudden action
čiùpt — expresses the idea of snatching, grabbing a little bit
čiũpt — expresses the idea of snatching, grabbing to a greater de-
    gree than *čiùpt*
drìbt — denotes the sound of sudden falling
glimžt — expresses the idea of grasping, grabbing for something
kìlst — denotes the action of lifting or raising something
kìšt — denotes the action of thrusting a little bit
kýšt — denotes the action of thrusting to a greater degree than *kìšt*
lèpt — denotes the action of falling
pèšt — denotes a slight tug or jerk
pliáukšt — denotes a sudden sound of hitting, striking
plýkst — denotes a sudden flash of flame
pliũpt — denotes a fall (into the water)
pókšt — expresses the sound of cracking
tìmpt — denotes a slight tug, a jerk
trìnkt — crash, smash (expresses the sound of crashing)
triókšt — crack (expresses the sound of breaking)
trũkt — denotes a strong, hard pull
trùkt — denotes a slight tug, a jerk
ũžt — denotes a sudden action (gust)

žìbt — denotes a small flash of light
žýbt — denotes a sudden, brilliant flash of light
žvìlgt — denotes a glance at something

Examples of their use in sentences are given below:

1) *Tìk triókšt iř nulúžo.* — It just went crack and broke.
2) *Pókšt iř nutrúko.* — Bang and it broke off.
3) *Žýbt, žýbt sužaibãvo.* — Flash, flash it lightened.
4) *Girdžiù—trìnkt trìnkt—kàžkas eĩna.* — I hear—crash, crash—someone is coming.
5) *Drìbt kepùrė añt žẽmės nudrìbo.* — Plop the cap fell on the ground.
6) *Šuõ úžt peř tvõrą.* — The dog leaped over the fence.
7) *Aš jį̃ ùž rankóvės pèšt.* — I tugged at his sleeve.
8) *Kýšt gálvą prõ durìs.* — He butted his head through the doors.

From the point of view of their meaning the interjections are closely bound to the verbs in *-telėti* which have a momentary aspect. Thus *pókšt* has roughly the same meaning as *pókštelėjo* '(it) cracked'; *žýbt* the same meaning as *žýbtelėjo* '(it) flashed'.

51.   ACCENTUATION. *Nouns and adjectives.*

In a short syllable only a short intonation is possible; the acute intonation is written *ìr, ìl, ìm, ìn, ùr, ùl, ùm, ùn* in groups beginning with either *i* or *u* followed by *r, l, m,* or *n*.

51.1 Nouns and adjectives of *the first accent class* have the stress on the same syllable throughout the declension. The acute intonation may be on any syllable of the stem, and the circumflex or the short intonation may be on any syllable of the stem except the penultimate. The stress is never found on an inflectional ending in nouns and adjectives of this class. For examples see 41.10, 41.11, 41.20, 41.21, 41.55, 42.3 and Lesson 5

51.2 Nouns and indefinite adjectives of *the second accent class* have the stress (which must have either the circumflex or short intonation, never the acute) on the final syllable of the stem except for the following cases where the stress is found on the inflectional ending: the nominative singular of nouns in *-à*, the

369

instrumental singular in -à, -è, -ù (but not in -mi); the locative
singular of nouns which have the nominative singular in -as; the
accusative plural and the nominative-accusative-vocative dual. For
examples see 41.14, 41.41, 42.3 (geležìnis) and the examples given
below:

	Singular	Plural	Dual
N.	rankà (2) 'hand, arm'	rañkos	rankì
G.	rañkos	rañkų	———
D.	rañkai	rañkoms	rañkom
A.	rañką	rankàs	rankì
I.	rankà	rañkomis	rañkom
L.	rañkoje	rañkose	———
V.	rañka	———	rankì

	Singular	Plural	Dual
N.	rãktas (2) 'key'	rãktai	raktù
G.	rãkto	rãktų	———
D.	rãktui	rãktams	rãktam
A.	rãktą	raktùs	raktù
I.	raktù	rãktais	rãktam
L.	raktè	rãktuose	———
V.	rãkte	———	raktù

51.21 Definite adjectives have the same stress pattern as their
indefinite counterparts with the following exceptions: the
masculine nominative singular ending -ỹsis has the circumflex
intonation, the feminine nominative singular ending -óji has the
acute intonation, the masculine and feminine instrumental singular endings -úoju, -ą́ja have the acute intonation, the masculine
and feminine accusative plural endings -úosius and -ą́sias have the
acute intonation, the masculine and the feminine nominative-accusative-vocative dual have the acute intonations -úoju and -íeji
respectively. For examples see 42.43.

51.3 In nouns and indefinite adjectives of *the third accent class*
the stress during declension may be either on the penultimate or the final syllable. In the nominative singular the stress
is always on the final syllable (with the circumflex intonation if
the syllable is long) except for nouns and indefinite adjectives
which have the nominative singular ending -as. In the genitive
singular the ending receives the circumflex intonation unless the
ending is -o, in which case the penultimate syllable is stressed.
In the dative singular the penultimate syllable is stressed except
for the masculine singular adjective ending in -ám which receives
the acute intonation. In the accusative singular the penultimate

syllable is always stressed. In the instrumental singular the penultimate syllable is stressed unless the final syllable of the ending is -*mi* in which case this final syllable receives the (short) intonation. In the locative singular the final syllable is always stressed giving -*è* unless the final -*e* is dropped in which case the preceding syllable (if long) adopts the circumflex intonation. In the vocative of nouns the final syllable is stressed with the circumflex intonation except for nouns which have the vocative ending -*e* or -*a* immediately preceded by a consonant (i.e. not -*iẽ*); such nouns have the stress on the penultimate syllable. In the nominative plural the penultimate syllable is stressed except for the endings -*ai* and -*i* which take the circumflex and short intonations respectively. The genitive plural ending is always stressed (with the circumflex intonation) and the dative plural ending is always stressed (with the acute or short intonation). In the accusative plural the penultimate syllable is always stressed. In the instrumental plural the final syllable is always stressed (with the circumflex or short intonation depending upon the ending). In the locative plural the final syllable is always stressed giving -*è* unless the final -*e* is dropped in which case the preceding syllable (if long) adopts the circumflex intonation. Compare the locative plural with the locative singular in this regard. In the nominative dual the stress is on the penultimate syllable. In the dative dual the (acute or short) intonation is on the final syllable. In the instrumental dual the circumflex intonation is on the final syllable. It must be kept in mind that in the third accent class whenever the stress falls on the penultimate syllable of disyllabic words the stressed syllable will have the acute intonation. See 41.12, 41.40, 42.1, 42.2, 42.41, 42.42, Lesson 5 and the examples given below:

	Singular	Plural	Dual
N.	galvà (3) 'head'	gálvos	gálvi
G.	galvõs	galvũ	——
D.	gálvai	galvóms	galvóm
A.	gálvą	gálvas	gálvi
I.	gálva	galvomìs	galvom̃
L.	galvojè	galvosè	——
V.	gálva	——	gálvi

	Singular	Plural	Dual
N.	kálnas (3) 'mountain'	kalnaĩ	kálnu
G.	kálno	kalnũ	——
D.	kálnui	kalnáms	kalnám
A.	kálną	kálnus	kálnu
I.	kálnu	kalnaĩs	kalnam̃
L.	kalnè	kalnuosè	——
V.	kálne	——	kálnu

51.31 Trisyllabic nouns and adjectives of this class having the acute intonation in the initial syllable of the accusative case are labeled 3[a] and tetrasyllabic (four-syllable) nouns and adjectives which have the acute intonation in the initial syllable of the accusative case are labeled 3[4a]. The play of stress is between the initial syllable (rather than the penultimate) and the final syllable. Otherwise it is the same as that described in 51.3 for disyllabic nouns and adjectives. See 41.51 and the examples given below:

	Singular	Plural	Dual
N.	dóbilas (3a) 'clover'	dobilaĩ	dóbilu
G.	dóbilo	dobilų̃	——
D.	dóbilui	dobiláms	dobilám
A.	dóbilą	dóbilus	dóbilu
I.	dóbilu	dobilaĩs	dobilam̃
L.	dobilè	dobiluosè	——
V.	dóbile	——	dóbilu

N.	kosulỹs (3a) 'cough'	kosuliaĩ	kósuliu
G.	kósulio	kosulių̃	——
D.	kósuliui	kosuliáms	kosuliám
A.	kósulį	kósulius	kósuliu
I.	kósuliu	kosuliaĩs	kosuliam̃
L.	kosulyjè	kosuliuosè	——
V.	kosulỹ	——	kósuliu

	Singular	Plural	Dual
N.	lygumà (3a) 'plain'	lýgumos	lýgumi
G.	lygumõs	lygumų̃	——
D.	lýgumai	lygumóms	lygumóm
A.	lýgumą	lýgumas	lýgumi
I.	lýguma	lygumomìs	lygumom̃
L.	lygumojè	lygumosè	——
V.	lýguma	——	lýgumi

N.	auksakalỹs (3[4a]) 'goldsmith'	auksakaliaĩ	áuksakaliu
G.	áuksakalio	auksakalių̃	——
D.	áuksakaliui	auksakaliáms	auksakaliám
A.	áuksakalį	áuksakalius	áuksakaliu
I.	áuksakaliu	auksakaliaĩs	auksakaliam̃
L.	auksakalyjè	auksakaliuosè	——
V.	auksakalỹ	——	áuksakaliu

Masculine Adjective

	Singular	Plural	Dual
N.	álkanas (3a) 'hungry'	alkanì	álkanu
G.	álkano	alkanų̃	——
D.	alkanám	alkaníems	alkaníem
A.	álkaną	álkanus	álkanu
I.	álkanu	alkanaĩs	alkaniẽm
L.	alkanamè	alkanuosè	——

Feminine Adjective

	Singular	Plural	Dual
N.	alkanà (3a) 'hungry'	álkanos	álkani
G.	alkanŏs	alkanų̃	——
D.	álkanai	alkanóms	alkanóm
A.	álkaną	álkanas	álkani
I.	álkana	alkanomìs	alkanŏm
L.	alkanojè	alkanosè	——

51.32 Trisyllabic nouns and adjectives of this class having the circumflex or short intonation in the initial syllable of the accusative case are labeled 3[b] and tetrasyllabic nouns and adjectives which have the acute intonation in the initial syllable of the accusative case are labeled 3[4b]. The play of stress between the initial syllable and the final syllable is the same as that described in 51.3 for disyllabic nouns and adjectives (except, of course, that the stress is on the initial rather than the penultimate syllable). See 41.52, 41.54 and the examples given below:

	Singular	Plural	Dual
N.	kãtinas (3b) 'male cat'	katinaĩ	kãtinu
G.	kãtino	katinų̃	——
D.	kãtinui	katináms	katinám
A.	kãtiną	kãtinus	kãtinu
I.	kãtinu	katinaĩs	katinam̃
L.	katinè	katinuosè	——
V.	kãtine	——	kãtinu

	Singular	Plural	Dual
N.	kirmėlė̃ (3b) 'worm'	kirmėlės̃	kir̃mėli
G.	kirmėlės̃	kirmėlių̃	
D.	kir̃mėlei	kirmėlė̃ms	kirmėlė̃m
A.	kir̃mėlę	kir̃mėles	kir̃mėli
I.	kir̃mėle	kirmėlėmìs	kirmėlė̃m
L.	kirmėlėjè	kirmėlėsè	——
V.	kir̃mėle	——	kir̃mėli

	Singular	Plural	Dual
N.	pasiuntinỹs (34b) 'messenger'	pasiuntiniaĩ	pãsiuntiniu
G.	pãsiuntinio	pasiuntinių̃	——
D.	pãsiuntiniui	pasiuntiniáms	pasiuntiniám
A.	pãsiuntinį	pãsiuntinius	pãsiuntiniu
I.	pãsiuntiniu	pasiuntiniaĩs	pasiuntiniam̃
L.	pasiuntinyjè	pasiuntiniuosè	——
V.	pasiuntinỹ	——	pãsiuntiniu

Masculine Adjective

N.	baɫzganas (3b)	balzganì	baɫzganu
	'whitish'		
G.	baɫzgano	balzganų̃	——
D.	balzganám	balzganíems	balzganíem
A.	baɫzganą	baɫzganus	baɫzganu
I.	baɫzganu	balzganaĩs	balzganiẽm
L.	balzganamè	balzganuosè	——

Feminine Adjective

	Singular	Plural	Dual
N.	balzganà	baɫzganos	baɫzgani
G.	balzganõs	balzganų̃	——
D.	baɫzganai	balzganóms	balzganóm
A.	baɫzganą	baɫzganas	baɫzgani
I.	baɫzgana	balzganomìs	balzganõm
L.	balzganojè	balzganosè	——

51.33 In the definite adjectives of all of the varieties of the third accent class the stress is in general on the same syllable as in the corresponding indefinite form. The following endings, however, require comment:

> The masculine nominative singular ending is *-àsis*,
> the feminine nominative singular ending is *-óji*.
> The masculine instrumental singular ending is *-úoju*,
> the feminine instrumental singular ending is *-ą́ja*.
> The masculine locative singular ending is *-ãjame*,
> the feminine locative singular ending is *-õjoje*.
> The masculine nominative plural ending is *-íeji*,
> the feminine accusative plural ending is *-ą́sias*.
> The masculine instrumental plural ending is *-aĩsiais*,
> the feminine instrumental plural ending is *-õsiomis*.
> The masculine locative plural ending is *-uõsiuose*,
> the feminine locative plural ending is *-õsiose*.
> The masculine nominative dual ending is *-úoju*,
> the feminine nominative dual ending is *-íeji*.

See 42.41 (*baltàsis*), and 42.42.

51.4 In nouns and indefinite adjectives of *the fourth accent class* there is a play of stress between the stem final syllable (which must have either the short or circumflex intonation) and the inflectional ending. To the learner the fourth accent class seems to be a kind of combination of the second and third accent

374

classes. In any particular case if the stress is required on the inflectional syllable by either the rules of the second or the third accent class, then the stress will be on the inflectional syllable. In other words the stress is on the case ending unless a stem stress is demanded for that same case in both the second and third accent classes (*dìdis* is an exception). See 41.13, 41.15, 41.22, 41.23, 41.31, 41.50, also Lesson 5, 42.1 (*saũsas, dìdis*), 42.2 (*puikùs, atidùs*) and the example given below.

	Singular	Plural	Dual
N.	laĩkas (4) 'time'	laikaĩ	laikù
G.	laĩko	laikū̃	———
D.	laĩkui	laikáms	laikám
A.	laĩką	laikùs	laikù
I.	laikù	laikaĩs	laikam̃
L.	laikè	laikuosè	———
V.	laĩke	———	laikù

51.5   The definite adjective has the stress on the same syllable as the corresponding indefinite form. See 51.21 and 51.33.

51.6   *Verbs.* In the present and past tenses the unprefixed verb will retain the stress on the same syllable throughout the conjugation if the third person has the acute intonation on the stem, cf. 43.11 and 43.12 (*dìrbti* and *mylė́ti*).

51.61   In the present and past tenses the unprefixed verb will shift the stress to the ending in the first and second persons singular if the third person has the short or the circumflex intonation, cf. 43.11, 43.12 (*matýti*), 2.1 (*ruõšti* and *skaitýti*) and 1.3 (*eĩti*).

51.7   In the present tense of prefixed verbs the stress generally either remains on the stem according to the rules of 51.6 or shifts to the end according to the rules of 51.61. The following exceptions must be noted.

51.71   The prefix *pér-* always takes the stress throughout the conjugation, no matter what the intonation of the root may be in the prefixed form.

51.72 The stress shifts to the verbal prefix or the negative particle *ne-* of any first or second conjugation verb with an -*i-*, -*u-*, -*a-* or -*e-* in the root followed immediately by a single consonant, e.g. *ùž-ima* '(he) occupies', *nù-meta* '(he) throws down', etc. Exceptions are *tùri* '(he) has' and *gãli* '(he) can' which do not shift the stress in the negated forms *netùri* '(he) does not have' and *negãli* '(he) cannot'.

51.73 The stress is shifted to any prefix of a first conjugation verb which has a root -*e-* immediately followed by -*m̃-*, -*ñ-*, -*r̃-*, -*l̃-* in the present stem if this -*e-* alternates with an -*i-* (or -*į̃-*) in the infinitive stem, e.g. *su-til̃pti* 'to find room enough' but *sù-telpa* '(he) finds room enough', *nu-pir̃kti* 'to buy' but *nù-perka* '(he) buys', *iš-bri̇̀sti* 'to wade out of' but *iš-brenda* '(he) wades out of'.

51.74 The stress is shifted to any prefix of a first conjugation verb which has the infinitive stem in -*ėti* unless this first conjugation verb has a present stem ending in a palatalized consonant, e.g. *ap-kalbė́ti* 'to slander' but *àp-kalba* '(he) slanders'.

51.8 In the past tense the stress is shifted to the prefix only for first conjugation verbs with the ending in -*ė* if the corresponding unprefixed form has a short or circumflex intonation in the third person, e.g. *dẽgė* 'it burned' but *ìš-degė* 'it burned out'.

51.81 If there is more than one prefix and the stress shifts, it will shift to the one immediately preceding the root, e.g. *nebepàneša* '(he) cannot carry any more'.

51.9 In the future tense the stress is the same as that for the infinitive and is constant on the same syllable throughout the conjugation. But an acute intonation is replaced by a circumflex in the third person, cf. 43.14 and 9.1.

51.91 A few monosyllabic verbs with the stem in -*ý-* or -*ū́-* shorten the stem syllable in the third person rather than substitute a circumflex stress, e.g. *bū́ti* 'to be', but *bùs* '(he) will be' etc.

52. The following charts give the noun endings according to the declension. If there is no number immediately under the ending this means that the ending is never stressed. If a stress is written above the ending, this means that the ending is stressed in that accent class the number for which is found immediately under the ending. Thus, for example, we find the second declension genitive singular ending *-õs* with the numbers 3 and 4 immediately under the ending. This means that the ending *-os* is not stressed in accent classes 1 and 2, but that it does receive the (circumflex) intonation in accent classes 3 and 4.

NB. For the accentuation of the pronouns, numerals, adverbs, prepositions, etc., consult the appropriate lessons, also the appropriate paragraphs of the Appendix.

S i n g u l a r

	1st Dec.	2nd Dec.	3rd Dec.	4th Dec.	5th Dec.
N.	as, ȳs, is	à, ì, ẽ	ìs	ùs	uõ, ẽ
	3	2 3 3	3	3	3 3
	4	3 4 4	4	4	4 4
		4			
G.	o	õs, ẽs	iẽs	aũs	eñs, ers
		3 3	3	3	3 3
		4 4	4	4	4 4
D.	ui	ai, ei	iai, iui	ui	iui, iai
A.	ą, į	ą, ę	į	ų	į
I.	ù	à, è	imì	umì	iù, ia, imì
	2	2 2	3	3	4 3
	4	4 4	4	4	4
L.	è, yjè	ojè, ėjè	yjè	ujè	yjè
	2 3	3 3	3	3	3
	3 4	4 4	4	4	4
	4				
V.	e, ȳ, i	a, e	iẽ	aũ	iẽ
	3		3	3	3
	4		4	4	4

Plural

	1st Dec.	2nd Dec.	3rd Dec.	4th Dec.		5th Dec.
N.	aĩ	os, ės	ys	ūs, iai		enys, erys
	3					
	4					
G.	ų̃	ų̃	ių̃	ų̃		ų̃
	3	3	3	3		3
	4	4	4	4		4
D.	áms	óms, ėms	ìms	ùms, áms		ìms
	3	3	3	3	3	3
	4	4	4	4	4	4
A.	ùs	às, ès	ìs	ùs		ìs
	2	2	1	2		4
	4	4		4		
I.	aĩs	omìs, ėmìs	imìs	umìs, aĩs		imìs
	3	3	3	3	3	3
	4	4	4	4	4	4
L.	uosè	osè, ėsè	ysè	uosè		ysè
	3	3	3	3		3
	4	4	4	4		4
V.	Same as nominative in all declensions					

53. VERBAL PREFIXES

1. *ap-* (*api-* appears before forms beginning with *p-* and *b-*).

A. It may denote that the action occupies the entire surface of an object or a whole series of objects. Examples: *ap-áugti* 'to become overgrown (with), to grow up all over (with)'; *ap-gaũbti* 'to cover, to wrap up completely'; *api-bérti* 'to strew all over, to sprinkle all over'; *ap-láistyti* 'to besprinkle, to sprinkle (water) all around'; *ap-ieškóti* 'to search everywhere, to ransack'; *ap-ródyti* 'to show everything, to show around'.

B. It may denote an action around, or passing by the object. Examples: *ap-eĩti* 'to circumvent, to go around, to avoid'; *ap-važiúoti apliñk ẽžerą* 'to travel around the lake'; *ap-keliáuti pasáulio šalìs* 'to travel through the countries of the world'.

C. It may denote that the action is completed only to a certain degree and does not encompass the object completely. Examples: *ap-draskýti* 'to tear, to scratch'; *ap-daužýti* 'to damage, to beat'; *ap-dáilinti* 'to polish, to beautify'.

D. It may denote the process of becoming something or the completion of an action. Examples: *ap-sir̃gti* 'to fall ill, to become sick'; *ap-kur̃sti* 'to become deaf'.

E. With reflexive verbs it may mean that the action is carried out to the end. Examples: *ap-si-gyvénti* 'to take up residence'; *ap-si-džiaũgti* 'to rejoice'.

2. *at-* (*ati-* appears before forms beginning with *t-, d-*)

A. It may denote arrival, coming to a certain place. Examples: *at-eĩti* 'to come, to arrive'; *at-nèšti* 'to bring, to carry here'; *at-važiúoti* 'to come, to arrive (by vehicle)'; *at-vỹkti* 'to arrive'.

B. It may denote separation or division or removal. Examples: *at-ką́sti* 'to bite off'; *at-kir̃sti* 'to cut off, to hew off'; *at-jùngti* 'to unyoke, to disconnect'; *at-skìrti* 'to separate, to detach'; *at-piáuti* 'to cut off, away'.

C. It may denote return to an original position, passage from one place to another. Examples: *at-áugti* 'to grow back, to grow again'; *at-gim̃ti* 'to be reborn, to be revived', *ati-darýti* 'to open', *at-rìšti* 'to untie', *at-gáuti* 'to win back, to get back, to retrieve'.

D. It may denote the completion of an action. Examples: *at--pìgti* 'to become cheap, to fall in price'; *at-bùkti* 'to become blunt, to become stupid'; *at-baĩgti* 'to finish, to end, to conclude'.

E. Reflexive verbs denote the intensity, the sufficiency or the absolute completion of an action. Examples: *at-si-miegóti* 'to sleep oneself out, to get one's fill of sleeping'; *at-si-rė̃kti* 'to shout oneself out, to shout a lot'; *at-si-džiaũgti* 'to get one's fill of rejoicing'.

3. *be-*

A. It may denote the duration of a characteristic or an action. Examples: *Sēnis võs bèkruta* 'The old man hardly gets around'; *Be-sė́dint šálta pasidárė* 'Sitting (for some time) one became cold'; *Sūnùs be-skaĩtąs, tėvas be-rašą̃s* 'The son is reading, the father is writing'.

B. It is used as a prefix for verbs with the meaning 'still' or it may be used with negative verbs to denote that there isn't any more of the object in question. Examples: *Kõ be-reĩkia?* 'What more is necessary?'; *Ne-be-reĩkia* 'It is no longer necessary'; *Ne-belỹja* 'It isn't raining any more'; *Ne-be-àtmenu* 'I don't remember any more'.

C. It is used as a prefix for verbs with the meaning 'only'. Examples: *Jìs víenas be-lìko* 'He remained alone (without anybody else)'; *Tíek iř̃ be-girdėjo* '(He) heard only so much'.

4. *į-*

A. It may be used to denote motion into a place or an object. Examples: *į-eĩti* 'to go into, to enter'; *į-važiúoti* 'to drive into'; *į-vèsti* 'to lead into'; *į-vèžti* 'to transport into'.

B. It may denote the beginning of an action which is carried out only to a slight degree. Examples: *į-plėšti pópierių* 'to tear some paper'; *į-kiř̃pti* 'to cut into something, to cut a little bit'.

C. It may be used with verbs formed from nouns or adjectives. Examples: *į-stìklinti* 'to glaze (a window)', cf. *stìklas* 'glass'; *į-ámžinti* 'to immortalize', cf. *ámžinas* 'eternal, everlasting'.

D. It may denote the ability to carry out an action. Examples: *Jìs daũg į-válgo* 'He can eat a lot'; *į-rékti* 'to be able to shout'; *į-matýti* 'to be able to see something, to see something clearly, to guess correctly'.

E. It may denote the completion of an action. Examples: *į-drėgti* 'to become wet through'; *į-tìkinti* 'to persuade'; *į-výkdyti* 'to carry out, to complete'; *į-si-žiūrėti* 'to look at (attentively)'.

5. *iš-*

A. It may denote motion out of something. Examples: *iš-varýti* 'to chase out of'; *iš-eĩti* 'to go out of'.

B. It may denote that the action covers the entire area or a whole series of objects. Examples: *iš-mìndyti* 'to trample all over'; *iš-láužyti* 'to break up everything'; *iš-miřti* 'to die out completely'.

C. It may denote an action lasting for a certain length of time. Examples: *iš-dìrbti* 'to work for a certain length of time'; *iš-bū́ti* 'to stay, to remain for a certain length of time'; *iš-budėti* 'to watch over for a certain length of time'.

D. It may denote ability to carry out an action. Examples: *iš-rékti* 'to be able to cry out'; *iš-dainúoti* 'to be able to sing a lot'.

E. It may denote completion or fulfillment of an action. Examples: *iš-mókti* 'to finish learning, to learn thoroughly'; *iš-áugti* 'to grow up'; *iš-lõšti* 'to win'; *iš-válgyti* 'to eat up, to empty (a plate)'.

6. *nu-*

A. It may denote motion away from something or some place. Examples: *nu-eīti* 'to go away'; *nu-plaūkti* 'to sail away'; *nu-skrìsti* 'to fly away'.

B. It may denote motion downwards. Examples: *nu-lìpti* 'to climb down, to get down'; *nu-liñkti* 'to bend down'; *nu-šókti* 'to jump down'.

C. It may denote severance from the main part of an object. Examples: *nu-im̃ti* 'to take off'; *nu-piáuti* 'to cut off'; *nu-gérti* 'to drink off'; *nukiřsti* 'to cut off'.

D. It may denote that the action was completed to the very end. Examples: *nu-mìrti* 'to die off'; *nu-dìrbti* 'to accomplish, to fulfill'; *nu-piřkti* 'to buy'.

7. *pa-*

A. It may denote that something is put under something else. Examples: *pa-kìšti* 'to push under, to shove under'; *pa-brùkti* 'to put under, to shove under'; *pa-lį̃sti (põ stalù)* 'to creep under (the table)'.

B. It may denote the completion of an action. Examples: *pa-rašýti* 'to finish writing'; *pa-darýti* 'to make, to do'.

C. It may denote that the action is lasting for a certain short, limited period. Examples: *pa-nèšti* 'to carry for a little bit'; *pa-šókti* 'to dance for a little while'; *pa-kalbéti* 'to talk for a while'.

D. It may denote attenuation of the action. Examples: *pa-dirbéti* 'to work for a little bit'; *pa-bégéti* 'to run a short distance (or a little while)'.

E. It may denote the ability or capacity to perform a certain action. Examples: *pa-eīti* 'to be able to walk'; *pa-lékti* 'to be able to fly (said of young birds)'; *pa-nèšti* 'to be able to carry'; *pa-skaitýti* 'to be able to read'.

8. *par-*

A. It may denote the idea of returning or coming back. Examples: *par-vèžti* 'to bring home (in a vehicle)'; *par-važiúoti* 'to come home (in a vehicle)'; *par-bégti (namõ)* 'to run home'.

B. It may denote falling to the earth. Examples: *par-mùšti* 'to knock down, to strike down'; *par-viřsti* 'to throw down, to overthrow'; *par-mèsti* 'to throw down, to bring to the ground'.

9. per-

A. It may denote motion across or through something. Examples: *pér-eiti* 'to cross, to go across'; *pér-lipti* 'to climb over'; *pér-šokti* 'to jump over, to leap over'; *pér-durti* 'to pierce through, to transfix'; *pér-šauti* 'to shoot through'.

B. It may denote separation or division. Examples: *pér-laužti* 'to break into pieces'; *pér-kirsti* 'to cut through, to cut in two'; *pér-piauti* 'to cut in two'; *pér-skirti* 'to separate, to divide'.

C. It may denote an action which takes place or is performed by an intermediary. Examples: *pér-duoti* 'to deliver, to transmit'; *pér-siųsti* 'to transfer, to remit'.

D. It may denote an action lasting for a definite period of time. Examples: *pér-nakvoti* 'to spend the night'; *pér-žiemoti* 'to spend the winter'; *pér-guléti (vìsą dieną)* 'to pass the whole day lying down'.

E. It may denote the repetition or the renewal of an action. Examples: *pér-dirbti* 'to do over again'; *pér-galvoti* 'to think over, to reconsider'; *pér-dažyti* 'to paint over; to paint another color'.

F. It may denote exceeding of the norm or going beyond a certain limit. Examples: *pér-si-stengti* 'to make too great efforts'; *pér-mokéti* 'to overpay'; *pér-pildyti* 'to overfill'.

G. It may denote success or victory in some venture. Examples: *pér-rékti* 'to outshout'; *pér-ginčyti* 'to overcome in an argument'.

10. pra-

A. It may denote movement by or past some place. Examples: *pra-eĩti* 'to pass by'; *pra-bégti* 'to run by'; *pra-važiúoti* 'to drive past, to ride past'.

B. It may denote movement through something or some place. Examples: *pra-dùrti* 'to pierce through'; *pra-piáuti* 'to cut through'; *pra-láužti* 'to break through'.

C. It may denote disappearance, loss or lack of something. Examples: *pra-léisti* 'to miss'; *pra-gérti* 'to drink away (one's money)'; *pra-gaĩšti* 'to be lost, to vanish, to disappear'; *pra-pùlti* 'to be lost completely, to vanish'.

D. It may denote the passage of a certain length of time in some activity. Examples: *pra-bùti* 'to be some place for a certain length of time'; *pra-miegóti* 'to pass one's time in sleeping'; *pra-guléti* 'to pass one's time lying abed'.

E. It may denote the beginning of an action. Examples: *pra-vìrkti* 'to begin to cry'; *pra-gýsti* 'to begin to sing'; *pra-kalbéti* 'to begin to speak'.

F. It may denote that the action was carried out to a certain degree. Examples: *pra-plãtinti* 'to spread out'; *pra-vérti* 'to open just a bit'; *pra-mókti* 'to learn a little'; *pra-si-žióti* 'to open the mouth a little bit'.

11. pri-

A. It may denote movement toward a place. Examples: *pri-bėgti* 'to run near (to), to run to'; *pri-eĩti* 'to go near to'; *pri-tráukti* 'to drag near, to drag close to'.

B. It may denote the action of fastening one object to another or annexing something. Examples: *pri-rìšti* 'to tie to, to bind to'; *pri-mègzti* 'to knit on to'; *pri-tvìrtinti* 'to fasten to'.

C. It may denote the direction of an action downward, from above. Examples: *pri-spáusti* 'to press down hard'; *pri-slégti* 'to depress, to press down'.

D. It may denote the idea of putting something into something else or filling something. Examples: *pri-pìlti* 'to pour into'; *pri-kiṁšti* 'to stuff into'; *pri-lýti* 'to be filled by rain'.

E. It may denote that an action was carried out only to a certain degree. Examples: *pri-gèsti* 'to burn with a weak flame'; *pri-vérti* 'to half-close'; *pri-si-bijóti* 'to be a little afraid of'.

F. It may denote that the action has been carried out to its completion. Examples: *pri-baĩgti* 'to bring to a complete close, to put an end to'; *pri-nókti* 'to ripen'; *pri-válgyti* 'to eat one's fill'.

12. su-

A. It may denote convergence or congregation. Examples: *sudéti* 'to put together, to compose'; *su-riñkti* 'to gather, to collect'; *su-bėgti* 'to run together, to converge'; *su-eĩti* 'to come together, to meet'.

B. It may denote dissection, dismemberment or division into parts. Examples: *su-daužýti* 'to break into parts, to smash to pieces'; *su-mùšti* 'to break to pieces, to smash'; *su-skáldyti* 'to split up, to cleave to pieces'.

C. It may denote the beginning of an action. Examples: *su-rìkti* 'to begin to shout'; *su-šnèkti* 'to begin to talk'; *su-žvìlgti* 'to begin to glitter'.

D. It may denote the attainment of the goal or the aim. Examples: *su-láukti* 'to wait for something (until it comes to pass), to attain one's goal in waiting'; *su-ràsti* 'to find (what one has lost)'; *su-sèkti* 'to trace down, to find out'.

E. It may denote the fulfillment or completion of an action. Examples: *su-témti* 'to get completely dark, to become night'; *su-ěsti* 'to eat up, to consume'; *su-galvóti* 'to think up, to contrive'.

13. *už-*

A. It may denote the direction up. Examples: *už-eĩti (añt kál-no)* 'to climb up (the hill)'; *už-lìpti* 'to climb up, to mount, to ascend'; *už-kélti* 'to lift up'.

B. It may denote that something is put on something else. Examples: *už-deñgti* 'to cover'; *už-kàsti* 'to bury, to cover with earth'; *už-sěsti* 'to sit down on'.

C. It may denote putting something behind something else or going behind something. Examples: *už-lį̃sti* 'to crawl behind'; *už-statýti* 'to place behind'; *už-stóti* 'to stand behind; to intercede'.

D. It may denote the completion of an action. Examples: *už-áugti* 'to come to full growth, to grow up'; *už-mokěti* 'to pay, to settle (an account)'; *už-mùšti* 'to kill'.

E. It may denote the begining of an action. Examples: *už-dainúoti* 'to start singing, to begin a song '.

NOTES:

1. Some verbs can have two prefixes if the first has coalesced with the root. Examples: **iš-pã-sakoti** 'to relate, to tell to the end'; **iš-par-dúoti** 'to sell out'.

2. The prefix does not give a new meaning to some verbs and therefore the verb means practically the same thing with or without the prefix. Examples: **grį̃žti - su-grį̃žti** 'to return'; **miřti - nu-miřti** 'to die'; **baĩgti - pa-baĩgti** 'to finish'; **ràsti - su-ràsti** 'to find'.

3. Some verbs may have practically the same meaning or the same meaning with either of two prefixes: **iš-áugti - už-áugti** 'to grow up'; **iš-nȳkti - pra-nȳkti** 'to disappear'; **iš-gȳti - pa-gȳti** 'to recover, to get better'; **iš-bálti - nu-bálti** 'to become white, pale'; **iš-si-gą̃sti - nu-si-gą̃sti - per-si-gą̃sti** 'to be frightened'.

4. Many verbal prefixes modify the meaning of the verb or show a distinct direction. Examples: **ap-eĩti** 'to circumvent, to go around'; **at-eĩti** 'to arrive'; **į-eĩti** 'to go into, to enter'; **iš-eĩti** 'to go out of'; **nu-eĩti** 'to go away'; **pa-eĩti** 'to be able to walk'; **par-eĩti** 'to come home'; **pér-eiti** 'to cross, to go across'; **pra-eĩti** 'to pass by'; **pri-eĩti** 'to go near to'; **su-eĩti** 'to come together, to meet'; **už-eĩti** 'to drop in, to visit'.

But in some few cases the prefix can change the real verbal meaning or give the verb an opposite meaning. Examples: **dúoti** 'to give' but **par-dúoti** 'to sell'; **nèšti** 'to carry' but **pra-nèšti** 'to report, to inform'; **laiměti** 'to win' but **pra-laiměti** 'to lose'; **ràsti** 'to find' but **pra-ràsti** 'to lose', etc.

54. VERBAL ASPECTS

Verbal aspect is that characteristic of the verb which shows whether the action has been completed or is still in progress. Thus for example for the imperfective aspect of *rašýti* 'to write' we find following forms: (3rd person present) *rãšo* 'he writes'; (3rd person simple preterit) *rãšė* 'he was writing, he was engaged in writing, he wrote'; (3rd person future) *rašŷs* 'he will be writing, he will be engaged in writing, he will write'. For the perfective aspect (here formed by the addition of the prefix *pa-*) of this verb, *parašýti* 'to write', we have the 3rd person simple preterit *parãšė* 'he wrote' and the 3rd person simple future *parašŷs* 'he will write'.

In Lithuanian the use of the verbal aspect depends on three things, viz. the structure of the verb, its lexical (real) meaning and tense.

As far as structure is concerned, most simple (unprefixed) verbs are imperfective, e.g. *rãšo, rãšė, rašŷs* and most compound (prefixed) verbs are perfective, e.g. *parãšė, parašŷs*, i.e. in general the prefix makes the verb perfective. But the addition of the iterative suffix *-inėti* makes such verbs imperfective again or perhaps neutral in regard to aspect. For example *sãkė* 'he said' and *rãšė* 'he wrote' are imperfective; *at-sãkė* 'he answered', *pér-rašė* 'he copied' are perfective; but *at-sak-inėjo* 'he kept answering', *pér-raš-inėjo* 'he kept copying' are imperfective.

As far as the lexical meaning of the verb is concerned, those verbs which denote a very short (momentaneuos) action can only be of the perfective aspect, e.g. *ràsti* 'to find', *šáuti* 'to shoot', *surìkti* 'to give a shout', *rìktelėti* 'to shout a little'.

As far as tense is concerned the duration of an action is important because we can only imagine a finished action in the past or the future. A finished action in the present would be in the past at the moment of utterance. Perfective verbs can then only be used with present tense endings in secondary functions, i.e. to denote (1) a general action which is not connected with any special time, e.g. *žẽmė apsìsuka apliñk sáulę peř 365 dienàs* 'the earth revolves around the sun in 365 days'; (2) the possibility of performing an action, e.g. *vaĩkas jaũ paskaĩto* 'the child already reads' or 'the child already knows how to read'; (3) the historical present, e.g. *Výtautas Didýsis sùmuša kryžiuočiùs 1410 mẽtais* 'Vytautas the Great defeats (i.e. defeated) the Knights of the Cross in 1410'; (4) the future, e.g. *einù iř pasakaũ* 'I shall go and I shall say' (where *einù=eĩsiu* and *pasakaũ=pasakýsiu* 'I shall say').

In addition the forms of the various tenses of the verb can be of different aspects. Therefore one must talk about the aspects of verbs in different tenses.

The Present Tense

Simple forms of the present tense are imperfective, e.g. *rãšo* 'he writes', *dìrba* 'he works', *eĩna* 'he goes'. Forming an exception to this are the punctual or momentary verbs with a meaning such as *rañda* 'he finds', *šáuna* 'he shoots', *suriñka* 'he gives a shout', *rìktelia* 'he shouts a little'. Since these forms do not actually denote a present time they are not imperfective.

Compound (prefixed) imperfective verbs are those which: (1) are not generally used without prefixes, e.g. *suprañta* 'he understands', *àtmena* 'he remembers', *pãsakoja* 'he relates', *pajẽgia* 'he is able (to)'; (2) change their basic meaning when they are prefixed, e.g. *kaĺba* 'he speaks', but *àp-kalba* 'he slanders' or *gáuna* 'he gets', but *ap-gáuna* 'he deceives'; (3) or modify the basic meaning of the verb, e.g. *bẽga* 'he runs', but *iš-bẽga* 'he runs out of' or *lìpa* 'he climbs' but *nùlipa* 'he climbs down'.

All other compound (prefixed) verbs are perfective and are used only in the secondary functions mentioned above.

The Simple Preterit Tense

A. Simple forms.

1. Most simple verbs are imperfective, e.g. *dìrbo* 'he worked', *rãšė* 'he wrote', *skaĩtė* 'he read', *kalbėjo* 'he spoke'.
2. A number of verbs are neutral from the point of view of the aspect, i.e. they can be either perfective or imperfective, e.g. *baĩgė* 'he finished', *dãvė* 'he gave', *pir̃ko* 'he bought'. For example, *kaĩ àš baigiaũ dárbą, pàs manè atėjo draũgas* could be translated either 'as I was finishing work a friend came' or 'when I finished work a friend came'.
3. Punctual verbs such as *diñgo* 'he disappeared', *rãdo* 'he found', *šóvė* 'he shot' and verbs with the suffix *-terėti*, *-telėti* are only perfective. Examples: *kur̃ diñgo màno pinigaĩ?* 'where did my money disappear?'; *jìs dróžė mán į̃ aũsį* 'he gave me a slap on the ear'; *jìs rãdo manè namiè* 'he found me at home'; *dìrstelėjau į̃ kalnẽlį ir̃ mataũ . . .* 'I glanced at the hill and I see . . .'; *móteris šýpterėjo, bèt niẽko neatsãkė* 'the woman gave a little smile, but answered nothing'.

B. Compound (prefixed) forms.

1. Most prefixed forms are perfective. Among these some are resultative, e.g. *padãrė* 'made', *pasãkė* 'said', *supùvo* 'rotted', *sunaikìno* 'destroyed'; others are ingressive, e.g. *prašnẽko* 'began to talk', *surìko* 'gave a shout'; still others are attenuative, e.g. *pagulẽjo* 'lay for a little bit', *pasėdẽjo* 'sat for a little while', *paskaĩtė* 'read a little'; and still others are terminative, e.g. *atẽjo* 'arrived', *išẽjo* 'went out', *nuẽjo* 'went away'. An example illustrating the difference between the imperfective and the resultative perfective is the following: *jìs daũg dãrė, bèt niẽko nepadãrė* 'he did a lot, but accomplished nothing'. In this sentence *dãrė* merely means 'engaged in a certain amount of activity' whereas *padãrė* implies a completed action or the attainment of a goal.

2. Some prefixed forms are neutral, i.e. they can be either perfective or imperfective, e.g. *àtminė* 'remembered', *suprãto* 'understood'. In a sentence such as *jìs àtminė manè* 'he remembered me' the verb *àtminė* could be either perfective or imperfective depending upon how one understands it. If one understands it as an action lasting over a long period of time, i.e. with the meaning 'he had me in mind', then it is imperfective. If, on the other hand, one understands it as meaning 'he (suddenly) realized who I was', then it is perfective.

3. A few are imperfective, namely those which are not used without prefixes or the prefix of which changes the basic meaning. Such are *pãsakojo* 'related', *pavydẽjo* 'envied', *atrόdė* 'seemed', etc.

The Future Tense

Roughly speaking one can say that the categories of the future tense parallel those of the preterit discussed above. Example: *jìs daũg darỹs, bèt niẽko nepadarỹs* 'he will do a lot, but will accomplish nothing'.

The Frequentative Past Tense

Just as in the preterit, verbs in the frequentative past tense may be either imperfective, neutral (i.e. either perfective or imperfective) or perfective.

A. Examples of the imperfective: *jìs dìrbdavo namiẽ* 'he used to work at home'; *jìs visadà pavydẽdavo* 'he always used to be envious'.

B. Examples of neutral verbs: (perfective) *kaĩ jìs ateĩdavo, visì atsistódavo* '(every time) when he came, everybody got (would get) up'. Here the action is perfective because it is a completed action, i.e. everybody got up after he came. (imperfective) *kaĩ jìs ateĩdavo, visì bėgdavome jõ pasitìkti* 'when he came (would come), everybody would run to meet him'. This is imperfective because the two actions, that of arriving and that of running are simultaneous. Here we see the dependence of aspect on tense: *ateĩna* 'arrives' is imperfective; *atėjo* 'arrived' is perfective; *ateĩdavo* 'arrived, used to arrive' is neutral.

C. Example of a perfective verb: *Jìs visadà laimėdavo* 'he would always win' or 'he always used to win'.

The Infinitive

In general one can find the same aspectual differences in the infinitive as in the preterit. It must be pointed out, however, that in many cases there is hardly any difference in meaning between the imperfective and the perfective infinitive. Examples: (imperfective) *prašaũ sėsti* = (perfective) *prašaũ atsisėsti* 'please sit down'. One should note here that it is possible to use a perfective infinitive as a complement of *baĩgti* 'to finish' or *pradėti* 'to begin' if the verb in question has no imperfective counterpart with the same meaning, e.g. *jìs pradėjo atsisvéikinti* 'he began to take leave'.

The Imperative Mood

We find the same categories in the imperative as in the preterit. For example, one might use the imperfective in the sentence *skaitýk lietùvių literatūrą* 'read Lithuanian literature' where the command is a general injunction to spend some time in the persuit of Lithuanian literary studies. On the other hand one might use the perfective imperative in the sentence *pérskaityk Ostráusko Kanarėlę* 'read Ostrauskas' (play) The Canary'. In the second case the object is more definite and the goal of the action is the completion of the reading of a specific play by K. Ostrauskas, a contemporary Lithuanian author. In some cases there seems to be no real difference in meaning between the perfective and imperfective imperatives. Thus one might say either (imperfective) *bučiúok rañką* or (perfective) *pabučiúok rañką* 'kiss the hand' without any real difference in meaning.

The Subjunctive Mood

Here again we find the same categories as in the preterit. Examples: (perfective) *àš parašýčiau tą knýgą, jéigu àš galėčiau* 'I would write (finish writing) that book, if I could'; (imperfective) *àš vìsą diēną rašýčiau, jéigu àš galėčiau* 'I would write all day (spend all day writing), if I could'.

The Compound Tenses

The same categories as we have in the preterit are to be noted here. It is most important here for the student to distinguish carefully between the perfect tenses and the perfective aspect. A perfect tense denotes the state or condition which is the result of a past action, whereas the perfective aspect denotes a completed action. Thus the various perfect tenses may have verbs in either the perfective or imperfective aspect. Examples: (present perfect tense, but imperfective aspect) *àš esù važinėjęs šìtuo keliù* 'I have traveled by this road'. In this case the imperfective verb *važinėti* 'to travel' denotes that it was a repeated action, but the perfect tense denotes that the speaker is in the condition of a man who has made the trip a certain number of times, (pluperfect tense and perfective aspect) *kaĩ jìs atėjo, àš jaũ buvaũ išvažiãvęs į̃ svečiùs* 'when he arrived, I had already left to go visiting'. Although any combination of tense and aspect is theoretically possible it is to be expected that the perfect tenses are more likely to be used with verbs of the perfective aspect. This is because 'a condition which has been attained' (the sign of the perfect tense) is more likely to be coupled with a completed action (the sign of the perfective aspect) than with an incomplete action (the sign of the imperfective aspect).

Some Lithuanian Proverbs

Kas ars, nepavargs; kas vogs, nepralobs. — (He) who ploughs will not grow tired; (he) who steals will not get rich.

Verkiu duona, tinginio valgoma. — Bread cries when eaten by a lazy person. (That is, a lazy person has no right to be fed.)

Kaip pasiklosi, taip išmiegosi. — As you have made your bed, thus will you sleep. (That is, one gets what one deserves, the results of one's actions must be endured.)

Ką pasėsi, tą ir piausi. — Whatever you sow, that will you reap. (Similar in meaning to proverb 3 above.)

Obuolys nuo obels netoli nukrinta. — Like father, like son. (Lit.: An apple doesn't fall far from an apple tree.)

A Short Introduction to Readings

It was not the intention of the authors to present here an anthology of some selections of Lithuanian literature: that would simply take up too much space. We have tried simply to add a few reading selections for those for whom other regular readings in Lithuanian are not readily available.

R e a d i n g s include the following:

1) *Kvailutis*, a folktale, a little simplified and adapted for easier understanding.

2) *Lietuvos monarchijos kūrimasis*, a short survey about the establishment of the Lithuanian monarchy in the Middle Ages.

3) *Vytenio ir Gedimino Lietuva*, a survey of the times of these two rulers of Lithuania. Both no. 2 and 3 have been taken from the book *Mūsų Lietuva*, edited by Bronius Kviklys. The language in these two selections has not been changed: it represents rather difficult expository prose. The student should not worry if he finds these selections a 'little' difficult.

4) *Tautinės šventės prasmė* is an editorial taken from the Lithuanian semi-weekly newspaper DARBININKAS. It is perhaps the most difficult prose selection.

5) Four Lithuanian folksongs: *Mēnuo saulužę vedē*; *Ūžkit, ūžkit, mano girnaitēs*; *Lēk, vanagēli*; *Dainuok, sesyte*. Although we have tried to select as simple folksongs as possible, the students will find them rather difficult to translate. However, there are translations of all of these folksongs available. See footnote 7 under *Dainuok, sesyte*.

6) Of the individual Lithuanian lyric poetry, we selected only four poems by four outstanding Lithuanian lyrical poets: Maironis, Mykolaitis-Putinas, Jonas Aistis and Kazys Bradūnas. The poems selected are again chosen primarily because their language is somewhat easier, not because we think that these four poems are the most characteristic poems of the Lithuanian lyrical poetry, or of the poets themselves. Reading and understanding poetry is a difficult task, even for the native speaker of the language,

therefore, we consider these poems only as a sample of "how Lithuanian sounds in a lyrical poem"...

Translations into English of all these poems are available. See footnote 7 under *Dainuok, sesyte.*

The notes are rather copious, but still the students will have to call upon their native instructor to understand fully the selections included herein.

KVAILUTIS

Vieną kartą gyveno toks ūkininkas, kuris turėjo tris sūnus: du protingus, o trečią kvailutį. Mirdamas[1] tiems protingiems sūnums jis paliko namus ir žemę, o kvailučiui — mažą veršiuką. Kvailutis papiovė tą veršiuką ir jo mėsą atidavė šunims, sakydamas:

— Šuniukai, pirkite[2] mėsą! Šuniukai, pirkite[2] mėsą!

O šunys jam atsakė:

— Mes norėtume pirkti, bet neturime pinigų.

— Jeigu neturite pinigų, tai imkite[2] be pinigų...

Šunys suėdė tą mėsą, o kvailutis grįžo namo. Jo broliai klausia jo:

— Kur padėjai veršiuką?

— Šunims išdalinau.

— Tai labai kvailai[3] padarei, — sako broliai. — Ar esi kur nors girdėjęs,[4] kad šunys kam[5] skolą grąžintų?

— Man grąžins, — tarė kvailutis.

Jis nusivijo ilgą botagą ir tuo botagu[6] pradėjo visus kaimo šunis mušti, šaukdamas[1]:

— Atiduokite[2] man pinigus! Atiduokite man pinigus!

Šunys išsigando ir išbėgo iš kaimo į mišką. Kvailutis, matydamas[1], kad jų pėsčias nepasivys, pasibalnojo brolių arklį, pasiėmė duonos[7] ir pradėjo šunis vytis. Miške kaip tik tuo metu[8] viename mažame namelyje gyveno plėšikai. Jie sėdėjo prie stalo, galando peilius ir skaičiavo pinigus.

Šunys, išsigandę[9] kvailučio botago, sušoko pro langą į plėšikų namelį. Šie, manydami[1], kad paskui šunis atbėgs ir žmonės, metė pinigus ir pabėgo į pačias tamsiausias miško vietas. Kvailutis pasiėmė visus pinigus ir tarė:

— Ačiū, šunyčiai, kad man už mėsą užmokėjote.

Kai apie tai išgirdo kvailučio broliai, tai išpiovė gyvulius ir išvežė į turgų, tačiau turguje niekas jų mėsos[10] nepirko, ir jie grįžo namo labai perpykę. Jie išvijo kvailį iš namų, kadangi jis jiems buvo pripasakojęs[11], kad mėsa labai pabrangusi.

Kvailutis eina, eina ir prieina dvarą. O ten gyveno tokia žiopla ponia. Ji ir klausia:

— Iš kur pats atsiradai,[12] kad aš niekad tavęs nesu mačiusi?[13]

— Iš dangaus nukritau,[14] — atsakė kvailutis.

— Ar nematei[15] ten mano sūnaus?[16] Kaip jis ten laikosi?

— Mačiau, mačiau: jam ten labai blogai.[17]

— Ar nenuneštum[18] mano sūnui pinigų?[19]

— Kodėlgi ne! Jeigu tik duosi, tai ir nunešiu.[20]

Ponia davė jam pinigų,[19] o tas ir eina sau toliau.[21] Netrukus sugrįžo to dvaro ponas. Jis tuojau suprato, kad koks gudruolis bus jo žmoną apgavęs.[22] Jis tuojau pasikinkė arklį ir ėmė apgaviką vytis. Pamatęs atvažiuojant poną, kvailutis pečiais parėmė pasvirusią obelį. Privažiavo ponas ir klausia:

— Ar nematei tokio žmogaus, kuris mano žmoną apgavo?

— Mačiau, kuriuo keliu[23] ir kurion pusėn[24] jis nuėjo. Aš tuojau jį pagausiu, tik palaikyk tamsta obelį, kad ji neišvirstų.

Laiko ponas obelį, o kvailutis įšoko į vežimą ir nudardėjo su pono arkliu. Grįžo ponas namo pėsčias, supratęs, kad kvailutis jį taip pat apgavo. Tada jis pasikinkė kitą arklį ir vėl šoko kvailučio vytis. Kvailutis jau buvo pono arklį pardavęs,[25] tik girdi — vėl jį kažin kas[26] vejasi. Jis išsitepė dumblu[27] veidą ir galvą, kad jo nepažintų,[28] atsisėdo prie kelio ir laukia. Kai ponas privažiavo, jis jam sako:

— Pone, ar negirdėjai naujienos:[29] karalius išleido raštą, kuriame parašyta,[30] kad po trijų dienų visus plikus kars. Laimė,[31] kad aš turiu vaistų,[32] nuo kurių per tris dienas plaukai atželia.

Tas ponas buvo plikas. Jis pradėjo kvailučio prašyti tų vaistų. Kvailutis ištepė jo galvą ir visą veidą dumblu[27] ir liepė jam tris dienas nejudėti iš vietos, o pats įšoko į jo vežimą ir nuvažiavo.

Sėdėjo ponas su tuo dumblu ant galvos tris dienas, o kai dumblas išdžiuvo ir reikėjo jį nukrapštyti, tai paskutinius pūkelius reikėjo nuo plikės nurauti. Grįžo jis namo be arklių, du kartus kvailučio[33] apgautas.

Matyt, esama[34] žemėje kvailesnių[35] už kvailutį.

NOTES:

1) Special active participle, cf. 26.4.
2) Imperative form.
3) Translate: 'did a foolish thing'.
4) **esì girdėjęs** (perfect tense) 'have heard'.

5) **kám** (here) 'to anyone'.
6) (instrumental case) 'with that whip'.
7) **dúonos** (genitive case) 'some bread'.
8) **kaĩp tìk tuõ metù** 'just at that time'.
9) **išsigañdę** (masc. nom. plur. of past active participle of **išsigą̃sti**) 'having become frightened'.
10) **mė̃sõs** 'meat' is in the genitive case as the direct object of **nepir̃ko** 'didn't buy', a negated verb.
11) **bùvo pripãsakojęs** 'had told'.
12) 'Where did you come from?'
13) **tavę̃s nesù mãčiusi** (perfect tense) 'I haven't seen you'.
14) **nukritaũ** (simple preterit of **nukrìsti**) 'I fell'.
15) **nemateĩ** (simple preterit of **matýti**) 'didn't you see?'.
16) **sūnaũs** 'son' is in the genitive case as the object of the negated verb **nemateĩ**.
17) **jám teñ labaĩ blogaĩ** 'he is having a bad time there' (lit.: 'to him there very bad').
18) **nenunè̃štum** (see Lesson 31) 'wouldn't you take'.
19) **pinigų̃** (genitive case) 'some money'.
20) future tense.
21) **eĩna sáu tuliaũ** 'continues on his way farther'.
22) **bùs . . . apgãvęs** (see Lesson 22) 'must have deceived'.
Future perfect tense used with meaning of probability.
23) **kuriuõ keliù** (instrumental case) 'by which road'.
24) **kuriõn pùsėn** (illative case) 'in which direction'.
25) **bùvo . . . pardãvęs** 'had sold'.
26) **kažiñ kàs** 'somebody or other'.
27) **dumblù** (instrumental case) 'with mud'.
28) **nepažìntų** (subjunctive mood, see Lesson 31) 'wouldn't recognize'.
29) **naujíenos** (genitive case as the direct object of a negated verb) 'news'.
30) **parašýta** (neuter form of past passive participle) — 'it is written'.
31) **Láimė** 'it is fortunate, it is lucky'.
32) **váistų** (partitive genitive) 'some medicine'.
33) **kvailùčio** (genitive case to express agent of a passive participle) 'by the fool'.
34) **ė̃sama** (neuter form of present passive participle of **bū̃ti**) 'there are'.
35) **kvailesnių̃** 'some who are more foolish'.

LIETUVOS MONARCHIJOS KŪRIMASIS

Nebuvo lengva lietuviams išlaikyti savo nepriklausomybę. Kai mes šiandien žvelgiame į Lietuvos gamtovaizdį, reta rasti[1] vietovę, kurios apylinkėje nebūtų piliakalnio. Kai kur dar ir vėlesnių — mūrinių pilių griuvėsiai tebestovi,[2] kaip taurūs liudytojai . . . Jie liudija, kad ne metus, ne dešimtį, bet ištisus šimtmečius lietuviams teko[3] atkakliai ginti savo kraštą, kaupiant[4] visas jėgas, naudojant[5] tuo laiku[6] jiems prieinamas techniškas priemones,[7] o svarbiausia,[8] parodant[9] jau organizuotos tautos ypatybes: laisvės meilę ir vienybės siekimą. Ir kai XIII amžiuje iškyla ryškus karaliaus Mindaugo asmuo, tai mes jau žinome, kad tai buvo tik pats vainikavimas lietuvių tautinio ir valstybinio brendimo, vykusio,[10] be abejojimo, ištisus šimtmečiu.s, nors ir neužrašyto[11] istorijos knygose atskirais vardais ir įvykiais.[12]

Mindaugas vainikavo ilgesnio laikotarpio lietuvių pastangas; pats buvo vainikuotas Lietuvos karaliumi[13] 1253 m. Porą metų anksčiau jis apsikrikštijo. Greičiausiai jis tai padarė politinių aplinkybių spaudžiamas, kai prieš jį buvo susidariusi[14] kaimynų koalicija. Jis buvo supratęs, kad Vakarų Europos kultūra yra aukštesnė, kaip to meto Lietuvos, kad ją reikės pasisavinti ir kad Vakarų Europos tautų bendruomenėje, kaip lygus narys, galės dalyvauti tik krikščioniška valstybė. Senoji lietuvių tikyba, kiek apie ją žinome,[15] buvo idealistinės krypties,[16] be ritualinių žiaurumų, palaikanti[17] bei puoselėjanti[17] ir krikščionybei priimtinus moralinius pagrindus.[18] O tačiau ji savo paskirtį mūsų tautos istorijoje jau buvo atlikusi ir turėjo užleisti savo vietą krikščionybei: visos aplinkinės tautos (vokiečiai, rusai, lenkai) jau buvo krikščioniškos. Deja, tie, kurie pasiryžo nešti krikščionybę į Lietuvą, taigi[19] kryžiuočių ir kalavijuočių ordinai, pasirinko tai misijai[20] atlikti kelią, susijusį su ginklo jėga bei politine okupacija. Lietuviai gynėsi nuo likimo, ištikusio prūsus, jotvingius, latvius, ir kartu gynėsi, nors gal kartais ir apgailestaudami, ir nuo krikščionybės, nešamos[21] lygiagrečiai su politine kalavijuočių-kryžiuočių priespauda.

Taigi ir Mindaugo Lietuvos pastatas, nors buvo pastatytas ant tvirtų pamatų, neišliko visas vėlesnėms kartoms.[22] Jo vienas stulpas—krikščionybė—sugriuvo su tragiška Mindaugo mirtimi. 1263 m. Mindaugas buvo nužudytas vidaus politinių priešų.[23] Sunku buvo rasti pasaulyje tautą, kur nebūtų buvę pralieta[24] kraujo[25] dėl valdžios. Neaplenkė toji dėmė ir Lietuvos, nors gal Lietuvoje ir mažiau tebuvo tokių įvykių kaip kitur.[26] *

---

* Taken from: Kviklys, Bronius, ed., Mūsų Lietuva, Lietuvių Enciklopedijos Leidykla, Boston, 1964, p. 49.

NOTES:

1) **rēta ràsti** 'it is rare to find'.
2) **tebestóvi** 'still stand'.
3) **lietùviams tēko** 'it fell to the lot of Lithuanians to'.
4) **kaũpiant** (special gerund, cf. 26.7) 'accumulating, building up'.
5) **naudójant** (special gerund, cf. 26.7) 'making use of'.
6) **tuõ laikù** (instrumental case) 'at that time'.
7) **jíems prieínamas tèchniškas príemones** 'the technical means available to them'; **jíems** 'to them'; **prieínamas** (fem. acc. plur. of the present passive participle of **prieíti**) 'accessible, available'.
8) **svarbiáusia** 'most important of all'.
9) **paródant** (special gerund, cf. 26.7) 'showing'.

10) výkusio (masc. gen. sing. of past active participle of výkti; modifies brendìmo) 'having taken place, which took place'.
11) neužrašýto (masc. gen. sing. of past passive participle of [ne]užrašýti; modifies brendìmo) 'not copied down'.
12) atskiraĩs vardaĩs iȓ įvykiais (instrumental plural) 'as separate names and events'.
13) karãliumi (instrumental singular) 'as king'.
14) bùvo susidãriusi 'has been created'.
15) kíek apiẽ ją̃ žìnome 'as much as we know about it'.
16) idealìstinės kryptiẽs 'of an idealistic bent, turn'.
17) Fem. nom. sing. of present active participle.
18) krikščionýbei priiȓtinus morãlinius pãgrindus 'morally acceptable bases for Christianity'; pãgrindus is in the accusative case as the object of palaĩkanti and púoselėjanti.
19) taĩgi 'that is'.
20) mìsijai is in the dative case as the object of the infinitive atlìkti.
21) nẽšamos (fem. gen. sing. of present passive participle of nèšti; modifies krikščionýbės) 'carried'.
22) neišlìko vìsas vėlèsnėms kartóms 'did not remain whole for later generations'.
23) vidaũs polìtinių príešų (the last two words in the genìtìvė case because they denote the agent) 'by interior political enemies'.
24) nebū́tų bùvę pralíeta 'would not have been spilled'; pralíeta is the neuter form of the past passive participle.
25) kraũjo is in the genitive case to denote a certain quantity.
26) mažiaũ tebùvo tokių̃ įvykių kaĩp kituȓ 'there were fewer such events than elsewhere'; tokių̃ įvykių is in the genitive case since it is governed by mažiaũ.

VYTENIO IR GEDIMINO LIETUVA

Mindaugui mirus,[1] Lietuvos valstybės rūmas smarkiai susvyravo. XIII a. antroje pusėje nuolat besikeičią valdovai, apie kuriuos kartais nedaug ką[2] daugiau težinome, kaip tik[3] jų vardus, atrodė vargiai beįstengs[4] išlaikyti vienybėje Lietuvos valstybę, kuriai[5] sujungti Mindaugas ir prieš jį gyvenusieji padėjo tiek vargo ir pastangų. Tačiau laimingu būdu Lietuva šį savitarpio kovų[6] (1263-1270) bandymą išlaikė. O po 1293 metų, kai Lietuvą pradėjo valdyti Vytenis, jau nenutrūko valstybės tęstinumo grandinė ligi pat Liublino unijos. Nebebuvo[7] Lietuvai[8] pavojaus[9] grįžti[10] į palaidą atskirų kilčių junginį, nors kitos rūšies pavojų ir vargų nestigo.

Kunigaikščių Lietuva! Apdainuota poetų,[11] išgarbinta rašytojų.[11] Kunigaikščių vardai yra mums[12] garbės vardai: jais[13] puošiasi Lietuvos jaunimas, vadinami kariuomenės pulkai, valstybės ordinai ir garbės ženklai. O tačiau klystume tardami,[14] kad jie vieni,[15] tie keli asmenys, sukūrė visa tai, kuo mes Lietuvos istorijoje pagrįstai didžiuojamės.[16] Ne, jie buvo tik valdovai, derintojai, sakytume, simboliai visų tautos luomų pastangų ir susiklausymo. Jie iškilo natūraliu geresniųjų atrankos keliu;[17] jie valdė nuo XIII a. pabaigos, nors ir ne šiandieninių, formaliai demokratiškų rinkimų būdu,[18] — pusiau paveldėjimo teise.[19]

Kunigaikštis Vytenis, be abejo, žinojo ir vertino Mindaugo žygius. Tik ką jis galėjo padaryti, pvz., krikščionybės įvedimo reikalu,[20] jeigu ordino grobuoniškas elgesys pasiekė tokias ribas, jog net pats Rygos arkivyskupas kvietėsi į pagalbą[21] *pagonį* Vytenį prieš ordino savivalę. Kryžiuočių ordinas, įsikūręs ir išaugęs kovose su turkais Palestinoje, į visus nekrikščionis žiūrėjo[22] tomis pačiomis akimis,[23] kaip į turkus. Vyteniui beliko[24] kovoti ir laukti šviesesnių dienų.

Vytenio brolis Gediminas, palikęs vardą dinastijai, davusiai visą eilę garbingų valdovų ne tik Lietuvai, bet ir Lenkijai (Jogailaičių vardu), ėmėsi kelti[25] Lietuvą visose tose srityse, kuriose ji buvo atsilikusi[26] nuo Vakarų Europos, visų pirma ūkio srityje. Iškilo Trakų ir Vilniaus pilys; augo, garsėjo, kaip tas Geležinio vilko[27] staugimas, naujoji Lietuvos sostinė Vilnius. Iš Vakarų Europos pakviesti[28] plaukė į Lietuvą amatininkai, pirkliai. Toji Vakarų Europa darėsi vis artimesnė. Štai ir tiesioginis ryšys[29] su popiežium užmezgamas. Krikščionybė vėl žymiai priartėja prie Lietuvos. Deja, Gediminas vėliau atsisako krikštytis. Tikrąsias šio atsisakymo priežastis vargu kada[30] sužinosime. Ligšioliniai aiškinimai, kad kalta toji pati kryžiuočių grėsmė, nepakankamai šį atsimetimą pagrindžia. Kaip ir daugeliu[31] istorinių atvejų, taip ir šį kartą gal norėtųsi[32] pageidauti, kad įvykiai būtų kitaip susidėstę. Tačiau šis ir kiti istoriniai faktai yra jau amžiams nebepakeičiami:[33] iš jų galime tik pasimokyti.

Kai Gediminas, tėvynę gindamas, žuvo kovoje su kryžiuočiais 1341 metais, jis paliko savo įpėdiniams sujungtą ir ūkiškai pakeltą valstybę,[34] paliko tačiau ir tas problemas, kurių jis nebespėjo išspręsti.*

---

* Taken from: B. Kviklys, ed., Mūsų Lietuva, Lietuvių Enciklopedijos Leidykla, Boston, 1964, pp. 49-50.

NOTES:

1) **Mìndaugui mìrus** — 'after Mindaugas died'; dative plus special gerund derived from past active participle, cf. 39.4 and 26.7.
2) **nedaũg ką̃** 'not much'.
3) **kaĩp tìk** 'except, but'.
4) **bejsténgs** (future used with modal meaning) 'would be able to'.
5) **kuriái** (fem. dat. sing.; dative case is used as the object of the infinitive).
6) **savìtarpio kovų̃** 'internecine struggles'.
7) **Nebebùvo** 'there was no longer'.

8) **Líetuvai** (dative case) 'for Lithuania'.
9) **pavõjaus** (genitive case with negation) 'any danger'.
10) **grĩžti** (lit.: to return). Translate the entire expression as: "There was no longer any danger that Lithuania might return . . ."
11) The genitive case denotes agent.
12) **mùms** (dative case) 'for us'.
13) **jaĩs** (instrumental case) 'with them'.
14) **klýstume tardamì** 'we should be mistaken to say'.
15) **jiē vienì** 'they alone'.
16) **taĩ, kuõ . . . didžiúojamès** 'that of which we are proud'.
17) **natūraliù geresniųjų atrankõs keliù** 'by the natural path of the selection of the best'; **natūraliù** in the instrumental case modifies **keliù**.
18) **nè šiandieninių, formaliaĩ demokrãtiškų rinkìmų būdù** 'not by means of contemporary formally democratic elections'.
19) **téise** (instrumental case) 'by right of'.
20) **krikščionýbès įvedìmo reĩkalu** 'as far as the introduction of Christianity is concerned';**reĩkalu** in the instrumental case means 'concerning the affair of' or 'relative to'.
21) **kviētėsi į pagálbą** 'asked for help (from)'.
22) **į visùs nekrikščiónis žiūrėjo** 'looked at all non-Christians'.
23) **tomìs pačiomìs akimìs** (instrumental case) 'with the same eyes' (i.e. the same way).
24) **Vytėniui beliko** 'it remained for Vytenis'.
25) **ėmėsi kélti** 'undertook to raise (to the level of)'.
26) **bùvo atsilìkusi** (pluperfect tense) 'had remained behind'.
27) **Geležìnio Vìlko**, literally 'Iron Wolf'. It is the symbol of the strength and fame of the city of Vilnius. There is a legend that Grand Duke Gediminas in his dream saw this 'Iron Wolf' howling. Since the howling iron wolf symbolizes strength and fame, it became the legendary symbol of Vilnius where Gediminas established his capital.
28) **pakviestì** (masc. nom. plur. of past passive participle) 'invited'.
29) **tiesióginis ryšýs** 'direct connection'.
30) **vargù kadà** 'who knows when, it is difficult to say when'.
31) **daūgeliu** (instrumental case) 'in a great number'.
32) **norėtųsi** (reflexive subjunctive) 'it might be wished'.
33) **nebepakeičiamì** (masc. nom. plur. of present passive participle) 'are no longer changeable'.
34) **sùjungtą iř ūkiškai pakéltą valstýbę** 'a united and economically improved state'.

TAUTINĖS ŠVENTĖS PRASMĖ

Kiekviena šventė yra surišta su praeitimi. Nešvenčiamas gimtadienis,[1] kai[2] kūdikis gimsta. Ir po keliolikos metų gimtinės arba vardinės[3] nėra tiek[4] reikšmingos, kaip[5] sulaukus[6] 50 ar 75 metų. Juo[7] tolimesnis įvykis, tuo šventė darosi svarbesnė ir iškilmingesnė. Praeitis nenustelbia, bet dar labiau pririša.[8] Kasmet minima,[9] ji pasidaro tvirta tradicija. Tuo būdu susidaro tautinės ir valstybinės šventės.

Lietuvoje nepriklausomybės laikais[10] pradžioje buvo tik viena iškilesnė Vasario 16 šventė. Ji priminė nepriklausomos Lietuvos valstybės atkūrimą. Kaip[11] valstybinė šventė, dabar rusų okupantų[12] neleidžiama[13] švęsti. Panaikinę[14] valstybės nepriklausomumą, naikina ir valstybines Lietuvos šventes. Taip[15] daro visuose kraštuose visi okupantai, ir iš to[16] jau gali juos pažinti. Užgniaužę laisvę, siekia užslopinti ir tos laisvės prisiminimą.

Tautos šventė, Rugsėjo 8, nepriklausomoje Lietuvoje buvo įvesta Vytauto Didžiojo metais[17] (1930), minint[18] jo 500 metų mirtį. Parinkta diena,[19] kurioje jis turėjo vainikuotis[20] Lietuvos karaliumi,[21] bet tas užsimojimas[22] pradžioje buvo sukliudytas lenkų,[23] o paskui mirties. Prieš mirtį vainikavimas buvo sutartas Vilniuje. Neįvyko tiktai iškilmės.[24] Tautos šventę Rugsėjo 8 norėta[25] pabrėžti ne tiek tą vainikavimą, kiek Lietuvos valstybės galybę[26] Vytauto Didžiojo laikais.[27] Vasario 16 priminė atkurtąją Lietuvos valstybę,[28] kuri buvo žymiai senesnė ir didingesnė. Tai tos pačios lietuvių tautos praeitis,[29] tiktai paskutiniais amžiais[30] aptemdyta nelaisvės.[31] Bet dėl to ne tiktai nereikia[32] senos praeities[33] pamiršti, bet prisiminimu ir jausmais[34] dar tvirčiau susirišti, nes tauta tiktai tada[35] stiprėja ir išlieka vieninga, kai[35] išlaiko vienybę su visa savo praeitimi.

Trumpas laikas buvo laisvėje tiem ryšiam[36] tvirčiau su Lietuvos praeitimi sumegzti.[37] Tautos šventė pasidaro visuotinė ir tradicinė tiktai per ilgesnį laiką,[38] o Lietuvą greitai vėl užklupo karas ir okupacijos. Okupantam svarbu,[39] kad tauta visai pamirštų, kas ji buvo, ir darytųsi lengviau jų pavaldoma.[40] Užtat naikinamos pavergto krašto šventės ir grūdamos svetimos.[41] Tai pavergtos tautos prievartavimas ir išniekinimas. Laikoma[42] niekingu daiktu, kai vieno tikėjimo žmogus spiriamas eiti į kito tikėjimo bažnyčią. Niekinga taip pat yra okupuotam kraštui primesti vergėjų[43] išgalvotas šventes, su kuriom[44] Lietuva nieko bendro neturi.

Rugsėjo 8 turi dar vieną neišraujamą lietuvių tautoje tradiciją ir šventę — tai Marijos Gimimo prisiminimą.[45] Nors ir religinės šventės Lietuvoje šėtoniškai užstelbtos, bet iš žmonių širdžių jų išrauti neįstengiama. Tai rodo dabar į Skiemonis[46] sutekančios[47] minios žmonių, o nuo seniau[48] į Šiluvą.[49] Rugsėjo 8 yra sena ir garsi šiluvinių atlaidų šventė.

Kai kam[50] seniau rodėsi, kad tautinė šventė lyg ir[51] norėta užstelbti religinę lietuvių tradiciją. Jei kas[52] tokią mintį turėjo, tai netoli matė. Religija ir tautybė nesikerta, o viena antrą remia. Tautinės šventės darosi visuotinesnės, kai turi ir religinį pagrindą. Antai, ne betkas[53] įstengtų ir išdrįstų iš airių tautos išplėšti šv. Patriko dieną, kuri yra tiek pat patriotiška, kaip ir religiška.

NOTES:

1) Translate as: "The birthday is not celebrated".
2) kaĩ 'when'.
3) vardìnės 'name-day'. The day of the patron saint for whom the person is named is frequently celebrated rather than the birthday.
4) nėrà tíek 'is not so'.
5) kaĩp 'as'.
6) suláukus lit.: 'having waited (and received)'. Here suláukus can best be translated by English 'after'.
7) juõ...tuõ 'the more...the more'. Here "The more distant the event, the more the holiday becomes more important and more solemn."
8) No direct object is required in Lithuanian as it would be here in English.
9) minimà is the present passive participle of minéti. It can be translated as 'commemorated' or 'celebrated'.
10) laikaĩs is the instrumental plural of laĩkas. Here it means 'in the time of' or 'during'.
11) kaĩp 'as'.
12) rùsų okupántų 'by the Russian occupiers'. The first genitive rùsų 'Russian' is used adjectivally to modify okupántų which is in the genitive case as the performer or the logical subject of a passive verbal construction.
13) neléidžiama is the present passive participle of neléisti. It is feminine nominative singular to agree with šveñtė. Here it can be translated as 'is not permitted, is not allowed'.
14) panaikìnę is the past active participle of panaikìnti. It is in the nominative plural to agree with the understood subject of the sentence okupántai. Here it can be translated as 'having destroyed, having ruined, having abolished'.
15) Taĩp dãro...visì okupántai 'all occupiers (subjugators) do this'.
16) iš tõ 'by this, in this way'
17) mėtais 'in the year (of Vytautas the Great)'.
18) mìnint is a special gerund derived from minéti. The whole expression may be translated as: "commemorating the 500th year since his death."
19) parinktà dienà 'a day was chosen'.
20) turėjo vainikúotis 'was supposed to be crowned'.
21) karãliumi is in the instrumental singular to denote capacity or station. Here it can be translated 'as king'.
22) užsimojìmas 'intention, plan'.
23) lénkų 'by the Poles'. Note the genitive case to denote the logical subject of the passive verb.
24) Neįvýko tiktaĩ iškilmės 'Only the ceremony did not take place'.
25) norėta is the neuter form of the past passive participle of norėti. Here it may be translated as 'it was wanted, they wanted'.
26) nè tíek tą vainikãvimą, kíek Lietuvõs valstýbės galýbę 'not so much the coronation as the power of the Lithuanian state'.
27) Výtauto Dìdžiojo laikaĩs 'in the time of Vytautas the Great'.
28) atkùrtąją Lietuvõs valstýbę 'the re-established Lithuanian state'. atkùrtąją is the feminine accusative singular of the past passive participle of atkùrti 'to re-establish'. It agrees with valstýbę, the word it modifies.
29) Taĩ tõs pačiõs lietùvių tautõs praeitìs 'This is the past of the same Lithuanian nation'.
30) tiktaĩ paskutìniais ámžiais 'only in recent times'.
31) neláisvės 'by servitude'. Note the genitive case functioning as the logical subject of the passive participle aptémdyta.
32) nè tiktaĩ nereĩkia 'not only must one not'. Note that here nereĩkia means 'one must not' or 'it is necessary that...not'.

400

33) Note the genitive case here as the object of a negated expression.
34) **prisiminimù iȓ jausmaȋs** 'by remembrance and emotions'. Note the instrumental case to express means.
35) **tadà ... kaȋ** 'then ... when'.
36) **tíem rýšiam** is a dative plural without the final **-s**.
37) The entire sentence is to be translated: "Freedom was too shortlived to associate these bonds more firmly with Lithuania's past." **Truȓpas laȋkas** is the subject, but it must be understood as 'too short a time'; **láisvėje** 'in freedom'; **tíem rýšiam** object of the infinitive **sumègzti** in the dative plural; **tvirčiaũ** 'more firmly'; **sù Lietuvõs praeitimȋ** 'with Lithuania's past'; **sumègzti** is an infinitive meaning 'to tie together, to knot'. Lit.: "A (too) short time was in freedom to knot these bonds more firmly with Lithuania's past."
38) **pèr ilgèsnį laȋką** 'in the course of a longer (period of) time'.
39) **okupántam svarbù** 'it is important for the occupiers'.
40) **darýtųsi lengviaũ jū̃ pavaȋdoma** 'would be more easily ruled by them'. **darýtųsi** is the third person subjunctive of **darýtis**; **lengviaũ** 'more easily' comparative degree of the adverb **lengvaȋ**; **jū̃** is the genitive plural of **jis** and refers to the occupiers; **jū̃** is in the genitive case since it is the logical subject of the passive verb **pavaȋdoma**, the present passive participle of **pavaldýti**. Note that the perfective verb **pavaldýti** here means 'to be able to rule. Literally it means: 'would become more easily by them to be ruled'.
41) **grūdamos svētimos** 'foreign (holidays) are forced (on the enslaved country)'; **grūdamos** is the nominative plural feminine of the present passive participle of **grūsti** 'to force'; **svētimos** is in the nominative plural feminine to agree with **šveñtės**.
42) **laȋkoma** neuter present passive participle of **laikýti**; 'it is considered, generally held'.
43) **vergėjų** 'by the enslavers'. The genitive here denotes the logical subject of **išgalvótas** 'having been invented, having been thought up'.
44) **kurioȓ** 'which'. Note the colloquial form of the instrumental plural (instead of **kuriomìs**).
45) **Marìjos Gimìmo prisiminìmą** 'the feast of the Birth of the Virgin Mary'.
46) **Skiemónys** is a little town (**bažnýtkaimis** or **miestėlis**) in north-eastern Lithuania. In Skiemonys it is alleged that the Virgin Mary appeared to a certain Ramutė Macvytė (then about 14 years old) in the year 1962. This has not been officially confirmed by the Church; nevertheless thousands of people flock to this field to bring flowers, sing hymns and pray every week. It is frequently turned into an emotional demonstration against Communism.
47) **sùtekančios** 'flocking'. This is the present active participle of **sutekėti**. It is in the nominative plural feminine to agree with **mìnios** 'crowds'.
48) **nuõ seniaũ** 'since an earlier time'.
49) **Šiluvà**, located in the county of Raseiniai in western Lithuania (Žemaitija), is a place where the Virgin Mary appeared to certain children and then to adults at the time of the Reformation when many Lithuanians were turning Protestant. In the Catholic National Shrine in Washington, D.C. there is a chapel dedicated to Our Lady of Šiluva.
50) **Kaȋ kám** 'to some people'.
51) **lýg iȓ** 'apparently, it is just as if'.
52) **kàs** 'somebody, someone'.
53) **nè betkàs** 'nobody'.

MĖNUO SAULUŽĘ VEDĖ

Mėnuo[1] saulužę vedė[2]
Pirmą pavasarėlį.[3]

Saulužė[4] anksti kėlės,
Mėnužis[5] atsiskyrė.

Mėnuo vienas vaikštinėjo,
Aušrinę pamylėjo.

Perkūns,[6] didžiai supykęs,
Jį kardu perdalijo.

— Ko[7] saulužės atsiskyrei?
Aušrinę pamylėjai?
Viens[8] naktį vaikštinėjai?[9]

NOTES:

1) **Mėnuo** 'moon'
2) **vėdė** 'married' (speaking of men)
3) **pavasarėlį**, a diminutive of **pavasaris** 'spring'. Lith. folk songs are full of diminutives.
4) **saulùžė**, dim. of **sáulė**.
5) **mėnùžis**, dim. of **mėnuo**
6) **Perkūns** (abbreviated form of **Perkūnas**): the meaning is 'the Thunder God', although today **perkūnas** simply means 'thunder and lightening'.
7) **Kõ**, here it means: 'why?'
8) **Víens═víenas** 'alone'.
9) Cf. fn. 7 of **Dainuok, Sesyte, The Green Oak**, p. 25.

ŪŽKIT, ŪŽKIT, MANO GIRNAITĖS

Ūžkit[1], ūžkit,
Mano girnaitės!
Dingos,[2] ne viena[3] malu.

Aš viena maliau,
Viena dainavau,[4]
Viena girnužes traukiau.

Ko[5] užsipuolei,
Jaunas bernyti,
Mane — vargų mergužę?

Juk tu žinojai,[6]
Širdies bernyti,[7]
Mane dvare nesėdint:[8]

Iki kelužių
Į purvynaitį,
Ik pažastaičių
Į vandenaitį . . .
Vargios mano dienužės.[9]

1) **Ūžkit** (2nd plur. imperative) 'roar'.
2) **dìngos** (3rd person present) '(it) seems (to)'.
3) **nè vienà** 'not alone'.
4) **dainavaũ** (1st singular past of **dainúoti**) '(I) sang'.
5) **kõ** (here) 'why'.
6) **tù žinójai** 'you knew'.
7) **širdiēs bernýti** 'oh lad of (my) heart'. Note that **bernýti** is in the vocative case.
8) **manè dvarè nesėdint** 'me in the manor house not sitting', i.e. '(you knew that) I wasn't sitting in the manor house'. **manè** 'me' is the direct object of **žinójai** '(you) knew'; **nesėdint** is a special gerund in the present tense.
9) Cf. fn. 7 of **Dainuok, sesyte, The Green Oak**, p. 40.

402

LĖK, VANAGĖLI

Lėk,[1] vanagėli,[2]
Per ežerėlį,
Tame[3] ežerėly
Verpetas sukas.

Pas tą verpetą
Rūtų darželis,
Tame daržely
Verkia mergelė:

Nėr man[4] motušės
Kraiteliui[5] kloti,
Nėr man tėtušio
Dalelei[6] skirti.

Nėr man brolelio
Žirgams[7] balnoti,
Nėr man seselės
Vainikui pinti.

Saulė motušė,
Saulė motušė,
Saulė motušė
Kraiteliui kloti.

Mėnuo tetušis,
Mėnuo tetušis,
Mėnuo tetušis
Dalelei skirti.

Žvaigždė seselė,
Žvaigždė seselė,
Žvaigždė seselė
Vainikui[8] pinti.

Sietynas brolelis,
Sietynas brolelis,
Sietynas brolelis
Lauku[9] lydėti.[10]

1) lėk is the 2nd sing. imperative of lėkti 'to fly'.
2) vanagėli is the vocative of vanagėlis 'hawk'.
3) tamè is the masc. loc. sing. of tàs 'that'.
4) mán is the dat. sing. of àš 'I'. Here mán can be translated as 'for me'.
5) Note that kraitėliui is a dative object of klóti.
6) Note that dalėlei is a dative object of skìrti.
7) Note that žirgáms is a dative object of balnóti.
8) Note that vainìkui is a dative object of pìnti.
9) laukù 'by the field, through the field' is in the instrumental case.
10) Cf. fn. 7 of Dainuok, sesyte, The Green Oak, p. 31.

DAINUOK, SESYTE!

Dainuok,[1] sesyte![2]
Ko[3] nedainuoji?
Ko rymai ant rankelių?
Rankelės užrymuotos!

Kur aš dainuosiu?
Kur linksma būsiu?
Yra darže iškada,
Daržely iškadužė:

Rūtos numintos,
Rožės nuskintos,
Lelijos išblaškytos,
Rasužė nubraukyta!

Ar šiaurys pūtė?
Ar upė patvino?
Ar perkūnas griovė,
Ar žaibais mušė?

403

Ne šiaurys pūtė,[4]
Ne upė patvino,[4]
Perkūns negriaudams
Su žaibais nemušė.

Barzdoti vyrai,[5]
Vyrai iš jūrių,
Prie krašto leidžiant,[6]
Į daržą kopiant,

Rūtas numynė,
Rožes nuskynė,
Lelijas išlakštė,
Rasužę nubraukė.

O ir aš pati
Vos išsilaikiau
Po rūtų pašakėliu,
Po juodu vainikėliu.[7]

1) **dainúok** is the 2nd sing. imperative of **dainúoti** 'to sing'.
2) **sesýte** is the vocative sing. of **sesýtė**, a diminutive of **sesuõ** 'sister'. **Sesýte** = 'sister dear, my dear sister'.
3) **kõ**, the genitive of **kàs**, may mean 'why'.
4) **Nè šiaurỹs pūtė, Nè ùpė patvìno** ' It was not the north-wind which blew, not the river that swelled up'.
5) **Barzdóti výrai** 'bearded men' refers to the Vikings who used to attack Lithuania in 9th - 10th centuries.
6) **leidžiant** special gerund of **leĩsti**. Here it means 'getting off, alighting'.
7) An English translation is to be found in **The Green Oak** by Algirdas Landsbergis and Clark Mills, The Voyages Press, New York (1962), pp. 38-39.

Maironis

SENOVĖS DAINA

Eina garsas nuo pat Vilniaus:[1] žirgą reiks[2] balnoti;
Daug kryžeivių nuo Malburgo rengias mus terioti.
Pasilik,[3] sesute, sveika! Nuramink širdelę!
Gal pargrįšiu nepražuvęs[4] į tėvų šalelę.

Daugel turto pas kryžeivius nuo senos gadynės;[5]
Auksu[6] žiba miestų bonės, šilko pilnos skrynios.
Aš parvešiu[7] sau iš Prūsų plieno kardą kietą,
Tau, sesyte, šilko skarą, diržą auksu lietą.[8]

Jau pavasaris išaušo, gieda vieversėlis, —
Nebegrįžta[9] nuo Malburgo mielas bernužėlis!
Saulė leidos, buvo kova, kraujo daug[10] tekėjo:
Mylimasis už tėvynę galvą ten padėjo.

Mano draugės gieda linksmos[11] ir šilkais[12] dabinas;
Man gi ašaros tik žiba[13] ir kapai vaidinas!
Nekalbėsi, bernužėli, man meilių žodelių,
Neužmausi aukso[14] žiedo[15] ant baltų rankelių.[16]

404

1) **nuõ pàt Vìlniaus** 'from Vilnius itself' (=important rumor!).
2) **reĩks** 'it will be necessary' (abbr. of **reikĕs**).
3) **pasilìk** 'stay, remain'; 2d sing. imperative of **pasilìkti**.
4) **nepražùvęs** 'not having perished'. Negated form of the past active participle, nominative singular masculine of **pražúti**.
5) In translating supply the phrase 'there is' or 'there are'.
6) **áuksu** 'with gold, like gold'. Instrumental singular.
7) **parvĕšiu** 'I shall bring back'. First singular future of **parvèžti**.
8) **dìřžą áuksu líetą** ' a gilded belt, a belt covered with gold'; **líetą** is the accusative singular masculine of the past passive participle of **líeti** (here) 'to forge' and modifies **dìřžą** 'belt'; **áuksu** is in the instrumental singular and is to be translated 'with gold, by means of gold'.
9) **nebegrĩžta** 'does not return'.
10) **kraũjo daũg=daũg kraũjo** 'much blood'.
11) **liñksmos** modifies **draũgĕs**.
12) **šilkaĩs** 'with silks'. Instrumental plural.
13) **mán gi ãšaros tìk žìba** 'my tears only glisten'.
14) **áukso** in the genitive case meaning 'golden, of gold'.
15) **žiẽdo** in the genitive case as the direct object of a negated verb.
16) Cf. fn. 7 of **Dainuok, sesyte, The Green Oak**, p. 69.

V. Mykolaitis-Putinas

RŪPINTOJĖLIS[1]

Dievuli mano, kas per[2] šviesios naktys!
Ir kas plačių padangių per[3] aukštumas!
O žvaigždės, žvaigždės! didelės ir mažos
Taip spindi, net graudu,[4] Dievuli mano.

Išeisiu, sau tariau,[5] ant lygaus kelio:
Ant lygaus kelio tai valia valužė,[6]
Ant lygaus kelio šviesiąją naktužę
Tai tik jaunam plačias dūmas dūmoti.[7]

Bet kam gi[8] tu, budrus Dievuli mano,
Prie lygaus kelio rūpestėliu[9] rymai?
Prie lygaus kelio, kur vargų vargeliai[10]
Vieni[11] per dienas dūsaudami vaikšto.

Dievuli mano, argi mūsų godos
Tave prie kelio iš dangaus atprašė,
Ar gal tos šviesios rudenio naktužės
Tave iš mūsų žemės išsapnavo?[12]

Priimki[13] gi mane, budrus Rūpintojėli,
Prie lygaus kelio šiąnakt padūmoti. —
O kad[14] aukštam danguj tos šviesios žvaigždės
Taip spindi, net graudu, Dievuli mano.[15]

405

1) The **rūpintojėlis** is a wooden sculpture of Christ who is seated and leaning on his elbow. Frequently such figures are located at crossroads in a
tree or on a small pole, or attached to a cross, and they appear to be
looking down at people who pass by.
2) **kàs pe̅r** 'to what an extent, what kind of, how great'. Used with the nominative case it is an idiomatic construction.
3) **kàs...pe̅r**, cf. fn. 2 above. Lit.: 'how great (are) the heights of the wide
spaces under the sky'. For understanding change the word order to: **kàs
pe̅r plačiu̅ padángiu̅ aukštùmas.**
4) **tai̅p spiñdi, nèt graudù** 'it shines so much that it is even sorrowful'.
5) **sáu tariaū** 'I said to myself'.
6) **tai̅ valià valùžė** 'that is freedom, real freedom'.
7) **tai̅ tìk jaunám plačiàs dūmàs dūmóti** 'it is only for the young to dream
broad reveries.'
8) **bèt kám gì** 'but why on earth'.
9) **rūpestėliù** 'in the form of a care'. Instrumental meaning 'as'.
10) **vargu̅ vargēliai** 'misery of miseries'.
11) **vienì** 'alone'.
12) **iššapnāvo** 'dreamed up, created by phantasy'.
13) **priiñki** 'allow'; 2nd sing. imperative of **priiñti** (usually: **priiñk**).
14) **kàd** 'how'.
15) Cf. fn. 7 of **Dainuok, sesyte, The Green Oak**, p. 76.

Jonas Aistis

ŠV. SEBASTIJONAS

Pakeldamas[1] akis aukštyn drebėjau,
Kad nepalaužtų valios man kančia[2]—
Įsmigo štai pirmoji vylyčia,
Ir nerimas, o Viešpatie, praėjo.

Kaip miela[3] — lyg[4] šilti lašai lašėja...
Lyg sąla sąnariai... Kaip gera[5] čia
Man laukt,[6] matyt su šypsena skaisčia
Ateinantį[7] iš tolo Atpirkėją.

Garbė ir šlovė Tau, o Visagali!
Maniau, kad reiks įtempti valią,
Bet štai Tu Pats manęspi ateini[8]...

O kiek šviesos![9] Net man akis gadina[10]...
Švelnaus skambėjimo skliautai pilni[11]...
Tik svyra jau galva, sunki kaip švinas[12]...

1) **pakéldamas** 'lifting'. Special adverbial active participle, cf. 26.4.
2) **kàd nepalāužtu̅ vālios mán kančià** 'that torment might not break my will'.
kančià is the subject of the verb **nepaláužtu̅**; **vālios** is in the genitive case
as the object of the negated verb; **mán** in the dative case is a dative of
interest.

406

3) **kaĩp miёla** 'how fine, nice'; **miёla** is the neuter form of the adjective.
4) **lýg** 'just as if'.
5) **gёra** 'good, nice'; **gёra** is the neuter form of the adjective.
6) **kaĩp miёla . . . kaĩp gёra mán láukt, matýt** 'how fine, how nice it is for me to wait, to see'; **láukt**=**láukti**, **matýt**=**matýti**.
7) **ateĩnantį** 'coming'. Accusative singular masculine of the present active participle of **ateĩti**; modifies **Atpirkёją** 'Redeemer'.
8) **manė̃spi ateinì** 'you come to me'; **manė̃spi** is an old allative case.
9) **kíek šviesõs** 'how luminous' (lit.: 'how much light').
10) **nèt mán akìs gadìna** '(it) even ruins my eyes, it blinds me'; lit.: '(it) ruins to me the eyes'.
11) **švelnaũs skambė̃jimo skliautaĩ pilnì** 'the arches are full of gentle sounding'; **skliautaĩ (yrà) pilnì švelnaũs skambė̃jimo**.
12) Cf. **Dainuok, sesyte**, fn. 7, **The Green Oak**, p. 80.

Kazys Bradūnas

KAD NEBŪTUM VIENA

Nuploviau[1] langą
Prie tavo lopšio,
Kad žvaigždės tekėtų,[2]
Tekėdamos mirgėtų,
Kad nebūtum viena,
Per naktužę viena.

Linguosiu gluosniu[3]
Prie lygaus kelio,
Kad paukštis nutūptų,
Nutūpdams čiulbėtų,
Kad nebūtum viena,
Kelionėje viena.

Kalnan[4] palydėsiu,
Smiltim[5] nubyrėsiu,
Kad vėjelis pustytų,
Pustydamas migdytų,
Kad nebūtum viena,
Žemelėje viena.[6]

1) **nuplóviau** (1st sing. preterit of **nupláuti**) 'I scrubbed'.
2) **Kàd žvaĩgždės tekėtų** 'so that the stars might rise'.
3) **Lingúosiu glúosniu** 'I shall sway in the manner of a willow'; **glúosniu** in the instrumental case denotes 'like, in the manner of a willow'.
4) **Kalnañ** (old illative case of **kálnas**) 'to the hill, up the hill'.
5) **smiltim̃** 'in the manner of, like'. Cf. the use of the instrumental case in **glúosniu** above.
6) Cf. fn. 7 of **Dainuok, sesyte**, **The Green Oak**, p. 97.

VOCABULARY

The number in parentheses following the Lithuanian nouns and adjectives denotes the accent class. For adjectives the feminine form is listed also. For nouns in *-is* the genitive singular is listed. The number in parentheses following the English meaning of the word gives the lesson in which the word appeared for the first time. This number has been omitted for words in the appendix and for common words. The letter A in parentheses shows that the word appears in the anthology.

In the main entry the verbal prefixes are set off by hyphens. Following the infinitive in parentheses are listed (1) the first person singular of the present tense, (2) the third person of the present tense, (3) the third person of the simple preterit and (4) the third person of the future tense.

ABBREVIATIONS

1st — first	poss. — possessive
2nd — second	prep. — preposition
3rd — third	pres. — present
acc. — accusative	pret. — preterit
act. — active	pron. — pronoun
adj. — adjective	prs. — person
adv. — adverb	sg. — singular
compar. — comparative	spec. — special
conj. — conjunction	superl. — superlative
dat. — dative	voc. — vocative
dim. — diminutive	
fem. — feminine	**A**
fut. — future	à, ã (interjection) — oh, ah I see (to
gen. — genitive	express surprise or understanding)
imper. — imperative	abejójimas (1) — doubt (A)
indecl. — indeclinable	abejõnė (2) — doubt (37)
inter. — interrogative	abì (used with fem. nouns) — both
interj. — interjection	(29)
instr. — instrumental	abìpus (prep. with gen.) — on both
loc. — locative	sides of
nom. — nominative	abù (used with masc. nouns) — both
part. — participle	(20)
plur. — plural	ãčiū — thank you (11)

administrãcija (1) — administration (37)

advokãtas (2) — lawyer, attorney-at-law (6)

ahã (interjection) — ah, so

ái and aí (interjection) — oh, alas, dear me (to express pain, fear, surprise)

aimán! (interjection) — unfortunately, what a pity

aíris (2) — Irish person (20)

áiškiai — clearly (21)

áiškinimas (1) — explanation (A)

áiškinti (áiškinu, áiškina, áiškino, áiškins) — to explain (17)

áiškus, -i (3) — clear (21)

Aizkrauklė — Aizkraukle (a village in Latvia)

ajè (interjection) — alas, dear me

àk (interjection) — alas, oh (moan)

akceñtas (2) — accent (22)

akėčios (noun used in plur.; 1) — harrow

akiniaí (noun used in plur.; 3b) — glasses, spectacles (23)

akìs -iẽs (fem.; 4) — eye (17)

akmenìnis, -ė (2) — stone, made of stone (34)

akmuõ, (gen. akmeñs; 3b) — stone

albãnas (2) — Albanian (noun) (20)

alfabètas (2) — alphabet (29)

Algirdas (1) — Algirdas, grand duke of Lithuania (37)

aliuminìnis, -ė (2) — aluminum (adj.)

alùs (4) — beer, ale (3)

amatiniñkas (2) — artisan, craftsman (A)

Amèrika (1) — America (5)

amerikiẽčių (gen. plur. of amerikiẽtis; used as adjective) — American

amerikiẽtis -čio (2) — American (5)

amžinaí — eternally (32)

ámžius (1) — age, century, eternity (23)

anàpus (prep. with gen.) — on the other side of, beyond

anàs, -à (4) — that one (over yonder), cf. 36.1

Anatòlija (1) — Anatolia (39)

ángelas (3a) — angel (15)

ánglas (1) — Englishman (5)

Anglija (1) — England (5)

ángliškas, -a (1) — English (22)

ánglų (gen. plur. of ánglas; used as adjective) — English (5)

anksčiaũ (compar. degree of ankstì) —earlier, before, originally (15)

ankstì — early (23)

anóks, -ia (1) — that kind of, cf. 36.1

anót (prep. with gen.) — according to

añt (prep. with gen.) — on (11)

antaí (interj.) — there (to bring the action closer to the speaker)

añtakis -io (1) — eyebrow (25)

ántis -ies (fem.; 1) — duck (17)

antrãdienis -io (1) — Tuesday (32)

añtras, -à (4) — second, other (15)

antràsis (masc. nom. sg. definite form of añtras) — second (15)

antróji (fem. nom. sg. definite form of añtras) — second (15)

anuõmet — at that time, in those days, then

ap-áugti (apáugu, apáuga, apáugo, apaũgs) — to become overgrown (with)

ap-dainúoti (apdainúoju, apdainúoja, apdainãvo, apdainuõs) — to praise in song (A)

apdairùs, -ì (4) cautious, clever (36)

ap-daužýti (apdaužaũ, apdaũžo, apdaũžė, apdaužỹs) — to damage, to beat

ap-draskýti (apdraskaũ, apdrãsko, apdrãskė, apdraskỹs) — to tear

ap-eíti (apeinù, apeĩna, apėjo, apeĩs) — to circumvent, to go around

ap-gailestáuti (apgailestáuju, apgailestáuja, apgailestãvo, apgailestaũs) — to regret (A)

ap-gaũbti (apgaubiù, apgaũbia, àpgaubė, apgaũbs) — to cover, to wrap up completely

apgáutas (masc. nom. sg. of past passive participle of apgáuti) — deceived (A)

ap-gáuti (apgáunu, apgáuna, apgãvo, apgaũs) — to deceive

apgãvęs (masc. nom. sg. of past active participle of apgáuti) — having deceived

apgavìkas (2) — deceiver, cheater (A)

apgãvo (3rd prs. simple preterit of apgáuti) — deceived

api-beřti (apìberiu, apìberia, apibėrė, apibeřs) — to strew all over, to sprinkle all over

apiẽ (prep. with acc.) — about, concerning, round about, near (15)

ap-ieškóti (apíeškau, apíéško, apieš-
kójo, apieškõs) — to search everywhere, to ransack

apýlinkė (1) — surroundings, area,
district (27)

apýrankė (1) — bracelet (34)

ap-júosti (apjúosiu, apjúosia, apjúosė, apjuõs) — to surround, to encircle (33)

ap-kalbėti (àpkalbu, àpkalba, apkal-
bėjo, apkalbės) — to slander

ap-keliáuti (apkeliáuju, apkeliáuja,
apkeliãvo, apkeliaũs) — to travel
through, around

ap-láistyti (apláistau, apláisto, apláis-
tė, apláistys) — to besprinkle

ap-lankýti (aplankaũ, aplañko, aplañkė, aplankỹs) — to visit (9)

ap-leñkti (aplenkiù, apleñkia, àplen-
kė, apleñks) — to spare, to pass
over (A)

apliñk (prep. with acc.) — around,
all around, along side of (16)

aplinkýbė (1) — circumstance (A)

apliñkinis, -ė (1) — neighboring,
close (A)

apliñkui — cf. apliñk (37)

ap-mókyti (apmókau, apmóko, apmókė, apmókys) — to train (37)

ap-rašýti (aprašaũ, aprãšo, aprãšė,
aprašỹs) — to describe (38)

ap-ródyti (apródau, apródo, apródė,
apródys) — to show everything

apsiaũstas (2) — coat (36)

ap-si-daužýti (apsidaužaũ, apsidaũžo,
apsidaũžė, apsidaužỹs) — to bang
about, to hurt oneself by banging
about on something; to hit each
other slightly while fighting

ap-si-džiaũgti (apsidžiaugiù, apsi-
džiaũgia, apsìdžiaugė, apsidžiaũgs)
— to rejoice (31)

ap-si-ginti (apsìginu, apsìgina, apsi-
gýnė, apsigiñs) — to defend oneself (33)

ap-si-gyvénti (apsigyvenù, apsigyvė-
na, apsigyvėno, apsigyveñs) — to
move in, to take up residence

ap-si-krìkštyti (apsikrìkštiju, apsi-
krìkštija, apsìkrikštijo, apsikrìkš-
tys) — to be baptized, to become a
Christian (A)

ap-si-nakvóti (apsinakvóju, apsinak-
vója, apsinakvójo, apsinakvõs) —
to spend the night, to stay over-
night, to get a place to spend the
night

ap-si-reñgti (apsirengiù, apsireñgia,
apsìrengė, apsireñgs) — to get
dressed (32)

apsùk (prep. with acc.) — around, by

ap-šaũkti (apšaukiù, apšaũkia, àp-
šaukė, apšaũks) — to proclaim; to
call (a person something) (23)

ap-témdyti (aptémdau, aptémdo, ap-
témdė, aptémdys) — to obscure, to
darken (A)

ap-važiúoti (apvažiúoju, apvažiúoja,
apvažiãvo, apvažiuõs) — to travel
around

ap-žiūrėti (apžiūriù, apžiūri, apžiūrėjo, apžiūrės) — to have a look at
(13)

ar̃ — interrogative particle; (conjunction) whether, or (20)

ar̃ nè? — is it not?, cf. 6.3

arbà (conjunction) — or (5)

arbà ... arbà — either ... or

arbatà (2) — tea (2)

arčiáusia (superl. degree of artì) —
closest (27)

ar̃gi — inter. particle ar̃ plus intensive enclitic gi (A)

arkivýskupas (1) — archbishop (A)

arklỹs (3) — horse (3)

armėnas (1) — Armenian (noun) (39)

ármija (1) — army (27)

artì (prep. with gen.) — near, close
by

ar̃timas, -à (3b) — near (35)

ãsmenys (nom. plur. of asmuõ) —
persons (A)

asmuõ, (gen.) asmeñs (irregular
noun, cf. 41.51; 3b) — person

àš — I (1)

ãšara (1) — tear (A)

aštuntãdalis -io (1) — one-eighth (24)

aštuñtas, -à (4) — eighth (29)

aštuonerì, aštúonerios (3a) — eight
(24)

aštúonetas (1) — (a group of) eight
(24)

aštuonì (used with masc. nouns; 3)
— eight (4)

aštúoniasdešimt (indeclinable) —
eighty (24)

aštuoniasdešìmtas, -à (4) — eightieth

aštuoniólika (1) — eighteen (16)

aštuonióliktas, -a (1) — eighteenth
(29)

aštúonios (used with fem. nouns; 3) — eight (4)
at-bė́gti (atbė́gu, atbė́ga, atbė́go, atbė́gs) — to run up, to arrive running (A)
ateĩnantį (masc. acc. sg. of present active participle of ateĩti) — coming, next (32)
at-eĩti (ateinù, ateĩna, atė́jo, ateĩs) — to come, to arrive (6)
ateitìs -iė̃s (fem.; 3b) — future (24)
ati-darýti (atidaraũ, atidãro, atidãrė, atidarýs) — to open (20)
atìdavė (3rd prs. simple preterit of atidúoti) — gave (A)
ati-dė́ti (atìdedu, atìdeda, atidė́jo, atidė́s) — to delay, to put off, to postpone (33)
atidė́tinas (participle of necessity of atidė́ti) — which should be delayed, postponed (33)
ati-dúoti (atidúodu, atidúoda, atìdavė, atiduõs) — to give back, to return; to give (14)
atidžiaĩ — carefully, attentively (36)
atidžiaũ (comparative degree of atidžiaĩ) — more carefully, more attentively (36)
atkakliaĩ — stubbornly, tenaciously (A)
atkópdama (special adverbial active participle of atkópti, cf. 26.4) — climbing up, rising (38)
at-kópti (atkópiu, atkópia, atkópė, atkõps) — to rise, to climb up (38)
atkraštỹs -čio (3b) — land bordering on a coast (35)
atkūrìmas (2) — re-establishment (A)
at-kùrti (àtkuriu, àtkuria, atkū́rė, atkùrs) — to re-establish (A)
atlaidaĩ (noun used in plur.; 3b) — church-festival (A)
Atlántas (1), or Atlánto vandenýnas (1) — Atlantic Ocean (10)
at-léisti (atléidžiu, atléidžia, atléido, atleĩs) — to forgive
at-lìkti (atliekù, atliẽka, atlìko, atlìks) — to complete, to perform, to accomplish (33)
atmintinaĩ — by heart, by memory (18)
at-nèšti (àtnešu, àtneša, àtnešė, atnèš) — to bring (26)
atóstogos (noun used in plur.; 1) — holidays, vacation (19)

atpirkė́jas (1) — redeemer (A)
at-plaũkti (atplaukiù, atplaũkia, àtplaukė, atplaũks) — to arrive (on board ship)
at-prašýti (atprašaũ, atprãšo, atprãšė, atprašỹs) — to ask (to come back, to come to) (A)
atrankà (3b) — selection, choice (A)
at-ràsti (atrandù, atrañda, atrãdo, atràs) — to find, to discover (29)
at-ribóti (atribóju, atribója, atribójo, atribõs) — to separate (35)
at-ródyti (atródau, atródo, atródė, atródys) — to seem, to appear
atródo (3rd prs. present of atródyti) — it seems, it appears (24)
atsãkymas (1) — answer (36)
at-sakýti (atsakaũ, atsãko, atsãkė, atsakỹs) — to answer (6)
at-si-dùrti (atsìduriu, atsìduria, atsidū́rė, atsidùrs) — to be exposed to, to get (into), to run (into)
at-si-gáuti (atsigáunu, atsigáuna, atsigãvo, atsigaũs) — to recover, to recuperate, to rise again (36)
at-si-gérti (atsìgeriu, atsìgeria, atsigė́rė, atsigeřs) — to have a drink, to get a drink (15)
at-si-guĺti (atsìgulu, atsìgula, atsìgulė, atsiguĺs) — to lie down; to go to bed (15)
at-si-kélti (atsìkeliu, atsìkelia, atsìkėlė, atsikeĺs) — to get up, to rise; to move into, to arrive (after moving (36)
at-si-kìšę (masc. nom. plur. of past active participle of atsikìšti) — protruding, protruded
at-si-kìšti (atsìkišu, atsìkiša, atsikìšo, atsikìš) — to stick out, to protrude
atsikráustymas (1) — arrival (35)
at-si-lìkti (atsiliekù, atsiliẽka, atsilìko, atsilìks) — to remain behind, to fall behind, to go more slowly (A)
atsimetìmas (2) — apostasy, falling away from (A)
at-si-miñti (atsìmenu, atsìmena, atsìminė, atsimiñs) — to remember, to keep in mind (21)
atsiprašaũ (1st sg. pres. of atsiprašýti) — excuse me (11)
at-si-prašýti (atsiprašaũ, atsiprãšo, atsiprãšė, atsiprašỹs) — to excuse oneself (11)

at-si-ràsti (atsirandù, atsirañda, atsi-rãdo, atsiràs) — to appear, to be found (A)

atsisãkymas (1) — refusal

at-si-sakýti (atsisakaũ, atsisãko, atsisãkė, atsisakỹs) — to refuse, to turn down; to resign (A)

at-si-sė́sti (atsisė́du, atsisė́da, atsisė́do, atsisė́s) — to sit down, to assume a sitting position

at-si-skìrti (atsìskiriu, atsìskiria, atsiskýrė, atsiskiřs) — to separate oneself from, to depart (39)

at-si-stóti (atsistóju, atsistója, atsistójo, atsistõs) — to stand up, to assume a standing position

at-si-svéikinti (atsisvéikinu, atsisvéikina, atsisvéikino, atsisvéikins) — to take leave of, to say goodby to

atsitìko (3rd prs. simple preterit of atsitìkti) — happened (5)

at-si-tìkti (atsitiñka, atsitìko, atsitìks. Used only in 3rd person) — to happen (5)

àtsiuntė (3rd prs. simple preterit of atsių̃sti) — sent (36)

at-sių̃sti (atsiunčiù, atsiuñčia, àtsiuntė, atsių̃s) — to send (31)

ãtskiras, -à (3b) — separate, single, individual (35)

atstõvas (2) — representative (36)

atvažiã́vęs (masc. nom. sg. of past active participle of atvažiúoti) — arrived (36)

at-važiúoti (atvažiúoju, atvažiúoja, atvažiãvo, atvažiuõs) — to arrive (3)

ãtvejas (1) — case (A)

at-výkti (atvykstù, atvỹksta, atvỹko, atvỹks) — to arrive (26)

ãtviras, -à (3b) — open (26)

at-žélti (àtželiu, àtželia, atžélė, atžéls) — to grow back (A)

áugti (áugu, áuga, áugo, aũgs) — to grow (16)

aukóti (aukóju, aukója, aukójo, aukõs) — to sacrifice (21)

áuksas (3) — gold (15)

auksìnis, -ė (2) — gold, golden, made of gold (13)

aukščiaũ (compar. degree of aukštaĩ) — higher (27)

aukščiaũ (prep. with gen.) — above

aukštaĩ — up, in a high place (38)

áukštas, -à (3) — high, tall (22)

aũkštas (2) — floor (in the sense of level, French étage, German Stockwerk) (20)

aukštèsnis, -ė (comparative degree of áukštas) — higher, taller (25)

aukštỹn — up, upward (A)

aukštóji mokyklà — university, college, institution of higher learning (28)

aukštùmas (2) — height, altitude, highness (23)

ausìs -iẽs (fem.; 4) — ear (17)

aũskaras (3b) — earring (25)

Austrãlija (1) — Australia

aušrìnė (2) — morning (star) (A)

autobùsas (2) — bus (3)

automobìlis (2) — automobile, car (18)

áutorius (1) — author (34)

ą́žuolas (3a) — oak (22)

B

bãdas (4) — hunger, starvation (15)

baĩgti (baigiù, baĩgia, baĩgė, baĩgs) — to finish, to end
(Note that this verb may take an infinitive as a direct object in Lithuanian, whereas in English we would have a participle; thus baigė́ vienyti means 'finished unifying') (14)

báimė (1) — fear

baisùs, -ì (4) — dreadful, terrible (27)

bàkst, bàst (interjection) — denotes the action of piercing something suddenly

balañdis -džio (2) — April (32)

balnóti (balnóju, balnója, balnójo, balnõs) — to saddle (A)

baĩsas (4) — voice (10)

báltas (1) — a Balt, a Baltic person (35)

báltas, -à (3) — white (11)

Bál tija — Baltic (10)

baltiniaĩ (noun used in plural; 3a) — underwear (23)

bañdymas (1) — trial, test (A)

bánkas (1) — bank (5)

bárkšt (interjection) — denotes the idea of rattling, clinking

bárti (barù, bãra, bãrė, bařs) — to scold, to reprimand

barzdà (4) — beard (25)

barzdótas (1) — bearded, with beards (A)

baseĩnas (2) — (swimming) pool (37)

bãtas (2) — shoe (25)

413

baũsti (baudžiù, baũdžia, baũdė, baũs)
— to punish
bažnýčia (1) — church (9)
bè (prep. with gen.) — without; in
addition to (4)
bè — inter. particle, cf. 38.5
bè ábejo — without a doubt (37)
bè tõ — besides; moreover (24)
bégti (bégu, béga, bégo, bégs) — to
run (10)
beĩ (conjunction) — and
beĩsteñgs (3rd prs. future of įsténgti
with prefix be) — will be able to,
would be able to (A)
be-lenktyniáudami (masc. nom. plur.
of special adverbial active participle of lenktyniáuti) — racing, trying to outdo each other (27)
bendraĩ — together, in common (37)
beñdras, -à (4) — common (13)
bendrìnis, -ė (2) — belonging to all,
common (13)
bendrúomenė (1) — community, society (1)
beñt — at least (33)
bernýtis -čio (diminutive of bérnas;
1) — lad, fellow (A)
berniùkas (diminutive of bérnas; 2)
— boy (37)
bernužėlis -io (diminutive of bérnas;
2) — lad, boy (A)
béržas (3) — birch (27)
beržėlis -io (diminutive of béržas; 2)
— little birch (10)
besìkalbant (special gerund of be-si
-kalbėti) — while (someone) is
(was, will be) still talking (26)
besikeičią (masc. nom. plur. of present active participle of be-si-keisti)
— changing (A)
bèt (conjunction) — but (11)
bèt kàs — someone, somebody; anybody; cf. 36.4 (A)
bèt kóks — any; cf. 36.5
bèt kurìs — anyone; cf. 36.5
bètgi (conjunction) — but, however
bevéik — almost (13)
bežiūrint (special gerund of (be)žiū-
rėti) — while (someone) is (was,
will be) still looking (26)
bý kàs — anybody; somebody; cf. 36.4
bibliotekà (2) — library (3)
bičiùlis -io (2) — friend (13)
bijóti (bijaũ, bìjo, bijójo, bijõs) — to
fear, to be afraid of (with gen.)
bìlįetas (1) — ticket (19)

biržėlis -io (2) — June (28)
blakstíena (1) — eyelash (25)
blauzdà (4) — shin (25)
bliñkt (interjection) — expresses the
idea of throwing something
blõgas, -à (4) — bad (5)
bókštas (1) — tower (26)
bonė̃ (3) — spire (A); (bonė̃ is a
Slavic loanword; use bókštas)
Bòstonas (1) — Boston (32)
botãgas (2) — whip, lash (A)
braidýti (braidaũ, braĩdo, braĩdė,
braidýs) — to wade (7)
bràkšt (interjection) — crash, bang
(expresses the idea of something
smashing)
brangióji (fem. nom. sg. definite form
of brangùs) — dear (32)
brangùs, -ì (3) — dear, expensive (8)
brendìmas (2) — ripening; coming to
age (A)
brolēli (voc. sg. of brolēlis) — brother, brother dear (11)
brolēlis (dim. of brólis; 2) — dear
brother, little brother (11)
brólis -io (1) — brother (1)
brúožas (1) — trait, characteristic
(39)
bū́čiau (1st sg. subjunctive present of
bū́ti) — I would be
bučiúoti (bučiúoju, bučiúoja, bučiãvo,
bučiuõs) — to kiss
bū́das (2) — character, manner (16)
bū́davo (frequentative past of bū́ti)
— it used to be, it was (12)
bùdinti (bùdinu, bùdina, bùdino, bù-
dins) — to wake up, to awaken (38)
budrùs, -ì (4) — vigilant, watchful
(A)
bū́dvardis -džio (1) — adjective (35)
bū́k (2nd sg. imper. of bū́ti) — be (11)
bùlvė (1) — potato (26)
bū́rỹs (4) — group, gang, platoon
(36)
burnà (3) — mouth (17)
Burtnieki — a place in Latvia; in
Lithuanian the nom. plur. is Burt-
niekai
bū́simas (future passive participle of
bū́ti) — future (33)
bū́simàsis (masc. nom. sg. definite
form of bū́simas) — future (20)
bùtėlis -io (1) — bottle (3)
bū́ti (esù, yrà, bùvo, bùs) — to be
(5)

414

bùtinas, -à (3a) — indispensable, necessary

bùtinaĩ — absolutely, indeed, certainly, without fail (36)

buvaũ (1st sg. preterit of bùti) — I was (12)

bùvo suprãtę (pluperfect tense of supràsti) — had understood (36)

bùvusios (fem. nom. plur. of past active participle of bùti) — having been (35)

bùvusių (gen. plur. of past active participle of bùti) — having been (35); former (36)

C

cementìnis, -ė (2) — cement, concrete (adj.) (23)

ceñtas (2) — cent (19)

ceñtras (2) — center (3)

Cìceras (1) — Cicero (a suburb of Chicago) (24)

cigarètė (2) — cigarette (16)

cìnkt (interj.) — crash (expresses the sound of breaking)

civilizãcija (1) — civilization (4)

cùkrus (2) — sugar (6)

Č

čèkis -io (2) — check (24)

čežéti (čežù, čėža, čežėjo, čežės) — to chirp, to twitter (25)

čià — here (1)

čiũkšt (interj.) — denotes a sudden action

čiulbéti (čiùlbu, čiùlba, čiulbėjo, čiulbės) — to sing (of a bird) (27)

čiùpt (interj.) — expresses the idea of snatching, grabbing a little bit

čiũpt (interj.) — expresses the idea of grabbing, taking

Čiurliónio Dailės Muziẽjus — Čiurlionis Art Museum (23)

D

dabař — now (5)

dabartìnis, -ė (2) — contemporary, modern, present-day (34)

dabartìs -iẽs (3b) — present time, contemporary time (24)

dabìntis (dabinúosi, dabìnasi, dabìnosi, dabìñsis) — to adorn oneself, to deck oneself out (A)

dáiktas (3) — thing, object (34)

dailė̃ (4) — art (23)

daĩlininkas (1) — artist (38)

dainà (4) — song, folk-song (10)

dainavaũ (1st sg. simple preterit of dainúoti) — I sang (A)

dainúoti (dainúoju, dainúoja, dainãvo, dainuõs) — to sing (6)

dãktaras (3b) — doctor (Ph.D. or M.D.) (6)

dalēlė̃ (diminutive of dalìs; 2) — portion, share (38)

dalỹkas (2) — affair; thing, matter (18)

dalìnti (dalinù, dalìna, dalìno, dalìñs) — to divide (24)

dalìs -iẽs (fem.; 4) — part (35)

dalyváuti (dalyváuju, dalyváuja, dalyvãvo, dalyvaũs) — to participate (A)

dangùs (4) — sky; heaven (6)

dantìs -iẽs (masc.; 4) — tooth (4)

dár — still, yet, even (2)

dár geriaũ — even better (13)

dár kařtą — once more, once again

dár vìs — still (14)

dárbas (3) — work, task, job (12)

darbýmetis -čio (1) — harvest time; working time (24)

darbiniñkas (2) — worker (34)

darbìnis, -ė (2) — work (adjective: clothes, etc.) (13)

darýdavo (3rd prs. frequentative past of darýti) — used to make, cf. 12.4 (6)

darýsiu (1st sg. future of darýti) — I shall do (15)

darýti (daraũ, dãro, dãrė, darỹs) — to do, to make

darýtis (daraũsi, dãrosi, dãrėsi, darỹsis) — to become; to make something for oneself (27)

dařžas (4) — garden, vegetable garden (8)

darželis -io (dim. of dařžas) — little garden (A)

daržóvė (1) — vegetable

daũg (adv. of quantity requiring gen. case) — much, many (3)

daũgel — many (A)

daũgelis -io (1) — many, several, quite a few (36)

daugiaũ (compar. degree of daũg) — more (13)

daugiáusia — mostly, for the most part (34)

daugýbė (1) — multitude, mass (31)

dáuginti (dáuginu, dáugina, dáugino, dáugins) — to multiply (24)

Dauguvà (3b) — river Dauguva (in Latvia) **(35)**

dãvė (3rd prs. simple preterit of **dúoti**) — gave

dãvusiai (fem. dat. sg. of past active participle of **dúoti**) — having given (A)

dažýti (dažaũ, dãžo, dãžė, dažỹs) — to paint (20)

dažnaĩ — frequently, often (8)

dažniaũ (compar. degree of **dažnaĩ**) —more frequently, more often (17)

debesėlis -io (dim. of **debesìs**; 2) — cloud, small cloud (6)

dėdė (2) — uncle (3)

dègti (degù, dẽga, dẽgė, dègs) — to burn (4)

degtùkas (2) — match (16)

dejà (interj.) — unfortunately, what a shame

dėkà (prep. with gen.) — thanks to, owing to

dėkóti (dėkoju, dėkója, dėkójo, dėkõs) — to thank (25)

dėkui Diẽvui — thank God (15)

dėl (prep. with gen.) — for, for the sake of, because of

dėl tõ — therefore (A)

dėlei — cf. **dėl**

délnas (3) — palm (of the hand); cf. kaĩp añt délno (38)

dėmė (4) — spot, blemish (A)

dėmesỹs (3b) — attention (36)

demokrãtiškas, -a — democratic (A)

dẽnis -io (2) — deck (of a ship) (21)

dėrintojas (1) — conciliator, harmonizer (A)

dėstyti (dėstau, dėsto, dėstė, dėstys) — to teach (20); to lay out

dešimčia (instr. sg. of **dešimtìs**) — (divided into) ten (35)

dėšimt — ten (4)

dešiñtas, -à (4) — tenth (29)

dešimtìs -iẽs (fem.; 3b) — ten (35)

dešinė (3b) — right (2)

dešininis, -ė (2) — right (25)

dėti (dedù, dẽda, dėjo, dės) — to place, to put (15)

dėtis (dedúosi, dėdasi, dėjosi, dėsis) — to pretend to be (23)

devynerì, devýnerios (3a) — nine (24)

devýnetas (1) — (group of) nine (24)

devynì (used with masc. nouns; 3) — nine (4)

devýniasdešimt (indecl.) — ninety (24)

devyniasdešiñtas, -à (4) — ninetieth (29)

devyniólika (1) — nineteen (16)

devynióliktas, -a (1) — nineteenth (29)

devýnios (used with fem. nouns; 3) — nine (4)

devintãdalis -io (1) — one-ninth (24)

deviñtas, -à (4) — ninth

dėžùtė (dim. of **dėžė**) — little box (16)

dideliamè (loc. sg. masc. of **dìdelis**) — (in the) large (3)

dìdelis, -ė (3b) — large (1)

didèsnis, -ė (compar. degree of **dìdelis**; 2) — bigger (32)

didìkas (2) — nobleman, noble (36)

didìngas, -a (1) — noble, dignified, majestic, grand (A)

didỹsis kunigáikštis — Grand Duke (27)

didỹsis (masc. nom. sg. of definite form of adjective **dìdelis**) — big (15)

didókas, -a (1) rather large (35)

didùmas (2) — size (19)

didžiaĩ — greatly, much (A)

didžiáusias, -a (superl. degree of **dìdelis**) — the biggest (10)

dìdžiojo (masc. gen. sg. of definite form of **dìdelis**, i.e. **didysis**) — (of the) big (23)

didžiúotis (didžiúojuosi, didžiúojasi, didžiãvosi, didžiuõsis) — to boast, to brag (A)

dienà (4) — day (6)

dienomìs (instr. plur. of **dienà**) — by days, during the days (16)

dienùžė (dim. of **dienà**; 2) — day (A)

Diẽvas (4) — God

dievažì, dievàž (interj.) — as sure as shootin', surely, by gosh (to express certainty)

Dievùlis (dim. of **Diẽvas**; 2) — God (A)

dinãstija (1) — dynasty (37)

dìngos (archaic 3rd prs. present reflexive of **dìngoti**) — it seems, it appears (A)

dìngoti (dìngoju, dìngoja, dìngojo, dìngos) — to think, to consider (A)

diñgti (dingstù, diñgsta, diñgo, diñgs) — to disappear

dìrbti (dìrbu, dìrba, dìrbo, diȓbs) — to work, to do (17)

dirbtìnis, -ė (2) — artificial (13)

dìrstelėti (dìrstelėju, dìrstelėja, dìrstelėjo, dìrstelės) — to glance at, to look briefly at

diȓžas (4) — belt (25)

dóleris -io (1) — dollar (3)

dovanóti (dovanóju, dovanója, dovanójo, dovanõs) — to give as a gift, to present someone with (something)

drabùžis -io (2) — (a piece of) clothing, clothes (24)

dramà (2) — drama, serious play (8)

draũgas (4) — friend (7)

draũgė (4) — (female) friend (A)

draũgiškas, -a (1) — friendly

draugiškèsnis, -ė (compar. degree of draũgiškas; 2) — more friendly, friendlier (27)

drebėti (drebù, drēba, drebėjo, drebės) — to shake, to quiver (25)

drìbt (interj.) — denotes the sound of sudden falling

dróžti (dróžiu, dróžia, dróžė, drõš) — to hit, to slap

druñgnas, -à (4) — bland, mild, lukewarm, tepid (38)

dù (used with masc. nouns) — two (19)

dukrėlė (diminutive of duktė̃; 2) — small daughter, little daughter (34)

duktė̃ -eȓs (3b) — daughter (7)

dūmai (commonly used in plural; 1) — smoke (20)

dūmà (3) — thought, reveries (a Slavic loanword) (A)

dum̃blas (2) — mud (A)

dūmóti (dūmóju, dūmója, dūmójo, dūmõs) — to think, to muse, to reason (A)

dúok (sg. imperative of dúoti) — give (15)

dúona (1) — bread (6)

dúoti (dúodu, dúoda, dãvė, duõs) — to give (7)

dùrys (used only in plur.; 2) — door (20)

dūsauti (dūsauju, dūsauja, dūsavo, dūsaus) — to sigh (A)

Dùsburgas — Peter of Dusburg, Peter von Dusburg (Duisburg) (35)

dušim̃tas, -à (4) — two-hundreth (29)

dvãras (4) — manor house (A); also (land) estate

dvėjetas (1) — (group of) two (24)

dvejì, dvėjos (4) — two (24)

dvì (used with fem. nouns) — two (17)

dvìdešimt (indecl.) — twenty (10)

dvidešim̃tas, -à (4) — twentieth (29)

dvýlika (1) — twelve (16)

dvýliktas, -a (1) — twelfth (29)

dvìratis -čio (1) — bicycle (21)

džiaũgtis (džiaugiúosi, džiaũgiasi, džiaũgėsi, džiaũgsis) — to rejoice (15)

E

ē, è, ě̃ (interj.) — hey (to call, to express surprise)

ēglė (2) — spruce (16)

egzempliŏrius (2) — copy (33)

eìk (2nd sg. imperative of eĩti) — go (7)

eĩkite (2nd plur. imperative of eĩti) — go (15)

eilė̃ (4) — series; line, row (A)

eilùčių (gen. plur. of eilùtė) — lines (38)

eilùtė (2) — suit (of clothes); line (of poetry) (24)

eĩna (3rd prs. present of eĩti) — (he, she) goes (2)

eĩname (1st prs. plur. present (or imper.) of eĩti) — (we) go; let's go (1)

eĩsmas (2) — traffic (36)

eĩti (einù, eĩna, ějo, eĩs) — to go (1)

ėjaũ (1st sg. simple preterit of eĩti) — (I) went (on foot) (12)

elgesỹs (3b) — behaviour (A)

ėmė (3rd prs. simple preterit of im̃ti) — took; began (A)

ėmėsi (3rd prs. simple preterit of im̃tis) — began, undertook (A)

ēsama (neuter form of present passive participle of būti) — there is, there are (A)

ēsamas, -à (present passive participle of būti; 3b) — being, is being (33)

ēsame (1st prs. plur. present of būti) — (we) are

esì apžiūrėjęs (2nd prs. sg. perfect tense of apžiūrėti) — (you) have looked over (13)

èstas (2) — Estonian (35)

esù (1st prs. sg. present of būti) — am (1)

esù bùvęs (1st prs. sg. perfect of būti) — (I) have been (13)

417

esù parãšęs (1st prs. sg. perfect of parašýti) — (I) have written (14)

etimològinis, -ė (1) — etymological (35)

Euròpa (1) — Europe (15)

ẽžeras (3b) — lake (24)

ežerėlis -io (dim. of ẽžeras; 2) — little lake (A)

F

fãbrikas (3b) — factory (19)

fãktas (2) — fact (A)

fìlmas (1) — film; movie (13)

fòrma (1) — form (39)

formaliaĩ — formally (A)

fòtelis -io (1) — armchair, easy chair (15)

frìgas (2) — Phrygian (noun) (39)

G

gãbalas (3b) — piece, chunk, hunk (34)

gabùs, -ì (4) talented, gìfted (6)

gadýnė (1) — era, epoch, age (34)

gadìnti (gadinù, gadìna, gadìno, gadìñs) — to spoil, to ruin, to damage (A)

gaĩla — (it is) too bad, a shame, a pity (9)

gailĕti (gailiù, gaĩli, gailėjo, gailės) — to feel sorry for (29)

gaĩsras (4) — fire, conflagration (5)

gaivìnti (gaivinù, gaivìna, gaivìno, gaiviñs) — to revive, to refresh, to comfort (38)

gál — perhaps (10)

gál iř taĩp — perhaps it is so; it may be so (13)

galándo (3rd prs. simple preterit of galą́sti) — were sharpening, sharpened (A)

gãlas (4) — end (37)

galą́sti (galándu, galánda, galándo, galą̃s) — to sharpen (A)

galĕti (galiù, gãli, galėjo, galės) — to be able, can (4)

galétute (2nd plur. subjunctive of galĕti) — you would be able (31)

galýbė (1) — might, power (A)

gãlima — (it is) possible (7)

galindas (1) — Galindian (noun) (Old Prussian tribe) (35)

galìngas, -a (1) — powerful (27)

galinìñkas (2) — accusative

galûnė (1) — ending (40)

galutinaĩ — finally, for good (37)

galvà (3) — head (19)

gamtà (4) — nature (37)

gamtóvaizdis -zdžio (1) — scenery (A)

gañdras (2) — stork (28)

garbĕ (4) — honor (A)

gárbinti (gárbinu, gárbina, gárbino, gárbins) — to worship (34)

Gaŕdinas — Gardinas, city in Southern Lithuania (35)

gardžiaĩ — heartily (to laugh) (31); gardžiaĩ válgyti — to eat eagerly, tastily

gárlaivis -io (1) — steamship (15)

gaŕsas (4) — rumor, sound (A)

garsĕti (garsĕju, garsĕja, garsĕjo, garsĕs) — to become famous, to become well-known (A)

gaŕsiai — loudly (16)

garsiáusias, -a (superlative degree of garsùs; 1) — the most famous (27)

garsùs, -ì (4) — famous (27)

gãtvė (2) — street (3)

gãtvės (nom. plur. of gãtvė) — streets (3)

gáusi (2nd sg. future of gáuti) — you will get (15)

gáuti (gáunu, gáuna, gãvo, gaũs) — to get, to receive (15)

gãvęs, -usi (past active participle of gáuti; 1) — got, gotten

gãvo (3rd prs. simple preterit of gáuti) — got (36)

gĕda (1) — shame (34)

Gedimináitis -čio (1) — descendant of Gediminas (37)

Gedìminas (2) — Gediminas (1316 - 1341), grand duke (king) of Lithuania (9)

gegužĕ (3b) — May (32)

gėlĕ (4) — flower (19)

geležìnis, -ė (2) — iron, made of iron 13)

geležìnkelis -io (1) — railroad (19)

geltónas, -a (1) — yellow (11)

geltóni (nom. plur. masc. of geltónas) — yellow (14)

gènijus (1) — genius (36)

geogrãfija (1) — geography (31)

gĕra (neuter form of gĕras) — (it is) good (10)

gerà (fem. nom. sg. of gĕras) — good (2)

geraĩ — fine, well, all right (7)

gĕras, -à (4) — good (11)

gérdavo (3rd prs. frequentative past

of gérti) — used to drink, cf 12.4 (6)

gerèsnis, -ė (compar. degree of gĕras; 2) — better (15)

geriaũ (compar. degree of geraĩ) — better (13)

gĕrimas (1) — drink (6)

germãnas (2) — Teuton, member of a Germanic tribe (39)

gerókai — considerably (39)

gérti (geriù, gĕria, gĕrė, geĩs) — to drink (6)

gerùmas (2) — goodness (19)

gérvė (1) — crane (10)

gì — emphatic enclitic particle, cf. 38.5

gýdyti (gýdau, gýdo, gýdė, gýdys) — to cure, to heal (25)

gýdytojas (1) — physician (6)

giedóti (gíedu, gíeda, giedójo, giedõs) — to sing (a hymn) (9)

gilèsnis, -ė (compar. degree of gilùs; 2) — deeper (27)

gilùs, -ì (4) — deep; distant (past) (8)

gimìmas (2) — birth (32)

gimináitis -čio (1) — relative (26)

giminĕ (3b) — relative, close relative (26)

gimtãdienis -io (1) — birthday (A)

gimtàsis, -óji (definite form) — native (12)

gim̃ti (gimstù, gìmsta, gìmė, gim̃s) — to be born (22)

gýnėsi (3rd prs. simple preterit of gìntis) — resisted, defended themselves (16)

giñklas (2) — arms, weapon (A)

giñtaras (3b) — amber (10)

gintarìnis, -ė (2) — amber, made of amber (25)

gìnti (ginù, gìna, gýnė, giñs) — to defend (23)

gìntis (ginúosi, gìnasi, gýnėsi, giñsis) — to defend oneself (16)

girdĕti (girdžiù, giȓdi, girdĕjo, girdĕs) — to hear (17)

gìrna (1) — mill-stone (A)

girnáitės (dim. of gìrnos; used only in plural; 1) — little mill-stones, quern (A)

girnùžės (dim. of gìrnos; used only in plural; 2) — nice little mill-stones, quern (A)

gìrti (giriù, gìria, gýrė, giȓs) — to praise (33)

gìrtinas, -à (participle of necessity of gìrti) — praiseworthy (33)

gìrtis (giriúosi, gìriasi, gýrėsi, giȓsis) — to brag (26)

gývas, -à (3) — alive, living (39)

gyvĕnimas (1) — life (36)

gyvĕnamas (masc. nom. sg. of pres. passive participle of gyvĕnti) — inhabited (35)

gyvĕnti (gyvenù, gyvĕna, gyvĕno, gyveñs) — to live (3)

gyvĕntojas (1) — inhabitant (23)

gyvĕnusieji (masc. nom. plur. of definite form of past active part. of gyvĕnti) — those who lived (A)

gyvulỹs (3a) — animal (13)

gyvúoti (gyvúoju, gyvúoja, gyvãvo, gyvuõs) — to get along, to live, to be (1)

glaũsti (glaudžiù, glaũdžia, glaũdė, glaũs) — to press close to (25)

glìmżt (interj.) — to express the idea of grabbing, grasping

glóstyti (glóstau, glósto, glóstė, glóstys) — to stroke, to pet (25)

glúosnis -io (1) — willow (A)

godà (4) — day-dream, dream, reverie (A)

gòlfas (1) — golf (38)

graĩkas (4) — Greek (person) (10)

gramãtika (1) — grammar (34)

grandìnė (2) — chain (A)

graudùs, -ì (4) — sad, sorrowful (10)

gražèsnis, -ė (compar. degree of gra̧žùs; 2) — more beautiful (27)

gražì (fem. nom. sg. of gražùs) — — beautiful, pretty (4)

gražiaĩ — beautifully (12)

gražiáusias, -a (superl. degree of gra̧žùs) — the most beautiful (27)

grą̧žìnti (grą̧žinù, grą̧žìna, grą̧žìno, grą̧žiñs) — to return (transitive) (31)

gražù (neuter form of gražùs) — beautiful (14)

gražùs, -ì (4) — beautiful, handsome, fine, pretty (6)

grĕbti (grĕbiu, grĕbia, grĕbė, grĕbs) — to rake (26)

greičiaũ (compar. degree of greĩtai) — faster, more rapidly (27)

greičiáusiai — in all probability, most likely; most rapidly (A)

greĩt (cf. greĩtai) — fast (34)

greĩtai — fast, right away, soon (8)

greĩtas, -à (4) speedy, rapid, fast (19)

grėsmė (4) — threat (A)

gretà (prep. with gen.) — side by side, near, by the side of

griáuti (griáunu, griáuna, grióvė, griaũs) — to thunder (6); also: demolish, destroy, tear down

grỹbas (2) — mushroom (28)

grynaĩs pinigaĩs (instr. plur. of grýnas pìnigas) — in cash (24)

grýnas, -à (3) — pure, clear (6)

griñdys (plur. form; 4) — floor (15)

grióvė (3rd prs. preterit of griáuti) — thundered (A)

griovỹs (4) — ditch, moat (33)

griuvėsis -io (2) — ruins, remains

grįžti (grįžtù, grįžta, grįžo, grįš) — to return (intransitive) (A)

grobúoniškas, -a (1) — predatory, rapacious (A)

grõžis -io (2) — beauty (37)

grūdamos (fem. nom. plur. of pres. passive participle of grūsti) — are crushed

grúodis -džio (1) — December (32)

grùpė (2) — group (34)

grūsti (grūdu, grūda, grūdo, grūs)— to knock to pieces, to pound, to drive violently

Gudijà (2) — White Russia (10)

gudruõlis -io (2) — crafty, clever person (A)

gudrùs, -ì (4) — clever, smart (7)

gulėti (guliù, gùli, gulėjo, gulės) — to lie, to be in a lying position (11)

guĺti (gulù, gùla, gùlė, guĺs) — to lie down, to assume a lying position (19)

gumà (4) — rubber; chewing gum (17)

H

hegzãmetras (1) — hexameter (38)

hetìtas (2) — Hittite (noun) (39)

Į

Į (prep. with acc.) — into, at, in (object of motion); (with expression of time) per, a (2)

į dẽšinę — to the right (2)

į svečiùs — as a guest

idant (conj.) — so that, in order that

idealìstinis, -ė (1) — idealistic (A)

įdomèsnis, -ė (compar. degree of įdomùs; 2) — more interesting (27)

įdomùs, -ì (4) — interesting

į-eĩti (įeinù, įeĩna, įėjo, įeĩs) — to go in, to enter (14)

ieškóti (íeškau, íeško, ieškójo, ieškõs) — to hunt for, to search for (16)

ìki (prep. with gen.) — until, till, up to, as far as; (with dative in certain fixed expressions, cf. 37.4)

ìki pasimãtymo — goodby (7)

įkypaĩ (prep. with gen.) — diagonally across

įkùrtas (masc. nom. sg. of past passive part. of įkùrti) — founded

į-kùrti (įkuriu, įkuria, įkūrė, įkuŕs) — to found

įlanka (1) — gulf, bay (35)

ilgaĩ — long, for a long time (4)

ìlgas, -à (3) — long

ilgèsnis, -ė (compar. degree of ìlgas; 2) — longer (27)

ilgiaũ (compar. degree of ilgaĩ) — longer (31)

ilgiáusiai — the longest (time) (37)

ilgiáusias, -a (superl. degree of ìlgas; 1) — the longest (15)

ìlgos (fem. nom. plur. of ìlgas) — long (3)

į-lìpti (įlipu, įlipa, įlipo, įlips) — to get in, to climb in, to climb up (24)

ilìras (2) — Illyrian (noun) (39)

ilsėti (ilsiù, iĺsi, ilsėjo, ilsės) — to rest (19)

ilsėtis (ilsiúosi, iĺsis, ilsėjosi, ilsėsis) — to rest (19)

im̃k (2nd prs. sg. imper. of im̃ti) — take (11)

im̃ti (imù, ìma, ėmė, im̃s) — to take, to pick up; to begin (11)

im̃tis (imúosi, ìmasi, ėmėsi, im̃sis) — to begin, to undertake (A)

ìndas (1) — Indian, inhabitant of India (39)

indoeuropiẽtis -čio (2) Indo-European (35)

indo-iranėnas (1) — Indo-Iranian (noun) (39)

inžiniẽrius (2) — engineer (6)

įnagininkas (1) — instrumental (3)

į-nèšti (įnešu, įneša, įnešė, įnèš) — to bring in, to introduce (into something) (14)

ýpač — especially (33)

ypatýbė (1) — characteristic, quality (A)

ypatìngai — especially (23)

ypatìngas, -a (1) — special; peculiar (9)

į́pėdinis -io (1) — successor (A)

iř — and; too, also (1)

iř taĩp — as it is, even so (22)

iř vìs — and for all this, all the time (32)

yrà (3rd prs. present of bū́ti) — is, there is, there are (1)

yrà jaũ bùvusi (pluperfect of bū́ti) — had already been (15)

į́rašas (1) — inscription (23)

iřgi — also (8)

įsìkerta (3rd prs. pres. of įsikiřsti) — thrusts itself between (35)

į-si-kiřsti (įsìkertu, įsìkerta, įsikiřto, įsikiřs) — to thrust oneself between (35)

į-si-kùrti (įsìkuriu, įsìkuria, įsikū́rė, įsikuřs) — to establish oneself, to settle down (in a place) (35)

į-smìgti (įsmingù, įsmiñga, įsmìgo, įsmìgs) — to strike, to be stuck into, to thrust into (intransitive) (A)

Ispãnija (1) — Spain

į́spūdis -džio (1) — impression (24)

į-sténgti (įsténgiu, įsténgia, įsténgė, įsteñgs) — to be able (A)

istòrija (1) — history (5)

istòrikas (1) — historian (35)

istòrinis, -ė (1) — historical (23)

įstrižaĩ (prep. with gen.) — diagonally across

ìš (prep. with gen.) — out of, from (5)

ìš anàpus (prep. with gen.) — from the other side of (37)

ìš kařto — at once, all at the same time

ìš kuř — from where; how (6)

ìš põ (prep. with gen.) — from under (37)

ìš tikrų̃jų — actually, really (36)

ìš tõ — by this, from this feature (A)

ìš tólo — from a distance (19)

iš-áiškinti (išáiškinu, išáiškina, išáiškino, išáiškins) — to explain (34)

iš-áugti (išáugu, išáuga, išáugo, išaũgs) — to grow (34)

iš-aũšti (išaũšta, išaũšo, išaũš) — to dawn, to break, to come forth (A)

iš-bandýti (išbandaũ, išbañdo, išbañdė, išbandýs) — to test, to try out (25)

iš-bė́gti (išbė́gu, išbė́ga, išbė́go, išbė́gs) — to run out (of) [a place] (37)

iš-dalìnti (išdalinù, išdalìna, išdalìno,

išdalìns) — to distribute, to divide up (among) (A)

iš-drį̃sti (išdrį̃stù, išdrį̃sta, išdrį̃so, išdrį̃s) — to dare, to venture, to attempt (A)

iš-džiū́ti (išdžiū́stu, išdžiū́sta, išdžiū́vo, išdžiū̃s; also: išdžiūvù, išdžiū̃va, išdžiū́vo, išdžiū̃s) — to dry out (A)

iš-eĩti (išeinù, išeĩna, išė̃jo, išeĩs) — to go out (of), to leave (14)

iš-galvóti (išgalvóju, išgalvója, išgalvójo, išgalvõs) — to invent, to think up (A)

iš-gárbinti (išgárbinu, išgárbina, išgárbino, išgárbins) — to glorify, to extoll (A)

iš-giřsti (išgirstù, išgiřsta, išgiřdo, išgiřs) — to hear, to hear about, to perceive, to learn of (16)

iš-gyvénti (išgyvenù, išgyvéna, išgyvéno, išgyveñs) — to live (for a certain length of time) (37)

išilgaĩ (prep. with gen.) — along (37)

iškadà (2) — damage, disaster, ruination (A)

iškadùžė (dim. of iškadà; 2) — damage, disaster, ruination (A)

iškilèsnis, -ė (compar. degree of iškilùs; 2) — higher, more exalted (A)

iškilmė̃ (1) — celebration, festival (A)

iškilmìngas, -a (1) — solemn, festive (A)

iš-kìlti (iškylù, iškỹla, iškìlo, iškìls) — to arise, to come about (A)

iškilùs, -ì (3b) — elevated, exalted, high (A)

iškyšulỹs (34b) — point of land, cape

iš-laikýti (išlaikaũ, išlaĩko, išlaĩkė, išlaikỹs) — to preserve; to withstand (39)

iš-lakštýti (išlakštaũ, išlãkšto, išlãkštė, išlakštỹs) — to tear apart, to cull, to destroy (A)

iš-léisti (išléidžiu, išléidžia, išléido, išleĩs) — to let out; spend; publish (35)

išliẽka (3rd prs. pres. of išlìkti) — remains, remain (A)

iš-lìkti (išliekù, išliẽka, išlìko, išlìks) — to remain, to be saved (with instr.) (36)

iš-lìpti (išlipu, ìšlipa, išlìpo, išlìps) — to get out of, to climb out (14)

iš-miegóti (išmiegù, išmiẽga, išmiegójo, išmiegõs) — to have sufficient sleep, to get enough sleep, to sleep well (26)

iš-mir̃ti (išmirštù, išmìršta, ìšmirė, išmir̃s) — to die out (39)

išmìrusiomis (fem. instr. plur. of past act. part. of **išmir̃ti**) — extinct, having died out (39)

iš-mókyti (išmókau, išmóko, išmókė, išmókys) — to teach (the perfective aspect here implies a favorable result) (22)

iš-mókti (išmókstu, išmóksta, išmóko, išmõks) — to learn (9)

iš-mùšti (ìšmušu, ìšmuša, ìšmušė, išmùš) — to break, to smash (20)

iš-naikìnti (išnaikinù, išnaikìna, išnaikìno, išnaikiñs) — to annihilate, to destroy (35)

iš-nèšti (ìšnešu, ìšneša, ìšnešė, išnèš) — to carry out (14)

išniēkinimas (1) — desecration, dishonoring (A)

iš-nýkti (išnykstù, išnýksta, išnýko, išnýks) — to disappear (15)

į-šókti (į̃šóku, į̃šóka, į̃šóko, į̃šõks) — — to jump into (A)

iš-par-dúoti (išpardúodu, išpardúoda, išpar̃davė, išparduõs) — to sell out (40)

iš-piáuti (išpiáunu, išpiáuna, išpióvė, išpiaũs) — to butcher up (A)

iš-pláuti (išpláunu, išpláuna, išplóvė, išplaũs) — to wash out, to deposit on shore (of seas, lakes, rivers)

iš-plė̃sti (išplečiu, ìšplečia, ìšplėtė, išplė̃s) — to expand, to extend (37)

iš-plė̃šti (išplė̃šiu, ìšplėšia, ìšplėšė, išplė̃š) — to steal, to rob; to tear out (of) (A)

iš-ráuti (išráuju, išráuja, išróvė, išraũs) — to extirpate, to pull out (A)

iš-riñkti (ìšrenku, ìšrenka, išriñko, išriñks) — to elect (23)

iš-sapnúoti (išsapnúoju, išsapnúoja, išsapnãvo, išsapnuõs) — to spend the night dreaming; to dream up, to create by phantasy (A)

iš-si-bùdinti (išsibùdinu, išsibùdina, išsibùdino, išsibùdins) — to wake up, to rouse oneself, to bestir oneself (38)

iš-si-dalìnti (išsidalinù, išsidalìna, išsidalìno, išsidalìns) — to divide up (36)

išsigañdo (3rd prs. simple pret. of iš-sigą̃sti) — got scared, became afraid (15)

iš-si-laikýti (išsilaikaũ, išsilaĩko, išsilaĩkė, išsilaikỹs) — to hold one's own, to stand firm (A)

iš-si-nèšdinti (išsinèšdinu, išsinèšdina, išsinèšdino, išsinèšdins) — to leave, to get out of town

iš-si-pešióti (išsipešióju, išsipešiója, išsipešiójo, išsipešiõs) — to pluck out (one's eyebrows) (25)

iš-si-reñgti (išsirengiù, išsireñgia, išsireñgė, išsireñgs) — to get ready, to set out (37)

iš-si-riñkti (išsìrenku, išsìrenka, išsiriñko, išsiriñks) — to choose for oneself (23)

iš-si-tèpti (išsìtepu, išsìtepa, išsìtepė, išsitèps) — to smear oneself with (A)

iš-si-tiē̃sti (išsitiesiù, išsitiẽsia, išsìtiesė, išsitiẽs) — to stretch (oneself) out (37)

iš-si-výstyti (išsivýstau, išsivýsto, išsivýstė, išsivýstys) — to develop (intransitive) (39)

išskýrus (special gerund of **išskìrti**) — except (29)

iš-skìrti (ìšskiriu, ìšskiria, išskýrė, išskir̃s) — to except, to exclude (35)

iš-skrìsti (ìšskrendu, ìšskrenda, išskrìdo, išskrìs) — to fly out (16)

iš-spausdìnti (išspausdinù, išspausdìna, išspausdìno, išspausdiñs) — to print (38)

iš-sprę́sti (išspréndžiu, išspréndžia, išspréndė, išsprę̃s) — to solve (A)

iš-studijúoti (išstudijúoju, išstudijúoja, išstudijãvo, išstudijuõs) — to study thoroughly (38)

iš-tekė́ti (ìšteku, ìšteka, ištekė́jo, ištekė́s) — to get married (of a woman) (26)

iš-tèpti (ìštepu, ìštepa, ìštepė, ištèps) — to smear completely (A)

iš-terióti (išterióju, išteriója, išteriójo, išteriõs) — to lay waste (35)

iš-tìkti (ištinkù, ištiñka, ištìko, ištìks) — to befall, to overtake (A)

ištìkusio (masc. gen. sg. of past act. part. of **ištìkti**) — which befell, having befallen (A)

ìštisas, -à (3b) — whole, entire (A)

iš-tį́sti (ištį̃stù, ištį̃sta, ištį̃so, ištį̃s) — to stretch, to grow long, to be long (35)

iš-ugdýti (išugdaũ, išùgdo, išùgdė, išugdỹs) — to raise, to nurture, to
develop, to expand (37)

iš-vadìnti (išvadinù, išvadìna, išvadìno, išvadiñs) — to name, to call
(23)

iš-varýti (išvaraũ, išvãro, išvãrė, išvarỹs) — to chase out, away

iš-važiúoti (išvažiúoju, išvažiúoja, išvažiãvo, išvažiuõs) — to depart, to
set off for, to drive out of (23)

iš-veřsti (išverčiù, išveřčia, ìšvertė,
išveřs) — to translate; to knock
down, to tip over, to overturn (38)

iš-vèžti (išvežu, ìšveža, ìšvežė, išvèš)
— to transport away (A)

iš-výkti (išvykstù, išvýksta, išvýko,
išvýks) — to leave (one place for
another place) (29)

iš-viřsti (išvirstù, išviřsta, išviřto, iš-
viřs) — to fall down (A)

iš-vìrti (išvérdu, išvérda, ìšvirė, iš-
viřs) — to cook, to cook up, to
complete cooking

iš-výti (išveju, ìšveja, išvìjo, išvỹs)
— to chase out (A)

itãlikas (1) — speaker of one of the
Italic languages (39)

į-tekėti (įteku, įteka, įtekėjo, įtekės)
— to flow into (15)

į-tem̃pti (įtempiù, įtem̃pia, įtem̃pė,
įtem̃ps) — to tighten, to pull tight
(A)

į-tráukti (įtráukiu, įtráukia, įtráukė,
įtraũks) — to drag into, to draw
into (14)

įvadas (1) — introduction

įvairùs, -ì (4) — various, different
(34)

įvedė (3rd prs. simple pret. of įvèsti)
— introduced, led into (36)

įvedìmas (2) — introduction (A)

įvestà (fem. nom. sg. of past passive
part. of įvèsti) — introduced (A)

į-vèsti (įvedu, įveda, įvedė, įvès) —
to lead into, to introduce to (36)

įvykis -io (1) — event, happening (A)

į-výkti (įvýksta, įvýko, įvýks; used
only in 3rd prs.) — to happen, to
occur, to take place (14)

ìžas (2) — floe; drift-ice (10)

J

ją̃ (fem. acc. sg. pronoun) — her (2)

jái (fem. dat. sg. pronoun) — to her,
her (2)

jám (masc. dat. sg. pronoun) — to
him, him (15)

jamè (masc. loc. sg. pronoun) — in
it, in him (18)

Japònija (1) — Japan

jaũ — already (6)

jaunà (fem. nom. sg. of jáunas) —
young (2)

jáunas, -à (3) — young (6)

jaunèsnis, -ė (compar. degree of jáunas; 2) — younger (27)

jaunìmas (2) — young people, youth
(33)

jaunỹstė (2) — youth (period of
time) (24)

jaũsmas (4) — emotion, feeling (A)

jãvas (4) — grain (28); crop (žiemì-
niai javaĩ — winter crops)

jėgà (4) — strength (37)

jéi (conj.) — if, in the case that (7)

jéigu (conj.) — if, in the case that
(9)

jì — (fem. nom. sg. pronoun) — she
(5)

jì dìrba — she works (2)

jį̃ (masc. acc. sg. pronoun) — him, it
(15)

jiẽ (masc. nom. plur. pron.) — they

jìs (masc. nom. sg. pronoun) — he, it
(5)

jõ (masc. gen. sg. pronoun) — his, of
him, its (7)

jõ nèrà — he is not here (there) (20)

jóg (conj.) — that

Jogáila — Lithuanian grand duke,
Polish king, sometimes known in
English as Yagailo or Jagellon (37)

Jogailáitis -čio (1) — member of the
family of Jogaila (Yagailo, Jagellon)

jojè (fem. loc. sg. pronoun) — in it,
in her (8)

jókio (masc. gen. sg. of jóks) — no,
none (13)

jóks, -ia (3) — no, not one, none; cf.
36.9 (13)

Jõnai (voc. sg. of Jõnas) — John (14)

Jõnas (2) — John (14)

jõs (either fem. nom. plur. or fem.
gen. sg. of pronoun jì) — they;
hers, her, its (10)

josè (fem. loc. plur. of pronoun) —
in them (16)

jótvingis -io (1) — Jatvingian (also
known as Sudovian) (35)

jų̃ (masc. or fem. gen. plur. of pronoun jis) — them, their, theirs, of them (18)

judesỹs (3b) — movement, motion

judḗti (judù, jùda, judḗjo, judḗs) — to move (A)

judrùs, -ì (4) — agile, active (27)

jùk — but, well (27)

jùms (dat. of jūs) — you, to you (18)

junginỹs (3a) — union (A); also: compound; combination

jungtìnis, -ė (2) — united (10)

juõ...tuõ — the (more)... the(more), by whatever amount... by that a-mount (A)

júodas, -à (3) — black (6)

Juodóji jūra — Black Sea (37)

juokáuti (juokáuju, juokáuja, juokã-vo, juokaũs) — to joke (13)

juõktis (juokiúosi, juõkiasi, juõkėsi, juõksis) — to laugh (7)

júos (masc. acc. plur. of pronoun) — them (18)

júosta (1) — belt, sash, ribbon, stripe (10)

jūra (1) — sea (10)

jūrės (poetic form of jūra; only used in plural; 1) — sea (A)

jūsų (gen. of jūs) — your, yours; of you (20)

K

ką̃ (acc. of kàs) — what, whom (20)

kabóti (kabaũ, kãbo, kabójo, kabõs) — to hang (intransitive)

kačiùkas (dim. of katė̃; 2) — kitten (9)

kàd (conj.) — that, so that; since, because; if (15)

kàd iř (conj.) — although

kadà — when (12)

kadà nórs — at some time or other (unspecified, perhaps never) (13)

kadà tìk — whenever (12)

kadángi (conj.) — since, because, as

kaĩ — when, as (12)

kaĩ kàs — some people; some, many a; cf. 36.4 (17)

kaĩ kóks — a few; cf. 36.5

kaĩ kuř — here and there (A)

kaĩ kuriẽ — some, some people; cf. 36.5 (19)

kaĩ kuriẽ iš jūsų — some of you (19)

kaĩ tìk — as soon as (15)

káimas (1) — village (9)

kaimýnas (1) neighbor (12)

kaimýnė (fem.; 1) — neighbor (11)

káina (1) — price (34)

kainúoti (kainúoju, kainúoja, kainã-vo, kainuõs) — to cost (14)

kaĩp — how, as (cf. also tíek)

kaĩp añt délno — as clear as day (38)

kaĩp nórs — somehow or other (38)

kaĩp tìk — except for, save for (A)

kairė̃ (4) — left; į̃ kaĩrę — to the left (2)

kairẽn — to the left (15)

kairùs, -ì (4) left (35)

kaklãraištis -čio (1) necktie (25)

kãklas (4) — neck (25)

kaktà (4) — forehead (25)

kalavijuõtis -čio (2) — a knight of the order of Sword Bearers (1201-1236 in Livonia); also known as Knights Templar, Knights of the Sword (36)

kalbà (4) — language; speech, dis-course (5)

kalbḗti (kalbù, kaĩba, kalbḗjo, kal-bḗs) — to speak, to talk (2)

kalbḗtis (kalbúosi, kaĩbasi, kalbḗjosi, kalbḗsis) — to talk to, to have a conversation with (26)

kalbiniñkas (2) — linguist, specialist in linguistics (35)

kalbìnis, -ė (2) — pertaining to lan-guage, linguistic (39)

kalbótyra (1) — linguistics (32)

Kalḗdos (used in plur.; 2) — Christ-mas (19)

kalḗjimas (1) — jail, prison (20)

kalendõrius (2) — calendar (32)

kálnas (3) — mountain (26)

kalnẽlis (dim. of kálnas; 2) — hill, little hill

kaĩtas, -à (2) — guilty, at fault (29)

kaltė̃ (4) — sin, trespass (21)

kalvà (4) — hill (40)

kám (dat. of kàs) — what good, for what, what do I need... for; for whom, to whom (15)

kambarỹs (3b) — room (11)

kam̃barius (acc. plur. of kambarỹs) — rooms (2)

kãminas (3b) — chimney, funnel, smokestack (21)

kam̃pas (4) — corner (20)

Kanadà (2) — Canada (5)

kančià (4) — pain, torment, agony (A)

kapaĩ (used in plur.; 4) — cemetery, graveyard (A)

karalỹstė (2) — kingdom (36)

karãliškas, -a (1) — royal (36)
karãlius (2) — king (10)
kãras (4) — war (16)
kar̃das (3) — sword (A)
kariáuti (kariáuju, kariáuja, kariãvo, kariaũs) — to be at war with, to fight (37)
kariúomenė (1) — army (37)
karõliai (used in plur.; 2) — necklace (25)
kárštas, -à (3) — hot (20)
kar̃štis -čio (2) — heat, hot weather (37)
kartà (4) — generation (A)
kar̃tą (acc. sg. of kar̃tas) — once, one time (25)
kar̃tais (instr. plur. of kar̃tas) — sometimes (23)
kar̃tas (2) — time, event, occurence (18)
kárti (kariù, kãria, kórė, kar̃s) — to hang (A)
kartóti (kartóju, kartója, kartójo, kartõs) — to repeat (29)
kartù — together (7)
kartù sù — together with (36)
kárvė (1) — cow (19)
karvẽlis -io (2) — dove, pigeon, Columba domestica (20)
kàs — who, what; some people; someone, anyone; cf. 36.2 (1)
kàs diẽną — each day, every day
kàs-nè-kàs — a few, not many; cf. 36.4
kàs nórs — something, something or other; cf. 36.4 (3)
kàs rýtas — every morning (25)
kasdiẽn — every day (25)
kasmẽt — every year, annually (A)
kàsti (kasù, kãsa, kãsė, kàs) — to dig (8)
katẽ (4) — cat (20)
kãtedra (1) — cathedral (9)
katràs, -à (4) — which one of two; cf. 36.2,2
Kaũnas (2) — Kaunas; sometimes known as Kovno in English (23)
kaũpti (kaupiù, kaũpia, kaũpė, kaũps) — to accumulate, to build up (A)
kautỹnės (used in plur.; 2) — battle, fight (36)
kavà (4) — coffee (3)
Kazìmieras (1) — Casimir (32)
kažì, kažìn — who knows, it's hard to say, cf. 38.5

kažìn kas — somebody, something; cf. 36.4
kažkàs — someone, something; cf. 36.4
kažkóks — some, some kind of; cf. 36.5
kažkurìs, -ì (4) — certain, some; cf. 36.5
kėdẽ (4) — chair (15)
keĩstis (keičiúosi, keĩčiasi, keĩtėsi, keĩsis) — to change; to succeed (in power) (37)
keĩtėsi (3rd prs. simple pret. of keĩstis) — changed (37)
kẽlė (3rd prs. simple pret. of kélti) — raised (16)
keleĩvinis, -ė (1) — passenger (23)
keleĩvis -io (2) — traveler (14)
kelerì, -ios (3b) — how many; cf. 36.6
keleriópas, -a (1) — of how many kinds, cf. 36.2,2
kẽlės (3rd prs. simple pret. of kéltis) — rose, got up (A)
kẽletas (1) — a few, several (38)
kelì, kẽlios (used in plur.; 4) — a few, some; cf. 36.6; how many; cf. 36.2,2
kẽlias (4) — way, road (12)
keliasdẽšimt — quite a few (lit.: several tens) (34)
keliáuti (keliáuju, keliáuja, keliãvo, keliaũs) — to travel (6)
kelìñtas, -à (4) — which, what (one); several, some; cf. 36.2,2 (32)
keliólika (1) — several (higher than ten, but less than twenty) (A)
keliõnė (2) — trip, voyage (21)
kelìs (acc. plur. of kelì) — some (14)
kẽlis -io (2) — knee (25)
kélnės (used in plur.; 1) — (pair of) trousers (23)
keĩtas (2) — Celt (39)
kélti (keliù, kẽlia, kẽlė, keĩs) — to raise, to lift up (16)
kéltis (keliúosi, kẽliasi, kẽlėsi, keĩsis) — to get up, to arise, to rise (26)
kelùžis -io (dim. of kẽlias)
keñkti (kenkiù, keñkia, keñkė, keñks) — to harm (with dat.) (17)
kẽpalas (3b) — loaf (15)
ker̃pasi (3rd prs. pres. of kir̃ptis) — get (the hair) cut (17)
Kęstùtis -čio (2) — Kestutis, grand duke of Lithuania (37)
ketìnti (ketinù, ketìna, ketìno, ketìñs) — to intend (27)

keturì (used with masc.; 3b) — four (4)

kėturiasdešimt (indecl.) — forty

keturiasdešim̃tas, -à (4) — fortieth

keturiólika (1) fourteen (16)

keturióliktas, -a (1) — fourteenth (29)

kėturios (used with fem.; 3b) — four (4)

ketverì, kėtverios (3b) — four (24)

kėtvertas (1) — four (24)

ketvirtãdalis -io (1) — one-fourth (24)

ketvirtãdienis -io (1) — Thursday (32)

ketvir̃tas, -à (4) — fourth (29)

ketvir̃tis -čio (2) — one-fourth (24)

kiaušìnis -io (2) — egg

kíek (adv. of quantity requiring gen. — how many; how, to what an extent; somewhat; as much as (17)

kíek laĩko — what time is it (32)

kíek vėliaũ a little later (36)

kiekvíenas, -à (3) — each, every (5)

kiẽmas (4) — yard (16)

kienõ (gen. of kàs) — whose, of whom, by whom (21)

kíetas, -à (3) — hard (A)

kilčių̃ (gen. plur. of kiltìs) — (of) tribes (A)

kilìmas (2) — origin (19)

kilminiñkas (2) — genitive (40)

kilomètras (2) — kilometer (24)

kìlst (interj.) — denotes the action of lifting or raising something

kìlti (kylù, kỹla, kìlo, kiĩs) — to rise (27)

kiltìs -iės (fem.; 4) — tribe (35)

kim̃šti (kemšù, kem̃ša, kim̃šo, kim̃š) —to stuff, to fill up, to cram (19)

kìnas (2) — movies, motion picture (5)

kir̃pti (kerpù, ker̃pa, kir̃po, kir̃ps) — — to cut (with scissors only) (17)

kir̃ptis (kerpúosi, ker̃pasi, kir̃posi, kir̃psis) — to have (something) cut (17)

kir̃stis (kertúosi, ker̃tasi, kir̃tosi, kir̃sis) — to disagree (violently); to fight, to bet, to argue (A)

kišėnė (2) — pocket (24)

kýšoti (kýšoju, kýšoja, kýšojo, kýšos) — to stick out, to protrude (26)

kìšt (interj.) — denotes the action of thrusting out a little bit

kýšt (interj.) — denotes the action of thrusting

kìtą diẽną (acc. sg.) — on the next day (24)

kitaĩp — otherwise, in another manner (18)

kitaĩp sãkant — in other words (24)

kìtas, -à (4) — other, next (10)

kitóks, -ia (1) — another kind of, a different kind of (34)

kitur̃ — elsewhere (32)

Klaĩpėda (1) — the city of Klaipėda, a Lithuanian harbor on the Baltic Sea; the Germans renamed it Memel after the river (35)

klãsė (2) — class (17)

kláusimas (1) — question (20)

klausinėti (klausinėju, klausinėja, klausinėjo, klausinės) — to question, to ask questions (21)

klausýti (klausaũ, klaũso, klaũsė, klaũsys) — to listen (0)

kláusti (kláusiu, kláusia, kláusė, klaũs) — to ask (questions) (6)

klebõnas (2) — pastor (38)

klėvas (4) — maple, maple tree (10)

klýsti (klýstu, klýsta, klýdo, klỹs) — to make a mistake, to err

klýstume (1st plur. subjunctive of klýsti, cf. 31.1 & 31.2) — we would be mistaken, we would make a mistake (A)

klónis -io (1) — valley, dale (38)

klóti (klóju, klója, klójo, klõs) -- to lay out, to spread out; to gather (dowry) (A)

klùbas (2) — hip; club (25)

knygà (2) — book (3)

knygàs (acc. plural of knygà) — books (2)

knygýnas (1) — book-store (11)

kõ (gen. of kàs) — why; of what (15)

kõ nórs (gen. of kàs nórs) — something (3)

koalìcija (1) — coalition (A)

kodėl — why (20)

kõgi (gen. of kàs gì) — what, whom; of what, of whom (20)

kója (1) — leg; foot (25)

kójinė (1) — sock, stocking (25)

kóks, kokià (3) — what, what kind of; some; cf. 36.2,2 (1)

kóks nórs — some, some kind of; cf. 36.5

kõl — until

Kolùmbas (1) — Columbus (32)
komèdija (1) — comedy (8)
koncèrtas (1) — concert (9)
kopà (2) — dune (21)
kópiant (spec. gerund of kópti) — climbing (A)
kópti (kópiu, kópia, kópė, kõps) — to climb (A)
kortėlė (2) — little card, sticker (24)
kostiùmas (2) — suit, clothes (37)
kovà (4) — battle, struggle, fight (A)
kóvas (1) — March (32)
kovóti (kovóju, kovója, kovójo, kovõs) — to fight (37)
kraĩgas (4) — roof top (20)
kraitėlis -io (dim. of kraĩtis; 2) — dowry (A)
kramtýti (kramtaũ, kram̃to, kram̃tė, kramtýs) — to chew (17)
kranksėti (kránksiu, kránksi, kranksėjo, kranksės) — to cackle, to caw (16)
krañtas (4) — bank, shore (22)
krãštas (4) — country; edge, border, shore
kraũjas (4) — blood (35)
krautùvė (2) — store (28)
kreĩpti (kreipiù, kreĩpia, kreĩpė, kreĩps) — to turn, to direct (36)
kreĩpti dėmesį — to pay attention (36)
krikščionýbė (1) — Christianity (A)
krikščiónis, -ė (1) — Christian (noun)
krikščióniškas, -a (1) — Christian (adjective) (A)
krìkštas (4) — baptism, christening (36)
krìkštytis (krìkštijuosi, krìkštijasi, krìkštijosi, krìkštysis) — to be baptized (A)
kryptìs -iẽs (fem.; 4) — direction, bent (4)
krìsti (krentù, kreñta, krìto, krìs) — to fall (19)
Kristijõnas — Christian (proper name) (38)
Krìstus (2) — Christ (39)
kryžeĩvis -io (2) — Teutonic knight (A)
kryžiuõtis -čio (2) — Teutonic knight (36)
krósnis -ies (fem.; 1) — oven (4)
krūmas (1) — shrub, bush, thicket (38)
kruopėlė (2) — little flake; little pill (25)

krūtìnė (2) — chest (25)
kūdikis -io (1) — baby (A)
Kùlmas (1) — Culmerland, today the city of Kulm (Polish Chełmno) on the right bank of the Vistula (35)
kulnėlis -io (2) — ankle (25)
kultūrà (2) — culture (4)
kūnas (1) — body, human body (25)
kunigaikštijà (2) — dukedom, principality (37)
kunigáikštis -čio (1) — duke, prince (15)
kùnigas (3b) — priest (19)
kuõ (instr. of kàs) — with what, by means of what (17)
kuomèt — when (23)
kúopa (1) — company (of soldiers) (23)
kúopinis, -ė (1) — collective (35)
kupė̃ (4) — coupé, train compartment (24)
kuř — where (1)
kuř čià — how on earth (38); also: where (is) here . . .
kuř nórs — somewhere, some place, anywhere, some place or other (37)
kurį̃ (masc. acc. sg. of kurìs) — which (18)
kuriaĩs mẽtais — which year, in which year (36)
kuriamè (masc. loc. sg. of kurìs) — in which (5)
kūrìmasis (noun with reflexive particle added) — creation (A)
kūrinỹs (3a) — creation; work (38)
kuriõs (fem. nom. plur. and fem. gen. sg. of kurìs) — which, who (16)
kurìs, kurì (4) — which, who; cf. 21.6 and 36.2,2 (5)
kurìs-ne-kurìs — certain, some; cf. 36.5
kurìs nórs — some; cf. 36.5
kuriuõ (masc. instr. sg. of kurìs) — along which, by which (12)
kuròrtas (1) — spa, health resort (21)
kuřšis -io (2) — Curonian (35)
kuršiškùmas (2) — Curonian character, 'Curonianness' (35)
Kuřšių Neringà (3b) — Curonian isthmus (a narrow isthmus on the Baltic Sea)
Kuřžemė (1) — Curland (35)
kvailaĩ — stupidly, foolishly (A)
kvaĩlas, -à (4) — foolish, stupid (A)
kvailèsnis, -ė (comparative degree of

kvaĩlas; 2) — more foolish, more stupid (A)
kvailỹs (4) — fool (23)
kvailùtis -čio (dim. of kvailỹs; 2) — fool (A)
kvepéti (kvepiù, kvẽpia, kvepéjo, kvepės) — to smell (good); to emit fragrance (34)
kviẽsti (kviečiù, kviẽčia, kviẽtė, kviẽs) — to call, to invite (20)
kviẽstis (kviečiúosi, kviẽčiasi, kviẽtėsi, kviẽsis) — to invite (for one's own benefit) (A)

L

labà dienà — hello, good day (22)
labaĩ — very, very much (2)
lãbas — a greeting similar to English 'hello' (13)
lãbas, -à (4) — good (13)
labiaũ (compar. degree of labaĩ) — more (27)
lãbiáusiai (superl. degree of labaĩ) — most of all, the most (27)
lagamìnas (2) — suitcase (24)
laĩ — may one, let one, cf. 38.5
laikaĩs (instr. plur. of laĩkas) — in the time of, during the time of (35)
laĩkas (4) — time; tense (of verbs) (8)
laikýti (laikaũ, laĩko, laĩkė, laikỹs) — to hold; to consider ... as; to maintain (25)
laikýtinas, -a (1) — retained; one (or something) which should be considered (as), or kept (35)
laikýtis (laikaũsi, laĩkosi, laĩkėsi, laikỹsis) — to get along (A)
laĩko (3rd prs. pres. of laikýti) — holds; considers (as) (A)
laĩkoma (neuter pres. passive part. of laikýti) — (it is) considered (A)
laĩkomas, -a (pres. passive part. of laikýti) — is considered as (35)
laĩkosi (3rd prs. pres. of laikýtis) — is getting along (A)
laikótarpis -io (1) — era (38)
laĩkraštį (acc. sg. of laĩkraštis) — newspaper (2)
laĩkraštis -čio (1) — newspaper (17)
laĩkrodininkas (1) — watchmaker (32)
laĩkrodis -džio (1) — clock, watch (13)
laĩkui bėgant — in the course of time (39)

láimė (1) — good fortune, good luck; it is lucky (10)
laimėjimas (1) — victory (37)
laiméti (laimiù, laĩmi, laimėjo, laimės) — to win (37)
laimìngai — happily, luckily, good luck (ii)
laimìngas, -a (1) — happy, fortunate, lucky (15)
laimìngi (masc. nom. plur. of laimìngas) — happy (2)
laimìngos keliõnės (gen. sg.) — bon voyage, have a good trip (27)
láipsnis -io (1) — degree (26)
láistyti (láistau, láisto, láistė, láistys) — to pour water on, to water (29)
láisvė (1) — freedom (23)
Láisvės Vařpas — Liberty Bell (23)
láišką (acc. sg. of láiškas) — letter (2)
láiškas (3) — letter (8)
laĩvas (4) — ship, vessel (21)
lángas (3) — window (11)
lãpas (2) — leaf (of a tree); sheet (of paper) (14)
lãpkritis -čio (1) — November (32)
lãšas (4) — drop (A)
lašéti (lašù, lãša, lašėjo, lašės) — to drip, to drop, to trickle (A)
lašiniaĩ (used in plur.; 3b) — bacon (23)
Lãtgala (1) — Latgal, Latgalia, Latgale (35)
Lãtvija (1) — Latvia (10)
lãtvis -io (2) — Latvian (person) (35)
laukañ — outside (as the object of motion), cf. 38.6
laũkas (4) — field (14)
laukè (loc. sg. of laũkas) — outside, outdoors (6)
láukti (láukiu, láukia, láukė, laũks) — to wait for, to await (14)
lazdà (4) — stick (7)
lẽdas (4) — ice (34)
léidžiant (spec. gerund of léisti) — descending, alighting (A)
léiskite (2nd prs. plur. imper. of léisti) — allow (7)
léisti (léidžiu, léidžia, léido, leĩs) — to allow (7)
léistis (léidžiuos(i), léidžias(i), léidosi, leĩsis) — to set (of the sun) (A)
lẽk (2nd sg. imper. of lẽkti) — fly (A)
lẽkštė (2) — plate, dish (12)
lẽkti (lekiù, lẽkia, lẽkė, lẽks) — to fly (A)

lėktùvas (2) — airplane (28)
lelijà (2) — lily (A)
lémpa (1) — lamp (8)
lempùtė (2) — (electric) bulb (15)
lēmiamas, -à (3b) — decisive (37)
lengvaĩ — easily
leñgvas, -à (4) — easy, light (21)
lengviaũ (compar. degree of lengvaĩ)
— more easily (A)
lénkas (1) — Pole, Polish person (35)
Lénkija (1) — Poland (10)
leñkti (lenkiù, leñkia, leñkė leñks) —
— to bend (7)
lenktyniáuti (lenktyniáuju, lenkty-
niáuja, lenktyniãvo, lenktyniaũs)—
to race, to compete (27)
lenktìnis, -ė (2) — bent, bending;
folding (13)
leñktis (lenkiúosi, leñkiasi, leñkėsi,
leñksis) — to bow, to bend (7)
lentà (4) — blackboard, board (17)
lentýna (1) — shelf (33)
lèpt (interj.) — denotes the action of
falling
lýbis -io (1) — Livonian (Finno-Ugric
people who lived near Riga; hence
the name Livland, Livonia) (35)
lydéti (lydžiù, lýdi, lydėjo, lydės) —
to accompany (23)
liēkana (1) remnant, remains (35)
Lielupe — river which is called Lielupe in Latvia but Mūšà in Lithuania (35)
líepa (1) — linden tree; July (10)
liēpti (liepiù, liēpia, liēpė, liēps) —
to order (A)
liēsti (liečiù, liēčia, liētė, liēs) — to
touch (15)
liēti (liejù, liēja, liējo, liēs) — to
pour; to forge (A)
lietìngas, -a (1) — rainy (28)
lietùs (3) — rain (6)
Lietuvà (3a) — Lithuania (23)
lietuváitė (1) — Lithuanian girl (10)
lietùvis -io (2) — Lithuanian (noun)
(6)
lietùviškai — in the Lithuanian (language); in the Lithuanian manner
lietùviškas, -a (1) — Lithuanian (adjective) (35)
lietùvių (gen. plur. of lietùvis) — used
in places where in English we
would use the adjective Lithuanian
(22)
Lietuvõs (gen. sg. of Lietuvà) —
Lithuania's, of Lithuania (3)
lìg — cf. ligi

lýg — like, similar to; as if (10)
lýg ir — apparently, just as if (A)
ligà (4) — illness, sickness (25)
lìgi (prep. with gen.) — till, until;
to, up to, as far as (12)
lygiagrečiaĩ — in a parallel manner,
likewise, similarly (A)
lyginamàsis, -óji — comparative (39)
ligónė (1) — sick woman, patient (25)
ligóninė (1) — hospital (19)
ligónis (1) — sick man, patient (19)
ligšiõl — up to now (21)
ligšiolìnis, -ė (2) — up to the present
(A)
lýgus, -i (3) — even, level, smooth;
equal to (sù) (37)
likìmas (2) — fate (A)
lìkti (liekù, liēka, lìko, lìks) — to
remain (16)
lìkusią (fem. acc. sg. of past act. participle of lìkti) — having remained,
remaining (36)
lingúoti (lingúoju, lingúoja, lingãvo,
linguõs) — to rock, to sway (A)
lìnija (1) — line (35)
liñk (prep. or postposition with gen.)
— to, towards, in the direction of
linkéjimas (1) — wish, greetings, regards
linkéti (linkiù, liñki, linkéjo, linkés)
— to wish (good luck, good fortune, etc.) (13)
liñksmas, -à (4) — gay, happy, cheerful (27)
linksmiáusias, -a (superl. degree of
liñksmas; 1) — the gayest, most
cheerful (27)
linksmýbė (1) — joy (38)
liñkti (linkstù, liñksta, liñko, liñks)
— to bend, to bow down (intransitive) (10)
liñkui — cf. link
lìpti (lipù, lìpa, lìpo, lìps) — to climb
(37)
lìtas (2) — lit (monetary unit of independent Lithuania) (19)
lýti (lýja, lìjo, lìs) — to rain (16)
lytìs -iēs (fem.; 4) — form (39); also
sex
Liùblino ùnija — Union of Lublin (A)
liūdesỹs (3b) — sadness, mourning
(10)
liùdijimas (1) — testimony; certifi-
cate; card; (driver's license) (35)
liùdyti (liùdiju, liùdija, liùdijo, liùdys)
— to bear witness, to witness (A)
liùdytojas (1) — witness (A)

liūtas (2) — lion

liuterõnas (2) — Lutheran (noun) (37)

lìzdas (4) — nest (16)

lopšỹs (3) — cradle (A)

lotỹnas (2) — Latin (noun) (39)

lotỹniškas, -a (1) — Latin (adj.)

lóva (1) — bed (26)

Liubãvas (2) — Löbau (Polish Lubów, Lubowo) (35)

lùbos (used in plur.; 4) — ceiling (15)

lúomas (1) — rank, class (A)

M

mačiaũ (1st sg. simple preterit of matýti) — I saw (12)

mãčiusi (fem. nom. sg. of past active part. of matýti) — seen (26)

maĩšas (4) — bag, sack (19)

maišýtis (maišaũsi, maĩšosi, maĩšėsi, maišỹsis) — to get mixed up; to be mixed together (??)

Malbùrgas (1) — Marienburg (A)

maliaũ (1st sg. simple preterit of málti) — I ground (A)

malõniai — pleasantly, nicely, good (12)

malonù — pleased (to make your acquaintance); said when one is introduced to someone (7)

malonùs, -ì (4) — nice, pleasant

málti (malù, mãla, mãlė, maĩs) — to grind, to mill (A)

mamà (2) — mama (5)

mán (dat. of àš) — me, to me, for me (7)

mán daugiaũ patiñka — I like better (lit.: it pleases me more) (13)

mán jõ reĩkia — I need it (lit.: it is necessary to me) (11)

mán nereikě̃s — I won't have to (9)

mán patiñka — I like (3)

manè (acc. of àš) — me (11)

manę̃s (gen. of àš) — me (11)

manę̃spi (allative of àš) — to me, to a place near me (A)

manýti (manaũ, mãno, mãnė, manỹs) — to think, to believe, to mean (7)

màno (poss. pron. or adj.) — my; mine; by me (1)

márgis -io (1) animal with variegated colors; frequently used as a dog's name (6)

marškiniaĩ (used in plural; 3a) — shirt (23)

martì, marčiõs (4) — daughter-in-law (3)

Maskvà (4) — Moscow (37)

mašinà (2) — machine (33)

màt (mataĩ) — to be sure, indeed; because, since; let one, may one (36)

mateĩ (2nd sg. simple preterit of matýti) — you saw (16)

matýt (abbreviation of matýti) — apparently, seemingly (16)

matýti (mataũ, mãto, mãtė, matỹs) — to see; apparently, seemingly (7)

mãtosi — it is visible, it can be seen (7)

máudymas (1) — swimming (7)

máudymosi (gen. sg. of máudymas plus reflexive particle -si) — of swimming, swimming (with adj. meaning) (37)

máudytis (máudausi, máudosi, máudėsi, máudysis) — to bathe, to go for a swim (7)

mãža — few (neuter adjective) (19)

mažaĩ — few (adverb)

mãžas, -à (4) — little, small (7)

maždaũg — approximately, more or less (22)

mažiaũ (compar. degree of mažaĩ) — fewer, less (A)

mažnè — almost, nearly (35)

Mažóji Lietuvà — Lithuania Minor (38)

medicinà (2) — medicine (5)

medìnis, -ė (2) — wooden (13)

mẽdis -džio (2) — tree (8)

medùs (4) — honey (6)

mė́gti (mė́gstu, mė́gsta, mė́go, mė́gs) — to like (6)

méilė (1) — love (15)

Mèksika (1) — Mexico (10)

mėlynaĩ (adv.) — blue, a blue color (20)

mė́lynas, -a (1) — blue (11)

meĩstis (meldžiúosi, meĩdžiasi, meĩdėsi, meĩsis) — to pray (9)

mė́nesį (acc. sg. of mė́nuo) — month (22)

meniù (indecl.) — menu (15)

mėnùlis -io (2) — moon (9)

mė́nuo, mė́nesio (1) — month; cf. 7.1, 41.5,3; moon (22)

mėnùžis -io (dim. of mė́nuo; 2) — (little) moon (A)

mergáitė (1) — girl (2)

mergė̃lė (2) — maid, maiden, girl (A)

mergùžė (dim. of mergà) — maid, maiden, girl (A)

mēs (1st plur. prs. pron.) — we (5)

mēs sù bróliu — my brother and I (27)

mėsà (4) — meat (17)

mèsti (metù, mēta, mētė, mès) — to throw (9)

mētai (used in plur.; 2) — year

Mētai — Donelaitis' famous poem, "The Seasons" (38)

mētas (2) — time, span of time (23)

mētė (3rd prs. simple preterit of mèsti) — threw (A)

metù (instr. sg. of mētas) — in the time of (37)

mētų (gen. plur. of mētas) — of years, years' (2)

midùs (4) — mead (a sweet drink made from honey) (6)

miēgamas, -à (pres. passive part. of miegóti) — sleeping (33)

miēgas (4) — sleep (15)

miegóti (miegù, miēga, miegójo, miegōs) — to sleep (9)

mielaĩ — with pleasure, gladly, willingly (9)

míelas, -à (3) — dear; kind, nice (14)

miēstas (2) — city (10)

miestè (loc. sg. of miēstas) — in the city (3)

miestēlis -io (2) small town (15)

migdýti (migdaũ, mìgdo, mìgdė, migdỹs) — to put to sleep, to lull to sleep (A)

Milãnas (2) — Milan (31)

mylėti (mýliu, mýli, mylėjo, mylēs) — to love (18)

mylià (2) — mile (24)

milijárdas (1) — billion (24)

milijõnas (2) — million (24)

mylimàsis, -óji (definite form of past passive part. of mylėti) — beloved one, dear person (A)

mýlime (1st plur. pres. of mylėti) — we love (2)

mylįs (masc. nom. sg. of pres. act. part. of mylėti) — loving (31)

Mìndaugas (1) — Mindaugas (ca. 1200-1253), king of Lithuania; also known in English as Mindovg (10)

minėti (miniù, mìni, minėjo, minēs) — to mention; to commemorate, to celebrate (33)

minėtinas, -a (part. of necessity of minėti) — worthy of mention (33)

minià (4) — crowd (A)

mìnimas, -à (pres. passive part. of minėti) — mentioned, being mentioned (A)

mìnint (spec. gerund of minėti) — commemorating, celebrating (A)

mìnkštas, -à (3) — soft (27)

mintìs -iēs (fem.; 4) — thought, idea (A)

mìnus — minus (24)

minùtė (2) — minute (11)

mirgėti (mìrgu, mìrga, mirgėjo, mirgēs) — to twinkle (A)

mir̃siu (1st sg. future of mir̃ti) — I shall die (15)

mir̃ti (mirštù, mìršta, mìrė, mir̃s) — to die (of human beings or bees) (10)

mirtìs -iēs (4) — death; deadlock (A)

mìsija (1) — mission (A)

mìškas (4) — forest, woods (12)

modernùs, -ì (4) — modern (22)

mókestis -čio (1) — tax (24)

mokėti (móku, móka, mokėjo, mokēs) — to know, to understand, to have a skill in; to pay (9)

mokyklà (2) — school (20)

mokỹklą (acc. sg. of mokyklà) — school (2)

mokinė (3a) — pupil (fem.) (2)

mokinỹs (3a) — pupil (masc.) (20)

mókyti (mókau, móko, mókė, mókys) — to teach (22)

mókytis (mókausi, mókosi, mókėsi, mókysis) — to study, to learn (14)

mókytoja (1) — teacher (fem.) (17)

mókytojas (1) — teacher (masc.) (1)

mókslininkas (1) — scientist (34)

morālinis, -ė (1) moral (A)

móteris -ies (fem.; 1) — woman (18)

mótina (1) — mother (2)

motùšė (dim. of mótina; 2) — mama, dear mother (A)

mozūras (2) — Mazur, Mazovian (a Polish tribe) (35)

mumìs (instr. of mēs) — us (19)

mùms (dat. of mēs) — us, to us, for us (8)

mūrìnis, -ė (2) — brick; stone (house) (13)

mùs (acc. of mēs) — us (14)

mùsė (2) — fly (34)

mūsų (gen. of mēs) — us; our, ours (11)

Mūšà (4) — a river which is called Mūšà in Lithuania, but Lielupe in Latvia

mūšis -io (2) — battle (37)
mùšti (mušù, mùša, mùšė, mùš) — to hit, to beat (32)
muziėjus (2) — museum (23)

N

nà (interj.) — well, there, now (encouragement, threat, surprise, displeasure)
nãgas (4) nail (25)
naikìnamas, -a (pres. passive part. of naikìnti) — destroyed, abolished (A)
naikìnti (naikinù, naikìna, naikìno, naikiñs) — to destroy, to abolish (A)
nãktį (acc. sg. of naktìs) — at night, during the night (9)
naktìbalda (1) — one who roves about at night (3)
naktìs -iẽs (fem.; 4) — night (8)
naktùžė (dim. of naktìs; ?) — night (A)
nãmas (4) — house; the plural form of this word is used with the singular meaning also; thus namaĩ can be translated house too; namaĩ also means 'home'
namẽlis (dim. of nãmas; 2) — little house, hut (A)
namiẽ — at home (2)
namìnis -ė (2) — domestic (13)
namìškis -io (2) — member of the household, inhabitant of the house, the home
namõ — home, homeward (directional meaning) (1)
Nãrevas (1) — Narew, a tributary of the river Bug in Poland (35)
narỹs (4) — member (39)
narsùs, -ì (4) — brave, courageous, bold (36)
naštà (4) — burden (33)
natūralùs, -ì (4) natural (A)
naudiniñkas (2) — dative (3)
naudóti (naudóju, naudója, naudójo, naudõs) — to make use of (A)
naujà (fem. nom. sg. of naũjas) — new (4)
naũjas, -à (4) — new (11)
naujíena (1) — news, piece of news (A)
nè — not; no; it may be used as a prefix to negate the meaning of the word to which it is prefixed; sometimes it may be translated by non-;

in looking for words in the vocabulary remove the ne- and hunt for the word under its stem form; if the verb is reflexive it will be necessary to remove the -si- also.
nè betkàs — not everyone, not everybody (A)
nè tìk ... bèt taĩp pàt — not only ... but also (28)
ne-ap-kẹsti (neapkenčiù, neapkeñčia, neàpkentė, neapkẹs) — to hate
neatsigãvo (negated 3rd prs. sg. simple preterit of atsigáuti) — did not recover (36)
nebenorẽsiu (negated 3rd prs. sg. future of norẽti) — I shall never want, I shall want no more (15)
nebeñt — except that, save that (38)
nebepakeĩčiamas, -à (negated pres. passive part. of pakeĩsti; 3) — no longer changeable, which no longer can be changed (A)
nebūtum (negated 2nd sg. subjunctive of bū́ti) — you may not be, you might not be (A)
nebuvaũ mãtẹs — I had not seen
nebùvo mãtẹ — they had not seen
nedìdelis, -ė (3b) — small (10)
negãli bū́ti — it can't be (25)
negaliù (negated 1st prs. sg. pres. of galẽti) — I cannot (4)
negù — than
néi — than (35)
neĩ ... neĩ — neither ... nor (13)
neįmãnoma (neuter of neįmãnomas) — it is inconceivable, it is unthinkable (38)
neįmãnomas, -a (1) — inconceivable; unthinkable (38)
neįsténgiama (negated neuter pres. passive part. of įsténgti) — it is not possible (27)
nekaĩp — than; not too well (27)
nekóks, -ià (3) — rather poor, bad; cf. 36.5
neláisvė (1) — captivity, slavery (A)
neléidžiamas, -à (negated pres. passive part. of léisti) — is not permitted (A)
neleñgva — it is not easy
Nẽmunas (3b) — a river in Lithuania, also known (in other languages) as Niemen or Memel (9)
nenúorama (1) — mischief-maker; unruly child (3)
nepadãro (3rd prs. pres. of padarýti)

— does not make; is unable to make; note the use of the perfective aspect to denote a general truth in **Pasaka apie l. u.**
ne-pagýdomas, -a (negated pres. passive part. of pagýdyti) — incurable
nepakañkamai — insufficiently (A)
nepriklaũsomas, -a (1) — independent
nepriklausomýbė (1) — independence (31)
nepriklausomùmas (2) — independence (A)
nĕr — shortening of nėrà; cf. nėra (A)
nėrà (contraction of ne plus yra) — is not, are not; there is not, there are not (2)
nereikĕdavo (negated 3rd prs. freq. past of reikĕti) — it did not used to be necessary, it was not necessary (12)
nėrimas (1) — anxiety, uneasiness (A)
Nerìs -iės (4) — Neris, a river in Lithuania on which Vilnius is located (15)
nèrvintis (nèrvinuosi, nèrvinasi, nèrvinosi, nèrvinsis) — to get nervous (32)
nès (conj.) — because (3)
nėsame (contraction of ne plus esame) — we are not (24)
nėsame bùvusios (negated 1st prs. plur. perf. fem. of bũti) — we have not been (24)
nėsate (contraction of ne plus esate) — you are not
nėsate bùvusios (negated 2nd prs. plur. perf. fem. of bũti) — you have not been (24)
nesìkerta (negated 3rd prs. pres. of kiȓstis) — are not in disagreement; do not intersect
nesirūpink (negated 2nd prs. sg. imperative of rūpintis) — don't worry (22)
nesù rãdęs (negated 1st sg. perfect of ràsti) — I have not found
nesurãdo (negated 3rd prs. simple pret. of suràsti) — he did not find (25)
nėšamas, -à (pres. passive part. of nèšti) — carried (A)
nėšdintis (nėšdinuosi, nėšdinasi, nėšdinosi, nėšdinsis) — to go, to run; nėšdinkis! — be off!, get away!

nešióti (nešióju, nešiója, nešiójo, nešiõs) — to wear (34)
nèšti (nešù, nĕša, nĕšė, nèš) — to carry (9)
nèt — even (10)
netaisyklìngai — incorrectly (22)
netèkti (netenkù, neteñka, netĕko, netèks) — to lose (33)
netolì (prep. with gen. or adv.) — not far, not far from, near (to); approximately (15)
netrùkus — soon, in a short time (22)
neturtìngas, -a (1) — poor (15)
neveȓtas, -à (4) — not worth (23)
nevisái — not wholly, not exactly (33)
niĕkad — never
niekadà — never (36)
niekadõs — never (8)
niĕkas — no-one; nothing (15)
niekìngas, -a (1) — frivolous; mean (A)
niĕko (gen. of niĕkas) — nothing; no one (15)
niĕko beñdra netùri sù — has nothing in common with (35)
niekuomèt — never (7)
niekuomèt daugiaũ — no more, nevermore (36)
niĕkur — nowhere (21)
nykštỹs -čio (3) — thumb (25)
Niujòrkas (1) — New York (22)
norĕčiau (1st sg. subjunctive of norĕti) — I should like (31)
norĕta (neuter past passive part. of norĕti) — it was wanted, (they) wanted (A)
norĕti (nóriu, nóri, norėjo, norĕs) — to want (5)
norĕtis (used in 3rd prs. only: nórisi, norėjosi, norĕsis) — to be wished (A)
nórs (conj.) — although, though; at least (15)
nósis -ies (fem.; 1) — nose (4)
nù (same as nà) (interj.) — now then (to express surprise, threat)
nũ (interj.) — now then (to urge on)
nu-baũsti (nubaudžiù, nubaũdžia, nùbaudė, nubaũs) — to punish, to fine
nu-byrĕti (nubyrù, nubỹra, nubyrėjo, nubyrĕs) — to be strewn about, to be scattered about (A)
nu-braũkyti (nubraukaũ, nubraũko, nùbraukė, nubraukỹs) — to brush off, to brush away (A)
nu-dardĕti (nùdardu, nùdarda, nudar-

433

dėjo, nudardės) — to rattle off, to rattle away, to go away rattling (A)

nu-dažýti (nudažaū, nudăžo, nudăžė, nudažỹs) — to paint (20)

nu-eĩti (nueinù, nueĩna, nuėjo, nueĩs) — to go away, to depart; to reach, to get to (14)

nu-galėti (nùgaliu, nùgali, nugalėjo, nugalės) — to overcome, to defeat (16)

nùgara (1) — back (25)

nu-krapštýti (nukrapštaū, nukrăpšto, nukrăpštė, nukrapštỹs) — to pull off, to scratch off (A)

nu-krìsti (nukrintù, nukriñta, nukrì- to, nukrìs) — to fall (39)

nu-liñkti (nulinkstù, nuliñksta, nuliñ- ko, nuliñks) — to bend down (15)

nu-lìpti (nùlipu, nùlipa, nulìpo, nu- lìps) — to climb down, to get off (14)

nùlis -io (2) — zero, null (24)

numýnė (3rd prs. pret. of numìnti) — trample down (A)

nu-mìnti (nùminu, nùmina, numýnė, numiñs) — to trample down (A)

nu-mìrti (numirštù, numìršta, nùmi- rė, numìrs) — to die (18)

numìrusių (gen. plur. of past act. part. of numiřti) — dead (38)

nu-nèšti (nùnešu, nùneša, nùnešė, nu- nèš) — to carry to, to take to; to carry off

nuõ (prep. with gen.) — from, away from; since (10)

nuõ tõ laĩko — since that time, since then (16)

nuõlat — all the time, continuously (21)

nuolatìnis, -ė (2) — constant, per- manent (37)

núopelnas (1) — merit (36)

núosėdos (used in plur.; 1) — residue (34)

nu-piáuti (nupiáunu, nupiáuna, nu- pióvė, nupiaũs) — to cut off, to sever (14)

nu-piřkti (nùperku, nùperka, nupiř- ko, nupiřks) — to buy

nu-plaũkti (nuplaukiù, nuplaũkia, nù- plaukė, nuplaũks) — to sail from ...to (15)

nu-pláuti (nupláunu, nupláuna, nu- plóvė, nuplaũs) — to wash off, to clear off by washing (A)

nuplóviau (1st sg. simple pret. of nupláuti) — I washed off (A)

nu-ramìnti (nuraminù, nuramìna, nu- ramìno, nuramiñs) — to calm, to console (A)

nu-ráuti (nuráunu, nuráuna, nuróvė, nuraũs) — to pull out (A)

nu-si-bósti (nusibósta, nusibódo, nusi- bõs) — to become bored with, tired of (subject in dative) (27)

nu-si-láužti (nusiláužiu, nusiláužia, nusiláužė, nusilaũš) — to break (one's arm, leg) (25)

nu-si-piřkti (nusìperku, nusìperka, nusipiřko, nusipiřks) — to buy for oneself (8)

nu-si-praũsti (nusiprausiù, nusipraũ- sia, nusìprausė, nusipraũs) — to wash up (27)

nu-si-rašýti (nusirašaū, nusirăšo, nu- sirăšė, nusirašỹs) — to copy out (for oneself) (37)

nu-si-šypsóti (nusišỹpsau, nusišỹpso, nusišypsójo, nusišypsõs) — to smile; to sneer (15)

nu-si-výti (nusìveju, nusìveja, nusivì- jo, nusivỹs) — to pursue, to run after, to drive after, to chase after; to make (a rope)

nuskýnė (3rd prs. simple pret. of nu- skìnti) — plucked, gathered (A)

nu-skìnti (nùskinu, nùskina, nuskýnė, nuskiñs) — to pluck, to gather (A)

nu-skrìsti (nùskrendu, nùskrenda, nu- skrìdo, nuskrìs) — to fly away (16)

nu-stelbti (nustelbiù, nustelbia, nu- stelbė, nustelbs) — to smother, to stifle (A)

nu-stóti (nustóju, nustója, nustójo, nustõs) — to stop, to cease; to lose (26)

nu-šálti (nušąlù, nušą̃la, nušãlo, nu- šaĩs) — to freeze (with frost-bite) (25)

nu-šókti (nušóku, nušóka, nušóko, nušõks) — to jump off, from

nu-tařti (nùtariu, nùtaria, nùtarė, nutař̃s) — to decide, to agree on (28)

nu-trū́kti (nutrū́kstu, nutrū́ksta, nu- trū́ko, nutrū́ks) — to be broken (A)

nu-tū́pti (nùtupiu, nùtupia, nutū́pė, nutū́ps) — to sit down (of birds) (A)

nu-važiúoti (nuvažiúoju, nuvažiúoja,

nuvažiãvo, nuvažiuõs) — to go, to get, to betake oneself (somewhere in a vehicle) (23)

nu-vèžti (nùvežu, nùveža, nùvežė, nuvèš) — to take (someone or something somewhere in a vehicle) (23)

nu-výkti (nuvykstù, nuvýksta, nuvýko, nuvýks) — to get, to go (somewhere) (23)

nužùdymas (1) — assassination (32)

nu-žudýti (nužudaũ, nužùdo, nužùdė, nužudýs) — to murder, to assassinate (36)

O

õ (conj.) — but, and; whereas, while (7)

õ (interj.) — o, alas, ah (to express surprise, shouting, displeasure)

obelìs -iẽs (fem.; 3a) — apple tree (A)

obuolýs (3a) — apple (13)

ohõ (interj.) — my goodness, oho (to express surprise)

ói (interj.) — ah, oh (to express pain, difficulty)

ojè (interj.) — oy (to express surprise, to call)

okupãcija (1) — occupation (A)

okupántas (1) — occupier, occupying force (A)

òpera (1) — opera

oraĩ (nom. plur. of óras) — weather (28)

óras (3) — air; weather (6)

òrdinas (1) — order (of knights); (military or state) decoration (38)

organizúoti (organizúoju, organizúoja, organizãvo, organizuõs) — to organize (A)

originãlas (2) — the original text (22)

Osà — Ossa, the right tributary of the Vistula (35)

P

pa-áiškinti (paáiškinu, paáiškina, paáiškino, paáiškins) — to explain (29)

pabaigà (3b) — end (A)

pa-baĩgti (pabaigiù, pabaĩgia, pàbaigė, pabaĩgs) — to finish

pabaigtùvės (used in plur.; 1) — feast celebrating the completion of some task (23)

Pabaltijýs (3b) — Baltic area, Baltic shores (34)

pabaudà (3b) — fine, punishment for an offense (36)

pabaudà ùž per greĩtą važiãvimą — ticket for speeding (36)

pa-bėgióti (pabėgióju, pabėgiója, pabėgiójo, pabėgiõs) — to run around a little bit (37)

pa-bėgti (pabėgu, pabėga, pabėgo, pabėgs) — to run; to run away, to escape (38)

pa-brángti (pabrángstu, pabrángsta, pabrángo, pabrañgs) — to become expensive (A)

pabrángusi (fem. nom. sg. of past act. part. of pabrángti) — become more expensive (A)

pa-brėžti (pabrėžiu, pabrėžia, pabrėžė, pabrėš) — to emphasize, to stress (A)

pa-bučiúoti (pabučiúoju, pabučiúoja, pabučiãvo, pabučiuõs) — to kiss

pabùdo (3rd prs. simple pret. of pabùsti) — woke up (15)

pa-bùsti (pabundù, pabuñda, pabùdo, pabùs) — to wake up (15)

pa-bũti (pabūvù, pabū́va, pabùvo, pabùs) — to be, to stay (for a certain period of time) (31)

pa-dalìnti (padalinù, padalìna, padalìno, padalìns) — to divide (18)

padalìnti (masc. nom. plur. of past passive part. of padalìnti) — divided (24)

padángė (1) — firmament, space under the heavens, skies (A)

pa-darýti (padaraũ, padãro, padãrė, padarýs) — to make, to do (12)

pa-dáuginti (padáuginu, padáugina, padáugino, padáugins) — to multiply (24)

padáuginti (masc. nom. plur. of past act. part. of padáuginti) — multiplied (24)

pàdeda (3rd prs. pres. of padėti) — help(s); put(s) (15)

pa-dėkóti (padėkóju, padėkója, padėkójo, padėkõs) — to thank (25)

pa-dėti (pàdedu, pàdeda, padėjo, padẽs) — to help; to put (7)

pa-dirbėti (padirbėju, padirbėja, padirbėjo, padirbės) — to work for a little bit, a little while (14)

pa-dovanóti (padovanóju, padovanó-

ja, padovanójo, padovanŏs) — to
give as a gift, to present (someone
with something)
pa-dūmóti (padūmóju, padūmója, pa-
dūmójo, padūmŏs) — to engage in
reverie for a certain period; to re-
flect (on), to think (A)
pa-dúoti (padúodu, padúoda, pàdavė,
paduŏs) — to give, to hand over;
to serve (36)
pagaĺ (prep. with acc.) — along, beside; according to
pagálba (1) — help (A)
pagaliaũ — finally (16)
pa-galvóti (pagalvóju, pagalvója, pa-
galvójo, pagalvŏs) — to think over
(31)
pa-gárbinti (pagárbinu, pagárbina,
pagárbino, pagárbins) — to adore,
to praise (34)
pa-gáuti (pagáunu, pagáuna, pagãvo,
pagaũs) — to begin (with infini
tive); to catch, to get (38)
pa-geidáuti (pageidáuju, pageidáuja,
pageidãvo, pageidaũs) — to desire,
to wish (A)
pa-gýdyti (pagýdau, pagýdo, pagýdė,
pagýdys) — to cure, to heal (25)
pagýdomas, -a (pres. passive part. of
pagýdyti) — being cured, curable
(33)
pagijìmas (2) — recovery (19)
pa-gìrti (pàgiriu, pàgiria, pagýrė, pa-
giŕs) — to praise (38)
pa-glabóti (paglabóju, paglabója, pa-
glabójo, paglabŏs) — to seize, to
take possession, to receive, to em-
brace (A)
pagónis -io (1) — pagan, heathen (A)
pãgrindas (3b) — basis, foundation
(A)
pagriñdžia (3rd prs. pres. of **pagrįsti**)
— provide(s) a base for (A)
pagrįstaĩ — justly, with reason (A)
pa-grįsti (pagrindžiù, pagriñdžia, pà-
grindė, pagrįs) — to provide a
basis for, to give a foundation to
(A)
pa-gulėti (pàguliu, pàguli, pagulėjo,
pagulės) — to lie down for a little
while, for a short time
pa-ieškóti (paíeškau, paíeško, paieš-
kójo, paieškŏs) — to seek, to search
for (31)
pa-ilsėti (pailsiù, paílsi, pailsėjo, pa-
ilsės) — to rest (19)

pa-im̃ti (pàimu, pàima, pàėmė, pa-
im̃s) — to take
pajėgà (3b) — (in sg.) ability, fac-
ulty; (in plur.) forces (37)
pajūris -io (1) coast, sea-shore, sea-
side (10)
pa-keĩsti (pakeičiù, pakeĩčia, pàkeitė,
pakeĩs) — to change (A)
pàkeliamas, -à (pres. passive part. of
pakélti) — capable of being lifted
(33)
pakeliuĩ — on the way to (39)
pa-kélti (pàkeliu, pàkelia, pakėlė, pakeĩs) — to lift up (7)
pa-kìlti (pakylù, pakỹla, pakìlo, pa-
kiĩs) — to rise (37)
pa-kiŕpti (pàkerpu, pàkerpa, pakiŕpo,
pakiŕps) — to cut (17)
pa-kláusti (pakláusiu, pakláusia, pakláusė, paklaũs) — to ask (one a
question) (?4)
pa-klýsti (paklýstu, paklýsta, paklý-
do, paklỹs) — to err, to make a
mistake; to stray, to lose one's way
pakraštỹs -čio (3b) — border, edge
(35)
pa-kviẽsti (pakviečiù, pakviẽčia, pà-
kvietė, pakviẽs) — to invite (A)
paláidas, -à (3) — loose, detached (A)
pa-laikýti (palaikaũ, palaĩko, palaĩkė,
palaikỹs) — to sustain, to support
(A)
pa-láukti (paláukiu, paláukia, paláu-
kė, palaũks) — to wait for
pa-láužti (paláužiu, paláužia, paláu-
žė, palaũš) — to break; to break
someone's resistance (A)
paleĩ (prep. with acc.) — along, by
the side of, beside
Palestinà (2) — Palestine (A)
pa-lydėti (palydžiù, palỹdi, palydėjo,
palydės) — to accompany (23)
paliẽsiu (1st sg. fut. of **paliẽsti**) —
I shall touch (15)
pa-liẽsti (paliečiù, paliẽčia, pàlietė,
paliẽs) — to touch (15)
pàlietė (3rd prs. simple pret. of **pa-
liẽsti**) — he touched (15)
palìk (2nd sg. imper. of **palìkti**) —
leave (11)
pa-lìkti (paliekù, paliẽka, palìko, pa-
lìks) — to leave (behind), to bequest (11)
palikuonìs -iės (masc.; 34b) — descendant (37)

pãmaldos (used in plur.; 3b) — religious service (9)

pamaldų̃ (gen. plur. of pãmaldos) — religious service (9)

pamataĩ (usually used in plur.; 3b) — foundation, groundwork (20)

pamãtėme (1st plur. simple pret. of pamatýti) — we saw (16)

pamãtę̃s (masc. nom. plur. of past act. part. of pamatýti) — having seen (A)

pa-matýti (pamataũ, pamãto, pamãtė, pamatỹs) — to see (24)

pamažù — slowly (2)

pàmečiau (1st. sg. simple pret. of pamèsti) — I lost

pa-mèsti (pàmetu, pàmeta, pàmetė, pamès) — to throw down; to lose (25)

pa-mylėti (or: pamìlti) (pamýliu, pamýli, pamylėjo, pamylės) — to fall in love with (A)

pamiñklas (2) — monument (38)

pa-miřšti (pamirštù, pamiřšta, pamiřšo, pamiřš) — to forget (A)

pamokà (3b) — lesson, 'home-work' (2)

pãmokas (acc. plur. of pamokà) — lessons (2)

panaikìnę (masc. nom. plur. of past act. part. of panaikìnti) — having destroyed (A)

pa-naikìnti (panaikinù, panaikìna, panaikino, panaikiñs) — to abolish (A)

panašùmas (2) — similarity (39)

panašùs, -ì (4) — similar (37)

panemunė̃ (34b) — region along the river Nemunas (35)

pa-peĩkti (papeikiù, papeĩkia, pàpeikė, papeĩks) — to scold, to admonish (38)

pa-piáuti (papiáunu, papiáuna, papióvė, papiaũs) — to butcher, to slaughter (A)

papióvė (3rd prs. simple pret. of papiáuti) — butchered, slaughtered (A)

paprastaĩ (2) — usually, generally (27)

pa-prašýti (paprašaũ, paprãšo, paprãšė, paprašỹs) — to ask (15)

pãpuošalas (34b) — ornament (10)

parãdas (2) — parade (31)

parãpija (1) — parish (38)

parašýta (neuter form of past passive part. of parašýti) — (it is) written (A)

pa-rašýti (parašaũ, parãšo, parãšė, parašỹs) — to write; to know how to write (8)

paraũdo (3rd prs. simple pret. of paraũsti) — became red (25)

pa-raũsti (paraustù, paraũsta, paraũdo, paraũs) — to become red (25)

pardãvę̃s (masc. nom. sg. of past act. part. of pardúoti) — sold, having sold (A)

par-dúoti (pardúodu, pardúoda, par̃davė, parduõs) — to sell (13)

par-eĩti (pareinù, pareĩna, parė́jo, pareĩs) — to come back, to come home (15)

parė́jo (3rd prs. simple pret. of par-eĩti) — came home, came back (15)

pa-rem̃ti (pàremiu, pàremia, pàrėmė, parem̃s) — to hold up; to support (A)

pargriáudama (fem. form of spec. adv. act. part. of pargriáuti, cf. 26.4) — throwing down, toppling down (38)

par-griáuti (pargriáunu, pargriáuna, pargrióvė, pargriaũs) — to throw down, to topple down (38)

par-grį̃žti (pargrį̃žtù, pargrį̃žta, pargrị̃žo, pargrị̃š) — to come back, to return (A)

pàrinktas, -à (past passive part. of pariñkti) — chosen, selected (A)

pa-riñkti (pàrenku, pàrenka, pariñko, pariñks) — to choose (A)

párkas (1) — park (9)

pa-ródyti (paródau, paródo, paródė, paródys) — to show (25)

par-si-vèžti (parsìvežu, parsìveža, parsìvežė, parsivèš) — to bring along (in a vehicle) (9)

pa-ruõšti (paruošiù, paruõšia, pàruošė, paruõš) — to prepare (29)

par-vèžti (par̃vežu, par̃veža, par̃vežė, parvèš) — to bring home (in a vehicle) (A)

pàs (prep. with acc.) — at, by, to, with, at the home of (6)

pasàk (prep. with gen.) — according to

pãsaka (1) — fairy tale, folk tale (12)

pa-sakýti (pasakaũ, pasãko, pasãkė, pasakỹs) — to say (17)

437

pǎ-sakoti (pǎsakoju, pǎsakoja, pǎsakojo, pǎsakos) — to tell (a story), to relate (12)

pasáulis -io (1) — world (36)

pa-sėdėti (pasėdžiu, pasėdi, pasėdėjo, pasėdės) — to sit for a little while, a little bit (37)

pa-sénti (pasénstu, pasénsta, paséno, paseñs) — to grow old (18)

pa-si-baĩgti (pasibaigiù, pasibaĩgia, pasìbaigė, pasibaĩgs) — to come to an end (intransitive) (20)

pa-si-balnóti (pasibalnóju, pasibalnója, pasibalnójo, pasibalnõs) — to saddle up (A)

pa-si-darýti (pasidaraũ, pasidãro, pasidãrė, pasidarỹs) — to make something for oneself; to happen; to become (26)

pa-si-dúoti (pasidúodu, pasidúoda, pasìdavė, pasiduõs) — to give in, to give up (27)

pa-síekti (pasíekiu, pasíekia, pasíekė, pasíeks) — to reach (7)

pa-si-im̃ti (pasìimu, pasìima, pasìėmė, pasiim̃s) — to take (for oneself) (29)

pa-si-kalbėti (pasìkalbu, pasìkalba, pasikalbėjo, pasikalbės) — to have a talk, to have a chat (9)

pa-si-keĩsti (pasikeičiù, pasikeĩčia, pasìkeitė, pasikeĩs) — to change (intransitive) (39)

pa-si-kinkýti (pasikinkaũ, pasikiñko, pasikiñkė, pasikinkỹs) — to harness up (for oneself) (A)

pa-si-kiřpti (pasìkerpu, pasìkerpa, pasikiřpo, pasikiřps) — to get (something, e.g. one's hair) cut, to have (something) cut (17)

pa-si-leñkti (pasilenkiù, pasileñkia, pasìlenkė, pasileñks) — to bow, to bend down (7)

pa-si-lìkti (pasiliekù, pasilìeka, pasìliko, pasilìks) — to remain, to stay behind (26)

pasilìkusius (masc. acc. plur. of past act. part. of pasilìkti) — who had remained, having remained (26)

pa-silsėti (also: pailsėti) (pasilsiù, pasìlsi, pasilsėjo, pasilsės) — to rest (15)

pasimãtymas (1) — seeing one another, meeting, 'date' (11)

pa-si-máudyti (pasimáudau, pasimáu-do, pasimáudė, pasimáudys) — to swim, to go swimming

pa-si-mókyti (pasimókau, pasimóko, pasimókė, pasimókys) — to learn (A)

pa-si-naudóti (pasinaudóju, pasinaudója, pasinaudójo, pasinaudõs) — to make use of, to take advantage of (39)

pa-si-puõšti (pasipuošiù, pasipuõšia, pasìpuošė, pasipuõš) — to dress up, to spruce up; to adorn oneself (14)

pa-si-riñkti (pasìrenku, pasìrenka, pasiriñko, pasiriñks) — to choose for oneself (36)

pa-si-rýžti (pasirýžtu, pasirýžta, pasirýžo, pasirỹš) — to determine, to resolve, to make up one's mind (A)

pa-si-ródyti (pasiródau, pasiródo, pasiródė, pasiródys) — to appear (15)

pa-si-ruõšti (pasiruošiù, pasiruõšia, pasìruošė, pasiruõš) — to get prepared, to get ready, to get finished (32)

pa-si-sãvinti (pasisãvinu, pasisãvina, pasisãvino, pasisãvins) — to adopt; to appropriate (A)

pa-si-sèkti (pasìseka, pasìsekė, pasìseks) — to succeed (in); logical subject in dat. (36)

pa-si-skùbinti (pasiskùbinu, pasiskùbina, pasiskùbino, pasiskùbins) — to hurry (32)

pa-si-svéikinti (pasisvéikinu, pasisvéikina, pasisvéikino, pasisvéikins) — to greet (26)

pa-si-tikėti (pasìtikiu, pasìtiki, pasitikėjo, pasitikės) — to have confidence (in one another) (36)

pa-si-tìkti (pasitinkù, pasitiñka, pasitìko, pasitìks) — to meet

pasiuntinỹs (34b) — envoy, ambassador

pa-siųsti (pasiunčiù, pasiuñčia, pàsiuntė, pasiųs) — to send (31)

pa-si-váikščioti (pasiváikščioju, pasiváikščioja, pasiváikščiojo, pasiváikščios) — to take a walk (26)

pa-si-výti (pasìveju, pasìveja, pasivìjo, pasivỹs) — to catch, to overtake (A)

pa-si-žiūrėti (pasižiūriù, pasižiūri, pasižiūrėjo, pasižiūrės) — to have a look at, to get a look at (5)

paskaità (3b) — lecture (32)

pa-skaitýti (paskaitaũ, paskaĩto, pa-skaĩtė, paskaitỹs) — to read for a while; to know how to read, to be able to read; to finish reading (14)

pa-skambinti (paskambinu, paskambina, paskambino, paskambins) — to ring up, to call up; to play (the piano) for a short while (13)

paskendęs (masc. nom. sg. of past act. part. of paskęsti) — sunken, hidden (10)

pa-skęsti (paskęstù, paskęsta, paskeñdo, paskęs) — to be drowned; to sink, to go down (10)

páskiras, -à (3b) — individual, separate, single (39)

pa-skìrti (pàskiriu, pàskiria, paskýrė, paskirs) — to appoint, to name (someone to some office) (23)

paskirtìs -iẽs (fem.; 3b) — task, appointed duty; destination (A)

pa-skõlinti (paskõlinu, paskõlina, paskolino, paskõlins) — to lend (31)

pa-skubėti (pàskubu, pàskuba, paskubėjo, paskubės) — to hurry (32)

paskuí (prep. with acc.) — after, behind

paskuí (adv.) — then, afterwards (23)

paskutìnis, -ė (2) — last, recent (34)

pa-sodìnti (pasodinù, pasodìna, pasodìno, pasodiñs) — to plant (26)

pastangà (3b) — pains, effort (A)

pãstatas (3b) — building, edifice (3)

pa-statýti (pastataũ, pastãto, pastãtė, pastatỹs) — to erect, to build (15)

pastatýti (masc. nom. plur. of past passive part. of pastatýti) — built, erected (15)

pa-stebėti (pàstebiu, pàstebi, pastebėjo, pastebės) — to notice (36)

pastógė (1) — attic, garret (20)

pasùkite (2nd plur. imper. of pasùkti) — turn (15)

pa-sùkti (pàsuku, pàsuka, pasùko, pasùks) — to turn (15)

pa-svéikinti (pasvéikinu, pasvéikina, pasvéikino, pasvéikins) — to greet (34)

pa-sveĩkti (pasveikstù, pasveĩksta, pasveĩko, pasveĩks) — to recover, to get better, to get well (25)

pa-svìrti (pasvyrù, pasvýra, pasvìro, pasvìrs) — to hang down, to sway from side to side (A)

pasvìrusią (fem. acc. sg. of past act. part. of pasvìrti) — having hung down, bent over (A)

pašakėlis -io (1) — place under the branches of a tree (A)

pãštas (2) — post-office (2)

pàt (particle) — very, even, right (15)

pa-taisýti (pataisaũ, pataĩso, pataĩsė, pataisỹs) — to repair, to make better; to correct (19)

patarìmas (2) — advice (13)

pa-tarnáuti (patarnáuju, patarnáuja, patarnãvo, patarnaũs) — to be of service, to render service

pa-tar̃ti (pàtariu, pàtaria, pàtarė, patar̃s) — to advise (12)

pa-tèkti (patenkù, pateñka, patěko, patèks) — to get to, to get into (34)

paténkintas, -a (1) — satisfied, content

pa-tìkti (patinkù, patiñka, patìko, patìks) — to please; to like (with logical subject in dat.) (13)

patiñka (3rd prs. pres. of patìkti) — pleases; like (13)

patõgiai — comfortably (37)

patriòtiškas, -a — patriotic (A)

pàts (masc.), patì (fem.) — intensive pronoun meaning myself, himself, yourself depending on context, cf. 44.3 (7)

pa-tvìnti (patvìnstu, patvìnsta, patvìno, patviñs) — to swell up, to rise (of a river) (A)

paũkščių (gen. plur. of paũkštis) — (of) birds

paũkštis -čio (2) — bird (23)

pa-váikščioti (paváikščioju, paváikščioja, paváikščiojo, paváikščios) — to walk about a little bit, to take a walk (6)

pavakarỹs (34b) — around evening, near evening (24)

pa-válgyti (paválgau, paválgo, paválgė, paválgys) — to eat (12)

pavardė̃ (3b) — last name, family name (24)

pavar̃gęs (masc. nom. sg. of past act. part. of pavar̃gti) — tired

pa-var̃gti (pavargstù, pavar̃gsta, pavar̃go, pavar̃gs) — to be tired, to be weary (15)

pavar̃gusi (fem. nom. sg. of past act. part. of pavar̃gti) — tired

439

pavãsaris -io (1) — spring
pavéikslas (1) — picture, painting (15)
pavéldėjimas (1) — inheritance (A)
pa-vėlúoti (pavėlúoju, pavėlúoja, pavėlãvo, pavėluõs) — to be late (32)
pàvergtas, -à (past passive part. of paveřgti; 3) — enslaved, subjected (37)
pa-veřgti (pavergiù, paveřgia, pàvergė, paveřgs) — to enslave; to subject (37)
pavėsis -io (1) — shade (37)
pavydėti (pavýdžiu, pavýdi, pavydėjo, pavydės) — to be jealous of, to envy (with dat.) (36)
paviřs (3rd prs. future of paviřsti) — — will become, turn into (15)
pa-viřsti (pavirstù, paviřsta, paviřto, paviřs) — to turn into, to change into (with instr.) (15)
paviřto (3rd prs. simple pret. of paviřsti) — it became, it turned into (15)
pavyzdỹs -džio (3b) — sample, example (33)
pàvyzdžiui (dat. sg. of pavyzdỹs) — for example
pavõjus (2) — danger (29)
pa-žaísti (pažaidžiù, pažaĩdžia, pàžaidė, pažaĩs) — to play a little bit (38)
pažastáitis -čio (dim. of pažastìs; 1) — armpit (A)
pa-žìnti (pažįstu, pažįsta, pažìno, pažìns) — to know (someone), to be acquainted with (someone); to recognize (24)
pažįstamas, -a (pres. passive part. of pažìnti; 1) — acquaintance; known, being known (26)
pažiūrėkime (1st plur. imper. of pažiūrėti) — let's take a look at (10)
pa-žiūrėti (pažiūriù, pažiūri, pažiūrėjo, pažiūrės) — to take a look at (10)
pa-žvelgti (pažvelgiù, pažvelgia, pàžvelgė, pažvelgs) — to glance, to look (39)
pečiaĩs (instr. plur. of petỹs) — with his shoulders (A)
pėdà (3) — foot (25)
peíkti (peikiù, peĩkia, peĩkė, peĩks) — to blame, to scold (34)
peílis -io (2) — knife (4)
peizãžas (2) — landscape (10)

pelė̃ (4) — mouse (37)
pelėda (1) — owl (16)
penkerì, peñkerios (3b) — five (24)
peñketas (1) — (a group of) five (24)
penkì (used with masc.; 4) — five (4)
peñkiasdešimt (indecl.) — fifty (24
penkiasdešiḿtas, -à (4) — fiftieth (29)
penkiólika (1) — fifteen (16)
penkióliktas, -a (1) — fifteenth (29)
peñkios (used with fem.; 4) — five (4)
penktãdalis -io (1) — one-fifth (24)
penktãdienis -io (1) — Friday (32)
peñktas, -à (4) — fifth (19)
peř (prep. with acc.) — through, across; during, throughout; (with expressions of time) within (6)
peř (adv.) — too, too much, to too great a degree (25)
peř ámžius — forever (23)
peř daũg — too much (17)
peř rãdiją — on the radio, over the radio (6)
pér-dalyti (pérdaliju, pérdalija, pérdalijo, pérdalys) — to separate, to divide (A)
pér-duoti (pérduodu, pérduoda, pérdavė, pérduos) — to hand over, to transmit, to give
pér-eiti (péreinu, péreina, pérėjo, péreis) — to cross (14)
per greĩtai — too fast (36)
per greĩtas, -à (4) — too fast, overly speedy (36)
peřka (3rd prs. pres. of piřkti) — buys (25)
pér-kelti (pérkeliu, pérkelia, pérkėlė, pérkels) — to move, to transfer (27)
Perkũnas (1) — god of thunder (23)
Perkũns (for Perkũnas; 1) — god of thunder; thunder and lightning (A)
pérlaužti (pérlaužiu, pérlaužia, pérlaužė, pérlauš) — to break into pieces (14)
pér-lipti (pérlipu, pérlipa, pérlipo, pérlips) — to climb over (14)
pérnai — last year
pérpykę (masc. nom. plur. of past act. part. of pérpykti) — angry, mad, indignant (A)
pér-pykti (pérpykstu, pérpyksta, pérpyko, pérpyks) — to become angry, indignant (A)

pérsikėlimas (1) — moving, removing (27)

pér-si-kelti (pérsikeliu, pérsikelia, pérsikėlė, pérsikels) — to move, to remove (to another place) (27)

pér-skaityti (pérskaitau, pérskaito, pérskaitė, pérskaitys) — to read through (29)

pėsčias, -à (3) — on foot, as a pedestrian (23)

pėstì (masc. nom. plur. of pėsčias) — on foot (23)

pèšt (interj.) — denotes a slight tug or jerk

petìs -iẽs (fem.; 4) — shoulder (25)

petỹs, péčio (alternate form of petìs; 4) — shoulder (A)

Pẽtras (2) — Peter

Petriùkas (dim. of Pẽtras; 2) — Pete, Peter (17)

pianìnas (2) — upright piano (20)

píenas (1) — milk (3)

piẽšti (piešiù, piẽšia, piẽšė, piẽš) — to draw (11)

pieštùkas (2) — pencil (14)

pietáuti (pietáuju, pietáuja, pietávo, pietaũs) — to dine (40)

pietìnis, -ė (2) — southern, south (35)

pietùs (acc. plur. of piẽtūs) — south; dinner (2)

piẽtūs (used in plur.; 4) — south; dinner, noon meal (2)

píeva (1) — meadow (10)

pigiaĩ — cheaply (12)

pìktas, -à (4) — angry (11)

pỹkti (pykstù, pỹksta, pỹko, pỹks) — to be angry (29)

piliãkalnis -io (1) — castle hill (hills and mountains in Lithuania where in ancient times stood castles, fortifications or warning towers) (21)

pilìs -iẽs (fem.; 4) — castle (15)

pìlkas, -à (3) — gray (21)

pìlnas, -à (3) full (39)

pìlti (pilù, pìla, pýlė, pìls) — to pour (19)

pìlvas (4) — belly (25)

pìnigas (3b) — money

piniginė (2) — purse, wallet, money-bag (25)

pìnti (pinù, pìna, pýnė, pìns) — to braid, to plait, to twist (A)

pýpkė (1) — pipe (19)

pirkià (2) — hut, wooden hut, cottage, dwelling house

pirklỹs (4) — merchant (39)

pir̃kti (perkù, per̃ka, pir̃ko, pir̃ks) — to buy (13)

pir̃m — cf. pirmà (37)

pirmà (prep. with gen.) — in front of, before

pìrmą kar̃tą — for the first time (21)

pìrmą vãlandą — at one o'clock (22)

pirmãdienis -io (1) — Monday (32)

pirmaeĩlis, -ė (2) — first-line, first-rate, first-class (37)

pìrmas, -à (3) — first (10)

pirmàsis (masc. nom. sg. of definite form of pìrmas) — first (10)

pirmiaũ (adv.) — first (31)

pirmiáusia (adv.) — first of all, in the first place (15)

pir̃štas (2) — finger; (kójos pir̃štas) toe (25)

pirtìs -iẽs (fem.; 4) — bath-house (26)

piūtìs -iẽs (fem.; 4) — harvest (36)

plačià prasmè (instr. sg. of platì prasmė) — in the broad sense (A)

plačiaĩ — widely (12)

plačiù keliù (instr. sg. of platùs kẽlias) — along the broad path, road (12)

plačiuõsiuose (masc. loc. plur. of definite form of platùs) — in the wide . . . (28)

plãnas (4) — plan; map (11)

platùs, -ì (4) — wide, broad (12)

pláukas (3) — (one strand of) hair; plaukaĩ translates English hair in collective sense (17)

plaũkti (plaukiù, plaũkia, plaũkė, plaũks) — to swim; to sail (8)

pleĩštas (2) — wedge (35)

plėšìkas (2) — bandit, plunderer, robber (A)

plevėsúoti (plevėsúoju, plevėsúoja, plevėsávo, plevėsuõs) — to flutter (in the wind) (31)

pliáukšt (interj.) — denotes the sound of sudden hitting, striking

pliẽnas (4) — steel (A)

plienìnis, -ė (2) — steel, made of steel (13)

plìkas, -à (4) — bald (A)

plìkė (2) — bald spot (A)

plýkst (interj.) — denotes sudden flash of flame

plytà (2) — brick (33)

pliũpt (interj.) — denotes sudden outpouring (of water)

pliùs — plus (24)

plónas, -à (3) — thin (33)

plótas (1) — expanse, space, area (35)

plùnksna (1) — pen; feather (11)

põ (prep.) — (with acc.) in, through, about; (with instr.) under; (with gen.) after; (with dat.) in certain fixed expressions, cf. 37.4; (with acc.) in distributive meaning, cf. 37.5

po kuriuõ — under which (15)

po tõ — after that (15)

poemà, poèmos (2) — poem (37)

poètas (2) — poet (23)

pókšt (interj.) — expresses sound of cracking

policija (1) — police (34)

policininkas (1) — policeman (15)

polìtinis, -ė (1) — political (36)

põnas (2) — mister, sir; gentleman (20)

ponià (4) — lady, Mrs. (11)

põpierius (1) — paper (11)

pópiežius (1) — pope (36)

porà (4) — a pair, a couple of, several (33)

porỹt — the day after tomorrow (10)

pra-bûti (prabūnù, prabūna, prabùvo, prabùs) — to be (for a certain length of time) (14)

pra-dėti (pràdedu, pràdeda, pradėjo, pradės) — to begin

pradìnis, -ė (2) — elementary, primary, initial (31)

pradžià (4) — beginning, start (28)

pradžiõs mokyklà — elementary school (28)

pra-eĩti (praeinù, praeĩna, praẽjo, praeĩs) — to pass by; to pass (14)

praeitìs -iẽs (fem.; 3b) — past (24)

praėjusią (fem. acc. sg. of past act. part. of praeĩti) — last, bygone (32)

praléido (3rd prs. simple preterit of praléisti) — spent (37)

pra-léisti (praléidžiu, praléidžia, praléido, praleĩs) — to spend (a vacation, one's life) (28)

pra-líeti (pralíeju, pralíeja, pralíejo, praliẽs) — to spill, to shed (A)

pra-linksmėti (pralinksmiù, praliñksmi, pralinksmėjo, pralinksmės) — to cheer up

pra-miegóti (pramiegù, pramiẽga, pramiegójo, pramiegõs) — to oversleep (32)

prãmonė (1) — industry; work, creation (38)

pra-mùšti (pràmušu, pràmuša, pràmušė, pramùš) — to beat through (14)

prancûzas (2) — Frenchman (22)

Prancûzijà — France (37)

pranešìmas (2) — report (32)

pra-nèšti (prànešu, pràneša, prànešė, praneš̃) — to announce, to report; to let (someone) know (6)

pra-plėsti (pràplečiu, pràplečia, pràplėtė, praplės̃) — to extend, to widen (37)

pra-ràsti (prarandù, prarañda, prarã-do, praràs) — to lose (14)

pra-si-dėti (prasìdedu, prasìdeda, prasidėjo, prasidės) — to begin (intransitive) (28)

prasmė̃ (4) — sense, meaning, significance (35)

prašaũ (1st sg. pres. of prašýti) — I ask, I beg; you are welcome (15)

prašýk (2nd sg. imper. of prašýti) — ask (15)

prašýti (prašaũ, prãšo, prãšė, pra-šỹs) — to ask, to request (someone to do something) (8)

pra-šnèkti (pràšneku, pràšneka, prašnė̃ko, prašnèks) — to begin to speak

pra-taŕti (pràtariu, pràtaria, pràtarė, prataŕs) — to utter, to say (15)

pra-važiúoti (pravažiúoju, pravažiúo-ja, pravažiãvo, pravažiúos) — to drive past, to travel past (37)

pra-viŕkti (pravirkstù, praviŕksta, praviŕko, praviŕks) — to begin to cry

pra-žûti (pražùvu, pražūva, pražùvo, pražùs) — to perish (A)

prēkė (2) — kind of ware, goods (36)

prekiáuti (prekiáuju, prekiáuja, prekiãvo, prekiaũs) — to trade (10) (with instr.)

prezideñtas (2) — president (23)

pri-artėti (priartėju, priartėja, priartėjo, priartės) — to approach, to come near to (A)

pri-dėti (prìdedu, prìdeda, pridėjo, pridės) — to add (24)

priẽ (prep. with gen.) — near, at; a place near (7)

prieĩnamas, -à (3b) — accessible (A)

pri-eĩti (prieinù, prieĩna, priẽjo, prieĩs) — to approach, to come near

prìėmė (3rd prs. simple pret. of pri-iḿti) — accepted (36)
príemiestis -čio (1) — suburb (6)
príemonė (1) — means (A)
príespauda (1) — oppression (A)
priẽš (prep. with acc.) — ago; before, in front of; against (16)
príešas (1) — enemy (33)
príetėmis -io (1) — dusk, twilight (10)
prievartāvimas (1) — violence, assault (A)
priežastis -iẽs (fem.; 3a) — reason (A)
pri-iḿti (prìimu, prìima, prìėmė, pri-iḿs) — to accept; to admit (someone) (24)
priiḿtinas, -à (3b) — acceptable (A)
pri-kiḿšti (prìkemšu, prìkemša, pri-kiḿšo, prikiḿš) — to stuff (19)
priklausą̃s (masc. nom. sg. of pres. act. part. of priklausýti) — dependent (33)
pri-klausýti (priklausaũ, priklaũso, priklaũsė, priklausỹs) — to belong (to) (with dat.) (19)
priklaũsomas, -a (pres. passive part. of priklausýti; 1) — dependent (33)
priklijúotas, -a (past passive part. of priklijúoti; 1) — attached (to), stuck (to) (24)
pri-klijúoti (priklijúoju, priklijúoja, priklijãvo, priklijuõs) — to stick to, to glue to, to paste to (24)
pri-mèsti (prìmetu, prìmeta, prìmetė, primès) — to impose upon (A)
pri-miñti (prìmenu, prìmena, prìminė, primiñs) — to call to mind, to remind (A)
pripãsakojęs (masc. nom. sg. of past act. part. of pripãsakoti) — told (A)
pri-pã-sakoti (pripãsakoju, pripãsakoja, pripãsakojo, pripãsakos) — to relate, to tell (a great deal) (A)
pri-pìlti (prìpilu, prìpila, pripýlė, pripìls) — to pour into (19)
pri-rašýti (prirašaũ, prirãšo, prirãšė, prirašỹs) to write a great deal; to write all over; to add (a few lines) (38)
pri-rìšti (prìrišu, prirìša, prirìšo, prirìš) — to tie, to bind (A)
prisiminìmas (2) — remembrance
pri-skìrti (prìskiriu, prìskiria, priský-rė, priskìrs) — to attribute to, to ascribe to (35)

privatùs, -ì (4) — private (34)
pri-važiúoti (privažiúoju, privažiúoja, privažiãvo, privažiuõs) — to approach (riding in a vehicle)
prõ (prep. with acc.) — past, by, through (9)
problemà (2) — problem (A)
profèsorius (1) — professor (6)
prókalbė (1) — proto-language (39)
prõtas (2) — sense, mind, reason; intellect, intelligence (19); sveĩkas prõtas — common sense
protìngas, -a (1) — intelligent, wise, sensible (31)
Prūsai (used in plur.; 1) — Prussia (36)
prūsas (1) — Prussian, Old Prussian; German (derogatory) (35)
Prūsija (1) — Prussia (39)
pùčiamas, -à (pres. passive part. of pūsti; 3) — blown, being blown (10)
puikùs, -ì (4) — fine, excellent (6)
pūkẽlis -io (2) — little piece of down, tuft of hair (A)
pulkas (4) — regiment (37)
pùlti (púolu, púola, púolė, puls) — to attack, to assault (36)
puodùkas (2) — cup (3)
púoselėti (púoselėju, púoselėja, púoselėjo, púoselės) — to cultivate, to foster (A)
puõštis (puošiúosi, puõšiasi, puõšėsi, puõšis) — to adorn oneself, to deck oneself out (10)
puřvas (4) — mud
purvynáitis -čio (dim. of puřvas; 1) — place where there is a lot of mud, marsh (A)
pusañtro — one and one-half (cf. 24.7,1)
pusaštuñto — seven and one-half (cf. 24.7,1)
pùsbrolis -io (1) (male) cousin
pusdeviñto — eight and one-half (cf. 24.7,1)
pùsė (2) — side; direction; one-half (11)
pusiáu (prep. with gen.) — half way up, half way along; (adv.) half way (A)
pusketviřto — three and one-half (cf. 24.7,1)
pùslapis -io (1) — page (29)
puspeñkto — four and one-half (cf. 24.7,1)

pùsryčius (acc. plur. of pùsryčiai) — breakfast (2)

pùsryčiai (used in plur.; 1) — breakfast (2)

pusseptiñto — six and one-half (cf. 24.7,1)

pusšēšto — five and one-half (cf. 24.7,1)

pūsti (pučiù, pùčia, pūtė, pùs) — to blow (10)

pustýti (pustaū, pùsto, pùstė, pustỹs) — to blow intermittently; to cause to drift (A)

pustrēčio — two and one-half (cf. 24.7,1)

pušìs -iês (fem.; 4) — pine (22)

pūtė (3rd prs. simple pret. of pūsti) — blew (A)

putódams — cf. putódamas

putódamas, -a (spec. adv. part. of putóti) — foaming (cf. 26.4) (38)

putóti (putóju, putója, putójo, putõs) — to foam, to froth (38)

pvz. (abbreviation of pãvyzdžiui) — for example (A)

R

rādijas (1) — radio (6)

raidė (2) — letter (of the alphabet) (16)

raitýti (raitaū, raĭto, raĭtė, raitỹs) to curl (the hair, a moustache, etc.) (25)

ramýbė (1) — quiet, peace (11)

ramùs, -ì (4) — quiet, calm (22)

rañdamas, -à (pres. passive part. of ràsti) — is found, being found (34)

rankà (2) — hand, arm (15)

rankēlė (dim. of rankà; 2) — little hand, arm (A)

rankóvė (1) — sleeve (25)

rañkraštis -čio (1) — manuscript (37)

rasà (4) — dew (39)

ràsti (randù, rañda, rãdo, ràs) — to find (10)

rasùžė (dim. of rasà; 2) — dew (A)

rašýti (rašaū, rãšo, rãšė, rašỹs) — to write (2)

rašýtojas (1) — writer, author (22)

rãšo (3rd prs. pres. of rašýti) — writes (2)

rãšomas, -a (pres. passive part. of rašýti) — being written, written; writing (33)

rãštas (2) writing, (written) work, (poetic) work; edict (38)

raudónas, -a (1) — red (7)

raukšlė (4) — wrinkle (25)

raūsti (raustù, raūsta, raūdo, raūs) — to become red (25)

reĭkalas (3b) — purpose, matter, 'business'; need (33)

reikalìngas, -a (1) — necessary (4)

reikēti (used in 3rd prs. only: reĭkia, reikējo, reikēs) — to be necessary; to need (with logical subject in dat.) (11)

reikšmē (3) — meaning, significance (35)

reikšmìngas, -a (1) — significant, meaningful (A)

réikšti (réiškiu, réiškia, réiškė, reĭkš) — to mean, to signify (22)

reĭkti or reikēti (used in 3rd person only: reĭkia, roĭkė, reĭks) — to be necessary (A)

relìginis, -ė (1) — religious (A)

relìgiškas, -a (1) — religious (A)

reñti (remiù, rēmia, rēmė, reñs) — to support (A)

reñgtis (rengiúosi, reñgiasi, reñgėsi, reñgsis) — to get ready (16)

renkì (2nd sg. pres. of riñkti) — (you) gather (25)

restorānas (2) — restaurant (11)

rētas, -à (4) — rare (A)

ribà (4) — boundary, border, limit (37)

ribótis (ribójuosi, ribójasi, ribójosi, ribõsis) — to border on, to be bounded by (35)

Rygà (4) — Riga (capital of Latvia) (35)

rýmai (2nd sg. pres. of rýmoti) — (you) are leaning (A)

rýmoti (rýmau, rýmo, rýmojo, rýmos) — to lean; remain leaning (upon) (A)

rinkìmas (2) — selection (A)

rinkinỹs (3b) — selection, collection (22)

ryšỹs (4) — connection, contact, relation (36)

ryškùs, -ì (4) — attracting attention, distinct (A)

rýtą (acc. sg. of rýtas) — in the morning (16)

rýtas (3) — morning (12); the plur. of rýtas, rytaĭ means 'east' (10)

rytìnis, -ė (2) — eastern (35)

rytój — tomorrow (9)

rytój vakarè — tomorrow night, tomorrow evening (9)

rituãlinis, -ė (1) — ritual (A)

rýtus (acc. plur. of rytaĩ) — east (10)

ryžtìngas, -a (1) — determined (36)

ródyti (ródau, ródo, ródė, ródys) — — to show (34)

ródytis (ródausi, ródosi, ródėsi, ródysis) — to seem, to appear (18)

ródos (3rd prs. pres. of ródytis) — it seems, appears (18)

Romà (2) — Rome (31)

romãnas (2) — novel; speaker of one of the Romance languages (11)

romėnas (1) — Roman (10)

rõžė (2) — rose (A)

rùdas, -à (4) — brown (14)

rùdenio (alternative gen. sg. of ruduõ) — of autumn, of fall (A)

rudeñs (gen. sg. of rudu̇õ) — autumn, fall (16)

rudì (masc. nom. plur. of rùdas) — brown (14)

rùdis -džio (2) — someone brown; frequently used as dog's name (6)

rudu̇õ -eñs (3b) — fall, autumn (cf. 41.51) (14)

rugỹs (4) — rye (Secale cereale) (19)

rugpiūtis -čio (1) — August (32)

rugsėjis -jo (1) — September (32)

rūkýti (rūkaũ, rūko, rūkė, rūkýs) — to smoke (a cigarette, a pipe, etc.) (25)

rūkti (rūkstù, rūksta, rūko, rūks) — to smoke (intransitive) (20)

rūmai (nom. plur. of rūmas; 1) — big house, palace (23)

rūmas (1) — palace (A)

ruõšia (3rd prs. pres. of ruõšti) — prepares, 'does' (2)

ruošìmas (2) — preparation (38)

ruõšti (ruošiù, ruõšia, ruõšė, ruõš) — to prepare (2)

ruõštis (ruošiúosi, ruõšiasi, ruõšėsi, ruõšis) — to prepare oneself, to be prepared (23)

rūpestėlis -io (dim. of rūpestis; 2) — concern, trouble, care (A)

rūpestis -čio (1) — care, worry (38)

rūpintis (rūpinuosi, rūpinasi, rūpinosi, rūpinsis) — to worry, to care, to be worried (22)

rūpintojėlis -io (dim. of rūpintojas; 2) — a small statue of Christ carved out of wood. It is usually set up in a tree or a small shelter of some type and Christ appears to be looking at those who pass by (A)

rùsas (2) — Russian (noun) (35)

rūšis -ies (1) kind, sort (A)

rūtà (2) — rue (a plant with yellow flowers and a strong bitter taste) (A)

S

sakaĩ (used in plur.; 4) — resin (do not confuse this noun with the 2nd sg. pres. of sakýti which is also sakaĩ)

sakinỹs (3b) — sentence (13)

sakýti (sakaũ, sãko, sãkė, sakỹs) — to say (6)

sakýtis (sakaũsi, sãkosi, sãkėsi, sakỹsis) — to say oneself to be, to say that one is

sakýtume (1st plur. subjunctive of sakýti) — we would say, we should say (cf. 31.1 and 31.2) (A)

sakúotas, -a (1) — resinuos (34)

salà (4) — island (27)

saldaĩnis -io (2) — candy (17)

saldìnis, -ė (2) — sweet, of a sweet kind (13)

saldùs, -ì (3) — sweet (12)

sálti (sąlù, sãla, sãlo, saĨs) — to grow sweet; to become fine, infinitely pleasant (A)

samanótas, -a (1) — mossy, overgrown with moss (10)

samdýti (samdaũ, sam̃do, sam̃dė, samdỹs) — to hire (21)

sąnarỹs (3a) — joint, member (of the body), knuckle (A)

sanskrìtas (2) — Sanskrit (39)

sántaka (1) — confluence (23)

sãpnas (4) — dream (15)

sapnãvo (3rd prs. simple pret. of sapnúoti) — dreamed (15)

sapnúoti (sapnúoju, sapnúoja, sapnã-vo, sapnúos) — to dream (15)

sąrašas (3a) — list (39)

sąskaita (1) — bill, check (3)

sąspara (1) — joint, dovetail (20)

sáu (dat. reflexive pronoun) — to oneself, for oneself, to himself, for himself, etc. (29)

sáulė (1) — sun (27)

saulėlė (dim. of sáulė; 2) — sun (38)

saulùžė (dim. of sáulė; 2) — sun (A)

saũsas, -à (4) — dry (28)

saũsis -io (2) — January (22)

saváitė (1) — week (22)

savẽs (gen. reflexive pronoun) — oneself, himself, etc. (29)

savimì (instr. reflexive pronoun) — oneself, himself, etc. (29)

savìtarpis -io (1) — mutuality (A)

savìvalė (1) — unruliness, self-will (A)

savù (instr. of sãvas) — its own, one's own (10)

sàvo (reflexive possessive) — This pronoun always refers to the subject of the sentence; if the subject is in the 1st prs. sg. it will be translated 'my'; if the subject is in the 2nd prs. it will be translated 'your', etc., etc. (6)

sąžinìngas, -a (1) — conscientious (38)

Sebastijõnas (2) — Sebastian (A)

sėdėti (sėdžiu, sėdi, sėdėjo, sėdės) — to sit (i.e. to be in a sitting position) (6)

sėjà (4) — sowing (36)

sėkantis (masc. nom. sg. of pres. act. part. of sèkti) — next (14)

sekmãdienis -io (1) — Sunday (9)

sėkmė (4) — success (13)

sèkti (sekù, sėka, sėkė, sėks) — to follow (after [with instr.]); to notice, to watch (with acc.) (14)

sèktis (used in 3rd prs. only: sėkasi, sėkėsi, sėksis) — to succeed, to come along, to get along (38)

sėlis -io (1) — Selonian (35)

semèstras (2) — semester (32)

senaĩs laikaĩs (instr. plur.) — in ancient times (10)

senamè (masc. loc. sg. of sėnas) — in the old … (3)

senãmiestis -io (1) — old part of the city (26)

sėnas, -à (4) — old (5)

senãtvė (2) — old age (24)

senėlė (2) — grandmother (9)

senėlis -io (2) — grandfather (9)

seniaĩ — for a long time; a long time ago (7)

seniaũ (compar. degree of seniaĩ) — before, earlier, heretofore (A)

seniáusias, -a (superl. degree of sėnas) — oldest (27)

senóvė (1) — antiquity; the past (10)

senóvėje (loc. sg. of senóvė) — in ancient times, a long time ago (6)

senóviškas, -a (1) — archaic (38)

septynerì, septýnerios (3a) — seven (24)

septýnetas (1) — (a group of) seven (24)

septynì (with masc.; 3) — seven (4)

septýniasdešimt (indecl.) — seventy (24)

septyniasdešim̃tas, -à (4) — seventieth (29)

septyniólika (1) — seventeen (16)

septynióliktas, -a (1) — seventeenth

septýnios (used with fem.; 3) — seven (4)

septintãdalis -io (1) — one-seventh (24)

septiñtas, -à (4) — seventh (29)

seŕga (3rd prs. pres. of siŕgti) — is sick (25)

sesėlė (dim. of sesuõ; 2) — sister, dear sister (A)

sėserį (acc. sg. of sesuõ) — sister (2)

sesýtė (dim. of sesuõ; 1) — sister, dear sister (A)

sėskite (2nd plur. imper. of sėsti) — sit, sit down (15)

sėsti (sėdu, sėda, sėdo, sės) — to sit, to assume a sitting position, to sit down (15)

sesuõ, -eŕs (fem.; 3b) — sister; cf. 41.52 (2)

sesùtė (dim. of sesuõ; 2) — sister, little sister (2)

sėti (sėju, sėja, sėjo, sės) — to sow (16)

siaũras, -à (4) — narrow (35)

siaurèsnis, -ė (compar. degree of siaũras; 2) — narrower, more narrow (35)

siaũros (fem. nom. plur. of siaũras) — narrow (3)

sidabrìnis, -ė (2) — silver, made of silver (13)

siekìmas (2) — striving for, trying to reach (A)

síekti (síekiu, síekia, síekė, síeks) — to reach; to strive for (25)

síena (1) — wall; boundary (20)

sietýnas (1) — the Pleiades (A)

sijõnas (2) — skirt (25)

sìlpnas, -à (4) — weak (27)

silpnèsnis, -ė (compar. degree of sìlpnas; 2) — weaker (27)

sim̃bolis -io (1) — symbol (A)

simfonìnis, -ė (2) — symphony (32)

siȓgti (sergù, seȓga, siȓgo, siȓgs) — to be sick, to be ill (19)

siuntinỹs (3b) — shipment; parcel, package (to mail) (22)

siū́ti (siuvù, siùva, siùvo, siùs) — to sew (33)

siùvamas, -à (pres. passive part. of siū́ti; 3) — being sewed; sewing (33)

skaičiúoti (skaičiúoju, skaičiúoja, skaičiãvo, skaičiuõs) — to count

skaĩčius (2) — number, figure (19)

skaidrèsnis, -ė (compar. degree of skaidrùs; 2) — clearer, more transparent (27)

skaidrùs, -ì (3) — clear, transparent, clean (27)

skaistùs, -ì (4) — fresh, bright (A)

skaitýti (skaitaũ, skaĩto, skaĩtė, skaitỹs) — to read (2)

skaitýtojas (1) — reader (33)

skaĩto (3rd prs. pres. of skaitýti) — reads (2)

skaĩtome (1st prs. plur. pres. of skaitýti) — we read (2)

skambėjimas (1) — sound, ringing (A)

skam̃binti (skam̃binu, skam̃bina, skam̃bino, skam̃bins) — to ring up, to call up; to play (a piano); to ring, to toll (13)

skaniaĩ — in a tasty manner (12)

skanùs, -ì (4) — tasty, good-tasting

skarà (4) — scarf, kerchief (A)

skaudėjimas (1) — pain, ache (37)

skaudėti (3rd person only: skaũda, skaudėjo, skaudės) — to ache (29)

skersaĩ (prep. with gen. or acc.) — across, athwart

skę̃sti (skęstù, skę̃sta, skeñdo, skę̃s) — to disappear into, to sink into; to be drowned (10)

skėtis -čio (2) — umbrella (25)

skyrẽlis -io (2) — compartment; division (24)

skìrstyti (skìrstau, skìrsto, skìrstė, skìrstys) — to divide, to apportion, to classify (39)

skìrti (skiriù, skìria, skýrė, skiȓs) — to name, to appoint; to bequeath, to assign (23)

skìrtumas (1) — difference (37)

skliaũtas (2) — arch, vault (A)

skolà (4) — loan (A)

skolìngas, -a (1) — indebted (14)

skorpiònas (2) — scorpion (34)

skraidýti (skraidaũ, skraĩdo, skraĩdė, skraidỹs) — to fly about, to fly to and fro (37)

skránda (1) — sheepskin coat (38)

skrybėlė̃ (3a) — hat (25)

skrynià (2) — big box (A)

skrìsti (skrendù, skreñda, skrìdo, skrìs) — to fly (28)

skrúostas (3) — cheek (25)

skruzdė̃ (4) — ant (34)

skubėti (skubù, skubì, skubėjo, skubės) — to hurry (13)

skubiaĩ — hurriedly (12)

skùbintis (skùbinuosi, skùbinasi, skùbinosi, skùbinsis) — to hurry (26)

skubùs, -ì (4) — hurried (12)

slãvas (2) — Slav, Slavic person (39)

smagùs, -ì (4) cheerful (12)

smãkras (4) — chin (25)

smalsùs, -ì (4) — curious (18)

smaȓkiai — violently, severely (16)

smiltìs -iẽs (fem.; 4) — sand (A)

smū́gis -io (2) — blow, stroke (36)

sniẽgas (4) — snow (5)

sniẽgs — cf. sniẽgas (38)

sõdas (2) — orchard, garden (15)

sodẽlis -io (dim. of sõdas; 2) — little garden; little orchard; back yard with some trees, flowers) (26)

sodýba (1) — homestead, settlement (35)

sodìnti (sodinù, sodìna, sodìno, sodìns) — to plant (8)

sofà (2) — sofa (15)

sóstinė (1) — capital city (3)

spãlis -io (also used in plur.; 2) — October; shive (of flax) (32)

spalvà (4) — color (39)

spalvìngas, -a (1) — colorful (28)

spáudžiamas, -à (pres. passive part. of spáusti; 3) — forced, under the pressure of (A)

spáusti (spáudžiu, spáudžia, spáudė, spaũs) — to squeeze, to pinch (of shoes); to make someone do something, to force someone to do something (25)

spė́ti (spė́ju, spė́ja, spė́jo, spė́s) — to have time to, to be able to (A)

spygliúotas, -a (1) — coniferous

spygliúotis -čio (2) — coniferous tree (34)

spindėti (spindžiù, spiñdi, spindėjo, spindės) — to glitter, to glisten, to shine (A)

447

spìriamas, -à (pres. passive part. of
  spìrti; 3) — is forced (A)
spìrti (spiriù, spìria, spýrė, spiřs) —
  to urge, to force; to kick (A)
spréndžiant (spec. gerund of sprᶒsti)
  — judging (35)
sprᶒsti (spréndžiu, spréndžia, sprén-
  dė, sprᶒs) — to judge, to decide
sritìnis, -ė (2) — regional, area, divisional (36)
sritìs -iẽs (fem.; 4) — region, area,
  field (35)
sriubà (4) — soup (3)
stãlas (4) — table (11)
statýbininkas (1) — builder, con-
  tractor (34)
statýti (stataũ, stãto, stãtė, statýs)
  — to build, to set up; to place, to
  put (15)
staugìmas (2) — howl, howling
stebᶒti (stebliû, stᶒbi, stebėjo, stebᶒs)
  — to observe, to watch
stebᶒtis (stebiúosi, stᶒbisi, stebėjosi,
  stebᶒsis) — to wonder, to be sur-
  prised
sténgtis (sténgiuosi, sténgiasi, sténgėsi, sténgsis) — to try, to make
  an effort (21)
stìgti (stingù, stiñga, stìgo, stìgs) —
  to lack, to be short of (with gen.)
  (A)
stìklas (4) — glass (6)
stiprᶒti (stiprᶒju, stiprᶒja, stiprᶒjo,
  stiprᶒs) — to become strong, to be
  strong (37)
stiprùs, -ì (4) — strong (27)
stógas (3) — roof (10)
stóras, -à (3) — thick, fat (33)
stóti (stóju, stója, stójo, stõs) — to
  stand up; (with prep. į) to enter,
  to begin (39)
stotìs -iẽs (fem.; 4) — station (2)
stovᶒti (stóviu, stóvi, stovᶒjo, stovᶒs)
  — to stand, to be in a standing
  position (11)
stovyklà (2) — camp (26)
strõpiai — diligently (31)
studeñtai (nom. plur. of studeñtas) —
  — students (1)
studeñtas (2) — (male) student (1)
studeñtė (2) — (female) student (2)
studeñtų (gen. plur. of studeñtas) —
  students (3)
studijúoti (studijúoju, studijúoja, stu-
  dijãvo, studijuõs) — to study (at
  a university) (3)

stulpas (4) — support, pillar (A)
sù (prep. with instr.) — with (6)
su-darýti (sudaraũ, sudãro, sudãrė,
  sudarýs) — to form, to constitute,
  to make up, to compose (14)
su-daužýti (sudaužaũ, sudaũžo, su-
  daũžė, sudaužýs) — to break to
  pieces, to smash
su-dėti (sùdedu, sùdeda, sudėjo, su-
  dᶒs) — to put together; to put in,
  to load in (14)
sudėtìnis, -ė (2) — compound (13)
sudiẽu (sudiẽ, sudiẽv) — good-bye
  (3)
sūdùvis -io (2) — Sudovian (an Old
  Prussian tribe) (35)
suᶒdė (3rd prs. simple pret. of su-
  ᶒsti) — devoured, ate up (A)
su-eĩti (sueinù, sueĩna, suᶒjo, sueĩs)
  — to come together, to congregate,
  to meet (14)
su-ᶒsti (suᶒdu, suᶒda, suᶒdė, suᶒs) —
  to eat up, to devour (A)
su-gaĩšti (sugaĩštù, sugaĩšta, sugaĩšo,
  sugaĩš) — to linger, to delay (38)
su-galvóti (sugalvóju, sugalvója, su-
  galvójo, sugalvõs) — to figure out
  (31)
su-gèsti (sugendù, sugeñda, sugᶒdo,
  sugᶒs) — to break down, to go bad,
  to be ruined (13)
su-grᶏžìnti (sugrᶏžinù, sugrᶏžìna, su-
  grᶏžìno, sugrᶏžìñs) — to return,
  to bring back (33)
su-griúti (sugriúvù, sugriúva [sugriū-
  na], sugriùvo, sugriùs) — to col-
  lapse, to fall to the ground (A)
su-grȋžti (sugrȋžtù, sugrȋžta, sugrȋžo,
  sugrȋš) — to return, to come back
  (16)
su-imti (sùimu, sùima, sùėmė, suim̃s)
  to arrest (34)
su-jùngti (sujùngiu, sujùngia, sujùn-
  gė, sujuñgs) — to unite, to put together (A)
sukaktùvės (used in plur.; 2) — anniversary (23)
su-kietᶒti (sukietᶒju, sukietᶒja, su-
  kietᶒjo, sukietᶒs) — to get hard, to
  harden (34)
su-kìlti (sukylù, sukýla, sukìlo, su-
  kiľs) — to rise (against) (36)
su-kliudýti (sukliudaũ, sukliùdo, su-
  kliùdė, sukliudýs) — to prevent, to
  hinder (A)

su-klóstyti (suklóstau, suklósto, su-klóstė, suklóstys) — to fold, to lay in layers (34)

suknėlė (2) — dress (25)

su-kráuti (sukráunu, sukráuna, su-króvė, sukraūs) — to load up, to load in (37)

su-krŷkti (sukrykiù, sukrŷkia, su-krŷkė, sukrŷks) — to quack, to cry out, to creak (10)

sùkti (sukù, sùka, sùko, sùks) — to turn (7)

sùktis (sukúosi, sùkasi, sùkosi, sùk-sis) — to revolve, to spin, to whirl about (26)

su-kùrti (sùkuriu, sùkuria, sukūrė, sukuřs) — to create, to found (4)

su-latvėti (sulatvėju, sulatvėja, sulat-vėjo, sulatvės) — to become Latvian (Lettish) (35)

su-láukti (suláukiu, suláukia, suláukė, sulaūks) — to wait (until some-one comes)

suláukus (spec. gerund of suláukti) — after (i.e. having waited) (A)

su-lietuvėti (sulietuvėju, sulietuvėja, sulietuvėjo, sulietuvės) — to be-come Lithuanian (35)

sulìg (prep. with instr.) — according to; about the size of, up to, as far as (19)

su-lìpti (sulimpù, sulim̃pa, sulìpo, su-lìps) — to stick together (25)

sumãnymas (1) — idea, thought (38)

sumanùmas (2) — cleverness, wis-dom, shrewdness (37)

su-maskõlinti (sumaskõlinu, sumas-kõlina, sumaskõlino, sumaskõlins) — to Russianize

su-mègzti (sùmezgu, sùmezga, sù-mezgė, sumègs) — to tie together, to knit closely (A)

su-mokėti (sumóku, sumóka, sumokė-jo, sumokės) — to pay (34)

su-mùšti (sùmušu, sùmuša, sùmušė, sumùš) — to beat; to crush (in a war); to win (a battle); to smash (36)

su-naikìnti (sunaikinù, sunaikìna, su-naikìno, sunaikiñs) — to destroy (37)

sūnėlis -io (dim. of sūnùs; 2) — son, little son

suñkiai (adv.) — heavily, hard (12)

sunkù (neuter form of sunkùs) — (it is) difficult (3)

sunkùs, -ì (4) — heavy; difficult (12)

sūnùs (3) — son (6)

súomis -io (1) — Finn, Finnish per-son (35)

su-pa-žìndinti (supažìndinu, supažìn-dina, supažìndino, supažìndins) — to introduce to (su with instr.); to acquaint (somebody with somebody else) (22)

supŷkęs (masc. nom. sg. of past act. part. of supŷkti) — angry (A)

su-pŷkti (supykstù, supŷksta, supŷ-ko, supŷks) — to get mad at, to get angry with (26)

su-pràsti (suprantù, suprañta, suprā-to, supràs) — to understand (2)

supràtęs (masc. nom. sg. of past act. part. of supràsti) — understood, having understood (A)

supràto (3rd prs. simple pret. of su-pràsti) — understood (36)

su-pūti (supūvù, supūva [supūna], supùvo, supùs) — to rot, to putre-fy (13)

su-ràsti (surandù, surañda, surãdo, suràs) — to find (25)

su-rìkti (surinkù, suriñka, surìko, su-rìks) — to begin to shout; to give out a short cry

su-riñkti (sùrenku, sùrenka, suriñko, suriñks) — to pick, to gather (19)

sūris -io (1) — cheese (37)

su-rìšti (sùrišu, sùriša, surìšo, surìš) — to bind together, to tie together (A)

su-rūdýti (surūdijù, surūdìja, surūdì-jo, surūdŷs) — to rust (13)

su-sėsti (susėdu, susėda, susėdo, su-sės) — to sit down, to sit down together (26)

su-si-darýti (susidaraū, susidãro, su-sidãrė, susidarŷs) — to originate, to have its origin, to be formed (39)

su-si-dėstyti (susidėstau, susidėsto, susidėstė, susidėstys) — to put/lay together; to compose (oneself); to develop

su-si-dùrti (susìduriu, susìduria, susi-dūrė, susidurs) — to collide (with each other) (18)

susiglaūdusių (gen. plur. of past act. part. of susiglaūsti) — pressed to-gether (26)

su-si-glaūsti (susiglaudžiù, susiglaū-džia, susìglaudė, susiglaūs) — to press together, to be close to each other (26)

449

su-si-jùngti (susijùngiu, susijùngia, susìjungė, susijuñgs) — to get oneself united with (sù) (36)

susìjusj (masc. acc. sg. of past act. part. of susýti) — connected with (sù) (A)

susiklaũsymas (1) — agreement, harmony (A)

su-silpnėti (susilpnėju, susilpnėja, susilpnėjo, susilpnės) — to weaken, to grow weaker (37)

su-si-pažìnti (susipažįstu, susipažįsta, susipažìno, susipažiñs) — to become acquainted with, to get to know (7)

su-si-ràsti (susirandù, susirañda, susiràdo, susiràs) — to find for oneself (11)

susir̃gęs, -usi (past act. part. of susir̃gti) — ill, sick

su-sir̃gti (sùsergu, sùserga, susir̃go, susìrgs) — to become ill (21)

su-si-riñkti (susìrenku, susìrenka, susiriñko, susiriñks) — to gather (intransitive), to meet (18)

su-si-rìšti (susìrišu, susìriša, susirìšo, susirìš) — to be tied together, to be bound together (A)

susiskìrstymas (1) — (systematic) division, grouping (35)

su-si-skìrstyti (susiskìrstau, susiskìrsto, susiskìrstė, susiskìrstys) — to be divided (35)

su-si-tar̃ti (susìtariu, susìtaria, susìtarė, susitar̃s) — to reach an agreement, to conclude an agreement (37)

su-sýti (susyjù, susȳja, susìjo, susȳs) — to be connected with (A)

su-si-tìkti (susitinkù, susitiñka, susitìko, susitìks) — to meet (each other) (7)

su-si-žeĩsti (susìžeidžiù, susìžeidžia, susìžeidė, susìžeĩs) — to hurt oneself, to wound oneself (25)

su-skaitýti (suskaitaũ, suskaĩto, suskaĩtė, suskaitȳs) — to count (17)

su-skìlti (suskylù, suskȳla, suskìlo, suskiĩs) — to branch out, to split (39)

su-slė̃gti (sùslegiu, sùslegia, sùslėgė, suslė̃gs) — to press together (34)

su-spė́ti (suspė́ju, suspė́ja, suspė́jo, suspė́s) — to be in time, to have enough time (to do something) (32)

su-stabdýti (sustabdaũ, sustãbdo, su-stãbdė, sustabdȳs) — to stop, to cause to stop (36)

su-stìngti (sustìngstu, sustìngsta, sustìngo, sustìñgs) — to get hard, to harden (34)

sustojìmas (1) — stop, bus-stop (15)

su-stóti (sustóju, sustója, sustójo, sustõs) — to stop, to halt (24)

susvyrãvo (3rd prs. simple pret. of susvyrúoti) — swayed, tottered (A)

su-svyrúoti (susvyrúoju, susvyrúoja, susvyrãvo, susvyruõs) — to sway, to totter (A)

su-šálti (sušą́lu, sušą́la, sušãlo, sušaĩs) — to get thoroughly cold (26)

su-šìlti (sušylù, sušȳla, sušìlo, sušiĩs) — to warm up (26)

su-šlamė́ti (sùšlamu, sùšlama, sušlamė́jo, sušlamė́s) — to rustle (10)

su-šókti (sušóku, sušóka, sušóko, sušóks) — to jump (A)

su-šùkti (sušunkù, sušuñka, sušùko, sušùks) — to shout, to call (25)

su-tar̃ti (sùtariu, sùtaria, sùtarė, sutar̃s) — to settle upon, to agree with (A)

su-tekė́ti (sùteku, sùteka, sutekė́jo, sutekė́s) — to flow together

su-tìkti (sutinkù, sutiñka, sutìko, sutìks) — to meet; to agree (35)

su-trukdýti (sutrukdaũ, sutrùkdo, su-trùkdė, sutrukdȳs) — to hinder, to prevent, to stop; to disturb (16)

su-trum̃pinti (sutrum̃pinu, sutrum̃pina, sutrum̃pino, sutrum̃pins) — to shorten

su-tvarkýti (sutvarkaũ, sutvar̃ko, su-tvar̃kė, sutvarkȳs) — to put in order, to straighten out, to arrange (37)

su-úosti (suúodžiu, suúodžia, suúodė, suuõs) — to smell, to catch the smell of something (17)

su-válgyti (suválgau, suválgo, suválgė, suválgys) — to eat up, to consume (25)

su-varvė́ti (sùvarvu, sùvarva, suvarvė́jo, suvarvė́s) — to gather by dripping (34)

su-važiúoti (suvažiúoju, suvažiúoja, suvažiãvo, suvažiuõs) — to come together (in a vehicle, in vehicles) (5)

su-viẽnyti (suviẽniju, suviẽnija, su-viẽnijo, suviẽnys) — to unify, to unite (36)

450

suviēnytas, -a (past passive part. of suviēnyti) — united (36)
su-vókietinti (suvókietinu, suvókietina, suvókietino, suvókietins) — to Germanize (35)
su-žinóti (sužinaū, sužìno, sužinójo, sužinõs) — to learn, to find out (A)
svajõnė (2) — dream (31)
svarbèsnis, -ė (compar. degree of svarbùs; 2) — more important (A)
svarbiáusia — most important of all (A)
svarbiáusias, -a (superl. degree of svarbùs; 1) — the most important (27)
svarbùs, -ì (4) — important (27)
svēčias (4) — guest (19)
Svedasaī (3a) — a town in eastern Lithuania
sveīkas, -à (4) healthy, sane, whole; hello; you (5)
sveikatà (2) — health (19)
sveikiaū — (it is) healthier, better (13)
svéikinti (svéikinu, svéikina, svéikino, svéikins) — to greet, to give regards to (14)
sveīkti (sveikstù, sveīksta, sveīko, sveīks) — to recover, to get better, to get well (25)
svētimas, -à (3b) — foreign (35)
svíestas (1) — butter (12)
svíetas (1) — (archaic) world (38)
svìrti (svyrù, svỹra, svìro, svìrs) — to sway, to bend down
svìrtis, -ies (fem.; 1) — water-pulley, water-lift (10)

š

šakà (4) — branch (15)
šakėlė (dim. of šakà; 2) — twig, little branch (34)
šalčių (gen. plur. of šaltis) — cold's, cold weather's (38)
šaldytùvas (2) — refrigerator (29)
šalėlė (dim. of šalìs; 2) — country, land (A)
šalià (prep. with gen.) — near, by, at the side of
šalìgatvis -io (1) — sidewalk (23)
šalìs, -iēs (fem.; 4) — country; side (10)
šalnà (4) — frost (26)
šáltas, -à (3) — cold (20)
šaltìnis -io (2) — source, well (35)
šaltis -čio (2) — cold (weather) (25)

šauksminiñkas (2) — vocative (3)
šáukštas (1) —spoon (33)
šaūkti (šaukiù, šaūkia, šaūkė, šaūks) — to shout; to call forth
šáuti (šáunu, šáuna, šóvė, šaūs) — to shoot
šeimà (4) — family (2)
šeimiñkė (2) — housewife; landlady; hostess (2)
šēšerì, šēšerios (3b) — six (24)
šēšetas (1) — (a group of) six (24)
šešì (used with masc.; 4) — six (4)
šēšiasdešimt (indecl.) — sixty (24)
šešiasdešiñtas, -à (4) — sixtieth (29)
šešiólika (1) — sixteen (16)
šešióliktas, -a (1) — sixteenth (29)
šēšios (used with fem.; 4) — six (4)
šeštãdalis -io (1) — one-sixth (24)
šeštãdienis -io (1) — Saturday (32)
šēštas, -à (4) — sixth (29)
šetõniškai — devilishly, satanically (A)
šiaīp — so, in this way, as it is; otherwise, else (35)
šiaīp taīp — with great effort, somehow or other, barely (15)
šiãnakt — tonight (A)
šiañdien — today (6)
šiandienìnis, -ė (2) — today's, contemporary (A)
šiàpus (prep. with gen.) — this side of, on this side of
Šiauliaī (used in plur.; 4) — city in northern Lithuania (10)
šiáurė (1) — north (10)
šiáurę (acc. sg. of šiáurė) — north (10)
šiaurìnis, -ė (2) — northern (35)
šiaurỹs (4) — north-wind (A)
šiēmet — this year (26)
šiēnas (4) — hay (26)
šykštùs, -ì (4) — miserly, stingy (39)
šìlas (4) — pine forest (10)
šilčiaū — warmer (37)
šilčiáusias, -a (superl. degree of šìltas; 1) — warmest (36)
šìldyti (šìldau, šìldo, šìldė, šìldys) — to warm, to heat (4)
šìlkas (4) — silk (A)
šiltas, -à (4) — warm (7)
šiluvìnis, -ė (2) — pertaining to Šiluva (A)
šiñtas (2) — hundred (19)
šiñtas, -à (4) — hundredth (29)
šiñtmetis -čio (1) — century
šiõ (gen. sg. of šìs) — of this (15)
šióks tóks — poor, of mediocre qual-

ity, bad (cf. 36.5)

šiomìs (fem. instr. plur. of **šìs**) — these (24)

šỹpsena (1) — smile (A)

širdìs -iẽs (fem.; 3) — heart (15)

širdė̃lė (dim. of **širdìs**; 2) — heart (A)

šìtas, -à — this, this one; cf. 36.1 (6)

šis, šì — this; cf. 36.1 (5)

šìtoks, -ia (1) — this kind of; cf. 36.1

šiuõ metù (instr. sg. of **šìs mẽtas**) — at this time, nowadays (23)

šlamė́jimas (1) — rustling sound (37)

šlamė́ti (šlamù, šlãma, šlamė́jo, šlamė̃s) — to make a rustling sound (10)

šlaunìs -iẽs (fem.; 4) — thigh (25)

šlovė̃ (3) — honor, glory (A)

šokolãdas (2) — chocolate (17)

šókti (šóku, šóka, šóko, šõks) — to rush, to jump; to dance (A)

štaĩ (interj.) — here, look here; expresses vividness, brings the action closer to the speaker

šùnį (acc. sg. of **šuõ**) — dog (7)

šunýčiai (nom. plur. of **šunýtis**) — dogs (A)

šunìms (dat. plur. of **šuõ**) — to the dogs (A)

šunýtis -čio (dim. of **šuõ**) — dog (A)

šuniùkas (dim. of **šuõ**; 2) — puppy, little dog (A)

šuñs (gen. sg. of **šuõ**) — dog (10)

šuõ, šuñs or šuniẽs (4) — dog; cf. 41.50 (7)

šv. — abbreviation for **šveñtas** (A)

švar̃kas (2) — jacket (25)

švarùs, -ì (4) — clean (25)

švelnùs, -ì (4) — gentle, mild, light (A)

šveñčiamas, -à (pres. passive part. of **švę̃sti**; 3) — celebrated (31)

šveñtas, -à (4) — saint, holy (A)

šventė̃ (2) — holiday, celebration (31)

švę̃sti (švenčiù, šveñčia, šveñtė, švę̃s) — to celebrate (31)

šviesùs, -ì (4) — bright, light, luminous (A)

švìlptelė́ti (švìlpteliu, švìlptelia, švìlptelėjo, švìlptelės) — to give out a little whistle

švìnas (4) — lead (A)

T

tabãkas (2) — tobacco (19)

tačiaũ (conj.) — but, nevertheless, still, however, in spite of that (6)

tadà — then, at that time (11)

taĩ (conj.) — so then (9)

taĩ (pronoun, expletive) — that, this (3)

taĩ gãlima matýti — one can see that (24)

taĩ ką̃ — and what...; and whom...; so what (are you doing...)

tai ką̃ gi — well, well; well now (13)

taĩ todėl — that's why (29)

taĩgi — therefore (19)

taĩgi ir̃ — so that even, thus even (35)

taikìngas, -a (1) — peaceful (37)

taĩp — yes; so, so much; thus, in this way (13)

taĩp, kàd (conj.) — so that (15)

taĩp, kaĩp — just as, such as (15)

taĩp pàt — also, too (2)

taĩp pàt ... kaĩp — just as ... as (17)

taĩs mẽtais (instr. plur. of **tiẽ mẽtai**) — in that year; in those years (days), then (36)

taisýklė (2) — rule (18)

tàkš — onomatopoetic word denoting striking or falling

tãlentas (1) — talent (19)

talkiniñkas (2) — helper, supporter (37)

tamè (masc. loc. sg. of **tàs**) — in that... (25)

tamsiáusias, -a (superl. degree of **tamsùs**; 1) — darkest (A)

támsta — (polite) you

tamsùs, -ì (4) — dark (12)

tánkus, -ì (1 or 3) — thick, dense, close (10)

Tãnenbergas (1) — Tannenberg (37)

tàpti (tampù, tam̃pa, tãpo, tàps) — to become (23)

tãrė (3rd prs. simple pret. of **tar̃ti**) — said (25)

tarnáuti (tarnáuju, tarnáuja, tarnãvo, tarnaũs) — to serve, to be of service (16)

tarnáutojas (1) — employee (33)

tar̃p (prep. with gen.) — between, among (10)

tárpas (1) — interval, span of time; surroundings, society (23)

tar̃ti (tariù, tãria, tãrė, tar̃s) — to say, to pronounce, to utter (15)

tàs, tà — that; cf. 36.1 (5)

taškė̃lis -io (2) — little dot (24)

táu (dat. of **tù**) — to you (8)

Taurãgnai (2) — town in eastern Lithuania

taurùs, -ì (4) — noble, sublime (A)

tautà (4) — nation; folk (35)

tautýbė (1) — nationality (A)

tautìnis, -ė (2) — national (A)

tavè (acc. of tù) — you (25)

tavęs (gen. of tù) — you (15)

tàvo (possessive of tù) — your, yours (19)

tè — take, here; cf. 38.5

teãtras (2) — theater (5)

tèchniškas, -a — technical (A)

tegù (particle introducing exhortation) — may, let (someone do something; cf. 38.5

teĩgiamas, -à (pres. passive part. of teĩgti; 3) — affirmed, thought to be true, affirmative, positive (35)

teĩgti (teigiù, teĩgia, teĩgė, teĩgs) — to affirm, to assert (35)

téisė (1) — right

teisýbė (1) — truth; that's right (27)

tèkti (tenkù, teñka, tēko, tèks) — to fall to one's share, to come to, to belong; to have to, to be required to (with logical subject in dative) (35)

telefònas (2) — telephone (2)

televìzija (1) — television (20)

teñ — there (20)

tenaĩ — there (15)

terióti (terióju, teriója, teriójo, teriõs) (archaic) to desolate, to lay waste, to ravage (A)

teritòrija (1) — territory (35)

tęstinùmas (2) — continuity (A)

tėtė (2) — father (term of endearment) (3)

tėtis -čio (2) — dad, father (term of endearment) (5)

tėtùšis -io — daddy, papa (A)

tėvaĩ (used in plur.; 4) — parents (19)

tėvas (3) — father (1)

tėvėliai (dim. of tėvaĩ; 2) — parents (14)

tėvėlis -io (dim. of tėvas; 2) — dad, daddy, father (19)

tėvýnė (2) homeland, fatherland (22)

tíek — as much as many; so many, so much; so

tíek daũg — so many (18)

tíek ... kaĩp — so (as) ... as (A)

tíek ... kíek — so much ... as (A)

tiẽs (prep. with instr.) — opposite to, in front of; near, by, at (23)

tiesà (4) — truth; also used as tag word with meaning 'isn't it?', 'aren't they?', 'aren't you?', etc. Like n'est-ce pas. (6)

tiesióg — straight ahead; directly

tiesióginis, -ė (1) — direct (A)

tiẽsti (tiesiù, tiẽsia, tiẽsė, tiẽs) — to straighten out, to make straight (37)

tìk — only (2)

tìk ką̃ — just now, a few moments ago (6)

tikėjimas (1) — religion, faith, belief (A)

tikėti (tikiù, tìki, tikėjo, tikės) — to believe, to trust (7) (with instr.)

tikėtis (tikiúosi, tìkisi, tikėjosi, tikėsis) — to expect, to hope for (7)

tikýba (1) — faith, religion (A)

tikraĩ — really, actually, indeed, for sure (7)

tìkras, -à (4) — real, true, certain; iš tikrųjų 'in reality' (7)

tiktaĩ — only (28)

tìkti (tinkù, tiñka, tìko, tìks) — to fit, to be suitable (33)

týliai — silently (16)

tìmpt — denotes a slight tug, a jerk

tinginỹs (3a) — lazy-bones, lazy fellow (14)

tiñkamas, -à (pres. passive part. of tìkti; 3) — suitable (33)

tinkąs, -anti (pres. act. part. of tìkti; 1;) — suitable (33)

týras, -à (3) — pure, clear, genuine (A)

tochãras (2) — Tokharian (39)

todėl — therefore (8)

tóji (fem. nom. sg. definite form of tà) — this, that; cf. 44.7 (A)

tókiu būdù (instr. sg.) — in this way, in this manner (16)

tóks, -ià (3) — such, such a; cf. 36.1 (11)

tõl — so far, so long (38)

toliaũ (compar. degree of tolì) — further, farther (10)

toliaũ (prep. with gen.) — beyond, farther than

tólimas, -à (3a) -- far away, distant (21)

tolỹn — farther on

Tolmìnkiemis -io (1) — place in Lithuania Minor (37)

tolókas, -a (1) — a bit far, rather far (37)

453

tõs (fem. gen. sg. or nom. plur. of tàs) — that, this (15)
totõrius (2) — Tartar (person) (37)
tradìcija (1) — tradition (A)
tradìcinis, -ė (1) — traditional (A)
trãgiškas, -a (1) — tragic (A)
trãkas (2) — Thracian (39)
tramvājus (2) — streetcar, trolley-car (23)
trankýtis (trankaūsi, trañkosi, trañkėsi, trankýsis) — to shake, to go on a rough ride (32)
traukinỹs (3a) — train (19)
tráukti (tráukiu, tráukia, tráukė, traūks) — to drag, to draw, to pull (A)
trečdalis -io (1) — one-third (24)
trečiādienis -io (1) — Wednesday (32)
trečias, -ià (4) — third (20)
trėjetas (1) — (a group of) three (24)
trejì, trėjos (4) — three (24)
trejì mėtai — three years
trijùlė (2) — triad, a group of three (35)
trýlika (1) — thirteen (16)
trýliktas, -a (1) thirteenth (29)
trinkt (interj.) — expresses the sound of crashing, smashing
triókšt (interj.) — expresses sound of breaking, cracking
trìs (acc. of trỹs) — three (14)
trỹs (4) — three (18)
trìsdešimt (indecl.) — thirty (24)
trisdešiṁtas, -à (4) — thirtieth (29)
triùkšmas (4) — noise, uproar, fuss (16)
triūsas (2) — labor, work (38)
trókšta (3rd prs. pres. of trókšti) — longs for (15)
trókšti (trókštu, trókšta, tróško, trõkš) — to long for, to wish for, to desire; to be thirsty (15)
trukdýti (trukdaū, trùkdo, trùkdė, trukdýs) — to disturb, to bother, to pester (11)
trùkt (interj.) — denotes a slight tug, jerk
trūkt (interj.) — denotes a strong, hard pulling
trūktinas, -a — scarce (35)
trumpaĩ (adv.) — short (17)
truṁpas, -à (4) — short (23)
trumpèsnis, -ė (compar. degree of truṁpas; 2) — shorter
truṁpinti (truṁpinu, truṁpina, truṁpino, truṁpins) — to shorten (17)

trùputį (acc. sg. of trùputis used as adv.) — a little bit, a little
trùputis -čio (1) — a bit, a morsel
tù — you (familiar) (7)
tūkstantas, -a (1) — thousandth (29)
tūkstantis -čio (1) — thousand (24)
tuõ (masc. instr. sg. of tàs) — that; right away, cf. tuojaū (25)
tuõ būdù (instr. sg.) — in that way, in that fashion (A)
tuõ metù (instr. sg.) — at that time (36)
tuõ tárpu (instr. sg.) — in the meantime (13)
tuõj — cf. tuojaū
tuojaū — right away, soon, immediately (11)
tuomèt — then, at that time (22)
tupėti (tupiù, tùpi, tupėjo, tupės) — to perch, to sit (of birds) (16)
tur būt — perhaps, it must be (24)
turėjo (3rd prs. simple pret. of turėti) — was supposed to (have been) (A)
turėti (turiù, tùri, turėjo, turės) — to have; to have to, to be supposed to, to be obliged to (5)
tuȓgus (2) — market; market-day (37)
turìstas (2) — tourist (15)
tuȓkas (2) — Turk, Turkish person (A)
tuȓtas (2) — wealth, property (18)
turtìngas, -a (1) — rich (15)
turtuõlis -io (2) — rich man (38)
tùščias, -à (4) — empty (31)
tvarkýti (tvarkaū, tvaȓko, tvaȓkė, tvarkýs) — to manage, to direct; to set in order (37)
tvirčiaū (compar. degree of tvirtaĩ) — more firmly, more strongly (A)
tvirtaĩ — firmly (36)
tvorà (4) — fence (37)

U
ugnìs -iẽs (fem.; 4) — fire (4)
ùi (interj.) — oh, ouch; expresses surprise, fear, pain
ūkininkas (1) — farmer (15)
ūkis -io (1) — farm; economy (9); žėmės ūkis — agriculture; píeno ūkis — dairy farming, etc.
ūkiškai — agriculturally; economically (A)
ùnija (1) — union (A)
universitètas (2) — university (23)
úoga (1) — berry (28)

úostas (1) — port, harbor (10)
ùpė (2) — river (7)
upýnas (1) — river-basin (35)
Upýtė (1) — a town in Lithuania
ūsas (commonly used in plur.; 2) — moustache (25)
ùž (prep.) — (with gen.) in (a certain amount of time), cf. 32.12; behind, across; (with acc.) for, in return for; than
už taĩ — in return for that (25)
už-áugti (užáugu, užáuga, užáugo, užaũgs) — to grow up (22)
už-darýti (uždaraũ, uždãro, uždãrė, uždarýs) — to close (15)
už-dègti (ùždegu, ùždega, ùždegė, uždègs) — to light, to turn on (15)
uždėk (2nd sg. imper. of uždègti) — turn on (lights) (15)
už-eĩti (užeinù, užeĩna, užėjo, užeĩs) — to drop in on; to go behind (14)
užėjote (2nd plur. simple pret. of už-eĩti) — you dropped in on (a person) (8)
užgniáužę (masc. nom. plur. of past act. part. of užgniáužti) — having suppressed (A)
už-gniáužti (užgniáužiu, užgniáužia, užgniáužė, užgniaũš) — to suppress, to quell (A)
už-imti (ùžimu, ùžima, ùžėmė, užiĩms) — to occupy (37)
už-kálbinti (užkálbinu, užkálbina, užkálbino, užkálbins) — to begin to talk to (24) (with acc.)
už-klùpti (užklumpù, užkluĩmpa, užklùpo, užklùps) — to come upon suddenly, to occur suddenly (A)
už-léisti (užléidžiu, užléidžia, užléido, užleĩs) — to cede, to give up (A)
už-máuti (užmáunu, užmáuna, užmóvė, užmaũs) — to put (a ring on a finger) (A)
už-mègzti (ùžmezgu, ùžmezga, ùžmezgė, užmègs) — to tie (36)
užmègzti ryšiùs — to get connected with, to initiate relations with (36)
už-migti (užmingù, užmiñga, užmìgo, užmìgs) — to fall asleep (15)
už-mir̃šti (užmirštù, užmir̃šta, užmir̃šo, užmir̃š) — to forget (14)
už-mokėti (užmóku, užmóka, užmokėjo, užmokės) — to pay up, to pay
už-mùšti (ùžmušu, ùžmuša, ùžmušė, užmùš) — to kill (36)

už-rašýti (užrašaũ, užrãšo, užrãšė, užrašỹs) — to note, to copy (A)
už-rýmoti (užrýmau, užrýmo, užrýmojo, užrýmos) — to become tired from leaning (A)
už-si-imti (užsìimu, ùžsiima, užsìėmė, užsiiĩms) — to be busy, to be occupied (14)
užsimojimas (2) — raising one's hand as if to strike; intention, aim, plan; range (A)
už-si-pùlti (užsipúolu, užsipúola, užsipúolė, užsipuls) — to attack (A)
už-slopìnti (užslopinù, užslopìna, užslopìno, užslopiñs) — to stifle; to suppress (A)
už-stel̃bti (užstelbiù, užstel̃bia, ùžstelbė, užstel̃bs) — to smother; to suppress (A)
už-sùkti (ùžsuku, ùžsuka, užsùko, užsùks) — to turn (in a certain direction) (39)
ūžt — denotes a sudden action
užtàt — that is why, therefore (A)
už-tèkti (užteñka, užtēko, užtèks) — to be sufficient, to suffice
ūžti (ūžiù, ūžia, ū̃žė, ū̃š) — to roar, to make a noise (A)
už-tìkrinti (užtìkrinu, užtìkrina, užtìkrino, užtìkrins) — to assure (37)
už-valdýti (užvaldaũ, užval̃do, užval̃dė, užvaldỹs) — to take over, to occupy (16)
už-válgyti (užválgau, užválgo, užválgė, užválgys) — to have a bite, to have a snack (15)

V

và (interj.) — look here; expresses command to look
vabzdỹs -džio (4) — insect (34)
vãdas (4) — leader (23)
vadìnamas, -a (pres. passive part. of vadìnti) — named, called
vadìnas (3rd prs. pres. of vadìntis) — that is, that means, i.e.; used as introductory statement for a clause (32)
vadìnasi (3rd prs. pres. of vadìntis) — he (she, it) is called (3)
vadìnti (vadinù, vadìna, vadìno, vadiñs) — to name, to call (23)
vadìntis (vadinúosi, vadìnasi, vadìnosi, vadiñsis) — to be called, to be named (6)

455

vadováujamas, -a (pres. passive part. of vadováuti; 1) — led by, under the leadership of (36)

vadováuti (vadováuju, vadováuja, vadovǎvo, vadovaũs) — to lead, to guide, to direct (36)

vagìs -iẽs (masc.; 4) — thief (18)

vagỹstė (2) — theft (34)

vagõnas (2) — (railway) car, wagon (23)

vaĩ (interj.) — oh! ah!

vaidilà (2) — priest (in pagan mythology); actor (3)

vaidìntis (vaidinúosi, vaidìnasi, vaidìnosi, vaidiñsis) — to appear as a specter (A)

vaĩkas (4) — child (19)

vaikẽlis -io (dim. of vaĩkas; 2) — little child (20)

vaikštinẽti (vaikštinẽju, vaikštinẽja, vaikštinẽjo, vaikštinẽs) to stroll about (A)

váikštyti (váikštau, váikšto, váikštė, váikštys) — to wander about (A) (usually used in the present tense only)

vainìkas (2) — crown; wreath (36)

vainikǎvimas (1) — coronation; crowning success (A)

vainikẽlis -io (dim. of vainìkas) — wreath, crown (A)

vainikúoti (vainikúoju, vainikúoja, vainikǎvo, vainikuõs) — to crown (36)

vainikúotis (vainikúojuosi, vainikúojasi, vainikǎvosi, vainikuõsis) — to be crowned (A)

vairúoti (vairúoju, vairúoja, vairǎvo, vairuõs) — to steer; to drive (18)

vairúotojas (1) — driver (36)

vairúotojo liùdijimas — driver's license (36)

vaĩsius (2) — fruit (6)

váistas (usually in plur.; 1) — medicine

vaĩzdas (4) — view; picture, portrayal (35)

vaizdìngas, -a (1) — full of beautiful images, poetical (38)

vajè (interj.) — oh, good heavens, ah; expresses surprise, exclamation

vǎkar — yesterday (8)

vakaraĩ (nom. plur. of vǎkaras; 3b) — west (10)

vakaraĩs (instr. plur. of vǎkaras) — in the evenings (23)

vǎkaras (3b) — evening; used in plural means 'west' (1)

vakarè (loc. sg. of vǎkaras) — in the evening (1)

vakariẽnė (2) — supper, evening meal (23)

vakariẽnę (acc. sg. of vakariẽnė) — supper (2)

vakarìnis, -ė (2) — western (35)

Vakarų̃ Euròpa — Western Europe (A)

vakaruosè (loc. plur. of vǎkaras) — in the west (10)

valandà (3b) — hour (16)

valdiniñkas (2) — public official; pǎšto valdiniñkas 'post-man' (6)

valdìnis, -ė (2) — official (A)

valdýti (valdaũ, vaĩdo, vaĩdė, valdỹs) — to rule (36)

vaĩdomas, a (pres. passive part. of valdýti) — ruled (36)

valdõvas (2) — ruler (36)

valdžià (4) — power, authority, rule, government (popular) (A)

valgyklà (2) — restaurant, diner (23)

válgyti (válgau, válgo, válgė, válgys) to eat (3)

válgomas, -a (pres. passive part. of válgyti; 1) — being eaten; eaten; edible (33)

valià (2) — will (15)

valiõ (interj.) — hurrah, hurray; expresses approval

valýti (valaũ, vǎlo, vǎlė, valỹs) — to clean (2)

vǎlo (3rd prs. pres. of valýti) — cleans (2)

valstýbė (1) — state (10)

valstýbinis, -ė (1) — governmental, government (A)

valùžė (dim. of valià; 2) — will, free will, freedom (A)

vanagẽlis -io (dim. of vǎnagas; 2) — hawk (A)

vandenáitis -čio (dim. of vanduõ; 1) — water (A)

vandenýnas (1) — ocean (10)

vanduõ -eñs (3a) — water; cf. 41.51 (15)

vařdas (4) — name (7)

vardìnės (used in plur.; 2) — name-day (the day of the saint for which the individual is named; sometimes celebrated rather than the birthday)

vardiniñkas (2) — nominative; the man whose name day is being celebrated (3)

vaȓgas (4) — misery, trouble, hardship, care, suffering (38)
vargdiẽnis -io (2) — poor fellow, poor guy
vargėlis -io (dim. of **vaȓgas**; 2) — trouble, care, sorrow (A)
vaȓgiai — hardly, scarcely (A)
vargìngas, -a (1) — poor, miserable, wretched; troublesome (15)
vaȓgšas (2) — poor fellow, poor guy (15)
vaȓgti (vargstù, vaȓgsta, vaȓgo, vaȓgs) — to suffer, to eke out a living (10)
vargù — hardly, with difficulty (A)
vargùs, -ì (4) — miserable, difficult (A)
várna (1) — crow (16)
vaȓpas (4) — bell (23)
vaȓtai (used in plur.; 2) — gate
vartóti (vartóju, vartója, vartójo, vartõs) — to use (35)
vãsara (1) — summer (13)
vasarìnis, -ė (2) — summer (24)
vasãris -io (2) — February (31)
vasárnamis -io (1) — summer house, cottage, villa (21)
važiãvęs, -usi (past act. part. of **važiúoti**) — traveled (22)
važiãvimas (1) — traveling (36)
važinėti (važinėju, važinėja, važinėjo, važinės) — to drive about, to ride about, to travel regularly
važiúoti (važiúoju, važiúoja, važiãvo, važiuõs) — to travel, to go (in a vehicle) (5)
vėdė (3rd prs. simple pret. of **vèsti**) — led; married (A)
vėdęs (masc. nom. sg. of past act. part. of **vèsti**) — led; married (6)
véidas (3) — face (25)
véidrodis -džio (1) — mirror (15)
veĩkalas (3b) — (artistic) work (38); **mókslo veĩkalas** — scientific work; **mẽno veĩkalas** — work of art
veiksmãžodis -džio (1) — verb (2)
veĩkti (veikiù, veĩkia, veĩkė, veĩks) — to do, to act, to be in effect (20)
veĩstis (veisiúosi, veĩsiasi, veĩsėsi, veĩsis) — to multiply, to proliferate, to breed (34)
vėjas (1) — wind (10)
vėjasi (3rd prs. pres. of **výtis**) — chases after, is chasing after (A)
vėjėlis -io (dim. of **vėjas**; 2) — wind (A)

vėl — again (8)
vėliaũ — later (27)
vėliava (1) — flag (31)
vėlúoti (vėlúoju, vėlúoja, vėlãvo, vėluõs) — to be late (32)
vėlùs, -ì (4) — late (A)
vėpla (1) — gaping fool, gaper, joker (3)
verčiaũ (compar. degree of **veȓta**) — (it is) better (38)
vérda (3rd prs. pres. of **vìrti**) — cooks (2)
vergėjas (1) — subjugator, enslaver, tyrant (A)
veȓkti (verkiù, veȓkia, veȓkė, veȓks) — to cry (A)
verpėtas (2) — whirlpool, vortex (A)
veršiùkas (dim. of **veȓšis**; 2) — calf (A)
veȓta (neuter form of **veȓtas**) — (it is) worthwhile (38)
vertìmas (2) — translation (22)
vértinti (vértinu, vértina, vértino, vértins) — to value, to deem of worth (A)
veržìmasis (noun with reflexive particle; 1) — push, drive (37)
vèsti (vedù, vėda, vėdė, vės) — to lead; to marry
vestùvės (used in plur.; 2) — wedding (23)
vežìmas (2) — carriage, wagon; transport (A)
vèžti (vežù, vėža, vėžė, vèš) — to transport, to carry (in a vehicle) (9)
vidaũs (gen. sg. of **vidùs**; used as adj.) — interior, inside (A)
vidùdienis -io (1) — noon, midday (24)
vidùj (prep. with gen.) — within, inside of
vidurỹs (3b) — middle, center (25)
viduȓnaktis -čio (1) — midnight (24)
viduȓvasaris -io (1) — the middle of the summer (24)
vidùs (4) — inside, interior (A)
Vìdžemė (1) — Livland, Livonia, western part of Latvia (35)
víeną (fem. acc. sg. of **víenas**) — one (2)
víeną rudeñs rýtą — one autumn morning (16)
víenas, -à (3) — one; alone (15)
víenas kìtas — a few (cf. 36.7); **víenas kìtą**, etc. — each other (cf. 36.8)

vienerì, víenerios (3a) — one
vienýbė (1) — unity, harmony, concord (A)
vienìngas, -a (1) — united (A)
vieniñtelis, -ė (1) — only (child); all alone (40)
viênyti (viêniju, viênija, viênijo, viênys) — to unite, to unify (36)
víens — cf. víenas (A)
vienúolika (1) — eleven (16)
vienúoliktas, -a (1) — eleventh (29)
viēšbutis -čio (1) — hotel (9)
viešpatāvimas (1) — reign (37)
Viēšpats -ties or -čio (1) — Lord, ruler, sovereign, master (A)
vietà (2) — place (15)
viētoj (loc. sg. of vietà) — in place of, instead of (15)
vietóvė (1) — place, locality (A)
vieversĕlis -io (dim. of vieversỹs; 2) — lark (A)
vỹkti (vykstù, vỹksta, vỹko, vỹks) — to take place; to go, to leave for; to succeed (in) (A)
vilà (2) — villa (31)
vylyčià (2) — (archaic) arrow (A)
viĩkas (4) — wolf (A)
vilnìs -iēs (fem.; 4) — wave (17)
Vilnius (1) — Vilna, Vilnius (3)
vinìs -iēs (fem.; 4) — nail (17)
výras (1) — man; husband (8)
vyrèsnis, -ė (2) — older (of a person), senior (27)
vìrk (2nd sg. imper. of vìrti) — cook (7)
vìrsiu (1st sg. fut. of vìrti) — I shall cook
viřsti (virstù, viřsta, viřto, viřs) — to turn into, to become (15)
viřš (prep. with gen.) — over, beyond; above
viřšininkas (1) — superior, boss (23)
viršùj — cf. viřš
viršum̃ — cf. viřš
viršùs (4) — top (26)
vìrti (vérdu, vérda, vìrė, viřs) — to cook (7)
vìs — always (8)
vìs (with compar. degree of adj. or adv.) — more and more ... (27)
vìs dėlto — nevertheless; in spite of that (25)
vìsa — everything (15)
visagãlis -io (2) — omnipotent person (A)
visái — completely (35)

vìsas, -à (4) — all, the whole, whole (5)
visì (masc. nom. plur. of vìsas) — everybody, all (2)
vìsiškai — completely, entirely; (with negative) at all (31)
vìskas (only in sg.; 1) — everything (5)
Výsla (1) — Vistula river (35)
vìso (masc. gen. sg. of vìsas) — in all (24)
vìso lãbo — all together; (24); (taking leave) good-bye, so long
visóks, -ia (1) — all kinds of, any kind of (18)
visóms kalbóms keĩčiantis — since (whereas) all languages change, cf. 39.3
vis tíek — all the same (11)
visuomèt — always (6)
visuotìnis, -ė (2) — general, universal (A)
visuř — everywhere (13)
vištà (2) — hen (24)
Výtai (vocative sg. of Výtas) — (oh) Vytas (11)
Výtas (1) — dim. of Výtautas (11)
Výtautas (1) — Vytautas (13)
Výtautas Didỹsis — Vytautas the Great; Vitovt (36)
Výtauto Dìdžiojo Kultū̃ros Muziē̃jus — The Vytautas the Great Museum of Culture (23)
Vytē̃nis (2) — Vytenis, grand duke of Lithuania (37)
výtis (vejúosi, vējasi, vìjosi, vỹsis) — to chase after, to hunt (A)
Viznà (2) — Wizna, a little town in Poland (35)
võgti (vagiù, vãgia, võgė, võgs) — to steal (18)
vókas (3) — envelope (16)
vókiečių (gen. plur. of vókietis; used as adj.) — German
Vokietijà (2) — Germany
vókietis -čio (1) — German (22)
võs — hardly, just, only (15)

Z

ziřzti (zirziù, ziřzia, ziřžė, ziřs) — to whine (9)
zoolõgija (1) zoology (15)
zoolõgijos sõdas — zoo (15)

ž

žadė̃ti (žadù, žãda, žadė̃jo, žadė̃s) — to promise (11)

žaíbas (4) — lightning, flash of lightning (A)

žaísdavome (1st plur. freq. past of **žaísti**) — we used to play (12)

žaísti (žaidžiù, žaídžia, žaídė, žaĩs) — to play (7)

žãlias, -à (4) — green (10)

žaliúoti (žaliúoju, žaliúoja, žaliãvo, žaliuõs) — to be green, to appear green, to become green (28)

žalùmas (2) — verdure, greenness (37)

žemaĩ — down, in a low place (38)

žemaítis -čio (2) — Samogitian, Žemaitis, Low Lithuanian

žẽmas, -à — low (27)

žẽmė (2) — earth, land (8)

žemėlapis -io (1) — map (10)

žemėlė (dim. of **žẽmė**; 2) — earth, land (A)

žemiaũ (prep. with gen.) — below, under, farther down than

žemỹn — down, downward (15)

žénklas (3) — sign (36)

žiaurùmas (2) — cruelty (A)

žibėti (žibù, žìba, žibėjo, žibės) — to shine

žibt (interj.) — denotes a small flash of light

žýbt (interj.) — denotes a sudden, brilliant flash of light

žydėti (žýdžiu, žýdi, žydėjo, žydės) — to bloom (22)

žíedas (3) — blossom, flower; ring (34)

žiemà (4) — winter (27)

žiemgãlis -io (2) — Zemgallian, Semgallian, Semigallian (35)

žýgis -io (2) — campaign, deed (36)

žìlas, -à (4) — gray (25)

žýmiai — considerably, noticeably (A)

žinaĩ (2nd sg. pres. of **žinóti**) — you know (13)

žinaũ (1st sg. pres. of **žinóti**) — I know

žynė (4) — good fairy (25)

žinià (4) — report, information; (plur.) news (32)

žinójęs, -usi (past act. part. of **žinóti**) — known (31)

žìnoma — to be sure, of course (28)

žìnomas, -a (1) — known, famous (36)

žinóti (žinaũ, žìno, žinójo, žinõs) — to know (a fact) (6)

žiõplas, -à (4) — slow-witted, gawky, silly (A); **žioplỹs** — gaper

žìrgas (3) — steed, splendid horse (A)

žirgẽlis -io (2) — (dim. of **žìrgas**) ancient Lithuanian roof ornaments in the stylized shape of a horse's head or the front part of a horse; dragon-fly; also: horse, steed (in folksongs) (10)

žìrklės (used in plur.; 1) — pair of scissors (23)

žiūrėti (žiūriù, žiūri, žiūrėjo, žiūrės) — to look

žiūrėti į (with acc.) — to look at (18)

žmogẽlis -io (dim. of **žmogùs**; 2) — little man, insignificant fellow (38)

žmogùs (4) — man, human being; cf. 41.42 (4)

žmonà (3) — wife (21)

žmónės (nom. plur. of **žmogùs**; 3) — men, people; cf. 41.42 (18)

žmoniũ (gen. plur. of **žmogùs**) — men, people (18)

žodėlis -io (dim. of **žõdis**; 2) — word (A)

žodýnas (1) — dictionary (22)

žõdis -džio (2) — word (21)

žolė (4) — grass; weed (25)

žolėlės (used in plur.; 2) — herbs; tea leaves (38)

žudìkas (2) — assassin (36)

žurnãlas (2) — journal (40)

žurnalìstas (2) — journalist, newspaper man (7)

žúti (žústu, žústa (žúva), žúvo, žús) — to die, to perish (36)

žùvus Mindaugui — after Mindaugas died; cf. 39.4 (36)

žvaigždė (4) — star (A)

žvejỹs (4) — fisherman (21)

žvelgti (žvelgiù, žvelgia, žvelgė, žvelgs) — to look at (A)

žvìlgt (interj.) — denotes a glance at something

žvìlgterėti (žvìlgterėju, žvìlgterėja, žvìlgterėjo, žvìlgterės) — to glance at, to look at

ENGLISH - LITHUANIAN

A

a — (in the sense of 'per') į
a lot — daũg (38)
about — (prep.) apiẽ (23)
acquaint — supažìndinti (2)
acquaintance — pažį́stamas (26)
afternoon — po pietų̃ (32)
again — dár kar̃tą (8)
ago — (prep.) priẽš (16)
alive — gývas (39)
all — vìsas (13)
almost — bevéik (23)
alphabet — alfabètas (29)
already — jaũ (2)
also — taĩp pàt (1)
although — nórs (40)
aluminum — aliuminìnis (13)
always — visuomèt (8)
am — esù, cf. 1.3
am afraid — bijaũ (cf. bijóti) (7)
am going — einù, cf. 1.3
amber — giñtaras (34)
America — Amèrika (10)
ancient times — senóvė (6)
and — iȓ (1)
answer — atsakýti (40)
answer a letter — atsakýti į láišką (40)
anything — niẽkas (i.e. 'nothing' when used in negative sentences, cf. 4.3) (12)
apple — obuolỹs (22)
are — cf. be (1)
area — sritìs (27)
around — (prep.) apliñk (16)
arrive — atvažiúoti (in a vehicle); atplaũkti (on board a ship); ateĩti (on foot); atvýkti (3)
arrive at — pasíekti (23)
art — dailė̃ (23)
as soon as — kaĩp tìk (40)
ask — (someone to do something) prašýti; (information of someone) kláusti, pakláusti (31)
assassinate — nužudýti (36)
at — (prep.) priẽ (7)
at a (the) university — universitetè (5)
at home — namiẽ (1)
at night — nãktį, cf. 22.3 (16)
Australia — Austrãlija (21)
automobile — automobìlis (16)
autumn — ruduõ (14)

B

back yard — sodė̃lis
bad — blõgas (27)
Baltic area — Pabaltijỹs (34)
bathe — máudytis (7)
battle — mū̃šis (37)
be — bū́ti, cf. 1.3
be able — galė́ti (32)
be adorned — pasipúošti (14)
be afraid — cf. fear (7)
be born — gìmti (39)
be called (named) — vadìntis (38)
be done (i.e. come to pass) — bū́ti, cf. 17.3 (40)
be green — žaliúoti (28)
be necessary — reikė́ti, cf. 9.5
beads — karõliai (34)
beat — mùšti (40)
beautiful — gražùs (1)
beautifully — gražiaĩ (12)
because — nès, kadángi, cf. 38.2 (13)
become — viȓsti (34)
become green — sužaliúoti (28)
bed — lóva (26)
beer — alùs (6)
before — priẽš (36)
begin — (transitive) pradė́ti; (intransitive) prasidė́ti (13)
bell — var̃pas (23)
belong — priklausýti (39)
berry — úoga (28)
better (adj.) — gerèsnis -ė (12)
better (adv.) — geriaũ (12)
bird — paũkštis (16)
birthday — gimìmo dienà (32)
Black Sea — Juodóji jū́ra (37)
blackboard — lentà (17)
blame — peĩkti (34)
blossom — žiẽdas (34)
blue — mė́lynas (11)
board — lentà (17)
book — knygà (5)
book-store — knygýnas (36)
Boston — Bòstonas (32)
both — (masc.) abù; (fem.) abì (23)
boundary — ribà (37)
bracelet — apýrankė (34)
branch — šakà (16)
break (a leg) — nusiláužti (kóją) (40)
break down — sugèsti (13)
breakfast — pùsryčiai (32)
brick — (adj.) mūrìnis; (noun) plytà (13, 33)
broad — platùs (22)

brother — brólis (1)
brown — rùdas (14)
build — statýti, pastatýti (27, 33)
building — pãstatas (14)
burn — dègti (4)
burns — dẽga (3rd prs. pres.) (4)
bus — autobùsas (3)
busy — užsiẽmęs (past. act. part. of
užsiiṁti) (14)
but — o, bèt (12)
buy — piṝkti (13)
by the side of — priẽ (7)
by bus — autobusù (3)

C

cackle — kranksẽti (16)
call (name) — vadìnti (37)
calm — ramùs (22)
can (be able) — galẽti (32)
can no longer — nebegãli (from 'ne-
be-galẽti') (17)
Canada — Kanadà (15)
candy — saldaĩnis (17)
cannot — negãli (3rd prs. pres.) (4)
cannot — negãlime (1st prs. plur.
pres.) (4)
cannot — negaliù (1st prs. sg. pres.)
(4)
capital — sóstinė (3)
capital of Lithuania — Lietuvõs sóstinė, cf. 3.1,2 (3)
car — automobìlis (16)
carry to — nunèšti (34)
castle — pilìs (23)
castle hill — piliãkalnis (21)
cat — katẽ (16)
cathedral — kãtedra (26)
caw — kranksẽti (16)
celebrate — švẽsti (31)
celebration — šveñtė (31)
center — ceñtras (40)
century — šiṁtmetis (33)
chair — kėdẽ (40)
chew — kramtýti (17)
Chicago — Čikagà (24)
child — vaĩkas (12)
chocolate — šokolãdas (17)
church — bažnýčia (9)
city — miẽstas (3)
civilization — civilizãcija (4)
class — klãsė (38)
clear — grýnas (6)
clever — gudrùs (7)
coffee — kavà (20)
cold — šáltas (I am cold, cf. 12.3) (8)
colorful — spalvingas (28)

come — ateĩti; cf. 17.3 (40)
comedy — komèdija (8)
comparative — lyginamóji (fem.)
(39)
compartment — skyrẽlis (24)
compose — sudarýti (19)
concert — koncèrtas (9)
confluence — sántaka (23)
coniferous — spygliúotas (34)
conquer — nugalẽti (16)
content — paténkintas (31)
continuously — nuõlat (22)
copy out — nurašýti (37)
country — krãštas (21)
Couronian Isthmus — Kuršių Neringà (21)
cousin — pùsbrolis (22)
create — sukùrti (4)
crow — várna (16)
culture — kultūrà (4)

D

dark — tamsùs (29)
daughter — duktẽ (15)
day — dienà (6)
decisive — lemiamàsis (37)
deep — gilùs (23)
descendant — palikuonìs (37)
describe — aprašýti (38)
destroy — sumùšti (36)
die — miṝti, numiṝti (18)
die out — išmiṝti (39)
difficult — sunkùs (27)
dine — pietáuti (40)
dinner — piẽtūs (40)
discover — atràsti (29)
distant — tólimas (27)
divide — padalìnti (18)
do — darýti, padarýti (7)
doctor — dãktaras; (physician) gýdytojas (6)
dog — šuõ, cf. 7.1, 41.50 (7)
donate — (pa)dovanóti (23)
door — dùrys (40)
down town — į miẽstą (20)
drama — dramà (8)
draw — piẽšti (11)
dreadful — baisùs (27)
drink — gẽrimas (6)
drink — gẽrti (6)
drive — važiúoti (20)
dune — kopà (21)

E

each — kiekvíenas (24)
ear — ausìs (17)

461

earlier — anksčiaũ (27)
earth — žēmė (40)
easiest — lengviáusias (29)
easy — leñgvas (27)
eat — válgyti (17)
eight — (masc.) aštuonì; (fem.) aštúonios (19)
eighteen — aštuoniólika (24)
eighth — aštuñtas (24)
eighty — aštúoniasdešimt (24)
eleven — vienúolika (24)
ending — galūnė (40)
England — Anglija (15)
English — (to speak in English) ángliškai (22)
enter — įeĩti (11)
entire — vìsas (13)
envy — pavydēti (36)
Europe — Euròpa
evening — vãkaras; In the evening —
vakarè (1)
ever — kadà (nórs) (2f)
every — kiekvíenas; kàs, cf. 32.4 (24)
every day — kas diēną (40)
every morning — kas rýtą (40)
everything — vìskas (18)
everywhere — visuř (13)
examine carefully — apžiūrēti (13)
excellent — puikùs (22)
expensive — brangùs (27)
explain — (iš)áiškinti, (pa)áiškinti
(29, 34)
extend — išplēsti (37)
eye — akìs (17)

F

factory — fābrikas (40)
fairy tale — pāsaka (12)
fall — cf. autumn (14)
fall — krìsti (19)
family — šeimà (19)
farm — ūkis (9)
farmer — ūkininkas (18)
fast — greĩt, greĩtai (27)
faster — greičiaũ (27)
father — tēvas (1)
fear — bijóti (7)
few — kelì (32)
field — laũkas (21)
fifteen — penkiólika (16)
fifth — peñktas (24)
fifty — peñkiasdešimt (24)
film — fìlmas (22)
find — ràsti; (pres. passive part. is
'rañdamas') (34)
fine — puikùs (22)

finish — pabaĩgti (29)
fire — ugnìs (4)
first — pìrmas (24)
five — (masc.) penkì; (fem.) peñkios (19)
flag — vēliava (31)
flow — tekēti (16)
fly out — išskrìsti (16)
fold — suklóstyti (34)
folk tale — pāsaka (12)
follow — sèkti (27)
food — maĩstas (17)
for the past two years — paskutiniùs
dvejùs metùs (40)
forest — mìškas (14)
forget — užmiřšti
forgets — užmiřšta (3rd prs. pres.)
(14)
form — fòrma, lytìs (40)
forty — kēturiasdešimt (24)
found — įkùrti (33)
four — (masc.) keturì, (fem.) kētu-
rios (19)
fourteen — keturiólika (24)
fourth — ketviřtas (24)
freedom — láisvė (23)
Friday — penktādienis (29)
friend — draũgas, bičiùlis (14)
from — iš (21)
full — pìlnas (28)

G

garden — sodas; (vegetable garden)
dařžas (14)
gather by dripping — suvarvēti (34)
German — vókietis (40)
German — (to speak in German)
vókiškai (40)
Germany — Vokietijà (21)
get on (train, bus, etc.) — įlìpti (24)
get out (of a train, bus, etc.) — išlìpti (26)
get tired — pavařgti (40)
get up — atsikélti (27)
girl — mergáitė (16)
give — dúoti; (imper.) dúok(ite), cf.
7.3
glass — stìklas (34)
go — eĩti, cf. 1.3; (imper.) eĩk(ite);
(in a vehicle) važiúoti; (go for a
walk) pasiváikščioti (1)
go away — nueĩti (23)
goes — (3rd prs. pres.) eĩna, cf. 1.3
go for a walk — pasiváikščioti (6)
gold, golden — auksìnis (13)

462

good — (adj.) gḗras; (adv.) malõniai; geraĩ (13)
grain — jãvas (28)
grammar — gramãtika (29)
grand duke — kunigáikštis (27)
grandfather — senẽlis (9)
grandmother — senẽlė (9)
grandparents — senẽliai (40)
Greece — Graikijà (39)
Greek — graĩkas (34)
green — žãlias (14)
greet — pasisvéikinti (40)
group — grùpė (39)
grow — áugti (14)

H

half — pùsė
hand — rankà (17)
hand over — pérduoti (21)
happen — atsitìkti (39)
happy — laimìngas, liñksmas (9)
harbor — úostas (21)
hard — (adv.) suñkiai (12)
harm — keñkti (17)
has — (3rd prs. pres.) tùri (7)
hat — skrybẽlė (40)
have — turẽti (7)
have been — esù bùvęs (1st sg. perf.),
cf. 13.4
have to (must) — turẽti (31)
haven't been — nesù bùvęs (1st sg.
perf. masc. with negation) (13)
haven't found — nesù rãdęs (1st sg.
perf. masc. with negation) (13)
he — jìs (3)
he likes — jám patiñka, cf. 3.6
healthier — (adv.) sveikiaũ (13)
healthy — sveĩkas (17)
hear — išgìŕsti; girdẽti (16)
heat — šìldyti (4)
heats — (3rd prs. pres.) šìldo (4)
heaven — dangùs (40)
heavy — sunkùs (27)
her — (possessive pron.) jõs, cf. 2.3
(5)
here — čià (1)
high — áukštas (27)
hill — kalvà (40)
his — (possessive pron. jõ, cf. 2.3 (6)
historical — istòrinis (23)
history — istòrija (37)
hold — laikýti, turẽti (40)
holiday — šveñtė
home (in the direction of, to) — namõ (1)
honey — medùs (10)

horse — arklỹs (11)
hospital — ligóninė (32)
hot — kárštas (15)
hour — valandà (16)
house — nãmas (1)
housekeeper — šeimininkė
how — kaĩp (7)
how long — kíek ilgaĩ (32)
how many — kíek (14)
Hudson river — Hudsono ùpė, Hud-
sonas (40)
hundred — šim̃tas (24)
hurry — skubẽti (13)
hurt — kénkti (i.e. harm, do damage
to) (17)

I

I — àš (1)
if — jéigu (40)
immediately — tuojaũ (23)
important — svarbùs (39)
impression — įspūdis (23)
in (a certain period of time) — ùž,
cf. 32.12
in a city — miestè (3)
in a suburb — príemiestyje (6)
in ancient times — senóvėje (6)
in my house — màno namè (4)
in the big city — dideliamè miestè
(3)
in the center of the city — miẽsto
centrè (3)
in the evening — vakarè (2)
in the library — bibliotèkoj(e) (3)
in the olden days — senóvėje (40)
in the river — ùpėje (7)
in the sky — dangujè (9)
in the stove — krósnyje (4)
in the street — gãtvėje (7)
in the summer — vãsarą, cf. 32.6 (14)
in this manner — tókiu būdù (16)
Indo-European — (gen. plur.) indoeuropiẽčių (39)
independence — nepriklausomýbė (31)
institution of higher learning — aukštóji mokyklà (40)
intend — ketìnti (27)
interesting — įdomùs (22)
into — į (with acc.) (7)
iron — geležìnis (13)
is — cf. be; cf. 1.3 (1)
is called, is named — (3rd prs. pres.
of 'vadìntis') vadìnasi (3)
is coming — (3rd prs. pres. of 'at-
eĩti') ateĩna (6)

463

is going — (3rd prs. pres. of 'eĩti')
eĩna, cf. 1.3
is not — nėrà (40)

J
Japan — Japònija (20)
John — Jõnas (14)
joke — juokáuti (13)
journal — žurnãlas (40)
July — líepa (37)

K
kilometer — kilomètras (24)
king — karãlius (14)
kingdom — karalỹstė (40)
kitten — kačiùkas (9)
Klaipeda — Klaĩpėda (15)
Knight Templar — kalavijuõtis (36)
know — žinóti (21)

L
lake — čžeras (40)
lamp — lémpa (40)
language — kalbà (20)
large — dìdelis (1)
last night — vãkar vakarè (8)
last year — praėjusiais mètais (40)
later — vėliaũ (40)
laugh — juõktis (7)
lazy-bones, lazy person — tinginỹs (14)
leaf — lãpas (14)
learn — išmókti (22)
leave (behind) — palìkti (18)
leg — kója (40)
lesson — pamokà (16)
let us go — eĩkime, cf. 7.3
letter — láiškas; (of the alphabet) raĩdė (5)
library — bibliotekà (3)
lie, to be lying down — gulėti (11)
lift up — kélti (26)
light — leñgvas (27)
like — (conj.) kaĩp (14)
like — mėgti, cf. 6.4 and 3.6
linden tree — líepa (16)
linguistics — kalbótyra (39)
Lithuania — Lietuvà (3)
Lithuania Minor — Mažóji Lietuvà (38)
Lithuanian — (adjective) lietùviškas; (masc. noun) lietùvis; (fem. noun) lietùvė (9)
Lithuanian — (to speak Lithuanian) lietùviškai (9)
little — mãžas (9)
live — gyvénti (3)

lives (3rd prs. pres.) — gyvèna (3)
long — ìlgas (21)
look (at) — žiūrėti (į) (18)
look (through) — žiūrėti (pro) (37)
loudly — gařsiai (16)
love — mylėti (7)
low — žėmas (27)

M
make — (pa)darýti (23)
make up — sudarýti (19)
mama — mamà (13)
man — žmogùs (4)
many — daũg (3)
mead — midùs (6)
meadow — píeva (21)
meet — sutìkti (21)
meet (each other) — susitìkti, cf. 7.2
midnight — viduřnaktis (32)
mile — mylià (24)
million — milijõnas (24)
minus — mìnus, bè (24)
minute — minùtė (16)
mister — põnas (8)
mix — maišýtis (34)
modern — modernùs (33)
Monday — pirmãdienis (9)
money — pìnigas (31)
month — mėnuo, cf. 7.1 & 41.53 (25)
moon — mėnùlis (9)
more — daugiaũ (31)
more healthy — cf. healthier (13)
morning — rýtas (8)
most beautiful — gražiáusias, cf. 27.4
mother — mótina (1)
mountain — kálnas (9)
mouth — burnà (17)
move — pérsikelti (27)
movies — kìnas, fìlmas (20)
much — daũg (12)
museum — muziẽjus (23)
my — màno (1)

N
name — vařdas (7)
narrow — siaũras (27)
native — gimtàsis, cf. 28.1 (11)
near — priẽ; (not far away from) netolì (14)
necessary — reikalìngas (4)
necklace — karõliai (34)
need — reikėti, cf. 11.2
neighbor — kaimýnas (12)
neither...nor — neĩ...neĩ (19)
Nemunas — Nėmunas (21)
nest — lìzdas (16)

never — niẽkad, niekadà; niekuomèt (6)
new — naũjas (4)
New York — Niujòrkas (25)
newspaper — laĩkraštis (5)
next week — kìtą saváitę (40)
nice (weather) — gẽras (óras) (40)
nicely — malõniai (12)
night — naktìs (8)
nine — (masc.) devynì; (fem.) devýnios (18)
nineteen — devyniólika (24)
ninety — devýniasdešimt (24)
ninth — deviñtas (24)
no — ne; (adj.) jóks (36)
noise — triùkšmas (16)
noon — vidùdienis (32)
nose — nósis (17)
not — ne
nothing — niẽkas (18)
novel — romãnas (11)
now — dabař (8)

O

oak — ą́žuolas (22)
object — dáiktas (34)
occupy — cf. take over (16)
o'clock — (hour) valandà, cf. 32.1,5 (40)
old — sẽnas (3)
older (of a person) — vyrèsnis
oldest — seniáusias, vyriáusias (33)
on — añt (11)
on top of — viršujè (26)
once — víeną kařtą (40)
one — víenas (16)
one-fourth — ketviřtis (24)
only — (adv.) tik; (adj.) vieniñtelis (6)
opera — òpera (16)
ordinarily — paprastaĩ (27)
other — kìtas (18)
our — mū́sų, cf. 2.3
out of — iš
outside — laukè (6)
owl — pelė́da (16)

P

page — pùslapis (29)
palace — rū́mai (23)
paper — põpierius (40)
parade — parãdas (31)
parents — tėvaĩ, tėvẽliai (14)
park — párkas (9)
part — dalìs (38)
pass — praeĩti (16)

passenger — keleĩvis (24)
past — prõ (9)
pastor — klebõnas (38)
pen — plùnksna (11)
pencil — pieštùkas (11)
people — žmónės (18)
perch — tupẽti (16)
picture — pavéikslas (23)
pine — pušìs (22)
plant — sodìnti (8)
play — žaĩsti (7)
pleasant — malonùs (12)
pleasantly — malõniai (40)
please — prašaũ, cf. prašýti (8)
plus — plius (24)
poem — poemà (38)
poet — poètas (23)
port — úostas (21)
praise — gìrti (34)
precious — brangùs (40)
prepare — ruõšti (40)
president — prezideñtas (25)
press together — suslẽgti (34)
pretty — gražùs (22)
print — išspausdìnti (38)
professor — profèsorius (6)
profound — gilùs (23)
property — tuřtas (18)
Prussia — Prū́sija (39)
pupil — (masc.) mokinỹs; (fem.) mokinẽ (2)
put in order — tvarkýti (37)

Q

quarter — ketviřtis (24)
question — klausinẽti (22)
quiet — ramùs (22)

R

railway car — vagònas (24)
rain — (verb) lýti; (noun) lietùs (6, 31)
rainy — lietìngas (28)
raise — kélti (16)
reach (arrive at) — pasíekti (23)
read — skaitýti; (imper.) skaitýk (ite); cf. 7.3 (3)
receive — gáuti (40)
red — raudónas (11)
relative — giminẽ (26)
remain — lìkti (38)
remember — atsimiñti (21)
repeat — kartóti (29)
resemblance — panašùmas (39)
resin — sakaĩ (34)
return — (su)grį̃žti (40)

rich — turtìngas (31)
ride — važiúoti (20)
rise (of the sun) — tekėti (40)
river — ùpė (7)
road — kēlias (12)
Roman — romēnas (34)
room — kambarỹs (11)
rot — supûti (13)
ruckus — triùkšmas (16)
ruins — griuvēsiai (24)
rule — valdýti (36)
run — bėgti (7)
Ruth — Rûtà (11)

S

sail — plaûkti (21)
satisfied — paténkintas (31)
say — sakýti (6)
says — (3rd prs. pres.) sãko (6)
scholar — mókslininkas (34)
school — mokyklà (Ω)
scientist — mókslininkas (34)
scold — bárti (33)
sea — jûra (21)
sea-shore — pajûris (34)
season — mētų laĩkas (14)
second — añtras (24)
see — matýti, cf. 2.1 (7)
sees — (3rd pers. pres.) mãto (7)
sell — pardúoti (13)
send — atsiũsti (31)
seven — (masc.) septynì; (fem.) septýnios (16)
seventeen — septyniólika (24)
seventh — septiñtas (24)
seventy — septýniasdešimt (24)
she — jì, cf. 2.3
ship — laĩvas (21)
shore — krañtas; cf. sea-shore (34)
show — (pa)ródyti (40)
sick — siřgęs, nesveĩkas (40)
sidewalk — šaligatvis (23)
silently — tyliaĩ (6)
sing — dainúoti, giedóti (40)
sister — sesuõ, cf. 7.1 and 41.52
(dim.) sesùtė (1)
sit, to be sitting —sėdėti; (of birds)
tupėti (6)
sit down — sėsti, atsisėsti (40)
sit down (together) — susėsti (26)
six — (masc.) šešì; (fem.) šēšios (19)
sixteen — šešiólika (24)
sixth — šēštas (24)
sixty — šēšiasdešimt (24)
sky — dangùs (6)
sleep — miegóti (16)
small — mãžas (9)

smart — gudrùs (7)
smell — (transitive) suúosti; (intransitive) kvepėti (17, 34)
so — taĩp (12)
so well as — taip geraĩ kaĩp (40)
somebody — kas nórs (36)
son — sūnùs (6)
soon — greĩt, greĩtai (8)
Spain — Ispãnija (20)
speak — kalbēti (9)
spring — pavãsaris (27)
spruce — ēglė (16)
stand — stovēti (11)
start — pradēti (40)
station — stotìs (15)
stay (for a certain period of time) —
pabûti (31)
steal (from) — võgti (iš) (18)
steamship — gárlaivis (21)
steel — plieninis (13)
still — (adv.) dár; (verbal prefix)
tebe- (37)
stone — akmuõ, cf. 7.1
stone —(adj.) mūrìnis (23)
stop — (su)stóti (40)
stove — krósnis (4)
street — gãtvė (3)
student — (masc.) studeñtas; (fem.)
studeñtė
study — mókytis, studijúoti (14)
study hard enough — rimtaĩ studijúoti (40)
study harder — daugiaũ studijúoti
(40)
suburb — príemiestis (6)
such (a) — tóks (36)
sugar — cùkrus (10)
summer — (noun) vãsara; (adj.) vasarìnis (14)
summer house — vasárnamis (21)
sun — sáulė (40)
swim — cf. bathe, travel (7)

T

table — stãlas (8)
take — im̃ti (26)
take a good look — apžiūrēti (13)
take a walk — pasiváikščioti (6)
take over — užvaldýti (16)
talk — kalbēti (23)
tall — áukštas (22)
tasty — skanùs (22)
tea — arbatà (6)
teach — mókyti, dēstyti (20)
teacher — (masc.) mókytojas; (fem.)
mókytoja (1)

tell — pãsakoti (12)
ten — dẽšimt (24)
tenth — dešiřtas (23)
than — negù; ùž (13)
that — (conj.) kàd; (pron.) tàs; cf. 36 (13, 31)
the fact that — (conj.) taĩ, jóg (34)
theater — teãtras (8)
their — jū̃, 2.3 (9)
there — teñ (19)
they — (masc.) jiẽ; (fem.) jõs (5)
thief — vagìs (18)
thing — dáiktas, dalỹkas (34)
third — trẽčias (24)
thirteen — trýlika (24)
thirteenth — trýliktas (33)
thirty — trìsdešimt (24)
this — (masc.) šìs; (fem.) šì, cf. 36 (27)
thousand — tū́kstantis (24)
three — trỹs (14)
through — peř (21)
thy — tàvo (40)
time — laĩkas; (event, occurence) kařtas (8)
tired — pavař̃gęs (23)
to — (someone's house, place of business) pàs; (a place) į̃ (26)
to school — į̃ mokỹklą (2)
to the university — į̃ universitẽtą (3)
today — šiañdien (6)
together — kartù (19)
Tolminkiemis — Tolmìnkiemis (38)
tomorrow — rytój (9)
too much — per daũg (13)
tooth — dantìs (17)
top — viršùs (26)
tower — bókštas (26)
town — miẽstas, miestẽlis (3)
trade — prekiáuti (34)
train — traukinỹs (24)
travel — važiúoti, keliáuti (14)
traveler — keleĩvis (24)
tree — mẽdis (14)
trip — keliõnė (31)
Tuesday — antrãdienis (40)
turn into — viř̃sti (34)
twelve — dvýlika (24)
twenty — dvìdešimt (24)
two — (masc.) dù; (fem.) dvì (14)

U

uncle — dẽdė (22)
under — põ (16)
understand — supràsti (26)

unify — suvíenyti (36)
university — universitẽtas (3)
University of Vilnius — Vìlniaus universitẽtas (40)
until — ìki, lìg (40)
up to — lìgi (37)
uproar — triùkšmas (16)
usually — paprastaĩ

V

vacation — atóstogos (28)
very, very much — labaĩ (1)
village — káimas (9)
visit — aplankýti (9)
voyage — keliõnė (31)

W

wage war — kariáuti (37)
wait — láukti (26)
waiting — laukią̃s, cf. 26.2
wake up — pabùsti (22)
walk — pasiváikščioti (6)
wall — síena (40)
want — norẽti (7)
wants — (3rd prs. pres.) nóri (7)
war — kãras (16)
warm — šiltas (7)
was — (3rd prs. simple preterit of 'bū́ti') bùvo (8)
wash up (on the shore) — išpláuti (34)
watch — laĩkrodis (13)
water — vanduõ, cf. 7.1 and 41.51
way — kẽlias (12)
we — mẽs (1)
we like — mùms patiñka, cf. 3.6
weaken — susilpnẽti (37)
wealth — tuř̃tas (18)
weather — óras (8)
week — saváitė (25)
well — geraĩ (22)
were — (3rd prs. simple preterit of 'bū́ti') bùvo (40)
what — (pronoun) kàs; (adj.) kóks (1, 7)
what is ... name — kaĩp vadìnasi (7)
what kind (of) — kóks (1)
what time — cf. 32.1 and 32.1,5
when — kadà, kaĩ (8)
where — kuř̃ (1)
which — kurìs (27)
white — báltas (11)
who — (interj.) kàs; (relative) kurìs (1)
whole — vìsas (27)

467

whose — kienõ (19)
why — kodėl (13)
wide — platùs, cf. 12.1
wife — žmonà (30)
will — valià (40)
win — cf. conquer (16)
window — lángas (11)
winter — žiemà (25)
with — sù (8)
with what — (instr. sg. of 'kas') kuõ (17)
without — bè (4)
without fire — bè ugniẽs (4)
wood, wooden — medìnis (13)

work — (noun) dárbas; (verb) dìrbti (8)
works — (written) rãštai (38)
world — pasáulis (40)
write — (pa)rašýti (8)

Y

year — mētai (25)
yellow — geltónas (11)
yesterday — vãkar (8)
yet — dár (40)
you — (sg.) tù; (plur.) jũs (1)
young — jáunas (6)
your — (sg.) tàvo; (plur.) jũsų (1)

GRAMMATICAL INDEX

(The numbers refer to paragraphs or lessons)

Also available from Hippocrene...

Lithuanian-English/English-Lithuanian Concise Dictionary
by Victoria Martsinkyavitshute
- Over 8,000 entries
- Comprehensive definitions
- Phonetics for both languages
- Concise, easy-to-use format
- Completely modern
- Parts of speech indicated

382 pages • 4 x 6 • 10,000 entries • 0-7818-0151-6 • W • $14.95pb • (489)

The above title is also available in a compact dictionary size...

Lithuanian-English/English-Lithuanian Compact Dictionary
400 pages • 3½ x 4¾ • 10,000 entries • 0-7818-0536-8 • W • $8.95pb • (624)

Art of Lithuanian Cooking
A Hippocrene Original Cookbook
by Maria Gieysztor de Gorgey

With over 150 recipes, this cookbook is a collection of traditional hearty Lithuanian favorites like Fresh Cucumber Soup, Lithuanian Meat Pockets, Hunter's Stew, Potato Zeppelins, and delicacies like Homemade Honey Liqueur and Easter Gypsy Cake.

176 pages • 5½ x 8½ • 0-7818-0610-0 • W • $22.50hc • (722)

All prices subject to change. **To purchase Hippocrene Books** contact your local bookstore, call (718) 454-2366, or write to: HIPPOCRENE BOOKS, 171 Madison Avenue, New York, NY 10016. Please enclose check or money order, adding $5.00 shipping (UPS) for the first book and $.50 for each additional book.